The Most of
Andy Rooney

The Most of Andy Rooney

A Few
Minutes with
Andy Rooney

And More by
Andy Rooney

Pieces of
My Mind

ANDREW A. ROONEY

GALAHAD BOOKS
NEW YORK

Published in 1991 by

Galahad Books
A division of LDAP, Inc.
386 Park Avenue South
New York, NY 10016

Galahad Books is a registered trademark of LDAP, Inc.

This edition is reprinted by arrangement with Atheneum
Publishers, an imprint of Macmillan Publishing Company.

Library of Congress Catalog Card Number: 86-47671
ISBN: 0-88365-765-1

Printed in the United States of America

CONTENTS

A Few Minutes with

ANDY ROONEY

by ANDREW A. ROONEY

CONTENTS

Ourselves

PREFACE

THE writing in this book was originally done for television. S. J. Perelman said the only difference in writing for television is that to make it look like a script, you only write on the right-hand side of the paper. There are other differences, though.

Words written for television are meant to be heard by the ear, not seen by the eye. People don't talk the way they write and they don't write the way they talk, so you have to make some adjustments. When a writer puts it down on paper, he's more concise than he'd be in conversation. He cuts out a lot of the hemming and hawing and backtracking that all of us do when we talk. This saves everyone time but the writer. He thinks out what he's going to say in advance and then tries to stick to the point.

When the same writer puts words down to be spoken by someone on television, on a stage or in a motion picture, he puts a little of the hemming and hawing back in to make it sound more natural. At best it comes out as a compromise between written and spoken English.

To be spoken aloud, the sentences have to be shorter and the writing simpler. You can't turn a clever phrase because if the audience doesn't catch it the first time, they can't go back and read it over again. At the same time, a viewer or listener expects more from something that's been written to be said than he'd expect to hear from a friend he meets on the street, so the writing has to be a little concentrated.

If it is concentrated and there are ideas in the writing, it has to be slowed down because all of us talk faster than we listen. Writing for television, you often follow an idea with a few words that don't mean much just to give listeners time to hear what you've said.

If I were teaching a class of young writers, I'd advise them to keep in mind what something sounds like when they read it aloud, even if what they are writing is for print. Anyone should be very suspicious of a sentence he's written that can't be read aloud easily.

I'm telling you all this because I assume that if you weren't interested you wouldn't have bought the book. I hope it's a good book. Publishers these days are often more interested in whether something will sell than whether it's any good. A book by anyone on a popular television broadcast will probably sell whether it's any good or not and that makes me nervous.

It wasn't hard to talk me into putting this book together. It is unsatisfactory for a writer to have his words said once and then disappear forever into thin air. Seeing our names in print lends to the dream all of us have of immortality. You can't ask more from something than immortality and money next week.

I use the phrase "putting this book together" because it's been written over a period of ten years. For print I've crossed out some things that didn't mean anything at all without the pictures that originally went with them, and I've put apostrophes back in words like "*Ive*, "*dont*" and "*isnt*" which *Ive* abandoned in writing for television. For the most part, though, these essays are printed as broadcast.

The writer doesn't have much stature in the visual arts and, being as I am a writer, that irritates me. The performers and the producers get more of everything than the creators in most cases. Television writing in particular has been considered a second-class art form and that's why so much of it isn't any good. Almost none of the good writers who have already established themselves in print have turned to television. This is part television's fault for not encouraging them and part their own fault. Some of them are afraid they don't know how to do it and they hesitate to risk their reputations trying.

Even within the television industry, writers tend to leave their work to become producers as if that was a higher calling. (I don't use the subjunctive much writing for television.) They get more power, more money and they no longer have to make fools of themselves putting it down on paper where everyone can see it.

If the normal law of supply and demand worked, there would be a lot more writers than there are. There are hundreds of producers, directors, publishers, editors, actors and salesmen waiting for one writer to put something down on paper so they can change it, duplicate it and sell it. Hollywood and Broadway—and television in both places—are desperately in need of good writers. There are enough actors looking for work today to do all the plays, television productions and movies that will be written for the next fifty years.

Nonfiction writing in television is almost nonexistent outside the hard-news area. Even though more than half the best-selling books and mass-circulation magazines are nonfiction, commercial television has never given it much of a chance because network executives don't think it will attract a crowd. They are wrong and they'll change their minds.

You don't know Bob Forte and Jane Bradford but the three of us have worked together for ten years. They are important to the things I've done, and I'd feel terrible if their names weren't somewhere in this book.

Now I want to check my dictionary to see whether this is a preface, a foreword or an introduction.

ANDREW A. ROONEY

Belongings

CHAIRS

THERE is so much that is unpleasant and dull about living that we ought to take every opportunity presented to us to enjoy the enjoyable things of life. None of us can afford to become immune to the sensation of small pleasures or uninterested in small interests. A chair, for instance, can be a small and constant joy, and taking pleasure from one a sensation available to almost all of us all the time.

It is relatively easy to say who invented the light bulb but impossible to say who built the first chair. They took one out of King Tut's tomb when they opened it in 1922 and King Tut died fourteen hundred years before Christ was born and that certainly wasn't the first chair, either. So they've been around a long time. If there was a first man, he probably sat in the first chair.

Chairs have always been something more than a place for us to bend in the middle and put our posteriors on other legs in order to take the weight off our own. They have been a symbol of power and authority, probably because before the sixteenth century only the very rich *owned* real chairs. The others sat on the floor at their feet in most countries.

A throne is the ultimate place to sit down and there are still something like twenty-five countries in the world that have thrones, and leaders who actually sit on them.

The Peacock Throne of Persia is one of the most elaborate, but I don't know what happened to that. It belonged to the King of Persia, but Persia is called Iran now and, of course, they don't have a king. The leaders they have now usually sit on the floor. I suppose this is their way of reacting against the idiocy of a throne but I hope they haven't discarded theirs. It was crusted with rubies and diamonds and was supposed to be worth $100 million twenty

3

years ago. In today's market I should think it would bring $500 million, although I don't know who it would bring it from.

I've seen pictures of it but, personally, I wouldn't give them $50 million for it, and if the average American housewife got hold of it, she'd probably put a slipcover over it.

I didn't mean to get off on thrones but some kings and queens have more than one. Queen Elizabeth has one in every Commonwealth country, presumably in the event she wants to sit down if she visits one of them. She has five in London alone and several more at palaces around England. I'd hate to have to reglue a throne.

If the United States had a king, I suppose there'd be a throne in the White House. Too bad there isn't, in a way. It could be more of a tourist attraction than the Washington Monument.

Theoretically the royal chair is never sat in by anyone but a nation's ruler, but it's hard to believe that a few of the cleaning ladies and some of the kids around the castle don't test it out once in a while. I can imagine the guards in a state prison fooling around in the electric chair, too. "Hey, Joe. Look at me. Throw the switch!"

The closest thing we ever had to a throne was that big rocking chair John Kennedy intimidated people with. A visiting dignitary could be disarmed by its folksy charm and overwhelmed by its size and mobility.

There's nothing else like chairs that we have in such great numbers. We know how many cars there are in this country and how many television sets, but we don't have the vaguest idea how many chairs there are. I'll bet if everyone sat down in one, there'd still be fifty empty chairs left over for each one of us.

Over the past fifty years the most used piece of furniture in the house has been the kitchen chair. Like anything that gains wide acceptance, it turns out to be useful for a lot of things it wasn't built to do. The kitchen chair is for sitting on, for throwing clothes over, for hanging jackets on, for putting a foot on when you're lacing a shoe, and as an all-purpose stepladder for changing light bulbs or for getting down infrequently used dishes from high and remote parts of kitchen cabinets. It has usually been painted many times, hurriedly.

If the kitchen chair isn't the most sat on, the one the American working man comes home to every evening must be. (The American working woman doesn't have a chair of her own.) It's the one

in which he slumps for endless hours watching football games on television. It's the one in which he is portrayed in cartoons about himself and it's usually the most comfortable chair in the house. It's a chair you sit in, not on.

It isn't so much that the American male takes this throne as his prerogative. It's that women don't usually like a chair that mushy. It's a comfortable chair, though, and for all its gross, overfed appearance, I'm not knocking it. It serves as a bed when it's too early to go to bed. It's a place where you can take a nap before turning in for a night's sleep.

In big cities you see a lot of overstuffed chairs being thrown away outside apartment houses. I always think of the old Eskimo women they put out on an ice floe to die.

The kitchen chair and the overstuffed living-room chair are the *most* sat on, and there are always a few chairs in every home that no one ever sits on. Everyone in the household understands about it. There are no rules. It is just not a chair you sit on. It may be in the hall by the front door, used mostly for piling books on after school. Or it may be silk brocade with a gold fringe, in the back bedroom. It may be antique and uncomfortable or imperfectly glued together and therefore too fragile for the wear-and-tear that goes with being sat on regularly.

Sometimes there is no reason that anyone can give why a chair

isn't sat on. It's like the suit or dress in the closet which is perfectly good but never worn. The unsat-upon chair in a home really
isn't much good for anything except handing down from one generation to the next.

In hotels they often put two chairs not to be sat in on either
side of the mirror across from the elevator on every floor.

There aren't as many dining-room chairs as there used to be
because there aren't as many dining rooms. Now people eat in the
kitchen or they have picnics in front of the television set in the
living room. It's too bad, because there's something civilized and
charming about having a special place for eating. It's a disappearing
luxury, though. These days everything in a house has to be multipurpose, folding, retractable or convertible.

Dining-room chairs on thick rugs were always a problem. They
made it difficult or impossible for a polite man to slide a chair under
a woman. As soon as any of her weight fell on the chair, the legs
sank into the pile and stopped sliding. If she was still eight inches
from where she wanted to be, she had to put her hands under the
seat and hump it toward the table while the man made some futile
gestures toward helping from behind her. It took a lot of the grace
out of the gesture.

The other trouble with a good set of dining-room chairs was
that at Christmas or any other special occasion when you wanted
them most, there weren't enough of them. This meant bringing a
chair or two in from the kitchen or the living room and ruining
the effect of a matched set.

If dining-room chairs are the most gracious, folding chairs are
the least. I suppose someone will collect those basic folding, wood
chairs they kept in church basements and sell them as antiques
someday soon, but they're ugly and uncomfortable. Maybe they
were designed to keep people awake at town meetings.

The Morris chair was invented by an English poet named William Morris. He's better known for his chair than his poetry. A man
takes immortality from anywhere he can get it, but it seems a sad
fate for a poet to be remembered for a chair. I make furniture myself and I hate to think of any table I've made outlasting my
writing, but I suppose it could happen.

Very few chairs survive the age in which they were designed.
The Windsor chair is one of a handful of classics that have. The
Hitchcock is another. If the time comes when we want to place a

time capsule to show people on another planet in another eon what we sat on, we should put a Windsor chair in to represent us. You have to choose something better than average as typical.

The rocking chair probably comes closer than any other article of furniture to delineating past generations from present ones. People sat in them and contemplated their lives and the lives of people they could see passing by from where they sat. People don't contemplate each other much from chairs anymore. When anyone passes by now, he's in a car going too fast for anyone to identify him. No one is sitting on the front porch watching from a rocker anyway.

Rockers were good furniture. They were comfortable and gave the user an air of ease and contentment. They give the person sitting in one the impression he's getting somewhere without adding any of the headaches that come with progress.

From time to time furniture makers say there's a revived interest in rocking chairs, but I doubt this. For one thing, the front porch has probably been closed in to make the living room bigger and anyway people don't want anything as mobile or folksy as a rocker in a living room filled with electronic gear.

Comfort in a chair is often in direct ratio to the relationship between the height of the feet and the height of the head. People are always trying to get their feet up. Very likely there is an instinct for self-preservation here because the closer anyone's feet are to being on a level with the head, the less work the heart has to do to get the blood pumped around.

During the years between World War I and World War II, everyone's dream of a vacation was a boat trip somewhere on the *Mauretania,* the *Leviathan* or one of the *Queens* to Europe. In their dreams, the man and the woman were stretched out in the bright sunshine on deck chairs in mid-Atlantic. Not many people go by boat anywhere anymore, though, and the deck or steamer chairs were redesigned and moved to the backyard. The wood in those deck chairs has been replaced by tubular aluminum and the canvas by plastic straps. They wouldn't have lasted five minutes on the deck of the *Mauretania* in a stiff breeze.

At some time in the last hundred years, we reached the point where more people were working sitting down than on their feet. This could be a milestone unturned by social historians. We have more and more white-collar people and executives sitting in chairs telling people what to do and fewer and fewer people on their feet actually doing anything.

The sitting executives found that they weren't satisfied not moving at all, so they invented a chair for executives that swivels, rolls forward, backward or sideways and tilts back when the executive, who used to have his feet on the ground, wants to lean back and put them on his mahogany desk.

In many offices the chairs provided for men and for women are symbols that irritate progressive women. The chairs often represent clear distinctions in the relative power of the sexes there. The executive male has his bottom on a cushion, his elbows on arm-rests. At the desk outside his office, the secretary, invariably a woman, sits erect in a typing chair about as comfortable as an English saddle.

It's a strange thing and probably says a lot about our rush through life that the word "modern" has an old-fashioned connotation to it when you're talking about design. I think of Art Deco as modern. It must be because what we call "modern" is just a brand-new design about to become obsolete. Someone is always coming up with what is known as a modern chair. It looks old and silly in a few years but is still referred to as modern.

There are modern chairs that have not become obsolete because

they're so good. Some of them are forty years old but they're still called modern. Charles Eames designed that plastic bucket seat on tubular legs that will not go out of style. Mies van der Rohe designed the Barcelona chair that you have in the outer lobby of your office if you're a rich company. That's going to last like the Windsor and the Boston rockers because it's comfortable and simply attractive.

Considering how much time we spend sitting, it's strange our chairs don't fit us better. No size 6 woman would think of wearing a size 14 dress but a size 48 man who weighs 250 pounds is expected to sit in the same size chair a 98-pound woman sits in. To some extent a chair in a room is considered community property, but in most homes a family arranges itself in the same way day after day when it settles down, and more attention ought to be given chair sizes.

Certain purposeful chairs have been well done but with no regard to the size or shape of the occupant. The electric chair, the dentist's chair, the theater seat or the airplane seat are mostly well designed, but again every chair is the same size. We're not. I suppose it would be difficult to sell theater tickets by seat size or for a dentist to have more than one chair depending on whose tooth ached. But the fact remains: people don't take the same size chair any more than they take the same size shoe.

Even though most public seating furniture must have seemed comfortable to the people who designed it, it seems to have been designed and sat on for the test under laboratory conditions. These conditions don't exist in a movie theater or on a crowded airplane.

In the theater chair, the shared armrest has always been a problem. The dominant personality usually ends up using the one on both sides of the seat in which he or she is sitting and the occupants of the adjacent seats get either none or one, depending on who flanks them on the *other* side. The shared armrest may be part of what's known as the magic of the theater, but it's a constant source of irritation to anyone watching a bad movie.

The average airplane chair is a marvel of comfort and we could all do worse than to have several installed in our own homes. The problem on board, of course, is the person in the seat next to you. The seats are usually lined up three across, and if the plane is full the middle seat can make a trip to Europe a nightmare. It is no longer a comfortable place of repose; it's a trap and you're in it.

At a time when all of us are looking for clues to our character, it's unusual that no one has started analyzing us from the way we sit in chairs. It must be at least as revealing of character as a person's handwriting and an even more reliable indicator of both personality and attitude than, say, palm-reading.

The first few minutes after you sit down are satisfying ones, but no matter how good it feels to get off your feet, you can't stay in one position very long. Sooner or later that wonderful feeling you got when you first took the weight off your feet goes away. You begin to twitch. You are somehow dissatisfied with the way your body is arranged in the chair but uncertain as to what to do about it.

Everyone finds his own solution for what to do with feet. No two people do exactly the same thing. The first major alteration in the sitting position usually comes when the legs are crossed. The crossing of legs seems to satisfy some inner discontent, the scratching of a psychosomatic itch deep inside.

It's amusing to see how often we use a chair designed to be used one way in a manner so totally different that even the originator could not have imagined it. We straddle a chair, sitting on it backwards with our arms where our backs are supposed to be and our chin on our arms; we sit sideways in a lounge chair with our legs draped over one arm and our backs leaning against the other arm. We rock back in chairs that are not rockers, ungluing their joints. We do things to chairs we wouldn't do to our worst enemy, and chairs are among our best friends.

You'd have to say that of all the things we have built for ourselves to make life on earth more tolerable, the chair has been one of the most successful.

WHO OWNS WHAT

IN AMERICA

W E USED to toast Pepperidge Farm bread for breakfast in my house; then the little company that made it was taken over by Campbell Soup, a big company, and I don't think the bread's as good as it used to be.

Whenever a big company takes over a small company, the product almost always gets worse. Sue me, but it's true. The take-over is so popular with big business it's hard to know who owns what in America.

Take, for example, the International Telephone and Telegraph Company. They do some telephone business, I guess, but they also own Sheraton Hotels, the Hartford Fire Insurance Company, the company that publishes *Who's Who in America* and the bakeries that make Hostess Twinkies.

Most of the tobacco companies have taken over so many other companies that they've dropped "tobacco" from their names. Philip Morris bought that fine old German beer Lowenbrau, which they now make in such fine old German cities as Fort Worth, Texas. Liggett, known for its Chesterfield cigarettes, owns J & B Scotch and the company that makes Champion barbells. The former Reynolds Tobacco Company owns Chun King foods, Hawaiian Punch and Vermont Maid syrup, which is 2% maple and not made in Vermont.

Who would you think owns Montgomery Ward? Sears, Roe-buck? Wrong. Mobil Oil owns Montgomery Ward.

Pepsi-Cola owns Wilson, which makes tennis balls. And don't

try to find a Coca-Cola in a Pizza Hut because Pepsi-Cola owns them, too.

General Mills, which bought Bruce Jenner, the champion of breakfasts, owns Lacoste, the company that makes the tennis shirt with the little alligator on it. General Mills also owns the game of Monopoly.

Hershey makes chocolate bars, but also owns the San Giorgio Macaroni Company.

Consolidated Foods makes Sara Lee cheesecake, which seems fitting, and Electrolux vacuum cleaners, which doesn't.

ABC, Number 1 in television, owns *Prairie Farmer* magazine, but CBS isn't worried. It owns *Field & Stream* and *Woman's Day*.

Recently the Kellogg Company paid $56 million for a company called Mrs. Smith's Pies.

Big companies love homey-sounding little names like Mrs. Smith's Pies. We decided to go to Pottstown, Pennsylvania, where the pies are made, to see if we could find out what Mrs. Smith is going to do with the $56 million.

ROONEY:
Pardon me, do you know where Mrs. Smith is?
MAN:
Mrs. Smith?
ROONEY:
Yeah.
MAN:
What Mrs. Smith is that?

WOMAN:
Right. No, look, go here to the end of the alley and make a right.

ROONEY:
Where's the main office, do you know? Will Mrs. Smith be there?
MAN:
A Mr. Smith?
ROONEY:
No. *Mrs.* Smith. Is it *Mr.* Smith's Pies?

ROONEY:
Hi. You're Mrs. Smith, are you?
WOMAN:
No, I'm not.

Rooney (in factory parking lot):
Is there a Mrs. Smith? Smith isn't around at all?
Man:
No, there's a . . . there's no Smiths connected with the company at this time. It's owned by Kellogg's.

Who owns what in America? Not Mrs. Smith.

SOAP

I WENT out and bought as many bars and cakes of soap as I could find in the local stores around me. Americans buy about two billion of them a year—eight or ten cakes for each one of us. I've been to a couple of countries where I doubt the whole population uses eight or ten cakes a year. Nasty American thing to say, isn't it?

The most expensive one I found was Bronnley. It's soap in a little sponge pillow. It was $7.50. I can't wait until I submit an expense account and the money people at CBS see this: one cake of soap—$7.50.

Chanel No. 5. Hand soap, it says. Wouldn't want to get any of it on your face, I guess.

Guerlain's. They make perfume, too. I don't like perfumed soap. Soap, like people, shouldn't smell like anything. If soap smells too much, I figure they're hiding something.

A lot of the expensive ones sound like something to eat. Milk 'n Honey—contains milk proteins and pure honey. You wouldn't want to wash up with impure honey. Oatmeal. Victorian Herb soap—soap or soup? Soap—made of lettuce juice, it says. "Lettuce juice is calmative to rough skin." This one "combines the natural smoothness of avocado with the goodness of honey." Cucumber & Glycerine. I guess of all the things I'd least want to wash up with, it would be cucumber. Here's one that looks like a lemon. Cocoa Butter. Pears. I know Pears. It's transparent—in case you want to see through your soap. I suppose if you were washing someone else's back.

These are all the exotic soaps, of course, the expensive ones, that not many of us use. They're too expensive for us. The ones most of us use are Dial, Lux, Camay, Dove, Palmolive. I don't know which the best-seller is.

I don't have much complaint with American soaps—any one of them. Oh, I have a few complaints. For one thing, most of its lifetime a cake of soap is too small. I brought one in from the house. It's not a cake at all. It's more like a thin cookie. It's not only too small, it's sharp around the edges. No one wants sharp soap. The fact is a cake of soap is only at its best for two or three days, while you can still feel the letters on it. I'd like to be rich enough to throw soap away after the letters are worn off.

A lot of these are different colors, too. They're green and brown. Soap should be white. Dishes, underwear and soap should all be white. When a person takes a shower and looks down, he doesn't want to see a lot of colors running off him.

And just one last comment. Are the soap manufacturers paying off the people who build soap dishes into showers? If they aren't, how come the soap holders are always placed so they take a direct hit from the shower water; then, for the rest of the day the soap just sits there dissolving in a puddle of water?

And how about slippery, too, you soapmakers? You make it slippery on purpose so we'll drop it in the water, don't you? Huh?

JEANS

ALL blue jeans were ever meant to be were comfortable pants to work in or hang around the house in, Saturday morning. What in the world has happened to blue jeans?

Do we really have to go to Paris to get a pair of blue denim pants designed—two legs, a fly and some belt loops? Who is this Sergio Valente, anyway, and what's he done with pants that's so different?

I don't understand it. Everywhere you go these days, you're faced with the rear end of some pretty model posing in some unlikely position, trying to sell you blue jeans. They're on the backs of the buses everywhere . . . although I shouldn't think anyone who could pay for Jou Jou jeans would *take* a bus.

The ads stare down at you from billboards all over town. He loves her pants. She loves his pants. There's an awful lot of panting going on in these jean ads.

How come they wear so much below the waist and so little above it in some of the ads? I should think they'd get cold.

Oh, I think I know *why* they don't wear much. It's because one pair of blue jeans looks so much like the next pair of blue jeans that the designer's trying to take our eyes off the pants by attracting us to look elsewhere.

Now even the old-time jean makers like Levi and Wrangler have put fly fronts on women's pants and they're going for the designer market, too. To hear the women talk—often upside down —in the television commercials, you'd think all they want in the *whole world* is a new pair of pants.

I don't care how the pants look upside down. What I want to know is: How do they look after they've been in a heap on the floor all night?

Most designers put their names on the back of the jeans somewhere. Gloria Vanderbilt or Calvin Klein are status symbols pinned to your tail. Frankly, I wouldn't want Gloria's name on my tail, and I'm surprised she'd want it there either.

There's no doubt all this advertising has sold a lot of blue jeans. You see them on the street everywhere. They've taken over from khaki and corduroy. Some blue jeans aren't even blue anymore. But if you look at the people wearing them in the streets, one problem is apparent: most Americans simply do not have the designers' ideal derrière. If all the women in America were built like jean models, it would be different. But the promises of the advertising greatly exceed the fact of the average American posterior.

Just an opinion.

WARRANTIES

Wに呼 do you do with all the owner's manuals, warranties and pieces of paper that come in the box when you buy something new? I never know what to do with them.

I bought a new blender last week and there were eight separate things to read in there. I'm having a good time opening my new toy and the first thing I get is a warning: "stop!" They don't want me to hurt myself. "To avoid injury," it says, "see your recipe book for assembly instructions."

Well, in the first place, I didn't know I had to put the thing together myself, and in the second place, why would they put the assembly instructions in the *recipe* book?

"Place stamp here!" That's something I'm suppose to mail back to them if something is missing. Why didn't *they* make sure nothing is missing? If I have to put something together myself, I *always* think something's missing.

Here's the important one: "Owner's registration card." They want your name, address, date of birth, color of eyes, where you bought it, why you bought it and how you paid for it. It's as if they thought you *stole* it.

"IMPORTANT DO NOT DESTROY!" See, that's why I don't dare throw any of this out . . . they tell me not to.

I dug up all the guarantees I found in drawers around the house. I've got more old warranty cards than drawers to put them in. Let's face it, though, anything that's apt to happen to an appliance like a blender isn't covered by the warranty anyway, so I never send them in. If it breaks, I'll buy a new one. That's the American way.

"Congratulations, you are now the proud owner of a new GE automatic slicer. With care it will give many years of faithful

LIMITED WARRANTY

LIMITED WARRANTY

LIMITED WARRANTY

service." They all say the same things. It doesn't matter whether you buy a radio, a power tool or a new refrigerator. You know:

"Read instructions carefully."

"Do not immerse in water."

"Keep out of the reach of children."

"Wash occasionally in a mild solution of soap and warm water."

I've got one for an automatic dryer. We threw the dryer away nine years ago, but I'm still holding on to the warranty and the owner's manual.

"Your new drill is an outstanding value, combining quality with versatility." They keep selling you on these things even after they've got your money. "Made from the finest materials available."

They usually promise these things won't break, too, but I notice they always include a list of places where you can get them fixed. Montana, North Dakota . . . there's never a place near me.

"If this item has to be returned, mail it back in its original container." They're kidding. They expect us to save all that stuff too? I'd have to take it all back to Japan to find someone who could put it back in the package it came in.

And one last bit of reading matter: "Batteries not included."

DIRECTIONS

Do you find it hard to follow directions?

I was thinking of installing one of those automatic garage-door openers over the weekend. The directions say, "Make certain the garage door is square and straight and that the garage floor is level." Directions always read like that.

Is everything in your house straight, square and level? If my house was straight, square and level, I would never have to fix anything. What we all need are directions that tell us what to do when everything is crooked, off-center and all screwed up.

You buy a can of paint. You get ready to go to work. The paint seems a little thick, so you read the directions between the drips running down the side of the can. It says, "Make certain the surface is absolutely free of dirt, dust, grease or rust."

If the surface was perfect, would I be painting it?

The recipe in the newspaper gives you directions. They say, "Have your butcher prepare three six-ounce pheasants."

What butcher? All I ever see is a lot of packaged meat in the refrigerator counter, with the fat and the bones hidden on the downside. I don't have a butcher any more than I have a straight, square and level house.

You call the airlines. Ticket-seller takes the information and then gives you directions. Says, "Be at the airport to pick up your ticket at least an hour before flight time."

Well, if I have to be out at the airport an hour in advance, I might as well take the *bus* from downtown to where I'm going.

Then I like the directions we get from those consumer-affairs people about how to handle these problems. "If you want to get your car repaired," they tell you, "get at least three estimates in writing."

Have you ever taken your car to a garage without knowing what's wrong with it and demanded a written estimate from the mechanic on how much he'll charge to fix it?

If the pain persists, see your doctor.

CATALOGS

Do you read the catalogs the stores send to your home?
The women's catalogs are the best. I love how natural-looking the models are. Just plain folks, aren't they? They could be the girl next door, right? Miss Average American Woman.

They put the models in such everyday settings, too. They're always perching them on rocks somewhere. It's something you see all the time, isn't it: three women in the back of a covered wagon in decorator-designed underwear?

"The mark of Halston is graceful simplicity." The model stands there in a graceful, simple pose. You wonder how long she could hold it without dropping dead.

I like the writing, too. Women's clothes are always "versatile." They do "double duty." A pair of tweed knickers can be turned upside down and made into a downy-soft wraparound for pool-side, according to the advertisements. An evening gown converts into a sleeping bag or a poncho or maybe a mountain-climbing ensemble.

"Eggplant polyester": this is a color? They never use the names of any real colors in these women's catalogs. They never use red, for instance. Everything's either claret or burgundy. They're always inventing new names for colors: "cranberry," "nutmeg," "sea foam," "celery," "cinnamon," "taupe"—whatever taupe is—"stone," "brick." You know: fine, but what color is it?

"Hugs the body." I don't know about you but I don't want clothes hugging my body. I like to leave some doubt about where my clothes end and my body begins.

The men in these catalogs all look a lot like me, I think. They're handsome, young, rugged, about 150 pounds and never a hair out of place. I relate to these guys; this is what we look like hanging

around the house watching television in a velvet lounge ensemble. Just perfect. Even if we're wearing overalls, we look as though we've just been dusted.

You notice the male models in the pictures usually only put four fingers in their pockets, too. They leave their thumbs out. I don't know what that does for them.

I like the gadget catalogs, too. They always have just what you need . . . cordless electric pepper mills, things like that. Whatever it is, you just set it and forget it. "No more muss . . . no more fuss."

And I like the folksy catalogs. They often have the picture of the company's president and founder in them.

"Our president has searched the world over to bring you this rugged, three-speed, reversible, glen-plaid eggbeater. Never needs oiling."

I love looking through all these catalogs. And just one more thing: "Please allow six to eight weeks for delivery."

SIZES

IT SEEMS to me we're mixed up about the way we designate the size of things.

Look at the boxes of soap flakes, for example. Which size would you think was bigger: the jumbo, the giant, or the king size? The king size looks bigger, but it turns out that the jumbo box weighs nine pounds, and the king size only five pounds. The giant box weighs two pounds.

Eggs: a jumbo egg is large, extra large is regular, large is a small egg and medium you need two.

This all comes to mind now because it's Christmas and some of us are trying to buy clothes for our friends as presents. Clothes sizes are the worst mess of all. I wear a size 8½ shoe but I wear a size 11 sock. Does this make any sense? On the same foot?

Why does every piece of clothing have a different size scale? Why do I wear a size 7½ hat but a size 16½ shirt collar? Doesn't that sound as though I could put my shirt on over my hat with my collar buttoned? Why is the average suit size for a man a 40 and the average dress size for a woman a 12? We're not *that* much bigger.

Every year I go into a store wanting to buy a present for one of my daughters. I know what she looks like but I don't see her every day anymore. The clerk says, "How big is she?"

I say, "Well, you know, about—well, you know, not very big."

"Is she my size?"

"Yeah, she's about your size, but not quite so—you know."

Well, the clerk doesn't know at all, of course, and I have very little chance of getting anything that fits. The average woman might wear a size 12 dress, 34 blouse, size 6 shoe, size 10 stocking and a size 7 glove. If you go to a real fancy store and want to buy something made in France, of course, that's different. A size 12 is about a 42, unless she's a junior.

Merry Christmas. You can always take it back.

MAIL

W HY IS IT we all look forward to the mail coming every day? It's as if we were always getting money or good news from someone. That's not what I get. I doubt if one out of every ten pieces of mail that comes to my house is anything I want. You know, what you'd call a real letter.

This comes to mind now because I just got the darnedest box of mail you ever saw. Some woman in New Jersey—her name is Alice—saved up all the mail she got last year asking for money and sent it to me.

How can I ever thank you enough, Alice? Alice didn't even open most of it. I've never met her, but you can tell a lot about her from the mail she's gotten: the Salvation Army, Boy Scouts of America, UNICEF, National Indian Youth Council. Alice is in favor of protecting the environment, too. You can tell that. She likes animals. All good groups, but why do they gang up on this poor woman? She told me in a letter that she gave to just one of these environmental groups and that one passed her name along to all the others.

Some of them realize you're going to throw their letter away without reading it, so they try to get your attention on the envelope: *"Please return the enclosed questionnaire within 10 days."* Under threat of death, presumably!

"LAST CHANCE!" one says. If there's one thing you can be sure of, it's that when an envelope comes saying last chance on it, they'll give you another chance later.

Here's one trick: if you want to know who gives your name away or sells it to someone else, the thing to do is to give yourself a fake middle initial when you send money to any organization; then every time a letter comes addressed that way, you'll know where it came from.

The thing that bothers me most, I suppose, is that if you give twenty-five dollars to a school or a college or some good cause, they'll turn around and spend fifty dollars trying to get you to give more. I see that Alice has given to the United Negro College Fund. I gave twenty-five dollars to the NAACP years ago, and I'll bet the NAACP and the United Negro College Fund have spent a hundred dollars in stamps trying to get more from me since then.

The postal service says that they handle 97 billion pieces of mail a year but that only 20 percent of that is mail from one citizen to another. The commercial mail business says it would cost us all a lot more if it wasn't for them.

I think I'm willing to pay.

Mr. Andy Rooney
60 Minutes
524
SAN DIEGO CA
PM
24 MAR
1981
15c
US Postage
B
SANTA ANA, CA 92725
30 MAR
1981
Mr. Andy Rooney
"60 Minutes"
524 W. 57th St. 10019
New York, N.Y.
. Andy Roo
o 60 Minut
4 West 57t
New York, N
Randy Collins
1587 Charles Ct.
Arcata, Ca. 95521
Mr. Andy Rooney
c/o 60 Minutes
524 W. 57th St.
N.Y. 10019
USA 2c

LETTERS

Eᴠᴇʀʏ night when I get home, there's a little pile of mail waiting for me. I used to think I'd find something wonderful in the pile, but I never do.

I got thinking about the kind of letters I wish I'd receive and never do. I had to write these myself.

> Dear Classmate:
>
> Just a note to tell you there won't be any annual fund-raising drive this year. Because of the warm winter, the University's fuel bill was less than expected and, by firing some of the dead wood on the faculty, they've been able to stay way under budget and won't need any money.
>
> Sincerely,
> Ham Davis, Class Secretary

Here's one from a restaurant I ate in the other night.

> Dear Mr. Rooney:
>
> In checking your bill, we noticed that the total was $57.30 for four people, not the $63.40 we charged you. Our check for $6.10 is enclosed.

This is one I never got from the New York City Police Department.

> Dear Sir or Madame:
>
> Please ignore the parking ticket which was placed on the windshield of your vehicle in error. We regret any inconvenience this may have caused you.

Here's one I'd like to get from an insurance company.

> Dear Rooney:
>
> You can drop dead as far as the Pilgrim Fathers Life Insurance Company is concerned. We've tried to sell you a

policy for the past twenty years. You've never answered one request for information about yourself yet. This is the last letter you'll ever get from us, fella!

Well, I sincerely hope so, Pilgrim Fathers.

And here's a letter I'd like to get from a contractor working on my house.

> Dear Mr. Rooney:
>
> Enclosed is the bill for the addition to your home. Our estimate for the job was $6,700, but because of problems we thought we'd have that we didn't run into, we were able to complete it for only $5,100.
>
> > Martin Construction Company

And after a year of getting letters like those, here's a little note I'd like to find in my mailbox just before Christmas, with a ten-dollar bill attached to it.

> Dear Mr. Rooney:
>
> It's been such a pleasure serving you this year that I want you to accept this little token of my appreciation.
>
> > Signed,
> > Your mailman

Nice?

MOST NEEDED

W HAT I've done here is make a list of The Most Needed
Things in America.
—To start with, we need a telephone that lets you know who's
calling before you answer it. I always think it's going to be someone wonderful and it almost never is.
—We need a car that gets fifty miles to a gallon, won't rust out
after two winters with salt on the roads and can't go faster than
the speed limit. I approve of the 55-mile limit but I often drive
faster than that. I shouldn't . . . and I wouldn't if I couldn't.
—America needs a new kind of politician. We need a Presidential
candidate who is smart enough not to want such a terrible job.
—We need an umbrella that doesn't have a handle up the middle,
right where you want to stand when it's raining.
—We need a prison in which to put our worst criminals. It should
be secure enough so they'd never get out, but comfortable
enough for them so the rest of us wouldn't feel terrible about
keeping them in it for the rest of their lives. It should be a self-
supporting community.
—I hate to suggest another public agency, but we need one whose
only job would be to keep a brief record of each of our lives.
When any one of us dies, that record will be filed away permanently. Anyone living in the distant future will be able to look
us up and find out a little about us. We've lost too many people.
—I call on Congress to pass two laws. The first would decree that
henceforth there would be no overlapping of professional sports.
Baseball, being a spring-and-summer sport, would have to end
before football, a fall sport, began.
—The second law would concern Congress itself. In the future,
we'd be able to write to Congressmen free of charge. It would
cost *them* money to write to us.

—The next item concerns television. We need a television set that turns off automatically when a show gets bad enough. If they can make fire alarms that smell smoke, I don't see why a device can't be made that would detect a bad television show.

—The last thing we need is some new national emergencies. I think we're all sick and tired of oil and inflation.

Those are some of the things we need in America.

RATINGS

I RATE things one to ten.
One to ten ought to be our standard for rating everything. We need just one system and that's the best one.

Most schools grade students' work as A, B, C, D or F . . . five grades. Teachers aren't satisfied with five, so they start giving C pluses and D minuses. With a plus and a minus for five grades, that gives you fifteen. It's too many. Fifteen is for people who can't make up their minds how to rate something.

Perhaps you ask, "What are some of the things *you* rate from one to ten?" Well, I'll tell you some.
· *Charlie's Angels,* I give a three.
· Wonder Bread, one.
· Zbigniew Brzezinski, six.
· Scotch Tape, seven.
· Nixon's book, three.
· Howard Johnson's peppermint ice cream, nine.
· Golden retrievers, ten.
· Kleenex, eight.
· Schenectady, New York, five.
· General Eisenhower, ten.
· President Eisenhower, four.
· Vladimir Horowitz, ten.
· Rochelle Hudson, four.
· MacNeil/Lehrer, nine.
· Two-dollar bills, three.
· Howard Cosell, one.

It's fun to do. You can sit around nights and make a game of it, making a list of things and rating them . . . *Time* magazine . . . Disneyland . . . the post office . . . California . . . airline food . . . *Star Wars.* I mean, the list is endless.

35

If we all used the one-to-ten system of grading everything in our lives, it would make decisions quicker and easier.

Prejudice has gotten a bad name recently but prejudice is a great help to us in our lives. If we know what we think and where we rate things, we don't have to waste a lot of time thinking them through again. I rate liver one. I *know* I dislike liver and I don't ever want to try another piece.

The way to end a cute piece like this would be for me to give it a rating from one to ten. I rate television people who put endings like that on pieces like this, two.

ADVERTISING

My grandfather told me when I was a small boy that if a product was any good, they shouldn't have to advertise it.

I believed my grandfather at the time, but then years later my mother said that when *she* was a little girl he had told her that they'd never be able to build an automobile that would go up a hill. So I never knew whether to believe my grandfather or not.

Like so many things, I've really never made up my mind about advertising. I know all the arguments for it and against it, but the one thing I'm sure of is that there ought to be some sanctuaries, some places we're safe from being advertised at. There ought to be some open space left in the world without any advertising on it, some pieces of paper, some painted surfaces that aren't covered with entreaties for us to buy something.

Advertising doesn't belong on license plates, for instance. Of the fifty states, twenty-seven of them have slogans trying to sell themselves to the rest of us. It's offensive and wrong. The license plate has an important function and it's a cheap trick to tack something else on it. Most of the legends the states put on aren't true anyway.

Rhode Island, for instance, says it's the "Ocean State." There are fifteen states with more ocean than Rhode Island has. If they want to say something on their plate, why don't they explain why they call Rhode an island when it isn't one?

Florida says it's the "Sunshine State." I like Florida, but why don't they also say that Miami has more rain than any city in the whole United States except for Mobile, Alabama?

North Carolina says it's "First in Freedom." It doesn't say anywhere on the license plate who they think is *second* in freedom. South Carolina? Michigan?

37

Connecticut says it's the "Constitution State." I called the license bureau in Connecticut and no one there could tell me why they call it the Constitution State. Connecticut is not the Constitution state, of course. *Pennsylvania* is the Constitution state. And Pennsylvania calls itself the "Keystone State." Does anyone really care?

Maine says it's "Vacationland." How would you like to drive a garbage truck for eight hours in Augusta with a sign hanging on the back that says "Vacationland"?

New Hampshire plates carry the pretentious legend "Live Free or Die." Some religious organization that apparently wasn't willing to die if they couldn't be free objected and taped over those words on all their license plates. The state said this was illegal and the case went to the Supreme Court. The Court ruled that the religious order did have the right to block out those words. New Hampshire would have saved us all a lot of time and money if they'd never put them on in the first place.

New Mexico calls itself "Land of Enchantment." This is not the kind of slogan that gets the work of the world done.

Hawaii says it's the "Aloha State." Hawaii ought to get over its palm-tree mentality and removing "Aloha" from its plates would be a good start. What sensible state would want to conjure up a picture of dancing girls draping flower ropes over the necks of visitors every time anyone thought about it?

Wisconsin "America's Dairyland"? Never mind that, Wisconsin, if you're dairyland why don't you tell us on your license plates what ever happened to heavy cream? That's the kind of stuff we'd like to read about when we're driving along behind a car from your state.

And then Idaho. How would you like to work hard, save your money and decide, when the kids were educated and the house paid for, to buy yourself a Mercedes-Benz. You plunk down your $28,000, the dealer screws on the license plate and there you are with your dream car, you drive away, and affixed to the bumper is the sign that says "Famous Potatoes."

"If a state is any good," I imagine my grandfather would have said, "it shouldn't have to advertise."

License-plate advertising is a small part of what we're faced with when we're driving. On the highways, trucks are turned into rolling billboards. The companies that own them look on it as easy advertising, too cheap to pass up. On major highways the commercials come along more often than on a late-night television movie.

On city streets, the billboards on Coca-Cola and Pepsi trucks are often double-parked while the driver makes deliveries. In most cities now, taxis and buses carry advertising. When you're paying a buck and a half a mile, you shouldn't have to carry a sign pushing cigarettes.

In California there's a company called Beetleboards. What Beetleboards will do for you is paint your Volkswagen, apply a commercial motif from a sponsor who is paying them and pay you twenty dollars a month to drive around in it.

And if you can understand businesses advertising their products on our roads, how do you account for the private citizens who use the back end of their cars to tell us about themselves or about some private campaign of theirs? A typical car or van in a parking lot outside a tourist attraction in Washington, D.C., will announce, through the decals attached to it somewhere, that the owner is insured by Allstate, boosts the Northern Virginia Ramparts—a team of some sort, I guess—is against forest fires because he has a little Smokey the Bear stuck to his car, gives to the International Convention of Police Chiefs and believes in God because his bumper sticker tells us so.

If someone has to take pride in having people know what insurance company gets his money, he's in trouble for things to be proud of.

A third of the cars on the road have reading matter stuck to them somewhere trying to sell the rest of us a place, an opinion or a way of life. Sometimes it looks as though half the cars in the United States have been to a roadside stand in South Carolina called South of the Border, and for some reason the entrepreneurs who have made tourist attractions out of caves love to slap "Visit Secret Caverns" on visitors' bumpers.

One of the most incredible commercial coups of the century has been pulled off by the designers who have conned women into thinking it's chic to wear a piece of apparel on which the maker's name is imprinted as part of the design.

The French luggage maker Louis Vuitton may have started the trend when he made the brown LV the only design on his product, but the women's fashion designers have taken it over. Bill Blass makes towels with his name all over them. Why would anyone want to take a shower and buff themselves dry on a piece of cloth bearing Bill Blass's name? Why would a woman go around with the name "Bloomies" on the seat of her underpants? Is there something I don't understand here?

Why would I or anyone else want to lay me down to sleep with my head on a pillowcase embossed with the signature of Yves Saint Laurent?

The first time I remember seeing a designer's name on something, the name was Pucci. It seemed amusing enough but now they're all doing it. Halston, Calvin Klein and Diane Von Furstenberg must all be wonderfully famous and talented, but if I buy anything of theirs I'd prefer to have it anonymous. If I got a scarf with Diane Von Furstenberg's name on it, which is unlikely, my first inclination would be to send it out to the cleaners to have them try to get it out.

The advertisers are coming at us from all directions all the time. If we were deer, a closed season would be declared on us to protect an endangered species. It just seems wrong to me that we're spending more time and money trying to sell some things than we are making them in the first pace. I'm an all-American consumer but there are just certain times and places I don't want to be sold anything.

MR. ROONEY
GOES TO DINNER*

Y OU SEE so many things that all of us have done badly that life can be depressing unless you look for some of the things we've done well. And there are some.

Take something as basic as eating, for example.

It's absolutely necessary that we eat to survive, but we could do that by stuffing food in our mouths with our hands, so we can congratulate ourselves for having turned eating into a civilized and often very pleasant little ceremony called either breakfast, lunch or dinner.

All of us enjoy the ceremony and one of the special treats we give ourselves once in a while is eating out in a restaurant.

There are 400,000 restaurants in the United States and if you ate three meals a day in restaurants for seventy years, you could only eat in 76,000 of them.

Obviously I haven't gone to all 400,000 restaurants in the United States to make this report. Chances are I didn't go to the one you like best or least. I didn't even go to the one *I* like best.

My job may seem good to some of you . . . but I've got a tough boss. Several months ago he gave me an order. "Travel anywhere you want in the United States," he told me. "Eat in a lot of good restaurants on the company . . . and report back to me."

I took money, credit cards and a lot of bad advice from friends and set out across the country.

* Broadcast April 20, 1976.

* * *

People argue about where the best restaurants are in the United States.

Boston, San Francisco and New Orleans have always had good places. Florida has had some for a long time. New York has a hundred that would be the best in town anywhere else. But there have been some changes for the better in places that didn't used to have *any* good restaurants.

The South is getting over Southern cooking, for instance. Places like Cincinnati, Kansas City, Pittsburgh, even South Bend, Indiana, have excellent restaurants. You can get a gourmet meal in Houston, Texas, or Phoenix, Arizona.

There are a few places that puzzle me, though. For instance, I don't suppose there's a place in the whole world that grows as much good food as Iowa does. They brag about it. And yet a gourmet tour of Iowa would be a nonstop trip.

The biggest trend is a leveling out that has taken place. It's harder to find that great little undiscovered place in a small town, but more often than before you can find a restaurant that serves at least

acceptable food. The Rotary Club usually meets there.

There's more dependable mediocrity than there used to be. It isn't going to be very good, but it isn't going to be very bad either. And because most of it's frozen, it's going to be the same in Maine as it is in Oklahoma.

What's happened to all the good and bad little independent restaurants, of course, is all the big chains and the fast-food places. Many independents have been driven out of business.

There are the big steak chains, for instance. They often serve beef treated with tenderizer and are called something like the Beef and Bourbon or the Steak and Stein. They and the fast-food places bring in billions of dollars a year. Most are owned by big corporations with other interests: Pillsbury owns Burger King, for example.

Hamburgers are the big seller, a lot more American than Mom's apple pie now because Mom isn't baking pies much these days. The chicken places have come up fast in the last ten years and there are pizza parlors everywhere. You don't have to go to Mexico to get a taco.

The biggest and most successful fast-food operation is, obviously, McDonald's. There are 3,232 of them—and counting. They've driven thousands of individually owned diners and cafés out of business. The drive-ins have been victims in a lot of areas.

A typical meal in McDonald's costs about $1.75. The hamburger is good ground meat, the French fries are excellent and the shake is an imitation milkshake made with thickeners to give the impression it's made with ice cream—which it isn't.

McDonald's restaurants are probably a reflection of our national character. They're fast . . . they're efficient . . . they make money and they're clean. If they're loud and crowded and if the food is wastefully wrapped, packaged, boxed and bagged . . . let's face it, Americans, that's us.

There's nothing really distinctive about American cooking. "American cooking" isn't even a phrase like "French cooking." That accounts for why our best restaurants serve someone else's native dishes.

Italian restaurants are most popular. Thirty-six percent of all Americans who eat out eat in Italian restaurants at one time or another. Thirty-five percent, according to the National Restaurant Association, eat in Chinese restaurants. French restaurants are most popular with people who make more than $25,000 a year.

But we have everything. In the last ten years there's been a population explosion of Japanese restaurants. They serve steak, shrimp or chicken along with bean sprouts and onions—and it's all cooked right there in front of you. The man doing the cooking is part chef . . . part show biz . . . and part Kamikaze pilot.

One of the good things about these places is they never serve you a piece of anything you can't eat . . . no bones, no fat. I've never been to Japan. For all I know, they don't eat like this over there. Someone told me there's a Benihana of New York in Tokyo.

Part of the fun of eating out is doing something different. Japanese is different. How many times in the last few weeks have you come home from work to find your husband fixing sukiyaki for you?

The other kind of Japanese restaurant is the sushi bar. Five years ago you couldn't have told me I'd ever eat a piece of raw fish. Now I'm addicted to sushi. Sushi is carefully boned and carefully sliced raw fish . . . tuna . . . squid . . . mackerel . . . eel . . . octopus . . . served with cold rice wrapped in seaweed. Sounds good, doesn't it? It's always attractively served on a board. It looks like a Japanese painting.

Scandinavian smorgasbord places are popular, too: Americans like the idea of helping themselves to all they want. It's as if they were getting something free.

I ate in one called the Copenhagen one day—with a friend. He's a smorgasbord expert.

WALTER CRONKITE:
This is a Danish something.

ROONEY:
Lingonberries.

CRONKITE:
That's right. That's what it is. That's the word I was groping . . .

ROONEY:
You were grasping for.

CRONKITE:
And they're marvelous.

ROONEY:
What is this pink stuff?

CRONKITE:
That pink stuff is some very interesting . . . pink stuff there. I think it's beets. I believe. I don't know. I'm not sure what that is. I've never taken it. It looks repulsive, to tell you the truth. How about shrimp? Beautiful shrimp?

ROONEY:

Yeah, I'll have a shrimp. I notice they leave the shells on them, though. I figure that's to make it hard so you don't take too many.

CRONKITE:

Any restaurant you go to where the dessert tray is brought in like this, every table the reaction is the same. People recoil. They're obviously making the statement to their friends. "I . . . I shouldn't. Oh, no, I shouldn't. Take that away. I don't want to even look at that."

ROONEY:

"But maybe I'll just have a little bit."

CRONKITE:

But then they come back.

WAITRESS:

And these are special ones over here. They're made of almond paste.

ROONEY:

I really shouldn't.

CRONKITE:

No, I shouldn't either . . . so have one.

ROONEY:

Oh, thank you.

Like everything else, there are trends in the restaurant business —fashions in what a restaurant looks like. Years ago, many good restaurants had those white tile floors with lots of mirrors around and waiters who worked there for a hundred years wearing white aprons that came to their ankles.

In the past twenty years restaurants have gotten very conscious. Too conscious, probably. In the sixties, most new restaurants with any pretensions at all looked like this. As you came in, there was usually a coat of arms in the lobby. The dominant color was red, the lights were low and there was often a candle on the table held in one of those small bowls covered with white netting.

The menu was predictable . . . steak, shrimp, chicken, filet of sole and South African lobster tail . . . meaning they didn't really have a chef.

They were pleasant enough and there are still a lot of them

around—but there's a new trend. In the trade it's called "the theme restaurant." Eating in one, according to the ads, is an adventure.

If you want to start a theme restaurant, you can go to J.B.I. Industries in Compton, California. They can make the inside of your place look like anything from a submarine to a men's locker room.

Carolyn Steinbach is production manager.

ROONEY:

How many of these do you do a year? How many restaurants do you design, roughly? Would you guess?

STEINBACH:

Well, we did something like three hundred and fifty last year.

ROONEY:

Could you show some of them to us?

STEINBACH:

Certainly.

ROONEY:

A pirate ship.

STEINBACH:

A pirate ship.

ROONEY:

Hey, what would it cost somebody to come up with a pirate ship in a restaurant like that?

STEINBACH:

Our pirate ship runs somewhere around six thousand dollars.

ROONEY:

Gosh, I'll be darned.

STEINBACH:

This is our tin goose . . . seating on both wings, seating behind the engine and then down the center of the—

ROONEY:

The kids get a kick out of this?

STEINBACH:

Right. They really relate well to something like this.

Out back, it looked like Santa Claus's workshop. We talked to president Jay Buchbinder.

ROONEY:

Well, now, wouldn't something like that make kids stay longer in a restaurant so the restaurant would have a smaller turnover?

I mean, is that a factor?

BUCHBINDER:

Well, it might even speed up the process of eating, because if you go in with little children, the children will want to play on the trains, so they might eat faster and then the parents will want to leave more quickly.

We've even tried to get design involved in the rest-room areas where people might say, "Well, gee, they have nice clean rest rooms. We'll stop there because the rest rooms are nice and we'll also buy our food." So everything goes as a total package situation.

ROONEY:

You don't make any little engines for the rest rooms or anything?

BUCHBINDER:

There can be little décors in the rest-room areas, little train plaques or little car plaques. So when you go into a fast-food operation, it's like going into a finer restaurant now. They're giving you every courtesy that you might have in a better restaurant.

Workmen were finishing a new plastic replica of an old airplane to ship to a McDonald's opening in Glen Ellyn, Illinois. We were curious about how a hamburger would taste eaten in a plastic airplane, so a few weeks later, after it had been installed, we went to Glen Ellyn.

ROONEY (to cashier):

Same price whether I eat it here or in the airplane?

CASHIER:

Yes.

ROONEY:

I guess I'll eat it in the airplane.

It seems as though everywhere you go they're trying to take your mind off the food. It's got so it's almost as though they were embarrassed to look like a restaurant.

The most successful theme chain is Victoria Station. Just five years ago three young Cornell Hotel School graduates started buying up old boxcars for a few thousand dollars each. Now they own 250 of them and they're using them in 46 restaurants around the country. In five years, sales went from nothing to $47 million.

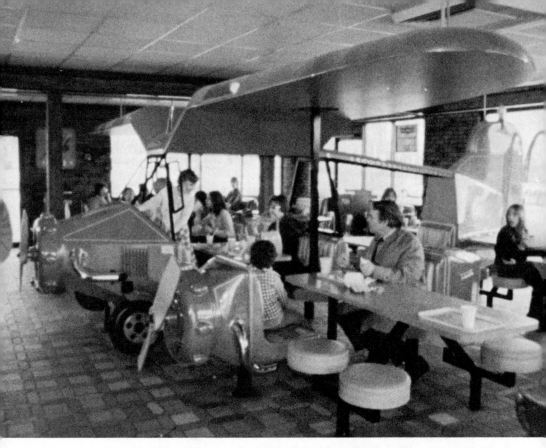

The difference between this and the all-American diner is that Victoria Station serves mostly roast beef and steak. And, of course, for cooking steak and roast beef you don't need a French chef; you need a smart American kid who can cook meat.

They also have a help-yourself salad bar. They've become very popular in American restaurants too. You come along and just help yourself to as much of everything as you want. I suspect that people might take a little more lettuce than they'd get if the waiter gave it to them. On the other hand, lettuce is a lot cheaper than help. And it sure saves on the help.

The food is pretty good at Victoria Station, but just as in most other gimmick restaurants, food takes second place.

As a person who likes to eat, I am just vaguely worried about the food business being taken over by entrepreneurs rather than by restaurateurs but even if it isn't the gourmet restaurants that are making the money, there are still a lot of impractical optimists who keep opening what they hope will be the perfect restaurant.

* * *

I'm seated at a table at the most expensive restaurant in the United States, the Palace in New York City.

Two of us just dined here. You don't eat at the Palace; you dine. And I have the check . . . brought on a silver platter. For two people: dinner . . . $179.35.

A lot of expensive restaurants are sneaky with their checks but there's nothing sneaky about the Palace. They lay it right on the line. Two dinners, $100. Two cocktails at $5 each, $10. A bottle of wine, $25. That was the second cheapest bottle on the menu, by the way. Tax. That all comes to $145.80. Plus 23% for service. That's $33.55 for tips, for a total of $179.35.

ROONEY:

I thought maybe you could tell me what it was I had if I went over the menu.

FRANK VALENZA, owner:

The first appetizer you had was the salad de Palace, which is fresh lobster with truffles, walnut oil, artichoke bottoms and a vinaigrette dressing.

ROONEY:

I thought it was pecan oil.

VALENZA:

No.

ROONEY:

Walnut oil, aha. Well, they fooled me there. And then I had—
this is the gazpacho?

VALENZA:

Gazpacho, very thin gazpacho, made with fresh vegetables and
a little garniture on the side.

ROONEY:

Made of what?

VALENZA:

Tomato, garlic, peppers, onions, all your fresh vegetables. But
just the essence of the vegetables.

ROONEY:

Garlic seasoned with a little tomato?

VALENZA:

Yes.

ROONEY:

And . . . fish.

VALENZA:

You had the fresh filet of sole filled with a mousse of salmon
with a crayfish sauce. And then we had a little sherbet to cleanse
the palate. Then, the main course, I believe you had the . . .

ROONEY:

The rack of lamb.

VALENZA:

Rack of lamb that was roasted with fresh aromatic herbs and
naturel au jus. And for dessert, a little chocolate truffle. It's ice
cream mixed with pastry cream. It's dipped in a very rich
chocolate with little nuts and then we put it in the freezer.

ROONEY:

Do you get people in here ever who are surprised at the cost?

VALENZA:

Once in a while. Saturday night a lady came by and asked the
price and I told her and she said, "I'm coming back with a boyfriend. I'm going to get a rich boyfriend to take me in." They
came down and made a reservation. They sat down. The gentleman opened the menu and there was the price and he jumped up.

He said, "Well, I just ate dinner and I thought this was just an after-theater snack." And we said, "Thank you, maybe another day." And the lady winked at me and she said, "Well, we'll try again."

Rooney (to camera):

The surprising thing about the Palace is how good it is. The food is excellent. As a matter of fact, I plan to come over here real often . . . and bring the kids.

Two of the best lunches I ever had, I ate standing up . . . and within an hour of each other. Both places serve the same thing, oysters. Felix's is on Iberville Street in New Orleans and the Acme Oyster House is right across from it.

Every restaurant has its own way of doing things and if you don't know what it is, it's easy to look dumb the first time you go in a place.

Rooney:

What is the difference between the ones that are three dollars a dozen and the ones that are two-seventy-five?

Man (cutting oysters open):

. . . table.

Rooney:

Oh, the table. If I eat them at the table, they're more? Are some of them harder to open than others?

Man:

Some of them are hard, some of them's easy.

Rooney:

But they're alive until you open them, is that right?

Man:

Yes, sir.

Rooney:

You mean I just ate a dozen live oysters?

It's always hard to find a good place to eat when you're driving in an unfamiliar part of the country, particularly if there are three or four people in the car who don't agree where you're going to eat. You get to one place and it looks fair but you decide to pass

it up. You drive ten miles and you wish you'd stopped there, usually.

The trouble with most country inns is the same thing that's wrong with so many restaurants. They're fake, an imitation of the real thing.

The food in most country inns now comes from the city . . . frozen.

Being good at picking a place to eat is a matter of experience . . . prejudice acquired over years of eating out. Deciding which restaurant *not* to go to is important. . . . There are little things you look for.

I have as many as fifty little reasons for steering clear of certain places. Just for example:

· I am very suspicious of a restaurant that says it is Polynesian and has flaming torches outside.
· If a Chinese restaurant serves chop suey and chow mein, I assume that it isn't very good . . . or very Chinese.
· Cute names on restaurants, such as Dew Drop Inn, suggest that the owners aren't very serious about their food. Watch out for places named after a new movie.

- Places that advertise "Home Cooking" don't interest me. If I want home cooking, I'll eat home.
- And I'm put off if there's a sign in the window saying "OPEN." Restaurants with OPEN signs usually leave them there even when they're closed.
- I'm not attracted to an establishment that puts more emphasis on liquor than on food.
- Usually I avoid a restaurant located in a shopping center.
- And if a restaurant is connected with a bowling alley, it isn't where I'm going to spend my money for food.
- I don't eat where there's music either. Sometimes two things that are great by themselves are ruined when mixed. Food and entertainment are best kept apart.
- It's hard enough to get waited on in a restaurant that thinks it has enough help without going to one with a sign in the window advertising for waiters.
- And when I stay in a hotel or a motel, I never eat in the restaurant attached to it unless it's snowing.

There are just as many things that attract me to a restaurant:

- I'm a sucker for a place bearing the first name of the owner. If it's called "Joe's," I go in.
- I'm attracted to a restaurant that has a menu written with chalk on a slate.
- And to me, a real sign of class is a restaurant that refuses to accept credit cards.

If you've always thought of a menu as just a list of the food a restaurant serves, you're wrong. Menus are a big business by themselves and a lot of restaurants spend a fortune making theirs look good.

We went down to a studio one day when they were filming a new cover for a Howard Johnson menu. The food was fixed in a kitchen near the studio. They try to be honest about it . . . but nothing ever looks *smaller* in the picture on the menu. For instance, they weigh the meat all right, but then they barely cook it so it doesn't shrink.

In the course of doing this report, we've looked through and collected several hundred menus. You can tell a lot about a restaurant from a quick look at its menu . . . even from the outside of it. For instance, if there's a tassel on the menu, you can add a couple of dollars per person.

Here's the Captain's Seafood Platter. The trouble with a restaurant called the Captain's Seafood Platter in Kansas City is that all the fish comes frozen, and by the time it's cooked in hot fat, you can't tell the oysters from the French fries.

The Lion's Paw . . . "Homemade Cheesecake." You always wonder whose home they mean it was made in.

Don Neal's Mr. T-Bone. He's a musician, I guess. This is the kind of a menu that's so cute you can hardly tell what they have to eat. "Rhapsody of Beef" . . . Roast Top Sirloin. "Symphony of the Deep" . . . Baked Lake Superior Whitefish. "Taste Buds in Concert" . . . Breast of Chicken Almondine.

Here's a place called the Bali Hai, a Polynesian restaurant. The "Pu-Pu Platter," they have. "Shrimp Pago Pago." I never know about the drinks in a place like this. Here's one called "Scorpion Bowl." I hate drinking from a glass with a naked girl on it.

This is a Spanish restaurant, La Corrida. Picture of a bullfight. They've just killed the bull, I guess.

I'm not a vegetarian, but I hate being reminded of the animals I'm eating. I'll eat almost anything, too, but there are a few things I'm narrow-minded about. Rabbit I don't eat, tripe, calves' brains, snails. I know I'm wrong, but I just don't eat them.

Karson's Inn in Historic Canton. This is one of those menus that tell you more about a town than you want to know. "Welcome to Karson's Inn in Historic Canton. . . ." It goes on and tells you all about how interesting Canton is.

Here's one from Troggio's in New Castle, Pennsylvania. This one tells you about how interesting New Castle is.

This is the Lamplighter, a family restaurant. It's one of those where they tell you about the family. "For over 50 years the Ferri Family has enjoyed serving the finest food to nice people like you. . . ." They like me.

This is another one: the Presuttis'. Mama and Poppa Presutti are on the cover there. And, yep, they tell you about the Presuttis here. "In 1933, Mr. and Mrs. S. Presutti converted their home into a restaurant." It goes on. You know, fine, but what have they got to eat?

This is something called the Shalako. It's one of those menus with a lot of writing in it. I always figure if I wanted to read, I'd

go to a library. It says "The Shalako is the most important religious ceremony performed by the Zuñi Indians." And it goes on for three pages. You can imagine a waiter standing there while you read this history of the Zuñi Indians.

Here's a place called the Parlour. I wonder where this is? Oh, there is no doubt where this is: "It is dusk in St. Paul. Sunset's fading light reflects a red ribbon on the meandering Mississippi River. The skyline is silhouetted against the blue-gray haze."

A menu.

We had a not particularly reliable survey made of menus and we have the results for you. According to the count we made, the most used words on menus were these, in order of frequency.

1. "Freshly"
2. "Tender"
3. "Mouth-Watering"
4. "Succulent"
5. "On a Bed of"
6. "Tangy"
7. "Hearty"
8. "Luscious"

9. "To Your Liking"
10. "Topped with"
11. "Savory"
12. "Tempting" and "Delicious" (Tie)
13. "Surrounded by"
14. "Golden Brown"
15. "By Our Chef"
16. "Seasoned to Perfection"
17. "Choice Morsels of"
18. "Delicately" and "Thick" (Tie)
19. "Crisp"
20. "Not Responsible for Personal Property"

"Freshly" was far and away the first.

"Savory," Number 11, was interesting. Actually, on menus where the dinner was more than $7.50, it was usually spelled with a "u." S-A-V-O-U-R-Y.

"Surrounded by." "Surrounded by" and "On a Bed of" are a lot the same, but "On a Bed of" actually beat out "Surrounded by."

"Golden Brown." Almost everything is "Golden Brown." Sometimes the lettuce is golden brown.

"By Our Chef." Even places that don't have a chef say "By Our Chef."

"Seasoned to Perfection." "Choice Morsels of." "Delicately" and "Thick" were tied for 18. Number 19 was "Crisp." And Number 20 on our list of most used words was "Not Responsible for Personal Property."

Wine menus. Last year was a very good year for wine menus.

Anyone who orders wine in a restaurant always wonders how much the same bottle would cost him in a liquor store. We thought we'd find out.

ROONEY (in liquor store):
What's the price of the Chauvenet Red Cap?
LIQUOR-STORE OWNER:
Six-ninety-nine.
ROONEY (from menu):
Chauvenet Red Cap . . . twenty dollars a bottle. This is at the restaurant called the Michaelangelo. Let's see. Liebfraumilch,

Blue Nun . . . ten dollars. (To liquor-store owner) What do you get for Blue Nun?

OWNER:

Three-eighty-nine.

ROONEY (from menu):

Mouton Cadet Rothschild, 1970 . . . twelve dollars. (To liquor-store owner) This Mouton Cadet. What do you get for that?

OWNER:

Three-ninety-nine.

ROONEY:

You don't lose any money on that, either.

OWNER:

No.

ROONEY (from menu)

Château Malijay . . . six-forty-five.

STORE OWNER:

That's a Côte du Rhône . . . one-ninety-nine.

ROONEY (from menu):

Here's a bottle of Pouilly-Fumé de la Doucette, 1971 . . . eighteen dollars. (To store owner) What do you get for that?

OWNER:

La Doucette, Pouilly-Fumé . . . We sell it for six-ninety-nine.

ROONEY (from menu):

This is a restaurant in Las Vegas. Here the Lancers Rosé is eleven dollars. (To store owner) Lancers Vin Rosé?

OWNER:

Lancers sells for four-twenty-nine.

ROONEY:

I always thought this was the kind of a wine where the bottle was worth more than the drink. I guess you wouldn't want to comment on that?

OWNER:

No. I'd rather not.

Everyone complains about wine snobs. Snobs of every kind have a bad reputation in America. No one understands that it's the snobs who set the standards of excellence in the world. There are art snobs, literary snobs, music snobs, and in every case it's the snobs who sneer at mediocrity. The gourmets are the food snobs. Without them we'd all be eating peanut-butter sandwiches.

Like the gourmets, wine snobs know what they're talking about. So if you're going to drink wine, get to know something about it. Be prepared to pay too much for a bottle of wine. Be your own wine snob . . . it's part of the fun.

A good rule of thumb is, if you can afford a wine, don't buy it.

I went to the National Restaurant Association Convention in Chicago and everywhere I wandered someone was pushing food or drink at me.

Everyone who sells anything to restaurants had an exhibit, so there were garbage cans . . . corn cookers . . . can openers . . . wall decorations . . . seating arrangements . . . and devices to keep bartenders from stealing.

Restaurants sell 20 percent of all the food eaten in the United States. They are first in the number of retail business places. In other words, there are more restaurants than any other kind of store. We did a lot of poking around at the convention and we got a frightening look at what some restaurants are going to be feeding us.

1ST EXHIBITOR:
  Well, this is a soy protein with about 60 percent protein and it goes into . . .
ROONEY:
  What does it do?
1ST EXHIBITOR:
  Well, it stretches out products like tuna salad by about 30 percent.
ROONEY:
  What do they use it in, in addition to tuna fish?
1ST EXHIBITOR:
  It goes into egg salads. It's used to extend all kinds of meats, either uncooked as meat patties or it might go into precooked entrees . . . sloppy Joes, chili con carne.
ROONEY:
  Is it any good?
1ST EXHIBITOR:
  What kind of a question is that?
ROONEY:
  Now, what is this here?

2ND EXHIBITOR:

These are our Morning Star institutional link-sausage-like flavor product.

ROONEY:

Sausage . . . like?

2ND EXHIBITOR:

Sausage-like flavor.

ROONEY:

They're artificial sausage?

2ND EXHIBITOR:

They're artificial sausage. They have no cholesterol, no animal fat.

ROONEY:

What *do* they have?

2ND EXHIBITOR:

Well, they're made out of various vegetable proteins . . . soy protein, wheat protein. We use egg albumen to hold it together.

ROONEY:

Are you a chef?

2ND EXHIBITOR:

No. I'm trained as a biochemist.

ROONEY:

Now what is this machine?

3RD EXHIBITOR:

This is a mechanical meat tenderizer.

ROONEY:

You put the meat on there?

3RD EXHIBITOR:

Put the meat on here. It'll pass through underneath the needle. The needle will come down and penetrate the meat and break down the tissue.

ROONEY:

So a restaurant could buy this and really buy less expensive meat?

3RD EXHIBITOR:

That's right.

ROONEY:

Now, I would call that orange juice canned. Not fresh.

4TH EXHIBITOR:

Fresh frozen.

ROONEY:

Fresh frozen. Right.

ROONEY (looking at ingredients):

Now, "standard chicken base." How do you pronounce that ingredient?

5TH EXHIBITOR:

It contains hydrolyzed vegetable protein.

ROONEY (reads ingredients):

"Salt, chicken fat, monosodium glutamate, dehydrated chicken, dextrose, dehydrated vegetable, spices and spice extract, bicalcium phosphate, citric acid."

5TH EXHIBITOR:

Right.

ROONEY:

That's chicken base?

5TH EXHIBITOR:

That's right.

ROONEY:

It tastes like chicken?

5TH EXHIBITOR:

Exactly. Four ounces of it tastes like an extra gallon.

ROONEY:

You put just four ounces of this hydro . . .

5TH EXHIBITOR:

And that's the basis for, in other words, if you want chicken noodle, you throw noodles in.

Rooney:

How many restaurants *don't* use anything like this?

5th Exhibitor:

Almost 100 percent of the restaurants use it. If they don't, then you're way on the other side of the . . . You can't exist today.

Rooney:

You mean without the artificial stuff?

5th Exhibitor:

It's not artificial really. You've got monosodium glutamate. You've got extracts. You've got fats. The real thing mixed with the chemical. This can feed or this can substitute or feed a thousand people per chicken, where you might have to take a hundred chickens. . . .

Rooney:

The chickens must love it.

5th Exhibitor:

You're a nice fellow.

Restaurants are one of the few good examples left of really free enterprise in America. There isn't much government control of them and the good ones prosper. The bad ones usually, though not always, go out of business.

The best restaurants are operated by people who like food better than money. The worst ones are run by people who don't know anything about food *or* money.

So that's our report on eating out in America. The camera crew is glad it's over because they say they're tired of spending their dinner hour watching me eat.

During the time we've been working on it, many friends and others here at CBS have been stopping me in the hallway to ask one question. It's a question I haven't mentioned so far in the broadcast. . . .

But the answer, as of this morning . . . fourteen pounds.

Surroundings

ON THE HOUSE

ONE of the most popular topics of conversation for home-owners is how much more their houses are worth now than when they bought them. It's a very dull topic and it's silly because we all know that if you sell a house for twice what you paid, you buy another for twice what someone else paid for that one. If you don't sell your house, it doesn't make any difference how much it's worth to anyone but you anyway, and not selling your house always seemed to make more sense to me.

There are 218 million people in the United States and 40 million houses for them to buy. There are as many different kinds of houses as there are different kinds of people: new houses, old houses, wooden houses, stone houses, brick houses, wonderfully substantial-looking houses and houses that blow away in the wind, houses all together in a row and houses all by themselves out in the middle of miles and miles of no-other-houses.

Most towns have one funny-looking house. Everyone laughs at it, but the people who live in it like it. Then there's the big house, owned by the rich grouch or by the widow of the man who owned the mill; the stately and beautiful home that everyone dreams of living in; the house that's just a little too obviously the product of a young architect's imagination.

Houses come in a variety of shapes, too. There are square houses, round houses, six-sided houses. There are even some eight-sided houses. A geodesic house is all sides and an igloo has none. Some houses are tall, some are short. There are houses that look like mushrooms and houses built like arches.

There are permanent little villages of comfortable homes nestled in the valleys across the country and contagious outbreaks of im-mobile mobile homes that pock the face of the landscape. If they're mobile, why don't they go?

People seem less sentimental about where they live these days. Maybe it's because not as many houses are homes or because they have no family in the cemetery in town. Maybe people are less sentimental about where they live now because they don't spend much time there. The new houses are efficient workshops, set up so that what has to be done can be done quickly, though without joy, so the people who own them can leave for someplace else. The getaway car is always ready in the driveway.

It used to be that home was a place to stay in and enjoy. The house had been built by a carpenter who did it from a plan in his head. There are rooms in those houses that weren't designed for anything special. There were usually four or five bedrooms, a living room, a parlor, a big kitchen, but then there were spare rooms. The builder didn't have any idea what you were going to do with your spare room. It wasn't his business. You could make up what the room was for as you went along living. There was always one floor above the top floor, too, the attic.

An attic was maybe the best place ever invented for a house and it's too bad they're a thing of the past. The family treasures from generations back were stored up there. Halloween costumes weren't

bought; they were made up from something dug out of a trunk in the attic.

Many of the old houses are deteriorating now, of course. They're too big to heat, too much to take care of. An old house takes a lot of love. A modern house doesn't take much love but it doesn't give much either.

Every town or city should have some rich people, but the big estates with expansive lawns are being chopped into tiny pieces for middle-income housing projects. No one has time to mow an acre of lawn and not many of us have the money to get it mowed for us. The people who have the money can't find anyone who wants to do it. Now a little patch of green will do. Mowing the lawn isn't much more than an extension of vacuuming the living room.

In hundreds of places, the biggest, grandest, most interesting house in town has been repaired, repainted, landscaped and restored to its original beauty . . . to be used as a funeral home.

Modern houses aren't so much built as they are produced. The houses are put up not one at a time but in clusters, each house having all the individuality of a slice of Wonder bread. It would be wrong to say there aren't some beautiful and livable modern

houses. Of course there are, just as there are miserable old houses. The trouble with so many modern houses is that someone else has decided where things are going to go. Everything is built in, recessed and right at your fingertips, even if that isn't where you want it.

The trouble with a house like that is finding a place to put the debris of your life that you love. Where do kids hide on each other in houses like that?

The next best thing to an attic they've stopped putting on houses is a porch. If they put anything out front now, it's a little cement square which has none of the grace of a porch even if you stick two plastic chairs on it.

People seem more backyard than front porch oriented now. There're turning their backs on a world they used to face. They're looking for privacy, hiding behind fences. What used to go on the front porch is taking place out back now behind the fence around the patio.

People seem to miss their front porches too. You see them inventing makeshift substitutes. There's something satisfying about sitting out in front of your very own house, watching the world go by. It's your house and there you are, out in front of it. You're available to be seen and can, in turn, watch the passing parade or just sit there, reading the paper, if there's no parade.

A porch made a perfect first step away from home for a child too young to cross the street. Wheeled toys rolled there in the rain, and on hot summer evenings young lovers rocked in their own breeze.

As the porch disappeared, we entered into a new era of garage-door dominance. This ranks as one of the major architectural and aesthetic disasters of all time. What you see when you look at a house like that is garage doors. The small area to one side of the garage doors is the house.

Almost all of the 40 million single-family houses in this country have garages, many of them built for two cars. The ultimate status symbol is a three-car garage. A three-car garage announces affluence.

It's a funny thing, though, no matter how many garages there are in America, it is very unlikely that more than a million of the 90 million cars we have ever gets put in one. For one thing, they don't fit. Almost no one can put even one of their cars in their two-car garage. The cars have been driven out by the lawnmowers, the bicycles and most important, of course, the indispensable junk. Sometimes people can't even get their car into the driveway leading to the garage. The worst thing, of course, is when you can't even get all the junk in the garage. Some people have even found the garage too valuable a space to be wasted on a car, so they convert it into a room.

A lot of people who are wonderfully good grounds-keepers landscape the exterior of their home and then ruin the effect by parking a battered hulk of a car or truck out front. As a matter of fact, you can usually tell almost everything about the people inside a house by looking at the outside of the house. There are people you know must live well-ordered lives. Their lawns are mowed and you know their checkbooks are, no doubt, balanced.

And then there are the more expansive types. They bite off more than they can chew with a house. They fill their lives and their backyards with just a little more than a life or a backyard can hold and their backyards runneth over.

The average American moves once every five years or thirteen times in his lifetime. That means that 20 percent of the population moves every year. They pick up their worldly possessions and take off. Everyone is going somewhere else.

I don't know why people are moving so often these days. No

house is perfect but you learn to live with it after you've been in one a few years. Like your own shortcomings, you find ways to ignore the imperfections of a house when it's your home.

There are reverberations of the past everywhere in a house you've lived in for a long time. It isn't a sad place, though, because all the things left undone hold great hope for future Saturday mornings. The house you live in isn't a potential real-estate listing in tomorrow's paper. It isn't a Holiday Inn or a temporary shelter to keep you warm and dry for the night before the hunt begins tomorrow. Your house is your home, an anchor, a place to go when you don't want to go anyplace.

STREET NAMES

WHAT would you think, just offhand, is the most common street name in the United States? Pretend you win a hundred dollars if you guess right.

You'd have to say that, overall, we haven't shown a lot of originality with the names we've given our streets. In most countries the great streets have great names. London has half a dozen of them: Bond Street, Fleet Street, Carnaby Street, Piccadilly; Paris has the Champs-Elysée; Berlin the Unter den Linden; Leningrad the Nevsky Prospekt.

What do we have? Michigan Boulevard. Sunset Boulevard. Some of our great streets don't even have names; they have numbers. In New York the classiest street in town is called Fifth Avenue; some of the numbers in New York are even dull. Forty-second Street. Would you write a song about a street with a name like that?

So, have you given any thought to the most common street name? Main? Wrong. Not even close. I'll give them to you in reverse order, like a Miss America contest. The fifth most common street name in America according to postal service records is (*music: sting*) Lincoln!

The fourth most common name is . . . Oak. Third, Maple. The second most common is Washington. And the winner, the single most frequently used name for a street in all the U.S. is . . . Park! Park Street, Park Avenue, Park Terrace, Park Something is the winner.

Of the twenty-five most common street names, seven are former Presidents, nine are trees. Franklin is the only person's name in the first twenty-five who wasn't a President. If you thought Broadway or Main were in there, you were really wrong. Main is thirty-second and Broadway isn't even in the first fifty.

Street names don't usually make much sense when you get thinking about them. If a street is named Wolf Lane, it's usually been a hundred years since anyone saw a wolf around there. Very often there's no view of the bay from Bay View, no oak trees left on Oak Street and no hill anywhere around most of Hillside.

These days there's nothing interesting about the way a street gets its name. What happens most often is that a developer comes along and builds a bunch of houses all in a row (and they're all made of ticky-tack). At some point he realizes that if he's going to advertise them for sale they have to have an address, so he thinks up a cute name for the street and for the rest of its life that's what it's called.

The names of streets in developments lack the same character the development lacks and are at least fitting in this respect. Developers very often try to lend class to an area by calling it something other than a street. They call it a lane, a terrace or a circle. They'll call it Dogwood Lane on the theory that you can ask more for a house on a lane than one on a street. A really exclusive street has bumps built into the road so no one can drive very fast. Built-in bumps are restricted to the classiest, most expensive development streets.

There is one mystery that remains unsolved in regard to street names in America. According to our count, Third Street was the seventeenth most popular street name. I accept that, but Second Street was nineteenth most common and what about First Street? First Street was thirtieth!

Now what in the world ever happened to all the First Streets in cities that have Second and Third Streets? And how come there are more Thirds than Seconds?

BANK NAMES

Thousands of you have written asking me to explain how they name a bank. How, you ask, do they come up with a name when they sit down and decide to start up a place for us to keep our money—or more accurately, a place for *them* to keep our money.

Well, it isn't like naming a child or a dog or even another business. A bank has to have a name that sounds important and honest, otherwise people would keep their money under the mattress where it belongs.

If a bank has connections in Washington, there's a law that says it has to call itself either National or Federal. After that, they can do what they want with their name and very few of them are satisfied with just one name like that, so they embellish it with something they feel makes it sound better.

They'll call themselves United National, Century National, Sterling National or Cosmopolitan National. National Bank of Pike City, National Bank of America, National Bank of Utah are all bank names. In Washington there's even a Hemisphere National Bank.

Just as banks are not satisfied being just plain National, neither are they happy being simply Federal. They prefer being Columbia Federal, Independence Federal, Metropolitan Federal or, perhaps, Central or Midwest Federal.

They may also be County or State Federal. This would seem to be a contradiction to many of us but not to the people who name banks. They don't seem to worry much about making sense with their names. It's just got to have the right ring to it. Perpetual Federal Savings is the actual name of a bank.

The greatest bank name in America and perhaps in the world is the National Home Permanent Federal Savings and Loan. That has just about everything anyone would possibly want in a bank name. They don't make it clear whether it's the savings or the loan that's permanent but that's one of the mysteries that keeps us all interested in banks.

If there is one tiny element missing in that name, it is the ever-popular bank word "American." Banks like being American-this, American-that. And then there are the banks that prefer simplicity to patriotism. Home Savings is a simple name. Or Farm and Home Savings. Would a bank named Farm and Home Savings cheat you?

Some banks get stuck with a name that sounded good a hundred years ago when they were founded but sounds sort of silly now. In New York there's a Dime Savings Bank. Once you pass forty, a dime isn't worth bending over to pick up if you drop one. You certainly wouldn't bother to take it to a bank to save it.

"Trust" is a word banks like in their names although it's a two-faced word. Banks use it in its financial sense and the rest of us think of it as meaning dependable. Banks like to have us think that about them and they are also suggesting they trust us—which we know isn't true.

Irving Trust . . . the National Savings and Trust . . . Bankers Trust. Bankers Trust is a big organization with a lot of customers, but who bankers trust is mostly each other.

Banks not only like being National, Federal, American, Home and Trusted, they also like being First. The First National Bank of Almost Anywhere, First Union Bank, First Savings and Loan. (In New York there's a Ninth Federal. This is strange because where there's a First Federal, there doesn't seem to be any Second, Third or Fourth Federal, let alone an Eighth. Bookkeeping error, probably.)

One of the newest banks is called the First Women's Bank. I suppose it won't be long before we get a Gay Trust.

Just as there are names banks favor, there are names they'd never think of using. Certain businesses seem to preempt groups of names for themselves. Acme, for instance, is most apt to be an exterminating service or a dry cleaner. You wouldn't call a bank the Acme Permanent Home Trust. AAA is a name reserved for car-repair shops and people who fix radiators.

Bel Air is popular everywhere as the name of a roadside motel. You wouldn't find a Bel Air Bank in any town that wasn't called

Bel Air itself. Nor would any financial institution call itself a Bankorama or Bankland or Bank City. Those are supermarket names.

Banks often spend a lot of money having a trademark designed for them too. They'll have something like a rolling wheel within an octagon that has all sorts of symbolic meaning to someone. The New York Bank for Savings uses a beehive as its symbol. This seems odd because we all know what happens to the bee. He works his tail off all summer saving honey for the tough times ahead and then some smart guy with a net over his head comes along and takes it all away from him.

And that's how banks are named.

FENCES

OUR brains have a way of jumping around a lot, thinking of one thing for a few seconds and then flitting off to think of another. For me as a writer, it's always been fun to see if I could stop one subject in my head for long enough to take a good look at it.

For instance, I was thinking about fences. There are as many kinds of fences in this country as there are people. You couldn't *count* all the kinds of fences there are. There are big fences, small fences, teeny-tiny fences.

The biggest difference between one fence and another fence is whether the fence was built to protect what's inside from what's outside or to protect what's outside from what's inside. To protect the people outside, for instance, a mean dog has to be fenced in.

It's a mystery why some fences are ever built at all. Most cemeteries have fences, even though no one outside really wants to get in and no one inside ever tries to get out.

Sometimes you can't tell what a fence is keeping in—or keeping out. You can't tell what a fence is protecting from what. You suspect that sometimes people just put up fences from habit, or as a show of strength or wealth. I hate anyone who has a fence that cost more than my house cost.

The best-looking fences are often the simplest. A simple fence around a beautiful home can be like a frame around a picture. The house isn't hidden; its beauty is enhanced by the frame. But a fence can be a massive, ugly thing, too, made of bricks and mortar. Sometimes the insignificant little fences do their job just as well as the ten-foot walls. Maybe it's only a string stretched between here and there in a field. The message is clear: don't cross here.

There's often a question about whether a barrier is a fence or a wall. Fences, I think, are thinner than walls. And, of course, there

are people who confuse us further by building fences on *top* of walls.

Every fence has its own personality and some don't have much. There are friendly fences. A friendly fence takes kindly to being leaned on. There are friendly fences around playgrounds. And some playground fences are more fun to play on than anything they surround. There are more mean fences than friendly fences overall, though. Some have their own built-in invitation not to be sat upon. Unfriendly fences get it right back sometimes. You seldom see one that hasn't been hit, bashed, bumped or in some way broken or knocked down.

One of the phenomena of fences is their tendency to proliferate. Note, if you will, how often one fence brings on another fence. People often seem to want their own fence, even if it's back to back, cheek by jowl with the neighbor's fence, almost as though the fence was put up to keep the fence out.

The other thing I thought about fences: I thought maybe the world wouldn't be very much changed if tomorrow morning . . . every fence was gone.

PUBLIC ART

IF YOU'RE putting up pictures in your own house, you can decide for yourself what looks good and how much you want to pay to have it look that way. Decorating a city with works of art is a lot harder.

Nothing in this country has changed more than our public art, and a lot of people don't like it. For a long while, the statues in little parks everywhere were in the image of traditional old American heroes, or perhaps some local hero known only to the people of the town where it stood. There were tens of thousands of Civil War statues put up, and tens of thousands more memorializing the doughboys of World War I.

Statues erected in honor of people who were heroic after 1930 are rare. Maybe heroes are rarer. Sculptors have always liked to make horses. Anyone looks heroic on a horse.

There was never much complaining about the money spent on heroic statuary. I suppose people aren't so apt to complain about art in honor of the dead.

That's not true about the new, modern sculptures being put up everywhere with both public and private money. It seems to many people that artists are trying too hard to be artistic. Most people like art to look like things as they know them to be. That's hard for an artist, and skeptics think that's why artists have changed what they do. If it doesn't look like anything we know, we can't complain that it doesn't look like what it's supposed to. It isn't *supposed* to look like anything.

A lot of the most modern work has been commissioned by the federal government. Most of us don't have very good taste in art, but government's taste is usually worse.

People who like the modern public art refer to it as a museum without walls.

Critics who *don't* like it call it nonsense and a waste of money.

A good artist tries to satisfy himself. That's a noble artistic idea, but when the artist is satisfying himself with public money, he has to satisfy some other people, too.

Many modern artists work in geometric shapes. They like angles, circles, cylinders. They mix them, balance them, stand them on end. Most of us aren't ready for it. We know the artist is trying to tell us something, but it's a foreign language and we don't understand what it is he's trying to say. We'd like to see the artist's idea written out on paper in English just once. A lot of us suspect the artist of not having any idea at all, beyond getting a government grant. We aren't sure enough, though, of our own artistic judgment to say so. We know from experience that the artist may be an artistic Einstein whose work is important and great and just beyond our comprehension.

The real question is this: Is America ready for art that's smarter than it is?

SIGNS

Someone's always trying to push us around with the signs they put up, aren't they? I mean, what's your reaction when you come up against this sign: "KEEP OUT"? Even if I don't want to go in, my reaction is always: "The hell with you, fella, I'm comin' in!"

I think most of us have some kind of reaction to every sign we see that isn't the one the people who put up the sign intended us to have. For instance, when I see this one: "NO PARKING AT ANY TIME. VIOLATORS WILL BE TOWED AWAY AT OWNER'S EXPENSE," I figure they're bluffing. They've had the sign up for nine years and haven't towed away anyone yet.

A lot of signs try to scare you into not doing something: "NO TRESPASSING." " WARNING: TRESPASSERS WILL BE PUNISHED." Or maybe they'll suggest you're going to get bit: "BEWARE OF DOG!"

Some signs are very polite. For instance, they'll try to sweet-talk you into not smoking: "THANK YOU FOR NOT SMOKING." Some are more direct: "SMOKING NOT PERMITTED." Some get tougher: "POSITIVELY NO SMOKING." "NO SMOKING—BY ORDER OF THE BOARD OF EDUCATION." Has any kid ever not done anything by order of the Board of Education?

Schools have a special, irritating way with signs. They pretend to be friendly—"WELCOME TO OUR SCHOOL"—but then tell you all the stuff you can't do: "NO BIKE RIDING, LACROSSE PLAYING, LOITERING, ETC." . . . Any kid reading it never would have thought of playing lacrosse on Sunday until he saw the sign.

I don't care much for signs with pictures of things on them: "DEER CROSSING," "CATTLE CROSSING." By the time I've figured out what it's a picture of, I'm past it.

I like signs there's no doubt about. I mean, this would only have one meaning: "IN." Here's a big new bestseller for people who make signs: "NO RIGHT TURN ON RED." We passed a law saying you *could* turn right on red; now we're putting signs up everywhere saying "Except here."

I always figure "NO THRU TRAFFIC" means it's a shortcut, but they don't want you to go that way. And "NO EXIT" *is* an exit, but they don't want you to go out that way.

There are a few signs you don't fool around with, such as "RADIATION." I mean, if you really didn't want anybody walking on your grass, that might be the one to put up.

A lot of signs are put up too late, of course. Usually by the time anyone puts up "NO DUMPING ALLOWED," people have been dumping there for ten years.

You know some signs don't really mean it. "SPEED LIMIT 5." I mean, there *is* no five miles an hour.

The fact of the matter is, most of us don't like to be told anything by a sign.

HOTELS*

O NE of the good things to do in life is stay in a hotel. People stay in hotels for two reasons. First, they're away from home and they need a place to sleep and leave their suitcases.

The second reason people stay in hotels is that a lot of them who are *not* neurotic and don't *mind* facing life most of the time, *enjoy* not facing it for short periods once in a while. A hotel is the ideal place for not facing life. Hotels have people who face life *for* you. All they ask of you is money.

There are about 75,000 places in the United States where more than twenty people can pay to spend the night. On an average night about two million Americans are doing that.

When people traveled on horseback or by carriage, there were roadside inns. An innkeeper was compelled by law to provide food, lodging and a place for your horse, all for one price. It was known

* Broadcast June 28, 1966.

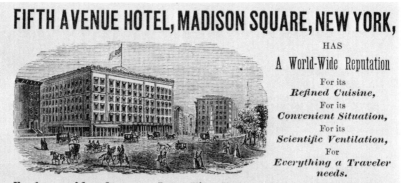

FIFTH AVENUE HOTEL, MADISON SQUARE, NEW YORK,

HAS

A World-Wide Reputation

For its
Refined Cuisine,
For its
Convenient Situation,
For its
Scientific Ventilation,
For
*Everything a Traveler
needs.*

Each corridor has an Iron Fire Escape from top to bottom.

Darling, Griswold, and Company, Proprietors.

as the "American Plan." Now you're more apt to find the American plan in Europe. "European Plan," more common in America, means no food and no lodging for horse or carriage.

The first real hotel in America was built in Washington, D.C., in 1793. It was called the Union Public Hotel. The City Hotel was begun the same year in New York. The first real hotel in Boston was the Tremont, built in 1827. In 1823, the 500-room National Hotel was opened in Washington. It was advertised as "The Palace of the People."

By 1850, railroad track connected most Eastern cities and was beginning to stretch west from Chicago. Wherever a train stopped, a hotel was built. In the small towns, the one hotel was a walk-with-bags from the station. Train was about the only way strangers came to town. Neither the trains, if they're still running, nor the hotels, if they're still standing, have changed much.

In the middle and late 1880s the first luxury hotels went up. They were great stone palaces built to last a thousand years. The trouble is, no one wants to stay in a thousand-year-old hotel. Most of them have outlasted their own usefulness. They are the hotels they don't build hotels *like* anymore. Plumbing killed them.

A few of them, like the Copley Plaza in Boston, are still standing. The Plaza in New York is another grand old holdout. The management of the Plaza has never felt the need to call attention to it with a sign bearing its name. Their feeling seems to be that if you don't know where the Plaza is, you probably don't belong there.

The Brown Palace went up in Denver in 1892. That's still up. Its cavernous lobby gives the appearance of being one of those British men's clubs with high-vaulted ceilings supported by marble columns.

All hotel lobbies used to be big. You could stand around and talk with friends in them, wander around looking at things or just sit in them and watch the new people check in. People who lived in the town used the hotel lobby as a meeting place.

Those people who used to sit around hotel lobbies are gone now. I guess they're up in their rooms watching television or at the airport catching a plane for home. Lobbies are just wide places by the registration desk in new hotels. There's no income from a lobby for the hotel management and they really don't want you sitting around in it anyway. They'd rather have you in the bar, drinking.

Most of the hotels you know best if you're more than fifty years old were built in the late 1920s. Name the best-known hotel in any city and the chances are it was built then. It's the one with the roof "from high atop" which those bands emanated on late-night radio broadcasts in the 1930s. It's where you took the girl for dinner if you were serious about her. It's where you arranged to meet someone if you were downtown. Those hotels lent continuity to the life of a city just by being there.

Before all of them were called Sheraton, Hilton or Statler, hotels had good names that meant something in a community. In my hometown, Albany, New York, the two hotels were called the Ten Eyck and the De Witt Clinton. You don't mistake those names for two hotels in Des Moines, Iowa. A landmark hotel was a point of orientation in a city. Things were a block from it or ten blocks and you turned left or right at it to get somewhere.

In the 1930s, during the Depression, there was no investment capital with which to build new hotels and no one had the money to stay in one if there had been. People started traveling more by car than by train, and a new institution came into being. It was first known as the "tourist cabin" or "motor court" and later as the "motel." Most invented names don't last as well as "motel" has.

Resourceful people who couldn't find work put up a few simple buildings by the side of the road, made the beds and sold the new traveler, the car driver, a night's sleep for a dollar or two.

The emphasis is on bedrooms in the hotels that have been built in the last twenty years. While there's no income from the people sitting in the lobbies and public rooms, 70 percent of every dollar taken in on a hotel bedroom is clear profit. Once the owners have it paid for, all they have to do is provide heat and someone to come in for ten minutes a day to make the bed. If the maid spends fifteen minutes, it's probably because she's watching a soap opera on your television set and wants to wait for a commercial before she moves to the next room. The emphasis on rooms gives a hotel a pigeonhole look from the outside—but they hold a lot of pigeons.

The hotel business has always gone through alternating periods of boom and bust. During the 1960s, they were in trouble and the hotels in the worst trouble were the big old ones downtown. Most of them were built on expensive real estate near the railroad station. It was still expensive in 1968, even though the railroad station was probably all but dead and the area had turned into a slum. The classy store that used to be a block's walk had closed and reopened in the new shopping area out on the edge of town.

A lot of those good old hotels were torn down between 1960 and 1970. They had old-fashioned plumbing, makeshift air conditioning and uneconomically large public rooms and hallways. They were gracious, but most people won't pay much for grace.

The people who used to come by train and stay for two days in a city started coming by plane. They stayed one night or not at all before they flew back out to sleep in their own beds at home. If they stayed overnight, they didn't stay downtown. They stayed in the new motel out by the airport.

Motels were the biggest problem the hotel business had, and a lot of hotel owners joined the trend. While they were tearing down great old hotels everywhere, they were erecting tacky new motels everywhere else. The real estate around all the crossroads of the major highways was bought up by motel entrepreneurs. If a traveler wants to get to a downtown hotel, he has to run a neon gauntlet of signs en route beckoning him into the roadside motel.

What motels have to offer is convenience. There they are. You register, drive your car to a spot near your room and take your own suitcases in. No one was ever really happy with bellboys. The question of how much to tip and whether you'd given him too much or too little was more than most people wanted to face.

No one has clearly defined the difference between a hotel and a

motel. If you carry your own bag to your room, it's almost certainly a motel, not a hotel. It's a motel if there's a Coke machine down the hall, an ice dispenser at the top of the stairs and a small, unused swimming pool in a center area. (A lot of people who never go in a pool won't stay in a place that doesn't have one.) It's a motel if you have to keep your curtains drawn all the time.

For a while, it was a hotel if it was vertical and more than ten stories high and a motel if it was horizontal and no more than two stories. That is no longer a dependable way to differentiate between them. They've lived together for so long now that hotels and motels have crossbred, and you can't always tell one from the other. The motel chains have built what look like hotels and called them "high-rise motels." The hotel people have tried to get in on the motel business by going to the perimeter of the city and building five-story "motor inns." They have neither the convenience of the motel nor the class of a hotel.

The big issue is the car. Something like 85 percent of all people arriving at motels or hotels come by car. Even if they fly in to the city, they rent a car at the airport.

In San Francisco one of the best hotel architects, William Tabler, designed a Hilton that tries for the best of both the hotel and the motel world. It's a hotel with a road up the middle so that you can spiral up the driveway in your car until you reach your own floor. You park, get out and carry your bag to your hotel room. Americans don't like to be far from their cars and this is the

next best thing to sleeping with it under your pillow.

Most of the great big old ramshackle wooden resort hotels are gone now. In their best days, they were filled with families who had packed a steamer trunk and come there to stay from July 1st to Labor Day. The father stayed for a month.

There are still a dozen of them left to remind us of what they were. The Greenbrier and the Homestead in West Virginia, the Mackinac Island Inn, the Cloisters on Sea Island, Georgia, the Lake Placid Club, and the Broadmoor in Colorado are all still hanging on. Across the bay from San Diego, the Hotel del Coronado, built in 1888, is a reminder to Californians that there was a real world there before they came.

Those grand old resort hotels were noted chiefly for their long stretches of porch lined with sturdy, wooden rocking chairs. One thing you have to say for those of us alive now, we aren't as satisfied just rocking as people used to be.

Hotels are built in most cities because there's a reason for people to come there and they need a place to stay. But then there are hotel cities where the number and quality of the hotels is part of the reason people are attracted to them. New York, Chicago, Miami, San Francisco have hotels that are themselves tourist attractions.

A good hotel room is nothing like home and that's the way we prefer it. It is refreshingly free of the miscellaneous paraphernalia that clutters our living room and our lives. Hotel managers flatter us with more towels for one day than we'd use at home in a week; they have our soap wrapped individually, put clean sheets on the bed every day and generally pretend they think we're used to being waited on.

A good hotel is a pleasure.

BASEBALL

I HATE baseball. I have always hated baseball. As a matter of fact, I have a hard time liking anyone who *does* like baseball.

To be honest with you, I'll tell you it may be because I was never very good at the game. I always threw a baseball like a girl. (Is that okay to say now, or does that suggest girls don't throw baseballs very well?) Let me put it another way. Billy Vroman's sister Olive threw a baseball better than I did.

But I have other reasons for not liking baseball, too. For one thing, the players all spit too much. Every time I try to watch a World Series game on television, someone's spitting at me. No game that can be played by a person with a wad of tobacco in his mouth is a sport.

Baseball has been called "The National Pastime." It's just the kind of game anyone deserves who has nothing better to do than try to pass his time. My own time is passing plenty fast enough without some national game to help it along. What does "pastime" mean anyway? And why doesn't it have two "t"s?

Maybe it's wishful thinking on my part but I think baseball is in trouble. It's been about ten years now since the President of the United States thought it was politically important for him to go throw out the first ball on opening day. All the balls are made in Haiti now, too, and most of the gloves are made in Taiwan.

It seems obvious to me that other sports are closing in on baseball and it's only a matter of time before the game will be squeezed out of the sports schedule. The professional basketball season doesn't end until a month after baseball starts, and football starts three months before baseball ends.

I don't like managers in sports either, and there is no other game where the manager is as important as in baseball. (I'll concede that

93

a football coach has no business calling plays.) But what's managing got to do with a game? They sit in the dugout like little kings, waving, gesturing, spitting. They rush out on the field to challenge a decision by an umpire even though no decision has ever been changed in the hundred years the game has been played. When a manager storms out on the field, does he think this is going to be the first time? Why do they let the managers out on the field at all?

Managers are so important to the game of baseball that Little League has become a big deal for fathers. The kids would rather go hit a ball around a vacant lot or dodge cars playing baseball in the street, but that wasn't good enough for the manager-type fathers of America. They had to draw up a set of rules, have a regulation ball field made and see to it that the kids played on schedule. Never mind whether they felt like playing baseball that day or not. There's a schedule.

The Little League teams are sponsored by the local laundry or the gas station and, of course, the fathers are out there managing. The funny thing about all this is that we started playing the game in Taiwan after World War II and the American soldiers stationed there condescendingly offered to teach the Taiwanese kids how to play. You know what happened, of course. By the late 1960s, the kids in Taiwan were playing so well that they came over here and won the Little League championship three years in a row. The "managers" of America rewrote the rules so Taiwan can't play in the Little League "World Championship" anymore.

Maybe they could get the President of Taiwan to throw out the first ball some year.

HOW TO WATCH FOOTBALL ON TELEVISION

Some of you don't like football. You have the mistaken notion that there's too much of it on television. This feeling can often be traced to the fact that you went to a college in the East where they actually let the students play on the team.

Well, of course there *is* quite a bit of football on television and it might be in order for me to suggest a few guidelines for watching it.

First, don't watch any pre-game shows.

Second, don't watch any post-game shows.

Third, don't watch any halftime shows. Try not to watch Howard Cosell at all. It's perfectly possible for anyone who knows the game to watch one without having anyone describe it to him.

For you casual football watchers who can take it or leave it, know which team you want to win. Find something about one of the teams you don't like and then root for the other team. It can be anything . . . you don't like the color of their uniforms . . . you once had a bad hotel room in the city the team represents . . . you've read where their middle linebacker is a dirty player or their quarterback is gay. Whatever it is, find something because an unreasonable prejudice against one of the teams is part of the satisfaction of watching football. It gets a lot of the hate out of your system.

People who don't like football don't understood people who do like it. There are some things these people ought to know. Remember this. The average football fan is a college graduate with an eighth-grade education. I, for instance, am a football fan. I'm a New York Giants fan and it hasn't always been easy. There have been times when I've thought about chucking it all in for ballet. I have a lucky Giant jacket I wear to the games, and some years I've worn it to eight home games and we've lost seven of them. How lucky can a jacket get?

There is something about being a football fan, though, that I recommend. Eight times a year, every home game, I make myself a tuna-fish sandwich, pour hot chicken broth in a vacuum bottle, put on some clothes too old to wear anyplace else and I take off for the game alone.

When I leave for the stadium, I don't have a care in the world. I have no encumbrances except my loyalty to a losing team. And if the Giants lose again this year and next, it won't make one damn bit of difference to my life.

I know that with all the games on television, a lot of you who don't like football but are basically good people anyway, are trying to understand those of us who do like football. You're trying to make some sense out of it. You see, that's where you're making your first mistake, right there. Being a football fan doesn't make *any sense at all* and that's the beauty of it.

POST SUPER
BOWL 1980

COULD I ask a little favor of some of you tonight? Please don't sit there saying you hate football and you're glad it's over. Don't say that. Some of us are very sad. There's a hole in our lives you could drive a truck through, as Frank Gifford might say.

Be kind to those of us who love football as we go through these agonizing weeks of withdrawal. Don't start out right away with saying cruel things. You know, things like, "You can unfasten your seat belt now, dear. The games are over." Or, "You remember your children, don't you? This is Donald. He turned nine while you were gone."

No one who has just lost a close friend wants to hear smart-aleck remarks. Just be patient and try to help us. We're going to be okay.

In another month or so, we'll be able to sit up and take food again at the dining-room table, instead of in front of the tube in the living room. We have a stack of Sunday papers we never got to read, but we have until next fall now to catch up on them. Next fall starts with the first pre-season game on August 8th.

We'll be back in touch with the world again pretty soon, too. Pat Summerall mentioned Jimmy Carter during the halftime show a few weeks ago. He is still President, isn't he?

Be patient with us now that football's over.

GOOD NEWS

ALL of us who work in television news are constantly being accused of emphasizing the negative side of everything. We get letters saying we never cover a story unless something terrible happens.

Tonight we've put together a little news broadcast to give you an idea of how it would look if you had it your way.

"I'm here by the Mississippi. It's raining but the river is not overflowing its banks.

"As a matter of fact, it doesn't look to me as though there's any danger of a flood whatsoever. People are not piling up sandbags. No one has been forced to evacuate his home and the Governor has not asked that this be declared a federal disaster area."

"O'Hare Airport in Chicago is one of the nation's busiest. At
11 A.M., a jet aircraft with 168 passengers and ten crew members
on board started down the long runway. The plane, headed for
London, took off without incident. It landed without incident too.
Everyone on board is now in London.

"One passenger on board that plane was quoted as saying he
didn't like the fake milk they served with the coffee."

"For a report from New York City we take you to our correspondent standing in front of the Plaza, one of New York City's
most luxurious hotels.

"This is the Plaza, one of New York City's most luxurious hotels.
CBS News has learned that last evening, after a night on the town,
the Shah of Franakapan and his semi-beautiful wife returned to
their hotel suite after depositing more than a million dollars' worth
of jewelry in the hotel safe. The jewels included the famous Cooch
Behar Diamond.

"This morning, when the safe was opened, all the jewelry including the famous Cooch Behar Diamond was right there where
they'd left it."

"In Florida, the orange crop was hit by another night of average
weather.

"The oranges just hung in there and grew."

"Oil industry officials announced today they were lowering prices
because they just don't need the money. One reason for their affluence is their safety records.

"The oil tanks behind me are very close to a residential area. If
they were on fire, smoke would be seen billowing up for miles
around. They aren't on fire, though; they're just sitting there."

"In Detroit, a General Motors spokesman announced today that
more than 174,000 Chevrolets made in the late fall of 1974 would
not be recalled. They are all perfect.

"At eleven-thirty this evening, CBS News will present a special
report listing the serial numbers of those cars."

And if that's what you want to hear, that's the way it was.
Good evening.

JULY 4TH STATISTICS

One of the things we can be sure of over the July 4th weekend is that news reports will keep telling us how many of us are going to die in automobile accidents.

This weekend, for instance, they estimate there will be about 800 motor vehicle deaths. During the weekend, while you're driving, the radio makes your drive more pleasant by giving you the play-by-play account of the death statistics.

I was curious about the car death figures and how they fit into the total picture of our demise in America. The Department of Health, Education and Welfare keeps these day-to-day statistics for the country on how many people die and what they die of every day.

On the July 4th weekend in 1976, for instance, 758 people were killed in car crashes . . . a terrible figure. In April, the weekend comes on the same four days of the month and only 555 people were killed in cars.

But now here's the interesting thing about these figures. On those four days in April, a total of 21,700 people died of *all* causes. On the four days in July, 19,600 died—2,100 fewer. Not only that, 86 more people died in the four days right *after* the July 4th weekend than during it.

It turns out that Fourth of July is really quite a *safe* weekend for us.

There were 30 fewer suicides over the Fourth. In the four days in April, 156 people died in accidental falls. Twelve fewer fell to their deaths over the Fourth. On the Fourth, there were 75 murders; on the fourth of April, 77 murders. Fewer people are watching television over the Fourth, too, so I suppose fewer die of boredom.

But, overall, fewer of us die from all causes over the July 4th weekend than on most weekends.

This suggests two things. One, no matter what we do, whether we're climbing ladders or driving cars, a lot of people die doing it.

And, second, considering the number of people driving somewhere over the Fourth, the chances are that, car for car, it's one of the safest weekends of the year to be going someplace.

COUNTERS

I'M the all-American consumer. My idea of a good time is to go out Saturday morning to buy something with some of the money I've made. My comment here is about the counters I encounter in stores—you know, the place where you pay your money to the cashier.

If you go to one of those department stores where you have to pay on your way out, the little alley by the cashier is so camouflaged with goods that it's hard to find. You have to look for the line of people.

Why don't the stores give us a break and leave us a little room so we can put our packages down while we fish out our money? When you come to a counter with an armload of things you're buying, you want someplace to put them down. You never know how long you're going to have to stand there with them. Of course, the worst thing that can happen is when the person in front of you is paying by check.

We all know *why* they don't leave us any space. It's because they're always trying to sell us just one more item before we get out the door. They're trying to get us to buy razor blades, film, a magazine with Jackie Kennedy's picture on it, a pair of rubber gloves, maybe gum or candy for the kids.

It isn't only supermarkets and department stores, either. All kinds of stores make it hard for you to pay because there's no counter space. You have to poke your money through a crack in a wall of merchandise. If you drop your change, it often falls down in with the cigarettes. In some small stores, it's hard to find any counter space *at all*. And if you do find it, you can't see much of the person behind it taking the money.

Drugstores clutter their counters with little bottles and boxes of pills. Even liquor stores often hide their cash registers behind bottles of slow movers. It may be good for the liquor business, but it's a pain in the neck to the customer.

Often the counters at the delicatessen department are not only crowded with junk; they're so high you can't see over them at all. What are delicatessen departments hiding back there anyway? You don't really know what you've bought until you get it home and unwrap it.

My question is this: If they want us to buy, why don't they make it easier for us to pay?

IN PRAISE OF
NEW YORK CITY*

I T's been popular in recent years to suggest that Nature is the
perfect condition, that people have done nothing to the earth
since they got here but make a mess of it. Well, that's true about
some places but untrue about others.

New York City is as amazing in its own way as the Grand
Canyon. As a matter of fact, you can't help thinking that maybe
Nature would have made New York City look the way it does
if it had had the money and the know-how.

When people talk about New York City, they usually mean
the part of the city called Manhattan. Manhattan is a narrow rock
island twelve miles long. Being an island is an important thing
about New York because even though no one thinks much about
it from day to day, they have to go to quite a bit of trouble to get
on it and off it. This makes being there something of an event and
people don't take it so lightly. New York isn't like so many places
that just sort of dwindle away until you're out of town. In New
York, it's very definite. You're either there or you aren't there.

The twenty-eight bridges and tunnels don't connect Manhattan
with New Jersey and the four other boroughs. They're for entering and leaving New York. Where from or where to is of secondary
importance. It may be some indication of the significance of the
event that it costs $1.50 to cross the George Washington Bridge
entering New York, nothing to cross leaving it.

The Brooklyn Bridge is a cathedral among bridges. Coming to
Manhattan across it every morning is like passing through the

* Broadcast February 1, 1974.

Sistine Chapel on your way to work. You couldn't be going to an unimportant place.

Although two million people work on the little island, only half a million of those who work there live there. As a result, a million and a half people have to get on it every morning and off it every night. That's a lot of people to push through twenty-eight little tunnels and bridges in an hour or so, but it's this arterial ebb and flow that produces the rhythm to which this heartless city's heart beats. There must be something worth coming for when all those people go to that much trouble to get there.

Although it isn't the outstanding thing about it to the people who live or work there, New York is best known to strangers for what it looks like. And, of course, it looks tall.

The World Trade Center has two towers, each a quarter of a mile high. The New York office worker isn't overwhelmed by the engineering implications of flushing a toilet 106 floors above the street.

The buildings of the city are best seen from above, as though they were on an architect's easel. It's strange that they were built to look best from an angle at which hardly anyone ever sees them. From the street where the people are, you can't see the buildings for the city. The New Yorker doesn't worry about it because he never looks up.

You have to talk about tall buildings when you talk about New York, but to anyone who has lived for very long with both, the people of the city are of more continuing interest than the architecture. There is some evidence, of course, that the New Yorker isn't all that separate from his environment. If dogs and masters tend to look alike, so probably do cities and their citizens.

The New Yorker takes in New York air. For a short time it trades molecules with his bloodstream and he is part city. And then he exhales and the city is part him. They become inextricably mingled, and it would be strange if the people didn't come to look like the city they inhabit. And to some extent like each other.

While the rest of the nation feels fiercely about New York—they love it or they hate it—New Yorkers feel nothing. They use the city like a familiar tool. They don't defend it from love or hate. They shrug or nod in knowing agreement with almost anything anyone wants to say about it. Maybe this is because it's so hard to say anything about New York that isn't true.

New Yorkers don't brood much, either. They go about their business with a purposefulness that excludes introspection. If the rest of the country says New Yorkers lack pride because they have so little to be proud of, the New Yorker shrugs again. He has no argument with the South or the Midwest or Texas or California. He feels neither superior nor inferior. He just doesn't compare the things in New York with those anywhere else. He doesn't compare the subway with Moscow's or with the Métro in Paris. Both may be better, but neither goes to Brooklyn or Forest Hills and for this reason doesn't interest the New Yorker one way or the other.

New York is essentially a place for working but not everyone works in a glass cube. The island is crowded with highly individual nests people have made for themselves. There are 100,000 Waldens hidden in the stone and steel caverns.

The places people work and live are as different as the people. If a Hollywood façade is deceptive because it has nothing behind it, a New York façade is deceptive because it has so much. You can't tell much about what's inside from what you see outside. There are places within places. Houses behind houses. Very often in New York ugliness is only skin deep.

New York is the cultural center of mankind, too. Art flourishes

in proximity to reality, and in New York the artist is never more than a stone's throw from the action. The pianist composes music three blocks from a fight in Madison Square Garden. A poet works against the sound of a jackhammer outside his window.

There are wonderfully good places to live in New York, if you have the money. A lot of New Yorkers *have* the money. Some of the grand old brownstones of an earlier era have been restored. There are no living spaces more comfortable anywhere. There are charming and unexpected little streets hidden in surprising places throughout the city. They attract the artist, the actor, the musician. The insurance salesman lives on Long Island.

The city is crowded with luxury apartments, so even if you don't own your own brownstone, there's no need to camp out.

The average living place is an apartment built wall to wall with other apartments, so that they share the efficiency of water and electricity that flows to them through the same conduits. They're neither slums nor palaces.

If you can afford $2,500 a month for a three-bedroom apartment, you can live in a living room with Central Park as your front yard.

Several hundred thousand people do have Central Park for a front yard and it's certainly the greatest park on earth. It's a world of its own. No large city ever had the foresight to set aside such

a substantial portion of itself to be one complete unbuilt-on place. It occupies 25 percent of the total area of Manhattan and yet any proposition to take so much as ten square feet of it to honor a Polish general or an American President brings out its legion of defenders.

There are crimes committed in the Park, but to say the Park is unsafe is like saying banks are unsafe because there are holdups. Life is unsafe, for that matter.

Most American cities have rotted from the center and the merchants have all moved to a place under one roof out in the middle of a suburban parking lot. Downtown was yesterday. New York is still vital at its core. It's the ultimate downtown. And if the biggest businesses are centered in New York so are the smallest.

Macy's, Gimbel's, Bloomingdale's are all here and so are the big grocery chains. But the place you probably buy your food is around the corner at a butcher's where you can still see both sides of a piece of meat.

If you want a rare and exotic cheese from Belgium, it's available or maybe you need a gear for a pump made in 1923. All there somewhere in the city. If you're seven feet tall, there's a store that'll take care of you or they can fit you with pants if you have a waist that measures sixty-four inches. There's nothing you can't buy in New York if it's for sale anywhere in the world.

Money doesn't go as far in New York but it doesn't come as far, either. All the numbers for all the money in American are handled in Wall Street on lower Manhattan. The banks, the businesses and even the government do most of their money shuffling and dealing there.

If a civilization can be judged on its ability not only to survive but to thrive in the face of natural obstacles, New York's civilization would have to be called among the most successful. For example, for what's supposed to be a temperate climate, New York has some of the most intemperate weather in the world. It's too hot in the summer, too cold in winter. During all its seasons, the wind has a way of whipping the weather at you and the rain is always coming from an angle that umbrella makers never considered.

The funny thing about it is that Nature and New York City have a lot in common. Both are absolutely indifferent to the human condition. To the New Yorker, accustomed to inconvenience of every kind, the weather is simply one more inconvenience.

New Yorkers learn young to proceed against all odds. If something's in the way, they move it or go under it or over it or around it, but they keep going. There's no sad resignation to defeat. New Yorkers assume they can win. They have this feeling that they're not going to be defeated.

People talk as though they don't like crowds, but the crowd in New York bestows on the people it comprises a blessed anonymity. New Yorkers are protected from the necessity of being individuals when being one serves no purpose. This blending together that takes place in a crowd is a great time-saver for them.

New York can be a very private place too. There's none of the neighborliness based solely on proximity that dominates the lives you share your life with in a small town. It's quite possible to be not merely private but lonely in a crowd in New York. Loneliness seldom lasts, though. For one thing, troubles produce a warmth and comradeship like nothing else, and New York has so many troubles shared by so many people that there's a kind of common knowingness, even in evil, that brings them together. There is no one with troubles so special in New York that there aren't others in the same kind of trouble.

There are five thousand blind people making their way around the city. They're so much a part of the mix, so typical as New Yorkers, that they're treated with much the same hostile disregard as everyone else. Many of the blind walk through the city with the same fierce independence that moves other New Yorkers. They feel the same obligation to be all right. "I'm okay. I'm all right."

It might appear to any casual visitor who may have taken a few rides about town in a taxicab that all New Yorkers are filled with a loudmouthed ill will toward each other. The fact of the matter is, though, that however cold and cruel things seem on the surface, there has never been a society of people in all history with so much compassion for its fellowman. It clothes, feeds, and houses 15 percent of its own because 1.26 million people in New York are unable to do it for themselves. You couldn't call that cold or cruel.

Everyone must have seen pictures at least of the great number of poor people who live in New York. And it seems strange, in view of this, that so many people still come here seeking their fortune or maybe someone else's. But if anything about the city's population is more impressive than the great number of poor people, it's the great number of rich people. There's no need to search for buried treasure in New York. The great American dream is out in the open for everyone to see and to reach for. No one seems to resent the very rich. It must be because even those people who can never realistically believe they'll get rich themselves can still dream about it. And they respond to the hope of getting what they see others having. Their hope alone seems to be enough to sustain them. The woman going into Tiffany's to buy another diamond pin can pass within ten feet of a man without money enough for lunch. They are oblivious to each other. He feels no envy; she no remorse.

There's a disregard for the past in New York that dismays even a lot of New Yorkers. It's true that no one pays much attention to antiquity. The immigrants who came here came for something new, and what New York used to be means nothing to them. Their heritage is somewhere else.

Old million-dollar buildings are constantly being torn down and replaced by new fifty-million-dollar ones. In London, Rome, Paris, much of the land has only been built on once in all their long history. In relatively new New York, some lots have already been built on four times.

Because strangers only see New Yorkers in transit, they leave with the impression that the city is one great mindless rush to nowhere. They complain that it's moving too fast, but they don't notice that it's getting there first. For better and for worse, New York has *been* where the rest of the country is going.

The rest of the country takes pride in the legend on the Statue of Liberty: "Give me your tired, your poor,/Your huddled masses . . ./The wretched refuse of your teeming shore. . . ." Well, for the most part it's been New York City, not the rest of the country, that took in those huddled masses.

Millions of immigrants who once arrived by ships stopped off in New York for a generation or two while the city's digestive system tried to assimilate them before putting them into the great American bloodstream. New York is still trying to swallow large numbers of immigrants. They don't come by boat much anymore and they may not even be from a foreign country. The influx of a million Puerto Ricans in the 1960s produced the same kind of digestive difficulties that the influx of the Irish did in the middle 1800s.

New York's detractors, seeing what happens to minority groups, have said there is just as much prejudice here as anywhere. New York could hardly deny that. The working whites hate the un-

employed blacks. The blacks hate the whites. The Puerto Ricans live in a world of their own. The Germans, the Hungarians, the Poles live on their own blocks. Nothing in this pot has melted together. The Chinese and the Italians live side by side in lower Manhattan as though Canal Street was the Israeli border. There's no intermingling, and in a city with almost two million Jews even a lot of *Jews* are anti-Semitic.

In spite of it all, the city works. People do get along. There is love.

Whether New York is a pleasure or a pain depends on what it is you wish to fill your life with. Or whether you wish to fill it at all. There is an endless supply of satisfaction available to anyone who wishes to help himself to it. It's not an easy city, but the cups of its residents runneth over with life.

It's a city of extremes. There's more of everything. The range of notes is wider. The highs are higher. The lows lower. The goods, the bads are better and worse. And if you're unimpressed by statistics, consider the fact that in 1972 the cops alone in New York City were charged with stealing $73 million worth of heroin. There are 1,700 murders in an average year.

Neither of those statistics is so much a comment on crime as it is a comment on the size and diversity of New York City.

No one keeps a statistic on Life. The probability is that, like everything else, there's more of it in New York.

THE DRAFT

THE argument about the draft is pretty dull because there are only two issues involved. One, should we have a draft at all? And two, if we have one, should we draft women?

The President could have considered a lot of other alternatives that would have made the argument more interesting, it seems to me. For instance, a sixteen-year-old boy wrote a letter to my hometown newspaper suggesting drafting *only* women. Well, now, *there's* an idea for you.

Men have been discriminated against in the draft for more than two hundred years. Maybe we ought to start an affirmative-action program, draft nothing but women until the total number of women drafted equals the total number of men who have ever been drafted. Even West Point would be all women with maybe eight or ten token men, just enough for an occasional newspaper feature story about how they're doing there.

Keep in mind, no one is saying men shouldn't serve in the Army at all. Far from it. There are certain noncombat jobs men are especially well qualified to do. Men make good medics, for example, because they're kinder, gentler, more sympathetic to someone in trouble. I think it would be safe to say that basically they're nicer people.

Wouldn't a proposition like that make the draft argument more interesting? Or how about using our free-enterprise system to attract people to the service? Offer to pay privates $50,000 a year, but only take the best applicants. There'd be plenty of applicants. This way we'd get good people and the Army and Navy wouldn't have to be so big.

There's more to the idea. Everyone wants to be an officer, no one wants to be a private, so privates would be paid the highest salary. As soon as a private was made a corporal, he'd only make $40,000 a year. A sergeant would make $35,000, and so on. By the time anyone in the Army got to be a general, she'd only be making $7,500 a year, something like that. There are *always* plenty of people who want to be the general.

Here's another idea. What about limiting the draft to people between the ages of fifty and sixty? A lot of us are in better shape now than we were when we were twenty and we're a lot smarter, too. Now, some fifty-year-olds might protest against registering for the draft, but wouldn't it be a relief to see someone other than *students* protesting for a change?

There are so many possibilities. What would you think about just drafting cigarette smokers? The ones who smoke more than a pack a day would serve in combat at the front lines, because . . . well, you know.

Well, something to argue about, isn't it?

POLITICAL PARTIES

A LOT of you probably aren't sure whether you're Republicans or Democrats. We have an election coming up shortly, and you ought to find out what you are. I thought it might help if I explained the difference between Republicans and Democrats.

Democrats believe the trouble started with Herbert Hoover, and was worse during the Presidency of Richard Nixon.
Republicans believe the trouble started with Franklin Roosevelt, and is worse than ever right now.

Democrats leave the dishes in the drying rack on the sink overnight.
Republicans put the dishes away every night.

Republicans play tennis.
Democrats bowl, unless they're Kennedy Democrats, in which case they play tennis too.

Democrats love television, and watch a lot of it.
Republicans hate television. They watch a lot of it too.

Democrats are baseball fans.
Republicans follow college football.

Democrats buy their food on payday once a week at the supermarket.
Republicans go to the grocery store every day.

Democrats usually write with a pencil.
Republicans use pens.

In the summer, Democrats drink beer.

Republicans drink gin and tonic. In the winter, they drink Scotch and soda.

Democrats drink beer.

Republicans think taxes are too high because of the Democrats. Democrats think taxes are too high because of the Republicans.

Republicans have dinner between seven and eight. Democrats have supper between five and six.

Democrats drink coffee with cream and sugar, from mugs. Republicans take theirs black—with cup and saucer.

Democrats don't seal the envelopes of their Christmas cards, which they sign by hand.

Republicans seal the envelopes of their Christmas cards, which have their names printed on them—unless they're very rich Republicans, in which case they sign them by hand. If they're very, very rich, they have someone else sign them.

Democrats believe people are basically good but must be saved from themselves by their government.

Republicans believe people are basically bad but they'll be okay if they're left alone.

A lot of Republicans are more like Democrats used to be, and a lot of Democrats are more like Republicans used to be. If you're still not sure what you are, you're probably a Democrat.

HOW WE ELECT
THE PRESIDENT

Most of us know how we elect our President, of course. It's a very simple democratic process. All it is is every American citizen over the age of eighteen votes for whomever he or she wants. That's all there is to it—practically all. There are a *few* little details.

For instance, first the voters pick the two people they want to run against each other, two outstanding Americans. This year it looks as though it'll be an old movie actor and a former peanut farmer.

Actually the voters don't choose those people, the members of the political parties do. It's called the primary system. The first primary is held in New Hampshire in February because it's—well, it doesn't matter *why* it's held there then, but it is.

So, beginning with New Hampshire, the two parties pick a candidate. They *sort* of pick a candidate. What really happens is they pick the delegates who will go to their party's convention. The delegates have to vote for the candidate the party members want them to—or at least in some states they have to. In other states, the delegates picked can vote for anybody they want to once they get to the convention. Then these thoughtful, handpicked Americans, who represent the whole country, solemnly decide who they want.

I think you can see how simple this system is that we have for electing our President. Once the candidates are chosen by the two parties, that's about it . . . unless, of course, there's a third party.

Now then, on November 4th all Americans go to the polls and vote for their choice. The person who gets the majority of the votes is President. That's *just about* it, anyway. The fact is, only about 54 percent of all Americans eligible to vote voted last time and the election was close, so you have to cut that figure in two, so only about 28 percent of us really voted to make Jimmy Carter President.

It doesn't matter, though, because the voters don't elect a President directly anyway. Actually, they're voting for *representatives* among the 538 people in the electoral college. They are the ones who *actually* vote to elect our President.

The people in the electoral college are chosen—well, they're chosen a lot the way New Hampshire was chosen to be the first primary state.

Let me read to you from the Constitution on how that works. It's called "Present Mode of Electing President and Vice-President by Electors." "The electors shall meet in their respective states and vote by ballot for President and Vice-President, one of whom, at least, shall not be an inhabitant of the same state with themselves."

" . . . one of whom shall not be an inhabitant of the same state with themselves."

Well, that's how we elect our President. Trust me.

POLLS

Y ou'll all be excited to learn that the results of the latest poll are in and I have them for you right here.

First you ought to know a little about the poll. The poll is about polls. It was prepared by me and I asked the questions of a broad cross section of nine Americans who work in the same office as I do.

Our first question was this, in two parts: In your opinion, which of the following polls are dullest and least accurate? Louis Harris/ABC, Gallup, Roper, CBS News/New York Times or NBC/Associated Press?

Seven of those polled thought they were all dull. Thirty-four percent said they thought the first two were most accurate *least* often. Fifty-six percent said that the last three were least accurate *most* often.

Second question: If the polls indicated that 90 percent of all Americans thought President Carter was doing a bad job, would you be more likely to vote for Teddy Kennedy?

Forty percent said "Maybe yes, Maybe no." Twenty-nine percent were undecided. Eleven percent said they didn't understand the question.

The remaining 22 percent said they'd rather have the Ayatollah Khomeini than Teddy Kennedy for President.

Third question: On Election Day the winners are often announced by the networks before the voting booths are closed. Does this lessen or increase your interest in voting?

Forty-one percent said "Yes." The rest of those polled said that if predicting was an exact science, weathermen wouldn't be wrong so often.

Fourth question: Have you ever been polled, has anyone in your immediate family ever been polled and do you care whether you're ever polled again? The answers to this question suggest some of those questioned weren't paying attention.

Twenty-three percent said "Walter Cronkite." Fifty-one percent said "Would you please repeat the question?" The rest told us to get lost.

Our last question was this: Even if the polls are accurate, do you wish they'd stop taking them? Here are the answers to that question:

"Yes," 50 percent. "No," 50 percent. "Undecided," 50 percent.

There's a margin for error on a question like this of about 50 percent one way or the other.

Finally, our poll indicated that if the next Presidential election were to be held this week, the winner would be the American public. It would save us all a lot of time and money.

DEBATES

Tonight's debate between the Presidential candidates won't be the only one, and I think it might be a good idea and make them more interesting if each of us kept a scorecard. I've drawn up a sample scorecard here. What you do is you give each candidate a mark of from zero to ten in each category.

APPEARANCE, for example. Give each candidate the score you think he should have for his appearance. If he doesn't appear at all, of course, he gets a zero.

INFLATION. From what they've said, how well do you think they'll handle inflation? You might also take into consideration whether the candidate sounds a little inflated himself.

NECKTIE. You'd want to consider color, how much you think it cost, how well it was tied and whether you think the candidate tied it himself or had a makeup person do it.

STALLING. Score them on whether or not they were evasive during the debate. If a candidate used a lot of phrases like "I think my position is clear on that," instead of saying what his position is, you'd give him a low mark.

ERA. ABORTION. GUN CONTROL. This is just one category here because they're the same thing. Everyone who is against one is against the others, and vice versa.

ENERGY. DEFENSE. HAIR. Reagan and Anderson both have good-looking hair. You might want to give them each an eight, unless you think Reagan dyes his brown; then you might want to give him only a two. If you think Anderson dyes his gray, give him a ten.

STANDABILITY. This is a difficult category, but it's important. You know how it is with some candidates? No matter what they say, you can't stand them. Mark them from zero to ten on standability.

So that's it. I've got just one more idea for the last debate. We'll all know what the candidates think by then, and we are, after all, electing a First Lady, too. So the last debate will be different. For half an hour, each candidate will argue with his wife.

POLLS 1980

THE election's long over, of course, and Ronald Reagan's been declared the winner. He got 43 million votes and Carter only got 35 million. But I'm still waiting to see who the *polltakers* say won the election. I mean, votes don't mean anything because they aren't scientific, like polls are.

I kept a file of a lot of poll stories over the past year. You probably read some of them.

"REPUBLICAN, INDEPENDENT VOTERS PICK FORD IN POLL"—Louis Harris. This was taken before the Republican Convention. Obviously, Gerald Ford was going to be the Republican candidate.

In August, "AP-NBC POLL SHOWS PREZ GAINING SHARPLY ON RON." This was before most of us even knew he was behind.

Time magazine's poll in September had them even at 39 percent.

According to Mervin Field, Reagan's lead in California began to shrink in September. He only won by 1.4 million votes in California.

"CARTER LEADS REAGAN IN ILLINOIS, POLL SAYS"—Carter 27 percent, Reagan 23 percent. The Chicago *Tribune* thought Carter was leading in Illinois, but admitted that 35 percent of the voters hadn't decided who to vote for yet. Apparently, 90 percent of the 35 percent decided to vote for Reagan.

In October, Carter was narrowing the gap in Virginia, according to the Richmond *Times-Dispatch*.

At the same time, he was gaining again in the ABC/Harris poll: Reagan 49 percent, Carter 46 percent. Carter sure did a lot of gaining in the polls.

The same day, the CBS/New York Times poll had Carter pulling even at 39 percent. They made it all very clear with a chart: "Carter found clear favorite among evangelicals." I always wondered, if you're born again do you get to vote twice?

Toward the end, they were all saying the race was about even. I took a little post-election poll myself. I asked one question of four people around the office. I asked them, "If the election was today, would you vote the same way you did?"

One person said he would; one person said he wouldn't; one person said he always got so confused in the voting booth that he couldn't remember who he'd voted for. The fourth person said she voted for Anderson and she'd do it again, too, because no matter what happens now, it isn't her fault.

I think all the polls this year make one thing very clear: the election was a lot closer than the unscientific voting would indicate.

THE CAPITAL

SOMEONE has written in suggesting we move the nation's capital out of Washington to somewhere in Kansas because that's closer to the center of the country. It's an old idea, but it might be worth considering.

If you've ever moved out of a house or an office, you know you have to go through all your old junk, and you end up throwing half of it away. There's no place on earth that needs stuff thrown away like Washington does.

The Capitol itself is a grand old building. We should certainly keep that. It could be taken down at its present location and put back up again in a wheat field in Kansas. Most of the big buildings we could leave. There's no need to take all those departments, agencies, bureaus and committees to Kansas. No need to take the Treasury Building, for instance. The Treasury is $790 billion in debt. Why take a building with nothing in it?

No need to take the Supreme Court Building either, I think. It's beautiful for a reporter to stand in front of, but it has a cold look. I think the Supreme Justices would seem less remote from all of us if they made their decisions from maybe rocking chairs on a comfortable front porch in Kansas.

The next question is this: What do we do with Washington? It's too good to throw away. The idea I like is to make Washington into one huge tourist-attracting Disneyland. It really wouldn't be much of a change.

The Pentagon could become a fun house. It's already a wonderful place to get lost in just as it is. Visitors could spend many happy hours playing in the Pentagon halls. The White House would be unchanged, except that the Presidents and their families would be represented by moving models—perhaps featuring a different Presidential family on each day of the month.

If we leave the old White House in Washington, of course, we'll need a new one in Kansas. Well, the President's always traveling around the country. Maybe the new White House should be a mobile home. That way, no matter where he went the President would know where his pajamas were.

MR. ROONEY GOES TO
WASHINGTON*

PEOPLE want to know what's going on in Washington. Last year 19 million Americans went there trying to find out. They spent most of their time lined up outside some place. The trouble with that is, like tourists anywhere, they leave no smarter about the place than they were when they came.

Several months ago CBS sent me to Washington to see what a nonpolitical reporter with no previous knowledge of that place could find out about it. It was a good assignment, like spending two months as a tourist in a foreign country with the company paying the bill.

The first thing I did in Washington was to try to find my way around. It's all right to say you're going to do some investigating, but it's embarrassing the first day when you go out the door and don't know whether to turn left or right to get to the White House.

I spent several days just looking around and taking pictures. No one can stand being a tourist for long, though, and the things I wanted to find out about Washington were the things the guide-books don't tell you.

Two and three-quarters million people are paid $35 billion a year to work for the federal government. I keep trying to find out exactly why it is our government has grown so big and why there are so many bureaus in the bureaucracy.

One of the reasons seems to be that almost every committee, every agency or every department is established by law, but there is never anything in that law about putting the agency out of

* Broadcast January 26, 1975.

business when its job is done. Once established, a government agency, like a government job, is practically immortal. If a committee or agency has a name that makes it sound out-of-date, it doesn't go out of business; it just changes its name.

We kept asking people if what they were doing was really necessary or if it was something the government ought to be doing for us in the first place.

We thought maybe Civil Defense was something out-of-date that we could do without. We had a nice talk with the Director of Civil Defense, John E. Davis.

The first thing we found out was, it isn't called that anymore.

DAVIS:

Two years ago we changed our name to Defense Civil Preparedness Agency. We wanted to be more inclusive, to look at natural disasters as well as preparation against survival from a nuclear attack.

Rooney:

People say that you're an agency in search of a mission.

Davis:

Quite to the contrary. This organization has taken on a currency role and I refer to the natural disasters that we have frequently occurring in practically all sections of the United States. There's none that escapes . . . tornadoes, hurricanes, earthquakes, winter storms. . . .

Rooney:

I'm confused about the Office of Emergency Preparedness in relation to you. Is there any overlapping there?

Davis:

We are the Office of— Oh, Office of Emergency Preparedness? Of course, that was a year ago in July, by Executive Order. It was separated and part of it now, of the Office of Emergency Preparedness, is called Office of Preparedness, which is in GSA, responsible generally for the continuity of government and certain emergency plans that were, had been associated with OEP. And part of it, the disaster relief generally, FDAA, Federal Disaster Assistance Agency, is over in HUD. And they administer the rehabilitation and have some responsibilities for assisting states as we do, but we have been assigned the mission of helping local communities prepare for these natural disasters. And that generally is where we get the authorities for what we're doing in the natural disaster field.

Rooney:

We've been looking at some of your literature that you've been publishing and we're particularly interested in this one, *Protecting Mobile Homes from High Winds*. Is telling people how to protect their mobile homes from tipping over a function of government?

Davis:

It's just one of these things that was done because of our professional knowledge and the fact that it was something that people wanted today.

Rooney:

I was taken with this one phrase in here. "Mobile homes meet a real need in our society: they are attractive, comfortable, and provide low-cost housing." Now, for a government booklet to say mobile homes are attractive . . . I never heard anybody call a mobile home attractive before.

Davis:

Well, it's—

Rooney:

Why would a government booklet call a mobile home attractive?

Davis:

Well, I think that this is a matter of opinion. Certainly the manufacturers of mobile homes and I imagine those that live in it—to them that is the case. And so it's all a relative thing.

Rooney:

What is your budget, your total budget?

Davis:

Eighty-two million dollars last year and it appears that it's under consideration by the Congress now and I think it will be approximately the same amount.

With the draft over, I thought our government might be saving money by closing the Selective Service Agency. We talked to the Director, Byron Pepitone, a retired Air Force colonel. We asked him what Selective Service was doing now that it wasn't selecting anyone anymore.

Pepitone:

We have become an organization in standby . . . much as an organization in the sense of insurance against an emergency. We're not inducting anyone, you see. The authority to do so has expired. But our staff and our offices have been reduced by a quarter, by three-quarters.

Rooney:

How much is your budget?

Pepitone:

In the spring of 1973, before inductions stopped, we were operating on a budget of approximately a hundred million dollars. Our request to the Congress for the fiscal year '75 forthcoming will be for forty-seven million dollars.

Rooney:

Is that the absolute minimum that it costs to do *nothing?* Not to draft *anyone?*

Pepitone:

Forty-seven million dollars is a very small amount to guarantee that should you have to augment that force, you have the capacity to do it in a timely fashion.

ROONEY:

What would happen to your operation if you spent only twenty million?

PEPITONE:

Well, my personal opinion is that if it gets much below the present level, we might just as well decide that we don't need it.

It's hard to show the size of government. It isn't as though you could get everyone who works for it to pose for one big class picture. And, of course, it hasn't always been this big, either.

In 1930, half of all government employees were mailmen. Now there are a lot more mailmen, but they represent only 25 percent of all goverment workers.

And back then, there was no such thing as a Department of Health, Education and Welfare. Our health, education and welfare were pretty much our own business. Well, of course, things have changed. Today, there are 127,000 HEW employees. The agency occupies space in fifty-seven buildings in the Washington area alone.

We thought it would be interesting to find out how many government buildings there are in the Washington area. We asked the General Services Administration for a complete list. They told us they didn't have one, but they could get us one for $150.

So we paid them $150 and here's the list they gave us. (*A computer printout unravels to the floor.*) This is a list of every government building in the Washington area.

I have another printout, too: "Real Property Owned by the United States." It's a list of every building our government owns all over the world. The CIA may have a pad or two in Budapest that isn't listed here, but substantially these are our real-estate holdings. Something like half a million buildings. Our government owns them.

The General Services Administration is an interesting operation. What it is, is a combination landlord and superintendent for all government buildings. If you work for the government and need a whole new building or just a box of rubber bands, you go to the General Services Administration.

Now, this is their catalog (*holding it up*). About anything you'd want is in here, and there are quite a few things you wouldn't want, too.

Here's a chair. They have sixteen different kinds of chairs, for instance. There are eighteen grades of government servants, so I suppose there's one chair for each grade . . . The bottom two grades must have to stand.

Here are the rubber bands, if you want rubber bands. This one here is Federal Specification ZZRoo1415. So the government's got just about everything you want if you work for it.

We wondered where all this stuff in the catalog came from so we went out to one of the General Services warehouses to look around.

(*Examining conveyor belt*) What would you like? Here's boxes of leather gloves. Mops. I imagine the mop handles will be coming along. Some kind of lock. String. There are two balls—for toilet bowls? A couple of dictionaries. You want a dictionary? Pans, pots, wrenches.

What would you like? Nameplates for executives' desks. Here's paint rollers. And where would the government be without—you thought this was a figure of speech—genuine government red tape.

I don't think there's anything more discouraging for a taxpayer who likes to think that he's doing something important for his country than to see something like this. You look at one of these boxes on the conveyor belt and you say to yourself, "There go my taxes . . . not democracy or freedom or a battleship or anything . . . just a box of stuff."

* * *

This chart, "Pay System Total General Schedule," shows all the ranks of Civil Service workers in government. There are eighteen grades and there are ten steps within each grade too, but we're not going to get into that.

And we aren't going to get into double-dipping either. In Washington, double-dipping is the practice of retiring from the Army, Navy or Air Force and then taking a job in Civil Service so that you get two salaries.

There are more government workers in Grade 5 than any other, 172,000. Each of them makes the minimum of $9,000. And it costs the government a billion and a half.

Grades 16, 17 and 18 all make $36,000. You'll see that Grade 16 is listed at thirty-five five, but actually Grade 16 makes $36,000 too . . . after he's been in the government for about twenty minutes.

It's one of the problems in government. All three top grades make the same, so there's not much advantage to getting to be the boss . . . except possibly you get to go home a little early on Friday.

If Civil Service worked the way it's supposed to work, it would be fine. It's supposed to go like this: If someone needs a certain kind of employee, he goes to his department's employment office and they find someone in their card file who fits his job description.

According to the people we talked to, it doesn't work ideally very often, though. Something like this is more apt to happen: Say I'm in a management position in government. I have a job open. My old college roommate needs a job but the description of the job in my office doesn't match his qualifications. He worked in the real-estate business for a while. He had a job in a bank once. His father is Italian. And he was editor of our college newspaper.

I want to help my old roommate, so I get him to apply to Civil Service. He puts down all his qualifications.

A short while later, I go to Civil Service and I say, "Say, that job I have is changed. What I need now is someone with newspaper experience to help our office with some real-estate dealings in an Italian neighborhood. He should have knowledge of mortgages and bank loans."

So someone at Civil Service takes that information, feeds it into a computer and, presto, guess whose name pops up? My old college roommate's.

The Civil Service payroll represents only half of what the government pays out in salaries every year, though. The names in a book called *United States Government Policy and Supporting Positions* represent something else. These are the people who work for government but are not Civil Service. In other words, these people were all appointed to their jobs.

This thing really makes good reading, too. Look at some of the titles in here:

—SECRETARY TO THE SECRETARY

—SECRETARIAL ATTENDANT TO THE SECRETARY

Secretary to the Secretary . . . .
Secretarial Attendant to the Secretary.
Chauffeur to the Secretary . . . .

Confidential Staff Assistant to Associate Director, Human Rights.
Congressional Relations Specialist . . . . .
Confidential Assistant . . . .
Policy Analyst . . . .
. . . . do . . . .
Congressional Relations Specialist . . . . .
Confidential Assistant to Assistant Director for P.R. & E.
Confidential Secretary to the Director . .
Confidential Assistant to Special Assistant to Director.
Confidential Assistant to the Director . .
Confidential Staff Assistant . . . .
Confidential Staff Assistant to the Associate Director, Congressional Relations.
Confidential Assistant . . . .
. . . . do . . . .
. . . . do . . . .
Confidential Staff Assistant . . . .
Private Secretary (Stenography) OEO Director.
Confidential Assistant . . . .
Confidential Staff Assistant . . . .
Confidential Staff Assistant to Assistant Director.
Confidential Staff Assistant to Assistant Director.
Confidential Assistant to the Associate Director Congressional Relations.
Confidential Secretary to the Director . .
Confidential Staff Assistant . . . .
Confidential Secretary to the Special Assistant.
Confidential Secretary (Stenography) . .
Confidential Secretary . . . .
Confidential Secretary to Associate Director, Congressional Relations.
Confidential Assistant to Special Assistant to Director.
Confidential Secretary (Stenography) . .
Confidential Secretary . . . .
Confidential Secretary to the Deputy Director.

Associate Deputy Administrator . . . . . .
Deputy Associate Administrator . . . . . .

Associate Administrator for Procurement and Management Assistance.
Special Assistant to Associate Administrator for Procurement and Management Assistance.

Deputy Assistant Secretary . . . .
Special Assistant to the Assistant Secretary.
Staff Assistant to the Deputy Assistant Secretary.
Private Secretary to the Assistant Secretary.
Private Secretary to the Deputy Assistant Secretary.

Assistant Administrator for Administration.
Deputy Assistant Administrator for Administration.

Confidential Assistant (Private Secretary) to the Secretary of Labor.
Assistant to Special Assistant to Secretary, Office of Legislative Liaison.

Special Assistant to the Secretary . . . .
. . . . do . . . .
Special Assistant to the Director, Federal Contract Compliance.
Assistant to Special Assistant to Secretary, Office of Legislative Liaison.
Special Assistant to the Secretary . . . .
Assistant to the Special Assistant to the Secretary for Communications.
Assistant to Special Assistant to Secretary, Office of Legislative Liaison.
Special Assistant to the Secretary . . . .

—CHAUFFEUR TO THE SECRETARY

Apparently the chauffeur doesn't have a secretary himself.

And then there are all the confidential people:

—CONFIDENTIAL STAFF ASSISTANT

—CONFIDENTIAL STAFF ASSISTANT TO THE ASSOCIATE DIRECTOR

—CONFIDENTIAL ASSISTANT

—CONFIDENTIAL STAFF ASSISTANT

Confidential, confidential, confidential . . . In Washington, a confidential assistant is the person who, if you don't want to know something, you go and ask him and he won't tell you.

There are also some beauties here:

—ASSOCIATE DEPUTY ADMINISTRATOR

—DEPUTY ASSOCIATE ADMINISTRATOR

And down further:

—DEPUTY ASSISTANT SECRETARY

—SPECIAL ASSISTANT TO THE ASSISTANT SECRETARY

—STAFF ASSISTANT TO THE DEPUTY ASSISTANT SECRETARY

—ASSISTANT ADMINISTRATOR FOR ADMINISTRATION

—DEPUTY ASSISTANT ADMINISTRATOR FOR ADMINISTRATION

And it goes on like that.

Government officials are always saying there aren't any more federal employees now than there were twenty years ago. This sounds good until you find out what the reason is.

The reason is an awful lot of government work in Washington is being done by private companies now, on contract.

I grew up thinking big government and big business were enemies. Well, imagine how surprised I was to find out they're really best friends . . . very close buddies. As a matter of fact, in Washington big business and big government get along so well it scares the life out of you.

The Department of Defense, for instance, has 80,000 people on its payroll who arrange contracts with private companies who actually do the work. There are hundreds of companies in Washington which do nothing but advise the government.

Here's a little example we looked into . . . a report on urban mass transportation presented by the Secretary of the Department of Transportation to the President of the Senate. At the time it was Gerald Ford. The letter accompanying the report says:

Dear Mr. President:

I am pleased to submit the Department's study of Urban Mass Transportation, needs and financing, etc.

Sincerely,

Claude S. Brinegar

Sec. Dept. Transportation

Well, now, you'd think this had been prepared by the Department of Transportation, wouldn't you? It wasn't. It was prepared by a private company called Peat, Marwick and Mitchell.

We got hold of the contract under which Peat, Marwick did this study. They were paid $260,564 for it. Would anyone know the study was done by Peat, Marwick? Would the Senate or the public know? Not from anything you could find in this study, because Peat, Marwick and Mitchell's name isn't mentioned anywhere in it. Not even in fine print.

The trouble with contracting is that it makes it even harder for all of us to find out where our money is going.

We tried for months to get someone at Peat, Marwick and Mitchell to talk to us about this. They refused. What are they hiding? There's no law they have to talk to us, of course, but, well, it *is* our money.

One of the obvious problems is that when a private company gives advice to the government in some special area and also has private clients in that *same* area, it seems very unlikely that the advice they give the government will do their *private* clients any harm.

Here's another example of contracting. We were looking through the *Commerce Business Daily* one day. I never heard of the publication before, but it's important to people in Washington doing business with the government. It lists contracts up for bids, contracts let, that sort of thing. We came on one small contract that had been given out. It said what the company was supposed to do: "Prepare guideline to be used for the rewriting of all Navy technical manuals to the ninth grade level."

A company called Biotechnology got the contract and were to be paid $65,622. Now that seemed interesting, so we set out trying to find out more about it.

First, we called Biotechnology. We didn't get far.

(*On phone*) "Andy Rooney, CBS News. Rooney, R-O-O-N-E-Y. . . . Well, check with him, will you, and see if he'll talk with

me. . . . He's not there right now, huh? Do you think he went somewhere? Is he apt to be in again today?"

(I'm always amazed at how a secretary can sit three feet from a guy and not know whether he's in or not.)

"Oh, you don't think he'll be back today. All right, put me on hold, fine. . . . I've been on hold before. . . . Out of the building, eh?"

(She's asking him whether he's in or not, I think.)

"What time is he apt to be in, do you know? Do you know what time he's apt to be in? . . . Around eleven . . . okay. Well, do you think if I call him around . . . He may go right to lunch from . . . instead of coming in at eleven. That's an early lunch. Do you know whether he has a lunch appointment or where he would be going? Will he call in and let you know whether he's coming in or not? . . . He wouldn't let you know about that. . . . And if he's *not* coming in, he won't tell you? Okay. Well, why don't I try you again at eleven then, and see if you know anything. . . ."

Several days later, much to our surprise, we got through to the company's president.

(*On phone*) "Andy Rooney, CBS News. How are you? I've been trying to get you for a long while. Would you be able to tell me, you know, who you're dealing with in the Navy? Is that a secret? (*Listens*) I just wondered, you know, if you could talk to us on camera someday about how it goes and what you do and that sort of thing? . . .

"Well, is the Navy apt to say they don't want any publicity at all on it? If you can get approval from the Navy, we could talk on camera. (*Listens*) Well, would you check it with them or should I?"

They told me they couldn't talk about it without Navy permission. So we went to the Navy. You haven't *seen* red tape until you deal with the Navy. We talked to them . . . a lot of them.

(*On phone*) "I was just trying to find out, you know, what was happening, what the Navy was doing with their manuals. . . .

"I had been trying to talk with some people at a company named Biotechnology. Are you familiar with them? . . . Yeah. I . . . you know, it just doesn't seem like anything very sneaky to me. I don't see why they wouldn't talk about it. They were reluctant to talk until they had gotten some sort of clearance from you people at the Navy.

"I then talked to a Mr. Shihda, and he referred me to a Mr. Tarbell, and Mr. Tarbell referred me to Mr. Cleverly. And then I guess he referred me to you. Do you think there would be any objection to my talking to the people at Biotech? . . . All right, thanks a lot, okay."

After weeks of phone calls, we reached someone in the Navy who said it was all right to talk to Biotechnology about it . . . if it was all right with them.

You won't be surprised to learn that Biotechnology still refused to talk to me.

We were really interested now and we were able to get hold of the Navy study on which that contract was based: "*Navy Enlisted Occupational Classification System (NEOCS) Study, Volume II.*" Armed with this study, we went to the Navy and had an interview with Admiral Frederick Palmer, the man in charge of implementing it.

Rooney:
   Are you having all the manuals rewritten to a ninth-grade level of comprehension, Admiral?

PALMER:

I think that needs a little explanation, because I think that you need to go further and find out ninth grade according to what standard.

ROONEY:

Has this contract been executed yet?

PALMER:

No.

ROONEY:

They haven't done the work?

PALMER :

No.

ROONEY:

We had tried to contact Biotechnology. Do you know Biotechnology?

PALMER:

No, I do not.

ROONEY (aside):

It just seems strange to us that the officer in charge of implementing this study never heard of Biotechnology or of the chart on page 51, dividing all potential Navy enlistees into four categories.

ROONEY (to Admiral):

I saw a report and it divided Navy enlistees into four categories: Socially Assertive Team Leaders; Uninvolved Reward Seekers; Active Manual Satisfaction Seekers; and Unrealistic Self-Improvement Seekers. You recognize them in the Navy?

PALMER:

I haven't the foggiest notion of what you're talking about. I hope I can get a copy of that to look into.

ROONEY:

Wasn't that in Volume II of your study?

PALMER:

I don't recall that at all.

ROONEY:

I think it was.

PALMER:

Do you have the page number of that?

Rooney:

No, I don't. It was known as the Grey study.

Palmer:

I'll sure look it up. I'll make a note of that right now.

Rooney:

If you had your report with you, I think it's probably in there.

Palmer:

Grey study. Volume II, you say. Thank you.

We're not drawing any conclusions about the Navy or this little company. They're probably both fine, but these contracts sure make it difficult for a citizen to find out where $65,000 goes.

And keep in mind that contract was only one of 583 that appeared in the *Commerce Business Daily* that day alone. We didn't have time to check the other 582.

Having struck out at both Peat, Marwick and Mitchell and Bio-technology, we went to a company called McKinsey.

McKinsey, though largely unknown to the public, is an important name in the high and inner circles of government. We'd all like to tell the government what to do once in a while. Well, McKinsey not only tells government what to do, but the government listens and pays them for the advice.

Robert Fry of McKinsey talked to us.

Rooney:

What would your contracts with government run to? A hundred thousand dollars? A hundred million dollars?

Fry (laughs):

Well, there was one with the Department of Transportation that we just finished, a study over there for Secretary Brinegar. That contract was quoted in Jack Anderson's column at three hundred and sixty-five thousand dollars—which I assume is about right.

Rooney:

Would you, at the same time, be doing work for General Motors when you were doing something for the Department of Transportation?

Fry:

Oh, I think the sense of your question is, could we be serving an industrial client. And the answer is yes. But we would be

serving it from a different office with different people. We have
internal controls to make sure that there's no conflict.

ROONEY:

What about just a list of the government agencies that you do
work for. Is that an available thing or is that a secret?

FRY:

Well, let me tell you some that I know have appeared in the
press or otherwise been mentioned publicly over the last few
years.

ROONEY:

In other words, there are some that you wouldn't . . .

FRY:

There are some I prefer . . .

ROONEY:

Prefer not to mention?

FRY:

Not to mention. We serve the Veterans Administration, the
Peace Corps, the Department of Transportation that I mentioned
earlier.

ROONEY:

But the ones that interest me most are the ones that you won't
tell me.

FRY:

That's a representative list. We serve the Office of Management
and Budget, the Treasury Department.

ROONEY:

Why wouldn't you tell me all of them?

FRY:

It's simply a practice of the firm that we're not the ones who
tell publicly who our clients are.

ROONEY:

In other words, the government would come to you and give
you this contract and say, "But don't tell anybody about it."

FRY:

No, they don't say that. I'm not trying to dodge your question.
I'm just being true to the standard practice of the firm, which
is a carry-over largely from the private sector. But we still observe
it here to the extent that our relationship with a client is not
widely known.

ROONEY:

Is there a way we could find out what McKinsey's total income for one year was from government contracts?

FRY:

Well, it would be in the several-hundred-thousand-dollar range.

ROONEY:

Well, that one you mentioned was three hundred and eighty-five thousand, so—

FRY:

Yes.

ROONEY:

It certainly would be several hundred.

FRY:

Yeah.

Power is always slipping away from most of us and into the hands of the very few. I guess we all worry about it, but if you spend some time in Washington, you get thinking that Congress, at least, isn't really very dangerous. Democracy still has the upper hand.

Almost everything we do is a fact before Congress knows what's happened. Take sex, for instance, or the economy, if sex offends you. Our national habits have changed in regard to both sex and money, but Congress didn't have a thing to do with either of them. We establish our own rules of how we live and all Congress can do is make them official and make them apply to everybody the same way.

Even if a congressman wanted to become some kind of a dictator, he couldn't do it. He's too busy. Congress is disorganized, overworked, and very little of what it does becomes law. If one congressman is *for* something, another is against it. We're lucky they don't get along because it offers all of us a great deal of protection.

We can't get cameras into the House of Representatives gallery, so we don't have film of a little argument that we saw break out one day between Congressman James Cleveland of New Hampshire and Congressman Pierre duPont of Delaware. We went to their offices later and talked to each of them about that.

ROONEY:

I heard you speak on the floor of the House a few days ago. You were trying to get money for people in a ski area. They said they were in trouble because it hadn't snowed much. Is protecting businessmen from the elements a function of government?

CLEVELAND:

I think so. I'm sure you're acquainted with flood insurance and disaster insurance. And I think that we have various federal programs to assist people that have been victims of some natural disaster.

ROONEY:

Is not-snowing a natural disaster?

CLEVELAND:

Well, apparently, it didn't fall within the provisions of any existing law, and that's why I got the amendment through that I did.

DUPONT:

My reaction to that is we've come to the ultimate in government now. . . . We're paying people because it isn't snowing where they live.

ROONEY:

But what do you say to Congressman Cleveland, who says there are five thousand people in New Hampshire who aren't going to eat well enough because it didn't snow—they need help.

DUPONT:

Well, you say, "Jim Cleveland, you're a good friend and you're a nice guy, but we shouldn't be paying people because it doesn't snow. If it doesn't snow, it doesn't snow, and that's one of the things that we live with."

CLEVELAND:

The ski industry is really quite important to northern New England and northern New York. It employs a great many people and it particularly employs a lot of college students who are attending colleges in those areas. It's weekend work for them when most of the action is—

ROONEY:

But that day on the floor of the House, I was sort of amused and I suppose you weren't. Congressman duPont said that it had been raining in Rehoboth Beach, Delaware, where he has a lot of constituents, and the people who sold bikinis were in trouble there and he wondered if they would be eligible for support because it was raining at the beach.

CLEVELAND:

Well, the answer is that if there was a prolonged period of rain and dismal weather, I would think that a resort-type area might be eligible for this.

DUPONT:

Well, the other thing you can say to him, although he probably wouldn't like it is, "Jim, if we start the subsidies this year, and it snows less next year, you'll be back for more. It's an endless program. And furthermore, if it *does* snow next year, you'll be back for this amount anyhow, because you'll say if we stop the subsidies now nobody will make any money, and the result is pretty soon we'll be paying people whether it snows or not."

Congressmen and women do most of their work in committee session. A lot of those are closed to the public but a lot are open too. Tourists ought to spend more time at these and less time hanging around down by the Washington Monument.

We listened in on about thirty committees. You often pick up interesting bits of information.

MR. MAGNUSON:

The price of wheat to the farmer is a very small item in the price of a loaf of bread whether it goes up or down.

CHAIRMAN:

That's very true.

MR. MAGNUSON:

And there are many occasions, I guess you've found out, where the price of wheat would go down and the price of a loaf of bread would go up.

CHAIRMAN:

Could you, for the record, and the record will stay opened . . .

In Washington, everything is for the record . . . which usually means, let's not waste time with it.

Washington is probably the only place in the whole world where there are more writers than readers. Everyone is writing something, having it duplicated or printed and distributing it to everyone else. No one, it seems, is actually reading much of it.

The U.S. Government Printing Office in Washington has committed more words to more paper than any other printing plant in the whole world. The *Congressional Record* alone is a monumental job of printing. Eight hundred and thirty Linotype operators and editors work all night putting it out every day.

We counted a more or less average day's *Congressional Record*. There were four thousand more than half a million words in it. And that's just for one day.

Let me read you the way Congress opens each session. First there's a prayer, uniting church and state, and then the Speaker of the House or the Senate makes a motion; in this case it was Senator Mansfield. He says, "Mr. President, I ask unanimous consent that the readings of the *Journal* of the proceedings of [the previous day] be dispensed with."

Well, consent is always given. Thank God. Because it would take sixty solid hours to get through reading just this one day's *Congressional Record*. And by that time, of course, they could have had three more sessions of Congress and three more editions of the *Congressional Record*, each containing half a million words.

*　*　*

Words. Behind the fireproof doors at the Federal Records Center are two and a half million boxes of words that probably ought to be burned.

(*Inside Federal Records Center*) These cardboard coffins are headed for the crypt. They're being saved not so much because they're important but because, like your own Sunday paper, someone couldn't stand the thought of throwing them out without reading them . . . and they couldn't stand the thought of reading them.

Filing costs the government $2.8 billion a year, about thirteen dollars apiece for every American.

Your name is in here somewhere . . . and so is your father's. The joke in government is that before you throw anything out, you Xerox it so you'll have a copy.

Not all government records are kept, though. The Pentagon is a regular secrets factory—and most of the secrets it produces every day are destroyed right where they're made. The Pentagon Disposal Center is the biggest secrets disposal mill in the whole universe. When people from a Pentagon office have papers they want

to destroy, they bundle them up, bring them to the disposal center, sign for them and stand by until they have been chewed and digested by the paper shredder.

According to a usually reliable Pentagon source, there are, in addition to the secrets, usually a few unfinished crossword puzzles that go in there to be uncycled.

ROONEY:
    About how much of this do you run through a day?
PAPER-SHREDDER SUPERVISOR:
    Well, on the average of ten to fourteen tons of dry paper.
ROONEY:
    And those are all *secrets?*
SUPERVISOR:
    All secrets as far as I'm concerned.
ROONEY:
    Boy, ten tons of secrets is a lot, isn't it?
SUPERVISOR:
    Yep.
ROONEY:
    Do you ever get curious about what's on those?

Supervisor:

No, sir. You get to the point where you don't pay any attention to what goes in.

Rooney:

And there's no possibility of anybody reading this, is there?

Supervisor:

I'd say. Take a look at it. (*Picks up wet pulp*) If you can read that, why, I'll give you my next month's salary.

You might think the government isn't aware of the proliferation of paperwork in its operation. Wrong. The government has had studies done of the problem . . . lots of them.

"We've had a study done"; that's what you hear all over Washington. Having a study done is an end in itself. Actually *doing* something about a study is something else.

We went in to talk to Mark Koenig, who was called Assistant Archivist for Records Management. He was sort of in charge of trying to cut down on government paperwork.

Rooney:

What's the cost of government paperwork?

Koenig:

The last estimate we had from the General Accounting Office is fifteen billion dollars a year.

Rooney:

Fifteen billion for paperwork.

The Paper Management Office tries to encourage people to cut down on paperwork by having a contest every year.

We have one of the letters sent out by a department head telling his people how to enter their nominees. It says: "The purpose of the award is to honor those Federal employees who have contributed significantly to the efficiency or cost reduction of Federal paperwork systems. Nominating procedures are described in the prospectus, but one change is necessary; six (6) copies of any nomination, rather than four (4), should be submitted."

Well, that's a bad start when you're trying to save paper.

The awards ceremony itself was a combination luncheon and cocktail party. It began at eleven-fifteen in the morning. It was a big event and very pleasant, but not in itself a good example of saving paper. There was paper everywhere you looked and in great quantity. You wonder whether maybe the paperwork award wasn't costing the government more in paper than it was saving it.

(*Music, military march*)

We weren't sure why the paperwork award ceremony was opened with a military color guard marching into the dining room . . . but, of course, we'd never been to a paper-saving award ceremony before, so what do we know?

This was the Super Bowl of paper-saving. We thought they were picking just one government money-saver, but it turns out there were lots of them. They gave out forty-one awards, some of them to as many as eight people. Actually, you could come away from this affair with the idea that the government wasn't *wasting* money at all on paper . . . that it was actually making money on it.

OFFICIAL GIVING AWARDS:

. . . during the last nine years have been responsible for savings in excess of one billion dollars. . . .

UNITED STATES GOVERNMENT

Memorandum

DEPARTMENT OF JUSTICE

Office of Management & Finance

TO : Heads of Offices, Divisions, and Boards of the Department of Justice

DATE: June 20, 1974

FROM Jack Rottman
Chief, Personnel Section
Operations Support Staff

SUBJECT: Tenth Annual Federal Paperwork Management Awards
Response Due: July 23, 1974

The Washington Chapter of the Association of Records Executives and Administrators, in cooperation with the National Archives and Records Service of GSA, is currently accepting nominations for the Tenth Annual Federal Paperwork Management Awards.

As mentioned in the attached prospectus, the purpose of the award is to honor those Federal employees who have contributed significantly to the efficiency or cost reduction of Federal paperwork systems or programs.

Nominating procedures are described in the prospectus, but one change is necessary; six (6) copies of any nomination, rather than four (4), should be submitted to the Personnel Section, Main Building, Room 6229 by COB July 23, 1974.

If you have any questions, contact Mr. Warren Oser on extension 4615.

Saving this kind of money, we could become a rich nation again.

(*Applause*)

VARIOUS VOICES:

"Congratulations."

"Thank you."

"You going to go and have a drink with us?"

"Say, that would be great."

"I'm not going back to the office."

"Oh, you're not?"

There's almost always someplace to go except back to work in Washington. There are a thousand little parties every week and it seems as though some people go to all of them.

In Washington, the amenities often take up more time than the business. The pace of the city is slower than in the cities that make something. There are more times out, more days off. "Lunch" doesn't always mean eating.

ROONEY:

You do this on your lunch hour?

1ST JOGGER:

Or, whenever.

ROONEY:

There's a lot of this going on in Washington. How come?

2ND JOGGER:

It just seems to be that way, I don't know.

ROONEY:

What's your job?

2ND JOGGER:

Over in the Pentagon.

ROONEY:

How many miles do you run a day?

3RD JOGGER:

Five.

ROONEY:

Five miles. Where do you work?

3RD JOGGER:

Pentagon.

Everything will still be here tomorrow. The government isn't *making* anything.

The United States government pays out something like $95 billion a year in subsidies. It seems as though every company and every professional organization has an office in Washington to represent its interests.

There's the National Soft Drink Association, the International Association of Fire Chiefs, the National Swimming Pool Institute, the Associated Telephone Answering Exchanges, the National Automobile Association, the Humane Society of the United States, the National Education Association, the National Rifle Association of America, the Society of American Foresters, the American Horse Council, the American Chemical Society, the Tobacco Institute. . . .

Almost every bill passed in Congress influences the distribution of money, and the game is to get more out of the government than you're putting in. A lot of people are winning the game.

Everyone knows the tax break the big oil companies get, but you don't hear much about the others. The lumber industry, for instance, gets a subsidy of $130 million. The federal government pays out $244 million to fourteen shipping companies. Every American seaman is subsidized for about $12,000. And that's in addition to what the shipping company pays the sailor.

And you don't have to look to the giants of industry either to find money being handed out. I was wandering through the Rayburn Congressional Office Building one day and came on an Association of Beekeepers trying to talk Congress out of some money.

MAN (*in cage with bees*):
But without the humble honeybee, agriculture couldn't survive. There's about ninety plants in agriculture—blueberries, apples, oranges, lemons, lots of other plants—where the honeybee is completely indispensable. We have to have the services of this little animal, again to bring the male and the female plants together.
ROONEY:
Are you a beekeeper?
1ST MAN:
No. We're honey processors.

ROONEY:

I see. And what is the purpose of this meeting?

1ST MAN:

The purpose is to educate the Congress on the needs of the honey people.

ROONEY:

How much help from the government does the honey business get?

2ND MAN:

If you want me to be very candid, we don't get as much as we would like. We would like to get more help, that's one of the reasons we're up here today.

ROONEY:

What sort of help do you need from the government?

2ND MAN:

Well, for instance, insecticide poisoning sometimes kills our colonies, and, of course, that stops our production.

ROONEY:

Are you reimbursed for that?

2ND MAN:

We are reimbursed for this.

ROONEY:

Have you personally gotten money from the government?

2ND MAN:

Yes, I have. On a couple of different occasions, very small amounts.

ROONEY:

And how much did you get?

2ND MAN:

Ah . . .

ROONEY:

Roughly?

2ND MAN:

Five hundred dollars.

Well, he isn't the only one who got a little something. It turns out that last year alone we paid a million and a half dollars to bee-keepers who said some of their bees had died under unfortunate circumstances. It's all perfectly legal. You don't have to be dishonest to get rich off the government.

One of the reasons many of us don't feel so good about government is we've had dealings with the people who work in it. Ideals like democracy are only pure and clear in a book or at a distance where you can't make out any of the details. Good government doesn't seem nearly so good when you're being run around by some junior clerk in the license bureau.

But we're determined not to be all negative. There *are* good things about Washington and there *are* some very good public servants.

We talked to some people who *aren't* heads of departments, *don't* have any big deals going and *aren't* in the headlines. They're just competent people working in government jobs.

Phillip Hughes of the General Accounting Office is one of them. He and his wife came here from Seattle twenty-five years ago and still live in the same house they bought then. On the three mornings a week he plays handball, Mr. Hughes doesn't get in till almost eight o'clock.

ROONEY:

Did you choose government as a career or did it just sort of happen to you?

HUGHES (laughs):

I guess I'm not real sure. I think, at least periodically, I rechose it. I'm a product of the Depression era, as most of us—all of us—my age are. And I was concerned when I was in college with the kinds of things that got us in the plight we were then in and about ways to get out of it.

That led me to get in the business of social and economic research and that got me into government. And I've been sort of plowing my way along ever since.

ROONEY:

Has there been any change in the attitude of people going into government?

HUGHES:

I think interest in government and the enthusiasm for it waxes and wanes depending on what's going on. I think the Kennedy and Johnson years brought a burst of interest on the part of young people in particular, and perhaps on everybody's part, in government—some feeling that government could save the world.

We've been disillusioned from that, those of us who were or who may have been at least partly convinced of it. But from my standpoint, I've found the government a continuing source of fascination. And an opportunity, at least at times, to feel that you have some grip on the world in which we live and on your own personal destiny and future.

ROONEY:

I'm interested in your saying that you're disillusioned. You mean from time to time you have been?

HUGHES:

Yes, I think we had more confidence in the sixties that good federal programs well administered could do things, could eliminate poverty, and so on. Those good programs won't do it by themselves.

ROONEY:

Is there too much government in America?

HUGHES:

Well, again, as a bureaucrat, that's a terrible question to ask me. But I guess I don't think so. There needs to be a central, at least a central source of inspiration, a source of exploration, and it seems to me government is really the only place to do that. But it needs to be done better than we've done it.

ROONEY:

In general terms, do you find the government represents the public interest or its own interest? Is it a self-perpetuating organization?

HUGHES:

Well, all organizations tend to perpetuate themselves . . . all organizations and individuals. That's the nature of the world. But I think government more nearly represents the public interest than any other entity that we have.

And I find it quite responsive. Most public servants, whether elected or appointed or bureaucratic, as I am in a sense, I think, want to respond to their perception of the public interest.

Now, nobody's perfect in perceiving it . . . but I think most of us in government try.

So that's some of what we found out about Washington.

Our society has become so interested in the visual aspects of everything it's easy to forget that there are no pictures of the most interesting things that go on in the world.

In Washington, it's not only hard to get pictures, it's hard to find out anything about *anything*. People hide things that there's no *reason* for them to hide.

Everyone has a public-relations person who is more interested in obscuring the truth than in revealing it. Every time you ask a question, they give you the impression they aren't thinking so much about what the *honest* answer is, but about what answer would make them *look* best. The truth doesn't enter into it unless it happens to coincide with their own best interests.

Now, that doesn't make government people unique, of course, but it makes you madder when you're being deceived with your own money.

It's very apparent that we all ought to know more about what's going on in Washington. The people who think *everything* is wrong down there are as far from the truth as the people who don't think *anything* is wrong.

It's not being run by evil people. It's being run by people like you and me.

And you know how we have to be watched.

Ourselves

D - DAY

IF YOU'RE young and not really clear what D-Day was, let me tell you it was a day unlike any other.

There've only been a handful of days since the beginning of time on which the direction the world was taking has been changed in one twenty-four-hour period by an act of man. June 6, 1944, was one of them.

We all have days of our lives that stand out from the blur of days that have gone by. This is one of mine, if I may impose it on you.

I landed on the beaches of France four days after D-Day thirty-five years ago. No one can tell the whole story of D-Day. Each of the 60,000 men who waded ashore that day knew a little part of the story too well. To them the landing looked like a catastrophe. Each knew a friend shot through the throat, shot through the knee. Each knew the first names of five hanging dead on the barbed wire offshore, three who lay unattended on the beach as the blood drained from the holes in their bodies. They knew whole tank crews drowned when the tanks were unloaded in twenty feet of water.

There were heroes here no one will ever know because they're dead. The heroism of others is known only to themselves.

Across the Channel in England, the war directors were remote from the details of tragedy. They saw no blood. From the statisticians' distant view, the invasion looked like a great success. They were right. We're always defeated by statisticians, even in victory.

What the Americans and the British and the Canadians—don't forget the Canadians—were trying to do was get back a whole continent that had been taken from its rightful owners. It was one of the most monumentally unselfish things one group of people ever did for another.

It's hard for anyone who's been in a war to describe the terror of it to anyone who hasn't.

"Here," the battleground guide says when the tourists come, "they fought the bloody battle for the beach." He talks on with a pointer in his hand to a busload of people about events that never happened, in a place they never were.

How would anyone know that John Lacey died in that clump of weeds by the wagon path as he looked to his left toward Simpson and caught a bullet behind the ear? And if there had been a picture of it—and there weren't any—it wouldn't have shown that Lacey was the only one who carried apples for the guys in his raincoat pocket.

If you think the world is rotten, go to the cemetery at Saint-Laurent-sur-Mer on the hill overlooking the beach. See what one group of men did for another, D-Day, June 6, 1944.

AN ESSAY ON WAR

W E ARE all inclined to believe that our generation is more civilized than the generations that preceded ours.

From time to time, there is even some substantial evidence that we hold in higher regard such civilized attributes as compassion, pity, remorse, intelligence and a respect for the customs of people different from ourselves.

Why war then?

Some pessimistic historians think the whole society of man runs in cycles and that one of the phases is war.

The optimists, on the other hand, think war is not like an eclipse or a flood or a spell of bad weather. They believe that it is more like a disease for which a cure could be found if the cause were known.

Because war is the ultimate drama of life and death, stories and pictures of it are more interesting than those about peace. This is so true that all of us, and perhaps those of us in television more than most, are often caught up in the action of war to the exclusion of the ideas of it.

If it is true, as we would like to think it is, that our age is more civilized than ages past, we must all agree that it's very strange that in the twentieth century, our century, we have killed more than 70 million of our fellowmen on purpose, at war.

It is very, very strange that since 1900 more men have killed more other men than in any other seventy years in history.

Probably the reason we are able to do both—that is, believe on one hand that we *are* more civilized and on the other hand wage war to kill—is that killing is not so personal an affair in war as it once was. The enemy is invisible. One man doesn't look another in the eye and run him through with a sword. The enemy, dead or

alive, is largely unseen. He is killed by remote control: a loud noise, a distant puff of smoke and then . . . silence.

The pictures of the victim's wife and children, which he carries in his breast pocket, are destroyed with him. He is not heard to cry out. The question of compassion or pity or remorse does not enter into it. The enemy is not a man, he is a statistic. It is true, too, that more people are being killed at war now than previously because we're better at doing it than we used to be. One man with one modern weapon can kill thousands.

The world's record for killing was set on August 6, 1945, at Hiroshima.

There have been times in history when one tribe attacked another for no good reason except to take its land or its goods, or simply to prove its superiority. But wars are no longer fought without some ethical pretension. People want to believe they're on God's side and he on theirs. One nation does not usually attack another anymore without first having propagandized itself into believing that its motives are honorable. The Japanese didn't attack Pearl Harbor with any sense in their own minds that they were scheming, deceitful or infamous.

Soldiers often look for help to their religion. It was in a frenzy of religious fervor that Japanese Kamikaze pilots died in World War II with eternal glory on their minds. Even a just God, though, listening to victory prayers from both sides, would be understandably confused.

It has always seemed wrong to the people who disapprove of war that we have spent much of our time and half of our money on anti-creation. The military budget of any major power consumes half of everything and leaves us half to live on.

It's interesting that the effective weapons of war aren't developed by warriors, but by engineers. In World War I they made a machine that would throw five hundred pounds of steel fifty miles. They compounded an ingeniously compressed package of liquid fire that would burn people like bugs. The engineers are not concerned with death, though.

The scientist who splits an atom and revolutionizes warfare isn't concerned with warfare; his mind is on that fleck of matter.

And so we have a machine gun a man can carry that will spit out two hundred bullets a minute, each capable of ripping a man in two, although the man who invented it, in all probability, loves his wife, children, dogs, and probably wouldn't kill a butterfly.

Plato said that there never was a good war or a bad peace, and there have always been people who believed this was true. The trouble with the theory is that the absence of war isn't necessarily peace. Maybe the worst thing Adolf Hitler did was to provide evidence for generations to come that any peace is *not* better than any war. Buchenwald wasn't war.

The generation that had found Adolf Hitler hard to believe, was embarrassed at how reluctant it had been to go help the people of the world who needed help so desperately. That generation determined not to be slow with help again and as a result may have been too quick. A younger generation doesn't understand why the United States went into Vietnam. Having gotten into the war, all it wanted to consider itself a winner was to get out. Unable to make things the way it wanted them, but unwilling to accept defeat, it merely changed what is wanted.

DWIGHT EISENHOWER, 1962: "I think it's only defense, self-defense, that's all it is."
JOHN KENNEDY, 1963: "In the final analysis it's their war. They're the ones that have to win it or lose it."
LYNDON JOHNSON, 1969: "But America has not changed her essential position. And that purpose is peaceful settlement."
RICHARD NIXON, 1974: "But the time has come to end this war."

There are a lot of reasons for the confusion about a war. One of them is that the statesmen who make the decisions never have to fight one themselves. Even the generals don't fight the battles.

Professional soldiers often say they hate war, but they would be less than human if they did not, just once, want to play the game they spent a lifetime practicing. How could you go to West Point for four years and not be curious about whether you'd be any good in a war?

Even in peacetime, nations keep huge armies. The trouble with any peacetime all-volunteer army is that the enlisted men in one are often no smarter than the officers. During a war when the general population takes up arms, the character of an army changes and for the better.

In the twentieth century there is open rebellion between the people who decide about whether to fight or not and some of the young men being asked to do the fighting. It hasn't always been that way. Through the years, even the reluctant draftees have usu-ally gone to battle with some enthusiasm for it. Partially the en-

thusiasm comes from the natural drama of war and the excitement of leaving home on a crusade. It's a trip to somewhere else, and with the excitement inherent in an uncertain return. It is a great adventure, with the possibility of being killed the one drawback to an otherwise exciting time in life.

There have been just and unjust wars throughout history but there is very little difference in the manner in which people have been propagandized to believe in them. Patriotism, sometimes no more knowing or sophisticated than pride in a high-school football team, is the strongest motivator. With flags enough and martial music enough, anyone's blood begins to boil.

Patriotic has always been considered one of the good things to be in any nation on earth, but it's a question whether patriotism has been a force for good or evil in the world.

Once the young men of a country get into a battle, most of them are neither heroes nor cowards. They're swept up in a movement that includes them and they go where they're told to go, do what they're told to do. It isn't long before they're tired and afraid and they want to go home.

True bravery is always highly regarded because we recognize that someone has done something that is good for all of us, certainly at the risk and possibly at the expense of his own life. But in war, the mantle of virtue is pressed on every soldier's head as though they were all heroes. This is partly because everyone else is grateful to him and wants to encourage him to keep at it. All

soldiers who come home alive are heaped with the praise that belongs to very few of them . . . and often to the dead they left behind.

In part, at least, this accounts for why so many men like being ex-soldiers. Once the war and the fighting are done with and they are safe at home, it matters not that they may have served in the 110th emergency shoe-repair battalion. In their own eyes, they are heroes of the front lines.

Even in retrospect, though, a nation has always felt an obligation to honor its warriors. The face of the earth is covered with statuary designed for this purpose which is so bad in many cases that were it not in honor of the dead, it would evoke not tears but laughter.

During and since World War II, the United States alone has bestowed ten million medals and ribbons of honor on its soldiers, many of them for acts calling for as little courage as living a year in Paris.

Bravery is as rare in war as it is in peace. It isn't just a matter of facing danger from which you would prefer to run. If a man faces danger because the alternative to doing that is worse or because he doesn't understand the danger, this may make him a good soldier but it is something other than bravery. Stupidity faces danger easier than intelligence.

The average bright young man who is drafted hates the whole business because an army always tries to eliminate the individual differences in men. The theory is that a uniformity of action is necessary to achieve a common goal. That's good for an army but terrible for an individual who likes himself the way he is.

Some men, of course, like the order imposed on them. They like the freedom from making hard decisions that mindless submission to authority gives them.

There is always more precision on the drill field back home than there is on the battlefield. Uniformity of action becomes less precise as an army approaches the front. At the front it usually disappears altogether. It is not always, or even usually, the best marchers who make the best fighters.

Everyone talks as though there was nothing good about war, but there are some good things and it's easy to see why so many people are attracted by it. If there were no good things about war, the chances are we would find a way not to have another.

A nation at war feels a unity it senses at no other time. Even the people not fighting are bound together. There is a sense of common cause missing in peacetime. Accomplishments are greater, change is quicker . . . and if progress is motion, there is more of it in wartime. A nation at peace is busy gratifying itself, overeating, overdressing, lying in the sun until it's time to eat and drink again.

If war brings out the worst in people as it has been assumed it does, it also brings out the very best. It's the ultimate competition. Most of us live our lives at half speed, using only as much of our ability as is absolutely necessary to make out. But at war if a man is actually fighting it, he uses all his brain and all his muscle. He explores depths of his emotions he didn't know were down there and might never have occasion to use again in his lifetime. He lives at full speed, finding strength he didn't know he had accomplishing things he didn't know he could do.

The best thing about war is hard to describe, is never talked about. Most of us get a warm sense of fellow feeling when we act in close and successful relationship with others, and maybe that happens more in war than any other time. There is a lonesomeness about life that no one who has experienced it likes to talk about,

and acting together for a common cause, men often come closest to what they ought to be at their very best.

It is paradoxical but true that in war when man is closest to death, he is also closest to complete fulfillment and farthest from loneliness. He is dependent, dependable, loved and loving.

And there is another thing about war. If there is love in us, there is hate too and it's apparent that hate springs from the same well as love and just as quickly. No one is proud of it but hate is not an unpleasant emotion and there is no time other than wartime when we are encouraged to indulge ourselves in an orgy of hate.

The worst of war is hell but there isn't much of the worst of it and not many soldiers experience even that much.

A soldier at war doesn't feel the need to answer any questions about it. He is exhausted by the battle.

He is busy destroying and it does not occur to him that he will have to help rebuild the world he is pulling down.

He often mistakes the exultation of victory for a taste of what things will be like for the rest of his life.

And they are only like that for a very short time.

YOUTH

THE other night on television someone was interviewing a former football player named Andy Robustelli. Andy said he thought there were more injuries in the game today because the young men playing weren't made of the same stuff they were when he played.

It reminded me that about the time Robustelli played I heard President Eisenhower, speaking in Abilene, Kansas, say that moral standards weren't as high among the youth as they were when he was planting sweet corn in his backyard there.

For as far back as I can remember, people have been saying the youth of the nation is getting soft and losing its moral fiber. I just doubt it. They certainly aren't wearing as much underwear but I doubt if there's any less moral fiber. I'll bet the very day Andy Robustelli put on his first jockstrap, some old athlete was saying athletes weren't what they used to be. I'll bet the day little Ike Eisenhower was planting that sweet corn, someone was saying kids wouldn't work anymore.

Last Thanksgiving some clergyman in Chicago was complaining about sexual freedom among the young. He said he wondered what the Pilgrims would think if they could see the dances the kids are doing today instead of the minuet.

Frankly, I think the pioneers would watch for a few minutes and then try to get with it. We are all evidence of the fact that the Pilgrim Fathers weren't always minueting. For every Pilgrim Father there was a Pilgrim Mother.

I think the reason for all these disparaging remarks by the old about the young is obvious. Because of the intimations of death in the color of their hair, the stoop of their shoulder or the sag of their chin, older people are at a disadvantage with the young and they know it.

Elders resent the suggestion, implicit in young people's attitude, that they are young as a matter of their own choice. As a result, older people try to get even by saying kids aren't what *they* used to be when they were kids.

It's just amazing how long this country has been going to hell without ever having got there.

HAIR

NEXT to death, commercial bread and the price of gas, I hate the idea of getting bald the most. I'm not really *getting* very bald yet and I'm pleased about that, but when I do, I'm not going to try and hide it. All anyone who's getting bald looks like when they try to hide it is like someone getting bald trying to hide it.

Some men let what little they have grow long and then spread it around. If someone wears a toupee—it looks like either a good toupee or a bad toupee, but it usually looks like a toupee. In the best toupee shops in the country, a good hairpiece costs about eight hundred dollars. Of course, over the long run, you make it up in haircuts.

I don't know *why* we're so sensitive about getting bald. A lot of men look good bald. They often look distinguished and important. Some men are even bald on purpose. It can even be a trademark.

Often the amount of hair on a man's head is sort of a political statement. You can tell a Reagan supporter from a Kennedy man.

One of the great mysteries of life is why some men have such an easy time growing hair on their face . . . and a hard time growing it on their head. You can't talk to a man about how he likes his hair. On the tennis court, Jimmy Connors looks terrible with long, stringy, wet hair. I suppose he likes the way it looks when he isn't playing tennis, although it doesn't look all that good then, either.

I'm very suspicious of a man who fusses much with his hair. It can be there or not be there, but he ought not to spend half his life arranging it. He ought to comb it once in the morning and maybe once in the middle of the day if he gets caught in the wind. Otherwise a man ought to leave his hair alone.

(*To camera*) Okay, cut. How was that? All right? How did— did I look all right on that? Let's—let's take it again.

EYEGLASSES

Do you wear glasses—yet, I mean? Because if you don't, you will. I never thought I would, but I do, for reading and writing.

I think most people fight wearing glasses and they ought to. We all have some obligation not to give in easily to deterioration of any kind.

It's a funny thing that even though most of us don't like the idea of wearing glasses because we don't think we look as good with them on, we don't think anyone *else* looks any *worse* wearing them. As a matter of fact, we all have friends who'd look strange if they *didn't* have their glasses on. They look like themselves with them; they'd look funny without them.

When I first got glasses, the doctor told me they wouldn't weaken my eyes. I mean, he said they wouldn't make me dependent on them. I don't think he knew what he was talking about. My eyes certainly got worse within a year after I started wearing glasses. I *was* dependent on them. Of course, I was a year older, too, so how are you going to know for sure which did it?

I got thinking about glasses because of an awful thing that happened to me two weeks ago. I was going out to dinner Saturday night, so I shaved twice that day. I was shaving away and feeling my face for whiskers, the way a man does, and sure enough I felt some. I *felt* them, but I couldn't *see* them.

I put my glasses on and, by golly, there they were—whiskers.

And that was the terrible thing that happened. I realized then that I need my glasses to shave with and I'm going to have to reorganize my whole system of getting up in the morning so I have glasses with me in the bathroom.

There are certain ways we all judge our own age other than by our birthdays, and I feel older now.

TYPES

THERE are only two types of people in the world, Type A and Type Z. It isn't hard to tell which type you are. How long before the plane leaves do you arrive at the airport?

Early plane catchers, Type A, pack their bags at least a day in advance, and they pack neatly. If they're booked on a flight that leaves at four in the afternoon, they get up at five-thirty that morning. If they haven't left the house by noon, they're worried about missing the plane.

Late plane catchers, Type Z, pack hastily at the last minute and arrive at the airport too late to buy a newspaper.

What do you do with a new book? Type A reads more carefully and finishes every book, even though it isn't any good.

Type Z skims through a lot of books and is more apt to write in the margins with a pencil.

Type A eats a good breakfast; Type Z grabs a cup of coffee.

Type A's turn off the lights when leaving a room and lock the doors when leaving a house. They go back to make sure they've locked it, and they worry later about whether they left the iron on or not. They didn't.

Type Z's leave the lights burning and, if they lock the door at all when they leave the house, they're apt to have forgotten their keys.

Type A sees the dentist twice a year, has an annual physical checkup and thinks he may have something.

Type Z has been meaning to see a doctor.

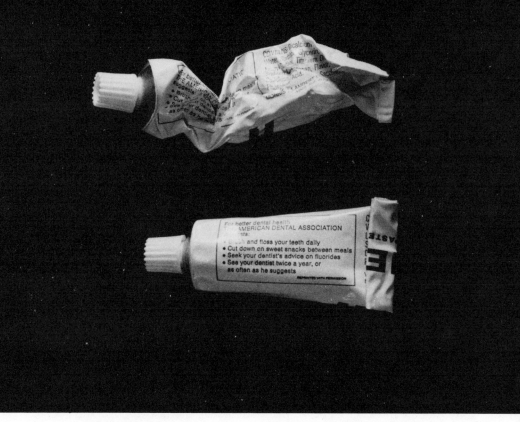

Type A squeezes a tube of toothpaste from the bottom and rolls it very carefully as he uses it, puts the top back on every time.

Type Z squeezes the tube from the middle, and he's lost the cap under the radiator.

Type Z's are more apt to have some Type A characteristics than Type A's are apt to have any Type Z characteristics.

Type A's always marry Type Z's.
Type Z's always marry Type A's.

SAVERS

JANUARY is the time of year we're all faced with a difficult decision. What do you do with the Christmas cards?

Some of them are too beautiful to throw out . . . others have names and addresses on them you want to keep. On the other hand, most of us are up to here in junk at this time of year and something has to go.

I'm a saver myself. I save everything. I don't think I've ever thrown away a pair of shoes, for example. I have shoes in my closet that hurt so much or look so terrible I'll never wear them again . . . but there they are.

I'm hooked on old peanut-butter jars, too. We don't eat much peanut butter in my house but I make up for that by saving old mayonnaise and jam jars, too.

Coffee cans. How can you throw out such a nice clean can with this tight-fitting plastic top? Who knows when I'll need how many for cleaning paintbrushes in turpentine? These are all from coffee we've made here in the office. I save them here, too, even though I don't have to paint my own office.

Sometimes I like the boxes things come in better than anything that comes in them. I keep old wine bottles, too. We don't drink any more wine than we eat peanut butter, but I keep the bottles on the shelf in the garage.

Up in the attic there are about six boxes and two big trunks with the really good stuff I've saved. I have things like the kids' old schoolwork papers, programs from school plays with their names buried somewhere down near the bottom with the angels . . . that kind of stuff.

There are two kinds of savers. The first is the practical saver

who keeps string, bags and old aluminum foil as a practical matter. And then there's the sentimental saver. The sentimental savers can't stand the idea of throwing out any memory of their lives.

Unfortunately, I'm both kinds.

TELEPHONES

I LIKE the telephone. It's a great invention. But there are a couple of problems with it. One problem is a lot of people like the telephone so much they use it even when they don't have anything to say.

One of my least favorite calls is from the person who dials my number, I pick up the phone and he says: "Hello, who's this?"

Who does he think it is—the Queen of England?

Most of us develop mannerisms on the phone—you know, with the instrument itself. For example, some people look off into the distance when they're on the telephone—big thinkers.

Other people seem to be trying to look over the wire so they can see the person they're talking to on the other end. They're very intense.

There are other telephoners who can't talk on the telephone unless they have a pad and a pencil in front of them. They do circles or squares or push-pulls. They doodle a lot.

I know several people around here who like to put their feet up on the desk when they talk on the telephone. They get so comfortable they hate to put their feet down.

There are certain people who have a knack for staying on the phone for hours without ever saying anything themselves. You know the type?

"Not really. Uh-huh. No, no. Yeah. Yeah. Yes. Yeah. Uh-huh . . . Who is this?"

Nervous executives like to stand when they talk. They often pace a lot. They have a long cord so they can move around. I think it gives them a feeling they're getting someplace in life.

And there are the cord-twisters. I hate to be the next one to use the telephone after a cord-twister's had it.

A lot of people can talk on the phone lying down. I can't do that. I have to at least get up on one elbow.

I don't know why the phone company has never come up with anything to solve the problem of how to talk on the phone when you're using both hands to do something else. A few newspaper reporters I've known were very good no-hands, usually with a cigarette in their mouth.

The person I really hate to get a call from is the semi-important executive who's too busy to make the call himself. You know how it goes: "Linda, get me Andy Rooney!"

I answer, and Linda says: "Please hold for Mr. Paley."

And there I am waiting for some guy I didn't want to talk to in the first place.

GENDER

OUR President won't face any more serious issue while he's in office than the crisis that exists with the English language.

A lot of women think they're getting a dirty deal when it comes to English usage and they insist that some changes be made. One trouble, of course, is that Americans don't go by any set rules of grammar. We're inconsistent about how we use words to indicate whether the person is a man or a woman.

We call men actors "actors." We call women actors "actresses."

On the other hand, we call men authors "authors" . . . women authors "authors."

Men waiters are "waiters." Women waiters are "waitresses."

Some of these problems just go away, of course. Years ago everyone called Amelia Earhart an "aviatrix." Well, you don't hardly see any aviatrixes anymore, or aviators either, for that matter. They're all just pilots now.

Some women insist we substitute "person" for "man" as a suffix on words. Recently a woman on Long Island went so far as to have her name officially changed from Goodman to Goodperson. Well, I'm not going to say whether I think that was right or wrong. I have absolutely no opinion about that kind of idiocy, but I don't think substituting "person" for "man" is the answer.

All of us want to do the right thing, but look what happens at a meeting when the chairman is a woman, for instance. There's always a confusion about what to call her.

WALTER CRONKITE:
    . . . Audrey Rowe Colom of Washington, D.C., who is the Chairperson of the National Women's Political Caucus . . .
BARRY GOLDWATER, JR.:
    Madame Chairman . . .

FEMALE VOICE:

. . . Chairwoman of the National Women's Political Caucus.

NELSON ROCKEFELLER:

And to Madame Chairman . . .

For a writer, the worst problem is what to use for the third person singular pronoun when you don't know whether the person is a man or a woman.

For instance, "Someone left *his* pen on my desk." Feminists resent the assumption it was a man, but it's too clumsy to say "Someone left *his or her* pen on my desk" every time.

What a lot of people do is avoid the problem by making an intentional grammatical error. They say, "Someone left *their* pen on my desk." Well, it was obviously only one person who left the pen but it bothers us less to make it plural than it does to offend women by using the universal "his."

Before the women's rights movement no one worried about it. "Man" in a general sense always meant women too. "Man the lifeboats" didn't mean women weren't welcome on board.

On the other hand, there were always certain inanimate objects we made feminine. A sailboat, for instance . . . "*She's* a beauty!" The lift-off of a rocket . . . "There *she* goes!" A train coming around the bend . . . "Here *she* comes!"

Strangely enough, even though we call a sailboat "she," we always say, "She had a four-man crew," even when two of the crew are women. It's really a mess and it has to be cleared up. One suggestion has been to reverse things for a while. Men would get the sailboats, the rockets and the trains coming round the bend. Women could have manpower, manhole covers, manslaughter. . . . As a matter of fact, as far as I'm concerned, if it would make them happy, they can have all of mankind.

DIRTY WORDS

I'D like to talk about dirty words.

There are about 490,000 words in the English language, and the Supreme Court says there are only seven of them we can't use on television because they're obscene. This comes to mind now because of the showing of *Gone With the Wind* on television.

When that picture was first made, it wasn't shown in some cities because at the end of the picture Clark Gable says the word "damn," a profanity.

"Frankly, my dear, I don't give a damn!" he said.

Now, of course, there aren't any words they don't use in the movies. It seems to me we're awfully confused over how we feel about obscenities. We don't use them on television, good newspapers don't print them and yet movies and widely read books and magazines use all of them.

I'm not confused about how I feel. I don't like obscenities and I don't use them. I don't even like to hear other people use them. This doesn't make me a wonderful person. We all decide which virtues to hold to and which to ignore. Not swearing's a minor virtue, but it's mine and I like myself for it. It's really more a matter of good and bad manners than anything else.

Why should anyone impose words on our ears that we don't want to hear, any more than they should throw food at our dining-room table?

I think a lot of dumb people do it because they can't think of what they want to say and they're frustrated. A lot of smart people do it to pretend they aren't very smart—want to be just one of the boys.

Women have been using more dirty words than they used to. I guess it gives them a feeling of being liberated. They want to be just one of the boys too.

Most people who use a lot of dirty words, or a few dirty words frequently, do it as a matter of habit. The words don't have any meaning to them when they say them.

There's certainly a place for obscenity and profanity in literature or any of the arts. When a novel's a mirror showing us to ourselves, it has to include some obscene things to make it true. But when writers start using more of it than people really use, that's not art; it's show business.

Not very funny tonight. Sorry.

MONEY

Every once in a while I wonder what in the world I've done with all the money I've made. Do you ever wonder that?

I began buying things with my own money in 1945, just after I was discharged from the Army. The other day I started making a list. This is very rough, but here it is.

Food for a family of six for 20 years, at two dollars a day per person, comes to $87,600. The kids have left home now, but my mother lives with us; that's three people for 15 years, at three dollars a day per person—food costs more now—comes to $49,275.

That's a total for food of $136,875.

It's hard to remember how many cars you've bought. I think I've bought 18 cars in 35 years for an average of maybe $3,500 a car. That's a total of $63,000 I've spent on cars.

We drive a total of about 50,000 miles a year. We have two cars. Gas costs $1.30 a gallon now, but it used to only cost 28 cents, so say an average of 35 cents a gallon. We get maybe 18 miles on a gallon of gas. So that's about 97,000 gallons of gas, at 35 cents a gallon, for a total of $34,000 we've spent on gas.

We bought the house in 1951 for twenty-nine five and, with a 20-year mortgage, the bank collected about $50,000 from me.

We put four kids through college, four years each at $6,000 a year apiece. That comes to a total of $96,000 for college. Sometimes I think we should have sent them to cheaper colleges and bought more expensive cars.

Heat, light, telephone, real-estate taxes, utilities in general, must have averaged $2,500 for 35 years. That's a total of $87,500.

Then there was miscellaneous: clothes, haircuts, crab-grass killer, sunglasses (I lose a lot of sunglasses), bourbon, beer, shoelaces, appliances, television sets. Say, $200,000 for miscellaneous.

Now I'm going to level with you, I've made a lot of money. You know, not a fortune, but more than most people. In 35 years, I suppose I made $1.25 million.

In addition to all these items, I guess I've paid about $400,000 in taxes. So, that's a grand total that I've spent of $1,067,375.

Now, tell me this. If I've made a million and a quarter and I've spent $1,067,000 . . . what the heck did I do with that other $183,000?

CALENDARS

THERE are half a dozen things that are basic to our lives that don't make any sense at all. They're basic and they're important, and why we don't change them I can't understand.

Take our calendar, for instance.

This is the beginning of the new year, right? Will someone please tell me how January 1st got to be the beginning of the year when we all know perfectly well it's right in the *middle* of the year?

The year actually ends just before the Fourth of July and it actually begins the day after Labor Day.

Here, look at this calendar for next year. Thanksgiving will be November 22nd . . . then a month and three days later we get Christmas . . . a week after that, New Year's.

We don't *need* three holidays that soon. When we need a holiday is in February, when everyone is sick and tired of winter.

Christmas obviously should be moved. No one knows for certain which day Christ was born on. And he certainly wouldn't mind if we celebrated Christmas in February. We could still make a week out of it without having New Year's Eve at the end of it. No one wants to go back to work again right after New Year's Eve.

If we moved Christmas to mid-February, that would make a lot more sense out of Thanksgiving. It's fun to get the whole family together for a turkey dinner at Thanksgiving . . . but not if it's just a month before the family gets together again for another turkey dinner at Christmas. There's just so much family or so much turkey anyone can take.

Now . . . about our summer vacation. Most of us take it in July or August—another thing that doesn't make sense. August is a nice name for a month but the weather isn't that good and the days are already getting shorter.

Here's the longest day of the year, June 21st. We should be on vacation while the days are almost at their longest but still getting longer. No one likes the feeling the days are getting shorter. It reminds us of our own mortality and that's nothing to be reminded of on vacation. *June* should be the principal vacation month.

So here's what I'm suggesting. Move the whole month of January, including my birthday, so that it falls between August and September.

Eliminate Labor Day altogether. Big Business doesn't have a day of its own and I don't think labor needs one. Under this new system, what was Labor Day will now be January 1st, New Year's Day.

There's still work to be done on days of the week too . . . but some other time.

VACATIONS

J ANUARY is the time of year a lot of people start thinking about their vacations. The one they took last summer is almost paid for and their thoughts are turning to where they're going to go this time.

It strikes me that the idea we have to *go* somewhere on vacation has gotten out of hand. The first day back at work, everyone wants to know "Where'd you go on your vacation?"

You're supposed to say, "The south of France" or "We went to the seashore," "We went to the mountains," "We took a raft trip down the Colorado."

The trip isn't good enough unless you can't afford it.

Why do we always have to take off? I mean, let's face it, going somewhere is never easy. It's not always any fun, either. Getting there is a pain in the neck and coming back is even worse. For one thing, your clothes don't fit in the suitcase anymore.

I don't know where we got the idea we have to go away for a vacation. I suppose the travel industry sold it to us. The travel business is the second largest industry in the United States. It's always trying to get us to go someplace *else* to spend our money when most of us don't have any trouble spending it right where we are. The industry tries to make us all feel cheap if we don't go on an expensive trip.

Well, I've got my plans all made for my vacation. I'm not going *anywhere!* How do you like that, travel industry? Show me all the luxurious accommodations you want, tempt me with pictures of bikini-clad girls with windswept hair on pearl-white beaches—I'm not going. I'm staying put is what I'm doing. We've all been tourists, and none of us likes being a tourist, so this summer I'll be somewhere I've never been on vacation—right where I live.

I know what I'm going to do, too. All year long I worry because I don't have the time to do all those little jobs around the house. Well, for my three weeks' vacation next year I'm going to stay home. I'm not going to do those little jobs then, either.

For vacation, I'm just not going to worry about them.

MR. ROONEY GOES
TO WORK*

(Police officer pulls Rooney to the side of the road.)

COP:

Hi!

ROONEY:

Hi, there.

COP:

Can I see your driver's license, please?

ROONEY:

Yep. We're doing a little story on working in America.

* Broadcast July 5, 1977.

Cop:

I see.

Rooney:

Are policemen working as hard as they used to?

Cop:

Well, I don't know. . . .

One cop in Janesville, Wisconsin, convinced us that he, at least, was working harder than was absolutely necessary.

When a writer sets out to report on something, he shouldn't have much of any idea in advance about what he's going to find out. That's nonsense, because of *course* he has some idea. The next best thing he can do is not let his preconceived ideas get in the way of what he actually *does* find out.

Last year some of us here at CBS thought we ought to do a report on "Work in America." It didn't seem as though anyone was working very hard and we were thinking of calling it "Goofing Off in America."

You know the story: everyone's leaning on his shovel; you can't get a plumber; they close at four o'clock; you have to make an appointment to have your car repaired two weeks before it breaks down; you read stories about strikes everywhere. . . . So I didn't go into this without an opinion.

To find out whether we were right or wrong, I set out across the country to talk to people and film them at work. I watched thousands of workers who didn't know I was watching. I talked to hundreds of them about their work. I talked to their employers and to their union leaders. In a few places they were reluctant to talk to me. For the most part, though, workers talked freely. They didn't seem afraid to say what they thought, even when the boss was standing there listening.

What follows is what one reporter found out about work in America.

The daily absentee rate in factories in the United States is about 5 percent. In other words, one out of every twenty workers is apt to be off the job any given day. On a nice summer Monday or Friday in Detroit, 15 percent of the workers are often officially "sick."

One out of every six Americans works for the federal, state or local government now. And there's general agreement, I think, that a government job brings out the *least* in people.

With vacations, three-day holidays, family emergencies and sick days, it seems as though a lot of us have as many days off as on now. Some of the new union contracts are calling for a work week so short they could make weekends obsolete.

So it's no wonder that there's a widespread opinion among Americans that Americans aren't working very hard.

WOMAN:

Well, I don't think that people do work hard . . . what they should work to get the money that they get.

ROONEY:

It's interesting that you would say that. I mean, you are in what would be called a blue-collar job, even though you have a white turtleneck sweater on. But do you think the young people are not working as hard as they used to?

WOMAN:

I don't think anyone is.

SUPERINTENDENT:

Some of 'em just have a "don't care" attitude. They just come and go. And years ago, why, everyone took pride in their work and of course they needed the money too. People have changed. That's for sure.

ROONEY:

Do you think young people are working hard? Other people your age? Are they working as hard as, say, your family did, or your grandparents?

COCKTAIL WAITRESS:

No, I don't think so.

ROONEY:

Given a thousand Japanese workers and a thousand American workers with the same tools, which group would produce the most?

TAIZO MATSUKAGI:

Ah, generally speaking, I would say probably Japanese.

FARMER:

I don't like to buy foreign material, but the Americans aren't doing so good on some of their stuff they put out. It isn't as good as it used to be. Too shiftless. I mean, they don't care. Years back, with the old machinery, the fellows that were building it took pride in what they were doing and they liked to have a

good product when they got done. But now they're shoving it too fast.

ROONEY:

Do you think that's something in the American character or is it just this desire to make money on the part of the big companies?

FARMER:

Well, I can't answer all them questions . . . 'cause I don't really know.

ROONEY (on Fort Lauderdale beach):

People working as hard as they used to?

MARCEL MULBERRY:

Not in my book. We're in the apple business way up in the
Champlain Valley, northern New York, and we have to get
imported help from the Bahamas now to help us harvest the crop.

ROONEY:

People just won't work?

MULBERRY:

Well, they just don't care to work anymore. The local people,
they'll come out a few hours and go home and be satisfied with
fifteen dollars. They just don't like the hard work. That's all.
They don't want to stay with it.

I read somewhere a statement made by a man named Sanford
Noll, Chairman of the Curtis-Noll Corporation. He said that the
trouble with the American worker is that he's making so much
money, he takes off on vacation whenever he feels like it. Well, that
was sort of a catchy remark, so we called Sanford Noll's office in
Cleveland to see if we could come there and talk to him.

His secretary told us he'd taken off for Fort Lauderdale and
wouldn't be back for six weeks. So we went to Fort Lauderdale
to find him.

SANFORD NOLL:

A certain group of people make enough money and that's all
they want. They're not looking to accumulate anything. They
just want to work to make enough to get the things that they
want out of life. And when they get a lot more, then a lot of
these people work less.

I think the younger workers are a result of a very affluent
society in which we live. . . . Their parents, who made very
nominal incomes twenty, twenty-five years ago, make very good
money now and they give their children the things they want
so that the motivation, the incentive, I think, has been curtailed.

ROONEY:

Then how do you go about motivating them?

NOLL:

Through a relationship with their supervisor, company newspapers, informing them as to what's going on. In that company
newspaper, everyone's birthday, everyone's anniversary is
printed. And through service awards.

ROONEY:

That's pretty sad as compared with giving them a raise. Isn't that the sort of thing the union objects to?

NOLL:

Well, we do both. . . . We have incentives where they can earn additional dollars if they meet certain standards.

ROONEY:

Labor says there's no sense doing that, because as soon as they attain those standards, you raise the standards.

NOLL:

Oh, I think a lot of that is hogwash. (*Laughs*)

ROONEY:

Does it do workers any good to work harder?

NOLL:

Yes, it does.

ROONEY:

It does *you* good, but does it do *them* good?

NOLL:

Yes, it does. Because it sets a pace and, by and large, the people respect the people that are working in a plant. Don't ever kid yourself that they don't. There's more respect for the people that are working than for the people who are goofing off.

William Winpisinger is the tough, friendly vice-president of the Machinist and Aerospace Workers Union. The day we talked to him, he was tough . . . I was friendly.

ROONEY:

A man named Sanford Noll said that American workers are making so much money they take off whenever they feel like it.

WINPISINGER (laughs):

I doubt they're even making as much money as he is.

ROONEY:

He was in Fort Lauderdale on vacation when he said that. What do you think about people like Sanford Noll?

WINPISINGER:

Well, it's people like him that make jobs for union officers like myself.

ROONEY:

There are statistics, for instance, in Detroit, and I imagine within your union, of how much more absenteeism there is on a Friday or on a Monday or on a nice summer day.

WINPISINGER:

There are some occupations that seem to develop that statistical base.

ROONEY:

Does a guy have a right to do that? How do you feel as a union person?

WINPISINGER:

Well, I think he has a right not to work if he doesn't want to work, yes.

ROONEY:

Are Americans working as hard as they could or should?

WINPISINGER:

I think so. I've always felt so.

ROONEY:

What do you say to people who say they aren't?

WINPISINGER:

I think the whole context of our times indicates a reduction of

manual labor. We don't work as hard as we once did perhaps in terms of what our fathers might say because of the tremendous automation of industry today that's taken a lot of the manual labor out of work.

I wonder if that's really true. I doubt it. Almost every Saturday morning, I know, I set out for the hardware store to find that magic tool, the one that's finally going to solve all my problems . . . make the grass easy to cut, snow easy to shovel, gutters easy to clean, wood easy to saw. You know how it is. Nothing seems to help. And, anyway, if it does and I do spend ten minutes less doing one thing, at the end of the day I spend ten minutes more doing something else. In other words, I don't *work* less. I *do* more.

The notion that the application of invention to labor will eliminate work is *wrong*. It always seems as though it's about to, but it never does. You know . . . they're going to invent a machine that'll take your job away. Right?

Well, the fallacy in the idea that science can contribute to permanent unemployment is that built into the idea is the belief that there's a specific amount of work to be done and that when that's accomplished, we'll be all finished with work.

Well, that's crazy. There's an infinite amount of work to be done, and as far as the unemployment question goes, that's one that we don't have to worry about. All the work will *never* be done by man *or* machine. And if it is ever done, it'll take another hundred years to clean up and put the tools away.

An amazing thing happened during the course of doing this research. I'm not a person who is easily convinced he's wrong, but after traveling across the country and visiting more than a hundred factories and other places of business and after seeing a lot of people leaning on their shovels when they should have been shoveling and then hearing people testify that they don't work hard . . . I have still become convinced, to my great surprise, that Americans *are* working their tails off.

I don't know why we're so convinced we aren't working. I think we all rate ourselves maybe against what we can do when we're at our very best, and of course we aren't at our best very often.

The other thing is, and I'm sure of this, I think a lot of that talk is part of the Good Old Days syndrome. You know . . . things aren't as good as they used to be . . . people don't work the way they used to . . . the snow isn't as deep . . . the roses aren't as red.

Our jokes and our talk are about getting out of work but the fact is, not many of us are happy unless we're working hard and getting some satisfaction from it.

Our lives are a lot different when we're at work than when we're at home, and we're at work a lot of our lives . . . so it makes a big difference to our total happiness whether we like our work or not.

ROONEY:

Do you hate your job?

AUTO WORKER:

No. No. Anybody that hates their job, whether they're in here or anyplace else, I think they're just hurting themselves. Because no matter what you're doing in life, you don't have to fall in love with it, but you shouldn't hate it.

ROONEY:
   Do you like working?
WORKMAN:
   Sure do.
ROONEY:
   What is your job?
MAN:
   Hauling rubbish. Cleaning up.
ROONEY:
   A lot of people wouldn't think that was a very good job, but
   you don't mind.
MAN:
   No, not at all. Not a bit. I can go to work when I get ready and
   go home when I get ready. If I don't feel like going today, I
   don't go.
AUTO-PRODUCTION-LINE WORKER:
   Oh, yeah, I like it. There's days I don't like it too . . . but
   there's days I do. There's worse jobs and better jobs.

ROONEY:

How do you feel about working? Do you like it or do you hate it or how do you feel?

TIRE WORKER:

Well, I don't know. I don't mind once I get here. Sometimes it's just hard getting here.

ROONEY:

How many of those shoes can you pack up in an hour?

WOMAN SHOE PACKER:

About twenty-five or thirty an hour.

ROONEY:

Twenty-five or thirty what?

WOMAN:

There's twelve in a box. Twenty-five or thirty an hour.

ROONEY:

Twenty-five or thirty boxes?

WOMAN:

Cases. Yes.

ROONEY:

That's a lot of shoes.

WOMAN:

Right.

ROONEY:

Do you ever get them in the wrong boxes?

WOMAN:

Not very often.

ROONEY:

You don't get the size eights in the size ten boxes.

WOMAN:

No. You have to watch all your sizes and stuff . . . and make sure that they match up.

ROONEY:

Do you like your work?

WOMAN:

Real well.

ROONEY:

You really like packing shoes?

WOMAN:

I really do. Very well.

* * *

Not only did we find an overwhelming number of people who *like* their jobs, but most people find a way to think that *their* job is just a little special, too.

ROONEY (watching white line being painted):
It's not a dull job?

STREET PAINTER:
No, not to say the least; not out here with the traffic going by, because you have some pretty close calls sometimes, you know.

ROONEY:
But you get satisfaction from your job?

STREET PAINTER:
Ah, yes, I definitely do. Because what we're building here is something that's going to last for who knows how long—hundreds of years. So, you know, it's like making history, in a way. You know what I mean? You know it's something that's going on right now and people will be able to see years and years from now.

WOMAN AT CLOTHES FACTORY:
Oh, I like my job. (Laughs) If I was sewing, I wouldn't like it because I don't like that type of work when you're sitting all the time.

ROONEY (on street):
Do you enjoy your work or are you just working for the money?

MAILMAN:
I enjoy talking to people, you know. Actually, I have—

ROONEY:
No, do you enjoy your work?

MAILMAN:
Yeah. I enjoy my work, yeah. I got this Watergate area down there and, you know, different types of people.

ROONEY (to trumpet tester):
Is that a good one?

TRUMPET TESTER:
It better be good 'cause I passed it already.

ROONEY:
Oh, I see. Well, now, you sound to me like a fellow who'd be in here whether you were getting paid or not. In other words, you're pretty wrapped up in your business, aren't you?

TRUMPET TESTER:
This is my life. This I love. I love this.

ROONEY (at shoe factory):
How long have you been at that?
SHOE WORKER:
Forty-two years.
ROONEY:
Same job?
SHOE WORKER:
Same job, yes.
ROONEY:
Do you like it?
SHOE WORKER:
Quite well, yes.
ROONEY:
You wouldn't want to do something else?
SHOE WORKER:
I don't believe so.
ROONEY:
You still enjoy it?
SHOE WORKER:
I still do, yes.
ROONEY (to second shoe worker):
When did you start?
GIRL (polishing shoes):
Two days after I got out of school, in '73.
ROONEY:
You've been doing it ever since.
GIRL:
Yeah.
ROONEY:
How long are you going to do it?
GIRL:
Ah, I don't know, probably quite a while.
ROONEY:
Do you like working?
GIRL:
Yes. It's pretty easy.
ROONEY:
But you wouldn't work if you didn't need the money?
GIRL:
Well, I think I would. It gets kind of boring sitting around all
the time. Nothing to do at home. It keeps me busy.

2ND WOMAN at Clothes Factory:

I've been here thirty-eight years 'cause I've enjoyed every minute
of it. I just love my work. (Laughs) Many of those years were
spent at the sewing machine and I like sewing very much. (Bell
rings.) That's the end of our break. We have to get back to
work.

ROONEY:

Well, I don't want to get you fired after thirty-eight years.
You'd better get back.

There's a common opinion that production-line work is dull,
monotonous and that everyone hates it. That's just not true. Some
production-line jobs that *look* dull don't *seem* dull to the people
doing them. And then, not everyone wants an interesting job,
either. There are people who like the predictability of the production line.

What happens is we all have problems at home we can't cope
with, things we don't get done, bills we can't pay, personal relation-
ships we can't handle. For some people those eight hours at work
on a repetitive job are like a day in the country. They're away
from their problems and the job provides a satisfying little feeling
of accomplishment every ten seconds.

There is companionship, and they're not only free from worry
while they're there, they're free to daydream because the job
doesn't take any thought after the first few thousand times they've
done it.

One of the revolutions that has taken place with hardly any of
us noticing it is in the matter of wages being paid to people doing
undesirable jobs.

Very often unemployment doesn't mean not being able to find
work at all. It means not being able to find the kind of job you
think you deserve.

It was always assumed that a job that took muscle paid less than
one that took brains. That's because there were more people *with*
muscle than with brains. These days everyone is getting so much
education that there are more dumb jobs to be done than there are
dumb people to do them.

For instance, it's easy to find plenty of high-school teachers now but hard to get someone to pick up the garbage . . . so the price for garbagemen goes up while teachers look for work. In New York City, for instance, the average teacher makes $17,000.

A garbageman, on the other hand, can cost the city $25,000 a year.

In relation to dirty jobs and hard work, I couldn't get Marcel Mulberry, the man I'd met on the beach in Fort Lauderdale, out of my mind. I was curious about whether he worked hard himself, so several weeks later I traveled 1,400 miles north to his apple orchard in the Champlain Valley.

I was surprised to find that Mr. Mulberry's regular employees think he's a good boss and that he himself works like a dog.

ROONEY:
What happened to your tan?
MULBERRY:
Well, it kind of disappeared when I got out in the north country here.
ROONEY:
How long do you spend down there in Fort Lauderdale?
MULBERRY:
Just a month.
ROONEY:
Is that what you work for, to be able to live a good life like that?
MULBERRY:
That's part of it, yes. I don't know. Of course, I've always been interested in agriculture, and producing food for the public has been a great pleasure for me all my life.
ROONEY:
You really resent people who don't work hard?
MULBERRY:
I guess most people who are in business do. And our crew here, they're all wonderful workers. They really seem to enjoy it and they're good. The regular people are all wonderful at it, but it's really hard to get people today to come out and do this farm work. We get all the local people we can, and it's quite a hard job to get them with the programs we have today, but—
ROONEY:
What do you mean, "the programs we have today"?

MULBERRY:

Well, lots of people are on unemployment and they don't care about going out and working at jobs like this, and we can't get enough local help to get the crop harvested. It just goes on the ground. A year before last we lost forty thousand boxes. Rotted on the ground.

We found one of the people not picking Mr. Mulberry's apples sitting in the sun not far from where we had originally found Mr. Mulberry on the beach in Florida.

BEACHCOMBER:

I generally work about six months out of the year and the rest I loaf.

ROONEY:

Does six months do it? Do you get enough money in that time?

BEACHCOMBER:

Enough for what I need. Yeah.

ROONEY:

But don't you think that people who have this great drive to do something, to build cars, to make things, have accomplished a lot for this country that you're enjoying?

BEACHCOMBER:

Hmm, yeah.

ROONEY:

You don't feel guilty at all about not contributing much to that?

BEACHCOMBER:

No, I can't say I do. Most of the things that people have and their wants are entirely different from what I want. I think there's entirely too much progress. I think that's why, to be blunt, things are screwed up today as they are, because there's just—things are just moving entirely too fast.

ROONEY:

What sort of things in life called progress have not been good?

BEACHCOMBER:

Look out in the street. The buildings along the beach. All the landmarks in the United States are being covered with condominiums and buildings. It's just destroying it.

ROONEY:

A lot of people are calling what you represent lazy, no-good loafers. Do you resent that?

BEACHCOMBER:

I don't much pay attention to it.

Who do you admire most or least . . . that young man or self-made Sam Braen? (*Shown walking his two poodles along Fort Lauderdale dock*) Sam is a cement-and-gravel tycoon from New Jersey. We found him walking toward his yacht in Florida.

SAM BRAEN:

I started when I was thirty-eight years old and I owed the bank five hundred dollars and fifteen years later I wound up owning the bank.

ROONEY:

People don't do that anymore?

BRAEN:

Naw. But I worked twenty-four hours a day. It takes something out of you. But when you get older, why, you can relax.

ROONEY:

What's wrong with people today? Why won't they work?

BRAEN:

Well, you know why, 'cause the giveaway program in the United States is too good.

ROONEY:

How did you start? Did you have money when you started? Your family have money?

BRAEN:

Naw. I didn't have two nickels to rub together.

ROONEY:

So you really made it all yourself?

BRAEN:

That's for sure. I bought myself a Ford truck in 1938, and I wound up owning seven hundred big ones . . . forty thousand dollars a throw.

ROONEY:

Who works best? Are there any groups that work better than other groups? Men? Women? Blacks? Whites?

BRAEN:

No. We have a good mixture of everything in our company.

ROONEY:

And they work about the same?

BRAEN:

Oh, sure. Out of the fifteen hundred employees, I would say, we always had at least two or three hundred colored, and they were darn good. They were in our asphalt departments. They came from the Asphalt Layers Union. And every time I went on the job, why, I'd throw them a fifty-dollar bill and say, "Here, boys, when you get too hot with that stuff on your feet" —you know, its three hundred and sixty degrees—"why, buy what you want with it." And they were real good workers, believe me.

ROONEY:

So you got along pretty well with your workers?

BRAEN:

Sure. Well, you have to get along, you know. If you can't beat 'em, you join 'em. Otherwise, they rip ya.

ROONEY:

Do you live alone on the boat?

BRAEN:

No. No. Got my wife.

Rooney (on board yacht):

Do you find people resenting you and people with wealth enough to buy a boat like this?

Mrs. Braen:

Well, it hasn't been what you would call an obvious resentment, but the feeling is there except for the workers in the yard who showed so much love for the boat. They worked so very, very hard in building her. But we created many jobs for them, too. For the average person who walks up and down the dock, looks at thing like this and says, "Boy, it must be easy." But it's far from easy.

My husband has worked very hard, provided a lot of employment for a lot of people in order to build this boat. And then, when we were building it, we employed a lot of people . . . the electricians, the people that built the engine, all of them, plus the wonderful woodworkers.

Rooney:

It's almost a public service you're doing, having a boat like this?

Braen:

Well, we like to feel that way. Of course, I think it would be very hard for the average citizen to understand that. But very frankly, yes, that's what it amounts to. I'm glad you said it.

Any economic system is supposed to provide a way for dividing the good things on earth so that no one group gets everything and no one group gets nothing.

The traditional enemies in our economy are business and labor. If it's true that the capitalist believes that things work best in an open market where everyone grabs all he can get for himself, then many labor unions are being attracted to that capitalist philosophy, because that's just what they're doing, grabbing all they can get without much thought about where it's coming from.

It's the opinion of most labor leaders that the only way to proceed is as though they were at war: Big Business versus Big Labor. Sometimes it's difficult for an objective observer to be sympathetic to *either* labor or business. They can both be so selfish, ignorant, power-hungry that you can't admire either one of them.

William Winpisinger typifies the labor leader who isn't going to change his views of how things ought to work any quicker than businessmen like Sam Braen or Sanford Noll.

ROONEY:

What changes would you make if you were president of, say, General Motors that would be beneficial to the worker?

WINPISINGER:

I have no idea. It's an area of expertise that I don't have, don't enjoy, and without knowing a good deal more about it than I do, I'd be unable to even make the wildest guess.

ROONEY:

Well, how can you fight these people without knowing what their problems are?

WINPISINGER:

I think, first and foremost, it has to be recognized that a union is cast in an adversary relationship, which I think is entirely appropriate. It's quite fashionable nowadays for people to go around trying to create schemes to reduce conflict, get the adversary relationship out of labor relations and everything else.

ROONEY:

It's almost as if you're afraid that if you knew all the facts, you couldn't be a good union man?

WINPISINGER:

No, not at all.

ROONEY:

But you didn't want to know anything about management problems?

WINPISINGER:

They're not my problems. I've got plenty of my own, to operate in behalf of the people who employ me. They don't employ me to run factories. They employ me to do a good job as a union officer and I try to do that.

Irving Bluestone is unusual. He's a soft-spoken intellectual who, as a vice-president of the United Auto Workers, nonetheless carries a big stick.

ROONEY:

I'm curious about the qualities that make a good union executive. Aren't they the same that make a good management executive?

BLUESTONE:

No, I don't think so. One must remember that the fundamental drive that motivates a manager of business or industry is profit.

ROONEY:

What's the fundamental drive that motivates you?

BLUESTONE:

I think trying to help others and to build a better society. There's a vast difference between that and the profit motive. I think what we're after, generally, is to improve the quality of work life in many, many different ways.

Most of us are suspicious of the kind of idealism that Irving Bluestone expresses, but I believe him and I also believe that a lot of American businessmen are idealists who are after something other than a buck.

We're all aware of how evil we can be sometimes, how rotten both labor and business often are. Fortunately, though, for all of us, we're still pleased with ourselves when we're virtuous.

ROONEY (at clock factory):

Why does a successful businessman like you, Mr. Miller, keep at it? Why do you get up every morning?

MILLER:

I enjoy the work. I enjoy coming to the factory and I've done this for so many years it's a part of me.

ROONEY:

Is your interest primarily in making money or making clocks?

MILLER:

My interest is in making clocks. And when we make clocks, we make people happy.

Jonathan Bainbridge represents a growing movement in this country—a move to get away from it all, to work outside the confines of a structured society and a regular job. Educated and worldly, Jonathan makes his living as a handyman. He lives with his wife, Suzie, and their child in an old barn that he's fixed up into an interesting home.

People like Jonathan Bainbridge are free in a sense many workers aren't. Since he left the security of getting a weekly paycheck for the freedom of working on his own, he answers to no boss but necessity.

ROONEY:

Can you hide from what you have been, what you started being?

JONATHAN:

Yes. I don't know if it's hiding. It's just finding another way of living.

ROONEY:

It looks like pretty hard work, though.

JONATHAN:

Yeah, but it's fun. It's your ideas that you see growing. Everything's organic. And in the city, it was just working, putting in time, and there wasn't much joy in that.

ROONEY:

You go along with that, Suzie?

SUZIE:

Oh, yeah. For sure.

ROONEY:

You really were doing a clockwork job?

JONATHAN:

Yeah. Clockwork in—in uniform with tie and white shirt and so forth. And it got to be too much.

ROONEY:

What was that job?

JONATHAN:

I was with Delta Airlines.

ROONEY:

And what were you doing?

JONATHAN:

I was a ticket agent at the airport, at Kennedy Airport.

ROONEY:

And how about the good ways of life, though, aside from your psyche. Have you had enough to eat?

JONATHAN:

Oh, yes. Yes. We do a large garden.

ROONEY:

I notice you drinking beer. You don't grow that, though.

JONATHAN:

No. No. When the money's coming in, there's enough beer. And as the money doubles, it goes out just as swiftly.

ROONEY:

Do you have any fears?

JONATHAN:

It's the same trip that it was in the city. You know? There isn't an escape. As things progress, there are going to be more wants and more desires for acquisitions.

ROONEY:

In other words, you notice some of the same things happening to you that happened to you in the city?

JONATHAN:

Yes. Very definitely. As a matter of fact, we have just received a loan to buy a new car. Now maybe that's our diploma. You know, we're back in the mainstream. It sort of felt that way. Whether it's for the better or the worse, I don't know.

Jonathan and Suzie Bainbridge may not be typical. Very few of the people who choose to work outside the system are typical of anything.

FRED STETTNER (with horse at the Stettner farm):

Here, Scarlet, come here.

ROONEY (aside):

For fifteen years, Fred Stettner worked in an office in New York City.

ROONEY:

How much did you know about horses in the beginning?

FRED:

Nothing.

ROONEY:

You didn't?

FRED:

Not a thing.

ROONEY:

You mean, you never grew up with horses at all?

FRED:

No. I grew up in the city.

ROONEY (aside):

Today he's working a lot harder for a lot less money and loving it. Seven years ago Fred and his wife, Enid, and their three children moved into this old farmhouse on a two-lane blacktop road three miles from a couple of towns in upstate New York you never heard of.

ROONEY:

And what were you trying to get away from?

FRED:

I would say the difficulty of living in the city . . . the problems that one has living in the city and raising children . . . a desire for a better kind of freer existence, I think, which you can find in a place like this.

ROONEY:

I have this theory that the same thing keeps happening to the same people. Doesn't the same thing happen to you as a couple here as it did in New York City?

ENID:

No. I don't think it does, because here we have something to work for together and we didn't in New York.

ROONEY:

What would happen if vast numbers of Americans decided to quit the production line at General Motors and find themselves a house out in the middle of nowhere and grow some things and keep some animals?

ENID:

Well, probably we wouldn't need as many cars. The value system would be totally different. It's a very different value system. We work so that we can live the life that we want. It's not just to accumulate goods.

FRED:

Although somehow we have accumulated a lot.

ENID (laughs):

We happen to have accumulated a lot of things. I find that people who are most interested in doing what we do are people who are in very high-pressure jobs.

ROONEY:

I look around at what you have here and I notice tremendous pressure. You had a kid you had to pick up from school and rush to some musical rehearsal thing.

ENID:

Right.

ROONEY:

You've got a house that needs cleaning. The dishes are in the sink . . . you haven't done them yet. You've got problems. You've got to go to town tomorrow. You've got a library meeting. I think you're still under pressure.

ENID:

We didn't say we weren't.

FRED:

But our lives won't fall apart if we don't do all these things.

ENID:

It's pressure that we don't mind. We enjoy this pressure. There's so much to do now. We are always busy. We are always doing something. But it's things that are meaningful to us. It's not imposed from the outside. It's imposed from within.

FRED:

I think that to work at something and do something that you're not really particularly interested in your whole life, just to wait until you're able to collect your Social Security and your pension, is . . . you miss the whole point.

The Stettners and the Bainbridges may live happily ever after where they are, but they'll always be city people living in the country. George LaPelle never lived anywhere but the country. George works around a lake where many people have vacation homes and he's exactly what the whole world needs . . . someone to take *care* of things.

There's nothing George can't do. Although there are a lot of things he *won't* do if he doesn't feel like it. We talked to him one day he didn't feel like it.

ROONEY:

What's that going to cost somebody to get a job like that done?

LAPELLE:

You want me to quote you a price?

ROONEY:

Not me. I don't have to pay for it.

LAPELLE:

I don't know. As I say, you don't know till you get down there and see what's gone underneath.

ROONEY:

You're pretty cagey about what it's going to cost somebody.

LAPELLE:

Well, certainly. I wouldn't tell you how much it's going to cost you.

ROONEY:

About how many hours do you put in a day?

LAPELLE:

Eight.

ROONEY:

Are you careful about that?

LAPELLE:

Careful? No. If I've got something else to do, I do eight here and maybe another four at home.

ROONEY:

You'd make more money if you worked nine hours, wouldn't you?

LAPELLE:

What am I going to do with the money?

ROONEY:

Spend it, I suppose.

LAPELLE:

Pay taxes on it.

ROONEY:

If you had your choice in the whole world, what would you be doing?

LaPelle:
Probably what I'm doing now.
Rooney:
You like it about as much as anything you can think of.
LaPelle:
Well, I certainly wouldn't be a politician.
Rooney:
What satisfactions do you get out of work? I mean, what is it
you like about it?
LaPelle:
Well, you accomplish a little something. Fix people up a place to
live or something.
Rooney:
You like that?
LaPelle:
Sure.
Rooney:
If you had a million dollars, what would you do?
LaPelle:
I don't know. You get me a million dollars and I'll let you know
afterwards.
Rooney:
Do you think you'd keep doing what you're doing?
LaPelle:
Oh, I'd do something, sure. I'd have to do something.
Rooney:
You've got a pretty nice house here?
LaPelle:
I've done all the work myself. Otherwise I wouldn't have it.
Rooney:
You've got two cars—a truck and a car.
LaPelle:
Yeah.
Rooney:
No worries.
LaPelle:
What do you mean, no worries? I've got everybody *else's* wor-
ries.
Rooney:
That's pretty much what you are, isn't it? When that phone
rings, it's someone else's worry?

LaPelle:

Yeah, that's about what it boils down to.

Rooney:

What's a typical phone call you're apt to get late at night?

LaPelle:

Oh, somebody's furnace don't run or somebody's water pump quit or their washing machine's bothering or something like that. Usually, you just plug 'em in or something and they start working.

Rooney:

What about young people? Do you think young people are working as hard as they used to?

LaPelle:

Most of them don't work at all.

Rooney:

Why's that, do you think?

LaPelle (laughs):

Too much education.

Rooney:

You think people who are more educated work less hard?

LaPelle:

Oh, sure.

Rooney:

There are some pretty nice places down on the lake. Do you ever get hating the people who own them?

LaPelle:

No. Why should I?

Rooney:

People with boats and a lot of money who don't look as though they work very hard?

LaPelle:

Well, that could include you, but you don't bother me too much.

As I understand it, and, of course, I may not understand it, if you're a capitalist, you believe in free enterprise. And what that means is, you think that if you work as hard as you can to get as much as you can for yourself, you'll be better off and so will everyone else.

If you build a factory and make a million dollars, you don't have to feel guilty about being rich; you can feel good about it, because in the process of making that million dollars, you've put 350 people to work in *your* factory.

The other extreme, socialism, is based on the idea that no one should get rich *or* poor. All the people should own all the businesses and the workers divide up the profits.

Socialism and capitalism seem to be living side by side in this country.

A lot of working people buy stock in the company they work for. The workers' pension funds are investing so much that within the next ten years they'll own a majority of the stock in all American corporations. Then who do the workers strike against?

So it's no longer a question of capitalism or socialism. Capitalism is taking socialism in as a business partner.

SWITCHBOARD OPERATOR:
   Lincoln Electric.

The Lincoln Electric Company in Cleveland makes half a dozen products that are too dull to tell you about unless you're an arc welder. But the Lincoln Electric Company itself is one of the most interesting in the whole country. They're very suspicious of reporters and cameramen, but we did get in.

They aren't making any top-secret weapons. What they're guarding so jealously is not any mysterious manufacturing process, either. It's their incredible record of success. They just don't want anything, including a lot of talk about it on television, to disturb it.

The company has the best worker-participation plan in the United States. No music. No swimming pool. No bowling alleys. No tricks. Just money.

ROONEY:
   Is it any secret what you make at Lincoln Electric?
1ST WORKER:
   Without the bonus, I'd say probably the average is ten to twelve thousand dollars a year.
ROONEY:
   And what would the bonus be?
1ST WORKER:
   Well, it'd probably be somewhere, roughly, just about 90 percent of that.

ROONEY:

In other words, you could make around twenty thousand dollars. . . .

1ST WORKER:

I think the average guy's probably making close to that.

ROONEY:

I guess that's why they want to work at Lincoln Electric?

1ST WORKER:

That's why they want to work here, right.

2ND WORKER:

Everybody makes pretty good money here. You enjoy it, you know. You enjoy some of the finer things in life. You know, some things that you probably would never have a chance to working someplace else.

ROONEY:

You mean, you're more apt to have two cars in your family than the average worker?

2ND WORKER:

More apt to, probably. More apt to take a vacation. More apt to have a savings account. Whereas, I suppose a lot of people don't have that nowadays, with the economy being what it is.

They do a lot of things differently at Lincoln and it's all directed toward increasing productivity. Most workers do more than one job. Some do a whole series of jobs that would keep ten men busy a lot of places.

By their own choice, the men work in a plant that's dingy, dark and it isn't air-conditioned. To make any changes would cost money . . . the workers' *own* money.

The offices where the paperwork for this multimillion-dollar-a-year operation is done at Lincoln Electric aren't much better. Most of the staff works in one large room and the manager is thrown in there with them.

All promotions at Lincoln Electric are made from within the company. Not some of them—*all* of them—and they're made on ability, not seniority. They don't end up with a lot of duds in high places because they've been there a long time.

There are no little coffeepots or transistor radios around here either. Each worker is rated every six months on four factors. His bonus depends on his ratings. Since 1934, the total bonus paid equals the total wages . . . and the wages are pretty good. No one at Lincoln Electric has been laid off since 1958. The workers are nonunion and have no interest in joining one.

ROONEY:

Is it a form of socialism?

1ST WORKER:

Oh, I wouldn't say it was a form of socialism. I would say it's more like a dictatorship in the fact that the heads of the company completely run it. But it's not a dictatorship, you know, in the fact that the men do have the freedom to have things changed. We have an advisory board. We can have things changed when we feel we need change, and that's one of the nice things, where you can talk with an official of the company.

ROONEY:

Like what? Give me an example.

1ST WORKER:

Well, a couple of weeks ago, I had a production problem on the line. I couldn't get it solved through the regular channels in the shop, so I went up and saw the president of the company.

ROONEY:

You just went in?

1ST WORKER:

I made a phone call and asked him if I could come in and see him, and he was glad to see me and I went up and talked to him, and he solved the problem and now we're running smooth again.

ROONEY:

You couldn't do that in many companies.

1ST WORKER:

I don't think you could do this in many factories. I worked for other companies that you couldn't even get to see the president to say good morning to him, let alone talk out the problems and get them solved.

3RD WORKER:

If you're going to have to get up at five-thirty in the morning, it's a good place to come.

ROONEY:

What's different about Lincoln Electric?

3RD WORKER:

Well, Lincoln Electric, as far as a manufacturer, is probably a perfect form of capitalism.

ROONEY:

Is it capitalism or is it socialism?

3RD WORKER:

No. It's capitalism. Look at the wages we make. It's strictly you get paid for what you do. And if General Motors would do that, we'd be able to buy new Eldorados for six thousand dollars.

The Donnelly Mirror Company in Holland, Michigan, has had a profit-sharing system called the Scanlon Plan for twenty years now. The Scanlon Plan, a watered-down version of Lincoln Electric's program, is the most widely used profit-sharing plan in the country.

Productivity at Donnelly is good, absenteeism rare and the workers seem to like it.

WOMAN WORKER:

I enjoy coming here, working with the girls. We have a real good time, a real good group.

It's hard for an observer to know when a profit-sharing plan is a superficial trick of management to get more production out of workers and when it's a genuine plan to benefit both workers *and* management.

Dick Arthur is an articulate middleman who makes his living as an industry consultant selling the Scanlon Plan to both management and labor.

ROONEY:

Are all these plans bringing us closer towards socialism in America?

DICK ARTHUR:

Just the opposite. I think America has had a tendency to go in the socialistic direction. The thing that we're teaching is probably the purest form of capitalism that could ever exist. Because we're in effect saying, "Hey, you want to share the loot, then produce. Either work harder or work smarter and you're going to get your share. And, incidentally, when you get your share, you're going to make me more, and you don't mind making me rich if I'm making you rich at the same time, do you?" And you say, "Hell, no, as long as I'm getting mine, too." For example, if they've been averaging 10 percent on sales we put our plan

in and say, "Okay, from now on everything that you make over
10 percent, we're going to split fifty-fifty."

ROONEY:

William Winpisinger, the union official we talked to, said:
"What's this everything over 10 percent? Why not start fifty-
fifty from the beginning?"

ARTHUR:

First place, you can't get an honest-to-God capitalist to do it,
so why waste your time talking about it? Second, it's impractical.
As a matter of fact, one of the things that we get really turned
on about this whole program is that it's a tremendous educational
process for people. They have to understand that the money
doesn't fall down from trees . . . that it costs money to build
buildings, to buy equipment, to buy tools, and a company has
to be making a fair profit. And I say, "Well, okay, what the hell
is fair?" If I can put my money in a bank and earn 5 percent
and sit with my feet on a footstool, certainly 10 percent working
my tail off is not exorbitant. And so there has to be a creaming
of the profits, so to speak, for the company.

Rooney:

You used the phrase "an honest-to-God capitalist." Who's harder
to educate . . . that honest-to-God capitalist or the hardheaded
union official?

Arthur:

My own personal experience is it's the capitalist. Okay. But I
think there's a reason. Perhaps you could even justify it.

Here you have a man that has put his money into a company.
It's *his* money. It's *his* investment. And so when you start saying
to him, "Hey, look, we want you to share some of the fruits of
your investment," he's hearing you from a different point of
view. Where a union official will say, "What the hell, the more
the merrier. You know, the more the troops get the better I can
look, so why should we fight it?" We do have union leaders who
do resist it sometimes but primarily because they see it as a threat
to their little kingdom.

We go into a plant where they've had a union and they've
had it for maybe thirty years, and we get union and management together, and we say, "Look, for the last thirty years,
management has exerted a tremendous amount of energy in how
to screw the union, the union has worked overtime figuring how
to screw management and in the meantime we're faced with
world competition, and I say let's all get together and screw the
French."

And to me, this is capitalism at its best . . . free enterprise at
its best.

There's something in the American character that likes to fool
itself. When a worker participates in profits, that's a form of
socialism, not capitalism. Americans fool themselves a thousand
ways, and they often end up believing what is simply not true.

For instance, no matter how much it amuses us to think we're
goofing off, and in spite of the evidence that in some places we
obviously are, the hard fact is that, man for man, woman for
woman, machine for machine, we're producing more than anyone
in the world.

We're producing 35 percent more than the Germans, 64 percent
more than the Japanese, and 85 percent more than the British. These
are not opinions, they're statistics.

I found out four things that surprised me during the course of assembling this report.

First, Americans are working hard even though it often seems as though they are not.

WORKER:
   Well, I can speak for my crew. We work pretty hard, I think.

Second, people like their jobs even though they often talk as though they do not.

WORKER:
   You hear some people complaining, but I can't see where they should. I think they should enjoy their work.

Third, workers don't hate the boss and they don't resent the money he makes, either. They'd rather have him drive a Cadillac than a Volkswagen.

Worker:

If it wasn't for these people, I wouldn't have a job. Right?

Fourth, and this was the biggest surprise of all to me, we're becoming a socialist nation within the framework of our free-enterprise system . . . whether anyone likes it or not.

If I'm wrong, I'm sure you won't hesitate to correct me.

UGLY

For a long time now a lot of us have excused ourselves for not knowing what is ugly and what is beautiful by saying to someone who does "That's what you think" or "Every man is entitled to his own opinion."

We set out to see whether it's true that everyone has a right to his own opinion. We wanted to find out whether beauty and ugliness are qualities of their own, independent of the person who looks at them.

Standards of beauty are set by those who know most about a subject. If other people who don't know as much about it see no beauty, we ought to be able to say they are wrong.

There are some subjects about which we all consider ourselves expert. What about standards of ugly, though? Who says what is ugly and what isn't . . . and for what reasons do they say it?

One of the disconcerting characteristics of ugly is that so many of us agree about *what* it is without being able to say *why* it is.

For instance, junk in any form strikes us all as offensive to the eye and ugly. America the beautiful may actually lead the world in ugly, and it seems to be because we have so much to throw away. Anything discarded is ugly. We make more cars, so we throw more away . . . and we are running out of ugly places to throw them, so we throw them anywhere and make *that* place ugly. Garbage or anything that has anything to do with garbage is ugly, and because garbage is a by-product of affluence, we have lots of it.

One of the things that seem to be true about ugly is that it is often associated with deterioration. Anything that doesn't look as good as it used to is on the way to becoming ugly. It is probably because anything that doesn't look as good as it used to is growing older and reminds us of ourselves and of death.

This idea, if it's true at all, doesn't account for everything ugly, though, because that factor is not always present. It is possible to make brand-new junk that is ugly. Not only that, but a lot of things which look good in their own place become ugly-looking someplace else. The object, itself unchanged, is changed by your reaction to it.

A woman's hair can be a thing of great beauty, one of her most attractive physical attributes. We are agreed. Now envision a well-set dinner table, with silverware, and candlelight. The soup is served. And this is the strange thing about ugly . . . take just one of the beautiful hairs from the woman's head and put it in the soup and both the hair and the soup are repulsive.

Almost anything out of place, anything that is not where it was meant to be, strikes us as ugly. Virgin snow in a country setting is beautiful. It is attractive on a ski slope. It can even be beautiful, freshly fallen, on a city. But in the city, snow quickly becomes used, out of place, dirty, dying . . . and ugly.

A smile is attractive and white teeth in a good mouth are beautiful. Take the teeth out of their natural setting and they are not beautiful, they are ugly . . . even when they're smiling. Teeth in

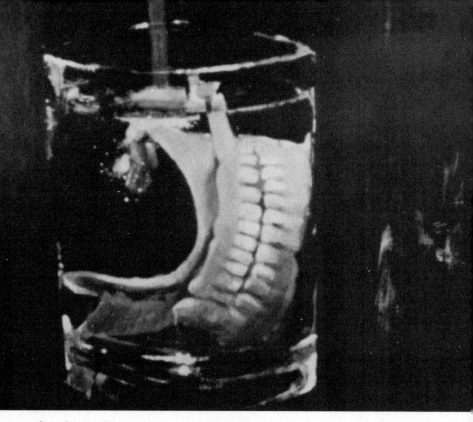

a glass have about them several of the attributes we associate with ugly. They represent an object out of place and they also suggest the losing battle we are all fighting against deterioration.

Life is beautiful.

Death is ugly.

It is always assumed that an interest in the beauty of Nature is a sign of goodness in a person. It is a strange assumption we make and neither do we understand why, generally speaking, we consider Nature to be beautiful.

Man is more apt to see beauty in symmetry and ugliness in disorder. Nature, superficially at least, appears to be disorderly. Left alone with Nature, man starts to rearrange what he finds there. He proceeds quite often with some principle of equation in his mind. He is driven by the notion that if he puts something on one side of anything, he ought to put another thing just like it on the other side. Then he calls it beautiful.

Symmetry is probably beautiful to a lot of us because we see in its design a clear plan. It suggests we can arrange and control our world . . . that we are not wet leaves in a stream of water. Our reaction to it is therefore pleasant and we call it beautiful.

There are further complications to this business of ugly which we do not completely understand. We would all agree that this abandoned gas station is ugly. No one has a single formula for ugly that fits every case, but the gas station has about it a good many of the characteristics which would be included in anyone's definition.

We have enlarged and framed one piece of the film showing the station. To our untrained eye it looks as artful as many pictures we have seen hanging in galleries. But if the gas station is ugly, is this a work of art and therefore beautiful?

And one hard question leads to another. If a scene that we all agree is ugly is graphically and accurately represented on canvas in oil paint, can *it* then be properly called a work of art and therefore beautiful?

There is a wide variety to ugliness. There are ugly things, ugly sounds, ugly people . . . and even motion can be ugly.

There is often something about movement that can suggest the thing is not working the way it ought to and this lack of grace is ugly. We all find grace and beauty in the purposeful design of a sailboat. Everything about how it has been made improves its

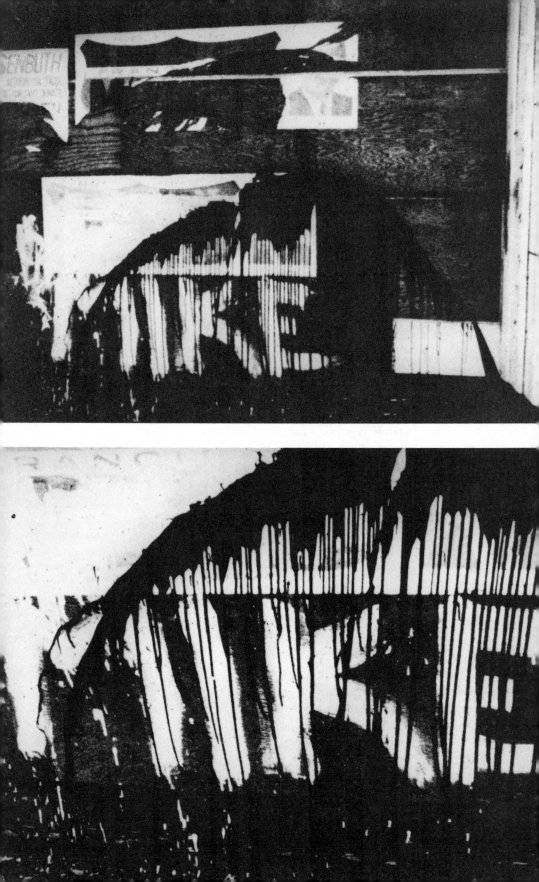

ability to be pushed swiftly through the water by the wind. It is an object of beauty, doing what it does best. Another boat, perhaps as well built but in another situation and another condition and no longer doing what it can do, is not beautiful. Rotting in the mud at low tide, it is an eyesore.

There is grace in the design of the *Queen Mary* . . . but the ultimately purposeful tugboats that push her and pull her . . . are they ugly or are they beautiful?

Why then do we find the hippopotamus, whose shape is as ideal as the trotting horse or the sailboat for doing what it does—wallowing in the mud—why do we find the hippopotamus one of the ugliest animals on earth?

And if we are repulsed by the hippopotamus, why are we attracted to elephants . . . or repelled by the grace of a snake?

Why is an alligator in a swamp ugly and repulsive . . . but an item of high fashion as a pocketbook on Fifth Avenue?

And what about man's closest relative in the animal kingdom, the ape? We're generally agreed he's ugly . . . but why are we agreed?

THE FACES OF CHRIST

Tomorrow is Christmas. It is the day Christians celebrate the birth of Jesus Christ, the Hebrew prophet they believe to have been the Son of God. Although Christ's teaching and his apparent goodness would seem to transcend the significance of what he looked like, almost a hundred generations of Christians have wanted some image toward which to direct their worship.

One of the difficulties in providing visualization of Christ is that no artist who lived when Christ lived drew any likeness of him that exists today. Neither was any physical description of Christ provided in the Bible.

Because the early Christian movement was disapproved of by public officials, Christ's followers used symbolic representations to conceal their affiliation. In an early church council these and other symbols were disapproved, and it was decreed that from that time onward Christ would be portrayed as a man.

The first efforts to picture Christ seem to have been Byzantine, meaning done in the city of Byzantium, the Turkish capital, once Constantinople, now called Istanbul. Many of them were mosaics, done in the third and fourth centuries. Christ was also frequently portrayed on the walls of the crypts in Roman cemeteries of that period.

The Old Testament Book of Isaiah says of the coming Messiah, "He was devoid of beauty and a sufferer."

Many of the earliest artists formed their concept of Jesus from this comment. A historian named Tertullian, who lived in the year 200, said of him, "There was nothing outstanding about Christ's flesh, and it was just this contrast with his personality which struck everyone. Far from emanating Divine radiance, his body had not even simple human beauty. The passion and the humility he suf-

fered left their mark, and it was deprived of all charm by his suffering."

Neither lay nor theological historians have been able to reconstruct any chronological order to most of the events in Christ's life. Although nothing at all is known of him for more than thirty of his thirty-three years, Renaissance artists were prolific in portraying the infant and child Jesus. Some of the world's most treasured artworks are those of Christ with his mother.

As the Christian movement spread and missionaries told the story, artists around the world painted the Jesus Christ they saw in their own mind. To the Christians of the Far East, he was Oriental; to the Indians, Indian; to the Africans, he was black— and who is to say otherwise if they see him so?

It is probable that if Christ had been born Roman or Greek, contemporary likenesses of him would have been painted or chiseled in stone.

The sophistication of modern religious belief, where there is any at all, prohibits a literal visualization of the idea of Jesus Christ. A picture of God as a bearded and benign elderly gentleman in a flowing robe is unacceptable now even to the true believer. As a result, Christ seldom inspires the imagination of the modern artist; and where he does, the image he paints is not apt to evoke much reverence. Skepticism has dissolved the pigment on the canvas, leaving in its place a blurred image. An artist, painting without a subject, illustrates his *own* state of mind.

The only description of Christ ever found purporting to have been written by a contemporary is not generally accepted as authentic, but it has been the basis of many great works of art. It was said to have been written by a public official in Jerusalem during Christ's lifetime. "There has appeared here in our time a man of great power named Jesus Christ. The people call him a prophet of truth, and his disciples the Son of God. He raises the dead and cures the sick. He is in stature a man of middle height and well-proportioned. He has a venerable face. His hair is the color of ripe chestnuts—smooth almost to the ears, but above them waving and curling, with a slight bluish radiancy, and it flows over his shoulders. It is parted in the middle on the top of his head after the fashion of the people of Nazareth. His brow is smooth and very calm, with a face without a wrinkle or a blemish, lightly tinged with red. His nose and mouth are faultless. His beard is luxuriant and uncreased, of the same color as his hair—not long, but parted at the chin. His countenance is full of simplicity and love. His eyes are expressive and brilliant. He is terrible in reproof, sweet and gentle in admonition, cheerful without ceasing to be grave. His figure is slender and erect. His hands and arms are beautiful to see. He is the fairest of the children of men."

Belief is a quality of its own. It is a virtue independent of that which is believed in. "The Christ head, the Christ face, what man will ever paint, chisel or carve it?" Carl Sandburg asked. "When finished, it would float and gleam, cry and laugh with every face born human. And how," the poet asked, "can you crowd all the tragic and comic faces of mankind into one face?"

And More by

ANDY ROONEY

Andrew A. Rooney

Contents

Introducing Andy Rooney

To begin with, here are some clues to my character. It seems only fair that if you're going to read what I write, I ought to tell you how I stand:

—I prefer sitting but when I stand, I stand in size 8½ EEE shoes. There have been periods in my life when wide feet were my most distinguishing characteristic.

—When it comes to politics, I don't know whether I'm a Democrat or a Republican. When I was young I was under the mistaken impression that all Democrats were Catholic and all Republicans were Protestant. This turns out to be untrue, of course, and I've never decided which I am. Those of us who don't have a party affiliation ought to be able to register under the heading "Confused."

—I like cold better than hot, rice better than potatoes, football better than baseball, Coke better than Pepsi. I've been to Moscow three times and don't like that at all.

—This morning the scale balanced at 203 pounds. I'm 5′9″. My mother always called me "sturdy" and said I have big bones. A little fat is what I am.

—I have an American Express card but often leave home without it and pay cash.

—The following are among the famous people I have met: Richard Nixon, George McGovern, Arthur Godfrey, Frank Gifford, Barry Goldwater, Art Buchwald, Jimmy Stewart and Carol Burnett. I have never met Teddy Kennedy although I've seen a lot of pictures of him.

—I have been arrested for speeding.

—I speak French, but Frenchmen always pretend they don't understand what I'm saying.

—It is my opinion that prejudice saves us all a great deal of time. I have a great many well-founded prejudices, and I have no intention of giving up any of them except for very good reasons. I don't like turnips and I don't like liver. Call it prejudice if you wish, but I have no intention of ever trying either again just to make sure I don't like them. I *am* sure.

—I don't like anything loud.

—Fiction doesn't interest me at all. I haven't read a novel since *Lorna Doone*. I meant to read Hemingway's *The Old Man and the Sea* when it came out, but I didn't. Fiction takes too long for the ideas contained in it. I'm not interested in being diverted from my own life.

—Good ideas are overrated. It makes more difference how a writer handles an idea than what the idea was in the first place. The world is filled with people with good ideas and very short of people who can even rake a leaf. I'm tired of good ideas.

—When I write, I use an Underwood #5 made in 1920. Someone gave me an electric typewriter, but there's no use pretending you can use machinery that thinks faster than you do. An electric typewriter is ready to go before I have anything to say.

—I know a lot about wood, ice cream, the English language and Harry Reasoner. In other areas I have some serious gaps.

—Writers don't often say anything that readers don't already know, unless it's a news story. A writer's greatest pleasure is revealing to people things they knew but did not know they knew. Or did not realize everyone else knew, too. This produces a warm sense of fellow feeling and is the best a writer can do.

—There's nothing mystical or magic about being a writer. A writer is just a person who writes something. There are almost no people who are not dentists who can fix teeth, but there are a lot of people who aren't professional writers who write very well. This is one of the reasons why being a writer is tougher than being a dentist.

—I admire people who don't care what anyone else thinks about what they do, but I'm not one of them. I care what people think and would not want you to know how much I hope you like what I write.

I:

MADE BY HAND

The Old Violin

I'M always on the lookout for something good about people. Often months go by.

There was a story last week about Roman Totenberg, a violinist whose violin was stolen last May after a concert. When he was young he'd lived on almost nothing to save enough to buy it, and it was not only of great sentimental value to him, but he'd used it to play for almost forty years. The musician was quoted as saying it was like having a child kidnapped, and he didn't know whether he'd ever play again with another instrument.

If the story ended happily and added to the flimsy proof we have that people are basically good, the thief would have read about the musician's grief and returned the violin. If he did, I never read about it, but even if he didn't, the story isn't all bad for people. Our affection for the tools we use is one of our nicest characteristics.

If you're a concert violinist, you like your violin, but it doesn't have to be that special. If you're a carpenter, I suspect you have one saw you have a special feeling for. If you do a lot of cooking, you probably have one pan you wouldn't trade for all the others.

Years ago I knew an elderly man who had whittled birds for a hobby most of his life. He had a knife his father had given him when he was fifteen and it was sharpened down to almost nothing, but it was still sharp and he was happiest when he had it in his hand. I suppose that knife was one of the most enduring things in his life. It was always there, always dependable, and there is no way to estimate the total pleasure it had given him over the years.

We all need some of the material things that provide continuity to our lives by always being there and always being the same. As a writer, I type a lot. The English language is often slippery, evasive and complex but my typewriter is simple, easy and dependable. It doesn't care how poorly I may be using the language. It knocks the words on the paper with a loud, comforting clack. I'm very fond of my typewriter, and if someone stole it I'd never write again.

Oh, I suppose I'd write again, because actually I have seventeen more like it. I buy every old Underwood #5 I find. I can write only

257

on this model typewriter, and I don't want to run out of them before I run out of time or things to say.

Most of us tend to be more sentimental about some of the tools we use than is absolutely necessary, but it's a charming fault. I even like the trait in myself. I have a shaving brush in the medicine cabinet in the bathroom that I carried with me through four years in the Army. It's spent time in Ft. Bragg, England, Normandy, Germany, and it has been to Berlin and Moscow. I've been shaving with an electric razor for twenty years now, but I wouldn't think of discarding that tired-looking old shaving brush. It served me well and every once in a while, when I've let my beard grow over the weekend, I'll lather up with it and shave with a blade just to let the brush know I haven't forgotten it.

Most of us get attached to our cars if we keep them for a few years. I've owned cars that I liked and felt terribly disloyal to them when I turned them in on a trade for a new one. It seemed so ungrateful of me just to dump them and leave them in the hands of some hardhearted secondhand car dealer. He wouldn't care. He'd sell them to anyone in order to make a buck for himself.

I wouldn't try to defend our attachment to inanimate objects on grounds of reason or logic, but you have to admit caring for the things that serve us is one of the few nice things we do.

Bathtubs

IT seems to me it's time to rethink bathtubs.

All of us seem to like the idea of having a bathtub, but we almost never take a bath in one anymore. We take a shower. A bathtub is, at best, a makeshift place to take a shower. It's hard to get into and out of gracefully, and there's no good way to arrange the curtain so that no water ends up on the floor.

The statistics on how much more water it takes for a bath than for a shower are overwhelming. The average bathtub holds about fifty gallons of water. The average shower spouts out two or three gallons a minute. In other words, if you put the plug in the tub and took a shower, it would take twenty minutes to fill it. That's a long shower, except for one of my kids. It must mean that a tub bath is very expensive to take.

We have two bathtubs in our house. In the past twenty years I suppose there have been fifty baths at the most taken in them by people. I say "by people" because Gifford, our English bulldog, was given hundreds of baths in the tub downstairs. It was known as Giffy's Tub.

It's easy enough to say shower stalls are better to have in a house than bathtubs, but if you have an old house it isn't that easy to switch over. It's probably easier to convert your furnace to coal. A bathtub is usually jammed in a small bathroom, and there's no way to take it out without breaking through a lot of expensive walls. After you get the tub out of its position in the bathroom, it probably won't fit through any of the doors in the house, either. You might as well be moving a piano.

Once you get used to a shower, it's hard to go back to the tub. On the few occasions I've taken a tub bath in the past ten years, I've emerged from the water wondering how much of the dirt and soap residue was left on me. I always have the feeling after a bath that I want to take a shower.

I wouldn't deny there is something luxurious about a tub bath. You feel warm and weightless in there and relatively immune from your problems with the cruel, cold outside world. It feels good to lie there, submerged, with the water just barely rippling over you. When the water begins to cool down, it's fun to see if you can turn on the hot water faucet with your feet without emerging into the cold to do it.

But those good features about a tub bath are outweighed by the bad. Washing a bathtub is no joke, and it's not what you feel like doing right after you get clean anyway. I don't know why they didn't design tubs with the drain at one end and the faucets at the other. With the water cascading in right over the drain hole, you're fighting an uphill battle when you try to wash the tub. The dirty water can't get out because the clean water is forcing it back, and it's hard to distribute the new, clean stream to the areas that need it.

One of the dumbest compromises I've ever seen is one you find everywhere. People want a shower, but they find the tub dangerous to get in and out of. They don't want to get rid of it, so they stick some nonslip strips of a sandpaperlike material to the bottom of the tub. It may make it safer, but it makes it impossible to use as a tub.

Who wants to go to all the trouble to take a tub bath and then sit there on corrugated strips of sandpaper?

Most hotels maintain combination shower-bathtubs. They have those strips in the bottom of the tubs. I'll bet years go by when no one takes a bath in some hotel room tubs. No one wants to *sit* in the same tub where so many others have stood.

If we're going to get rid of bathtubs and replace them with shower stalls, we're going to have to find something to do with a lot of old bathtubs. According to the last census, there are fifty-four million bathtubs in the United States.

Getting rid of fifty-four million tubs is going to be a real challenge, but if I knew fifty years ago what I know now and could have borrowed the money from my father to swing the deal, I'd be a rich man today. I'd have bought up every one of those big old wooden iceboxes that antique dealers are selling today for $800.

Bathtubs may be the wooden iceboxes of tomorrow!

Old Clothes

My clothes are in a terrible mess. The truth of the situation I'm in came home to me last night when I washed a batch of nineteen socks. The laundry does my shirts and my wife does my underwear along with the household stuff, but I have a few pairs of good wool socks and I don't like to have them go through the washing machine, so I let them pile up until my sock drawer is empty, then I wash them all at once.

Last night I hit a new high in unmatched socks. I ended up with seven odd socks. Seven out of a possible nineteen! I'm going to give up trying to wear socks in pairs. If they're both brown or both blue, they're going to be a pair from now on. I'm not going to worry about whether they're exactly the same or not. I've never known anyone who hated me because of my socks. If I was looking for a job, I suppose I'd wear matched socks, but I'm not and that's the end of it.

It isn't just my socks, either. As I look in my closet and my bureau drawers, all I see is disaster. Two weeks ago I had on my good new brown suit, and by mistake I put a felt-tipped pen without the top on it into the inside breast pocket. The cloth of the suit absorbed the ink from the pen, and the first time I knew what I'd done was late in the day when I found a blue spot the size of a fifty-cent piece on the front of the suit just below the outside pocket.

Everyone around the office had a different idea about what I should do. One said soak it in lemon juice. Well, I don't usually carry a lemon around with me, so I couldn't do that. Someone else suggested cold water. They said I should keep it wet until I got it to a cleaners. I did that.

On the way home I stopped in at two cleaners. Both of them said they couldn't do anything with it because it was wet.

The next day I left it at a third cleaners and he got the ink out, but the suit will never be the same. It's no longer my good new brown suit I could go anywhere in.

About half the shirts in my drawer are size sixteen, and I haven't been comfortable in a sixteen for four years. Sixteen-and-a-half is my size. It looks as if I have plenty of shirts, but when I go to pick one out in the morning, I get one with a frayed collar, a missing button or the one with the brown-suit ink on it. If everything else is perfect, it's a sixteen.

This morning, after I found two socks that were reasonably close to looking the same in dim light, I put my shoes on. I'm always aware when a shoelace could go any day, but in all my life I've never had the sense or foresight to change my worn shoelaces before they break just as I'm rushing to get somewhere.

I buy about five new neckties a year. I buy expensive ties at the post-Christmas sales, but I seem to lose or ruin more than five ties a year. There must be eight or nine very good silk ties with little spots on them hanging on the back of my tie rack. I keep ones with spots on them in a special place. I never throw them out and I never wear them. On several occasions I've sprayed them with that cleaner that has chalk powder in it. It often removes the grease spot and leaves a white chalk mark that nothing will take out.

Downstairs in the hall closet I have half a dozen coats. Half a dozen may seem like a lot but it isn't if you've been using the same closet for thirty years and never threw a coat away. This morning I needed a warm raincoat. The prediction was for rain possibly turning to snow, with temperatures ranging in the mid to low thirties. One of my trenchcoat-type coats has two buttons missing and isn't warm enough. The other has a lining that zips in, but the zipper's stuck and I can't get it all the way in or all the way out.

There are days when I wish I was rich enough to throw out every single piece of clothing I own and go out with a couple of thousand dollars and start all over. Just to be safe, I might buy size seventeen shirts.

Hangers

IT has always seemed to me that the President, Congress and news people spend too much time worrying about the problems that are here today, gone tomorrow, and too little time on the problems that endure, year after year, life after life.

I'll just give you one example. There aren't enough places to hang things.

If I had my way, the building code would decree that there be at least three doorknobs on every closet door. We all know a doorknob is the best and easiest place to hang something. Why is there only one to a door? Builders act as though the only purpose of a doorknob is to open a door.

A doorknob has a lot of advantages over the standard wire hanger, in addition to its ready availability. For a man, those wire hangers are hopelessly inadequate. Look at the facts:

If a man is going to wear the same pants tomorrow that he wore today, the chances are he'll want to leave the belt through the loops and some loose change and maybe even a few miscellaneous bits of hardware in his pockets.

The weight of these objects invariably causes the trousers to slide from the thin wire crosspiece of the hanger and drop to the floor. (There are wood hangers with various attachments designed to hold pants. They're good but someone takes these.)

The last place people want to hang clothes is their clothes closet. Closets are mean, inconvenient, often dark and always overcrowded. If a person's closet isn't overcrowded, you can bet that person needs a psychiatrist.

On the sagging crossbar of a clothes closet, wire hangers cluster together, wrapping their grubby little hooks around each other in an orgy of togetherness.

Doorknobs are not the only place around a house to hang something, of course. There are lots of other good places before you have to resort to putting something away in a closet.

The one place to hang a pair of loaded pants, far superior to all others, is from the top drawer of a dresser. Place a few inches of the bottom of the pant legs in the drawer and close the drawer on them just above the cuff, thus trapping them for the night. Nothing could be simpler.

Many people don't understand why cuffs were put on pants. Cuffs give a bureau drawer something to grab hold of. To eliminate cuffs on pants is a step in the wrong direction. Cuffless pants may slip from the drawer.

The best place to hang a suit coat is over the back of a chair. This is not only convenient, but there is something dramatic about a coat hung over the back of a chair.

If you are forced, by some unfortunate domestic circumstance like a neat husband or wife, into putting things away, there are still ways to avoid using hangers.

Most closets have a few hooks on either side. The best way to use these to get the most out of them (by getting the most on them) is by starting with the lighter items first. Several short-sleeved sport shirts make a good base. It is much easier to hang a pair of corduroy work pants over two sport shirts than it would be to hang one sport shirt over two pairs of corduroy pants.

Many four-poster beds are still in use, and they provide wonderful hanging space. During the winter, when you plan to put on substantially the same clothes in the morning that you took off at night, the bedpost by your feet is hard to beat as a place to hang them. They're close, convenient and in the middle of the night, who cares how they look?

There's no doubt of the shortage of places to hang things in America today, but with perseverance and ingenuity, and perhaps some help from Washington, we should be able to keep stuff off the floor.

Glue

I see where the Air Force is experimenting with a new glue they hope will hold some of their airplanes together. They think they may be able to replace the rivets in the fuselage with glue and save weight and money in the process. I hope the Air Force has more luck with glue than I've ever had.

The trouble most of us have with glue can't be blamed on the gluemakers. It isn't their fault. We just ask too much of glue and, of course, they encourage us to overestimate what it will do by showing us pictures of a drop of it lifting an elephant. I can't get a dish to hold together, and they're lifting elephants with it. Ed White, the football player, can't pull apart two blocks stuck with it.

It's interesting how often sticking things together and making them stay that way comes up in our lives. In my lifetime, I've had a lot to do with glue and the experiences have almost always been disappointing. I was disillusioned by glue early in life. One of the other kids in first grade told me his mother said you could make things stick together with a paste made of flour and water. Mixing flour and water never worked for me as a kid.

Maybe I just have no knack for glue. It's hard to remember a time in my life when the local hardware store wasn't pushing some new miracle bond, but none of them has ever proved to be miraculous for me.

This Air Force story says they glue two surfaces together and then put them in "an ovenlike pressure vessel at 250 degrees for an hour." Well, I just don't happen to have an ovenlike pressure vessel I can heat. Maybe that's why half the stuff I glue together comes apart.

Around the office I use paper cement. It's fun to play with and it works if it's the right consistency. The problem is, I only use it once a month or so, and it keeps getting too thick in the jar. We have a one-gallon can of paper cement thinner, and over the period of a year I use more thinner than I use cement.

In my cellar I glue a lot of wood together. I've tried the catalyst powder glue that you mix with water, I've tried the two-part epoxies, white casein-based glue, contact cement, hyde glue and the new superglues. Glue and I were simply not meant for each other. If I clamp four mortised legs into a tenoned frame and let the glue set, I find one leg is an inch shorter than the other three because the clamps were too tight in one direction. The glue has dripped down the legs and, all in all, I've made a mess of my project. Our Defense Department would be in sorry shape if I was gluing together planes for the Air Force in my basement.

When it comes to fixing things that are broken, I've had even less success with glue. If the rung of a chair is loose, you have to take the chair apart, put glue in all the rung holes and then try to find a way to clamp uneven surfaces together.

Whenever some china treasure is broken in our kitchen and assigned to me to repair in the cellar, I align the parts and apply the glue. There is no way to apply clamps to a plate, so I hold the pieces together for as long as I can. When I relieve the pressure, it always turns out that the two pieces I've glued together are no longer aligned.

The only thing I can do is give the Air Force my best advice. My advice is for them to consider some other way. Elastic bands, for example, are infinitely better than glue. I've seldom asked an elastic band to do something it couldn't handle. String or rope is a possible alternative to glue. If the Air Force wants to lift a one-ton elephant with a drop of something, I suppose they can use glue, but if they want to hold something together, I'd recommend almost anything else.

Wrappings

D EPENDING on what mood I'm in, I find it either irritating, funny or civilized when I think about how we protect protective coverings in this country.

When I come home from the grocery store and start to unpack, I am always unfavorably impressed with the layers of protective or decorative wrappings we cover our food with.

There is hardly anything we buy that doesn't come in at least two wrappings, and then several of them are assembled by the cashier at the checkout counter and put into a small bag. Then several of the small bags are grouped together and put into a big bag. If you have several big bags with small bags in them, they give you a cardboard box to put the-packages-in-the-little-bags-in-the-big-bags in.

A lot of things we buy wouldn't really need any protective wrapping at all. The skin of an orange protects an orange pretty well for most of its natural life, but we aren't satisfied with what nature has given it. We wrap ten of them in plastic or put them in a net bag, and we put the plastic bag in a paper bag. The orange inside the skin, inside the plastic which is in a paper bag, must wonder where it is.

A box of cookies or crackers often has waxed paper next to the cookies, a cardboard box holding the cookies and then waxed paper and a decorative wrapping around the cardboard box. What seems to be called for here is some stiff, decorative waxed paper.

We have always wrapped our cars in an incredible number of protective layers. We put fenders over the wheels to protect ourselves from flying dirt. Then we put bumpers front and back to protect the fenders. We proceed from there to put chrome on the bumpers to protect them from rust, and we undercoat the fenders to protect *them* from the dirt they're protecting us from.

We paint the car to protect the metal, wax the paint to protect that and then we build a two-car garage to protect the whole thing. If it was a child, it would be spoiled.

I'm laughing, but I'm a protector of things myself. I use wood preserver before I paint lumber, and when I buy a raincoat I always spray it with Scotchgard or some other silicone water resister. Over the years, I'll bet I've spent more on Scotchgard than I have on raincoats.

A good book is designed with a hard cover to protect its contents. The hard cover is protected from dirt and abuse by a dust jacket. A lot of people who are very careful with books cover the dust jacket with a plastic cover of its own.

A relative of ours bought a new couch recently because she liked the fabric it was covered with. She liked it so much she didn't want it to get dirty, so she bought a slipcover to put over it and she laid little oblong pieces of cloth over the arms where the wear is heaviest to protect the slipcover. She called them antimacassars.

We may never again see the fabric she's protecting.

Sizes

At some point we've got to take some time out and rethink sizes. I'm not a person who likes a lot of uniformity in his life, but we could save time, trouble and space if there wasn't so much variation in the size and shape of things.

Suitcases, for example, should be made in standard sizes. There should be just four. For advertising purposes the makers could call them HUGE, GIANT, LARGE and REGULAR. HUGE would be a big suitcase, GIANT would be a normal size, LARGE would be small and REGULAR would be a small bag used for personal items you wanted to keep with you on the trip.

If suitcases were made in only four standard sizes, we could save fifty percent of the space they now take up in airplane luggage compartments. At home we could have whole closets of space and the predictably shaped suitcases would make packing the trunk of a car a pleasure.

Envelopes should come in no more than three sizes. I'm no defender of the U.S. Postal Service, but it's ridiculous to ask them to handle hundreds of different size envelopes. Some envelopes are hardly bigger than the stamps they bear, while other envelopes are too big to fit in the average mailbox.

The Postal Service might start the ball rolling by making their stamps in standard sizes, too. Stamps should be graduated in size according to price. All stamps for first-class letters should be the same size and shape year after year.

Making stamps of the same denomination in different sizes is as foolish as it would be to make some dimes the size of nickels and some the size of quarters just because they had a new picture of someone on them. It would be a convenience to all of us if we could depend on the size and shape of a twenty-cent stamp. I know stamp collectors like it, but I'm not even sure we need all these inventive designs on new issues of commemorative stamps. We ought to know what a stamp is without having to study it to determine what it will send for us.

Car bumpers should all be the same size and the same height above the road. Some steps have been taken in this direction, but too many bumpers still do not meet. It makes it difficult to start a car by pushing it with another in winter, and it makes for a lot of bashed radiators and trunks all year round.

And while car manufacturers are at it, I wish they'd agree that the key with the square end was always the ignition key and the one with the round end was always the trunk key. Regularly, one major manufacturer decides to reverse that. I'd rather see them save their creative drive for some other feature in their cars.

Boxes of cookies and crackers that we keep on our kitchen shelves need not be so inventively different as they are. Like odd-shaped suitcases, it makes them very difficult to store in a limited space.

I suppose it would be wrong to try to impose standardization on them, but I wish bottles, magazines, receipts and ice cube trays came in just a few standard sizes, too. As it is, they take up too much room. You can't stack them, file them neatly or keep them on the same shelf, because they don't fit together.

Too often the shape and size of things is determined not by any-one thinking of how the item will be used, but by someone in the advertising department whose only consideration is how to sell it.

Letter Writing

THERE ought to be a five-cent stamp for personal letters. Letter writing is one of the good things about a civilized society, and it should be encouraged. It's a shame that everything is conspiring against letter writing. Our whole postal system has deteriorated to the point where mail is no fun at all. The excitement we used to feel about the arrival of the mailman is gone.

It costs twenty cents for a regular stamp now. That's a terrible number, and you don't dare buy a roll of twenty-cent stamps be-cause you know it's going to change before you get used to it and certainly before you use up a roll.

I object to the fact that it costs me more to send a letter to a friend than it costs some fly-by-night real estate operator to send me a phony brochure in the mail telling me I'm the provisional win-ner of a $10,000 sweepstakes. I don't like strangers knocking on my door trying to sell me something, and I don't want my mail clut-tered with advertising. If anyone wants to accuse me of feeling that way because I make a living from the advertising found in news-papers and on television, go ahead and accuse me of it. It isn't true.

I don't get five good, genuine, personal letters a year. The time is coming when the letter written with pen and ink and sent as a personal message from one person to another will be as much of a rarity as the gold pocket watch carried on a chain. It's a shame.

There is something special about a personal letter. It's better than a phone call, no matter what the telephone company says. A phone call disappears into the air as soon as the receiver is put back on the hook. A good letter can last a lifetime.

Some of my most precious possessions are letters that have been written to me sometime in the past. I don't have a single memorable phone call stored in a box in my attic or basement. I've never thrown away a good letter and, like any real treasure, I don't even have to look at them to enjoy having them. I *know* I have them.

The telephone calls come and go. They make no permanent impression on me and have no place in my memory.

A personal letter is a good thing because you say things you can't say in a crowd and might not even say to the person face to face. If you feel like it, a letter allows you to take yourself and your thoughts more seriously than you would dare take them in conversation. And you can say things without interruption.

A good letter is, in many ways, the exact opposite of a political speech. A politician addressing a crowd has to talk so broadly and generally about the issues in order not to offend any one of the thousands of people listening that he usually ends up saying nothing. A letter can be specific, and if the writer has some bias or prejudice, he can even reveal his true self by letting this show. Writing a friend, you shouldn't have to be careful. Abraham Lincoln's letter to his stepbrother telling him he wasn't going to loan him the eighty dollars he asked for tells you more about Abraham Lincoln than the Gettysburg Address does.

Some of our best history has come that way, from personal letters of famous people that scholars have dug up. You get a better idea of what someone is really like from a personal letter they weren't expecting you to read than you get from a carefully considered public statement they've made. We say real things in letters.

There are several reasons why we aren't writing many personal letters. We don't write letters with news of the family because we already have that by telephone; we don't write secrets because we're all so aware that they may fall into the wrong hands and end up in print; and we don't write awkward love letters much anymore because we're afraid of sounding silly. Love letters were almost always silly, but only in retrospect. The moment it is opened and read, a love letter is never silly. That's the other good thing about a personal letter. If you know each other well, it doesn't have to make absolute sense to anyone else.

Personal letters should go for a five-cent stamp.

Missing the Newspaper

WHEN I'm on vacation I can go for days without watching television, but I hate to miss my newspaper. I'm spending this part of my vacation thirty miles away from the nearest big city, and it's a major trip to get the papers. I don't want just *any* paper, either. I like my own bed, my own chair in the living room, my own place at the dinner table and my own newspaper. Reading a strange newspaper is like being in the hotel room you're usually in when you're reading it. It may be good but you're not at home with it. In the hotel room you can't find the bathroom in the middle of the night, and in the newspaper you don't know where they hide the sports page.

One way or another, I manage to get the paper on vacation. During the eight days we recently spent in France, I didn't see an American newspaper at all, with the exception of one issue of the Paris *Herald Tribune*. As a result, there's going to be a hole in my information storage system for the rest of my life. I know because I have some others just like it from times past when I've missed the newspaper.

"What do you mean he's dead?" I'll say. "When did he die?"

"Must have been a year ago. Last summer. Sometime in July."

Then it all dawns on me. The movie star, the sports figure or the poet passed away on one of those days I never got to read the newspaper.

There are going to be all sorts of little stories and events about which I'll be ignorant because of having missed those eight days of history. It's okay to say you can go to the library and look at the files of the old papers, but you don't get at doing that any more than you get at reading those parts of the Sunday paper you set aside to read later.

Once you get familiar with your own newspaper, you know how you want to read it. The trouble with a strange newspaper is, you have to read it the way the editor intended you to and *that's* no way to read a paper, as we all know. Fortunately, newspaper editors are too worldwise to have their little hearts broken by readers, but it must hurt them to see what people do with their day's work. Readers ignore stories the editors spent a lot of time and money on, and readers have their own ideas about which are the most important stories.

Editors try to assemble a newspaper in some logical, orderly way for an illogical, disorderly public. We ignore the editors' order. We don't read the stories they think are important first and then proceed to the dessert. We go right for the cake and ice cream first and come back to the meat and potatoes if we have time. A lot of times we don't have time. Each reader reedits the paper his own way.

I often take a train to work when I'm working, and there are important-looking executives going to town to deal with the world who get on, sit down, open the paper to the crossword puzzle or the ball scores and never once look at page one. The world could have come to an end during the night, but they aren't going to know about it until they get to the office and their secretaries tell them.

Editors know this, of course, but there's nothing they can do about it. They can't lead the paper with the crossword puzzle because even the man who is most interested in that wants the news on the front page whether he ever reads it or not. *Buying* the paper gives him the feeling he's read it.

In some ways I'm careful with money, but when it comes to buying newspapers, I'm profligate. Saturday mornings I buy two copies of the same newspaper. It costs me fifty cents instead of a quarter, but may save our marriage. I used to hate it when I had to sit there waiting for my wife to finish one section of the paper so I could read the jump of the story I'd started in the other section. And when I settle down with the paper, it spoils the pleasure of it for me when someone says, "Can I see a section of the paper?" I want the whole thing or none of it.

Now I have to make that damn thirty-mile drive.

Dictionaries

W<small>HEN</small> I look up something in the dictionary, it's never where I look for it first.

The dictionary has been a particular disappointment to me as a basic reference work, and the fact that it's usually more my fault than the dictionary's doesn't make it any easier on me. Sometimes I can't come close enough to knowing how to spell a word to find it; other times the word just doesn't seem to be anywhere in the dictionary. I can't for the life of me figure out where they hide some of the words I want to look up. They must be in there someplace.

Other times I want more information about a word than the dictionary is prepared to give me. I don't want to know how to spell a word or what it means. I want to know how to use it. I want to know how to make it possessive and whether I double the final consonant when I add -ing to it. And as often as I've written it, I always forget what you do to make a word that ends in *s* possessive. "The Detroit *News'* editor"? "The Detroit *Newses* editor"? I suppose the Detroit *News's* editors know, but I never remember and the dictionary is no help.

I have at least twenty words that I look up ten times a year. I didn't know how to spell them in high school and I still don't. Is it "further" or "farther" if I'm talking about distance? I always go to the dictionary for further details. I have several dictionaries and I avoid the one farthest from me. Furthest from me?

I am even nervous about some words I should have mastered in grade school. I know when to use "compliment" instead of "complement," when to use "stationery" and not "stationary" and "principle" not "principal," but I always pause just an instant to make sure.

You'd think someone who has made a living all his life writing words on paper would know how to spell everything. I'm not a bad enough speller to be interesting, but there are still some words I look up in the dictionary because I'm too embarrassed to ask anyone how they're spelled. I've probably looked up "embarrassed" nine times within the last few years, and I often check to make sure there aren't two *s*'s in "occasion." "Occassion" strikes me as a more natural way to spell the word.

Sometimes people use words that are wrong because they sound better than the right ones. I often do that. I wouldn't think of using the word "data" as a plural word, which it is. You wouldn't catch me saying, "All the data are in" even though it's proper. I often find myself using the word "hard" when I should be writing "difficult." It's hard to stick to the rules when the rules make you sound more formal than you want to be. I seldom use the subjunctive "were" for "was."

I've had several letters this year from literate readers accusing me of using the word "like" as a conjunction when I should be using the word "as," as in the phrase, "I don't know President Reagan like Nancy does."

That's wrong and I know it, but I can't bring myself to do it right, like in the phrase, "I don't know President Reagan as Nancy does." It just seems to weaken the statement.

The dictionary doesn't help much with the word "like" when I look there for some justification for misusing it. My Webster's starts this way: "like *adj* (ME, alter. of *ilich*, fr. OE *gelīc* like, alike; akin to OHG *gilīh* like, alike; . . . all fr. a prehistoric Gmc compound whose first constituent . . ." Come on, Webster, give us a break. Never mind the ilich, the gelic and the gilih, just tell it like it is.

The trouble with dictionaries is, they tell you more about words than you want to know without answering the question you have.

Design

Last summer I made a chair. The wood was maple and cherry, and I invented what kind of a chair it was as I went along. When I finished, the chair looked great, but it has one shortcoming. It tips over backwards when anyone sits in it.

My design was better than my engineering.

Most of us are so engrossed in whatever it is we do with our days that we fail to consider what anyone else is doing with theirs. I

attended a meeting in Washington D.C. a short time ago and everyone there but me was a designer of things. I never knew there were
so many. I came away realizing that designing what a product will
look like is a substantial part of any business. There are thousands
of people who spend their lives doing it.

Everything we use has been designed, well or poorly . . . your
car, your toaster, your watch. When Alexander Graham Bell finished inventing the telephone, all he had was wires. Someone had to
decide on the shape of the instrument it would be housed in, and
they came up with that great old standup telephone. That was industrial design.

There is usually trouble between engineers and designers. Most
designers are creative artists who tend to ignore the practical aspects
of a product. Most engineers, on the other hand, don't usually care
much what a product looks like as long as it works.

The only time the consumer wins is when design and function
blend together in one harmonious unit that looks great and works
perfectly. We know it doesn't happen often.

A lot of artists who can't make a living selling their paintings
or anything else that is commonly called art often turn to commerce. Sometimes they are apologetic about having to make a living, but they ought not be. If they are bad artists that's one thing,
but if they are competent or even talented artists they ought to
take a lot of satisfaction from being able to provide the rest of us,
who don't have their talent, with some visual niceties. Making the
practical, everyday world good-looking is not a job to be embarrassed about.

It may even be that industrial design and commercial art are
more important than art for art's sake. Art always appeals to me
most when it has had some restrictions placed on it. I like art that
solves a problem or says something a new way. Uninhibited, free-
form, far-out art never seems very artistic to me. Artists who can
do anything in the whole world they want to do don't usually do
anything. Even Michelangelo was at his best when he had a ceiling
to paint.

The danger industrial designers face is that they'll be turned into
salesmen. The first rule of industrial design should be that the product must look like what it is, not like something else. If something
looks like what it is and works, it's beautiful and no amount of
dolling it up will help it. This accounts for why bridges are so
attractive to us. The best bridges are built from plans that come
from some basic engineering principle that hasn't been altered by a
salesman who thinks he could get more people to cross it by making

it a different shape. I always liked the Shredded Wheat box for the same reason.

The best-designed packages are those whose first priority is to contain the product. The ones we are all suspicious of are the packages that are too big and too fancy for what they were built to contain. We are tired of false cardboard bottoms and boxes twice as big as they need to be to hold something.

The original green six-ounce Coca-Cola bottle was one of the great designs of all time. It was perfect in almost every way and has, naturally, been all but abandoned. The salesmen took over the bottle from the designers, and now it's too big or not a bottle at all.

I hope our industrial designers can maintain their artistic integrity, even though they have turned to commerce, because what worries me about all this is the same thing that worries me about that chair I made. Too often we're making things that look better than they are.

Four Cars

My daughter Emily has scraped together enough money to buy herself a new car—which takes some scraping these days—so she's going to get rid of her 1968 Volkswagen.

I've always wanted to own a Volkswagen Bug, so I told her I'd buy it from her for whatever the dealer offered her in trade on her new car. Emily likes the old car and the idea of having it in the family, where she can keep an eye on it, appeals to her.

Now, if you think of me as a homespun type with simple tastes who walks to the store for the paper Sunday morning, you're going to be disappointed to hear that Emily's Volkswagen would give me four cars. And that's just for two of us. I know that sounds rich and wastefully American, but I don't spend a lot of money on cars, and owning more cars than you can drive at any one time has a lot of advantages. It can even save money.

I'd love to be rich enough to have the perfect car for every occasion and forget about ever buying another new one. I probably drive 25,000 miles a year. If I could spread those miles over half a dozen cars, they'd never wear out.

If I get Emily's Volkswagen, it's going to create some confusion in the driveway. My wife now owns a 1978 Saab. She loves it and I hate it. She loves it because it's small, nicely made in many ways and gets her where she's going on very little gas. I hate it because the windows are hard to roll up, it turns like a truck and it can't get out of its own way on the road.

The car I drive the most is a 1977 Ford station wagon. It's a great car if you can afford the gas and find a parking space big enough to take it. I'm always carrying wood or tools or suitcases from here to there, and it's very handy to be able to dump everything in that huge rear area. It's coming up to 70,000 miles on the speedometer though, and I don't know what to do next. If gas goes to two dollars a gallon, I suppose I'll just have to throw it away, because *nobody* will want it.

My third car is a little beauty called a Sunbeam Tiger. I've owned it since 1966. It's one of those small green sports cars you've seen around, but this one is special. It has, packed under its bonnet, a Ford V8 289cc engine. The car is so small and the engine so big that it will, as my son Brian says, "blow the doors off anything on the road."

I'd give the Tiger to Brian, but I feel he's getting a little too old for a toy like that. And I don't drive it very fast anymore myself, because the engine has always been better than the body. I have a nervous feeling the body could fall off the engine at any time. I don't really drive it much at all anymore. It's too cold in winter and too hot in summer, and I won't take it out when there's salt on the road or when it's raining because it leaks. It's not a family car.

If I don't get Emily's Volkswagen, I'll be needing a new car in another year. I'd *like* to buy an American car. I feel about the U.S. auto industry the way you feel about one of your children who has done something really dumb or wrong. You're disappointed and disillusioned, but you still love it. You want to forgive and forget.

It might be practical for a group of friends on a block to get together and form their own car pool. A "hertz," they could call it. If four families owned eight cars, they could have just about everything they'd need for any occasion. Each family would have one basic car that it kept in its own driveway. The other four—or even six—vehicles would be kept in a communal parking lot. There might be a Jeep, a convertible sports car, a pickup truck and a big expensive car for special occasions. It could be a diesel Cadillac for long trips or maybe even an old Rolls-Royce if the group had a sense of humor and money. They might even want one motorcycle. They'd probably want at least one plain ordinary extra utility car.

But that doesn't solve my problem. Emily says there's some body rot in the Volkswagen, so I'm going to look at it. She always was too honest for her own good.

Advertising

M Y 1977 Ford station wagon has eight cylinders, a wonderfully powerful engine and an insatiable appetite for unleaded gas. It's a great car, if Ford wants a testimonial, and obviously I'll never have another like it.

It has 83,872 miles on it now, and for the past few weeks I've been wondering whether I should have it serviced and fixed up or buy something new and smaller. It costs me twenty dollars to fill the wagon with gas, which it consumes at the rate of something like fifteen miles to the gallon. I say "something like" because I'm not one of those people who figures out exactly how much a car gets to the gallon.

Last Tuesday I decided to call the Ford place. There were two numbers listed in the phone book, one for "Sales," the other for "Service." I was making a big decision right there when I decided which number to call. I called "Service."

Saturday is the best day for me to do something like take a car in, so I asked the service manager if I could bring it in the following Saturday. Service managers always have a way of making you feel unwanted, and he seemed pleased to be able to tell me they were closed Saturday and wouldn't be able to take me until a week from Thursday.

I didn't make a date. Instead I called the other Ford number under "Sales."

"Are you open Saturday?" I asked.

"Yes, sir," the cheery voice said at the other end of the phone. "We're here Saturdays from eight in the morning 'til nine in the evening, and Sundays from noon until six."

Now, if I can *buy* a car on Saturday, why can't I get one *fixed* on Saturday? What's going on here, anyway?

I think I know what's going on, of course. We're selling things better than we're making them, that's what's going on. Fixing things hardly enters into our economy at all anymore. Whatever breaks we discard and buy a new one like it.

I make my living writing for newspapers and television, both of which are sustained by advertising, so I may be taking my economic life in my hands when I say so, but I think advertising has been carried too far.

Too many bright young men and women are turning their talent to packaging and selling things; too few of them are going into the business of *making* anything. The advertising agencies in New York, Chicago and Los Angeles are filled with bright, creative people pushing products on us that they know or care little about. If their agency loses an account for one thing, they can switch to selling a competing brand or another product without missing a beat. Their techniques are the same whether they're selling extra strength horse-feathers or roll-on headache remedies. They don't care what they're selling, they just know how to do it. They could sell us new, improved sawdust if that's what their client wanted to move.

Advertising has been a force for good in the American economy over the years. It has made us all aware of new products and has pointed out the differences in others. It has helped the economy by creating a market and thus jobs. Advertising has helped make the United States what it has been and that's good. It seems now to be making us what we're becoming and that isn't so good.

I sat on a plane next to a man in the small computer business last week. He told me his company spends more on travel and enter-tainment than they do making their product.

"Our product costs twelve percent of our budget," he said. "The rest goes for packaging, selling, travel, things like that."

I asked him if he thought that was right. He did, but I didn't.

They used to say no amount of advertising could sell an inferior product, but I'm not sure that's true anymore. We're being sold products on every hand that aren't good enough, by clever, per-suasive advertising. I'm tired of great television commercials that are better than the programs they're sandwiched into; I'm tired of new products that are here today, by virtue of a big advertising cam-paign, and gone tomorrow, and if I buy a new car I'd like to buy it from a place where the mechanics work as hard and are as well paid as the salesmen.

Commercials

THE television set is on. Bob Hope is doing a commercial for a local bank in the Los Angeles area.

Why would Bob Hope do a commercial, I wonder to myself. There are three possibilities I can think of: 1) He needs the money. 2) A friend asked him to do it. 3) He owns the bank.

Of the three, only the last seems like a realistic possibility. I just can't figure it out.

Why does any successful person with a good reputation sell his name and that reputation by giving, as though it were his own, a favorable opinion about a product or service that has been written for him by an advertising agency?

The strange thing in my mind about all this is that I resent endorsements by some people and not by others. For instance, it doesn't bother me at all to see Robert Young doing Sanka commercials. Sanka keeps me awake, but their commercials are well done. I never thought of Robert Young as anything but an actor speaking someone else's words anyway.

There are dozens of people who have disappointed me by taking money to say something nice about something. In the past ten years, many of my heroes have been lost to me. I was at the air base in England during World War II when Jimmy Stewart was awarded the DFC for his heroic work as a B-24 bomber pilot. When I watched him in motion picture roles after the war, I knew there was something of honest substance behind that acting facade. And then one evening he suddenly popped up on my television screen and laid it on real heavy for a tire company. For money? Say it ain't so, Jimmy!

American Express has, singlehandedly, removed half a dozen heroes from my list. When their effective don't-leave-home-without-it commercials featured former North Carolina Senator Sam Ervin, what I had remembered as his homey, dry brilliance during the Watergate era turned to dust in my mind.

For years I braved the rain, the snow, the bitter cold to attend every New York Giants home game in hopes that the great Fran

Tarkenton would get enough help from his teammates to win one. Little did I know that while I was fighting the traffic to get back home before my wife left it, Fran was down in the locker room primping with a hair shampoo. Or is he just saying he did that for money?

I worked for John Houseman years ago. The eminent Shakespearean producer, director, actor and star of the TV show "Paper Chase," is now shilling for a brokerage house and a carmaker.

John worked with Orson Welles in their early days in the theater and maybe something rubbed off on each of them, because Orson is now doing those unctuous wine commercials. Welles has always been called a genius, but if those commercials are the work of genius, I don't understand the word. "Lousy" is the word that comes to my mind. If John and Orson needed money, why didn't they come to me?

And if I could ever understand an entertainer or an athlete selling his word for money, I will never understand an ex-astronaut or a former vice-presidential candidate like William E. Miller doing it.

Senator Bill Bradley, who may have been more help to a basketball team than anyone who ever played the game, refused millions of dollars in offers to endorse products when he was with the New York Knickerbockers. If I lived in New Jersey, this alone would be reason enough for me to vote for him.

When a person we respect for knowing how to do something transfers that respect to a product he knows little or nothing about, it is something other than honest.

New Products

MONEY is not my game, so I don't often read the *Wall Street Journal*, but someone on the train I take got off at the stop before mine the other night and left the paper on the seat next to me, so I looked through it. The *Wall Street Journal* gives you sort of a digest of the news you get on television.

One small story in there said that the companies that make things are coming up with fewer new products this year than last. The paper suggested this was bad, but I thought it was good. You can carry freedom of choice too far in a grocery store, for example. I don't want all the big companies squeezing out all the little upstart companies, but I don't want to be faced with ten different brands of what is substantially the identical product, either.

Our kitchen sink got stopped up last Saturday and I went to the grocery store for a can of Drāno. I don't know why Drāno. I'm just familiar with what the can looks like, and I was surprised to find a whole shelf filled with products that were supposed to free a clogged sink. There were powders, liquids and pellets. They came in cans, tubes, bottles and plastic. All of them said that if they didn't work, call your plumber. That always makes me suspect that they probably won't work on my problem. I found myself wishing the grocer had taken it upon himself to test the products for me so that he could have become expert enough to narrow my choices to just two or three.

I ended up with a can of Drāno, as always. I don't know whether any of those new, improved products were any better or not. I figured they were all more or less the same.

Genuine innovation is something we all like. That's what we mean by the line "Build a better mousetrap and the world will beat a path to your door."

The trouble is, too many big companies have been making the same old mousetrap and trying to get us to come to their door by painting it a different color or calling it the Official Mickey Mousetrap. That's not innovation, but that's what too often passes for a new product.

The automobile manufacturers of America are in trouble because we wanted something genuinely different and they gave us the same old mousetrap with electrically operated windows. The Japanese came up with some really new ideas in cars and people are buying them. When Volkswagen switched from the Bug to the Rabbit, the difference was more than new bumper stickers. You can tell a Saab from a Toyota, but you can't tell a Chevrolet from an Oldsmobile unless you own one.

Too many "new" products are coming from the sales departments of companies rather than from the engineering division. I hope Americans are tired of being tricked. A lot of good U.S. companies spend big money on product development, on good design, on engineering or improved chemistry. They have good, serious professionals working to make real improvements, not cosmetic changes, but for all the effort that is put into making the product better, it is hardly ever as much money as is put into selling it.

It has always seemed to me that, over the long run, we do one thing about as well or as poorly as we do something else in America. We have some national traits that show through our work no matter what our work is. Sometimes it's good, sometimes it isn't.

For instance, take two products as different as those produced by Detroit and the television industry. Our cars and our television, for all my complaints, are in many ways the best in the world, but they both suffer from the same things. They're big, fluffy and tend to imitate the other products in their market. Two situation comedies on competing networks are apt to be as much alike as an Oldsmobile and a Chevrolet.

Putting the same product in a new package isn't what I call a new product. When an advertisement tells me what I'm buying is "new and improved," I always wonder exactly what the improvement is and whether I was a sucker for having bought the product last year before they fixed whatever was wrong with it.

I don't care what the *Wall Street Journal* says, I like the idea of fewer new products on the market. What we ought to do is keep making the old ones until we get them right.

Quality?

IT is unceasingly sickening to see someone make a bad product and run a good one out of business. It happens all the time, and we look around to see whose fault it is. I have a sneaking feeling we aren't looking hard enough. It's *our* fault, all of us.

If it isn't our fault—the fault of the American people—whose fault is it? Who is it that makes so many bad television shows so popular? Why were *Life, Look* and the *Saturday Evening Post* driven out of business in their original forms while our magazine stands are filled with the worst kind of junk? Why are so many good newspapers having a tough time, when the trash "newspapers" in the supermarkets are prospering? No one is forcing any of us to buy them.

Around the office I work in, they changed the paper towels in the men's room several months ago. The new ones are nowhere near as good as the brand they had for years, and it takes three to do what one of the old ones would do. Somebody in the company decided it would look good if they bought cheaper paper towels. It is just incredible that smart people decide to save money in such petty ways.

I had a friend whose father owned a drugstore in a small town in South Carolina. It was beautifully kept and well run. My friend's father was an experienced druggist who knew the whole town's medical history. During the 1950s, one of those big chain drugstores moved in selling umbrellas, plastic beach balls, tote bags and dirty books, and that was the end of the good, honest, little drugstore.

We are fond of repeating familiar old sayings like "It's quality not quantity that matters," but we don't buy as though we believe that very often. We take the jumbo size advertised at twenty percent off—no matter what the quality is. I'm glad I'm not in the business of making anything, because it must be heartbreaking for the individual making something the best way he knows how to see a competitor come in and get rich making the same thing with cheap materials and shoddy workmanship.

America's great contribution to mankind has been the invention of mass production. We showed the world how to make things quickly, inexpensively and in such great numbers that even people who didn't have a lot of money could afford them. Automobiles were our outstanding example for a long time. We made cars that weren't Rolls-Royces but they were good cars, and just about everyone could scrape together the money to buy one.

Somewhere, somehow, we went wrong. One by one, the good carmakers were driven out of business by another company making a cheaper one. I could have cried when Packard went out of business, but there were thirty other automobile makers that went the same way, until all that was left was General Motors, American Motors, Chrysler and Ford. And in a few years we may not have all of them.

We found a way to mass-assemble homes after World War II. We started slapping them up with cinder block and plywood, and it seemed good because a lot of people who never could afford a home before were able to buy them.

They didn't need carpenters who were master craftsmen to build those homes, and young people working on them never really got to know how to do anything but hammer a nail.

We have a lot to be proud of, but there is such a proliferation of inferior products on the market now that it seems as though we have to find a way to go in another direction. The term "Made by hand" is still the classiest stamp you can put on a product and we need more of them. We need things made by people who care more about the quality of what they're making than the money they're going to get selling it.

It's our own fault and no amount of good government, bad government, more government or less government is going to turn us around. The only way we're going to get started in the right direction again is to stop buying junk.

II:

OLD FRIENDS

Neat People

Neat people are small, petty, nit-picking individuals who keep accurate checkbooks, get ahead in life and keep their cellars, their attics and their garages free of treasured possessions. They just don't seem to treasure anything, those neat people. If they can't use it or freeze it, they throw it away. I detest neat people. I was in a neat person's home several weeks ago and he took me down into his cellar. He must be making a dishonest living, because there was nothing down there but a few neatly stored screens and the oil burner.

I feel toward neat people the same way I used to feel toward the brightest kid in our class, who was also a good athlete and handsome.

My dislike for the tidies of the world is particularly strong this week because I realized Sunday that my desk is such a mess I can't find anything, my workshop looks like a triple-decker club sandwich with tools on top of wood on top of plans on top of sandpaper on top of tools on top of wood. If I need a Phillips screwdriver, it's easier to go out and buy a new one than to find any of the three I already own.

How do neat people do it? I hate them so much I don't want any help from them, but I would like to follow one around someday and see how they live. I bet they don't do anything, that's how they keep everything so neat. They probably do all sorts of dumb stuff like putting things back where they belong. They probably know which shelf everything is on in the refrigerator; they could probably put their finger on the nozzle to the garden hose.

What do you do with all that stuff I have cluttering my cellar, Neat People? Did you throw away the hammer with the broken handle? Mine is still down there.

What about the twenty feet of leftover aerial wire and the small empty wooden nail keg? Don't tell me you were so heartless that you tossed that out. You don't even appreciate the fact that you never know when you're going to have a good use for an empty wooden nail keg. That's how dumb you Neat People are. I, on the other hand, have been ready with an empty nail keg for the past twenty years. That's about how long it's been in the cellar, right there in the way if I ever need it.

You probably throw out broken plates and glass pitchers that can't be repaired, don't you? Tell the truth. I don't. I keep broken plates because I can't stand to throw them out. I'm waiting for them to make glue that will really mend china and glass, the way the ads say the glue will now.

Many years ago a man who owned a hairbrush factory gave me a bushel basket of odds and ends of rosewood. They're beautiful little pieces and I've never figured out what to do with them, but I wouldn't neaten up my cellar by throwing them out for anything.

My wife says the old bookcase I took out of the twins' room in 1973 should be thrown out. She gets a little neat every once in a while herself. Thank goodness that never happens to me. That's why I still have that bookcase.

We have four children and I'm not saving much money, but should I ever die, I'd like to leave the kids something. I have nineteen cans of partly used paint, some dating from the late fifties, in the cellar. I don't want them fighting over my estate when I go, so I think I'll make a will and divide the paint among them. I want it to have a good home.

My Closet

I've *got* to throw out some clothes.

My clothes closet in the hall outside our bedroom is at capacity. It looks like a New York City subway at rush hour in there. Clothes hang from hangers so tightly packed together that I can't get one out without removing several simultaneously.

You can laugh if you want, but it's no joke. This thing with my clothes is getting serious. I have three suits, five pairs of pants and a dozen sports shirts that would keep a poor person warm all winter, and I haven't worn them in ten years. They're too good to throw out and I don't like them enough to wear them, that's the problem. Or maybe they don't fit. That's another problem. Maybe they'll fit me later in the year. After I lose a little weight? I've been thinking that for more than ten years, and it hasn't happened yet.

I don't think you can hedge on throwing clothes away. I've given some to the Salvation Army, the Goodwill and other charitable organizations and it makes me feel good, but I seriously doubt whether the stuff I give them makes anyone else feel good. Is there someone living on welfare who really wants the jacket to a white tuxedo I bought for a wedding in 1957? Can someone use a double-breasted pinstripe suit with padded shoulders and bell-bottom trousers I thought looked great on me when I looked at myself in the store mirrors seventeen years ago? The press is still good in the pants and there isn't a spot on it. I just don't think there's a place for the suit in the give-away market.

There probably ought to be a law passed saying you can't buy a new piece of clothing without throwing one out. Maybe the law could work like deposit bottles. The store would have to give you something back on an old suit or dress when you brought it back. That way you wouldn't have the awful feeling you get when you throw something out that has a lot of wear left in it.

It isn't the money that keeps me from throwing clothes out. It's sentiment. I remember all the good times I had in that brown sports jacket. It came through at the elbow years ago and I've worn it to a few football games in the last five years, but I really can't go anywhere in it unless I'm wearing an overcoat I'm not going to take off.

I have thirty-four pairs of shoes. That sounds like a Liz Taylor kind of statistic, but I may even be cheating a little, because if I told you forty-three it would sound ridiculous. It isn't hard at all to accumulate forty-three pairs of shoes if you never throw a pair away. As a matter of fact, if you buy two pairs a year for twenty-five years, it isn't hard at all. Would you believe fifty-three?

When I say shoes I mean shoes, sneaks, loafers, moccasins, snow boots, workshoes, ski boots, black dress shoes for New Year's Eve, huaraches I bought in Mexico and the three pairs of shoes I actually wear.

You probably wonder what my clothes closet looks like. Well, it's sad when the kids leave home, but something good comes out of everything, and if Brian hadn't headed out on his own several years ago and, for all practical purposes, abandoned his closet, I don't know what I'd be doing for space. I've taken over. He has half a dozen abandoned pieces of footwear in there himself and at least ten odd jackets, ski pants and high school football jerseys, but they don't bother me much. I push them way to one side, and when he comes back at Christmas I like him to feel at home, so I stuff all my things back in my own closet or put them down cellar and move what he has left in there to the center of the clothes pole so he won't notice anything has changed.

I don't know what to do. I just can't bring myself to heap faithful old clothes on top of the garbage can, and it seems contemptible of me to think I'm doing anyone any good by giving them to the poor. When Brian comes home, I'm always nice to him. I tell him to take whatever he wants.

He never takes anything.

Throwing Things Out

TODAY is a turning point in my life.

From this day forward, I am not adding one single thing to my collection of possessions. If I bring something new in the front door, I'm going to throw something old out the back door.

The simple fact of the matter is, everything's full. My desk drawers are full and the top of my desk is heaped high with paper.

My two-car garage long ago passed the point where I could get one car, let alone two, into it. Now I can't even open the garage door from the driveway side and walk through it to the door leading to the kitchen. I have to go around.

When the oil-burner man came to give the furnace its annual physical, he said I couldn't have all that stuff piled so close to it. That's easy for an oil-burner man to say, but where would he put it? Where would he put the outdoor chair with the broken leg that's too good to throw away and that I'll probably get at fixing someday? There's no space left anywhere in the cellar except too close to the furnace.

The attic isn't any better. The attic is only high enough in the middle, under the peak of the roof, for me to stand up straight in, but I've hoisted boxes of old letters, books and suitcases filled with papers into it and shoved them over to the side where I have to get down on my hands and knees to shove them under the eaves.

The four kids have all left home, but they didn't leave home with much of their stuff. There is evidence of the eighteen or twenty years they spent in the house in closets everywhere. Parents entertain some foolish notion that they're loved and wanted just because children leave clothes behind when they strike out on their own. The kids, for their part, are about as sentimental about their closet at home as they'd be about a locker in a bus station. I love them, but when they come home for Thanksgiving and Christmas, I'm going to sneak out to their cars at night while they're sleeping and fill the trunks with old sneaks, small clothes and school papers of theirs that they've been storing at home. I'm going to stuff the cute, misshapen clay ashtrays they made in Miss Evans' pottery class into the crevices behind the front seats of their cars. I'm going to make Ellen take those 37 books in Russian she brought home from college.

In the kitchen, the drawers are piled so high with knives, forks and kitchen gadgets for cutting carrots into interesting shapes that something often sticks up too high and prevents a drawer from opening.

My life runneth over and I'm going to do something about it. Beginning today, I solemnly swear on a stack of old Garry Moore scripts, I will not bring one single item into the house or office without casting out some equivalent space-taker. If I buy a new tool, I'm going to throw out an old one. If I buy a new shirt, I'm going to throw out an old shirt.

I am no longer going to save the brown bags the groceries come in. I have a lifetime supply of old brown bags. I am going to cast out coffee cans, elastic bands, book matches, broken toasters, old snow tires and perhaps, just perhaps, my stack of old *Life* magazines.

I'm clearing out my life, beginning today . . . tomorrow the very latest.

Pennies

I think I'm finally about to get rich and I want to tell you about it. It may not be too late for you to get in on it.

My secret is pennies . . . one-cent U.S. coins. Very shortly now it looks as if the United States Mint is going to start making a new one-cent coin that will be made of zinc instead of copper. And you know what's going to happen then. Real copper pennies will start disappearing until there are practically none left, and the ones that are left will be very valuable to collectors.

Now for the good part. I am *already* a collector of pennies. Here's a case where I've really got a head start toward cornering the penny market of the future. Someone sold a 1922 Lincoln penny last year for $16,500. There must have been something special about it, but that's the kind of markup I'm looking for in the near future on the pennies I'm holding.

Here's a brief assessment of my net worth in pennies:

—I know for a fact there must be at least eighteen of them on the floor toward the back of my clothes closet in between several pairs of old shoes I don't wear anymore.

—There are two pairs of khaki pants and one pair of corduroy that I haven't been able to get into for the past few years. I'm certain to find another ten to fifteen pennies in the pockets of those.

—Up until now I've been waiting until I decided to turn in my old car before bothering to fish down in there behind the front seat cushion, but I know darn well there's a comb down there and it'll surprise me if there aren't at least twenty pennies.

—We have about ten suitcases among us in the family, and there's certainly a treasure in pennies down inside those little ruffled pockets of the suitcases.

—My real worth is up on my dresser and in a glass jar hidden between the dresser and the wall. I put the pennies from my pocket in an ashtray every night, and when that's full, I dump them in a glass jar. I've been doing that for eight or ten years. I must have three or four hundred genuine copper pennies in the jar.

Beginning today, I'm going to start being even more careful about saving my pennies . . . not that I approve of hoarding, mind you. I hate people who hoard things. Or, at least, I hate everyone but myself who hoards things. If I can save ten dollars' worth of pennies a week for the next six months before they start to disappear, that will give me twenty-six thousand of them, in addition to the stock I already have around the house.

This will be the first time I've ever been rich, although I've come close several times before. If I'd kept some of those old Benny Goodman records I had in high school, they'd be worth a fortune today. But I didn't keep them.

When I was about eight years old I started saving Indianhead pennies. I'm not sure what happened to those. I suspect my mother used them one day to pay for the laundry.

If I'd hung onto that old 1941 Ford phaeton I bought for $150 in 1951, I could get $10,000 for it today from an old-car collector.

The Lionel electric train I practically gave away twenty-five years ago would get me a bundle today.

So, I've been close before and I'm not going to let it slip away from me again. I've learned my lesson about holding onto things that will get valuable with time. I figure that if I can get together thirty thousand pennies now and hold onto them for thirty years, they'll be worth a dollar apiece and I'll sell them to a numismatist for a nice piece of change.

I'll be ninety-one.

Painting

WE had the cellar room painted last week. It's the playroom, but we've never played much of anything but records in it. I do much of my writing in it, and the walls are lined with books and binders with old scripts in them. The slide projector is down there, and there's always some debris left from the last showing we had with that.

What I resent most about the whole painting operation is that we paid to have it done, but I did most of the hard work. I moved my desk, moved two four-drawer files, moved a couch, six chairs and two storage chests and then took roughly five hundred books off the shelves and nineteen paintings and pictures off the walls. The painter came in, threw a drop cloth over the island of stuff I'd piled in the middle of the room, slapped on a coat of paint with a roller and left. There I was with a lot of heavy lifting to do and hundreds of tough decisions to make. This was obviously a time to weed out some of the literary dead wood.

I have won some awards of which I am proud, but do I hang the plaques and citations back on the walls again? Do I put the statuettes back on the bookshelves? They make me reluctant to ask guests to come down there. It must seem to them as though I've lured them to my trophy room with the promise of a slide show. On the other hand, do I bury these artifacts of success if I am really proud of them? I don't know what to do.

And what about the books? Do I keep all these books? I hate to throw one away, but do I really need *How to Cook and Eat in Russian?* The recipes are in both English and Russian. Here's Martha's fourth-grade arithmetic book, with some of her answers penciled into the exercises. It's a legitimate memento, no doubt about that, but if I keep the arithmetic book, do I also save the geography book in which she has written all sorts of nine-year-old-girl remarks?

I had to empty out the closet at the foot of the stairs too. We keep some overflow kitchen things in that. Here's one of those cute, overpriced wood cheese boards with a place for a knife. Someone gave us this for Christmas years ago. We'll never use it, but it's too good to throw away. Someone will throw it away someday, but it won't be me. I wish I hadn't been reminded it's still there. There's other stuff here, too . . . an espresso coffee maker that seemed like a good idea to buy once . . . an electric iron which I'm not going to take the time to check out . . . some cheap pie tins I must have saved from a take-out pizza place . . . several ugly flower vases. I guess I'll just dump all this stuff back in there and sort it out some other day.

I suppose I could get rid of this table . . . except that it's about the first thing I ever made when I started woodworking.

I'm certainly not going to get rid of any of my old typewriters just because the place was painted.

There must be more than one hundred pens and pencils now that I've collected them from drawers, table tops and from underneath couches and chair cushions. I almost never write with anything but a typewriter, but you don't throw away a good pencil.

What I'd like to do is, I'd like to sneak into that painter's house someday, pile all his furniture in the middle of his living room, put a nice fresh coat of paint on his walls and leave. I'd put a note on the kitchen table telling him I was so pleased with the job he did on my playroom that I wanted to do something nice for him in return.

I don't know why I never learn about jobs like this. If I'm going to pay for help I know exactly what I need. I need someone to come in, move all those books and all that furniture. *I'll* slap the coat of paint on the walls, and then the workmen can come back in, put everything back where it belongs and make all those hard decisions for me.

Now, a job like that I'd be willing to pay real money for.

The Refrigerator

Would anyone want to buy two lambchops, the front quarter of a cooked chicken, half a package of green beans, a loaf of bread and five plastic containers, the contents of which are unknown to me?

A recent check reveals that we have these items in our freezer. They'd be a good buy for someone. The lambchops are circa 1976. That was a good year for lambchops. Some of the stuff in the plastic containers will probably turn out to be beef cooked with vegetables in a Chinese manner. One or more might be just plain fat, though. We had a roast beef one night a year or so ago. I poured the fat off the pan before making the gravy, and I think I put it in the freezer to make it easier to dispose of and then forgot to dispose of it.

This one-time-only opportunity for some lucky person is available now because my wife and I cleaned out the freezer the other night. These were the things we thought were too good to throw away. In order to make room for this year's Thanksgiving and Christmas leftovers, we had to throw away last year's.

Years ago, I used to think it would be wonderful to buy whole sides of beef and whole boxes of cans of frozen orange juice. In the summer we would pick our garden fresh vegetables, follow directions on how to preserve their garden fresh character and then freeze them and thumb our noses at the supermarket manager all winter as we withdrew what we wanted each day from our laden larder.

When we first got a refrigerator that was half freezer, I had dreams of instant gourmet dinners. When the best foods were cheapest, we'd buy heavily. When it amused me to cook something fancy, I'd do it in my leisure time and then stow it away and amaze guests months later with my instant culinary expertise.

Ha! Ha! to all of that.

What do we use the freezer for? Ice cubes. That's about it. Ice cubes and perhaps a frozen vegetable or a can of frozen orange juice once a month. I'd trade three quarters of the space in the freezer for another burner on the stove any day.

The people who use their freezers the way they were intended are the people who put up pickles, make homemade chili sauce and have a root cellar. When we stow something in the freezer, it's Good-bye Charley. It might as well be up in the attic with the kids' sixth-grade geography books or down in the cellar under the old Christmas tree stand we don't use anymore since I bought a new one.

The people who are organized enough to label every item they put in the freezer and recall it on demand like a book on a library shelf are a marvel to me. There are a few labels on some of the containers in our freezer, but I suspect that some of them are containers we used for something else and never changed the label on when we changed the contents. When you're cleaning up the kitchen, it's easy to stick things in the freezer with plans to label them the next day.

To tell you the truth, the main section of our refrigerator isn't in great shape either. It's cluttered with all kinds of odds and ends too good to throw away but not good enough to make a meal of.

Part of the clutter comes from an uncertainty about what you keep in a refrigerator (which we still tend to call the icebox). Ketchup, mustard, jam and jelly? I think the commercial brands are all preserved for eternity, but once we open a jar, we keep it cold. We keep the opened can of coffee in the icebox.

Next year I'm going to get my finances in better shape, do my Christmas shopping early, keep a diary for tax purposes and keep track of what's in the refrigerator. Ha!

Lazy?

Lazy? I can't make out whether I'm lazy or not. Sometimes I just don't have the ambition to think about it. When my mother used to ask me to go out and get some wood for the fireplace in the cottage at the lake, I'd always come banging back in through the screen door with more than I could comfortably carry because I didn't want to have to go back out for more.

My mother always said, "That's a lazy man's load."

I don't think of myself as being lazy because I get up early every morning and go to work and I work a long day, but there's no doubt about it, certain jobs I'm faced with bring on a feeling I'd rather go lie down than do them.

It doesn't seem to have anything to do with physical labor. Some of those jobs I don't mind getting at. If I had a friendly family psychiatrist, I'd ask him to explain to me exactly what it is about some jobs that turns off my ambition. For instance:

—I don't mind washing the dishes at all, but if the dishes have been put in the dishwasher, I hate the job of emptying it.

—We have screens and storm windows in the garage that haven't been touched in years because I so dislike the job of putting them up and taking them down. Once you've passed through one whole season during which both were needed without getting them up, it's easier to pass through the next one, too.

—I'll tie a broken shoelace together in three places before facing the fact that I have to pull the whole thing out and replace it with a new one.

—I don't mind replacing a light bulb, but I dislike the job of getting the ladder out and putting it away again if it's the fluorescent lights on the kitchen ceiling.

—There's some theme here because, while I don't do it very often, I don't mind vacuum-cleaning a rug. I even enjoy it sometimes, but then I can hardly bring myself to unhitch the vacuum cleaner and put everything back in its place in the closet. If I'm vacuuming upstairs and have to put the vacuum cleaner away *downstairs*, I especially hate it. When my ship comes in, I'm going to buy a second vacuum cleaner so we'll have one on each floor. Of course, then I'll have to buy a bigger house with another closet upstairs to keep it in.

—We have never moved, because I couldn't possibly face the job of packing up my toys. We've lived in the same house since 1952 and I see no prospect of ever leaving it. It would be too hard.

—There is something satisfying about emptying a waste backet or taking out the garbage. Neither is my favorite job, but I don't mind doing those things. What I'm often too lazy to do is take the waste baskets back where they came from.

—After a long weekend when I've played tennis, done some painting or woodworking, gone to a party and just lounged around the house, I've often gone through three or four changes of clothes. By Sunday night the bedroom looks like the counter of the men's department of a clothing store after a half-off sale. My clothes are scattered everywhere, hanging from doorknobs and draped over chairs and tables. When it comes to putting clothes away, I'm incredibly lazy.

—If we return from a trip late Sunday afternoon or evening, I'll bring some of the stuff in out of the car, but then I'll sit down and watch television or start reading something, leaving the car half full in the driveway. Packing a car is just as hard work as unpacking it, but I do one without complaining and often avoid the other for days.

—Writing letters doesn't bother me as a job. It's addressing them and taking them to the mailbox that I find difficult.

—I don't mind writing my column the first time, but if it isn't good enough or if it's too messy to send out, I'm often too lazy to do it over.

Old Friends

THE next time we have friends at the house over a weekend, I'm going to make sure it isn't *old* friends. I want our next house guests to be friends we don't know well enough to be perfectly at ease with—not that I didn't enjoy having Barbara and Quintin, mind you. It's just that we all know each other so well that no one holds back.

"Boy, you got a lot of work to do around this place," Quintin said.

Well I *know* I have a lot of work to do and I *know* I'm not going to do a lot of it, and I don't need a good friend telling me about it.

"I drove up to Montreal to get my paint," Quintin said. "They can still make paint with lead in it up there, and it lasts a lot longer. That's why all the paint is peeling on your house. Paint made in the U.S. isn't good anymore."

He thinks perhaps I haven't *noticed* the house needs painting?

"I nearly broke my neck on those stone steps out by the back porch," he said. "That slab of stone on top is rocking. Can't you jam another little stone or something under there so it doesn't rock? Someone's going to get killed."

Quintin thinks perhaps I haven't been meaning to stabilize that stone for four years now since the frost heaved it?

"That's a good aerial you've got on your television set," he said. "Of course, you're on high ground here so you get a good picture.

Why don't you get yourself a decent-sized television set so you can see it?"

Saturday night we had some other friends over for a drink and dinner. Barbara and Quintin wanted to help.

"Sure," I said. "You can put the glasses and the ice and the bottles out on the table on the front lawn."

"Which glasses?" Barbara said.

I told her where the glasses were and she started taking things out.

"There are only seven of these glasses and there are going to be eight of us," Barbara said.

"I know, I know," I said. "We used to have twelve of them. You have to use one jelly glass. I'll drink out of that one."

"Don't fall on that loose stone step as you go out," Quintin said to Barbara. "What about chairs for out front?" he asked me.

I told him there were some old ones up in the garage if he wanted to get a couple of those.

Quintin is a willing helper. He went out to the garage and he was gone for about ten minutes before he returned carrying two aluminum chairs with broken webbing.

"You mean *these?*" he asked incredulously.

Those were the ones I meant. I knew the webbing was broken. If the webbing hadn't been broken they wouldn't have been in the garage in the first place.

"Boy," he said, as he put the chairs down, "I thought my garage was a mess. How do you ever get a car in there? You got stuff hanging all over. You ought to have a garage sale . . . and sell the garage." He laughed. Friends can be so cruel.

"Why don't I make the salad dressing," Barbara said to my wife. "Is this the only vinegar you have?" she asked, holding up a bottle of supermarket house brand, El Cheapo vinegar. "I guess I'll use lemon instead of vinegar," she said.

"Here come the first guests," Quintin said. "There sure isn't much space for them to park in that driveway of yours."

"I'll go greet the guests," Barbara said.

"Don't break your neck on that stone step as you go out," Quintin yelled after her.

Housing Subtractions

ONE of the secrets to getting ahead in the world is to anticipate trends. If you can figure out what a lot of people are going to be doing next, you've got a head start on the future. This is true about things large and small. The knack for looking ahead and seeing what's coming next is as helpful in choosing a line to stand in at the supermarket as it is in investing in the stock market.

I heard the first evidence of what I'll bet is going to be a trend of the future, and I can't wait until I figure out a way to cash in on it and finally get rich. I know there's going to be big money in it, and it's just a matter of my figuring out exactly what business to go into to make a killing.

We were sitting around with some friends when I first realized what the future held for a lot of Americans. One couple mentioned a loan they were trying to get at the bank to make their house smaller. Do you think you read that wrong? You did not. They've talked to a contractor about putting a subtraction on their house. They've lived in it for twenty-two years, and every few years when they had saved enough money they added a room or a wing or a bathroom to the house, and they are tired of it. They had three kids, all of whom are either at college or married and away from home now, and they don't need all those rooms no one ever uses, and the husband says it's foolish to try to heat it. They estimated they spent $571 last winter heating three rooms no one ever went in.

They talked about buying a new, smaller home, but they ran into the classic problem there. They figured they could get $75,000 for their old house and buy a smaller new one for $50,000. It turns out they could have gotten $50,000 for their old house and would have had to pay $75,000 for a smaller new one.

If you look at half the houses in this country with an analytical eye, you can see ugly additions that have been made to them. The classic farmhouse in America extends back into the growing area because when children grew up and married, they didn't want to live with their parents, but they didn't have any place to go. They were still going to be working right there on the farm, so an addition was put on out back the main house.

When their children grew up, the grandparents were still around and enjoying the main house. The grandchildren didn't want to live with their parents either, so another addition was tacked on.

As a matter of fact, "tacked on" is the dominant American architectural school. Most houses have had something added that doesn't really fit the way the house was intended to look originally.

I was thinking what we could do to our house by way of subtractions. We have a playroom we put in about twenty years ago, and I don't offhand ever recall anyone playing down there. That could come out. We could make it a storage room for junk we've collected. That's what we really need the room for these days. If we want to play, we'll go outdoors.

When this new idea of making houses smaller spreads across the country, specialists in house subtractions are going to be springing up everywhere. Plumbers will be advertising: "TAKE THAT UNNECESSARY BATHROOM OUT OF YOUR HOUSE! SAVE HEAT, WATER AND ELECTRICITY. FREE ESTIMATES."

"DO YOU LIVE IN A BIG BARN?" the contractors will advertise. "LET US CUT YOUR HOUSE IN TWO, MAKE IT THAT CUTE, COZY LITTLE HOME YOU'VE ALWAYS LONGED FOR."

The small-house revolution could be a great thing for this country. For a long while now, houses have been taking up more room than they deserve. You drive through the average city or even the average village these days, and the houses are so close together and there are so few empty lots left that there's no place for the kids to play but in the street. They cut down all the trees in the wooded area to build a new housing development, and the lot down the street that used to be vacant has been built on. Not only that, the houses on both sides of the new house added wings, so there's only twelve feet between them. What used to be a vacant lot is just two narrow alleys now.

I think there's a possibility we made the same mistake with our houses that we made with our automobiles. We built them too big and added too much junk to them. The house of the future will be smaller, tighter, more compact. It will be more like a Dodge Omni or a Volkswagen Rabbit than like a Lincoln Continental.

Teaching from the Classifieds

Everyone says kids aren't being taught to read and write the way they used to be taught. Maybe the trouble is that they *are* still being taught the way they always have been. The trouble may be that our schools aren't being practical enough. Children still read Shakespeare, Dickens and Ralph Waldo Emerson as their writing role models. If they're going to be successful in our world, maybe young students ought to study more practical examples of English usage.

A course based on the classified advertising section of any newspaper would provide lots of examples of how we actually use the English language in practical situations. A study of the classifieds would also give students the same kind of mind-expanding exercise that translating from French into English gives them now.

One semester could be devoted to studying and translating the Houses for Sale section of the classifieds, and a second semester could be spent studying the Automobiles listings.

I have just made a comprehensive review of the classified pages of twenty newspapers. The single most frequently used word in the car ads is "loaded." I was surprised at this finding, because the last time I looked at classified ads for autos the most frequently used word was "creampuff." I don't see "creampuff" at all anymore. This would be a good lesson for children. Like so many words in our language—words like "whippersnapper," "humdinger," "dreamy," "soused" and "pickled"—"creampuff" served its purpose for a while as a linguistic fad and then disappeared into the never-never land of lost expressions.

The word "loaded" is a good example of how complex the English language can be, and kids might as well understand that at the beginning. Only recently the word was most used not to describe a secondhand car, but as a synonym for "soused" or "pickled." Now "loaded" is a synonym for "many extras," "custom features" and "fully equipped."

Studying the classifieds would help prepare children for the real world, because they'd learn that things are not always what they seem. Here, for instance, are a few translations for phrases from the automobile section:

PHRASE	MEANS
Asking $3,500	Will take $2,700
$3,500 or best offer	Glad to get $2,500
Good station car	Don't try to go far in it
Runs good	Runs
Runs excellent	Runs
Runs well	Runs
Body needs work	Body rotted out
1981 model only 1100 miles	A lemon
Mint condition	Still some paint on it

Here are a few translations children might be taught from the housing ads:

PHRASE	MEANS
Owner willing to sacrifice	For sale
Transferred, must sell	For sale
Wooded area	Tree in front of house
Heavily wooded area	Two trees in front of house
Landscaped	Has a bush on the lawn
Beautifully landscaped	Two bushes out front and one on the side
Cozy, intimate	A really small house
Secluded	Out in the boondocks
30 minutes from downtown	Out beyond the boondocks
2 ½ baths	Includes the birdbath out back
Wall-to-wall carpeting	House has no real flooring

That's the homework for tonight, children.

Che-Wee

EVERY so often I'm struck with how dumb I am about something, so I buy a book that's going to solve my stupidity problem. They never help much.

Your Income Tax Made Simple is just as hard for me to understand as my income tax was in the first place.

The Handyman's Guide to Electricity doesn't do anything for me. I'm still a little nervous about changing a light bulb.

I'm not much of a bird-watcher, but we have a place in the country and I thought I ought to get to know a little more about the pretty little things flitting around our trees. All birds look like sparrows to me. There are big sparrows, small sparrows and gaily colored sparrows. But they all look like sparrows. Last summer I realized this was a know-nothing attitude, so I bought two bird books. They were filled with every conceivable kind of sparrow.

One pleasant afternoon, I picked a quiet spot near a tree where the birds usually hung out, carried a chair there and sat with the bird books opened on my lap.

You know, of course, what happened. There had never been a time in all the long history of that particular place where I'd chosen to sit when so few birds came by. There were chipmunks and a woodchuck down at the far end of the garden waiting for me to leave so he could go get the vegetables, but for hours there were no birds.

Several days later, I tried again and finally saw a bird circle in for a landing on the limb of the tree. Quickly I started leafing through the first bird book and found something called an American Redstart that I thought looked hopeful. On closer inspection I wasn't so sure. The bird was making some noise, so I went to the section of the book that describes the sound an American Redstart makes.

Listed under SONG, the first book said, "Che-wee, che-wee, che-wee with the final note slurred down . . ."

Hmmm. Under American Redstart the second book said, "VOICE: A series of rich, piping whistled notes."

This bird of mine didn't seem to be putting any commas or hyphens in what he was saying, and if he was singing "Che-wee, che-wee, che-wee," I couldn't tell whether it was rich, piping and slurred down or not. The neighbor's lawnmower was going, for one thing.

I have never been able to identify a bird from a bird book, a fern from a fern book or any star or set of stars, with the exception of the Big Dipper, from a book on astronomy.

My wife likes expensive rugs. She doesn't buy them, she just likes them. I've tried to get to know something about rugs from glancing through a book she has, and although she has dragged me into a thousand rug stores over the years, I still can't tell a Kaftari from a 500-knot Moolagian.

Whereas I know nothing about birds, ferns, shells or electricity,

I know quite a bit about wood. I can usually identify a board and have had a few nasty rows with antique dealers who were calling mahogany veneer solid walnut. But as good as I like to think I am with lumber, I know I'm not at all good identifying a standing tree.

There must be ten tree-identification books on our shelves. I can tell the books apart, but I can't separate the trees. Once I get past a few basic ones like birch, maple, elm and pine, I'm lost. I wouldn't know a sycamore if it fell on me. The bark and leaf samples in my books don't look like the bark and leaves on my trees.

Books on grammar and usage don't help me much either. If I'm looking for correct usage in some specific grammatical situation, I can never find help.

For example, in the first paragraph of this essay I said ". . . so I buy a book that's going to solve my stupidity problem." Then I added "They never help much." I felt that, strictly speaking, I should have said "*It* never helps much," referring to just one book. I was really referring to all the books I'd bought though and, grammatical or not, "they" seemed better. I don't know whether I was right or wrong and can't find any example close to it in any usage book I own, che-wee, che-wee, che-wee.

Loyalty

FOR years I kept my money in the same bank and filled my car at the same gas station. I liked the idea that I was loyal.

Over the years there's been a big turnover in bank personnel, and it occurred to me that when I went there, no one in the bank knew I was a loyal customer but me. It was the same with the gas station. I flattered myself into thinking they appreciated my business. When they gave me my change and said, "Thank you, have a nice day," I thought they were thankful and wanted me to have a nice day because I was such a good customer. Several years ago I realized I was kidding myself. The gas station had changed hands three times, and they didn't have the vaguest idea that I'd been buying my gas there for seventeen years.

Lately I've been banking and buying gas at my own convenience. I buy gas at the station nearest me when I need it or I drive to one

I know is a penny cheaper. I've changed banks twice recently because they opened a branch a block closer to my office. Give me a toaster or move in next door and you have my allegiance. Loyalty got me nowhere.

I suppose both gas stations and banks would object to being linked together, but they serve the same purpose in my life. When I run out of gas or money, I have to go to a place where I can get more. Gas stations used to compete for my business by offering free air, free water and a battery and oil check. Now you're lucky if the attendant bothers to put the gas cap back on.

Banks used to care about my business. They knew me. I didn't have to bring my birth certificate, a copy of my listing in *Who's Who*, and four other pieces of positive identification to cash a check for twenty-five dollars. If I wrote a check for more money than I had, Mr. Gaffney used to call and sound real angry. But he *did* call. He knew where to find me. No one at the bank knows me anymore. I went in yesterday to pick up a new Master Charge card that was supposed to be there, but they wouldn't give it to me because I hadn't brought the letter with me that they sent saying the card was ready.

If the bank doesn't know me by name, the feeling's mutual, because I don't know my bank's name anymore, either. It usually changes before I've used up all the checks they've sent me with the old name on it. My bank seems to keep acquiring other banks—with my money, I suppose—and they throw the other bank a bone by putting some little part of its name in with their primary name.

My bank's name was originally the Chemical Bank, plain and simple. They changed it to Chemical National Bank, then Chemical Bank and Trust Co., then they acquired the Corn Exchange Bank and my checks said the Chemical Corn Exchange Bank. I always liked that best, but it didn't last. They bought another bank, dropped the "Corn" and called themselves Chemical Bank New York Trust Co. This was unwieldy, and I was pleased several years ago when they renamed the bank once again. The new name? The Chemical Bank.

There is a bank in New York called the Irving Trust Company, and I've always sort of hoped they'd buy my bank and call it Irving's Chemical Bank.

It's too bad everything is as big and impersonal as it is now. I'm sorry to have lost personal touch with the people running the establishments where I do business, but if they don't care, I can't afford to be sentimental. When I was a little boy, we patronized Evans Grocery Store. It had oiled wood floors, and Mr. Evans always gave me a free candy bar when I brought him the check for the month's groceries. The supermarkets were just getting started, and eventually, of course, they ran almost all the little neighborhood grocery stores out of business. My mother kept buying things from Mr. Evans, even though the same loaf of bread was two cents cheaper at the new supermarket. She wanted to help him survive, but apparently the two cents wasn't enough, because he didn't make it for long. He never got to be Evans New York Chemical Corn Grocery Store.

Love Thy Neighbor

IT seems to me that neighbors are going out of style in America. The friend next door from whom you borrowed four eggs or a ladder has moved, and the people in there now are strangers.

Some of the old folklore of neighborliness is impractical or silly, and it may be just as well that our relations with our neighbors are changing. The biblical commandment to "Love Thy Neighbor" was probably a poor translation of what must have originally been "Respect Thy Neighbor." Love can't be called up on order.

Fewer than half the people in the United States live in the same house they lived in five years ago, so there's no reason to love the people who live next door to you just because they happened to wander into a real estate office that listed the place next door to yours. The only thing neighbors have in common to begin with is proximity, and unless something more develops, that isn't reason enough to be best friends. It sometimes happens naturally, but the chances are very small that your neighbors will be your choice as buddies. Or that you will be theirs, either.

The best relationship with neighbors is one of friendly distance. You say hello, you small-talk if you see them in the yard, you discuss problems as they arise and you help each other in an emergency. It's the kind of arrangement where you see more of them in the summer than in the winter. The driveway or the hedge or the fence between you is not really a cold shoulder, but it is a clear boundary. We all like clearly defined boundaries for ourselves.

If neighbors have changed, neighborhoods have not. They still comprise the same elements. If you live in a real neighborhood you can be sure most of the following people will be found there:

—One family with more kids than they can take care of.

—A dog that gets into garbage cans.

—One grand home with a family so rich that they really aren't part of the neighborhood.

—A bad kid who steals or sets fire to things, although no one has ever been able to prove it.

—People who leave their Christmas decorations up until March.

—A grouchy woman who won't let the kids cut through her back-yard.

—Someone who doesn't cut their grass more than twice a summer.

—Someone who cuts their grass twice a week and one of the times always seems to be Sunday morning at 7:30.

—One driveway with a junky-looking pickup truck or trailer that's always sitting there.

—A family that never seems to turn off any lights in the house.

—A teenager who plays the radio too loud in summer with the windows open.

—Someone who leaves their barking dog out until 11:30 most nights.

—One mystery couple. They come and go but hardly anyone ever sees them and no one knows what they do.

—A couple that has loud parties all the time with guests that take an hour to leave once they get outside and start shouting good-bye at each other.

—Someone who doesn't pull the shades.

—A house with a big maple tree whose owners don't rake the leaves until most of them have blown into someone else's yard.

It is easier to produce nostalgia about a neighborhood than about a community, but a community is probably a better unit. A neighborhood is just a bunch of individuals who live in proximity, but a community is a group of people who rise above their individual limitations to get some things done in town.

Home

ONE Saturday night we were sitting around our somewhat shopworn living room with some old friends when one of them started trying to remember how long we'd lived there.

"Since 1952," I said. "We paid off the mortgage eight years ago."

"If you don't have a mortgage," he said, "the house isn't worth as much as if you did have one."

Being in no way clever with money except when it comes to spending it, this irritated me.

"To whom is it not worth as much," I asked him in a voice that was louder than necessary for him to hear what I was saying. "Not to me, and I'm the one who lives here. As a matter of fact, I like it about fifty percent more than I did when the bank owned part of it."

"What did you pay for it?" he asked.

"We paid $29,500 in 1952."

My friend nodded knowingly and thought a minute.

"I'll bet you," he said, "that you could get $85,000 for it today . . . you ought to ask $95,000."

I don't know why this is such a popular topic of conversation these days, but if any real estate dealers are reading this, I'll give them some money-saving advice. Don't waste any stamps on me with your offers to buy. You can take me off your mailing list.

Our house is not an investment. It is not a hastily erected shelter in which to spend the night before we rise in the morning to forge on farther west to locate in another campsite at dusk. Our house is our home. We live there. It is an anchor. It is the place we go to when we don't feel like going anyplace.

We do not plan to move.

The last census indicated that forty million Americans move every year. One out of every five packs up his things and goes to live somewhere else.

Where is everyone moving to? Why are they moving there? Is it really better someplace else?

If people want a better house, why don't they fix the one they have?

If the boss says they're being transferred and have to move, why don't they get another job? Jobs are easier to come by than a home. I can't imagine giving up my home because my job was moving.

I have put up twenty-nine Christmas trees in the bay window of the living room, each a little too tall. There are scars on the ceiling to prove it.

Behind the curtain of the window nearest my wife's desk, there is a vertical strip of wall four inches wide that has missed the last four coats of paint so that the little pencil marks with dates opposite them would not be obliterated. If we moved, someone would certainly paint that patch and how would we ever know again how tall the twins were when they were four?

My son Brian has finished college and is working and no longer lives at home, but his marbles are in the bottom drawer of his dresser if he ever wants them.

There's always been talk of moving. As many as ten times a year we talk about it. The talk was usually brought on by a leaky faucet, some peeling paint or a neighbor we didn't like.

When you own a house you learn to live with its imperfections. You accommodate yourself to them and, like your own shortcomings, you find ways to ignore them.

Our house provides me with a simple pleasure every time I come home to it. I am welcomed by familiar things when I enter, and I'm warmed by some ambience which may merely be dust, but it is our dust and I like it. There are reverberations of the past everywhere, but it is not a sad place, because all the things left undone hold great hope for its future.

The talk of moving came up at dinner one night ten years ago. Brian was only half listening, but at one point he looked up from his plate, gazed around the room and asked idly, "Why would we want to move away from home?"

When anyone asks me how much I think our house is worth, I just smile. They couldn't buy what that house means to me for all the money in both local banks.

The house is not for sale.

III:

EATING AND LIVING

Fresh Fruits and Vegetables Incorporated

Iт's a funny thing that all of us get up every morning and set out to make progress, because when you think about some of the things progress has brought us, it isn't all that desirable sometimes.

We have a summer vacation place about a hundred fifty miles north of New York City, and to get there we pass through parts of the Hudson Valley that grow some of the best fruit and vegetables the world produces. The season is very limited and the crops are small, but when the strawberries come, there are none better. Shortly after that, the raspberries appear. They are gone in ten days, but when you can get them, they are as subtle and delicate a flavor as anything our taste buds can savor.

There is one roadside vegetable stand we patronized for years. We would stop there on every trip and load up with whatever fruit or vegetable was at its best. After the berries were gone, the corn came and along with it yellow squash, zucchini, green beans and peas. For a brief period every year I could imagine becoming a vegetarian. That's how good they were. These were local fruits and vegetables at their best, nothing imported from elsewhere, nothing frozen.

It is sad for me to report to you that progress has set in at our vegetable stand. We always waited with anticipation for those great, red-ripe, thin-skinned tomatoes. Last week we stopped at the stand, and they had tomatoes all right, but not the tomatoes that took me four miles off course to buy. These were the pink, perfectly formed, tough, tasteless variety. They give the impression that they weren't so much grown as manufactured. The only thing they're good for is as decoration on a salad plate. You can't actually eat them. They're to be used like parsley in a restaurant that serves small portions but wants to fill the blank spaces on the plate.

The virtue of these square tomatoes is that they can be picked by machine and shipped for thousands of miles over a period of months without deteriorating. I suspect it wouldn't hurt one of them much if one of the trucks behind the picking machines ran over it. The driver might think he'd hit a rock, but no real damage would be done to either the truck or the tomato.

My vegetable stand—my *former* vegetable stand now—had also decided to stock oranges from Florida, raspberries from California for $2.79 a half pint, and melons from Arizona. If I'd wanted melons from Arizona or tomatoes from California, I'd have stopped at the supermarket near home before I left for the place in the country.

The same thing has happened to roadside stands everywhere, even in California. Making a living from the good things grown locally is too tough a business so they branch out, and first thing you know, every roadside stand in America will carry the same things. I suppose some conglomerate will come along and buy up a few hundred roadside stands and make a chain out of them. The chain might be called Mom's Roadside Stand or Fresh Fruits and Vegetables Incorporated. They wouldn't bother handling the things the local farmers grew, because it would be too much trouble. Instead they'd be selling prepackaged products from the big commercial growers hundreds or even thousands of miles away.

If I am ever elected to Congress, I think I'll try to get a law passed making tomatoes and melons illegal, except for certain months of the year. I have spent more money on hard, tasteless melons and tomatoes in the last ten years than I've spent on toothpaste, shoelaces and typewriter ribbons combined. I never learn. I look at these things and my memory of how good they used to be in season makes me reach for my money.

My law would also prohibit a roadside stand from calling itself a vegetable or fruit stand if it also sold commercially made candy bars, souvenir ashtrays, gum, canned goods or homemade bread that wasn't made at home.

The federal government has sponsored research that has produced a tomato that is perfect in every respect, except you can't eat it. We should make every effort to make sure this disease, often referred to as "progress," doesn't spread.

Ice Cream

Because of the seriousness of our national and international situations, I'd like to say some things about ice cream.

The three things I have spent the most time thinking about and working with are words, wood and ice cream. Of those three things, it is possible that I'm best with the last.

Several times a year I fly into a rage as I'm reading a newspaper or magazine article on how to make ice cream. You may notice my hands are shaking this minute. The August issue of a good magazine about food called *Bon Appétit* arrived in the mail, and I've been reading a long feature story in it.

On the cover the story is called "The Best Homemade Ice Cream." Inside, the story is called "Ice Cream Greats." Magazines have gotten in the habit of calling their articles by one name on the cover and by a different name in the table of contents so they're hard to find. But this is not my complaint. My complaint is about their advice on how to make ice cream.

Under the heading "Easy Basic Vanilla Ice Cream," the writer gives this recipe: "2 cups half and half, 2 cups whipping cream, 1 vanilla bean, 8 egg yolks, ⅔ cup sugar, 4 tablespoons unsalted butter."

This recipe is not easy, it's not basic and it is not ice cream, it's frozen custard. The writer gets off to a bad start with me right away when she recommends "half and half." The assumption everyone makes is that it's half milk and half cream, but no one really knows what either half is.

I will tell you right now what easy, basic vanilla ice cream is. It is as much heavy cream as you can afford, enough sugar to make it sweet and enough pure vanilla extract to make it taste like vanilla. That is absolutely all you need to make great vanilla ice cream, and anyone who tells you something different hasn't made as much ice cream at home as I have.

I don't know why advice on how to make ice cream has been so bad over the years. The freezers they're selling have gotten a lot better just recently, but articles on how to make it are as bad as ever. When I was young, there were five kids in my summer group. We often made ice cream on hot evenings and it was no big deal. We'd decide to make it at 8:00, have it made by 8:30 and have the whole freezerful eaten by 8:40. The five of us ate it right out of the can with long spoons. It cut down on the dishwashing.

In the days before homogenized milk, about four inches of cream came to the top of each bottle. The five of us came from three families. We'd go to each icebox and take the top off whatever milk bottles were there, being careful to refill each skimmed bottle to the top with milk from another skimmed bottle. We thought this gave our parents the illusion that we hadn't taken the cream.

We used about a quart and a half of liquid, and if we didn't have enough cream, we filled in with milk or a can of evaporated milk. So, don't tell me about easy, basic vanilla ice cream that has eight egg yolks, half a stick of butter and a vanilla bean in it.

Bad or difficult ice cream recipes anger me for an obvious reason, I guess. We all like other people to enjoy what we enjoy, and these recipes are scaring people off homemade ice cream. I'd like everyone to enjoy making it and eating it as much as I do.

The first recipe in this magazine article after basic vanilla is one for "Prune and Armagnac Ice Cream." What would you serve with that, white clam sauce or ketchup? The magazine doesn't even give a recipe for the best ice cream to make in August, peach. To make peach ice cream, add mashed peaches to cream and sugar. Please don't put a lot of other stuff in it.

Part of the fascination of making ice cream is the physical principle involved. I know so few physical principles I get great satisfaction in knowing this one. The outside container of an ice cream freezer is wood or plastic. The container that holds the mixture is metal. You pack ice mixed with salt around the metal container. Salt converts ice to water without lowering its temperature. Any action like this consumes energy (heat). Neither wood nor plastic conducts heat the way metal does, so the energy to accomplish the conversion of the ice to water is drawn from the mixture inside the metal can, and when its heat is gone, it's frozen.

I'm not as sure about that, of course, as I am about how to make ice cream.

Donuts

WHEN I was about ten years old, my mother went on a donut-making binge. It lasted almost a year. Two or three times a week she'd heat up the oil, make the batter and start dropping them in. I even recall that she also cooked the part she had cut out of the center, as a little round ball, and I liked those best.

We had never had donuts before that and we never had them again afterwards, but for one year, boy! did we have donuts.

I mention this not to tell you about my mother's donuts, but to illustrate something that seems to be true of most of us in relation to food and cooking. We get hooked on a few things we like to eat or know how to prepare, and we have them over and over again until we're sick and tired of them. Americans are creative about most things but not with food.

Our own kids won't have their mother's donuts to kick around when they look back at their childhood, but they're not going to be able to forget those beef stew years, the applesauce cake era or my own popover period.

My most recent kick has been Chinese. For more than a year now I've been stir-frying everything in ginger and garlic and adding soy sauce. My bread-making drive seems to have waned, I'm not making lasagna or Caesar salads the way I used to, but I'm stir-frying up a storm when I get dinner.

I don't know why we get stuck on something that way. There are so many cooking styles open to us with what we have in our refrigerators and on our kitchen shelves that it's a shame we limit our menus as we do.

All you have to do to realize how insular we are about cooking is to consider how different meals taste in other countries, even though they have been prepared from basically the same ingredients we use.

A good Chinese cook could take the ingredients most of us have in our refrigerators and produce half a dozen dishes that would be unrecognizably delicious to our taste buds.

The French can produce gourmet meals out of substantially the same bag of groceries from which both the English and the Germans would cook something tasteless and lead-weight. (I didn't write this to make friends.)

I've often thought it would be fun to have a cooking event in the Olympics. You'd put ten cooks, each from a different country, in similar kitchens stocked with similar food supplies. When the referee said "Go," each cook would look around to see what he could produce for dinner in two hours. We might also have a breakfast and lunch competition. It would be fun to see how different the meals turned out even though they were made from the same ingredients.

During WW II, the U.S. Army was supplied with absolutely first-rate food that was more often than not ruined in preparation. The standard for Army units that were moving around but not actually in combat was something called the Ten-in-One ration. The solidly packed boxes were designed to serve ten men for one day. Each box had all the staples including meat but, of course, no fresh vegetables, milk or eggs. A lot of American soldiers learned that if they could find some friendly French woman to whom they could turn over the ration, both they and the French woman's family could eat better.

It was always best not to ask any questions or count. The French woman added fresh eggs, vegetables and genius, and deducted from the box the things the French couldn't get for themselves under wartime conditions. There was more sugar in the package than most soldiers wanted, for instance, and she would take most of that.

The mystery about all this is, with international travel so common, why there hasn't been more of a coming together of cooking. Why isn't there an international style of cooking that borrows the best from each culture? Why haven't we learned to use more of the Chinese tricks for making food taste good? How come the Germans have lived next door to the French all these years without having acquired any of the magnificent French knack for preparing food?

And, for that matter, how come they never have donuts in Peking, like mother used to make?

Holiday Recipes

My question is this. Does anyone actually *make* those holiday dishes recommended in the home sections of newspapers and magazines?

I don't want to start trouble with the editors of other sections of the newspaper, but aren't some of those recipes a little far out? Leftover turkey in aspic with cherries? Turkey pie with ripe olives flavored with rum? Turkey with oyster sauce?

I suspect I know what you editors over there are doing to us. You're just trying to shake us up a little. You think we're too set in our ways about the holiday meals we have, and you're trying to make it more interesting for us.

It's an unfortunate fact that there is something a little wrong about the meals we have on Thanksgiving and Christmas. They're great but they're the same. I don't know about your house, but at our house on both occasions we have turkey, stuffing, mashed potatoes and gravy, squash, creamed onions, two kinds of cranberry sauce and dessert. The only difference in the two meals is the dessert. At Thanksgiving we have mince and pumpkin pie. At Christmas we have several kinds of cake and homemade peppermint stick ice cream.

Every family has a dish or two of its own or some special variations of the traditional ones, but basically we all have the same feast. We like it that way, too. We enjoy reading about nine new and different ways to stuff a turkey, but we aren't going to stuff ours any one of the new ways. We're going to stuff ours the way we always have.

You editors and recipe writers think we're all dissatisfied with having the same meal twice on two occasions so close together, and you're trying to get us out of our rut. We're not going to budge an inch, though.

The good thing about all those recipes is that they make wonderful reading. A lot of people who are not in what is called the Smart Set enjoy reading about those people who are. A lot of people who aren't out of work get a kick out of the classifieds, and other people who aren't looking for a house wouldn't miss the real estate section. That's what saves it for you home section editors. We love your stuff. All of us who wouldn't think of switching from turkey for Thanksgiving and Christmas enjoy studying the details of how to prepare pheasant with braised endive and black grapes as "a delightful holiday change."

Just this one year alone I have rejected quail with truffles and foie gras, roast goose with haricot beans and guinea hen with juniper berries as an alternative to turkey. My wife is thoroughly familiar with our dinner and Christmas is not a day to get clever in the kitchen.

The fact is that Americans like to ask for advice and they even enjoy being given advice, but they hate to take any of it. We're always asking someone what they think or how we ought to do something, but just as soon as they've gone we do it the same way we always have.

Recipes are difficult to use. I do some cooking, but I don't use recipes much, because there's always something in one that either I don't understand or I question. Do they mean I mix all these ingredients together first and *then* add the other stuff . . . or do I mix this in with that now and put the other stuff aside until later?

Only good cooks should use recipes probably. It's the exact opposite of what you'd think. A good cook can look at a recipe, understand it as you would a sentence in a foreign language, and then put the recipe away and make the dish. The good cook doesn't have to go back and read the recipe line for line, because he understands it.

But keep those exotic recipes coming at us, food editors. Just one thing. If we come over to your house after Christmas, we better not catch you eating plain, cold, sliced turkey.

Diets

Is there anyone left who is confused about which foods are fattening and which foods are not?

Thumb through the papers or the magazines and, nine times out of ten, you'll find a new, improved, easy, foolproof, delicious way to lose weight and still eat all you want of your favorite foods—as long as they're raw carrots, cottage cheese, gelatin and grapefruit without seeds.

"Five Wonderful Ways to Lose Weight!"

"A Diet That Can't Fail!"

"Our Computerized Diet. Lose Weight by the Numbers."

"Take Off Pounds with the Amazing Chicken Fat Diet."

"Why Movie Stars Are Switching to the All-Chocolate Diet."

I've had enough advice myself. As an overweight American, I'd like to give some advice back to the people who write diets: knock it off, will you?

We *know* why we're fat. We eat too much, that's why. Telling us how to lose weight is like telling an alcoholic how to keep from getting drunk. It's like telling a teenage girl what not to do if she doesn't want to get pregnant.

We aren't ignorant of what causes these things. Drunkenness is brought on by alcohol, pregnancy by sex and overweight by food. What kind of any of those is of relative unimportance. That's why I've never been able to take diets seriously.

A typical day's diet will read something like this:

Breakfast: One prune
                 ¾ oz crust wholewheat bread
                 Black Sanka

  Lunch: *Two* prunes
                 ¼ cup peanut butter
                 6 grams cottage cheese
                 2 licks of a lollipop

  Dinner: ¾ cups lambchop
                 37 calories of rice
                 2 tsp chocolate chip ice cream, chips removed

I just don't need to have dinner broken down for me into units of measurement I don't understand. And which the food wouldn't understand either. All I have to do to lose weight is not eat so much.

The best weight-losing story I ever heard came out of a program conducted by a Midwestern university years ago. I've forgotten the university but I remember the story well.

They asked for twenty grossly overweight volunteers who wanted to slim down. When the volunteers came forward, they were asked to go back home and keep careful records of every single thing they ate for the next three weeks.

At the end of three weeks, the volunteers came with their records and were housed at the university under strict supervision. They were allowed no visitors and, to prevent cheating, they couldn't leave the building. For a second period of three weeks, each volunteer was fed everything he or she had put on the record as having eaten in the previous three.

If they said they ate a hamburg and apple pie for lunch, they got a hamburg and apple pie for lunch. If they admitted they snacked on a Hershey bar in midafternoon, they got a Hershey bar in midafternoon.

At the end of the second three-week period, the volunteers, eating under strict supervision, had lost an average of twenty pounds apiece. One woman lost thirty-five eating exactly what she said she'd been eating all along.

The moral is clear. When it comes to overweight and diet, we kid ourselves a little and lie a lot to our friends.

The Andy Rooney Upside-Down Diet

THE two biggest sellers in any bookstore are the cookbooks and the diet books. The cookbooks tell you how to prepare the food and the diet books tell you how not to eat any of it.

The quickest way for a writer to get rich is to write a diet book. A cookbook is more difficult. With a diet book all you need is one bad idea and a lot of statistics on what has how many calories. If you want to make the book thicker, you put in a whole series of typical meals that adhere to your idea.

As someone who's been eating too much all his life, I think I'm as qualified to write a diet book as anyone, and as a writer I'm twice as ready to get rich. Not only that, I have an idea. My book would be called *The Andy Rooney Upside-Down Diet Book.*

My theory is based on the idea that the average overweight person has to change his eating habits drastically. The overweight man or woman has fallen into a pattern of eating that is making him or her fat, and the only way that person is going to lose weight is for him to turn his eating habits upside down.

The appetite itself (I'll say in the Foreword to my book) is a strange mechanism. Our stomach often signals our brain that it's ready to have something sent down when our body doesn't really need anything yet.

As I understand it—and you don't have to understand things very well to write a diet book—the appetite is depressed as the blood sugar level rises. The trouble is that the blood sugar level rises slowly as your digestive processes start taking apart the food you've consumed, so that you can still feel hungry for quite a while after you've had enough because your blood sugar level hasn't caught up to your stomach.

So much for theory. Here, in brief, is my diet. You'll want to buy the book later, I imagine.

Basically, what I'm suggesting you do is reverse the order in which you eat things at a meal, and change the habits you have in regard to what you eat for what meal.

Forget cereal, pancakes or bacon and eggs for breakfast. We're going to start the morning with a bowl of chicken soup. Chicken soup will serve a dual purpose. It's nourishing, not fattening, and because it's a hot drink you won't need coffee. If you don't have coffee, you won't need sugar. No one is going to be tempted to put sugar in chicken soup.

The beauty of my diet—and I want them to make this clear on the jacket of my book—is that you don't have to deny yourself anything. Eat absolutely anything you feel like eating. The magic of my diet is in making sure you don't feel like eating much.

Before dinner many of us consume what we call appetizers. Don't take appetizers off your diet if you like them, just don't eat them first. In our *Upside-Down Diet Book* we'll be laying out more than one hundred weight-losing model meals. A typical breakfast might consist of half a grape, a bowl of chicken soup and plain butter, no toast.

Lunch might consist of ketchup, a Fig Newton, two Oreo Creme Sandwiches and lukewarm Ovaltine. In other words, Eat All You Want, but Change What You Want.

Your main meal will be dinner. Classic cuisine has called for an appetizer first, soup, a fish dish, meat, vegetables and potatoes, followed by cheese and then dessert. We're going to ask you to shake that up if you want to lose weight.

Each of our Upside-Down Diet meals will start with a bowl of ice cream or a chocolate eclair. Follow this with a small fish dish or oysters, clams or shrimp with a chocolate sauce. This will have the effect of raising your blood sugar level abruptly, and by the time the main course of oatmeal, corn flakes or Fruit Loops with buttermilk comes, you may not want any at all.

I don't want to be greedy, but after the book is published I have high hopes that it will be made into a movie.

Living Is Dangerous to Your Health

We're all bombarded from every side with bad news about what's good for us, aren't we?

How often does a day go by that you don't hear about something else you eat or do or don't do or wear or own that's bad for your health? At least once a week they announce another item on our diet that's suspected of causing cancer. If it doesn't cause cancer, it brings on heart attacks.

The fact of the matter is, *life* is bad for you. For one thing, living brings on age, and we know how debilitating age can be. It's something everyone should avoid.

I wouldn't be surprised if the government started making us wear little labels that said CAUTION: THE SURGEON GENERAL HAS DETERMINED THAT LIVING IS DANGEROUS TO YOUR HEALTH.

No matter what we do, they scare us to death for doing it.

We take a little vacation to lie in the sun and get some rest, and what happens? We can't get any rest, because we keep remembering being warned that too much sun produces skin cancer.

In order to lose some weight, because we've been warned of the dangers of being fat, we start using substitutes for sugar. Next thing we know they're warning us that cyclamates, which we never heard of before, are a principal ingredient in some sugar-free food and drink, and because there is evidence that they're bad for mice, we ought to stop using them.

Periodically they issue a report on which cars are the most dangerous to drive. Which cars are you most apt to be killed in if you have an accident? Naturally the answer is that the most dangerous cars are the small, foreign, gas-saving machines we've all been buying to save money. You're safest in the big, fat, expensive gas guzzlers. Would the people in charge of announcing bad news have had it any other way?

There are doctors who say that jogging is so tough on the hip, knee and ankle joints that people ought to find some other way to exercise.

It's almost as though someone was out to get us just as soon as they see us taking pleasure from anything.

The reason I bring this up at all is because I finally read some good news. It was announced at an annual conference of the American Heart Association. A group of doctors attending that conference said that a moderate amount of alcohol every day might help prevent heart attacks.

There were other doctors present who *didn't* think alcohol was good for you and I personally tend to doubt it myself, but what difference does that make? At least it's good news, and if it's good news, who cares whether it's true or not—right, America?

The Scientific Community doesn't think it's loved or understood by the rest of us. If the Scientific Community wants to do something about that, I can think of a lot of announcements it could make that would endear scientists to us.

I was thinking about a few things they could expect to read about themselves if they played their cards right:

DOCTORS REPORT CHOCOLATE CANDY BENEFICIAL TO PROSPECTIVE FATHERS.

SCIENTISTS DETERMINE LARGE QUANTITIES OF MAPLE WALNUT ICE CREAM PREVENT COLD SORES IN MICE.

HIGHWAY STATISTICS SUPPORT PSYCHIATRIST VIEW THAT FASTEST DRIVERS HAVE FEWEST ACCIDENTS.

OVERWEIGHT ELK FOUND TO BE LESS SUSCEPTIBLE TO SNOW BLINDNESS.

These are the kind of encouraging signs we want to have from those people who announce things. We've had enough bad news for a while. If Geritol causes hangnails in women more than fifty, we don't want to hear about it.

Doctors

TODAY I'd like to talk about something I'd rather not talk about, doctors.

What I have in mind is that bit of advice each of us reads or hears fifty times a day. It's just three little words: "See your doctor."

The reason I don't like to think about it is . . . well, maybe you're not going to believe this but, see . . . I don't *have* a doctor.

When I was young, Dr. Traver gave me some shots. When I was fourteen, Dr. Van Loon removed my appendix, and more recently when I broke my collarbone in a skiing accident, it was stuck together at a hospital in Vermont by a competent resident whose name I have lost. In 1978 Dr. Bienfield repaired a rent in my intestinal wall.

So, all in all, I've had good medical attention, but I do not have a doctor I can call my own, and I wish they'd stop telling me to go see him.

Even the yearly physical checkup is a problem. Over the years I've had a few checkups, but never by the same doctor, and I'm always reluctant to make an appointment with one for anything so vague as "a checkup." I have this recurring nightmare of what will happen when I present myself at the doctor's office.

"Good morning, Doctor," I say in this dream.

"Good morning, Patient #17. What seems to be our trouble?"

"We don't have any trouble," I say, falling into the medical "we." "We just thought we ought to have a checkup."

"Don't you know how busy doctors are these days?" the doctor snaps at me. "We heal the sick and mend the wounded. If there's nothing wrong with you, don't waste a busy man's time."

"But, Doctor," I say, "they told me to 'See your doctor.' "

"Nurse!" he shouts. "Give the patient his pants and show him the door. And find out if he wants the bill sent to his home or his office."

A doctor wouldn't say any of those things, of course, but if he did he'd be putting his finger on a universal problem. The day has come when each of us needs a basic medical education of our own just to be smart enough to know what's wrong with us so we can choose the right specialist to go see. If you have a heart attack and rush to see an orthopedic surgeon, you are making a big mistake.

Doctors don't like to admit we know anything about our bodies. They hate having us guess what our trouble is, because we're wrong so often. The fact of the matter is, though, that very often the dumbest patient knows a little something about his condition that the doctor doesn't know. When I broke my collarbone, I knew just a little something about broken collarbones that the resident who fixed it will never know until he breaks his.

I was skiing with a friend who is a psychiatrist when I fell, and he didn't have any idea how to fix the bone, and on the trip to the hospital he worried about how the pain was affecting my psyche.

That's what any specialist does. He interprets syndromes in terms of his own specialty.

If we go to a doctor with a pain in the neck, his approach to our problem depends on what kind of a doctor he is. The thoracic surgeon wants to know whether we smoke, the ophthalmologist inspects the possibility that faulty eyesight, poorly corrected with the wrong glasses, might be the trouble. The orthopedist thinks our bad posture may have led to deterioration of the spinal column which has manifested itself in a neck condition. The brain surgeon is most apt to think that the persistent pain in the neck comes from above, while the internist wants to know if we've been passing blood.

I like doctors. The ones in my class who became doctors were the smartest kids. As much as I respect them though, I still say it's awfully hard to pick the right one. Every time I read that advice "See your doctor," I find myself wishing someone would give me one for Christmas.

Too Many Doctors?

I KEEP reading statistics I don't believe. There was a story out of Washington last week saying that by the year 1990, there will be too many doctors in the United States. Sure. And gas will be back to twenty-seven cents a gallon.

Someone is dreaming if they think there are *ever* going to be too many doctors. A day doesn't go by when I don't have a question or a problem for a doctor, but I haven't been to one in four years now because they're so busy I hate to bother them.

There won't be too many doctors until every one of us, including each doctor, has a doctor of his own. When that time comes, each of us will get the kind of medical attention we'd like to have—the kind the President of the United States gets.

Now, maybe this article meant that there would be too many doctors for the *doctors'* own good, not for *our* own good. Maybe the story was put out by some medical group that figured doctors might make less money if there was a change in the supply of medical services that came closer to meeting the demand for them.

To tell you the truth, I wouldn't feel terrible if business got just a little worse for doctors.

I can't believe anyone really thinks there will ever be too many doctors. Maybe they mean there are going to be so many by 1990 that we won't have to sit around in their waiting rooms for two hours. It could even mean that a good doctor could live a normal life and work a normal day without feeling that he was abandoning a lot of dying patients every time he took a day off.

Here's the way I'd like to have my telephone conversations go when I call a doctor's office.

VOICE: Hello. Dr. Keller's office.

ME: Hello. This is Andy Rooney. I'd like to make an appointment with Dr. Keller sometime this year.

VOICE: Why, certainly. Any time. This is Dr. Keller. What seems to be our trouble?

ME: Sorry to bother you, Doctor. I thought I'd get your nurse's secretary.

VOICE: Oh, gosh, my nurse hasn't had a secretary for more than a year now . . . since about 1989. We aren't too busy anymore, you know. As a matter of fact, I gave my nurse the day off.

ME: Could you see me before Christmas then, Doctor?

VOICE: Sure could. What are you doing right now? I'm just sitting here doing the crossword puzzle myself. I don't have another appointment until two thirty.

Well, I should live so long to have a conversation like that with a doctor. No statistic can convince me there'll ever be too many of them. Science is discovering new things we're dying of faster than they're curing the old ones. They may have licked yellow fever, diphtheria, mumps, smallpox and whooping cough, but now we have a whole new set of things that are killing us. There's plenty for doctors to do until they lick this ugly business of dying.

If by any chance I'm wrong and the time actually comes when there are too many doctors, there are a lot of repairs I'm going to have made on my body. First, I'm going to have that mole removed from behind my ear. I've been meaning to do something about that since I was twenty-four. And I'm certainly going to get some attention for my right foot and ankle from a good orthopedics man. Something's wrong in there with the ligaments.

I often worry about my blood pressure, and years ago I was rejected when I tried to give blood because my white corpuscles were wrong. They either sank or floated when they were supposed to do the opposite. They didn't want my blood. I'd go to a doctor about that.

I've got a dozen little problems that could stand some medical attention, and when the day comes when I can see a doctor without standing in line, I'll have them attended to.

You, I suppose, don't have any problems at all.

Doctors and Doorknobs

Doctors should never talk to ordinary people about anything but medicine. If I were a doctor, I'd never go to another party where there were anything but other doctors present.

When doctors talk politics, economics or sports, they reveal themselves to be ordinary mortals, idiots just like the rest of us. That isn't what any of us wants our doctor to be. We want our doctor to be an intellectual giant who knows all about everything. We don't want him to be someone who has a lot of petty little theories about what's wrong in Washington, or what play the coach should have sent in Sunday when it was third and nine on the twenty-four.

Saturday night, I was talking to a doctor at a party, and he was telling me that the nurses situation is getting desperate.

"Young women just don't want to do that kind of hard work anymore," he said. "A lot of the good ones are quitting," he told me, "because they like nursing but can't take the paperwork." Another thing, he said, was that a lot of nurses resented doctors and often thought they knew as much about a patient as the doctor did.

Well, first thing you know we were arguing about how little a nurse is paid compared to a doctor and how a lot of women ended up as nurses when they should have been doctors and vice versa. I won't tell you which side of the arguments I was on, but neither of us distinguished ourselves. It was the kind of conversation that makes me realize doctors are only mortal men, and it's always a disappointment. I'm looking for a god in my doctor.

Surgeons I meet worry me. When I get talking politics with a surgeon who has done a hundred and fifty open-heart operations, I usually wonder how he ever did it without killing the patients. It turns out he's just as dumb as I am. His opinion of the current Administration is the same as the one I heard from the man who runs the shoeshine stand in the station last week, and I certainly wouldn't want the shoeshine man fooling around with my heart valves through an incision in my chest.

Years ago, my wife and I were spending the weekend in the house of an old college friend of hers whose husband was an orthopedic surgeon. One morning I started out the front door and the knob came loose. It just twisted around in my hand, so the doctor went down cellar to get a few tools. The doorknob was obviously on the critical list.

All I could think, as I watched him attack the problem, was how happy I was to be a houseguest and not a patient. He fussed with that doorknob for more than half an hour before he got an ill-fitting setscrew in there to hold it. I'd give that doorknob another three days. Here was a distinguished surgeon who had replaced the heads of two hundred femurs with stainless steel balls that enabled patients to walk once again free of pain in their hips, but he couldn't figure out how to fix that one lousy doorknob. What do you make of this?

One problem medical men and women have is one we all share with them. To be really expert in our chosen field takes more than one type of skill, and a person who has one doesn't necessarily have others. The young medical student who masters the details of anatomy and gets the best marks in his class is not necessarily manually dexterous. The dentist who has the ability of a good cabinetmaker to put together perfect, tight-fitting parts that hold together in a person's mouth was not always—or probably even usually—the dental student who finished at the top of his class.

A doctor can't help it if he isn't born with dexterous hands, but if he also has a lot of dumb opinions about the world, the least he can do is keep them to himself so we don't get wondering about his hands.

IV:

PREJUDICES

Street Directions

Where do streets go in a strange city and where do they come from?

If America wants to save gas, it ought to start over with its street signs and give everyone directions on how to give directions. It would not do this country any harm at all if there were college courses on the subject of direction giving.

Someone will say, "Go down here and turn left at the third traffic light. Keep going until you run into a dead end at Sixteenth Street, then bear right."

Those are simple enough, so you set out to follow directions. Within ten minutes you're at the corner of Broad and 4th streets, hopelessly lost. You never saw a Sixteenth Street. You feel either stupid and frustrated for not being able to follow simple directions or you feel outraged at the person who gave them to you.

I've often wanted to go back, find the guy and grab him by the throat. "All right, fella. You told me to turn left at the third traffic light and then keep going until I hit a dead end at Sixteenth. You were trying to get me lost, weren't you? Confess!"

It wouldn't be any use though. I know what he'd say. He'd say, "That's not counting this light right here. If you count this light, it's four."

Or he'd say, "Maybe it's Eighteenth Street where the dead end is . . ." or "You see, Sixteenth Street turns into Terwilliger Avenue after you cross Summit Boulevard."

Whatever his answer is, it's hopeless. He didn't mean to mislead you and you didn't mean to get lost, but that's what usually happens.

You can't lay all the blame on the people giving directions. People don't *take* them any better than they give them.

My own ability to retain directions in my head ends after the first two turns I'm given. Then I usually say to whomever I'm with, "Did he say right or left at the church on the right?" If there are seven or eight turns, including a couple of "bear rights" and a "jog left" or two, I might as well find a motel room and get a fresh start in the morning.

The superhighways that bisect and trisect our cities now aren't any help at all in finding your way around. Streets that used to lead across town in a direct fashion now end abruptly where the highway cut through. Finding the nearest entrance to the super-highway, so you can drive two miles to the next exit in order to get a block and a half from where you are, is the new way to go.

If they do start college courses in direction giving, I hope they devote a semester to arrow drawing for signmakers. It seems like a simple enough matter, but it is often not clear to a stranger whether an arrow is telling you to veer off to the right or to keep going straight.

Different towns and cities have different systems for identifying their streets with the signs they erect. Some have the name of the street you are crossing facing you as you drive past. Others identify the street with a sign that is parallel to it. This is more accurate, but you can't see it. And if you don't know which system they're using, it's further trouble.

There are cities in America so hard to find your way around that, unless you're going to live there for several years, it isn't worth figuring them out.

Many cities, like Washington, pretend to be better organized than they are. They have numbers and they use the alphabet just as though everything was laid out in an orderly fashion.

New York City, for example, has numbered avenues that run longitudinally up and down the island. What the stranger would never know is that in midtown the names go from Third Avenue to Lexington, to Park, and then to Madison before the numbers start again with Fifth Avenue. Where did Fourth Avenue go? Sorry about that, that's what we call "Park."

And then "Sixth Avenue" is next? Well, not actually. New Yorkers call it "Sixth," but the official name and the name on the signs is "Avenue of the Americas." No one calls it that but the post office.

I have long since given up asking for directions or reading maps. I am one of that large number of lost souls who finds that, in the long run, it's better simply to blunder on until you find where you're going on your own.

The 55 MPH Speed Limit

You'll all be pleased to read that I'm not going to give you an opinion on (1) gun control, (2) abortion or (3) the Equal Rights Amendment. Just trust me that I'm in one hundred percent agreement with you on these issues. I can't imagine how any right-thinking person could possibly believe other than we do. I trust, in turn, that if you're for one, you're for them all. If you're against one, you're *against* them all.

The fourth most controversial issue is the matter of the fifty-five mph speed limit. I'm going to comment on that because, while it gets people yelling and hollering at each other a lot, it doesn't bring out quite the same dirty, bitter, low-down kind of viciousness in nice people that those other issues do.

I stand unequivocally equivocal about it. I'm firmly of two minds. It's a law I hate and break all the time, but if I had been in Congress when it passed into law, I'd have voted in favor of it. To be honest with you, I think everyone *but me* should be limited to driving fifty-five mph.

Even though I'd have voted for it, it seems to me the law is too general to cover every driving situation. It ought to be more flexible. I know people who are safer driving seventy-five than my sister is driving thirty-five. She's basically a good person, but she's a lousy driver. She could never roller skate, either. Does my sister get to drive as fast on the highway as Richard Petty or Mario Andretti?

If fifty-five is safe for a competent driver, we ought to have a lower limit for incompetent ones. It's ridiculous to suggest that all of us have equal skill at the wheel of a car. There's no reason to think there's any less difference between a great skier and a bad one than there is between a good driver and my sister. The two skiers shouldn't have to come down the mountain at the same speed.

Besides the difference in the competence of drivers, there's the difference in road conditions. The fifty-five mph speed limit is too fast on a narrow, winding macadam road with traffic, even if it's legal. It isn't fast enough on a six-lane highway that stretches for a hundred straight miles in Wyoming. Why should the speed limit be the same in both places?

There's some evidence that the speed limit has saved both lives and gas. The National Safety Council estimates eight thousand lives were saved last year. If it's true, that's a persuasive argument. The trouble with the statistic is that people are driving a lot less than they were five years ago because of the cost of gas. If people drive less, fewer of them die driving. If no one ever drove at all, of course, no one would ever die in an auto accident, but the government isn't prepared to go that far. Where it stops and starts protecting us from each other is a very difficult decision for the government to make. It would be safer if no one ever crossed a street, too. That would make some life-saving statistic if we all avoided crossing a street for one year.

I've always objected to any law making it compulsory for me to wear a seat belt for my own safety. Passing a law to keep me from going too fast in order to protect *other* people's lives is one thing, but when the government passes a law making something mandatory *for my own good*, the government has gone too far. My life is none of the government's damn business. I'll save it or spend it as I please.

If Congress was serious about the fifty-five mph speed limit, it would have taken one effective step years ago. It would have made it illegal for anyone to sell a car that can *go* faster than fifty-five. What sense does it make to be producing cars that will go a hundred thirty miles an hour when there isn't a road in the country you can legally drive them on that fast?

And that's where I stand on the speed limit, straddling the solid white line.

Prejudices

WE are all warned that prejudice is a bad thing, but it is very hard to separate prejudice from experience. If the same experience produces the same result for you time after time, you get so you know what to expect. You prejudge what the results will be. There are a million little prejudices I have, and I have no intention of giving them up. For instance, it has been my experience that:

—It's not much of a sale if the sign says EVERYTHING MUST GO!

—He doesn't want to talk to you if the secretary says, "Just a minute. I'll see if he's in."

—If you haven't already seen the movie on television tonight, it probably isn't anything you want to watch.

—When the phone rings after ten at night, it's usually a wrong number.

—No envelope with one of those little windows in it ever contains anything as good as you'd hoped for.

—If the literature in your hotel room can name all the places of interest in the city, it isn't a very big city.

—If it takes longer to ride than to walk, you're in New York City. If it's too far to walk, you're in Los Angeles. If it's too steep to walk, you're in San Francisco.

—The person conducting the interview on television is in trouble if he starts a question by saying, "Tell me, exactly how did you get started?"

—You'd better rinse the soap off quickly if you're in the shower and the water is only warm and the cold water faucet is all the way around to off.

—Television shows with what are advertised as "All Star" casts are no better than movies with "All Star" casts used to be.

—If you can see the bottom of the cup in a cup of black coffee, the coffee isn't worth drinking.

—The older the paper money is, the farther you are from a big city.

—When you get a piece of mail saying you've won something, you haven't won anything.

—The gas station that doesn't have a big sign up saying how much it's getting per gallon is charging more than the station down the street.

—There's no sense thinking a ballpoint pen will start to write again once it runs out of ink and starts to skip.

—Most of the people in the cafeteria between 2 and 3 PM are overweight.

—If the announcer on the television show you're watching says "Stay tuned for more of our show" at eight minutes to the hour, it means the show is over and you're about to see eight minutes of commercials and promotions for other shows and the credits for the program you just watched.

—When a government official announces the price of something may go up "by as much as four to six cents in the next five months," the price of whatever it is will rise ten cents in the next two weeks.

—If the restaurant isn't overcrowded, there's probably a better one in town.

Sound and Noise

THEY'RE tearing down a nine-story building just outside my office window. It doesn't look as though it's going to be a short job either, because when they finish jackhammering this to the ground, they're going to start riveting up a new one. Obviously I've either got to get used to it or move.

I think the trick is to get thinking of it as a sound instead of a noise. The difference is hard to define, but a noise is mindless and irritating, while a sound can be soothing. I've known people who live in the city who can't sleep when they go to the country because of the crashing silence.

I like the sound of someone whistling on his walk to work, but if someone starts whistling around the office, my mind comes to a halt and I can think about nothing except how irritating the noise is. I start psychoanalyzing the whistler, trying to think why it is he or she feels compelled to make this noise by forcing a stream of air through pursed lips.

On the other hand, I've worked in newspaper city rooms filled with people moving, yelling and typing and I can continue to work, absolutely oblivious to the pandemonium around me.

A horn honked unnecessarily or more than once for any reason is noise. Every time someone behind me blows his horn the instant the light turns green, I turn red.

A ringing telephone can be a welcome sound or an irritating noise, depending on the circumstances. I've gotten over that feeling that it may be someone wonderful calling me every time the phone rings, but there is still a sense of anticipation we're all programmed to have when we hear the phone. Even when I know it's not for me, I can't stand to have a phone ring without answering it.

A barking dog is a noise, not a sound. There are almost no times of day when I can stand to hear a dog bark. Part of it is that you have the feeling the dog wants something it isn't getting and if you like dogs, that bothers you. It's like a crying child.

One of the most inexplicable noises is a soft one. It's the one each of us hears when we're staying alone in a house at night. Who *are* those people we always hear creeping up the stairs to our bedroom? The house never makes a noise when there's someone else in it with us.

There are good sounds and bad noises everywhere. Bullfrogs in the distance down by the pond are a great sound; so is Dave Brubeck, Segovia, Pavarotti or Horowitz. Even Frank Sinatra is a good sound if you're in the mood for him. The most intrusive sound being inflicted on most of us by a few of us these days is the loud radio or stereo tape player blaring out rock music.

Sounds are important in a war. In 1944 the 1st Infantry Division, the Big Red One, was our most warwise fighting force. It didn't panic. It did what it had to do. At one point in the move across France, a green infantry division was moved in on the 1st Division's flank. One company of that division ran across an arsenal of German weapons. When the 1st Division found German weapons, they destroyed them. These inexperienced soldiers were intrigued with the handy little German Schmeisser machine guns and, during a brief fire fight in the middle of the night, started using them against their former owners. Hearing that familiar sound on their flank and assuming the presence there of the enemy, a mortar unit from the 1st Division calmly turned its weapons in that direction and dropped shells until there was silence. Tragedy of war.

Everyone should think twice before making a noise.

The Theater

IT seems like some kind of cultural shortcoming on my part, but I've never liked the Theater. By "the Theater," I mean plays acted out on stage before a live audience. There is a mystique about it for people who love the Theater that I've never understood.

You might as well know right now that I don't care whether I ever see *Hamlet* again or not. I hate going to a Shakespeare play, and I feel terrible about myself because of it. I simply think Shakespeare reads better than he plays now. If I have time to do it carefully, I enjoy reading Shakespeare from time to time, but I'm not smart enough to take much from it when the words are being spoken by an actor on stage. I just sit there, amazed that he could memorize all that, but I'm not really hearing what he says. I've been to the Theater when I wanted to stand up and yell, "Hey, wait a minute, will ya! I don't get it. Say that over again, slowly this time."

If you live in or near New York, which I do, you are very aware of the Broadway Theater. It's the Big League and I like having it there, but I seldom attend anymore. I have two rules about the Theater, and they have kept me away from it for most of the last five years.

My first rule is "If you can buy tickets, don't go." The hit shows are always sold out, and while there may be an occasional gem being ignored, most of what's left is third rate. Most of the hits are second rate.

The second rule that keeps me away from the Theater concerns the reviews. If the reviewer spends most of his column telling me how good the acting is, I know the play is a dog. When the critic starts his review by saying something like "Coleen Handley is an absolutely marvelous Darcy in Wambly Frobisher's production of *Winterthorne*," I know I don't want to see it.

The problem for me is, I don't *like* good acting. Good acting annoys me even more than bad acting. If I'm aware of how good the acting is, it's bad for me. It is my opinion that the audience should not notice how good the acting is and as soon as it does, something's wrong with it. The actors are overacting.

It seems to me there are too many actors and not enough writers. There are thousands of actors standing around New York and Hollywood, ready to grab any part that's written. Why are there so many actors and so few writers? I have a sneaking suspicion it's because acting is easier and more lucrative than writing. (You, of course, have a right to have a sneaking suspicion that I think writers ought to get more money and attention because I'm one of them.) The actor's name is up there in lights. The actor gets the big contract. All the writer gets is trouble from the producer and the director who want to change his work.

There's no doubt, I suppose, that my complaint about the Theater is a personal one. They do not give much importance to writing, and if writing isn't important, and I'm a writer, then I'm not important.

There is no doubt either that the writer has been considered of little relative importance to Broadway plays recently. Of the thirty-five current productions listed in the newspapers, only about ten display the writer's name. Three of them are usually Neil Simon. The writer in most cases is anonymous. The hottest thing on Broadway recently was something called *42nd Street*. Everyone knows it was produced by David Merrick because they've seen dozens of television and newspaper interviews with him, but I have no idea who wrote it or whether, as a matter of fact, it was written at all.

If I could turn off a bad play and go to sleep, the way I do with bad television, I'd go to the theater more often.

Bilingual Education

W HEN I listened to President Reagan's denunciation of federal programs designed to support bilingual education in the United States, I would have stood and cheered if I hadn't been a little embarrassed about agreeing with such a conservative, hard-hat opinion.

"It is absolutely wrong," Reagan said, "and against American concept to have a bilingual education program that is now openly, admittedly dedicated to preserving their native language and never getting them adequate in English so they can go out into the job market and participate."

He was referring, of course, to the large number of children in our school system who speak only Spanish and, to a lesser extent, to the large number who speak only "Black English." This may not be much of a problem in your home town, but it is if you live in Los Angeles, Miami or New York.

The very concept of language calls for one system of word use to be spoken and written by everyone interested in communicating with one another. If we're going to understand each other, we all have to agree on what words stand for what ideas. You could suddenly decide to call a chair a franakapan if you wanted to, but no one would know what you meant. In English we call a chair a chair and all English-speaking people understand.

It is wrong for any large number of people to decide they want to speak another language because they already speak it and because it's part of their heritage. It's part of what Spanish-speaking people should have been willing to give up when they came here.

Language is an emotional issue, which is why a lot of people will be irritated by what I just said. Some of us may learn two or three languages in our lifetime, but we're only sentimental about the one we picked up by osmosis from our parents when we were small children.

English-speaking people, especially Americans, have always been accused of being pigheaded in their refusal to do business in anyone else's language. We've been accused of using our economic and military muscle to shove our language down foreign throats. There's been no doubt we were often guilty of some form of national conceit, but as far as the English language goes, we probably have a lot to be conceited about. It is a very good, very useful tool. It is certainly the biggest and probably the most precise language on earth.

If we've been overbearing as soldiers, tourists or businessmen when it came to insisting everyone who wanted to talk to us speak in English, we have been more democratic about accepting foreign words into our language. We've taken in foreign words just as we've taken in immigrants. We don't have the same hang-ups about the purity of our language as the French do, for instance, and as a result, English is a more useful language than French. Evidence that we are not language snobs is the fact that something like seventy-five percent of all the words we use are derived from some other language.

There is a good case to be made for English as the one international language if the day ever comes when we have one. Not only is English the language with the most words, but it seems also to be the language most acceptable to other people.

If a vote were taken among all the people in the world and they were asked to choose five languages in order of preference, each nationality would no doubt rank its own language first, so there wouldn't be any agreement on the first choice, but the majority of people of other nations would beyond doubt make English their second choice.

Spanish is a magnificent language with a great literary tradition and a sound to it that is better than English, and I can understand anyone's reluctance to give it up. "Black English" is not a language at all. Some great words and expressions have come from it, and they'll be taken into standard English along with so many other good words English has adopted. After that it should be rejected and abandoned as soon as possible—just as anything called Black Arithmetic would be if it claimed 2 × 2 equals 5.

Color

THERE are some ideas I stick with even though I'm vaguely aware that I may be wrong.

Last week I was watching a golf match on television and I noticed one of the players was using a yellow ball. For no reason at all, I disliked it. I thought it was out of place. Golf balls, in my little mind, are white.

In this one case I decided to force myself to change my opinion. Why should golf balls be white? I remember seeing the results of a study made years ago that proved that the color yellow was easiest to see. That alone is reason enough to make golf balls yellow. Tennis balls have been yellow for about ten years. You can hardly buy a white tennis ball now.

I don't know how we get our feelings about color. Why does blue stand for melancholy? How come we "see red" when we're angry? Yellow has always been a synonym for cowardice. That's an awful thing for a nice color like yellow to have associated with it.

I remember how slow I was coming around to calling Negroes blacks. About twelve years ago I was asked to write a television documentary and the producer, a friend named Perry Wolff, was calling his series "Of Black America." I remember telling him I thought using the word black for Negro was a passing fashion and wouldn't last. I was wrong, of course. Now the word Negro seems old-fashioned and I wouldn't think of using it.

I have a lot of color prejudices to get over. I dislike seeing women wear anything but red lipstick; I'm not keen on any color for underwear except white; I don't want to offend a lot of publishers who have spent a lot of money on color presses, but I like my newspapers black and white.

The color of something is probably not a very important feature of it, but our first impression of anything comes more from its color than its shape. We've been propagandized to react to colors. We've used the color red so often for danger or as a signal to stop that we don't pay much attention to it anymore. The backs of some cars show a string of red lights that brighten up a hundred times in a ten-mile drive, and we become so inured to their signal of danger that they're meaningless. Red has become meaningless because all the roadside signs trying to attract our attention use it, too. We just can't pay attention to all the reds we see vying for our eye's attention, so we ignore some we shouldn't. Maybe there ought to be a law limiting the use of red.

My favorite color is dark green, but I forget why. I think I may have been in love with a girl who said her favorite color was dark green when I was about ten. My wife grows a lot of flowers, and my taste for color is a little more sophisticated than it used to be. If I hadn't been saying my favorite color is dark green for so long now, I might say it's something else. I just hate to change. It's one of the few questions in my life I'm settled on.

How flowers come up out of the same ground different colors is certainly one of the ten major mysteries of life. You put two seeds in the ground and they look identical. You put a shovelful of manure in the earth around them and for a few weeks or months everything remains brown. Suddenly two thin green shoots appear. In another few weeks the two shoots have emerged from the manure, both smelling great and both looking great, but one is a red rose and one is yellow. How do they do that? Why do they smell the same and look different?

There are things we all learn in school and then intentionally ignore because, while they may be true, they don't fit our sense about them. I remember being told that white isn't a color because it's the absence of any color. Black, on the other hand, is a mixture of every color of the spectrum. I don't care. I still think of white as a color and it's at its best as snow. If they could only figure out a way to have snow come down on cities black and gradually turn white as it gets driven over, walked on and pushed around.

I only watched that golf game with the player using the yellow ball for about three minutes—and look where it got me.

Snow

THERE are about half a dozen potentially calamitous events I worry about. None of these has ever taken place and may never, but I worry that they might.

I refer to such big events as Earth being bumped into by a star bigger than it is, or Earth gradually getting too hot or too cold to live on. This is the sort of thing I mean. When I worry, I worry big.

The worry that always nags at me at this time of year is the possibility that, little by little, as we run out of ways to heat homes, factories and offices, everyone in the United States will move to someplace warm.

It has happened to a slight degree already, of course, but I'm not talking about retired people going to Florida for the winter months. I'm not talking about the people who decided long before there was an energy shortage that they like it down there. I'm talking about all of us *deserting* the Northeast, the Midwest and the Northwest.

I have these terrible nightmares about great empty cities and suburbs where zoning boards are no longer in cahoots with real estate operators and builders, because there are no people to build or buy. We're all down there huddled together in the Sun Belt. Boston would be inhabited by a few hundred hardy caretakers who slept with their mukluks on through the winter months. There would be no heat or water in the buildings, and the wind would whistle through the empty corridors of the Quincy Market.

Syracuse, Pittsburgh, Cleveland would be ghost towns, and people would migrate back to the Great Plains states for just a few warm weather months in order to plant and harvest quickly before they have to leave again to survive.

Well, fortunately for us all, this great event isn't any more likely to happen than the sun is likely to grow cold soon. Fortunately for Florida, California and Texas, ninety-eight percent of this country's population will *not* be moving there. There will be a trend in that direction, but for the same reason the Eskimos have never abandoned the Arctic Circle for the Virgin Islands, the people of Minneapolis will not be migrating to New Orleans.

There is something perverse in the nature of people who live under difficult weather conditions, and it seems to do good things for their character. This is not to say that the people of Maine are necessarily possessed of more character than the people of Georgia, but they do have an admirable ability to hold their ship to the wind in the worst weather. If this generality were not true, nothing ever would have been accomplished in Buffalo.

It is also strange but true that the farther north you get in the United States, the less attention people pay to bad weather in the winter. If Washington, D.C. gets an inch and a half of snow, the city is paralyzed for days. Commerce and government cease to operate.

In Glens Falls, N.Y., on the other hand, two feet of snow may not make page one of the newspaper. They shovel out and go about their business as usual. Just for fun I called the Board of Education in Glens Falls, and they said that in the 1978–79 school year, their schools were closed for just three days because of snow.

In Philadelphia, two hundred miles south of Glens Falls, where they have substantially less snow and no rural dirt roads to plow, schools were closed for five days because of snow.

It's apparent that the people who have the most snow get good at knowing how to handle it. Many people in the upper North seem actually to enjoy and derive strength from the rollercoaster extremes of the seasons. The rigors imposed by snow and cold weather in the most northerly sections of the country produce something in the body that moves it.

So, I can relax and stop worrying. Everyone in the Snowbelt is not going to abandon it and ruin the warm and lovely South by crowding into it.

Hot Weather

I detest hot weather. That's easy enough for me to say in the middle of a heat wave, but I'll say the same thing on the coldest day of the year.

Somehow we don't worry quite so much about the people subjected to relentless heat as we would if they had been through a flood or a hurricane. There are no pictures of it for television, and millions suffer silently.

Even though there are no pictures of heat and no one dies instantly as they might in a storm, in some ways heat may be worse than other natural disasters. In terms of physical damage to material things like houses and cars, the hurricane and the flood are worse, but when you're talking about the human spirit, a heat wave is worse. People join together and work shoulder to shoulder with a great sense of camaraderie to fight the effects of a flood or a snowstorm, but in oppressive heat all effort is impossible.

Half a dozen memories of the worst heat I've ever experienced come to my mind when it gets hot.

My first month in the Army was spent at Fort Bragg, North Carolina, in August. I will never forget having to stand at attention for hours on the red clay drill field on that one-hundred-degree day. The commanding colonel of our artillery battalion made a maddeningly slow inspection tour of the full field packs we had laid out on the ground, and our company was the one he came to last. Nine men fainted or decided to drop to the ground so they'd be carried off.

Later in World War II, I flew with the 8th Air Force on bombing raids over Germany and I traveled across Europe with the First Army, but I never had that bad a day again.

When I go to bed at night, I often toss and turn without being able to go to sleep for as long as fifteen or twenty seconds. Insomnia has never been one of my problems. I can go to sleep when I'm worried, I can go to sleep with a headache and I can even go to sleep when I have one too few blankets over me on a cold night. There's just one thing that keeps me awake, and that's heat.

Late at night in those early Army days at Fort Bragg, I lay awake in the barracks thinking about ice water. One night I couldn't stand it any longer. I got up, waited for the guard on duty in the company street to pass, then I slipped out the door and crawled under the barracks. The barracks were built on stilts, and there was plenty of room to walk in a low crouch. Underneath, I made my way the length of the barracks to the next company street and waited silently again for the guard to pass. It was as though I was a German infiltrator about to blow up the base, but all I wanted was ice water.

I made my way under three barracks until I came to the post exchange. It was 2 AM by then and the PX had closed at nine. But there was something I knew. Every night as they cleaned up, they dumped all their ice on the ground outside the back door. I finally arrived, undetected, and there it was, just as I had hoped. Cakes of ice that had originally been so big that even in the heat they were still huge chunks glistened. I took two cakes so big I had to hold them braced on either hip. It was cold and wet but wonderful, as the icy water soaked through my pajamas.

It took me ten minutes to get back to the barracks and my friends were glad to see me. As a matter of fact, I do not recall a time in all my life when I was so great a hero to so many people.

We broke the ice into pieces, filled our canteen cups with them and then added water. For more than an hour, ten of us sat silently on our bunks in the sweltering heat, drinking that beautiful ice water.

I'm one of the privileged class who lives and works mostly in air-conditioned buildings. For us, hot weather is like a heavy rainstorm. We get out of our air-conditioned car and rush a short distance to an air-conditioned house. During the workday we move quickly from air-conditioned building to air-conditioned building, as if to keep from getting wet in the rainstorm.

I feel terrible for the people I read about being subjected to awful heat, and I always wish I could bring them ice water.

Weathermen

U NLESS there's been a flood, a hurricane or three feet of snow, we aren't interested in a weather *report*. What we want is a prediction. We know what the weather has been like. We want to know what's coming next. And we don't want to be told it's raining, either. We want better information than we can get from looking out the window.

I suppose we expect too much of weathermen. We often malign them, but I think they have it coming.

Most newspapers give the weather forecast in just a few lines, but television and radio forecasts aren't usually that direct. If the local secondhand-car dealer wants to sponsor the weatherman, he needs a show that lasts longer than five seconds, so the weatherman has to stretch it out. He has the same information the newspaper has, but he has to make it last longer.

If the weatherman came on, smiled and just said, "Cloudy with showers late this afternoon," the secondhand-car dealer would feel cheated and his one-minute commercial would be out of proportion to his five-second show.

This has led to the extended weather report on local television news broadcasts. Some of them are good some of the time, but usually they are too long. For one thing, it doesn't matter how normal the weather has been today and is going to be again tomorrow, the weather report has to fill the time allotted to it.

Anchormen and weathermen, with nothing much to say about the weather, get involved in a lot of cute small-talk. The weatherman gives us some pseudo-technical talk about high and low pressure areas just to reassure us that he knows more about weather than we do.

All we want to hear is whether we ought to take along a raincoat or not, and he's telling us that something has dropped from 31.2 to 31.1 and is headed our way from Canada. Nothing ever heads our way from Mexico.

I'm suspicious of this, too, because it seems to me weathermen are imprecise with their geography. When they make those sweeping chalk marks to indicate fronts, three or four hundred miles one way or the other never seems to bother them. They'll draw big half circles to show us what the weather's going to be around the Great Lakes area, but it doesn't seem to matter to them if the chalk catches a little bit of Nebraska and a corner of Tennessee.

The necessity for consuming more time than a weather forecast actually takes is the cause of weathermen and women having acquired all sorts of irritating habits on the air. They'll say, for instance, "I'm sorry to have to tell you, ladies and gentlemen, that the weekend doesn't look good. Sunday is going to be a rainy, cold, dismal day."

In the first place, I'm not interested in whether he's sorry to have to tell us or not. I don't mind being told it's going to be cold and I want to know if it's going to rain, but when the weather expert tells me it's going to be a "dismal" day, he's gone too far.

"Dismal" is a state of mind, not a condition of the weather, and there is no way in the world that a weatherman can predict how a cold, rainy day is going to affect my state of mind.

If it's a Sunday and I have a fire in the fireplace and wish to settle down and read the paper instead of doing all those dirty jobs outside that I'd have had to do on a clear day, "rainy" might be just what I want for weather. The house is warm and cheery, and it gives me a good feeling that I am able to protect my family and myself from the elements. There is nothing "dismal" about it. Rainy and cold, yes, but "dismal" is none of the weatherman's business.

Weather reporters feel compelled to predict our reaction to conditions all the time, and they give us a lot of advice, too. "It'll be bitter cold and windy today, folks, so bundle up."

Is he giving us the weather forecast or advice on how to stay warm? Is he afraid we'll leave home in our shirt sleeves if he tells us the temperature is below zero but neglects to advise us to dress warmly?

"There's ice on the roads today and many of the roads are slippery, listeners, so please drive carefully."

Does he think we're idiots? Does he think we don't know ice is slippery? Does he think that if he simply told us the roads were icy without telling us they were slippery, we would ignore conditions and break our necks?

I have nothing against weathermen. I just wish they'd stick to the weather.

Sleeping on My Back

ONE of the great disappointments of my life is that I can't sleep on my back. I wish I was six feet tall and I wouldn't mind if I was handsome, but I'd trade either for being able to sleep on my back.

I've thought of going to a doctor, but what doctor do you go to for something like that? They're all busy doing heart by-pass operations, fixing broken bones and analyzing our psyches. They don't have time for why I can't sleep on my back. Obviously I'm not going to die of it.

Going to sleep is one of the things I don't have any trouble with at all if I lie on my side. I can drink two cups of strong black coffee after dinner, read, work, watch a little television and sometimes even take a little nap before going to bed, but it still doesn't keep me from falling asleep. I can hit the pillow at 11:14 and be asleep by 11:15. Unless I have to get up to go to the bathroom, I don't wake up until my clock radio goes off at 6:15 the next morning. That's if I don't lie on my back.

If I've been doing a lot of physical work that day or if I've played tennis, it often feels good at night to lie supine and relax every muscle in my body deliberately. That's when I get in trouble. It feels good to my body but terrible to my brain. I can't sleep and I begin thinking evil or depressing thoughts. I begin wondering how long I have to live, whether the furnace will blow up and whether that noise I hear downstairs is someone trying to break in.

Everything goes wrong when I lie on my back.

There doesn't seem to have been any grand plan made for how we're supposed to lie down and sleep. The body is shaped much better for standing or sitting than it is for lying down. Our hips are wider than our legs, and our shoulders stick out so much farther than our head that the head has to be supported by a pillow to keep it from dropping off at an uncomfortably sharp angle. There's nothing good to do with the arms.

Ever since prehistoric man laid himself down on a bundle of branches in his cave, we've been putting something soft under us before we go to sleep. If we lie down on some hard surface that doesn't give at all, our own weight bears down on the parts of us underneath and hurts or cuts off the circulation. It's related to why horses and elephants sleep standing up.

Bedding is pretty good in our country. Mattresses are usually firmer than those you find abroad. I spend quite a few nights away from home every year and I have a lot of complaints with the heating system and the lack of fresh air in hotel and motel rooms, but the beds are almost always fine. Doctors recommend a firm bed for anyone with a bad back. I'm sure it's good advice, but when doctors give it I think they're assuming people sleep on their backs, even though the doctors themselves don't. Most people don't, because they have my problem.

There's nothing much worse than lying awake in the middle of the night, staring at your life. One of the worst things about not sleeping is, you don't get any sympathy. The next morning you may say "I couldn't sleep," but no one feels sorry for you and sometimes they don't even believe you. The strange thing is that the following morning, even though you were sure at the time that you were awake from 2 AM until 5 AM, it's often hard to believe yourself. There's an unreal quality to being awake all night.

I've only had half a dozen sleepless nights in my life, and when I'm having one I always end up on my back. In addition to not sleeping, I have these black thoughts. I've often thought that I'd like to be buried on my side.

Airlines

ALTHOUGH no airline has ever written to me asking for advice, I'm going to give them some while a cross-country flight I just made is fresh in my mind.

The good thing you have going for you, airlines, is that we are all somewhat exhilarated by the thought of going to a distant place. I'm not a chronic airline knocker, but getting there these days is too often an unpleasant experience and, for your own good, I don't want you to take the magic out of it.

You do a lot of things well. You seem to try hard. I like the way one airline will give us information about another over the phone or at the counter, even when there's no business in it for them. Your facilities are usually clean and your employees courteous, but there are some things I want to talk to you about.

You seem to understand that all of us hate standing in line at the ticket counter at the airport, for example, but what you don't seem to realize is that we wouldn't hate it so much if we were absolutely sure we were standing in the right line and that it was necessary for us to stand in it at all. Which line is which? Can we go directly to the gate? Are we really checked in? You aren't going to give our seat away, are you? Which one of all these sheets of paper in this envelope is really the ticket? How many times do we have to show things to people before we get on the plane, and whom do we have to show what to? Help us with these matters.

It's a good feeling once we are actually on board and seated, but it takes too long to get there. It takes too long to get off, too. Couldn't you board and unload through two doors?

One of the reasons it's taking too long is that you're letting people carry too much junk on board. They take junk on board because it is still taking too long to retrieve a bag that's been checked through.

I was in Los Angeles last week and the return flight to New York was one hour and fifty-five minutes late taking off. I don't know why you didn't give us any explanation, but as soon as we got in the air the pilot came on and thanked us for our patience and understanding. I had not been patient and understanding at all, and I resent the pilot's assumption I was. As a matter of fact, I was damned *impatient*, if the pilot wants to know the truth.

There's something else I want to tell you about your pilots, too. Most of us hate the folksy ones. One of the best ways to pass time in flight is by sleeping. Last week, about half an hour out of Los Angeles, I was sound asleep and blissfully unaware of the discomforts of a crowded flight when the pilot blasted me awake over the intercom.

"There's a good view of the crater formed when that meteorite hit the Earth near Winslow, Arizona, over there to our right, ladies and gentlemen. The walls of the crater are 525 feet high."

Thanks a lot, Captain. I happen to be on the *left* side of the plane and can't see a thing. Where were you when we wanted to know why our flight was two hours late? Not only that, you told me to buckle my seat belt for my own comfort and convenience. I happen to think you wanted me to keep it buckled for *your* convenience, so I wouldn't stand up and get in the stewardesses' way. But that's another story. So what am I supposed to do? Get up and lean over someone on the right side of the plane or try to go back to sleep?

I can't complain much about your stewardesses. They aren't as young or as pretty as they used to be and this seems like a step in the right direction, but I do have one or two suggestions. Will you please tell them to stop making that announcement where they say, "If there's anything we can do to make your flight more enjoyable, please don't hesitate to call on us."

The chances are she's got a planeload of people and we'll all be lucky if she has time to throw lunch at us. We've got about as much chance of getting special attention from a stewardess as we'd have getting the only floor nurse in the middle of the night in a crowded hospital.

And another thing. Stop having her ask us if we want cream in our coffee. I don't know whether you airlines have noticed or not, but none of you serve cream anymore. You serve a white liquid plastic for the coffee.

You notice I haven't complained about your food. Actually I feel sorry for the chefs who design and prepare your meals. It is obvious they start with good ingredients and do well by them in the kitchen, but bricks wouldn't stand up to what happens to airline food between the hangar where it's fixed and the passenger's tray table. So, a last bit of advice. Keep the food simple. Don't try to serve us scrambled eggs on a flaming sword.

Air Fares

IF the airlines don't stop flimflamming us with the kind of numbers we're more used to seeing in secondhand-car lots, they could bring back the railroad train.

It is almost impossible for the average person to find out what the best deal is for him when he wants to fly somewhere. Air fares are so variable that many airlines ticket agents can't keep up with them. There doesn't seem to be any relationship between what it costs an airline to fly a person from one place to another and how much they charge for that service. The airlines are playing some game, but we don't know the rules and they won't tell us what they are. It isn't the sort of thing that gives us any confidence in air-lines, and I often find myself hoping their mechanics are more dependable than their prices.

What follows is the transcript of a telephone call I made to an airline, as closely as I can recall it:

AR: Could you tell me how much the fare is from New York to Los Angeles?

VOICE: Thank you for calling Ace Amalgamated Airlines, Your Stairway to the Stars. All our agents are temporarily busy. Please don't hang up. You will now hear Beethoven's Sixth Symphony by the Akron, Ohio, Symphony Orchestra, conducted by Sir Clarence Schimmel. Your call will be placed in our computer and will be answered automatically by one of our agents as soon as one is available. Thank you.

(At this point I held on to the phone through the first two movements of Beethoven until an agent broke in.)

AGENT: Hello, this is Linda, may I serve you?

AR: Yes, how much is the air fare from New York to Los Angeles?

AGENT: When did you wish to depart, sir?

AR: I don't wish to depart at all until I find out whether I can afford it. How much is it?

AGENT: Will we be traveling Economy or First Class?

AR: It's not "we," it's "me." I'd like to go tourist.

AGENT: Ace Amalgamated no longer offers a tourist class, sir. Would you like Coach, Economy, Super Saver, Super Coach, Super Duper Coach, or a seat with room in front of you for your legs?

AR: I read an advertisement that you have a one-way fare for $149.

AGENT: Yes, sir, but that's only available in Los Angeles if you're in New York . . . and vice versa. And you have to have bought your ticket at least three years in advance. And you have to stay at least eight days but not nine.

AR: Well, what's the cheapest fare from New York to Los Angeles that I can get now?

AGENT: If your plans call for an extended visit in California, we offer our Family Plan.

AR: What's the Family Plan?

AGENT: This is reserved for economy-minded travelers who don't mind being in the middle seat when the window seat and the aisle seat are occupied by a family . . . a mother and father and two small children.

AR: How much is first class?

AGENT: Regular or economy first class?

AR: What's the difference?

AGENT: Regular first class features all the champagne you can drink and food you can't eat at all. Our Economy First Class Special is $329 roundtrip. This includes an all-expense-paid trip to Disneyland, lunch with Carol Burnett and a reporter from the *National Enquirer*, and a room at the Y in Beverly Hills.

AR: I'll take that.

AGENT: I'm sorry, sir. Our Economy First Class Special is sold out. Actually we only had one seat allotted to that and the pilot's mother is using it. Are there any other reservations we may make for you while you're in the Los Angeles area?

AR: I think I'm all set.

AGENT: Thank you for calling Ace Amalgamated Airlines. If your future plans call for air travel, please call on us again.

Coaches

THE word "coach" has taken on a new meaning and I don't like what it means anymore.

A coach used to be the person who helped organize a team and then showed the young people how to play the game. Not anymore. Now the coach dominates every aspect of the game. The players are incidental. They have nothing to say about strategy and the coach manipulates them the way a general moves elements of his army at war.

Basketball and football coaches seem to be the most objectionable. In a televised basketball game you can always see the coach stalking up and down the sidelines, waving his arms in wild gestures and screaming at both players and officials.

"Shut up and sit down!" I want to yell at them. As a matter of fact I have yelled that at them, even though we don't have two-way television in our house yet.

Last season the coach of Princeton and the coach of Columbia got into a fight after their basketball games. I'd fire both of them.

There have been two recent cases where coaches have been fired for striking players. You wonder how long it had been going on before someone caught them doing it in public. What kind of a way is this to play a game for fun? The kind of sportsmanship a lot of young athletes are learning from their coaches is going to make them eligible for competition on the pro tennis circuit with such world-famous good sports as John McEnroe and Jimmy Connors.

Baseball is the only game where they face the fact and call the person running the team the manager. He's the one who runs out on the field, sticks his nose up against the umpire's nose and tells him off.

The coaches in other sports have learned how to do that too. They always complain loudly about a referee's decision. No decision by the officials in all the history of sports has ever been changed because a coach or manager complained about it, but they still do it during every game.

The intrusion of the coaches into football is ludicrous. Deciding what play would be most effective at any point in the game is an important part of knowing how to play football. It is a decision that should be made on the field, by one of the players appointed to do that. Traditionally the quarterback called the plays. Now most of the plays in professional football are called by the coach on the sideline, who gets advice from a man at the top of the stadium with whom he's in touch by telephone. High school and college coaches are, more and more, sending in plays.

It was about twenty-five years ago that Cleveland Browns' coach Paul Brown started shuttling two players in and out. After each play was over, the man standing next to him on the sidelines was told what Brown wanted the team to do next. He'd run in and make the announcement in the huddle. After the play, he'd run back out and the second man would run in with more instructions.

It has not been so long ago that it was illegal for anyone on the sideline to give advice to any of the players. When a substitute came into the game, that player couldn't join the others in the huddle for the first play. The teammate next to him whispered into his ear as they went to the line of scrimmage so he'd know what the play was. This seems like the way it ought to be. There is no doubt in the world that the rules of football should be changed to exclude the coach from making decisions about what to do next on the field.

The whole point of sports is fun. It is a diversion from the seriousness of life. We all make decisions every day that make a real difference to our happiness and our prosperity. Sports should provide a relief from that pressure. Sports don't make any difference. Vince Lombardi was absolutely wrong when he said, "Winning isn't everything, it's the only thing."

If a coach sets out to win, with no concessions made to fun or sportsmanship or more important factors in a young person's life, that coach can be a winner. I don't know any way that can be controlled but it always seems to me it's almost like cheating.

And please don't write and tell me there are a lot of good coaches. I know that, and they agree with me.

Tipping

I'D be just as happy if they passed a law tomorrow making tipping illegal.

There are all sorts of things wrong with tipping. It puts both tipper and tippee in a bad position. Why should anyone have to depend on what I choose to give them for their services? Who am I to leave a dollar grandly under my plate for the waiter as if I was doing him a big favor? I hate tipping. Why shouldn't an employer have to pay an employee a decent wage?

The first thing wrong is that most of us don't know who to tip or how much. We don't know what the person we're tipping expects from us. We don't want him to think we're cheapskates, and we don't want to look as though we're from out of town by tipping too much. Most of us tip out of fear more than gratitude. We're not moved to give away money by any sense of being thankful to the person who provided us with service. We just know we're supposed to do it.

I eat in a lot of restaurants during the course of a year, and the tip I leave the waiter or waitress very seldom bears any relationship to the quality of service I get. I leave the same tip for good service as I do for bad. Occasionally when service is really terrible, I'll shave the tip to the socially acceptable minimum but never below that. I'm a coward when it comes to tipping. Dr. Joyce Brothers would certainly point out that I hate tipping because I hate myself for tipping the way I do.

Years ago George Bernard Shaw ate in a restaurant in New York and the service was terrible. The waiter ignored him, got the orders mixed up and was rude. After the meal, Shaw paid the check and as he was leaving he looked the waiter in the eye and dropped a fifty-dollar bill on the table.

"This is what I tip for *bad* service," Shaw said.

The word "TIPS" is supposed to have come from the first letters of the words To Insure Prompt Service. I don't know whether that's true or not. All I know is it doesn't help the service at all and we ought to drop the custom.

There are a lot of small towns in the United States where no one would dream of tipping someone. That's the way it ought to be, but in the big cities you're expected to tip half the people you meet. In a hotel there are always a lot of people doing things for you that you'd rather do yourself, because they're looking for a tip. When there are nine taxicabs in a line outside the hotel, I don't need a doorman whistling his head off to get me one. I resent tipping doormen for doing almost nothing.

A friend of mine spent several days at the fancy Greenbrier Hotel in West Virginia once, and as he was leaving he held out a dollar to a doorman who hadn't done anything for him and said, "Do you have some change?"

The doorman looked at my friend and said, "Sir, at the Greenbrier, a dollar *is* change."

Several times a year, I find myself in an expensive restaurant that has a washroom attendant. I'm perfectly capable of washing and drying my own hands without having an attendant hand me a towel, and I think the establishment should pay someone to keep the place neat and clean without making the clients pay for it with tips. The attendant usually has four or five dollar bills in a dish, as if that's what you're expected to leave.

I don't have my shoes shined anymore because it costs too much with tip. I've never known how much to give the captain in the restaurant with a washroom attendant and if I have to slip a headwaiter ten dollars for a good table, I'm going to eat someplace else.

I'd like to put an end to all tipping, but I don't dare start the movement all by myself.

Gambling

THERE's nothing more satisfying than getting mad. I thoroughly enjoy it once in a while, and I want to thank the New York State Department of Taxation and Finance for getting me off to a great angry start today.

This morning I got up early and turned on the radio to make sure the world hadn't come to an end during the night. (I always do that because if the world does ever come to an end, I think I'll just go back to bed.) As usual, the world hadn't come to an end, and right after the weather report there was a commercial, paid for by New York State taxpayers, saying what a good idea it was for everyone who wants to get rich to gamble on a numbers game, the New York State Lottery. The New York Off Track Betting Commission has comparable advertising telling everyone what a good idea it is to bet on horses.

Well, gambling on numbers or betting on which horse will run fastest is *not* the way to get rich, and New York State ought not to suggest to its citizens that it is.

When these gambling bills were proposed before the state legislature, the argument for them was that people were going to gamble anyway so the state might as well take gambling away from the crime mob, run it honestly and make the profit itself. How come, I'd like to know, if people are going to do all this gambling naturally, the state has to buy radio and newspaper commercials to try to get them to gamble?

Why don't those commercials tell people what chance they have of winning in the state lottery? The state takes forty-five cents of every dollar bet. Does that sound like a good deal to you? Who but the dumbest and most desperate among us would take a chance like that?

The radio stations give the winning numbers every day, giving favorable publicity to big winners. I think the radio stations ought to announce the names of the *losers* every day. That would be some list!

All you have to do to see who this kind of betting appeals to is to stand outside a New York State Off Track Betting parlor any day of the week and watch the people who spend their time hanging around hoping to get lucky. They are the duds, the derelicts and the human disasters. Why does the state prey on these poor devils who can't take care of themselves?

New York State pays millions of dollars a week in welfare to its indigent citizens. Does it make any sense for the state to hand out money for food and lodging one day and take it away the next at the betting window so the state will have money for the welfare payments again the following week? It is absolutely the dumbest thing I ever heard of. This is robbing Peter to pay Peter.

How can we teach kids that hard work is the way to success if they hear radio commercials paid for by their government suggesting that the way to get rich is to bet money on a horse or a number? How can Americans who profess to believe in such classic virtues as honesty, thrift, hard work and intelligent action allow any part of the government they formed to run a gambling operation?

Gambling is a destructive force. People who spend their money on that don't spend it somewhere else. The man who blows twenty dollars at the OTB parlor doesn't have it to buy a new pair of sneaks for his son. What good does that do for the legitimate businessman who runs the shoe store or for the man's son?

I like to gamble. I go to Saratoga once a year and even Las Vegas has a terrible fascination for me. If blackjack was whiskey, I could become an alcoholic. I'm glad no casino is readily available to me because I need to be protected from myself. But for our own government to promote and make money by taking it away from the weakest among us in a gambling operation is the lowest form of taxation.

Now, I've been angry for today. I feel good and I can get at the day's work.

Oil Eaters

Dᴉᴅɴ'ᴛ you put gas in the car yesterday, dear?"
"Yes. I had it filled. What's the matter?"
"I can't get it started and the tank says empty."

This is how I envision the beginning of the end of the world.

The Supreme Court has just ruled that a new form of life invented by man can be patented and sold for profit. The scientists at General Electric came up with a new organism that eats gas or oil and turns it into carbon dioxide and protein. When the oil is gone, the inventors say, the new organism dies. Maybe!

The scientist, Ananda Chakrabarty, invented this new microorganism with a great plan in mind. He thought that when there was an oil spill in the ocean, a small colony of these little devils of his could be released in it. They'd start multiplying and eating all the oil they could find in the ocean. When they had licked their plate clean, they'd all die of starvation and that would be the end of them and the oil pollution.

But let's look at another scenario. One sunny day these organisms are gulping down all the oil they can eat when one of them decides they need leadership. He gets himself elected president of the new bacterial group and decides his followers ought to look ahead to the time when the oil spill is gone and they won't have anything more to eat. They develop a long-range plan.

A special task force made up of the youngest and most athletic bacteria gets itself a huge piece of floating debris. It is actually the door off the captain's cabin of the oil tanker that sank and left the oil slick.

They load up the door with a three-week emergency ration of oil to eat and set off exploring for new oil. They drift for weeks and things begin to look grim. Then one night they see the lights of a huge oil tanker bearing down on them. They jump into the water and, with their little feet kicking away, push the door into the path of the oncoming ship. Sure enough the tanker hits the door and all the microorganisms, a little weak now because their eating oil is almost gone, clamber up the sides of the ship and scamper down into the hold. There, in huge holding tanks, is a sight for sore microorganic eyes! Millions of gallons of good eating. The organisms get straws from the ship's galley and have themselves their first square meal in weeks.

When the ship gets to port, its oil is almost gone. The shipping magnate accuses the captain of having sold it en route. The captain insists there must be a leak in the tanks. With barely enough fuel left to get them back to the Middle East, the tankers leaves port to get another load.

By the time the SS *Ayatollah Esso* has reached port again in the Mediterranean, the oil-eating microorganisms are near starvation and the ship itself barely makes it to port. No sooner is it tied up at the docks than the pipes are coupled to its tanks and a new load of oil starts pouring in.

That small hardy band of microorganic green berets who started their trip so long ago on the captain's door are sick of the sea by now. They want a more secure life and a more certain source of eating oil.

Like salmon swimming upstream to multiply, Dr. Ananda Chakrabarty's Supreme Court blessed bacteria fight their way back up through the pipeline until finally, after almost giving up against the tide of oil rushing at them, they make their way down the oil-drilling rig and enter upon a placid, underground ocean of oil from which all oil company blessings flow.

Here in this land of plenty the organisms get religion and are told by their leaders to multiply and grow and go forth and populate the land.

They do this until they have entered into every oily place on the face of the earth and have consumed it all and there is no more to eat and the furnaces grow cold and the oil company profits cease to flow and the cars won't go. And a great silence falls upon the land.

Vacations in Outer Space

WE'RE getting into space none too soon.

There's just no doubt about it, we're running short of everything here on earth and we need some of that room there in outer space. No one knows how big outer space is, of course, nor if it ends, what's just beyond it.

When John Young arrived back on earth after that first space-shuttle mission, he said that interstellar travel was not far off. I certainly hope so, because one of the things we're in most desperate need of is some new place to go on vacation.

We're all looking for some places to go that everyone else hasn't already been to, and they're getting scarce here on earth. There's a mountain behind a cottage we have on a lake in northern New York State, and it used to be a great adventure to climb it. We never went up or down the same way twice, and we were often lost and sometimes scared for short periods during the climb, but it was never dull. Now there are four well-marked trails with color-coded signs pointing the way, and when you reach the top, the rocks at the summit are littered with orange peel, Styrofoam cups and discarded soft-drink cans. The adventure has been taken out of the trip. There are three other parties of climbers up there with you, and one member of one of them has brought a portable radio which is tuned to a rock music station in Albany.

The word "pioneer" in relation to geography can be retired from the language. Every place has been walked on and is not far from the federally funded highway.

All the good and remote places to go have been discovered and ruined. Yellowstone National Park gets so many visitors at times that they have to close the gates as if it was a rock music festival. I remember when it was chic for Americans with money to go to the magnificent crescent-shaped beach at Acapulco and return bragging about this wonderful place they'd found in Mexico. Today you can hardly find the beach if you go to Acapulco because it's hidden from the road by a solid phalanx of hotels.

There are travel agents who will book you a trip down the Amazon through the wilds of South America, but the Jungle Lodge at Iquitos, Peru, provides most of the civilized comforts of a Holiday Inn. I haven't been up there, but I wouldn't be surprised to find an Igloo Hilton at the North Pole. A few years ago we rented a quaint, thatch-roofed cottage on Galway Bay for a week and all our neighbors in adjacent cottages were, as we were, American tourists.

A friend of mine just returned from "a trek" to Mt. Everest. It was complete with Sherpa guides who carried all the heavy stuff and an American doctor who got his trip free in exchange for his services in the event they were necessary.

We can put the word "adventure" away with "pioneer," because there isn't much of it left. The trip down the Colorado in a rubber raft is safe enough to be taken by a President's wife and a quota of Secret Service agents. To fit the definition of the word "adventure," a trip ought to have an element of danger or uncertainty, and there aren't many places left to go that have either.

Travel agents find themselves in a paradoxical situation because people come in wanting something different and exciting, but then they want the travel agent to arrange things so carefully that all the elements of risk and surprise are taken out of the trip. They want to go someplace man has never set foot before, and when they arrive, they want to go up to their room, take a shower and rest a while before going out to some good restaurant that serves American food for dinner.

All we can hope is that the spaceship Columbia is the covered wagon of the future, and that it will open the way for long weekends and summer vacations in the unexplored wilds of outer space where prefab picnic tables have not yet been provided.

On Conservation

M Y grandfather was right and wrong about a lot of things, but he was never undecided. When I was twelve, he told me we were using up all the good things on earth so fast that we'd run out of them.

I've worried about that. I guess we all have, and I wonder whether it's true or not. The real question is, will we run out of the things we need to survive before we find substitutes for them? Of course, we're going to run out of oil. Of course, we're going to run out of coal. And it seems very likely that there will be no substantial forests left in another hundred years.

Argue with me. Say I'm wrong. Give me statistics proving there's more oil left in the ground than we've already used. Tell me there's coal enough in the United States to last seventy-five or a hundred years. Make me read the advertisements saying they're planting more trees than they're cutting.

I've read all those arguments and I'll concede I may be wrong in suggesting impending doom, but if doom is not exactly impending, it's somewhere down the line of years if we don't find replacements for the basic materials we're taking from the earth. What about five hundred years from now if one hundred doesn't worry you? What about a thousand years from now? Will there be an oak tree left two feet in diameter? How much will it cost in a hundred years to buy an oak plank eight feet long, two inches thick and a foot wide? My guess is it will cost the equivalent in today's money of a thousand dollars. A piece of oak like that will be treasured as diamonds are treasured today because of its rarity.

I don't think there is a more difficult question we're faced with than that of preservation. A large number of Americans feel we should use everything we have because things will work out. They are not necessarily selfish. They just don't believe you can worry about the future much past your own grandchildren's foreseeable life expectancy. They feel someone will find the answer. Pump the oil, mine the coal, cut the trees and take from the earth anything you can find there. There may not be more where that came from, but we'll find something else, somewhere else, that will be a good substitute.

The preservationists, on the other hand, would set aside a lot of everything. They'd save the forests and reduce our dependency on coal and oil in order to conserve them as though no satisfactory substitutes would ever be found.

It's too bad the argument between these groups is as bitter as it is, because neither wants to do, intentionally, what is wrong. The preservationists think business interests who want to use what they can find are greedy and short-sighted. Businessmen think the preservationists are, in their own way, short-sighted. (One of the strange things that has happened to our language is that people like the ones who run the oil companies are called "conservatives," although they do not approve of conserving at all.)

All this comes to me now because I have just returned from Hawaii and seen what havoc unrestricted use can bring to an area. To my grandfather, Honolulu would probably look like the end of the world if he could see it now.

We have just about used up the island of Oahu. Now we're starting on Maui. Is it right or wrong? Do the hotels crowded along the beach not give great pleasure to large numbers of us? Would it be better to preserve the beauty of Hawaii by limiting the number of people allowed to be there? Would it be better if we saved the forests, the oil and the coal in the world and did without the things they provide? If there is middle ground, where is it?

The answer will have to come from someone smarter than I am. I want to save oil and drive a big car fast. I want to cut smoke pollution but burn coal to save oil, and I want to pursue my wood-working hobby without cutting down any trees.

V:

QUESTIONS FOR THE PRESIDENT

What About a King?

EVERYONE complains so much about the political campaign for the presidency that I was wondering if it might not be a good idea for us to consider another form of government, one that would allow us to have some kind of leader other than a President.

What about a king?

It seems to me a king might be good. For one thing, no one takes a king very seriously anymore. We need a leader we don't take so seriously.

A king would sure save us a lot of trouble every four years. Once you've got yourself a king or a queen, you're all set for life. His or her life, that is. And when something *does* happen to a king, there isn't a lot of worrying about whether they were careful enough when they elected the Vice President. There is no vice-king. They just give the crown to his oldest kid or his next closest relative.

There was actually some talk of having a king here when Franklin Roosevelt was elected for a fourth term, although most of that talk came from his enemies, who said it as a bitter joke. If we had made Roosevelt king, King Franklin, we would have saved ourselves nine long, nasty political campaigns since then. When Roosevelt died in 1945, the throne would have been turned over to his son James. That is, if his mother, Eleanor, had allowed him to have it. King James would still be reigning now at age seventy-four.

It would also have been easy for us to switch over to a monarchy right after World War II. Eisenhower would have made a logical king. Had we made that change, we would now have King David. Julie Nixon Eisenhower would be a princess by marriage—although if Eisenhower had become king, Nixon never would have been President, and Julie and David might never have met and married.

We wouldn't have to make a lot of expensive changes to install a king. He could live in the same quarters the President lives in. We'd simply call it the White Palace. The changing of the guard might give a boost to tourism in Washington.

It just seems to me that a king or queen doesn't give you the same kind of trouble a President gives you. For one thing, a king doesn't really do much, and we're all agreed that one of the things we need is people in Washington who do less.

A king isn't the only alternative to our President. If we're really tired of these political campaigns every four years, we might look into a dictatorship. Dictatorships have acquired a bad name because we've had some bad dictators in recent history. What we'd have to have, of course, is a *good* dictator.

Dictatorships are an old concept. During the great years of the Roman republic, they used to get themselves a dictator every once in a while when things weren't going too good. They'd give this fellow complete control over everything for six months. He'd straighten out the country and then the Romans would return to their democracy. It's people like Hitler, Mussolini and Franco who ruined the image of the wise and benevolent dictator. What we could use is a real Mr. Nice Guy.

In the Soviet Union they've done several clever things that have largely blunted criticism of the management often found in dictatorships. First, young Russians are taught from birth that theirs is the best system, so when little Russians grow up, it doesn't occur to many of them that it stinks. Second, the Soviet dictatorship is no longer personified; it is a dictatorship by committee. A committee is harder to really hate than one man.

The only other alternative I can think of to a presidency is a junta and I don't think any of us would want a junta. For one thing, we don't know how to pronounce it.

Presidential Candidates

PRESIDENTIAL candidates act as though there was a lot of difference of opinion among us as to what we wanted to hear from them. I don't think there is. I know what I'd like to hear one of them say, and I suspect a lot of the rest of you would like to hear some of the same things.

First, a presidential candidate ought to be a man or woman who doesn't really want the job, who knows he isn't smart enough to do it and says so.

If a candidate is so conceited as to think he's got the brains it takes to solve this country's problems, I don't want to have anything to do with him. Of course he can't solve our problems. If he's honest, he'll tell us he's just going to do the best he can to keep everything from going to hell.

He ought to admit he's never going to be able to balance the budget and that he'll have to find some sneaky ways to raise taxes while he's talking about lowering them.

I don't mind if the candidate has an attractive wife (or husband), but I hope she's the kind of woman who doesn't want to get into the act all the time. If we wanted a wife (or a husband) for President, we'd have elected one.

To be perfectly honest, I'd be happy if my candidate didn't have any children, brothers or sisters. I know this makes me sound as though I hate dogs, but I just don't think we need kids or brothers of the President confusing us about what we think of him.

I wouldn't mind hearing my man admit that one of the reasons he's running for office is that he needs work. The job pays $200,000 a year plus a lot of fringe benefits. He gets a nice house to live in and someone to do the dishes.

When my candidate comes on television just before Election Day, I know just what I'd like to hear him say:

"Good evening, voters.

"Hope I look okay. I don't usually have my hair this slicked down, but I just took a shower and this is the way they told me I ought to look. This is a new suit I'm wearing, too. Sure hope I got all the tags off.

"There are a few things I want to say right off. If I'm elected, there are a lot of idiots who contributed money to my campaign and the chances are, I'm going to have to give jobs to some of them. You ever been in that kind of spot? I don't know what else to do. I'll try to put them in jobs that won't hurt much. Ambassador to Liechtenstein, that sort of thing. I mean, what's $40,000? Am I right or am I wrong?

"If I get in tomorrow, I'm going to knock off with those tours of the White House, too. Who wants people with muddy feet tramping through their house all day? It isn't like they were going to buy the place from me, you know.

"One more thing, before I get to some of the good stuff. I got this friend who'd do anything for me, you know what I mean? He may not be the smartest guy in the world and he's been involved in a few . . . well, nothing dishonest really but a little, like, well, shady deals.

"But what I want to say about him is, he's my friend and he can help me and I'd appreciate it if the press would stay off his back.

"I don't know a damn thing about foreign policy. I hate Mexican food, and I don't know how to use chopsticks. The only time I've been out of the country is ten days I spent in Puerto Rico on vacation. If you call that out of the country.

"There are two more things I want to tell you. First, I hadn't been to church in nine years before I started running for this office and, second, if elected I don't want the Secret Service around all the time.

"I have a pretty good wig and a false nose and about once a week my wife and I would like to slip out the back door of the White House and eat dinner alone at a little bistro we like over in Georgetown.

"Who knows, I might even tie one on once in a while."

Now, this is a candidate I could vote for with confidence.

Republican or Democrat

I F I say I am neither a Republican nor a Democrat, it seems to me it shouldn't make anyone angry. It does, though. What seems to happen is that when I say that, *everyone* gets mad at me. My Republican friends think I've lost my marbles and my Democratic friends think I've sold out to the enemy.

The fact is, though, I am neither. I have absolutely no inclination to sign up with any party or to vote their ticket right down the line, either. I'm against whoever is in office. That's not a party.

I can usually spot a liberal Democrat or a conservative Republican at one hundred feet, and I have no trouble at all when they come close enough so I can hear them talk. It doesn't matter whether the subject is sports, fashion, oil, politics, religion or breakfast food. I know one when I hear one. I credit my perception to my neutrality. I'm neutral against both extremes.

Most Democrats are considered to be liberals and most Republicans are thought of as conservative, but a strange thing has happened in relation to the word "conservative." In the first place, liberals are more conservative in matters of the land and our total environment. They want to save it. The traditional political conservatives, on the other hand, are not for conserving much of anything. They think all the trees and oil should be used.

The second paradox in relation to the word "conservative" is that most Republicans no longer fit the classic definition. "Conservatism," Thorstein Veblen said, "is the maintenance of conventions now in force."

In the 1930s, when Franklin Roosevelt was trying to curb our free enterprise system by imposing government on capitalism, Republican conservatives fought him. They wanted to maintain the status quo. They lost, though, and things did change. We no longer have that same free enterprise system. Government is in on the distribution of money at every level. Republicans want to get the government out. They are the revolutionaries who want change. Liberal Democrats wish to maintain things the way they are. *They* are, by definition, the conservatives.

Not knowing whether I'm a Democrat or a Republican sometimes gives me an insecure feeling of inferiority, and I've often tried to lay out in a clear way what I think Republicans believe and what I think Democrats believe. If I could do that, I might be able to take sides. I like liberals better than conservatives, but conservatives make more sense.

Democrats (I think to myself) are liberals who believe that people are basically good, but that they need government help to organize their lives. They believe in freedom so fervently that they think it should be compulsory. They believe that the poor and ignorant are victims of an unfair system and that their circumstances can be improved if we give them help.

Republicans (I think to myself) are conservatives who think it would be best if we faced the fact that people are no damned good. They think that if we admit that we have selfish, acquisitive natures and then set out to get all we can for ourselves by working hard for it, that things will be better for everyone. They are not insensitive to the poor, but tend to think the poor are impoverished because they won't work. They think there would be fewer of them to feel sorry for if the government did not encourage the proliferation of the least fit among us with welfare programs.

The President and the Press

THIS is not so much about Ronald Reagan as it is about journalism.

President Reagan told a reporter for the *New York Times* that he was always amazed at people who spent half an hour or less with him and then went away and psychoanalyzed him and drew negative conclusions about his ability to be President.

It's easy to understand the outrage most people in politics feel toward the press and television news. The media are always badgering them, prying into private matters, emphasizing things they wish they'd never said and even making misstatements of fact about them.

Fortunately for the nation, the press works a lot like our democracy. People vote for various candidates for various reasons, many of them wrong. Some of their reasoning is faulty or is based on misinformation or on no information at all, but the funny thing is that for a lot of wrong reasons, we elect a lot of right people.

The news media work somewhat the same way. No one reporter has all the story or has it all right. Most stories are inaccurate, but in different ways. In total, the public ends up with a somewhat confused picture of the candidate, but one that is close to the truth.

I don't think there is much difference between the public perception of Ronald Reagan and the whole truth of what he's like. Most of us don't swallow the real nasty stuff or the stuff that endows him with greatness. The same could be said for Jimmy Carter. He didn't like what was said about him, but I think the public got an accurate picture of what he was like.

Our Presidents don't seem to appreciate the public's ability to take in, sort out and then spit back about ninety-eight percent of everything it is told. If one reporter spends half an hour with Reagan and concludes that he is incompetent, not many readers are going to accept that as the last word. Some other reporter will be presenting evidence that suggests Reagan might make the best President since George Washington. The public isn't going to swallow that either. The public gets a picture that is a composite drawing. It sees in the picture what it wants to see and doesn't see anything else. How else do you account for the deification of Ted Kennedy by some people and the vilification of him by others exposed to the same information?

Years ago I was the writer of a one-hour documentary about Frank Sinatra. Several of us went to his home in Palm Springs to film and for two days saw quite a bit of him. Exposed to his charm firsthand, it was easy to understand his popularity.

When Walter Cronkite interviewed Sinatra for the report, he asked some hard questions about incidents in his past. He asked about mob associations, women and attacks Sinatra was reported to have made on newsmen or photographers. Sinatra was angry in response. He went point by point down a long list of things that had been said about him. He claimed, in quite a convincing way, that every one of those stories was untrue.

I always believed him. I suspected that the events had not taken place precisely as the public had been led to believe they had; but I also came away with an even stronger conviction about the journalistic process.

The public has a more accurate idea of what Frank Sinatra is really like than Frank Sinatra has of himself.

I think the public also knows almost exactly what Ronald Reagan is like. Under the same circumstances, that's the sort of thing that would make any one of us nervous and irritable.

Reagan's Gray Hair

CLOSE observers reported that Reagan's thick black hair showed definite patches of gray during his West Coast vacation." That's how a paragraph read in the *U.S. News and World Report*.

Shame on you, *U.S. News and World Report*. You're a good magazine with an important-sounding name and you ought not to dabble in drivel. What's going on in California, Poland, Afghanistan? That's what we sent you out to report back on, not the color of the President's hair.

President Reagan is seventy-one years old, he's got one of the hardest, most important jobs in the world, and he's got all that brush to clean out at the ranch. Of *course* he's getting gray.

What about George Washington, *U.S. News?* I don't see you

taking pot shots at the Father of our country and his hair was not only gray, it was white. I believe there were formal occasions when he wore a powdered wig. You'd have some time with Ronald Reagan if he showed up for a press conference with a powdered wig, wouldn't you? And did you get on President Eisenhower's back because he was bald? I don't know what's got into you.

The trouble is, you're playing into the hands of the people who are making a big deal about the color of a man's hair. If you keep talking about the President getting gray as if this was some kind of awful thing, Mobil Oil will be taking over Grecian Formula for its growth potential.

The American public already thinks the press does too much negative reporting and the press ought to save it for important things, not derogatory chitchat.

How would you like it, *U.S. News and World Report*, if I started criticizing your magazine for its petty faults? Just let me ask you a few questions:

—What's with your title, *U.S. News and World Report?* Is there any reason you didn't name your magazine *U.S. Report and World News?*

—How come you always slap the sticker with the subscriber's address on it right over some important word on the cover? Do you do this on purpose, or is it just careless? Which would you rather we believed?

This is the way you go after one of our Presidents. Now how do you like it? Let me ask you some other questions:

—How come your magazine is dated September 7 if I read it September 1? Don't you have a calendar over there in your editorial offices, or are you just trying to make your magazine seem up-to-date by putting an advance day on it? No comment?

—One of the stories you have headlined on your cover says "An Expert Tells: Which Diet is Best for You?" You're *U.S. News and World Report* and you're doing *diet* stories? Doesn't that sound more like *Reader's Digest* or *Cosmopolitan* magazine to you? Do you also run recipes and advice on how to have a satisfactory sex life? Is that considered U.S. News or a World Report?

—And one more question before I let you go. You don't exactly put out a magazine that would appeal to teenagers. How many of your subscribers are seventy years old or older? Of those subscribers seventy years old, how many of them don't have gray hair?

Those are just a few of the questions I'd like to ask *U.S. News and World Report*. If I make a story out of it, maybe I'll run it with pictures of what the editors' wives wore at their last party.

The Presidential Breakfast

THE President had breakfast the other morning with a group of influential congressmen.

Isn't that job tough enough without scheduling breakfast with a lot of people you probably don't even want to talk to during the day? When did he shave? When did he read the paper? When did he do his thinking if he had breakfast with a lot of people and had to start talking first thing in the morning?

There are a few moments in each of our lives that should be preserved for ourselves alone, and breakfast is one of them. I don't want to talk to anyone at breakfast, and I'll bet the President doesn't either. Breakfast is not a social or even a family occasion on a weekday. Saturday or Sunday may be a different matter, but if I'm going to work, I don't want to diffuse my already limited ability to solve the problems I face at the office by getting into an argument about whether to paint the back bedroom or not.

Why would anyone ever schedule a business breakfast? Who can be gregarious over grapefruit? I can't help wondering, too, if it was a fake breakfast or a real one. Hadn't the President already had a little something before he sat down with all those people? I'll bet he had. I'll bet most of the congressmen had eaten, too. You couldn't get up in the morning knowing you were going to meet with the President of the United States, shower, shave or put your makeup on, drive half an hour to the White House, wait for the crowd to assemble and keep clearly in mind what you wanted to say without first having started up your system with a fast-breaker.

If the people who came to the breakfast had, indeed, already had breakfast, this gets an important meeting off to a start already tainted with falseness.

There are so many reasons why a breakfast meeting is wrong. The things we eat for breakfast don't lend themselves to conversation the way lunch or dinner items do. Dinner comes to us on a plate and we go at it in an established way. Breakfast is different. Someone ought to watch the toast, for example. You can't make toast in the kitchen and bring it out because it's cold by the time it gets to the table. The toastmaster not only has to make certain the toast doesn't burn, he has to anticipate who will want toast next and how much he should make because the average appliance makes only two slices at a time. Does the President make the toast? If so, how can he think about world affairs?

A lot of Americans eat cereal for breakfast. There are hundreds of kinds of cereal, but people who eat it regularly don't want anything else but what they're used to. Does the White House stock Grape Nuts if that's what the senator from Pennsylvania wants? He's not going to be happy with Post Toasties if he likes Grape Nuts or Cheerios. A Shredded Wheat person will simply not take Wheaties as a substitute.

Even if the White House kitchen can provide the cereals everyone wants, the problem isn't over. You can't discuss foreign affairs and eat cereal. No one wants soggy corn flakes, so once you pour the milk on, you have to stick at it until it's gone.

I suppose we don't know as much about each other's breakfast habits as we know about other eating habits. We all have lunch or dinner with other people quite often, but we seldom have breakfast except alone or with the family.

I think most Americans are grab-it-and-run breakfast eaters. The people who sit down to bacon and eggs, grits or fried potatoes and apple pie are rare now. Pancakes and sausage are Sunday morning. Even within a family, eating habits differ. When our family eats breakfast together, I gulp down my fresh orange juice while my wife dawdles—it seems to me she dawdles—over half a grapefruit. My mother wants coffee first. Brian sits there and stares a lot. Emily wants cereal, Martha toast. Ellen sits there asking how we can eat at that hour.

I don't know how the White House could possibly handle all the breakfast idiosyncrasies a bunch of congressmen would have.

I just hope the people who make up the President's schedule don't arrange any more breakfast meetings for him. He deserves his preserves in peace. The best breakfast advice I ever heard was very simple, and the President can have it: "Never work before breakfast and if you have to work before breakfast, have a little breakfast first."

Inside the White House

CONSIDERING how hard a man works to get himself into the White House, it's funny that once he gets there he can't wait to leave. I felt sort of sorry for the President when it looked as though he and Nancy weren't going to be able to get away to their ranch in California for Thanksgiving, but they finally made it.

Just about everyone who goes to work has a little trip to make to get there and then to get back home at the end of the day. We don't think of the process of getting ourselves to our place of work as a wonderful experience every day, but I suspect the President would like the White House better if he didn't have to live where he works. A trip back and forth to the office or the plant adds a little drama and punctuation to the day. When you get there, you're at work, and when you leave, you're off. There's nothing that definite for a President living upstairs over his office. They can always call him and ask him to drop down for a minute. As a result, I think all our Presidents have felt confined by the White House and they've all been anxious to take off for someplace else.

I wish I had a key to the White House so I could get in there and snoop around when the President and Nancy are away. I'd head straight for the private living quarters on the second floor. The public rooms for tourists don't interest me.

It's none of my business, mind you, I know that, but you can't hate me for being curious. There are all sorts of little things I'd like to know. I'd look at the edge of the coffee table in front of the television set to see if there was any evidence that the President props his cowboy boots up on it nights when he's watching the news broadcasts or an old movie.

What do they keep on the night table next to the bed? Any favorite book, or the crossword puzzle maybe? They don't strike me as crossword puzzle types, but you can't ever tell. What's in the drawer of the night table by the bed? A couple of letters from the kids? Or is the presidential bedroom a sterile affair without the personal junk lying around that gives all our bedrooms their special personality? Do they have so many people cleaning up after them that there's none of the typical bedroom debris at all? That's probably the case and that's why they can't wait to get away from it.

I wonder if the President's valet always lays out his clothes for him or does it only on state occasions? I'd like to look in the President's closet or his bureau drawers, just to see if he has some special old shirts in there that he wears on Saturday when he's lying around the house. The President often wears a sports shirt on unexpected occasions, and I'll bet he picks them out himself. No valet can pick out a sports shirt for anyone. (I don't actually *have* a valet myself, but I wouldn't think he could, anyway.)

I'd look in the refrigerator, too. I wonder what a President and his wife keep in their own private refrigerator. I've always thought the jelly bean thing was mostly for public consumption, but they've both probably got something special they like stashed away in the icebox. I can't imagine getting so important that I wouldn't want my own soft drinks there. What does the President eat Sunday afternoons when he's watching the game on television? That's the kind of information I'd be after if I could get into the White House and look around while Ron and Nancy are away.

I just think a look backstage at the White House would give me a better idea of whether Reaganomics will work or not. I wouldn't take anything.

Questions for the President

THERE are some things about any President of the United States we never get to know. Partly it's because it's none of our business, but partly it's because no one ever asks the President those questions. If I could have a fifteen-minute interview with Ronald Reagan, here are some of the things I'd ask him:

—First, Mr. President, what are the three things you'd least like to talk about?

—Is being President as good as you thought it would be?

—What do you hate most about it?

—Do you think you could ever go back to making movies?

—If one of the big studios offered you ten million dollars and a piece

of the action to make a film in 1985, would you be tempted to accept the offer instead of running for reelection? Twenty million dollars?
—Have you sneaked out of the White House at all without any protection?
—Who's the biggest jerk you've met in government? Democrat or Republican?
—How's the lung, still hurt? Not even when you laugh about it? You remember that joke?
—How much money do you carry on you? Ever have a chance to spend any of it?
—Could we just have a look at what you carry in your pockets and in your wallet?
—You like the water on the warm or on the cool side when you take a shower?
—I'm tired of this jelly bean thing. How do you feel about it?
—You dress beautifully except for your shirt collars. You have a fifteen-and-a-half neck, but you wear a size seventeen collar. How come?
—How many suits do you own? Do you know? How many pairs of shoes, or have you lost track of this sort of thing since you've been President? Does a President ever wear out a piece of clothing?
—You often read without glasses. Do you wear contacts?
—Would you just briefly explain the difference between Afghanistan and Pakistan?
—How do you handle your mail? Don't you miss going to the front door for it? Is it embarrassing not to have time to read letters from old friends? Do you ever sit down and write a letter to an old friend who hasn't written you, just for the hell of it?
—How's your spelling? Your arithmetic?
—I mean this as a general question. I'm not suggesting you're dumb, but how do you account for the fact that the smartest person in the United States doesn't get elected President? What do *you* have that the smartest person doesn't have that makes us all want you for the job?
—Tell me what you think of when I mention the following names:

John Dean
Henry Kissinger
Billy Martin
Jesus Christ
Jean Harlow. She would have been exactly your age.
Jacqueline Kennedy Onassis. Ever met her?
Picasso

Linda Ronstadt
Mike Wallace

Thank you, Mr. President!

The First Lady

THERE are two things I wouldn't want to be in this life. I wouldn't want to be the Queen of England's husband and I wouldn't want to be the President of the United States' wife. Other than that, I'd be willing to try anything.

Both of them are really terrible jobs, even though I imagine you get all you want to eat. Prince Philip seems to handle his position with a casual charm that keeps the press off his back, but our First Lady, no matter who she is, always gets it from reporters. Mamie Eisenhower, for example, was considered to be nice but a dud as a First Lady, because she never had any strong opinions or did anything that stirred up controversy. Rosalynn Carter, on the other hand, was accused of having too many opinions because she sat in on Cabinet meetings sometimes.

Our First Ladies are asked to be the impossible. Broadcast reporters and newspaper people expect them to be busy saints. They're expected to have strong opinions but not express them. They're expected to be good hostesses in the White House without spending any money. They're expected to be beautifully dressed without buying any new clothes.

Nancy Reagan is currently getting the same kind of criticism that Jacqueline Kennedy got when she was in the White House. You can tell from the way Mrs. Reagan keeps herself that she's used to having things right. She has good and expensive taste in clothes, furnishings, food and decorations. It's not a serious defect in her character.

It is my opinion that reporters write stories picking on First Ladies because they think people *like* hating our First Lady. They think the public will object to the President's wife buying the best dinner settings available for the White House if they cost six hundred dollars each. The reporters are probably wrong. It's a strange thing about Americans, but even the ones living on food stamps don't resent rich people and they especially don't resent the President and his wife living well.

I'm soft on First Ladies. I don't know what's wrong with me, but I've liked just about all of them that I can remember. I even like Ronald Reagan better now than I did before I knew he and Nancy like each other as much as they seem to. It's nice.

If I'm ever elected President, the nation is going to be in for a shock with its new First Lady. If reporters think they have something to write about with Nancy Reagan, wait until my Marge moves in. She just isn't the type who'd make a lot of adjustments in her life-style, and the press is going to love it.

If I ever made a speech in front of the fireplace the way Franklin Roosevelt and Jimmy Carter did, my wife would be apt to walk in right in the middle of it and tell me to go out and get more wood. If I made some important policy statement she disagreed with, she certainly wouldn't hesitate to tell anyone who asked that I was out of my mind.

I know darn well she wouldn't spend half her day in the White House Rose Garden greeting Girl Scout troops, because she plays tennis three days a week, has French Club on Tuesdays, bridge on Wednesdays and she comes into New York to go to the Philharmonic every Friday. She does our bookkeeping nights. There's just no way she's going to hang around the White House to shake hands to get me in good with foreign dignitaries if she's got something she wants to do. And if she's ever First Lady and does what she did last week, the press will have a field day. She paid $350 for four tiger maple chairs that aren't even new.

As I anticipate the kind of First Lady my wife would make, I know how President Reagan must feel when they get after Nancy.

Shortsightedness

THERE are days when I wouldn't get out of bed if I started thinking about long-term, serious problems. Fortunately I have the ability to worry about the small things that I might be able to handle if I get up. Instead of worrying about whether I'll ever save enough money to die on, I'll worry about whether there'll be enough hot water for a shower or enough coffee left in the can for breakfast. These are the kind of worries I can handle.

Our political leaders do the same thing with their problems. The President of the United States, for example, has only a very short time to pay off on his campaign promises so, when he gets up in the morning, he goes to work on trying to get the economy off the ground by Christmas. He doesn't worry about whether the world we know on earth may come to an end in the year 2000 through a series of nuclear explosions.

The mayors of our cities have to worry about feeding and housing the poor this winter and paying the police more money for the fight against crime. The mayor can't get up worrying about how to raise fifty million dollars to completely reconstruct the sewer system that engineers tell him will be totally inadequate in 1995.

It's a good thing and a bad thing that we're so shortsighted personally and publicly. It would be wise but depressing if we spent all our time worrying about problems in their order of real importance.

This occurs to me today because some recent news stories have forced me to think about a lot of long-term problems I don't like to think about. Some of them are national problems, some local. Some will have to be solved with public money, others, if they're solved at all, with private money. Like what? Like these:

—The cost of making all public facilities available to handicapped people in wheelchairs has been found to be so expensive in some American cities that programs to build kneeling buses and ramps everywhere where there are now stairs have been abandoned. Where do I stand on this issue? Why, I'm in favor of doing everything possible for the handicapped, of course. If it costs every American five thousand dollars in additional taxes? One thousand dollars? A hundred dollars? If it comes to hard cash, how much of it am I willing to give to support my sentiment? Very tough question and anyway, I've got to take a shower.

—The General Accounting Office says that forty percent of all our 514,000 bridges are in need of repair. Most of them were built in the 1920s and 1930s, right after we got the automobile, and naturally they're getting old and rickety. The General Accounting Office says we could spend forty-one billion dollars fixing our bridges. Am I for safe bridges? You bet I am. Would I increase taxes to get that much or reduce, say, Social Security benefits by twenty-five percent to get the bridge-fixing money? Before I answer that question, I think I'll make the coffee.

—Chemical dumps all across the country are slowly polluting basic underground water sources, and it could cost billions to clean them up.

—Real safety for nuclear plants could make them so expensive that they'd be economically impractical.

We know how to solve these tough, long-term problems, but either we don't have the money to pay for them or we're not willing to sacrifice any of life's pleasures today for our safety and security tomorrow.

But before I worry anymore about these important matters, I think I'll go out and make sure I can get the car started.

Why No "Good" News?

Last week I spoke to a group of people in San Diego, and by any standard you'd have to say they were above average. They were asking me questions about things I didn't know a whole lot about, but they didn't seem to mind and we were all having fun until one fellow got up and asked me the question that people in the news business are asked most often:

"How come you never report any of the good things that happen in this country?"

I say it's a question, but it's usually asked of news people in such a manner as to suggest they are the agents of a foreign government trying to bring down the United States of America.

There's something that people who ask that question don't understand, and I don't suppose anything I say here is going to help, but I'm going to say it anyway.

In the first place, news by its very nature is often negative. News is change, a deviation from what's normal or the way things have been. Mount St. Helens in repose is normal, and when it doesn't erupt you won't find pictures of it on page one. When it erupts it is a news story because it's an abrupt change that has a negative effect on the lives of a lot of people. You could say the same of a shipwreck or Congress. Congressmen are honest, for the most part, and it is only news when one of them steals and is caught.

My questioner in this case went so far as to suggest newspapers and television journalism ought to seek out stories that show America in a good light. In other words, he thinks we should put news to work creating an effect. We should choose our stories not for their news value, but for the impression they will have on readers.

I'm sure this man is good to his wife and children and works hard at his job, but he doesn't know a damned thing about what makes this country great and free. Who would he suggest choose these "good" stories about America? Could anything so important be left to editors? Wouldn't it be better to have a government agency oversee the choice? There's plenty of precedent for this around the world. Our government agency could take a trip to the Soviet Union to see how they do it there. It isn't as oppressive as we think. They just don't let the journalists create a lot of negative ideas in people's heads by letting them report "bad" stories. For instance, Russian readers never have to read about an airplane crash. Aeroflot, the Soviet airline, is run by the government, and why undermine confidence in the government—right, Ivan? Russians didn't have to worry about wheat production falling twenty percent below predictions in the Soviet Union this year either, because that bad news wasn't reported in the papers. They'll find out about it soon enough when there's not enough bread to go around this winter.

It's difficult for anyone in the news business to understand how anyone can think news ought to be used for any purpose but to inform. As soon as it is used to promote one good cause, such as patriotism, by having positive allusions to that cause inserted in its news columns, that's the end of a free press, and first thing you know Spiro Agnew is running against George Wallace for President.

There's no doubt about it, news is tough to take here sometimes. In a single day's paper, you can read of one politician calling another a liar, you can read of murder, drug busts, bribery of elected officials, dishonest police and twelve percent inflation, but if some Americans find it more difficult to believe this is a great country because of the negative stories they read about it, that's their problem. It's right for us all to love America because you have to love your own in the world, but we ought to love it enough and believe in it enough to know that it will stand up in open competition with any country in the world, even when all the unpleasant facts about it are known.

War Games

No coach of a professional team ever tells his players or the owners of the team that the opposition is going to be easy this year. That's not the way to motivate the players or the way to get the owners to spend more money on the team.

That's why our Army and Navy people are always telling us how dangerous and well armed the Soviet Union is. They figure the best way to get their budget raised is to scare us to death.

Every American probably ought to go to the toilet just once in Moscow. It would put the whole threat Russia poses for us in better perspective. When I see one of their tanks or one of those giant weapons they have rolling over the cobblestones in Red Square, I always wonder whether they're any better made than their toilets. Plumbing is one of the many modern inventions the Russians have not mastered. I am hard put to explain how they ever got a man in space and can only conclude that they still have enough German scientists left over from World War II to help them accomplish it.

Everyone who has ridden in a car made in the Soviet Union, raise his hand! What did you think? Would you compare it to a prewar Pontiac? How about a late model Hupmobile? Their best car, the Zev, is most like a cheap imitation of the last Packard, made in 1958.

It is simply impossible to be impressed with Russian technology if you go there. Almost everything that's impressive is impressive for its size—like the Russian army—not its excellence. With the possible exception of vodka, I can't think of a single thing they do better than anyone else in the world.

I don't suppose the military men on either side would like the idea, but what we ought to do is stage a sort of military Olympics with the Russians. I've drawn up a tentative schedule of events. The networks would be allowed to bid for the rights to televise the games and that income would be used to help defray defense costs.

—One-hundred-meter dash for tanks. This would be a test of speed.
—Combination marathon and steeplechase for tanks. This race of 26 miles 385 yards would be over an obstacle course. The unmanned tanks would be shot at periodically to judge their resistance to at-

tack. They'd also be judged on their gas mileage, endurance and how they looked under parade conditions.

—Guided missiles. Each nation would designate a target area somewhere in a deserted part of its country where no further damage could be done. We might indicate the Russians' target could be the South Bronx. Each country would see how close their missile with a small warhead on board could come to the target.

—Nuclear submarines. In this contest the competition organizers would put an empty freighter in the middle of the Pacific. We and the Russians would each start a nuclear sub from a neutral corner of the ocean. The first one to torpedo the freighter and leave the scene without looking for survivors would be the winner.

—The spy contest. Each country would be given twenty-four hours in which to hide a top secret document. The whereabouts of the document would be known by just ten people, and each contestant would be given a set of clues. Five spies from each country would be provided with false passports and American Express cards. They could try to buy one of the ten people or offer them sexual favors according to the sexual preference of their choice. The first spy team to find the other country's documents would be the victor.

These military Olympics might be held between any two countries when war between them became inevitable. Syria and Israel could save themselves time, money and bloodshed by having one now. Instead of attacking each other, nations would hold a contest to determine who would have won if they'd fought each other for real.

I'd love to see us take on the Russians in a contest like this. I've been to the bathroom in Russia.

The Russians

THERE are certain things in each of our lives that we look on with pride. Four years ago I was refused permission to enter the Soviet Union with a film crew for the purpose of making a television documentary. How's that for a feather in my cap? How many of my friends can say they were refused admission to Russia? I find ways to drop it into conversations all the time.

But I am deeply puzzled by the Russians. I can't make out what I think of them or decide what kind of people they are. My first contact with them was towards the end of World War II when the Allies were driving east and the Russians west, across Germany. On April 25, 1945, the armored division with which I was traveling as a reporter met the Russians coming from the opposite direction at the town of Torgau on the Elbe River.

For me the significance of seeing the beginning of the end of the war was overshadowed by the drama of the meeting of Russian and American soldiers, and by something that made Torgau a very special town. Torgau, it turned out, was the site of the huge Hohner harmonica and accordion factory, and that accident of wartime geography influenced my first impression of the Russians in an unreasonably favorable way.

Russian soldiers, free for the first time in years of having an enemy in front of them, went berserk. They smashed their way into the Hohner factory and took thousands of harmonicas and accordions. There was nothing exceptional about this. American soldiers often did the same thing. What made this exceptional was that half the soldiers in the Red Army seemed to know how to play an instrument.

Russian refugees who had been caught in Germany followed along behind the U.S. forces as they advanced, and when these displaced persons, many of them women, met the Russian soldiers it was a monumentally emotional moment. It was comparable, in many ways, to our entrance into Paris eight months earlier.

One of the refugee women must certainly have been a prominent soprano before the war, because the impromptu concert that began in the streets of Torgau with her great voice rising above the chorus of a thousand harmonicas and accordions was the most memorable musical experience of my lifetime.

The Russian soldiers seemed wonderfully free-spirited and uninhibited to me at first. The following day a small contingent of us crossed the Elbe to where the bulk of the Red Army was bivouacked, and it was a sobering experience. The Russian soldiers were free-spirited there, too. They just didn't seem to give a damn about life—theirs or anyone else's.

Many had acquired bicycles in their long drive across Germany, and they were riding them aimlessly around their camp. Each of them carried a short, badly made but effective little automatic rifle slung over his shoulder. I saw one Russian soldier grab a bike from another and start across a field with it. The one from whom the bike had been taken dropped to one knee, unslung his weapon and started firing close to the ground at the tires of the bike. They were wildly, irresponsibly, dangerously free-spirited. That was the first time I ever saw that element of the Russian character, but I've seen it on every level a lot of times since then. It is always chilling.

It may not sound, from what I've said, as though I'm puzzled at all about the Russians, but I am. I have met so many of them I liked and have so often been struck by the fact that, of all other nationals I know, they are most like Americans. They have produced great music and great literature which all of us enjoy and understand. Why can't we talk to them?

And there is another paradoxical side to the Russian character that provides me with some comfort when I watch their May Day parade of weapons cross the cobblestone Kremlin Square. When you pass a convoy of Russian vehicles, twenty percent of them have pulled over to the side of the road, broken down.

I have a sneaking suspicion the average Russian soldier knows more about harmonicas than engines.

The Coldback Problem

Imagine this:

The Soviet Ambassador to the United Nations comes before the General Assembly to plead for help with a special problem. It seems people from other countries keep sneaking across the border into the Soviet Union. Russia is such a wonderfully prosperous country, with Liberty and Freedom for all, that everyone wants to go there.

The problem is especially acute where Little Diomede Island, part of Alaska, is within two miles of Siberia across the Bering Strait. Americans keep paddling out from Nome in their kayaks and then swimming the last two miles to Russia in the middle of the night. In Russia, these illegal immigrants from the U.S. are known as "coldbacks."

Day after day, there are newspaper stories detailing the harrowing exploits of Swedish boat people who set out from Stockholm to cross the stormy waters of the Baltic Sea. Once in Poland, the

Swedes make their way on foot through Lithuania to freedom in the land of milk and honey, Russia.

In Moscow, a committee has been formed to try to help free Bob Hope, who has been placed in a detention camp in a remote section of Wyoming because of the bad jokes he's been making about the President of the United States. Hope has gone on strike, refusing to tell any more jokes at all until he's free to make bad ones.

The Free Hope Committee in Moscow has invited Bob to come to Afghanistan to entertain Soviet troops for Christmas, but U.S. authorities are afraid to grant him a visa because of the possibility he'd defect.

The U.S. doesn't want to be embarrassed again the way it was immediately after the World Series, when the New York Yankees went to Murmansk to play an exhibition game. At that time Dave Winfield, Ron Guidry, owner George Steinbrenner and two utility infielders to be named later chose to stay in Murmansk. They said they got better publicity in the newspapers there.

In Kansas, farmers are complaining because Russia is dumping cheap, high-quality wheat on the American market. Russian farmers, whose crops exceeded expectations again for the sixth straight year because of technological advances, are being encouraged by their government with price support programs that have enabled many of them to become multimillionaires.

In the case of many of the poorer Third World countries, the Russians have been giving their grain to help feed the hungry there, out of the goodness of their Communist hearts.

President Reagan decides that after a couple of years in office, he deserves a good vacation. He and Nancy go to Sochi, the Russian resort on the Black Sea. The President says the trip will be half work, half play. While he's in the Soviet Union, he hopes to be able to learn something about the way the Russian economy works so that he can apply some of those successful principles to our economy here at home when he returns . . . *if* he returns. Pictures show Brezhnev and Reagan lying around on the beach having some good laughs together.

In Israel, Menachem Begin makes a special plea to the nation, in an attempt to stem the flow of Jews leaving to seek freedom in the Soviet Union. Meanwhile, along the border separating Mexico and the United States, all customs officials and border police have been removed from their posts. Mexicans who used to come here as illegal aliens no longer wish to gain entry to the U.S. Their dream is to save enough money to make it to Moscow.

When these events come to pass, I'll believe we have a serious problem with the Soviet Union, but while everyone is trying to get out of there and into here, I'll continue believing they have more of a problem with us than we have with them.

VI:

OCCASIONS

Memorial Day

S o far, it looks as though we're all going to die someday.

That goes for you young people reading this, too. Don't think for a minute that you're going to get out of it, because you aren't.

It doesn't give us much to look forward to, and the Memorial Day weekend isn't much help. If we're all remembered after we go the way those who have gone before are remembered by us now, things don't look too good.

Like everything else you can think of—and for better or for worse—Memorial Day isn't what it used to be. A lot of Americans are vague about its origin and purpose, because the federal government has jiggered the day around in order to make it more convenient for the living. The hell with the dead.

It was originally called Decoration Day and was established specifically in 1868 to honor the soldiers who died in the Civil War. Friends, relatives and patriots used to decorate their graves with flowers. (The word used in the books I looked this up in is "strew." They used to "strew" flowers on the graves. That appeals to me. Flowers are very often too carefully organized in vases for my taste. It is presumptuous of anyone to try to improve on nature's natural and random arrangement of flowers.)

As years went by, the day became one on which everyone made a specific point of remembering their dead by visiting the cemeteries where they were buried and often putting flowers on the graves.

Uncle Bill always put flowers on Auntie Belle's grave every Decoration Day. Then he'd stand there and tears would come to his eyes.

Not many of us put flowers on the graves of our dead friends anymore, and with the price of flowers what it is, certainly no one strews them.

I'm always touched when I see someone doing it or when I pass a cemetery and see evidence that they have done it, but I'd like to make an announcement: I'd prefer that no one put flowers on my grave if I have one. I don't like the idea of flowers dying on top of me.

Visiting a cemetery on Memorial Day is an intense experience. It's a good thing to do, but it's hard to bring yourself to do it because, for most of us, cemeteries are just too sad to contemplate. They bring to mind thoughts we'd prefer not to think.

I've talked myself out of visiting cemeteries, and I hope it isn't because I find it so sad. I say to myself I don't go because I find it's meaningless. You're no closer to the person you loved (I say to myself) when you're there by their grave than you are when you're anywhere else. If you wish to honor them by thinking about them, you can do that anywhere.

A visit to a cemetery on Memorial Day or any other day does force the memory, though, and sometimes that's a good thing to do. I don't care about the flowers, but I'd like very much to have someone remember me long and often. Each of us hopes for this. We have some kind of dream of immortality, but we know in our hearts that at best we'll only be remembered for a generation or two.

I remember my father and mother, of course, and I remember their fathers and mothers. But who remembers my grandfathers' and grandmothers' grandfathers and grandmothers? Or theirs? Not me, and in the long hard history of the world, that isn't much time.

It's all too much to consider—and too depressing.

I suspect the best thoughts of old friends come not on specific days set aside for remembering them, but from the things we used to do with them and from the special way we do things because that was the way *they* did them. The life they lived is now part of our own.

It's about the only kind of memorial that means much.

The Summer List

Y ou can complain a lot about how bad things are and about all the changes we've made for the worse, but there's just no doubt about it, we've moved summer up by a month in the last twenty-five years and that's not all bad.

I use the word "summer" loosely. By summer I mean the beginning of the time of year when you're more apt to knock off a little early on Friday and be a little later getting at things Monday. You start watching less television, you put more miles on the car, and you take some time off work to plan your vacation. I mean, let's face it, friends. Who are we kidding? *Everyone* is cheating on vacation days now. If you get three weeks, you somehow manage to connect it to a long weekend, two sick days, one plain goof-off day and you make it into a month. Everyone's doing it.

Summer used to start on July Fourth, but those days are long gone. We're a month into summer by the time the Fourth of July comes along now. That may be the time we *officially* start our vacation, but usually we've been stealing a day here and a day there from the boss long before that. It probably accounts for why the Japanese took the car business away from Detroit, but I don't want to get nasty just when we're all about to enjoy ourselves.

I was relaxing over the Memorial Day weekend making plans for some jobs I want to do around the house this summer. It's a good list:

—The windowsills on the back side of the house where the sun hits are in bad shape. I ought to scrape and sand them down to bare wood and put two coats of paint on them.

—This would be a good time to go through those closets and throw out the stuff I don't want. I particularly want to get at the closets where we keep the suitcases.

—The lock on the kitchen door doesn't work very well. Maybe I better replace that or fix the one that's there.

—We really need another bookshelf downstairs. I'll make that and put it in. If I put it in the room with the television set, I guess I better take everything out of there first and paint the room before I make the bookshelves.

—One of the cars has been dripping grease or something on the garage floor all winter. They have a kind of detergent that cleans it up. I'll clean up the garage floor. While I'm out there, I'll clean out the garage, too. I don't think anyone's ever going to use that cheap plastic toboggan. I'll keep the two Flexible Flyers in case we ever have grandchildren and snow the same year.

—This would be a good time to go through those boxes of old newspapers I've kept. That takes a while, of course, because when I look at the paper I usually can't remember why I kept it and I have to read the whole thing.

—That strap holding the television aerial on the roof looks loose, and the aerial is facing a little more south than it used to. We don't get as good a picture as we did. I'll get the ladder out and get up there and straighten it out.

—Some of those bushes around the house have gotten out of hand.

I'll clean them out of there. I'll pile the branches and junk from the garage out back, and then maybe I'll rent a small truck and take it all to the dump someday.

—One of the first things I guess I'll do is feed the lawn. Lime and fertilizer. Before I do that, I've got to take the one wheel that doesn't work off the spreader and oil or grease the bearing. As a matter of fact, before I fix the wheel or fertilize the lawn, I really ought to feed the maple trees. I'll pound a crowbar about a foot deep into the lawn around the perimeter of the trees and pour tree food in them.

I've had a tough winter and I deserve a little time off, so I don't want to rush into these things. Maybe the first thing I'll do is lie down and take some weight off my feet. After all, that list was good enough for last year and the year before. It'll be good enough for next year, too.

Thanksgiving

WE need a good, quiet, low-key holiday once in a while, and that's what Thanksgiving is.

It's unfortunate that we've diminished the importance of the word "thanks" by using it so often when we don't really mean it. We say it so many times during the average day that there isn't much left to say when you really appreciate something someone has done for you, and want to thank him or her with a word of appreciation.

What we've done is to invent a lot of superlative forms of the word. We say "Thank you very much," "thanks a lot," "how can I ever thank you" and "thanks a million." A million what is not clear.

For the most part, polite people use these phrases as a matter of common courtesy. We can't hate people for being courteous but, the fact is, we're filling the air with junk phrases. When the man who fills my tank with gas for $19.75 gives me my quarter change and says, "Thank you very much. Have a nice day," my inclination is to say, "I'd trade your kind words in for a windshield wash."

The sign over the pump in one gas station I've been to several times says, "No charge if we fail to smile and say thank you." That's fine, but they no longer have an air pump. What I want is less thanks for my patronage and more service.

The junk phrase that has begun to irritate me is the one being uttered as a matter of course by checkout cashiers. You lug a load of groceries to their counter, unpack your cart, put it on the moving belt and they say "Will that be it?"

What do they mean "Will that be it?" Of course that'll be it. If it wasn't it, I'd have picked up what was "it" and put it in front of them with everything else.

Yesterday I bought about fourteen items in a supermarket, and the cashier gave me the inevitable four words. I said, "Yes." I gave her a twenty and a ten to pay the $26.50 I owed. She carefully doled out my change of $3.50, and when she finished I just stood there with the change in the palm of my hand and said, "Will that be it?"

The cashier looked at me as if I'd said, "This is a stickup."

"Will that be it?" I repeated.

"What do you mean?" she asked.

"I mean," I said, "will that be it? Just like when you ask me 'Will that be it?'"

The cashier just shook her head, relieved that I was just crazy, not violent.

"Have a nice day," she said nervously and looked at the next customer.

When it comes to the "Thanks" in Thanksgiving, I hope we don't use it without any thought the way we so often use the word. I've often thought it ought to be called "Appreciation Day," but I realize that just doesn't have the same fine sound to it that "Thanksgiving" does.

Most of us go through the average days and weeks of our lives using those meaningless junk phrases that have no real thought behind them. It takes a toothache, the loss of a job or a death in the family to make us recall how good things were when our teeth didn't ache, when we were employed and when everyone in the family was healthy.

The trick to being happy is to stop and think occasionally, during normal times, how good things are going. At this very moment at Thanksgiving, my teeth don't hurt, I'm making a living and my family is fine. I'm just going to take the day off and sit around appreciating how lucky I am, and I hope you can do the same.

Have a nice day.

The Christmas Holidays Limitation Act

F<small>OR</small> everything there is a season and a time for every purpose under heaven," it says in the Bible.

That was obviously written by some ancient sage who didn't anticipate that there would be so much money to be made off professional football in July and January. Money seems to be the only thing that affects the seasons anymore.

There may once have been "a time to plant and a time to harvest that which is planted," but now the natural season for things is ignored. The seasons are becoming a blur on the calendar. Between rushing into the next season too soon, the way they do with fashions in store windows, staying with the last season too long, the way the professional sports teams do, and completely ignoring the seasons, the way the fruit and vegetable purveyors try to, we're losing the four-season definition of our years.

Last weekend I went into the department store over on the highway nearest our home looking for a leaf rake. (We don't burn leaves any longer and I approve, but it makes fall a less clearly defined season of the year, too.) It turned out the store didn't have any leaf rakes, because they'd cleared out their garden department to make room for Christmas tree ornaments.

In order to help preserve the Christmas season, I propose a Christmas seasons law. It would be called the Christmas Holidays Limitation Act. Here are some of its provisions:

—Capital punishment would be mandatory for anyone caught selling Christmas ornaments before Thanksgiving.

—Magazines would be precluded from issuing three Christmas editions, the first in October. No magazine dated "December" or calling itself "Christmas Edition" could be made available before December 1.

—Mail order houses would have their mail boxes taken away from them if they sent out brochures offering Christmas gifts before Labor Day.

—Every Christmas tree sold would have to be dated, like a quart of milk. The tree would be tagged with the exact day on which it was cut down.

—It would henceforth be illegal for any store to have a sale sooner than two weeks following Christmas Day.

—There would be stiff penalties for any individual caught mailing out Christmas cards before the tenth of December.

—Insurance companies, funeral homes, hardware stores and real estate operators would be forbidden from mailing out anything to anyone that said "Merry Christmas" on it.

If this Christmas Holidays Limitation Act is made into law, it could be expanded at a later date to include provisions that might help preserve the integrity of all our seasons.

If we can't make this a law, perhaps the following item should be added to an updated Ecclesiastes: "There's a time for Christmas holiday celebration and a time when it's too early to celebrate the Christmas holidays."

Christmas Trees

THE people who think Christmas is too commercial are the people who find something wrong with everything. They say, for instance, that store decorations and Christmas trees in shopping areas are just a trick of business.

Well, I'm not inclined to think of them that way, and if there are people whose first thought of Christmas is money, that's too bad for them, not for the rest of us.

. If a store that spends money to decorate its windows has commerce in mind, it doesn't ruin my Christmas. If I pay nine cents more for a pair of gloves from one of the good stores that spent that much decorating its windows to attract me inside to buy them, I'm pleased with that arrangement. It was good for their gross and my Christmas spirit. I stay away from the places that pretend they're saving me money by looking drab.

I like Christmas above any time of the year. It turns gray winter into bright colors and the world with it.

I like the lights and the crowds of people who are not sad at all.

They're hurrying to do something for someone because they love them and want to please them and want to be loved and pleased in return.

In New York City, the big, lighted Christmas trees put up along Park Avenue for three weeks every year produce one of the great sights on earth.

There is a kind of glory to a lighted Christmas tree. It can give you the feeling that everything is not low and rotten and dishonest, but that people are good and capable of being elated just at the thought of being alive this year.

When I'm looking at a well-decorated Christmas tree, no amount of adverse experience can convince me that people are anything but good. If people were bad, they wouldn't go to all that trouble to display that much affection for each other and the world they live in.

The Christmas tree is a symbol of love, not money. There's a kind of glory to them when they're all lit up that exceeds anything all the money in the world could buy.

The trees in our homes do not look like the ones in public places and they ought not to. They look more the way we look, and we are all different. They reflect our personalities, and if someone is able to read palms or tea leaves and know what a person is like, they ought to be able to tell a great deal about a family by studying the Christmas tree it puts up in the living room.

Christmas trees should be real trees except where fire laws prohibit them from being real. It is better if they are fir or balsam, but Scotch pines are pretty, often more symmetrical and sometimes cheaper.

Nothing that is blue, gold, silver, pink or any color other than green is a Christmas tree.

A lot of people are ignoring the Christmas tree tradition, but just to review it, it goes like this:

You put up the Christmas tree Christmas Eve. You do not put it up three weeks in advance or three days in advance.

If you have young children, you put them to bed first.

As the children get older, you let them help decorate the tree.

As they get even older, you *make* them help decorate the tree.

When the tree is decorated, you put the presents around it.

You do not open presents Christmas Eve.

The first one down in the morning turns on the Christmas tree lights.

The best Christmas trees come very close to exceeding nature.

If some of our great decorated trees had grown in a remote forest area with lights that came on every evening as it grew dark, the whole world would come to look at them and marvel at the mystery of their great beauty.

So, don't tell me Christmas is too commercial.

Christmas Thoughts

Some Christmas thoughts:

—A Tuesday is the ideal day for Christmas. It gives us Sunday to sit back and think about what last-minute things we have to do Monday.

—You know you've left your shopping until too late when the clerks and the shopkeepers are in the back of the store drinking eggnog when you come in.

—If your Christmas tree fits in the living room easily, it isn't big enough.

—One person in a household is almost always a better wrapper and string tier than anyone else. It's usually a woman, and the presents she receives don't look as good because someone else wrapped them.

—When children grow up, leave home and marry, parents often think about moving to a smaller house. The fact is they need a bigger house when sons and daughters start coming home for Christmas with wives, husbands, and children of their own.

—There are always fleeting moments of depression at Christmas. If they're only fleeting, you're lucky.

—The perfume counters in stores seem bigger than ever this Christmas. I assume we can count on people smelling better in the near future.

—One of the most glorious messes in the world is the mess created in a living room where eight or ten people have just opened their Christmas presents. It should not be cleaned up too quickly.

—It's difficult to know when to put the turkey in.

—There are always a few presents that resist being wrapped at all. It is impossible to wrap a bicycle.

—Lunch doesn't fit very well into the Christmas Day schedule.

—Sometime during the afternoon of Christmas Day, the people in our house divide themselves between those who feel they need exercise and those who think they'll take a little nap. I personally like to get some exercise and then take a nap.

—I'd hate to be President on Christmas Day.

—Someone always leaves one gift upstairs or in a drawer somewhere and forgets to give it until late in the day.

—None of the tricks they tell you about helps keep the needles on a tree. You either have a good tree that was cut recently or a dry tree that was cut last month.

—Christmas trees stacked for sale are one of the happiest Christmas sights. The same trees, still there, unsold, the day after Christmas are one of the saddest.

—Dogs seem to love Christmas.

—Kids don't get electric trains as much as they used to.

—We always get at least three Christmas cards with names we don't recognize.

—Last year I read Charles Dickens' "A Christmas Carol" and couldn't get over how good it was. I guess everyone else knew but me.

—It's too bad that anyone has to go anywhere at all on Christmas, but there's usually some little bit of business to be done, even if it's only picking up someone at the station or getting the newspaper.

—Someone always thinks something has been thrown out with the wrappings, but it turns out not to be true. It was under something else.

—I have always ignored advice on how to carve a turkey, but last year I read where you could remove the whole breast and then slice it down, across the grain. Pretty good idea. Now if they'd produce a turkey with less white meat and more dark, my family would be pleased.

—I'd hate to work in a department store the day after Christmas, even more than I'd hate to be President Christmas Day.

—Is there an American alive who can put something back in its original wrapping and package if it was originally put there by a Japanese?

—Every year there are a few people for whom I see dozens of things but then there's someone else on my list for whom I can find nothing satisfactory.

Favorite Presents

WHAT are the best Christmas presents you ever got?

I was trying to recall my favorites.

My parents gave me a Buddy-L truck that was strong enough for me to sit on when I was five or six and I can still remember everything about it. That was certainly one of my best presents ever.

A year or two later they gave me a little steam engine that actually worked. It ran from a boiler that was heated with a can of Sterno. The steam made the wheels go round, but I'm a little vague about what the wheels did once you got them going. It was a wonderful little toy, but in retrospect I think my uncle, who was there that Christmas, had more fun with it than I did. It certainly didn't compare with my Buddy-L.

Another uncle used to give me some dumb thing he found in his attic. I never liked whatever it was, but he usually gave me a five-dollar bill and a twenty-dollar gold piece too. At the age of ten or so I preferred the cold cash to the gold piece because, of course, my mother never let me spend that. I don't know what ever happened to all those gold pieces he gave me. I suspect my mother might have cashed them in one of those years they were having a tough time. Mom wasn't very sentimental about things like Indian head pennies or gold pieces that I'd saved.

Considering that I got dozens of presents every Christmas, it's not very nice of me to have forgotten all but a few. I remember the year I got an Iver Johnson bicycle and the year I got a pair of high leather boots with a jackknife in a little pocket on the side of the right one.

Once you get over being a kid, there's no telling what Christmas presents are going to strike you as exceptional. I have a cashmere scarf a friend gave me about twelve years ago. It looked just like any other scarf when I got it, but I've never lost it and I've worn it a lot on very cold days. Scarves don't normally turn me on when I get one as a present, but this one has been special.

My four kids, grown now, have been great gift-givers. There's no reason I should be surprised, but I always am at how intimately they know me. It's fun to get a present you weren't expecting that indicates that the person who gave it to you knows you thoroughly well. (Most of us are modest enough to be grateful to be liked by anyone who knows us well.)

Brian gave me a Japanese dovetail saw last year that must have been hard to find. I still use the pasta maker Emily got for me five years ago, and I love the wood-identification book that Ellen found. It has little samples of more than a hundred different kinds of wood, describing their properties. Martha and Leo gave me a whole *case* of tennis balls. I love anything in wholesale amounts, but it had never occurred to me to buy a case of tennis balls.

One of my great all-time presents was given to me by Arthur Godfrey in about 1954, when I was working for him. He gave me a woodworking tool called a Shopsmith. It must have cost about two hundred and fifty dollars at that time, and I couldn't have been happier if I'd been six again getting that Buddy-L. I still have it and use it every single weekend of my life and often on a week night.

I realize how personal all this is. I even understand that a reader wouldn't care specifically about my scarf or my Buddy-L. When you write something like this, you hope it will be understood that the specific examples represent something more universal. By which I mean, I'm sure you've all had your own equivalent of my Buddy-Ls, tennis balls and five-dollar bills.

Whoopie!

THE compulsion people feel to have fun New Year's Eve has always irritated me, because I'm not any good at it. A little fun goes a long way in my life, and very often *fun* isn't what I most feel like having. Fun means to me gay, lighthearted, thoughtless activity. There are other ways I prefer to spend my time, and before you decide I sound pretentious, I'll tell you that I'd include sleeping as one of the other ways.

We have gone to the same New Year's Eve party with the same people for twenty-five years now. I always enjoy seeing those old friends; it's the fun part of the evening that I hate. Someone always feels obliged to break balloons and blow horns, and I have a terrible time trying to act as though I am having a good time. I always have this strong urge to go home and go down cellar with a good piece of wood and see what I can make of it. Unfortunately for me, my wife is able to throw herself into the fun in a genuine way, so I can hardly leave or even act as though I'm not having a good time.

I don't kid myself that hating New Year's Eve is any virtue I have. I'm envious of people who like it. Hating it has nothing to do with brains either, because I notice that some of the smartest people are capable of acting like the biggest idiots New Year's Eve.

People who like New Year's Eve are usually good dancers. They learn new steps easily because they aren't afraid of making fools of themselves by trying them. (This is the same ability that enables some people to pick up a foreign language quicker than others. I am a very slow learner of both new dance steps and foreign languages.)

New Year's Eve rings a false bell in my brain because it seems contrived. The best kind of fun is the kind that comes unexpectedly. As soon as you plan to have fun or set out to go somewhere and pay money for it, you're usually disappointed. Fun, like love, is something you either fall into, or you don't. It can't be arranged. And that's the trouble with the New Year's Eve kind of fun. It's phony. There's nothing spontaneous about it. The noisemakers were bought at the five-and-ten. The confetti was cut by machine and sold in boxes. The fun is compulsory, and if you aren't having any, you're a bad sport and a party-pooper.

It is fitting that the traditional New Year's Eve drink is champagne, because if there's anything I hate worse than compulsory fun, it's bad champagne, and I think it's all bad; some of it is just worse than others. I am uneducable when it comes to champagne. By the time it is served, I've usually had two drinks of bourbon, and when I put a glass of bubbling white wine down on top of those, it assures me an uncertain tomorrow. It is not the way to start the New Year.

There are always people who are left out of the New Year's Eve festivities. I suspect there are almost as many people who sit home alone as there are revelers (I think the word is). I wish I could convey to these people how lucky I think they are. They are able to view the whole idiotic ritual on television, thinking their own thoughts, feeling melancholy or lonely if they wish, but at least they are in command of their own situation. They can go to the icebox;

they can sit there staring; they can go to bed at 11:47 and forget the whole thing.

That's what I'd like to do some New Year's Eve. Whoopie!

Proverbs for the New Year

AT the beginning of a new year, I tend to get philosophical. When I get philosophical it's usually in a very minor way. I don't review Spinoza, Plato or Aristotle. I get thinking about proverbs and truisms, the philosophy of nonintellectuals.

This year I got thinking that some of those old sayings aren't true.

Take, for example, the saying "Beauty is in the eye of the beholder."

I happen to think that is not true at all. Some things are beautiful and some are not. If you don't know which is which, that is your shortcoming, or mine, but the quality of the object is unchanged. We all have different experiences that influence our attitude toward something, but the fact is that the world's most knowledgeable art experts would not disagree very much on which are the best paintings. You can say "Beauty is in the eye of the beholder" or you can say "That's your opinion," but once two people know all about a subject, they almost always agree. We disagree on things when one person knows more than the other.

"A penny saved is a penny earned." There's another truism that isn't true anymore. A penny saved won't be worth as much next year as it is this year. That's one reason why the government is going to let savings banks pay higher interest rates.

"You can't judge a book by its cover." Says who? Have you spent much time in a bookstore lately? If you see a book jacket with the title *Weekend Date*, bearing a picture of a buxom young woman wearing a dress with a neckline ending at her navel, you are not apt to mistake the book for an instruction manual on how to solve Rubik's Cube.

Of course you can tell a book by its cover.

"Haste makes waste." Baloney. Haste usually saves time. Most of us move too slowly. The fastest workers are the people who know how to do the job best. I can fuss with a little job of carpentry for days, but if we get a professional carpenter in to make some china closets in the dining room, he's finished before I'd have figured out where to put them. Haste only makes waste if you don't know what you're doing.

"To the victors go the spoils." I guess that used to be true in ancient times when one nation invaded another and took what it wanted, but it doesn't seem true any longer. The Germans and the Japanese lost the last great war, but they're doing better than the winners. "To the victors go the headaches" is more like it.

"You can't teach an old dog new tricks." It may be conceit on my part, but I think I've learned some things about writing that I didn't know ten years ago. And I wasn't a kid ten years ago, either. We all get set in our ways, but some of the ways we get set in are right. We refuse to learn new tricks sometimes because we're satisfied with the old ones we know. You *can* teach an old dog a new trick if you want to. Here's one old dog who is still learning some new ways to roll over.

"Seek and thou shalt find." Not in the bottom drawer of my dresser you won't find. I've looked and it isn't there.

"Don't put all your eggs in one basket." This may be good advice, but I've never been able to take it. I don't like to spread anything too thin, not my time, my money or my interest. I like to know where all the eggs are. I just try hard not to drop the basket.

"Crime doesn't pay." We all hope this one is true, but sometimes we have to wonder.

"Two can live as cheaply as one." How about that for a dated proverb? Even if two could live for the same amount of money as one, you'd hardly call it cheap. Two *can't* live as cheaply as one, either. Two can live for about twice what one can. Maybe even a little more.

I don't mean to put you off proverbs. There are still a lot that are true. We just ought to weed out the ones that aren't and stop saying them.

Resolutions

THE holidays are over and I assume we're all ready to stop goofing off and get down to work. I was so busy watching football over the long New Year's weekend that I never did get at making any resolutions for this year, but they're ready now. I hereby resolve:

—Not to try to lose weight or go on any diets. I know the diets don't work and there's no sense pretending they might.

—That trying to balance my bank statement is a waste of time. If there's a swindler in the bookkeeping department at the bank, I doubt if he's going to pick my account to steal from. In the future I'm going to assume the bank is right.

—To forget about trying to be in bed by 11 PM every night. I've worried about it for years and I'm not ging to worry about it anymore. On the average night I miss by twenty minutes. Many nights I miss by half an hour, and occasionally I don't get to bed until 12:30. In the future when that happens, I'm just going to enjoy it and find someplace to sleep on the job the next day.

—That the cellar and garage are fine the way they are. And so is the attic. Every Saturday morning for years I've awakened and started to make plans to clean them out. I hereby resolve not to suffer through another year of guilt about the mess in the basement, the garage and the attic. I like them the way they are and I'm going to leave them that way.

—Not to try and keep either a diary or careful income tax records. I've started both of these half a dozen times in the past ten years and never got past March with them, so what I did keep was a waste of time, because three months of records gets you you-know-where with the IRS. Next year I'll fake the whole twelve months.

I further resolve that:

—I'm not going to try to stand up any straighter in 1982 than I naturally stand, which is a little bent over. People have been nagging at me to "stand up straight" for as long as I can remember. My mother started at me when I was nine. I'm tired of worrying about it. Take me as I am, a little stoop-shouldered, or don't take me at all.

—There are books that I've always thought I should read and I never have. I'm not going to read them this year, either. *The Brothers Karamazov, The Grapes of Wrath, Moby Dick* and *A Farewell to Arms* will have to wait.

—There may be a day I miss reading the newspaper, too, and I'm not going to kid myself this year by leaving it on the coffee table as if I was going to get at it tomorrow or the next day. I know damn well I'm not going to read it then either, so if I haven't read today's paper by the time tomorrow comes, I'm throwing it out this year . . . whether it has my column in it or not.

—I'm not going to worry about never having been to Spain. I didn't go to Spain last year, I didn't go to Spain ten years ago and I'm not going to Spain next year, either. There are just too many places I've never been to to start worrying about one.

—No matter what time I go to bed, I'm not going to resist falling asleep on the couch at 9:30 PM in front of the television set. I've spent hundreds of miserable hours trying not to fall asleep watching terrible television shows, and I'm not going to do it anymore. If I feel like taking a little nap before going to bed, I'm going to take it.

—I'm not going to try to improve my tennis game. My tennis game is just fine the way it is, and any attempts I've ever made to make it better have failed.

At long last I have become convinced we are what we are. I am what I am and no amount of resolve will change me.

VII:

RICH AND FAMOUS

A Cat Story

THERE are certain things writers don't say about themselves, even if they're relatively honest, because they feel there's no sense going out of their way to lose friends.

It is for this reason that I've never revealed that I don't love cats, and I wouldn't be telling you now except that last weekend I had an experience with a cat that I can't get out of my mind.

It is necessary to say that I spend time in my woodworking shop only on Saturdays and Sundays, and the shop is half barn and half garage. When I finish working, I have to move a lot of wood and tools to the back and sides to get my car in. Early Saturday morning I took the car out and started moving my tools into place, when a full-grown gray cat scampered past me and out the door. It startled me, but there are mice in the rafters so I assumed it had been back there trying to kill one. A cat's idea of a good time is to kill something.

As I started to work, I heard the barest suggestion of a meow from behind a pile of lumber. I stopped and stood absolutely still until I heard it again. I may not like cats but I'm not stupid about them, and I realized that the cat had not been back there killing mice but having kittens.

I carefully moved some lumber and uncovered a grocery store–sized box that I'd left old clothes in. For a minute in the shadow I saw nothing but an old wool jacket, but then something small and white moved. It was four inches long, pure white and had a cocoonlike look. It was a kitten a few minutes old.

I instantly forgot that I hated cats. I felt terrible. For an instant I froze as the whole terrible truth dawned on me. There was only *one* kitten! I had interrupted the mother in the process of having a litter. No one hates cats so much that they wouldn't feel bad under these circumstances.

My enthusiasm for woodworking was gone, and I withdrew from the barn to think about what to do. It was cold and obviously the kitten wouldn't survive without its mother. I left the door open and went down to the house to call a neighbor who is not really a farmer but lives as one. She's a kindly person, but she's been around animals a lot and I think it makes you less sentimental about them. She said the best thing to do was to put the kitten in a plastic bag with a rock tied to it and drop it in the lake down the road. She was only thinking of the kitten, she said. She didn't want it to suffer.

I guess you have to face things like that if you live on a farm, but I don't live on one and I don't have to. I knew if I did that I'd never get it out of my mind as long as I lived.

For the next half hour I puttered around the house, with just an occasional glance up toward the barn, until my wife came home from the store. I told her I wanted to show her something and explained that I had a big problem without telling her what it was.

We tiptoed into the barn and crept up on the box. The kitten was gone!

The mother cat had gone somewhere else to have the rest of her litter and then sneaked back into the grocery box in the barn for the white one and carried it to safety.

I'm still not crazy about cats, but I'm sure mighty grateful to that one, and if I ever see that little white kitten around and can get close to it, I'm going to tell it what a good mother it has.

An Address to My Family on Economics

(Following is a transcript of Mr. Rooney's comments to his family at the dinner table the other evening.)

I AM speaking to you tonight, following your mother's beef stew, to give you a report on our family's economy. You won't like it and I don't like it. As a matter of fact, I hate it. Let's face it, we're just about broke.

The economic lesson I wish to make clear to you tonight is that we're putting out too much and taking in too little. I'm not going to subject you to my checkbook. Take my word for it, I was overdrawn twice last month. We're in worse shape than at any time since the operation on Brian's appendix.

So much for the details. Now I want to draw up the broad outlines of our new program for you. First let me say that it is with great reluctance that I am raising my own allowance. In order to do that, I am increasing the self-imposed debt limit of what I borrow from the bank, from the $21,000 I now owe on mortgages, car payments and miscellaneous emergency loans, to a new ceiling of $30,000. This will give me the necessary capital I need to accomplish the programs that I feel are necessary if this family is to survive. Also, I want to pay my dues at the club with some of it.

There is no quick fix, to borrow an expression from one of our economy's most successful businesses. We're going to have to start by cutting the least important programs we now maintain in this family. Money for education is going to be eliminated. I'm certain none of you wishes to be the product of a welfare society, and I am therefore giving each of you the opportunity to become self-made men and women. It's time to recognize, too, that it would be foolish for the women in the house to go out and get a lot of education that would qualify you for jobs you can't get. I am therefore asking you girls to limit yourselves to a high school education.

It's time to recognize we've come to a turning point. For too long we've overlooked the fact that the family, any family, has a built-in tendency to grow. We've come to the end of that, too. The population of this family is six now. It seems like just a few short years ago it was two. This is an increase of three hundred percent, during which time my income has increased eleven percent.

What happened to the family dream of owning this house without the bank being in on it with us? I'm sure you're getting the idea that things are going to be a lot tougher around here. For many years now, you have complained about the regulations that have been imposed on you by me. That's all a thing of the past. You can go anywhere you want when you want to. Just don't ask me for any money to get there on. And don't go there in the Joneses' Rabbit diesel, either.

For too long now, we've been falling behind the Joneses. We're inflated and they're not. We have three cars, they have two. We put an addition on this house, they closed off their attic and den. No man is prouder of his family's capacity for work than I am but, frankly, you're all lousy workers. We are no longer competing effectively with the Joneses. In the winter, we're pouring gasoline into our snow blower, they're out there shoveling whether it snows or not.

In two weeks, I'll be talking to you again about the specifics of how you've got to cut back on what you spend and how I've got to spend money to make money.

Travelers Checks

Every night on television, we're faced with these people in the commercials who have gone somewhere without any real money and are in a panic because they can't find the imitation money they took with them instead.

My question is this: Why do people keep losing their travelers checks? It seems to me there can be only two reasons: (1) The people who buy travelers checks tend to be more careless about things than the rest of us, or (2) there is something basically wrong with the way travelers checks themselves are designed that makes them easy to lose.

I should think all this scare talk about losing them would be very bad for the people in the travelers check business, because the basic idea I get from the television commercials is that, while you may be able to get your money back, it would probably have been easier if you'd just taken money in the first place and been damned careful what you did with it.

On television, when the person or persons who lost the checks comes up to the tour guide or the hotel manager, the person in a position of authority always says, "What kind were they?"

They almost always seem to be American Express. Now, American Express always seemed like a pretty good company to me and I think it's high time top management looked into the reason for so many losses. When American Express goes to the trouble of returning money to the loser, it must take a lot of man-hours and machinery. This must add to what they have to charge for the travelers checks in the first place. If they could get to the bottom of this problem of why all these people are losing them, they could charge less.

Losing something is one of the least pleasant experiences in life. It's frustrating because you can't strike out at it. The thing is just gone, that's all, and you don't know where. There's often something traumatic about an unnecessary loss that you don't get over. I don't buy travelers checks because I'd rather just lose the money if that's what's going to happen. Money would be less personal than checks with my name on them.

Maybe it would be a good idea if American Express gave a course on where to hide things in a hotel room. That could cut down on thefts. Putting money in the pages of the Bible is one way to hide it in a hotel room. I have a friend who carries a waterproof plastic container. He puts his money in that and hides it in the water closet behind the toilet, if the room has one. Sometimes I put my extra money in with the clean towels. There are a lot of good hiding places in a hotel room.

There are two ways to lose something, of course. You can lose it through your own carelessness, by forgetting where you put it, or someone can steal it. Neither way is any fun, but if it's stolen, at least you have the pleasure of hating someone anonymously. If you lose it yourself, it's hard to find anyone to blame.

I've lost a lot of things in my life. The things I lose most often that don't worry me very much are sunglasses, gloves and umbrellas. I often wonder who has ended up with all those gloves I've lost. Somewhere I suppose there is someone as good at finding things as I am at losing them.

The first thing I remember losing was a Boy Scout knife my father bought me when I was about eight. It was a bitter day. There was no American Express office near our summer camp, and they wouldn't have replaced my Boy Scout knife anyway.

The most dramatic loss I ever suffered was when I fell asleep in a helicopter while photographing the *Queen Mary*. My arm hit the lever that opened the door. The door flew open and my camera and tape recorder dropped into the water below. A jacket with my money and credit cards drifted down the freeway nearby. We landed, and a watchman for the *Queen Mary* said he knew of a diver who might find my camera. I said I guessed it wasn't worth it and I was more worried about the jacket anyway. Within minutes a Richfield Oil truck pulled up and the driver waved at me. "Saw the whole thing," he laughed. "Here's your jacket."

If American Express sold jackets instead of travelers checks, it would have made a beautiful commercial.

The Rich

THERE are always things in the newspaper that I can't understand in terms of how they affect me, personally. For instance, the other day I was reading about the tax cut. The reporter said that some people were complaining that it helped the rich and hurt the poor. Naturally I was trying to figure out, reading the story, which category the writer thought I was in.

I got thinking about how to tell the rich from the poor. It's harder than it used to be. It used to be anyone making over $18,000 was rich, but these days I suppose you're eligible for food stamps if you're only making $18,000.

There are some dependable ways you can tell when someone is rich. If someone doesn't carry any money, the chances are he's loaded. I'm not sure about rich women, but I know rich men don't usually have a nickel with them. Years ago I had a friend named Steve Schlesinger who had made a bundle on the Red Ryder comic strip by selling it to newspapers and to Hollywood for Grade B movies. Steve would go into any restaurant in the world, order drinks and dinner for a party of ten, and then worry about what to do about money when the check came, because he never carried credit cards or cash.

Another way to tell a rich person from a poor person is one I learned years ago when I worked for a morning news broadcast. We often had important people on it as guests, and I began to notice one thing that the rich men had in common. They never wore overcoats.

Nelson Rockefeller must have been on the show five times on different winter days, and he never wore an overcoat or carried one. It was a long while before I realized he was so rich he didn't need one. He was never out in the cold, because all he ever did was walk the ten feet from his chauffeur-driven limousine to the building, and anyone can stand that much cold. For all I know, Rockefeller didn't even own a raincoat or an umbrella. Most of the restaurants a rich person would eat in would have canopies that extended to the street.

Bankruptcy seems to be another sign of great wealth. You never hear of any poor people going bankrupt. It's always the rich.

There are dozens of ways to tell when someone is rich . . . they keep the same car for ten years, they're slow to pay their bills, they're bad tippers and all they read in the newspaper is the stock market report and the sports page. In France you're considered rich when the company starts mailing your check to you twice a month instead of paying you in cash every week. That still leaves me uncertain about whether I'm rich or poor. My check is mailed but it's mailed every week and it's a darn good thing, too, because I need the money.

An Equerry

THE royal family doesn't carry any money in its pockets. That's the single most interesting piece of information I know about British royalty. When Prince Charles goes someplace, he doesn't have a shilling on him because he has someone who takes care of money for him.

He can complain all he wants about his lack of privacy, but he has to admit that never having to worry about money makes up for a lot. Kings, princes and even presidents have valets who lay out their clothes and butlers who bring fruit, toast and coffee to their bedrooms in the morning. I know they all have chauffeurs who drive them where they want to go and a lot of places they don't want to go. Those are all things I don't mind doing for myself. I don't need any help reaching in the bottom drawer for my underwear or putting sliced bread in the toaster, but I sure would like to have one of those guys follow me around and take care of paying for everything.

The prince has something called equerries. Equerries used to just take care of the royal horses, but now they do a lot of odd jobs around the palace for a prince, and one of them is taking care of the cash.

Can't you imagine how handy it would be to have someone like that? You go to the supermarket, load up the cart with everything that strikes your fancy, including several expensive gourmet items you'll probably never use. You trundle your cart up to the line at the checkout counter, then you just drop it and squeeze past the other customers. When the cashier looks up at you, you motion over your shoulder with a jerk of your thumb and say, "My equerry will take care of this. Put the eggs in a separate bag, please."

Not having to carry money would make life so much easier. Just not having to decide what to do with the pennies, nickels and dimes that collect on top of the dresser would be a relief.

I often make a forty-mile drive from New York City to Connecticut. There is a one-dollar toll bridge, one forty-cent road toll and another thirty-five-cent one. You can use the automatic toll gates only if you have the exact change. That means to go through all of them without waiting in line at the manned gates, you have to plan in advance to have six quarters, two dimes and a nickel or some comparable combination. That takes a lot of planning. If I were a prince, I'd have no problem. My equerry would have change coming out his ears.

My equerry would be an expert on tipping, too. I've traveled a lot and eaten in a great many restaurants, but I'm never sure what I should tip anyone. My equerry would know. I'd never worry about whether I'd tipped the right amount again. My moneyman would know exactly what he ought to give the bellboy, the porter at the airport and the waiter in the restaurant. When I went to a fancy restaurant with a waiter, a captain and a headwaiter, he'd know what to give each of them. I never have. On those occasions, I'd start to leave the restaurant and as I passed the outstretched palms, I'd just smile and say, "Thank you. It was very nice. My equerry will grease that."

The idea of a money handler appeals to me especially this week, because Tuesday I did what I haven't done in years. I actually got stranded in a small town in upstate New York without enough money to buy gas to get home. I asked several gas stations if they'd take a check or one of my credit cards. They gave me the kind of look that made me feel half my size. I went into the branch of a bank whose president in the main office fifty miles away had been a classmate of mine in high school. If you don't want to feel like a jerk, don't try to get a teller to cash a check by explaining to him that you know the president of his bank.

The thing to do in a case like this is to get yourself an equerry, like Prince Charles.

Awards

Most of us have an award we've been given, collecting dust somewhere around the house. It may be a bronze medal for a third-place finish in a camp swimming meet or a citation of merit for having collected more than a thousand dollars for some charity, but everyone can point with pride to something he or she has won in a lifetime.

I'm as susceptible to the pleasure of being given an award as anyone, but award-giving worries me. There is often a fine line between who's being honored, the individual getting it or the organization giving it. A lot of times the presence of the recipient does more honor to the giver than the getter.

This doesn't seem to me to be the way awards were meant to be given. Something's gone wrong. During the last month of his tenure as the CBS News anchorman, Walter Cronkite attended something like eighteen dinners, lunches or special awards ceremonies in his honor.

Cronkite is too nice a man to decline when someone says they want him to show up at one of their functions so they can honor him, but he must have gotten awfully tired of it. He must also have wondered, at least once or twice, if the honor wasn't being bestowed on him principally as a means for the sponsoring organization to sell a lot of tickets to the dinner.

I'm even a little suspicious of an award I've just been offered. During my college years I belonged to a fraternity that I'm not going to name. I enjoyed being with a good group of guys, but when I left college I had no interest in maintaining any relationship with it.

It wasn't as easy to drop the association as I thought. The national group started mailing letters to me almost immediately after college. They wanted me to pay my dues so that I'd get the monthly magazine and continue as "a member in good standing." I didn't want to stand anywhere with them, but they continued to follow me with hundreds of pieces of mail over the years. They sent things like too-good-to-pass-up group insurance pitches, brochures with great buys on watches and jewelry bearing the insignia of the organization, and travel package offers.

I got so fed up with mail from the organization that I started returning everything with my name on it, marked "deceased." The mail stopped coming.

Recently, the fraternity discovered me again on television. They think I'm wonderful and they want to reward me. They want me to be an honored member and they want me to come to their annual banquet to accept an award.

One of the good things about me is that I'm not as nice a person as Cronkite. I don't *want* their award and I'm not going to their banquet to accept it, because I'm just egotistical enough to think there's some question about who'd get the most out of my being there. While I'm not exactly Walter Cronkite, the organization offering me the award isn't exactly the Nobel Prize Committee, either.

Colleges have been in the business for years of giving awards to people they think can do them the most good. If you look at the roster of people to whom any university is giving its honorary degrees, you'll notice more of them are rich than smart. College authorities always sprinkle a few legitimate academic people in their list of honorees, but they never pass up the man who flunked out after his second semester but went on to become chairman of the board of his company and a multimillionaire.

On a bookshelf in my house, there's a small, tarnished cup with most of its thin plating of silver gone now. I won it for writing an article in my school magazine when I was fourteen, and I wouldn't swap it for any award in the world. When they gave it to me, they meant it.

A Realist's Horoscope

THE astrologists who say they can predict what our day is going to be like, based on the position of the stars in relation to the date of our birth, don't usually hit it with me. For one thing, they're unrealistically optimistic. I've been doing some gazing myself recently, and I'm going to take a shot at some horoscopes. This is more apt to be the way things will go:

Aries (Mar. 21–Apr. 19) You are a wonderfully interesting, honest, hard-working person and you should make many new friends, but you won't because you've got a mean streak in you a mile wide.

Taurus (Apr. 20–May 20) Take advantage of this opportunity to get a little extra sleep, because you're going to miss the bus again today anyway. You will decide to lose weight today, just like yesterday.

Gemini (May 21–June 20) A day to take the initiative. Put the garbage out, for instance, and pick up the stuff at the dry cleaners. Watch the mail carefully, although there won't be anything good in it today, either.

Cancer (June 21–July 22) This is a good time for those of you who are rich and happy, but a poor time for those of you born under this sign who are poor and unhappy. To tell you the truth, *any* day is tough when you're poor and unhappy.

Leo (July 23–Aug. 22) Your determination and sense of humor will come to the fore. Your ability to laugh at adversity will be a blessing because you've got a day coming you wouldn't believe. As a matter of fact, if you can laugh at what happens to you today, you've got a sick sense of humor.

Virgo (Aug. 23–Sept. 22) Learn something new today, like how to spell or how to count to ten without using your fingers. Be careful dressing this morning. You may be hit by a car later in the day and you wouldn't want to be taken to the doctor's office in some of that old underwear you own.

Libra (Sept. 23–Oct. 23) Major achievements, new friends and a previously unexplored way to make a lot of money will come to a lot of people today, but unfortunately you won't be one of them. Consider not getting out of bed today.

Scorpio (Oct. 24–Nov. 21) You will receive word today that you are eligible to win a million dollars in prizes. It will be from a magazine trying to get you to subscribe, and you're just dumb enough to think you've got a chance to win. You never learn.

Sagittarius (Nov. 22–Dec. 21) Your efforts to help a little old lady cross a street will backfire when you learn that she was waiting for a bus. Subdue impulse you have to push her out into traffic.

Capricorn (Dec. 22–Jan. 19) Play your hunches. This is a day when luck will play an important part in your life. If you were smarter, you wouldn't need so much luck and you wouldn't be reading your horoscope, either. You are a suspicoius person, and it will occur to you that astrologers don't know what they're talking about any more than your Aunt Martha.

Aquarius (Jan. 20–Feb. 18) You are the type of person who never has enough money to do what you want. Don't expect things to get any better today, either. As a matter of fact they might get worse. Intensify your relationship with your bank and any friends you have who might be able to lend you a few bucks.

Pisces (Feb. 19–Mar. 20) You will get some very interesting news of a promotion today. It will go to someone in the office you dislike and will be the job you wanted. Don't lend anyone a car today. You don't have a car.

Returning to College

IF I thought I'd live to be a hundred, I'd go back to college next fall. I was drafted into the Army at the end of my junior year and, after four years in the service, had no inclination to return to finish. By then, it seemed, I knew everything.

Well, as it turns out, I *don't* know everything, and I'm ready to spend some time learning. I wouldn't want to pick up where I left off. I'd like to start all over again as a freshman. You see, it isn't just the education that appeals to me. I've visited a dozen colleges in the last two years, and college life looks extraordinarily pleasant.

The young people on campus are all gung ho to get out and get at life. They don't seem to understand they're having one of its best parts. Here they are with no responsibility to anyone but themselves, a hundred or a thousand ready-made friends, teachers trying to help them, families at home waiting for them to return for Christmas to tell all about their triumphs, three meals a day. So it isn't gourmet food. You can't have everything.

Too many students don't really have much patience with the process of being educated. They think half the teachers are idiots, and I wouldn't deny this. They think the system stinks sometimes. I wouldn't deny that. They think there aren't any nice girls around/

there aren't any nice boys around. I'd deny that. They just won't know what an idyllic time of life college can be until it's over. And don't tell me about the exceptions. I know about them.

The students are anxious to acquire the knowledge they think they need to make a buck, but they aren't really interested in education for education's sake. That's where they're wrong, and that's why I'd like to go back to college. I know now what a joy knowledge can be, independent of anything you do with it.

I'd take several courses in philosophy. I like the thinking process that goes with it. Philosophers are fairer than is absolutely necessary, but I like them, even the ones I think are wrong. Too much of what I know of the great philosophers comes secondhand or from condensations. I'd like to take a course in which I actually had to read Plato, Aristotle, Hume, Spinoza, Locke, John Dewey and the other great thinkers.

I'd like to take some calculus, too. I have absolutely no ability in that direction and not much interest, either, but there's something going on in mathematics that I don't understand, and I'd like to find out what it is. My report cards won't be mailed to my father and mother, so I won't have to worry about marks. I bet I'll do better than when they *were* mailed.

I think I'd like to take a one-semester course in reading and interpreting the Bible. I haven't known many people who have actually read the Bible all the way through in an intelligent way, and it comes up so often, I'd like to be pressed to do that. There was a course in Bible at the college I attended, but I didn't take it. It was taught by the organist, and I'd want someone better than he was.

There are some literary classics I ought to read and I never will, unless I'm forced to by a good professor, so I'll take a few courses in English literature. I took a course that featured George Gordon Byron, usually referred to now as "Lord Byron," and I'd like to take that over again. I did very well in it the first time. I actually read all of *Don Juan* and have never gotten over how great it was. I know I could get an A in that if I took it over. I'd like to have a few easy courses.

My history is very weak, and I'd want several history courses. I'm not going to break my back over them, but I'd like to be refreshed about the broad outline of history. When someone says sixteenth century to me, I'd like to be able to associate it with some names and events. This is just a little conversational conceit, but that's life.

If I can find a good teacher, I'd certainly want to go back over

English grammar and usage. He'd have to be good, because you might not think so sometimes, but I know a lot about using the language. Still, there are times when I'm stumped. I was wondering the other day what part of speech the word "please" is in the sentence, "Please don't take me seriously."

I've been asked to speak at several college graduation ceremonies. Maybe if I graduate, they'll ask me to speak at my own.

Haircuts and Frank Costello

How many times have you had your hair cut?

My hair is beginning to curl in back and obviously I have to go to the barber today. I don't like going to the barber. Having someone fooling around with my hair isn't unpleasant, but when it's over I never look the way I'd hoped to look. I want to look great and I never do.

One of the problems for most of us is that we really look best when we need a haircut the worst. When you have it cut off, it gives you a brand-new, shorn look that you don't want. Women who have just too obviously come from the hairdresser never look good to me. I'd rather have them a little rumpled and windblown.

I always tell the barber the same thing: "Don't take much off." While he's snipping away I think he's not taking enough off, but the next morning, after I've taken a shower, it looks as though he took too much. I've decided the reason for this is that when he combs it for the way he cut it, it looks fine, but after a night's sleep I go back to combing it *my* way and it doesn't look the same at all. It doesn't fit the haircut he gave me. Some of the strands of hair that I put on the right of my part were cut to go on the left of my part, and vice versa.

In spite of quite a bit of dissatisfaction, most of us are loyal to a barber. Women are a little more fickle. They get mad at their hairdresser every once in a while and move to another. Manny has been cutting my hair for about eight years now and I wouldn't think of going to anyone else, even though I pass ten barbershops to get to his. "Manny" is an unlikely name for a barber, but I'm comfortable with him, even though I don't know his last name.

It takes a while to break in a new barber, and I suppose it takes even longer to break in a hairdresser. I originally went to Manny when my former barber retired, and I was apprehensive because there was a sign in the window that said "Men's Hair Styling." I didn't want my hair "styled," I wanted it cut. I don't want to tell you how much it costs. It always costs more if the barbershop claims to style your hair instead of just giving you a haircut.

The first barber I ever had was named Kelly. Just as I don't know Manny's last name, I didn't know Mr. Kelly's first. I was young, and he was just "Mr. Kelly" to me. A haircut cost thirty-five cents then, and I hated getting one. I had to sit there in a line of chairs Saturday morning while the other kids were out playing. There were always a few kids getting their hair cut Saturday, and Mr. Kelly took us in order. We each moved up one chair when he finished the kid he was working on. Every once in a while a grown man would come in Saturday morning, and Mr. Kelly would put him right in the chair ahead of all of us kids. It never occurred to me at the time that it was wrong. In retrospect I doubt that the adult was going to do anything more important with the rest of his Saturday morning than I was going to do with mine.

The most interesting place I ever got my hair cut was in a big hotel barbershop in New York. They charged the same as everyone else, but the shop was very classy and they had twenty barbers. Every time I went there to have my hair cut, Frank Costello, the mob leader who was later gunned down but survived to die a natural death, was holding forth. He was having his shoes shined, he was getting a shave and having his nails done, all while the barber snipped lightly at the hair on his head.

About the fourth time I went there I said to my barber, "Gee, it's a coincidence but every time I've come in here, Costello has been here too."

"He comes in here every day and stays all morning," the barber told me.

Everyone who worked there liked Frank Costello. He was a great storyteller and a big tipper. He even began saying hello to me with a big smile, so I kind of liked him too.

We all have our good points and our bad points. Frank Costello was a gangster responsible for dozens of murders and half the crime in the United States during the 1940s and 1950s, but, on the other hand, he was good to his barber.

The World Affairs Test

IF you read the papers much, you read recently that according to a test given to three thousand college students on a hundred and eighty-five campuses, American young people are ignorant about world affairs.

According to the study, paid for by the federal government and Exxon, two of the richest organizations in the world, the students averaged a score of less than fifty percent correct on one hundred and one questions.

I sent for a copy of all the questions that the Educational Testing Service and the Council on Learning produced for the $630,000 it cost, and they mailed me a book two hundred and eighty-nine pages thick that included not only the questions and the answers, but a lot of high-flying conclusions by the people who gave the test.

I'd like to send the whole thing back to the Educational Testing Service with a failing mark. It may or may not be true that college students aren't very knowledgeable about world affairs ("global understanding," the testers always call it), but the testers ought to go back to the fourth grade and start all over again learning how to write a sentence in plain English.

As an example of a question that must have given some smug satisfaction to the person who wrote it, but would be considered tortured English by anyone reading it, consider Question #72:

> Each religion below is correctly matched with countries in *each* of which it either predominates or has a significant minority following EXCEPT
>
> 1—Christianity . . . Greece, Lebanon, the Philippines, Ethiopia.
> 2—Islam . . . Saudi Arabia, the Soviet Union, Indonesia, Nigeria.
> 3—Buddhism . . . Japan, Thailand, Vietnam, Sri Lanka (Ceylon).
> 4—Hinduism . . . India, Pakistan, Afghanistan, Kampuchea (Cambodia).

If the object of the test was to make students stop to figure out what the question was, that's a good question. If the object was to test them on their knowledge of foreign countries, it is unnecessarily complicated. I suspect if you asked Henry Kissinger that question, he'd reply "Vhat?"

How about this as a substitute: "Which religion listed below is not usually associated with all the countries after it?"

The correct answer, by the way, according to the testers, was #4. Must have something to do with Kampuchea.

Before they start the test, the students are asked a lot of personal questions. To give you some idea of how the whole thing is going to go, the first personal question is this: "1. Age (in years)."

I can't for the life of me think how the testers thought the students were going to answer that question except in years, but I suppose that's why I've never been given $630,000 to administer a test.

In an introduction, the project director begins by writing, "While the required breadth of content coverage seems to have been the surprise in development of the knowledge or cognitive area, method was unquestionably the potential stumbling block of affective measurement."

Could you play that over once more, professor, for the kids in the back of the class? The professor has about ten words he's in love with. He loves any "perception," but especially "self-perception." He prefers "replicate" to "duplicate," and he never passes up a chance to drop in "cognitive" or "component." He doesn't call the test a "test," he refers to it as "the survey instrument." He never talks about radio and television. He calls them "the electronic media."

I personally thought his most devastating criticism of American college students was when he said, "The estimates reveal deficits in knowledge and affect through comparisons with explicit criteria and reasonable implicit criteria."

You get an A in Government Grants, professor, but an F in English.

We Need More Time

THE object, I think, is to get as much living into your life as possible. Most of us live at half speed most of the time, and we lose a lot of good living that way. We goof off or don't have a plan, or for one reason or another don't do much on many of our days.

A lot of us will live more than eighty years, but say we have just eighty years. That's 29,220 days. Maybe if we had a chart with every one of those days numbered and painted on a wall in a backroom or down in the cellar, and crossed one of them off every day, we'd be more careful to live them fully.

It seems to me that science could help us. There are a lot of things that take too long. Sleeping, for instance, takes too long. The average person sleeps seven hours a day, and some need eight. Why can't scientists develop something that makes us sleep faster? Should that be so hard? They've compounded all these mind-bending drugs that do nothing but get us in trouble; isn't there something they could make that would give us a night's sleep in a couple of hours? I wouldn't want it to be any shorter than two hours, because the whole business of getting ready to go to bed and lying there thinking for a little while before you fall asleep is a very pleasant process and a good part of a full life. I'd like it if I could get it all out of the way in two hours, though, so I could wake up refreshed and get back at all the wonderful things I like to do that I can only do when I'm awake.

There are several other things that take too long, too. I'd like to be able to get some exercise faster every day. I play tennis once or twice a week, but the exercise is incidental to the fun playing tennis. I don't want to cut down on the hour and a half tennis takes me. I want to be able to give all my muscles a workout in about ten minutes on the days I don't play.

Telephone calls take too long, and that's something we can all do something about. It takes too long to get started and too long to end the average phone call. Someone should rewrite the etiquette of the phone call and eliminate all the "How are you's?", the

"What's new with you's?" and the "Have a nice day's." We could each save a week a year by shortening our phone calls.

Dressing ourselves takes too long. I don't know whether any study has ever been done or not, but I suspect that women are able to get dressed quicker than men. The average man who wears a coat and tie puts on ten pieces of clothing. They're all different and present different problems in draping them over the body. With the exception of the brassière, women's clothes are simpler and easier to put on. A man's two shoelaces alone more than make up for the time it takes a woman to hook up a brassière. A lot of women go out into the world with only five pieces of clothing on. If men are going to save time for living by cutting down dressing time, men's clothes have got to be simplified and some of them eliminated.

There are some things that take a lot of time that might seem like a waste that are not. Sitting and staring, for example, is not wasting time. We all need to do more of that and you can't speed up staring, and I wouldn't want to if I could.

It just seems to me that science hasn't always put its effort in the right direction. We all need more time for living, and if they can't work it out so we each get at least one hundred good years, then they ought to find a way for us to get more into the years we have.

Morning People and Night People

ARE you consistently dumber during some hours of the day than others? I certainly am. I'm smartest in the morning. You might not think so if you met me in the morning, but that's the fact. After about 11:30 AM, my brain begins getting progressively duller, until by late afternoon I can't remember my middle name. It is morning as I write. My middle name is Aitken.

Each of has his best hours. The people who have to have a cup of coffee to activate their brain in the morning are the slow starters. I have a cup of coffee to get my body going, but my brain starts up without it.

It's always best if what we are coincides with the way we wish we were. It doesn't happen often to most of us, but both morning people and night people seem to be pleased with themselves the way they are.

I know I'm pleased to be a morning person. I think it's best. I associate it with virtue. It works out best for me, too. Not perfect, but best. I get to work very early, taper off around noon and have a very unproductive period between about 1:30 and 4:30. Unproductive periods are important too, you know.

Somewhere around 4:30, my brain begins to stage a mild comeback, but by then it's time to quit and go home.

I feel sorry for the people who think best in the evening and I'd like to tell you why. Night people awaken grudgingly. They dread getting up but eventually drag themselves out of bed, put themselves through their morning ablutions and stumble to work hating every minute of it. By noon their metabolism is finally moving at the same speed as the current of activity that surrounds them and they begin to blend in. It is now lunchtime.

In the early evening, after the sun has gone down and the rest of the world is settling in, they're ready to go. They waste some of their smartest hours, when they should be most productive, watching some of the dumbest shows on television.

Prime time television was designed for those of us who are smartest in the morning. By 8 PM, we've lost most of our critical faculties, and "Dallas" and "Laverne and Shirley" are just perfect for our level of intellectual activity. Even if we don't like them, they don't bother us enough to make it worth our while getting up to turn them off.

The night people sit there doing the crossword puzzle or reading the paper and grumbling because there's nothing on the tube worth watching.

It seems apparent to me that we ought to rethink the whole pattern of our daily lives. We've got to make some changes.

If each of us really does need seven hours' sleep, it would probably be better if we took it in shorter periods. I often get more sleep than I need or want all in one piece during the night. Even when I go to bed at 11:30 and get up at 5:45, which is my habit, there's something wrong with just lying there in one place for six hours and fifteen minutes.

I'll bet it would be better for both our brains and our bodies if we took our seven hours in sections instead of all at once. Say we slept for three hours between 1 AM and 4 AM, two hours from noon until 2 PM and another two hours between 7 PM and 9 PM.

This would give us the same seven hours, but better distributed over the twenty-four-hour period.

There are some problems that would have to be worked out, of course. The reason all of us now try to get what is known as "a good night's rest" is not because that's the way our bodies like it, but because the whole civilized process of going to bed and getting up is such a time-consuming activity that we couldn't afford to do it three or four times a day. And, of course, if it took the night people a couple of hours to get going again after each sleep period, they'd be less help than they are now. A personal opinion, you understand.

And, of course, there are other questions that would have to be resolved. When, for instance, would we change our underwear, take a shower and make the bed?

Rules of Life

WHAT follows are some rules of life:

—Don't pin much hope on the mail, and when the phone rings, don't expect anything wonderful from that, either.

—If everyone knew the whole truth about everything, it would be a better world.

—Any line you choose to stand in during your life will usually turn out to be the one that moves the slowest.

—The best things in life are not free, they're expensive. Good health is an example.

—If you wonder what anyone thinks of you, consider what you think of them.

—Don't take a butcher's advice on how to cook meat. If he knew, he'd be a chef.

—Anything you look for in the Yellow Pages will not be listed in the category you first try to find it under. Start with the second. Keep in mind cars are under A for "automobiles."

—Not everyone has a right to his own opinion. If he doesn't know the facts, his opinion doesn't count.

—If you think you may possibly have forgotten something, there is no doubt about it. You've forgotten something.

—Happiness depends more on how life strikes you than on what happens.

—The model you own is the only one they ever had that trouble with.

—Hoping and praying are easier but do not produce as good results as hard work.

—Wherever you go for whatever reason, it will turn out you should have been there last week.

—When you buy something, it's always a seller's market. When you sell something, it's always a buyer's market.

—The same things keep happening to the same people.

—Enthusiasm on the job gets you further than education or brains.

—Money is not the root of all evil.

—Every so often you ought to do something dangerous. It doesn't have to be physical.

—Patience is a virtue. Impatience is a virtue, too.

—All men are not created equal but should be treated as though they were under the law.

—The people who write poetry are no smarter than the rest of us, and don't let them make you think they are.

—Patriotism is only an admirable trait when the person who has a lot of it lives in the same country you do.

—Apologizing for doing something wrong is nowhere near as good as doing it right in the first place.

—If you want something you can't have, it is usually best to change what you want.

—The only way to live is as though there were an answer to every problem—although there isn't.

—New developments in science and new inventions in industry don't usually improve our lives much; the most we can hope is that they'll help us stay even.

—You may be wrong.

—You should be careful about when to go to all the trouble it takes to be different.

—It is impossible to feel sorry for everyone who deserves being felt sorry for.

—One of the best things about life is that we are happy more than we are unhappy.

—Not many of us are able to change our lives on purpose; we are all permanent victims of the way we are, but we should proceed as though this were not true.

VIII:

WHAT WE DO

Don't Do It Yourself

WHAT we need is a Don't-Do-It-Yourself Movement in this country. A lot of us are sick and tired of doing it ourselves. We'd like someone else to do it for us and we're willing to pay them. In the future, the man-of-the-house, whether he be male or female, would only do the odd jobs he felt like doing. If he didn't feel like doing them, he'd call someone and they'd come. *This* is how to create employment.

I'm not any kind of economist. When they print those graphs in the business sections of the newspaper, I can't make heads or tails of them. I don't care whether the chart goes up and down in columns, sideways in bars or roller-coaster style across a sheet of graph paper. I don't understand them. But I have a basic idea of what makes money go 'round.

Money goes 'round when *you* have something that *I* want, and I work hard enough making something other people want, to pay you for what you have. It's that simple. If I make paper and you fix cars, it's silly for you to try to make your own paper or for me to try to fix my own car. Neither of us is ever going to get to Europe that way.

What we have to do is draw the line. Neither of us will any longer waste our days off botching some job we don't know how to do. We will call for help and then retire to the living room with a drink to watch television. When the job is done we will pay for it.

Each of us has to get over the notion that the other person is getting paid too much for what he does. We can no longer be surprised when an experienced carpenter asks eighteen dollars an hour and averages five hundred dollars a week. Or whatever the figures are. What we have to do is pay him and then set out just a little earlier in the morning and hope we can bring home at least five hundred dollars a week to stay ahead.

The professionals have to do their part, too, if this Don't-Do-It-Yourself Movement is going to get off the ground. Some jobs are considered too small for an expert to bother with. That's where you professionals have to swallow your pride. Even if it's only a leaky faucet, come anyway. I'm not going to suggest electricians should drop by to change a light bulb, but when the chain-pull switch goes in the closet, don't turn down the job because any idiot ought to be able to fix it. I'm the idiot and I can't fix it.

They talk about the shortage of scientists and doctors, but have the people who talk about it tried to get anyone to fix one broken windowpane? Or to fix the flue in the fireplace? These are the experts America is short of. We've put them out of business by doing it ourselves. You can get men to erect a steel and granite skyscraper and you can go to the Yellow Pages and locate someone who will install a plate-glass window, but where are the professionals who will put a new pane in the basement window?

If the law of supply and demand really works, we're going to be paying more for a bricklayer in a few years than for an atomic scientist. That's because the Do-It-Yourself Movement has had us all laying our own bricks these past twenty years and putting bricklayers out of business. Thousands of bright young people are going to MIT every year, but how many are learning to lay a brick?

Trying to get an electrical appliance fixed is harder than trying to get a brick laid. If something small is wrong with anything, you're in big trouble. If the breakdown is major, you're lucky. It has to be sent back to the factory. They don't fix it. They don't know how, either. They remove the faulty part and replace it with a new lifetime self-lubricating built-in factory-sealed unit.

We've got to encourage the small operators in our neighborhoods to fix things for us. We shouldn't have to try to do it ourselves, and we shouldn't have to send it to the factory. I'm tired of buying oil by the quart at the supermarket instead of having it changed at the gas station. I'm even tired of putting shelves in the closets in my house. I don't care how small the job is. I'm willing to Not-Do-It Myself and pay an architect $27.50 for fifteen minutes' advice on where to have the carpenter I'm going to call put the shelves.

Tony

My relationship with Tony has lasted twenty-five years now, and I don't know whether to end it next spring or not.

I got thinking about it over the weekend, when I was raking

the last of the leaves out from under the bushes. The place just doesn't look as good as it used to.

The house isn't huge and it's on about two-thirds of an acre, and when we first bought it I spent several hours every week getting the lawnmower fixed and cutting the lawn, in that order. In about the fifth year I decided cutting the grass was something I didn't want to do any more of. I found Tony. Tony had an old pickup truck, a big, battered mower, and although it seemed like a lot of money to spend just because I was too lazy to cut my own lawn, I turned the whole thing over to him.

For four years, he cut the grass at the original price, but I noticed that toward the end of that year, he had a helper with him quite often. At the beginning of the fifth year, Tony said he was going to have to charge more. I wasn't happy, but it seemed reasonable that his prices should go up like everything else, so I agreed.

It was a satisfactory arrangement for fifteen years. By then Tony was in his middle sixties and still able to work hard, but he had a brand-new truck now, a new gang mower, a lot of other equipment and three people helping him.

I wasn't usually home when the lawn was cut, so all I ever saw were the results. The lawn always looked better on Tuesdays, but I began to notice he wasn't getting as close to the trees as he used to. The grass in the slate walk was left long and weedy, and very often he wasn't cutting the grass on the other side of the hedge by the road at all.

One Tuesday I stayed home because I had an appointment with the dentist later in the morning. I was wasting time, puttering around the garage, when an old truck swept into the driveway. Three men jumped out, rolled an old mower down the ramp,

I watched from the garage window, amazed at what I saw. While one of them sped around major parts of the property on the mower, a second made a few swipes at some tall weeds on the edge of my wife's garden and the third got back into the truck and smoked a cigarette.

In twenty minutes they had the mower back up the ramp, ready to leave.

I came out of the garage and walked to the truck.

"Where's Tony?" I asked them.

"He don't come no more," the one smoking said. "He's too busy. Too much work. He's in other truck."

"You didn't do a very good job," I said. "What about the tall grass you left over by the cellar door?"

"Next time," he said. "We get it good next time. Rained Friday and we way behind. Too much work."

I offer this story because it's only my house and my lawn, but it says a lot about what has happened to America. Everyone is an entrepreneur. Figuring a way to make a buck comes ahead of thinking about how to do the job better. Tony realized that if he hired another crew, got more customers and did the job quicker and sloppier, he could make more money.

So, I don't know what to do next spring. Tony will call with another price increase, I know that. I also know the job won't be very well done. He's charging me roughly four times as much as he charged when he started cutting my lawn.

To tell you the truth, I'd tell Tony I'm going back to cutting the grass myself again next year, except for one thing. I'm making about four times as much myself as when I first hired Tony.

Waiting for the Floorsander

I SENSED something was wrong the minute I walked in the kitchen door. Two small tables from the living room were over by the refrigerator, and the big Chinese lamp from the table with the magazines on it was next to the radiator in the kitchen. There was a pile of papers and magazines on top of the radiator.

What was wrong was that my wife had made arrangements to have the living room and dining room floors sanded and she was getting ready. All I wanted to do was sit down, have a drink and watch the news. All she wanted me to do was help move the furniture out of the living room and roll up the rug. She wanted me to disconnect the television set and move that, too.

I don't like to think and lift on the same day. My days for lifting are Saturday and Sunday. During the week I try to do my thinking or, at least, worry over why I am *unable* to think. This lifting request led to a confrontation between my wife and me, the details of which I'd prefer not to talk about.

Now, two days later, we have reestablished relations because we have a common enemy. He is listed in the Yellow Pages as John the Floorsander. We are plenty mad again today, but this time not at each other. We're mad at John the Floorsander because he never showed up.

The compromise arrived at the other night was that I *did* sit down and have a drink and watch the news, but then, after dinner, I violated my rule about not *lifting* on *thinking* days by moving the furniture out of the living room.

At nine yesterday morning my wife called me at the office, something she does only in times of life's most serious emergencies. She announced that "the men" hadn't come yet. I asked if she had called John the Floorsander's number. She said she had but that she got an answering machine. The answering machine doesn't do floors.

At ten she called back to say they still hadn't arrived, but that she had reached *Mrs.* John the Floorsander, who said they'd be there shortly.

There was something ominous about the rest of the day for me. My wife never called again to say that they had come or they hadn't but I know her well. She was home, burning with anger. She was too mad and frustrated to talk at all.

When I got home my worst fears were realized. The floors were just sitting there like always, dark brown, worn, stained and unsanded. The house was a shambles, with pieces of furniture balanced on top of each other, out of their natural habitat. There was no place to sit, no place to drink, no television set to watch.

Now I'm thinking of suing John the Floorsander. I wonder what chance I'd have if I sued him for forty-eight dollars? My wife waited for him full time between 8 AM and 2 PM before she gave up and left the house the other day. That's six hours. Would eight dollars an hour be too much to ask for her waiting time? She's college-educated, a former mathematics teacher and as good at waiting as anyone else. Certainly her waiting time is worth forty-eight dollars.

Why is it that the people we call for help with jobs around the house so consistently fail to show up when they've said they would? They assume our time is worth nothing to us. Is this some kind of occupational disease that spreads from plumber to tree surgeon to television repair man to floorsander? I'm resigned to the fact that doctors don't make house calls, but do I have to bring my house to the floorsander?

And even when they come, your problem is always so difficult, highly unusual, time-consuming and hard-to-get-at that they're unable to do it until next month.

What We Do

WE know very little about each other when it comes to the work we do. I have some very good friends in the business world, but I don't really know how they spend their days. People often come up to me and ask me what I do. They know I write "those little columns in the newspaper" and they know I appear on television, but they ask what I *really* do.

The confusion comes, I think, because whatever it is we *really* do doesn't take very long. If someone digs a ditch with a steam shovel, he isn't actually digging for much of the day. A woman who takes care of a family and a home isn't usually doing anything at any specific moment that she could tell anyone about. A football player who makes half a million dollars a year as a running back probably isn't actually running in a game for an hour a year.

We all understand a writer when he's typing, a business executive when he or she is making decisions and a ditchdigger when he's digging. It's what each of us does with all the rest of our time that we don't understand about each other.

My father spent his life selling paper mill felts. The felt is vital to papermaking because it keeps the wet sheet of pulp flat while it rolls over hot steel rollers and dries, but until he took me on a trip with him through the South, I never understood why he was away for two or three weeks at a time.

He would travel for hours to get to a paper mill and then wait for hours more, as salesmen often do, to see someone important enough to make an expensive purchase. More than half the time, they didn't buy anything and that was the end of the day for him. It might take him two days to get to the next mill, and they might not buy anything either.

There's always a lot of unexplained time in any job, and if you aren't the one doing the job, you're never going to understand it. I mention all this because most of us are unfair in our assessment of the work others do. It often seems to us that we're working hard while other people are goofing off.

This lack of understanding most of us have for other people's work accounts for why we usually think our own job is pretty interesting, but that our neighbor's job is dull. It's hard to believe, but most people like what they do. They aren't just putting in their time to make a living. I have visited a lot of factories and talked with men and women doing repetitive jobs on a production line. Those of us who don't work on a production line feel sorry for those who do, but those who do don't feel sorry for themselves. More often than not it gives them a feeling of satisfaction every time they put a piece of something together.

My father loved to sit around talking to other people in the paper business. I remember spending hundreds of hours at the dinner table when he had business guests, listening to details that bored me to death. All of us do that. We like talking to people who do the same thing we do. The political conventions are great fun for anyone in the news business because there are so many other news men and women there to talk to. The great AP columnist Hal Boyle was a good friend of mine. I was standing in a group with him one day and a woman said, "You must meet a lot of interesting people in your business."

Hal had met every important person who had lived in the world between 1934 and 1974. He looked at the woman with a little smile on his face and said, "I do . . . and most of them are other newspapermen."

My father would have said the same thing, but he would have thought most of them were other papermakers.

I have a feeling that most people who don't like what they do wouldn't like anything they did, no matter what it was.

Breaking in a New Boss

I'M not looking for sympathy, but I'm breaking in a new boss, and you all know how trying that can be. He seems like a nice, bright young fellow. He's got all kinds of education and I think he shows promise. He's got a lot to learn about being my boss though. How to be my boss is not a course they teach in college.

Because being a boss is such a terrible job, I try to look at it from their point of view. One of their biggest problems is that most of us have had a lot more experience being bossed than they've had bossing, and that gives us the upper hand. I started out being bossed as a private in the Army and I've had at least one boss over me ever since, and sometimes I've had dozens. I can't tell you how many bosses I've had. Bosses come and go in my life and I keep plugging away at the same job no matter who it is. Eventually the boss gets involved in some upper-level political intrigue in the company, and he gets fired or promoted or moves into limbo in a special office they have for limbo bosses, and another boss moves in over me.

A new boss usually feels he ought to be decisive and take command. He wants to show who's boss. He doesn't really know what he's doing, though, and he doesn't want to make any serious mistakes, so he starts moving people from the third floor to the second floor and vice versa. This causes some grumbling, but is called reorganization. Often the boss will bring in a friend and appoint him his assistant. The assistant is then my boss, too.

The relationship between bosses and workers has changed. Bosses don't fire people the way they used to. Usually there's a union, a contract, a company tradition or the threat of having the firing called discrimination, so bosses don't get to do much firing anymore. For instance, this new boss of mine would have a devil of a time firing me, although if I'm fired after he reads this, you'll know I was wrong.

The trouble for my boss is that while we've just had a little disagreement, I know how to do something that makes money for the company and he wants to keep me doing it. He just wishes I was nicer to bosses. He likes me but I make his blood boil, and when he goes home at night I imagine he complains about me to his wife.

My new boss is only kind of a junior boss and that must be hard on him, too. *He* has a boss and even *his boss* has a boss, so that puts him well down the boss ladder. He's in charge of me, but his boss has been a great old friend of mine for thirty-five years, and I even have reason to believe that his boss's boss, the boss of all bosses at the company, thinks highly of my work. That's an untenable position to put a junior boss in, and my heart goes out to him.

It seems to me all of us ought to be able to hire our own bosses. Who, after all, knows more about the kind of person who would make us a good boss than we do? You can't buy the kind of experience I've had with bosses, and if you did buy it, you'd probably want your money back.

I'd choose a boss who didn't ask dumb questions, who didn't

have meetings and who protected me from making a fool of myself. I want a boss who isn't honest with me all the time. If I write something that isn't very good, I want to hear him say, "Very good!"

In spite of a little trouble here at the start, I think I'm going to like this new boss. I certainly wish him all the luck in the world with me.

Job Applicants

I T'S easy to mistake words for thoughts when you're writing anything. I write so much and make the mistake often enough myself that I'm very aware of it in other people's writing.

Every year at this time a lot of bad writing comes my way from recent college graduates looking for jobs. What these kids really want is *my* job, but they're smart enough to avoid actually saying that, although many of them give the impression that they really wouldn't be satisfied with my job. They'd take it just to get a start in the business.

Today I got a letter from a young man graduating from college, and he had his own stationery with his name and address embossed on it. Classy for a kid out of work, isn't it? He told me he had written for his college newspaper, majored in economics and thought "60 Minutes" was a good television show, so he'd like to work on it as a writer or producer. I don't have the heart to tell him "60 Minutes" producers don't have their own personal stationery, or he probably wouldn't want to work there.

Here's an exact quotation from another letter:

"I am interested in participating at a television station because the dynamics occurring within a communications environment are those which interest me and have a direct relation to my long-range career objective."

Another letter from a young woman graduate says, "The enclosed résumé enumerates my relevant credentials and skills, specific experiences and related interests."

Come off it, will you, kids? This is your old friend Andy. I'd like to help. I think it's great when people want to get in the same business I'm in. It means we've made it look good to you and that's flattering, but you're never going to make it with prose like that. You meant to sound important, but it came out pretentious.

Almost every letter I see refers to the job seeker's "skills and talents." Just having skill and talent doesn't sound very impressive to them, I guess, so they lay it on me and make both of them plural for added effect.

There are not many of us who don't know the desperation of not having a job. Everyone else is inside and part of something. You are outside and all alone. You feel like the only unemployed person in the world and wonder if anyone ever went through his or her whole life without being able to get a job.

Being faced with the necessity for getting a job is a frightening prospect for a young person just out of college. The chances are the graduate has been brought along under the protective financial wing of loving parents, but at the moment of graduation there is an unspoken understanding. "It would be nice if you got a job now." They aren't throwing their offspring out of the house, but there is a pressure to go to work that everyone understands. It produces a kind of terror that I am familiar with, but there is no reason it should produce so much bad writing.

One summer when I was in college, I got a job helping a rigger in a big paper mill. We did heavy odd jobs, and the man I worked with knew how to do everything, it seemed to me. One day our job called for him to run a steam shovel. He just climbed on board and went to work with it.

Later, we were sitting on a pile of bricks eating our lunch, and I asked him how he learned to operate a steam shovel. He told me, and what he said was a lesson for young job seekers who say they can't get a job because they have no experience and can't get any experience without a job.

"I read an ad in the paper," he said. "This guy was looking for someone to run a steam shovel. I got the job and climbed up there and started fooling with the pedals and the hand levers. About an hour later, the boss knew for sure I didn't know what I was doing and I got fired. A week later, I got another steam shovel job and I only lasted four days, but by this time I knew a lot about how they worked. The third job I got, I kept because I had all this experience."

Somehow that approach to a job appeals to me more than a letter from someone who enumerates his relevant credentials and skills, specific experiences and interests.

My suggestion would be that they all learn how to shovel first.

Fired

There's something wrong with anyone who's never been fired from a job. If I'm ever in a position to hire someone, I'm going to be very suspicious of anyone who comes in looking for work with a résumé that doesn't include the information that he or she got the ax a couple of times either for incompetence or insubordination.

What's all this resignation business? Doesn't anyone get fired anymore? You read the business pages of the paper, and presidents of corporations are always resigning. From a cushy $250,000-a-year job? Come on, fellas. We're not business tycoons, but we're not that dumb. You got canned.

The whole business of resignation is false, and it's part of a new philosophy we seem to have adopted. There aren't any losers anymore.

At children's birthday parties, they play games in the cellar or the backyard, and the parents having the party give away prizes. It doesn't matter how well or poorly a child plays a game, he'll probably get a prize anyway, because the adults don't want to damage his little psyche by making him think he might not always win in life.

Most high school teams in any sport have co-captains now. Sometimes they have more than two. No one wants to hurt the feelings of a good player by choosing someone over him for the job. Sometimes the professional football teams have six or eight men trot out on the field for the coin-tossing ceremonies. They're all co-captains. Not a loser in the crowd.

I hope we never decide not to hurt the feelings of one of the presidential candidates by electing co-Presidents. One President is plenty.

Last week I read where someone won $34,000 for finishing second in a golf tournament. Second! Imagine making $34,000 for *losing* a game of golf!

The President is always saying he's "sorry" to have to accept someone's resignation. If he was really sorry he shouldn't have accepted it. All of us are using the word "sorry" too lightly. We're always saying we're sorry when we aren't really sorry at all. It's all part of the same refusal to face things as they are.

We're excusing everyone for everything. A boy of seventeen kills the man who runs the candy store for $1.35 and a Tootsie Roll.

The boy's parents find a bloody hammer under his bed and they confront him with it.

"I'm sorry," the boy says. "I killed him, but I didn't mean to do it."

The father looks at the mother with tears in his eyes and says, "At least he's honest."

The next day the neighbors are interviewed by a television reporter. They all say he was a nice quiet boy who always went to church. They don't bother to say that he was a bully, that he'd been stealing all his life and that he was rotten through and through.

We keep letting ourselves off the hook. No one wants to judge anyone else by strict standards for fear he'll be judged by them too. No one wants to say to someone on the job, "You just aren't good enough. You're fired."

Big Business

THERE is no more interesting or important work in the world than being a reporter. That's my opinion, of course, and being at least in part a reporter myself, it's natural I'd think so.

The word "reporter" isn't quite right for the job, though, because it only describes half of it—the half where you tell the reader or the listener what you've learned. The other half of a reporter's work isn't described by that word. That's the part where he or she collects the information before telling everyone about it. That's the hard part.

A good reporter ought to be part detective, part puzzle solver and part writer. A reporter has to find the facts, piece them together so they make sense and then put them down on paper in a manner that makes them clear to everyone else.

People often complain about inaccuracies in news stories. They talk as if reporters were deliberately inaccurate or in on some conspiracy, and this is almost never the case. No reporter sets out to write a distorted or inaccurate story. They sometimes come out that way because reporting is hard and some reporters aren't good enough. They also come out that way because a lot of people are very secretive and tell the reporter what they'd like to have printed, not what the facts are.

This all comes to me now, because this morning I got a letter from a boyhood friend I haven't seen in thirty-five years. I knew him as "Bud," but now his letterhead says his first name is "Cornelius" and he's vice-chairman of a big corporation in Oregon. He was a wonderful friend when I was young, but I don't think I know him at all now. After some personal words, he went into a tirade against the news organizations.

Being attacked by businessmen isn't a new experience for most reporters. I heard Lewis Lapham, then editor of *Harper's Magazine*, attacked one evening by a Texan with huge coal interests in Montana.

"You people know nothing about business," the businessman yelled at Lapham.

"You're right," Lapham yelled back, "and it's probably a damn good thing for business."

When businessmen say newspapers and television don't cover business very well, it makes me nervous because in many cases I think it's true. It is also true that it is business's own fault. Information about any business in town is almost impossible to get. They say they have a right to privacy, and I agree with that, but they're being stupid by not being more open, and I'll bet they *won't* agree with me.

It is possible now, because of the Freedom of Information Act, to get information out of government. It has been a great thing for the American public but, of course, there is nothing like that requiring business to reveal *its* business. Some businessmen claim they are secretive so their competition won't find out what they're doing and how, but that seldom stands up to inspection. The competitor usually knows *all* about the business across town. As a matter of fact, the plant manager used to work for Acme and one member of the Board of Directors of Allied is a former vice-president of Acme.

The average business keeps its operation a deep, dark secret mostly out of habit. If the secret is not dark, at least that's the impression they give the American public. It is Mike Wallace standing in front of the locked gates saying, "They refused to talk to us." It suggests there is something evil going on in there, and nine times out of ten there is not. The average businessman in America takes as much pleasure and pride from making a good product as he does from the money, but you'd never guess it from the public image he projects.

You could take the books and the production plans of any good company in America and print them on page one of the local newspaper, and it wouldn't alter the operation one bit. That includes printing the salary of every maintenance man and executive in the place. Business is simply too secretive about everything. They don't have anything more to hide than the rest of us.

The corporate public relations people who do the best job for their company are the ones who lay it on the line. They tell you the truth, even if it hurts a little. The ones who do their companies the most damage are those who try to hide little mistakes or keep information secret that would be better made public even when there is no law demanding it.

The American public is as suspicious of Big Business as it is of Big Government, and what I'd like to say to my old friend Bud is, business would do itself a favor and get better reporting in newspapers and on television if it opened up. If the company is making a good product for an honest profit, the truth won't hurt it.

Rebels

I T used to please me to think of myself as a rebel and a nonconformist, but all the pleasure has gone out of it now. These days the nonconformists outnumber the conformists. Rebels are a dime a dozen. It's got so it's more conventional to be unconventional than it is to be conventional.

Causes are hard to come by. There is a definite shortage of them, especially for young people, and it seems to me the government ought to step in and do something about it. One of the most discontented people in the world is the rebel who wakes up in the morning and finds there isn't anything he wants to be against. This has led to a serious situation among the youth of America.

Not since the Viet Nam War has there been a cause worth getting riled up about. The no-nukes, the militant antiabortionists, the gays and the pro-marijuana groups get together and stir things up once in a while, but none of these issues has caught the public imagination on such a broad scale as long hair or the Viet Nam War did in the 1960s.

I don't know when disillusionment began to set in for me as a rebel. I guess it was back then in the sixties. Sentimentally I was on the side of the protesters, but I often argued with them. They didn't really want me on their side anyway. I was forever being suspicious that our government might just possibly have been doing the right thing, and they didn't like that in me. And, of course, I was the wrong generation.

It is only natural to defend anything of your own, and I defended my own generation. It angered me when they suggested that my generation spent all its time making money and war, and theirs did nothing but make peace and love. You can take only so much of having your generation knocked without fighting back.

There were times when I admired Jane Fonda and times when I thought she was making a fool of herself and ought to shut up. When she made me mad, I got even with her by thinking of the almost completely nude pictures of her that appeared in *Playboy* magazine years ago. It's hard to take an angry political statement seriously from a naked woman.

The rebels of the 1960s decided our school system was wrong and they forced a change; they decided our marriage convention was silly and they changed the rules; they changed our sex mores and our attitude in world affairs. You just have to hope they were right, but honestly, things don't seem a lot better than they were before they got at them.

They've dropped the whole thing now, of course. Rebels are always so preoccupied with the revolution that they don't have time to look into what's going to happen if they win.

Maybe all this soured me on being a rebel myself. I like to think that I'm really not tired of rebelling, but that I'm just smarter than I used to be about what I rebel against.

You have to decide which battles to fight, which to abandon. There are a thousand causes to whose aid I would gladly come if I had the time and the ability, but I do not have enough of either.

Conformity can be very relaxing and a great time saver. Rebellion against everything takes up a lot of your life. I've been enjoying orthodoxy in moderate amounts. Sometimes I just blend in with the crowd and let myself be carried along in the mainstream of life like a 1979 Ford doing fifty miles an hour in the right lane of a crowded highway.

Everyone Else Is Doing It

I SAW the driver of a panel truck throw a paper cup and a napkin out the window onto a New York street yesterday and it angered me. I was driving myself, so I pulled up beside him at the next light and yelled, "You dropped something back there!"

He got my message and he gave me one in return.

"Whaddya want me to do, take it to the dump? This whole town's a dump."

In other words, everyone else was doing it, why shouldn't he.

"Everyone else is doing it" seems to be the single most persuasive reason most of us give ourselves for doing something we really shouldn't do. If enough people do something that's wrong, it often becomes acceptable practice.

A U.S. corporation tries to sell a few hundred million dollars' worth of its product to a foreign country with a corrupt government. It offers the potentate in charge of buying things a few million dollars to keep for himself if he'll buy the goods because, the corporation explains to itself, "that's just the way everyone does business over here."

A competitor sends a salesman overseas to the same country, and he reports back to his main office that everyone is making under-the-table deals and that it isn't considered unusual there. If they want to make a sale, he reports, they'll have to slip the potentate a few million themselves. It's the same paper cup and the napkin thrown in the street. If everyone else is doing it, why not?

The college football season is starting, and nowhere are ethical procedures more consistently violated. College teams should be made up of students who come to a school for an education and who play football for fun. The very first time one of the teams in a hot college rivalry lowered its standards just a hair to admit a high school boy who failed biology but ran the hundred-yard dash in 9.8 seconds, amateur football was done for in that league.

In the news business, the newspaper that embellishes the truth and emphasizes the stories that appeal to our lesser instincts will invariably sell the most papers. It is difficult for a competitor not to follow along on the theory that "everyone else is doing it."

There is a constant edginess among executives in network television news organizations, because if one of them ever decides to lower its journalistic standards and give people what they'd like to watch instead of what they ought to know, that network will very soon take the major part of the audience. If that happens, will the others follow? They probably will, and that will be the end of high quality television news. It has already happened in local television news in many cities.

I don't know why "everyone else is doing it" is such an attractive idea to a nation that prides itself on its individuality as ours does. We start leaning on the idea when we're kids. If our mother tells us to go to bed at eight thirty, our argument is that we ought to be able to stay up until nine because "everyone else does." Right or wrong doesn't enter into our thinking. Not only that, but if a mother learns that a lot of kids actually *do* stay up until nine, she's more apt to let hers do it too.

This isn't much of a column today, but I wanted to get one out in a hurry. I've been reading some of the other columnists and everyone else is doing it.

In Defense of Incompetence

This will be in defense of incompetence. There's so much of it going around, I think we have to find ways to turn it to our advantage.

Maybe as a start, we ought to stop knocking it. Incompetence has always had a bad name. People speak of it as though they alone, in all the world, were free of it, when in actual fact incompetence is a God-given gift with which all mankind is endowed. And you can throw womankind in there, too, if mankind offends you.

First we have to realize that incompetency is already a major industry in the United States. It is unlisted on the New York Stock Exchange, but certainly there's nothing we produce in such quantity.

If competency on the job replaced the slovenly, half-done work we get now, the service industry in America would shrink to nothing. Television repair shops, kitchen appliance service departments and automobile mechanics would go out of business. Unemployment figures would climb. Even incompetency in the repair business itself can't be reduced substantially without endangering the whole economy. If they fixed things right in the first place, we'd never have to come back to have them fixed again. Competency would take the bread out of their children's mouths.

If builders built houses right, if insurance agents sold the right policies the first time, and if bankers and stock brokers gave the right advice, we'd all be rich and trouble free, and there'd be no work in the world for anyone. Incompetency in every field of endeavor creates jobs.

If we were all good drivers, insurance agents would be out of work and there would be no need for auto body shops. If we were competent in caring for our own bodies, we'd need half the doctors, half the medical facilities we have now.

I'm really warming up to this defense of incompetency. Some of my best friends are incompetent. Who needs friends who make you look bad by going around doing things right all the time? I have friends whose incompetence is their most likable characteristic, and I've had bosses who were so incompetent that they were laughably lovable.

I see evidence of the advantages of my own incompetence every day of my life. A month ago, I decided to take some money I had and put it in the stock market. I kept looking at the stock charts and I asked for advice from people who know about that sort of thing, but I never got at doing anything about it. One day last week stock prices dropped an average of seventeen points and they've been going down almost every day since. Once again I was saved by my own ineptitude.

Americans have been complaining about incompetence in government for many years now. They may think things are bad, but they don't know what bad government is until they have a thoroughly efficient one that does everything it says it's going to do. If we had elected competent people for every job in Washington, this nation would be revolting now. Adolf Hitler's Third Reich was probably the most competent the world has ever known.

Do we really want an Internal Revenue Service so good and efficient that they catch every nickel and dime we deduct that we shouldn't deduct? Do we want police enforcing the letter of the law every time we drive twenty-seven mph in a twenty-five mph zone?

I contend that we do not, and I say that an efficient, thoroughly competent government is not only dangerous but un-American!

Fortunately, I don't think there's much chance that the level of incompetence in all of us will decline in the foreseeable future. In the past four months I've visited six universities, lecturing and visiting classrooms. Take my word for it, a lot of incompetent teachers are turning out large numbers of incompetent students ready to take their rightful place in our bungling world.

Voluntary Prayer

L ET's call the Town Hall Meeting of America together and discuss this question of voluntary prayer in public schools. I'll make a few prefatory remarks:

I think we're all agreed that Americans approve of prayer in our public schools. They are agreed that it is right and proper to pray to God.

Americans are also agreed, I think, that the prayers should be those from the Presbyterian prayer book. Right? Do I hear a dissenting voice from up there in Vermont? You don't think the prayers should be Presbyterian?

Well, fortunately, everyone has a right to his own opinion in America, even left-wing Commies from Vermont.

You with your hand up there in Illinois, what do you think the prayers should be? You think the prayers in public schools should be Catholic prayers? I'm not sure everyone's going to go along with you on that, sir.

I think perhaps the best thing would be if we had a kind of neutral prayer. God will understand, and that way we won't offend anyone.

I see a hand raised out there in California. Ask your question. You want to know which way the children will face when they pray? Oh, come now, sir. The children will face their teacher. What are you saying, Mecca? Mecca? Of course they won't be facing Mecca. Please sit down, sir. We will not be praying to Allah. . . . Well, there may be five hundred million Muslims in the world, but not here in the good old United States of America, and we'll be praying to the real God in our schools here. Please sit down. Give someone else a chance to speak.

Over there in Texas, yes. Who *is* the real God? Aren't we agreed that he's a white male in his middle to late sixties with a long white beard and flowing robes?

Sir, I don't think this is any time to discuss theology. Yes, over there in Ohio. Will there be religious freedom in our schools? Of course there'll be religious freedom. The children will be free to be Presbyterian, Baptist, Lutheran, Methodist, or Episcopalian.

Freedom *from* religion? I don't think the Constitution promises any such thing. Freedom *of* religion is what it says. If a child doesn't want to bow his head and pray with the others because his father and mother are troublemakers, all he has to do is raise his hand and demand his constitutional rights to be excused, and he may leave the room. If the other children make fun of him, that's something we can't control.

Church of the Latter-Day Saints? Jehovah's Witnesses? The Unification Church? We would naturally consider the rights of these sects, but I think there's such a thing as carrying freedom of religion too far.

Yes, you down there in Florida with the funny little black hat on. Jewish prayers? Of course, the Jews will be able to have their own prayers. If Jewish boys and girls don't wish to pray in the standard, proper and right way to our God with the rest of the kids, all they have to do is say so. We'll fix up a place for them to pray in Miss McClatchy's second grade room next to the gym.

Are there any other questions? Does God hear prayers if you say them silently, alone and without bowing your head? I really can't answer that question. I'm just a moderator, not a clergyman.

Just one more question, then we'll have a show of hands.

Will you repeat your question, madam? If the children pray in school, will they be taught arithmetic in church? I don't think we have time for smart-aleck questions, so I'll take one more.

What about keeping religion and government-supported schools apart? I gather what you're suggesting, if I may rephrase your question, is a separation of church and state. It's an interesting new idea, but I think we'll take it up at our next meeting.

The meeting is adjourned.

IX:

LIFE, LONG
AND SHORT

Saturdays with the White House Staff

Every Saturday morning I make a list of Things to Do Today. I don't *do* them, I just make a list. My schedule always falls apart, and I realize that what I need is the kind of support the President gets. Here's how Saturday would go for me if I had the White House staff home with me:

7:15–7:30—I am awakened by one of the kitchen staff bringing me fresh orange juice, toast, jam and coffee.

7:30–7:45—The valet lays out my old khaki pants, a clean blue denim shirt and my old work shoes. I dress.

7:45–8:00—The newspaper is on my desk, together with a brief summary of it prepared overnight by three editors.

8:00–8:15—My mail has been sorted with only the interesting letters left for me to read. Checks for bills have been written and stamps put on envelopes. All I have to do is sign them. The Secretary of the Treasury will make sure my checks don't bounce.

8:15–8:30—Staff maintenance men have left all the right tools by the kitchen sink, together with the right size washers. I repair the leaky faucet.

8:30–8:45—While I repaired the faucet, other staff members got the ladder out of the garage and leaned it against the roof on the side of the house. While two of them hold it so I won't fall, I clean out the gutters. They put the ladder away when I finish.

8:45–9:00—Manny, my own barber, is waiting when I get down from the roof and he gives me a quick trim.

9:00–9:15—Followed by four Secret Service operatives, I drive to the car wash, where they see to it that I go to the head of the line.

9:15–9:30—On returning from the car wash, I find the staff has made a fresh pot of coffee, which I enjoy with my wife, who thanks me for having done so many of the little jobs around the house that she'd asked me to do. Two insurance salesmen, a real estate woman and a college classmate trying to raise money call during this time, but one of my secretaries tells them I'm too busy to speak to them.

Long before noon, with my White House staff, I've done everything on my list, and I can relax, read a book, take a nap or watch a ballgame on television.

I'm dreaming, of course. This is more the way my Saturdays *really* go:

6:00–7:30—I am awakened by a neighbor's barking dog. After lying there for half an hour, I get up, go down to the kitchen in my bare feet and discover we're out of orange juice and filters for the coffeemaker.

7:30–8:30—I go back upstairs to get dressed, but all my clean socks are in the cellar. They're still wet because they weren't taken out of the washing machine and put in the dryer. I wait for them to dry.

8:30–9:30—Now that I have my shoes on, I go out to the driveway to get the paper. Either the paperboy has thrown it into the bushes again or he never delivered it. I drive to the news store and get into an argument about why the Raiders beat the Eagles.

9:30–10:30—The mail has come and I sit down in the kitchen to read it. The coffee was left on too high and is undrinkable. The mail is all bills and ads. I don't know how much I have in the bank, and I don't have any stamps. I don't feel like doing anything. I just sit there, staring.

10:30–11:30—I finally get up and go down cellar but can't find the right wrench for the faucet in the kitchen sink, and I don't have any washers anyway. I try to do it with pliers and string but finally give up.

11:30–12:30—I don't feel like digging the ladder out from behind the screens so I drive to the car wash, but there are twenty-three cars in front of me. Later, at the barbershop, Manny can't take me today.

I go home, get out of the car and find the left front tire is soft. I go into the house and sit down to stare again as my wife comes in and complains that I never do anything around the house.

Waiting

Today I stood in line for seventeen minutes to cash a check for seventy-five dollars. I'd given this company, a bank, all my money to hold onto for me until I needed it, and today, when I needed some of it, it took me that long to get it back.

This is a good example of the kind of things that makes so many of us smile when we read that banks are having a hard time. We're glad. It fills us with pleasure to read about their troubles. They've made us wait so often over the years that nothing bad that happens to a bank makes us do anything but laugh. "You had it coming, bank." That's what we think.

Waiting is one of the least amusing things there is to do. Short waits are worse than long waits. If you know you're going to have to wait for four hours or six months, you can plan your time and use it and still have the pleasure of anticipating what you're waiting for. If it's a short wait of undetermined length, it's a terrible waste of time.

I've read all the proverbs about waiting and patience:

"All things come to him who waits."

"They also serve who only stand and wait."

"Patience is a virtue."

I don't happen to believe any of those old saws. *Impatience* is a virtue, that's what I think. Shifting from one foot to the other and tapping your fingers on something and getting damn mad while you stand there is the only way to behave while you're waiting. There's no sense being patient with people who make you wait, because they'll only make you wait longer the next time. The thing to do is blow up . . . hit the roof when they finally show up.

Some people seem to think they were born to get there when they're ready, while you wait. Banks are not the only big offenders in the waiting game, so are doctors. Some doctors assume their time is so much more important than anyone else's that all the rest of us ought to wait for them, "patiently," of course. What other profession or line of business routinely includes in its office setup something called "the waiting room"?

In New York City many of the parking garages have signs over their cashier windows saying, "No charge for waiting time." What a preposterous sign! What it means is that they can take their time getting your car, but you don't have to pay them anything while you wait for it. I always tell them that *I* have a charge for waiting, and I think doctors ought to start knocking ten dollars off their bill for every half hour we spend in their waiting rooms. The doctor who tells all his patients to come at nine o'clock ought to be sent back to the hospital to spend another year as a resident.

All of us admire in other people the characteristics we think we have ourselves. I don't have any patience, so it's natural, I guess, that I don't admire it in other people. Sometimes I reluctantly concede it works for them, but I still don't think of it as a virtue. I secretly think that people who wait well are too lazy to go do something. Just an opinion, mind you. I don't want a lot of patient waiters mad at me.

The funny thing about that word "waiter" is that those who make a living as waiters are about the most impatient people on earth. You can't get a waiter to wait ten seconds. You go in a restaurant, he hands you a menu eighteen inches long with fifty dishes to choose from, and in three seconds he starts tapping his pencil on his order pad to let you know how impatient he is.

I'd make a great waiter. I can't wait at all.

Some Notes

WHAT follows are some notes I made on the backs of a wide variety of pieces of paper over the past few weeks. The ideas struck me as either true or funny when I first put them down.

—They always ask you to use the revolving door, but they don't make them any easier to push.

—You can't sleep late, cut wood, watch football, eat dinner and still finish all the Sunday paper.

—Several times a year I see pictures in a magazine or items in a column from Hollywood about a round bed. Do they make round electric blankets, and where do they keep the Kleenex?

—The average American, I read, is growing three-quarters of

an inch every twenty-five years. At that rate, I'll be six feet tall when I'm 210 years old.

—I don't stay to the end of civic meetings at the town hall, because they always end up in an argument about who has the floor and what motion they're voting on. Someone usually moves to table the motion on the floor, and someone else gets up to say you can't move to table a motion, because there's already a motion on the floor. That's when I get lost and leave.

—When someone isn't watching where he's going and bumps into me and almost knocks me off my feet, I almost always say "Pardon me."

—The newspapers often referred to Kennedy as JFK, to Lyndon Johnson as LBJ, to Roosevelt as FDR and to Truman as HST, but no one ever called Jimmy Carter by the initials JEC, and now I notice no one is using RWR for Ronald Wilson Reagan. What causes this?

—There's nothing people like better than being asked an easy question. For some reason, we're flattered when a stranger asks us where Maple Street is in our own home town and we can tell him.

—It's been my experience that, despite the old saying, barking dogs *are* more apt to bite than dogs that don't bark.

—I'd give $10,000 to have had some of the money I have now back in 1956 when I was dead broke.

—The back of my closet is filled with clothes that I'll be able to wear again just as soon as I lose ten pounds. On the other side of those on the pole is another, older bunch of clothes. I'll be able to wear those again just as soon as I lose twenty pounds.

—Farmers always seem to have a lot of big expensive equipment sitting all around, rusting. Are farmers really poor? How much do those machines cost? Are they paid for? Are they still any good? Why are they out there, rusting?

—When an argument comes up, I usually repeat what I thought yesterday or ten years ago. I don't very often think it through again to decide how I feel about it now.

—If you wait until you're absolutely certain before you do something, you never do it.

—Johnny Carson is largely a rumor to me. I guess he's good, but I've almost never seen him. We usually go to bed by 11:30 week nights. I'm always surprised at the ratings they say late night television shows get.

—If you gave a calf the homogenized, ultrapasteurized product they sell to humans as milk now, I wonder if it would recognize it as something that came from its mother.

—I'm not very punctual, but I like to keep my watch exactly on time to the second. That way, I know how late I am. Watches, by the way, are better than they were twenty years ago. I hate myself for it, but I've finally given up carrying my great gold Hamilton railroad watch in favor of a battery-operated quartz watch. It keeps better time. It's nice to know something is better than it used to be.

Memory

WHAT does AWACS stand for again, do you remember? Advance Warning something. Advance Warning American Command Ship? That's not it. I'll have to ask someone or look it up. And who was Lyndon Johnson's Vice President? You ought to remember a simple thing like that and I ought to myself, but I don't. There are times when I'm overwhelmed by my vast lack of memory. The other day I forgot my home phone number, and we've had it for thirty years.

I remember reading that we all start losing brain cells that make up the memory when we reach about age twenty, but this debilitating influence the years have doesn't seem to have much to do with my problem. I couldn't remember anything when I was eighteen, either.

Being tall and being able to remember things are probably the two most desirable human characteristics I don't have. Because I am neither tall nor able to remember things, I look for ways to diminish the importance of height and memory.

Just for example, memory of the past is not nearly so much fun as anticipation of the future and it's almost always sadder. Sadness is one of the principal ingredients of memory, and there's just so much of that anyone wants to bring on himself on purpose by sitting around remembering.

Another thing, as much as I'd like to have a good memory sometimes, it seems to me that people with good memories for names, exact times and dates are dull. They're not only dull, they can be a real pain in the neck to be around.

The trouble with people with good memories is that they keep wanting to show it off to you by remembering things you don't want to hear. Everything reminds them of something they've done before. I have one old friend I hate to see, because every time we're together he starts talking about World War II. I enjoy reminiscing once in a while, but do-you-remember-the-time-we stories don't hold my attention for long. I'd rather wait until I'm all through living and *then* review my life and times. Right now, I'm busy with today.

Last week, I met a friend I used to work with when I wrote for Arthur Godfrey. He repeated a story I've heard him tell fifty times. I've seen him twice a year since 1960, and I'd heard the story eight times before that.

It looks now as though those of us who can't remember anything may be saved. They're starting to sell small computerized memory banks for personal use. That's what I want when they get them pocket-size. I want to be able to reach in my pocket and enter the question, "What do the initials AWACS stand for?" and get an instant answer. I think I'll give one to my old friend for Christmas, too. If he enters the question, "Have I ever told this story to Andy before?" he'll get back the answer, "Yes, fifty times."

You often hear people say "I'm terrible with names," as if it was something to be proud of. I'm terrible with names, but I'm embarrassed about it, because I know it means I just don't care enough to make a point of remembering. That isn't nice or anything to be proud of.

My memory of my own past gives me a strange feeling, and I suppose everyone feels the same. When I look back at what I did a long time ago, it's hard to think of it as me. I see it clearly, but it's as if someone else was doing it. It's only my memory of me that's doing those things. It's like looking at the water in a river. The river looks the same all the time, but the water is always different.

I don't feel too bad about my bad memory—although I'd be happy if I could remember who Lyndon Johnson's VP was.

Trust

Last night I was driving from Harrisburg to Lewisburg, Pa., a distance of about eighty miles. It was late, I was late and if anyone asked me how fast I was driving, I'd have to plead the Fifth Amendment to avoid self-incrimination. Several times I got stuck behind a slow-moving truck on a narrow road with a solid white line on my left, and I was clinching my fists with impatience.

At one point along an open highway, I came to a crossroads with a traffic light. I was alone on the road by now, but as I approached the light, it turned red and I braked to a halt. I looked left, right and behind me. Nothing. Not a car, no suggestion of headlights, but there I sat, waiting for the light to change, the only human being for at least a mile in any direction.

I started wondering why I refused to run the light. I was not afraid of being arrested, because there was obviously no cop anywhere around, and there certainly would have been no danger in going through it.

Much later that night, after I'd met with a group in Lewisburg and had climbed into bed near midnight, the question of why I'd stopped for that light came back to me. I think I stopped because it's part of a contract we all have with each other. It's not only the law, but it's an agreement we have, and we trust each other to honor it: we don't go through red lights. Like most of us, I'm more apt to be restrained from doing something bad by the social convention that disapproves of it than by any law against it.

It's amazing that we ever trust each other to do the right thing, isn't it? And we do, too. Trust is our first inclination. We have to make a deliberate decision to mistrust someone or to be suspicious or skeptical. Those attitudes don't come naturally to us.

It's a damn good thing too, because the whole structure of our society depends on mutual trust, not distrust. This whole thing we have going for us would fall apart if we didn't trust each other most of the time. In Italy, they have an awful time getting any money for the government, because many people just plain don't pay their income tax. Here the Internal Revenue Service makes some gestures toward enforcing the law, but mostly they just have to trust that we'll pay what we owe. There has often been talk of a tax revolt in this country, most recently among unemployed auto workers in Michigan, and our government pretty much admits if there was a widespread tax revolt here, they wouldn't be able to do anything about it.

We do what we say we'll do; we show up when we say we'll show up; we deliver when we say we'll deliver, and we pay when we say we'll pay. We trust each other in these matters, and when we don't do what we've promised, it's a deviation from the normal. It happens often that we don't act in good faith and in a trustworthy manner, but we still consider it unusual, and we're angry or disappointed with the person or organization that violates the trust we have in them. (I'm looking for something good to say about mankind today.)

I hate to see a story about a bank swindler who has jiggered the books to his own advantage, because I trust banks. I don't *like* them, but I trust them. I don't go in and demand that they show me my money all the time just to make sure they still have it.

It's the same buying a can of coffee or a quart of milk. You don't take the coffee home and weigh it to make sure it's a pound. There isn't time in life to distrust every person you meet or every company you do business with. I hated the company that started selling beer in eleven-ounce bottles years ago. One of the million things we take on trust is that a beer bottle contains twelve ounces.

It's interesting to look around and at people and compare their faith or lack of faith in other people with their success or lack of success in life. The patsies, the suckers, the people who always assume everyone else is as honest as they are, make out better in the long run than the people who distrust everyone—and they're a lot happier even if they get taken once in a while.

I was so proud of myself for stopping for that red light, and inasmuch as no one would ever have known what a good person I was on the road from Harrisburg to Lewisburg, I had to tell someone.

My Looting Career

T HE story said a U.S. federal judge had ruled that two paintings worth three to five million dollars apiece had to be returned to Germany because they had been stolen from a castle there by an American soldier who was one of the occupying American forces in 1945.

The judge was probably right, but I hope he understood. The paintings weren't stolen, they were looted. The word looting didn't have the same evil sound to soldiers then as it has to civilians now. Looting was a wild, lawless, uncivilized thing to do, but I saw enough of it during World War II to understand how even a relatively civilized soldier could do it.

Here they were, fighting for their lives in a country whose people were responsible for their being there in the first place. Here was a house—call it a castle if you want—only recently occupied by the Germans whose guns had poked out its windows with the intention of killing Americans. The house was a shambles. It was not a person's house. It was the abandoned stronghold of the enemy. The former owners were gone, forever probably. Dead maybe, but certainly gone, and anyway they were Germans. Why not rummage through these rooms, this wine cellar, those drawers? If you didn't do it because of some feelings it was wrong, would the ten thousand soldiers that followed you through that house in the days to come also honor the possessions of the departed owners? Ten thousand honest, thoughtful, sympathetic soldiers without an acquisitive instinct among them? Hardly.

Of course it was not right, but you couldn't expect an American soldier under those circumstances to determine that kind of right from that kind of wrong.

I was a young correspondent for *The Stars and Stripes* at the time. Looting didn't bother me as much as the family photographs of the owners scattered on the floor by the soldiers rooting through the trunk or the bureau drawer. The people in the pictures didn't look like enemy. They looked like people.

My only looting excursion had a paradoxical ending for me. I guess no one will bring charges against me now if I tell you about it. I went into Cologne behind the tanks of the Third Armored Division and got several good firsthand stories for the paper about the fighting down by the Cathedral. I watched as our soldiers got to one of the great wine cellars in all Europe, the one in the bowels of the Excelsior Hotel. They didn't ask for the wine steward.

The following morning I headed for the rail yards just outside town. I had covered the Eighth Air Force raids from England before the invasion, and we had bombed Cologne so often I was curious about what effect the raids had had on train service.

I wandered alone among miles and miles of freight cars, some of them broken open by shells, some of them on their side and some untouched. Finally I pulled myself up into one whose middle door gaped open. It was stacked to its top with square wooden boxes. They were small, about eighteen inches on a side, but each must have weighed fifty pounds.

The stenciled marks on the side of the boxes said GUMMI SCHLAUCHE DER FAHRRADER 144. My German was terrible, but I realized that each box held 144 inner tubes for bicycle tires. I don't suppose there was a scarcer or more highly prized item in all of Belgium than the inner tube of a bicycle tire, and I was staying in a hotel in Liège, Belgium, taken over for correspondents. I got one box on my shoulder, leaving perhaps a thousand more in the freight car, and carried my pure gold up the bank to my jeep. Triumphantly, I drove back to Liège with my loot. Certainly the tubes were worth the equivalent of ten dollars each.

Well, I never found out, and I didn't have to wait for a federal judge to order me to return them. I left them in the jeep in the garage overnight and they were stolen.

So much for my looting career.

Weapons

THERE's always a lot of high level talk about how the next war will be fought. They don't talk much about *if*, but about *how*. Some people feel that if we arm ourselves with a lot of nuclear weapons, the Russians will never dare attack us. Others feel by doing that we are only asking the Russians to make more nuclear weapons themselves and eventually both countries will use them.

I just don't know. I've never owned a nuclear weapon myself. As a matter of fact, the most lethal weapon I ever had was a slingshot I sent away for when I was a kid. It was advertised in a magazine and it looked great in the ad, but when it came, I found I didn't really like it any better than the slingshot Alfie Gordon and I had made for ourselves out of some rubber bands and the crotch of a small tree.

Arming yourself as a kid is not that different from the way it is for a nation. If the kids on the next block have a new weapon, you've got to get one like it.

I didn't live in a tough area of town and we didn't have gang wars, but still, we were aware of weapons. In the spring we all had water pistols. Water pistols may be the best weapons ever made, because they're accurate, inexpensive and ammunition is readily available. It isn't like having to get yourself heavy plutonium or whatever it is they arm nuclear warheads with. All you need is a puddle.

They have that new nuclear weapon now that kills all the people in the area but doesn't damage the buildings. This must certainly rank with the greatest inventions of all time, but I still think that a shot right in the face or down the back of the neck with a well-aimed water pistol would be more help to mankind in the long run.

We had cap pistols, too, and there must be a mandatory death penalty now for carrying a cap pistol, because I haven't seen one for sale in years. I was lucky enough to have been born during the era that saw the introduction of the repeater, a cap pistol that could be loaded with a roll of caps. Up until that time, you had to insert a cap in front of the hammer for each shot. This, too, was considered a great advance in weaponry when I was young.

I don't know what position the National Rifle Association takes on bean blowers. Water pistols were our spring weapons, cap pistols our summer guns, but in the fall we switched to bean blowers. A bean blower was a metal tube about fourteen inches long with a hole through it about three-eighths of an inch in diameter. On one end it had a wood mouthpiece. You filled your mouth with white beans, positioned one in front of the mouthpiece with your tongue and then exhausted your lungs in an explosive puff. The bean shot out the tube and hurtled toward the target.

For several years this seemed like the ultimate weapon to us. It hurt more than the water pistol and it had a range of up to fifty feet, whereas even the most expert marksman couldn't hit anything with a water pistol at more than fifteen feet.

The weapons makers, perfectionists that they are, wouldn't quit with the bean blower though. By the time I was nine, the bean blower was obsolete, replaced by a more accurate weapon with greater range and greater hurt power. It was, of course, the pea shooter. It may not seem like much to those of you who don't comprehend weaponry, but the pea shooter represented a great step forward in our arms race on Partridge Street. The opening in the pea shooter was only half the size of the opening in the bean blower, so it not only hurtled the projectile faster, but the projectile itself, a small, hard green pea put fear in the hearts of the enemy over on Western Avenue.

There was only one weapon so fearful we hardly dared talk about it. For us it was as though they had made an atomic bomb encased in a cannister of bubonic plague. It was the dreaded BB gun. So armed, I might have conquered the world bounded by Madison, Western, Partridge and Maine. Unfortunately, my mother would never let me have one, and it has led to the greatly weakened position I find myself in today.

Joe McCarthy

No one is ever satisfied with the obituary notice printed on the occasion of the death of a friend or relative. It isn't good enough or complete enough. I suppose it is because, in the death notices of our friends, we see our own.

Joe McCarthy died recently, and the notices in the two papers I read were not right.

"Joseph W. McCarthy," one of them said, "was known for his books on the Kennedy family." Joe wrote two books about the Kennedys, but that isn't what he was known for at all. He was known to millions of soldiers during World War II as the editor of *Yank*, the best and most literate publication any army ever had.

Joe was working for the Boston *Post* as a sports reporter when he was drafted in 1941. He was assigned to the last mule pack artillery outfit in the Army, and by reporting his experiences with the animals, the guns and the people he met, he set the tone for the lighthearted literary tradition that emerged from the war.

I was a reporter for *The Stars and Stripes* when I first met Joe. He had come to London to see how things were going with the biggest of the twenty-one editions of *Yank* that he supervised. After the war he became editor of *Cosmopolitan*, vastly different then from now, and at one point hired me and my coauthor Bud Hutton to return to Europe as correspondents for the magazine.

Every writer needs an editor, and Joe was perfect. We turned in material another editor might have thrown in the waste basket, but Joe never lost patience. He talked it over with us, pointed out what was wrong and how it could be fixed. It always looked good when it was finally printed with our names on it, but by then it was as much Joe's piece as it was ours.

During the 1950s, when I was struggling to make a living as a free-lance writer, I used to drink with Joe in Toots Shor's. By then he was a free-lance writer himself and doing very well, although he was somewhat disillusioned with the magazine business. He gave me some advice about free-lance writing that I've never forgotten.

"Making a living as a free-lance writer isn't very hard," he said. "Find out what the editor wants, how long he wants it and get it to him the day he has to have it. It doesn't have to be any good."

Joe's writing was always good. He had an easy grace about himself that came through in anything he wrote.

There are stories I heard yesterday I can't remember at all, but Joe used to tell stories twenty years ago that I'll always remember.

He never got over his Irish youth in Cambridge, the town so dominated by Harvard and its sister college, Radcliffe. During his freshman year at the less well-known Boston College, Joe fell in love with a Radcliffe girl who came from a wealthy, social background. He took her out several times and left her with the impression that he was a Harvard student.

It is necessary to say, for those of you who don't know, that Harvard and Radcliffe share a campus and that Hasty Pudding is the name of a prestigious Harvard club known then for its inventive initiation rites.

In an effort to help himself through college and, incidentally, to scrape together a few dollars for another date with his Radcliffe friend, Joe took a Saturday job as a helper collecting trash in Cambridge.

One Saturday in the spring, his truck route took him along the fringe of the Harvard campus. Who should come bouncing along the street, as Joe was heaving a full can of garbage onto the truck, but the Radcliffe girl he had been trying to impress.

She saw him and Joe knew it. He didn't avoid her. He looked her right in the eye, smiled, gave her a big wink and said, "Hasty Pudding!"

The late A. J. Liebling, the journalist's journalist, often spoke of the advantage to a person of dying at the peak of his obituary value. Joe McCarthy, though only sixty-four, had not been in good health and had not written much for several years. If Joe had died at the end of World War II, he would have been on page one of every paper in the country.

It is very sad for those of us who knew him, but even if his obituary today were bigger and better, it wouldn't have said what we all thought about him. He was such a sweet guy.

Planning Ahead

WOULD you like a calendar that runs from January 1, 1981, to December 31, 1990? Someone has just sent me one and I'm throwing it out. I do not wish to contemplate that distant future. I am not going to plan my life so far ahead, and I don't care to think about where I'll be when I'm ten years older than I am today.

The passing of time is depressing to me, and planning for something six months in advance makes time pass even faster. I have no interest in rushing through the 1980s in order to get to some event I've put on my ten-year calendar for the year 1990.

The best thing that's happened to me in this regard is to have had a President elected who is nine years older than I am. It makes me feel great and gives me reason to hope I haven't even reached my peak yet. Ronald Reagan isn't going to be doing a lot of talking about the year 2000, because he'll be eighty-nine then. He's not going to be initiating programs that come to fruition in fifteen years because he'll want to see the programs he starts finished. I'd be surprised if Reagan has one of these ten-year calendars I'm throwing out.

This feeling I have is nothing new to me. I had it when I was twenty-five. Insurance salesmen were always talking to me about what I'd need when I was fifty and sixty, and I didn't want to hear what they said. I bought some insurance from them, but I did it more because I thought that's what everyone was supposed to do than because I really wanted it. I guess it pays off in the feeling of security it gives me, though. If I were to die tomorrow, my wife wouldn't have to worry. She'd be taken care of. Between the $1.35 a month she'd get for the rest of her life and some money her parents left her, she'd be comfortable.

All of us have to plan ahead as though our lives were going to proceed according to plan, but they never do. It's a good thing, too, because one of the best things about life is how unpredictable it is. No calendar, no digital watch that shows the time in three zones and goes off at 6:30 every morning can make the course of our lives any more certain. The certainty of uncertainty is the only thing that keeps us out of the hands of the computers.

My rule is not to plan on being anywhere more than three months in advance, and at that distance only when the circumstances are unusual.

I know people who have planned their whole lives in advance. They've stayed with the same company for twenty-five years in jobs they hated, just waiting for the day they were eligible for a pension. That's what I'd call planning your life away. Spending the best years of your life gritting your teeth and just getting through one day after another waiting for the time you can retire to nothing seems like an awful waste of life. It would serve one of these people right if, the day after they retired, a rich distant relative died and left them a million dollars and their pension meant nothing to them.

I know in my heart and mind that I'm wrong not planning my life more carefully, but I lack the ability to do it, so I take my pleasure from being disorganized. I delight in long distance plans that go wrong for other people, because it reduces them to my level. I don't like insurance companies or the people who take polls or the smart-money people on Wall Street whose businesses are based on statistical evidence that this or that will happen. We are all somewhat defeated by the evidence of our own predictability, but I refuse to accept defeat gracefully.

Life, Long and Short

I CHANGE my mind a lot about whether life is long or short. Looking back at how quickly a son or daughter grew up or at how many years I've been out of high school, life seems to be passing frighteningly fast. Then I look around me at the evidence of the day-to-day things I've done and life seems long. Just looking at the coffee cans I've saved makes life look like practically forever. We only use eight or ten tablespoons of coffee a day. Those cans sure represent a lot of days.

Used coffee cans are the kind of statistics on life that we don't keep. Maybe if we kept them, it would help give a feeling of longevity. Maybe when each of us has his own computer at home, we'll be able to save the kinds of statistics the announcers use during baseball games.

It's always fun, for instance, to try to remember how many cars you've owned. Think back to your first car, and it makes life seem longer. If you're fifty years old, you've probably owned so many cars you can't even remember all of them in order. I've also wondered how many miles I've driven. That's a statistic most people could probably make a fair guess at. If you've put roughly seventy-five thousand miles on twenty cars, you've driven a million and a half miles. You've probably spent something like twenty-five thousand dollars on gas.

It's more difficult to estimate the number of miles you've walked. Is there any chance you've walked as far as you've driven in a car? I'm not sure. You don't go out on a weekend and walk four hundred miles the way you'd drive a car. On the other hand, every time you cross a street or walk across the room, you're adding to the steps you've taken. All those little walks every day must add up to a lot of miles, even if you aren't a hiker.

And how much have you climbed? I must have lifted myself ten thousand miles straight up with all the stairs I've negotiated in my life. There are seventeen nine-inch steps in our front hallway and I often climb them twenty times a day, so I've lifted my two hundred pounds two hundred and fifty feet on the stairs in the house in one day alone. That doesn't include the day I climbed the Washington Monument with the kids or the time my uncle took me up the Statue of Liberty.

And how many pairs of shoes have I worn out walking and climbing all that distance? I'm always looking for the perfect pair of shoes and I've never found them yet, so I buy more shoes than I wear. There must be six old pairs of sneaks of mine in closets around the house. All in all, I'll bet I've had two hundred fifty pairs of shoes in my life. Easy, two hundred fifty.

How long would your hair be if you'd never cut it? Everyone has wondered about that at some time. What length would my beard be if I hadn't shaved every morning? And, it's a repulsive thought, but I suppose my fingernails would be several feet long if I hadn't hacked them off about every ten days. I don't know. Does hair stop growing once it gets a few feet long? I don't ever recall seeing anyone with hair ten feet long. My hair must grow at least an inch a month. That's a foot a year. I've certainly never seen anyone my age with hair sixty feet long.

This is the kind of thinking that helps make life seem longer to me. When I think of how many times I've been to the barber or even to the dentist, life seems to stretch back practically forever.

The one statistic I hate to think about is how many pounds of food I've consumed. Pounds would be an unmanageably large number. I'd have to estimate it in tons. I must have eaten ten tons of ice cream alone in my lifetime.

It makes life seem long and lovely just thinking about every bite of it.

Age

I AM sixty now. I hate it and I constantly inspect my brain and my body for signs of decline. I don't see it yet, but I suppose others do. There must be some. I played three sets of tennis today and I never played better. As a matter of fact, I never played that well.

Oh, I notice a little falling apart in the face when I look in the mirror to shave, but it's no worse a look than I had when I looked too young at twenty-five. The only really disturbing thing about that is that to detect the deterioration in the face, I need my glasses now.

I am most surprised at my physical stamina. I played a lot of football in high school and college and, watching games on television, I dream of what it would be like to get in for a few plays. I think I could, but I guess I'd be in for an awful surprise—still, I tend to run up a flight of stairs two at a time. I don't walk. I feel in shape. People haven't started saying how good I look for my age yet. That's a good sign.

It surprises me to consider how long the body lasts. I've been doing all these things I do with it for a long time now. And without much servicing, either.

I suppose I'll be the last one to know, but I haven't detected any deterioration in my ability to do what I do for a living, either. I write, of course. It still bothers me to look at something I wrote five years ago. I don't usually like it. I have a feeling I've learned a lot since then and wouldn't say it that way now. Is the time ever going to come when I read something I wrote a few years ago and say to myself, "I couldn't write it that well today"?

This is a recurring thought I've had for as long as I've written for a living. The things I wrote last year never seem very good, but that thought doesn't usually occur to me as I'm writing them. Some kind of protective thing that goes on in the brain, no doubt.

My hands look older. There are some veins showing through now and a few brown spots. I hadn't noticed them until I heard the commercials on television telling me about some salve that gets rid of them. I can't believe the salve is very good for you if it makes brown spots in your skin go away. The salve certainly doesn't make you any younger, and youth is the only thing that would really help. If they ever make a jar of that, I'll have some.

Even though my feeling that I haven't deteriorated much mentally or physically in the last forty years may be an illusion, I am convinced that there is enough truth to it to be cause for rejoicing. Forty adult years of full strength and mental capacity isn't bad.

What worries me is that physical deterioration is a lot more apparent than mental deterioration. There's no mirror I'm going to be able to look in, even with glasses, and be able to determine that my brain has brown spots.

I still expect Ben Hogan or Sam Snead or at least Arnold Palmer to win the U.S. Open again, but of course none of them will. There is too, too solid evidence that the body can't do at forty what it did at thirty. Let alone seventy. The evidence of what the brain can and cannot do with added age is not so clear.

My hero as a writer is E. B. White. He's eighty-two now and living in Maine. I know him some, not well, and I'd like to ask why he isn't writing much anymore. Has he said what he wants to say, or does he feel he can't say it as well anymore? Or is it just that he wrote to make a living and doesn't have to do that now?

When I'm eighty-two, I hope I can read what I wrote when I was sixty and think it wasn't very good.

The Body

THE only consolation you can find when you look in the mirror at yourself is that everyone is funny-looking, lopsided, blemished or seriously flawed in appearance, one way or the other. What makes us nervous, of course, is that we see in ourselves our own special flaws, and we inspect them so carefully and think about them so much that they often seem worse than other people's.

I often look at a body other than my own and wish I could swap. The trouble is, if I got myself the perfect body today, the chances are that in a few months I'd have it looking like the one I have now. The way we look has some connection with the way we are. It goes further than "you are what you eat." I suspect "we are what we think," too. The way we think affects our eating, our walking and every move we make, and this shapes the body as much as the genes we were born with. Of course, the genes we were born with affect the way we think, so we're all trapped with being the way we are. It's hard to get out of it.

I'm not complaining about the body I got in the deal. If I did the right things with it, it wouldn't be bad at all. Even abusing it the way I have, it seems to be standing up pretty well. Yesterday I stacked a pile of lumber that must have weighed a total of five thousand pounds. I can play three sets of singles without dropping dead on a tennis court, and my wife still asks me to take the tops off jars. I don't notice much I can't do at sixty that I could at forty. Someone else might, but I don't, and with this body, I'm the one that counts.

The worst thing that's happened to me is that I now weigh more than two hundred pounds. My mother always called me "sturdy." At 5'9", two hundred pounds is too much. "Big bones," my mother said. I used to believe my mother, but for the last thirty-five years I've faced the fact that I'm overweight. I still avoid thinking of myself as fat. I suspect there are some people who *don't* avoid thinking of me that way, but they keep it from me.

The best thing that's happened to me, as far as appearance goes, is that I still have most of my hair. I suppose if I got bald I might try and lose some weight, so having hair may shorten my life. I'm telling you all these things about myself not because I think you care about *my* problems, but it might interest you to translate them in terms of your own.

Almost everyone has some physical handicap. It might be one they were born with or one they acquired along the way. My biggest handicap is an ankle I tore up skiing fifteen years ago. I don't have much strength left in the right ankle or the foot because of torn ligaments that never reattached themselves to the bone. (That's correct, isn't it, doctor?) Three years ago I went to Joe Namath's doctor with it. He measured my thigh and calf, and pointed out that my right leg was substantially smaller than my left because I wasn't using the muscles in my right leg. I couldn't, because if I did, my foot and ankle collapsed.

But we're all in this thing together. If you get to know someone well enough or talk to him or her long enough, they get talking about what's wrong with their body. The marvel is that we're all so different with so many different things wrong with us, but nonetheless we manage to drag ourselves out of bed mornings.

The real question we all face is this: How much time do we want to spend taking care of our bodies as compared to the time we spend using them? The body seems to work pretty well if we just go about our business without paying a lot of attention to it. If I play tennis, I play to win at tennis, I play to win at tennis, not to exercise. That's a byproduct. I find joggers, as a group, nice people, but a little intense and more consumed with attention to their own bodies than is absolutely necessary.

Body Building

THE smartest people I've ever known were always excessively interested in their own bodies. They were right, of course, but they were often a pain in the neck to other people. I remember when someone accused the brilliant Eric Sevareid of being a hypochondriac. Eric just looked up slowly and said, "Hypochondriacs get sick too, you know."

The only time my body attracts my attention, other than those times when it's sick, is when a muscle is sore from overuse. That's the case today. The muscle in my right thigh is sore because I was trying to do deep knee bends yesterday on one leg. It's a good feeling in a way because it reminds me that I have muscles.

I've never really known what to do about my muscles. I'd like to look and be more muscular than I am, but there are so many of them I never know which ones to try to build up. Those body-building people go after all of them, but that's a full-time job and they end up looking like freaks in their perfection. The thing that's wrong with them is that they have developed those muscles with no intention of doing anything with them except showing them off.

The muscles that look best are the ones that have developed because of some natural activity the person engages in, not the ones built up by exercises designed for the purpose. I admire the muscular forearm of Billie Jean King and the biceps of the man who picks up our garbage twice a week. (I wish he didn't spill so much, but that's another matter.)

I've often set out on some body-building program of my own, but except for one three-year period when I was in school and did a hundred pushups a day, it's never lasted long. Each of us has good and bad body parts, and one temptation with muscles is to work on the ones that are already your best. I have strong shoulders and legs but weak feet and hands, but it's a lot more interesting to me to work on my legs than my feet, even though my leg muscles would be a lot more use to me if I had the feet to go with them.

Two years ago I bought a ten-pound dumbbell and started

lifting it to my shoulder one hundred times with each hand to strengthen my arm muscle. I brought it to the office and was doing it there, but someone stole the dumbbell about a year ago and I haven't given those muscles any attention since. You really can't, that's the trouble. It's easy enough to say, "It only takes fifteen minutes a day," but it takes more than that. It takes having your mind more on your muscle than on your brain.

I like natural exercise. I wish it was illegal for people to build up muscles deliberately, because they start beating you at whatever you're doing and you have to start building yours. I think of jogging as a natural exercise. I hate doing it myself and don't, but I love to see others jogging. On the days when I drive in to work in New York City, I always see a hundred great-looking women trotting along the drive by the East River. They look great not because they are necessarily beautiful, but because they look so alive and so determined to do the right thing. I'm moved by their muscles.

The real question is, how much time can we spend on our bodies? We all know they're important, but my feeling is we should use them and not fuss with them so much. I play tennis twice a week and usually run up any flight of stairs I'm faced with, but that's all the exercise I get in a normal week. Any week I try to do one-legged knee bends is not normal for me. If I'd spent more time on my muscles, I'd look better, but I'd have spent a lot less time writing, woodworking, cooking, reading and napping. Much as I yearn to look more muscular, it's not worth it.

Self-improvement

W̲ᴇ have chairs in the house no one has sat on in years. We have beds no one has slept in, except at Christmas, since the kids went away to college. We have dishes no one eats off and glasses no one drinks from. I can understand all that, but why we still have that piano in the living room, I'll never understand.

The piano itself must have forgotten what music sounds like by now. It's a magnificent piece of wood, but it hasn't been played in ten years, and then only for one night when an old school friend was at the house. He was the one who always played the piano when we were in high school, too.

Last weekend I got staring at the piano, and I walked over and picked up the lid of the piano bench and started looking at the sheet music and books stored in the compartment. There, yellow with age, was Schirmer's *Beginner's Piano Lesson Book* with my name on it.

I remember that whole sorry incident. When I was a freshman in college and playing a lot of football, I got worried about the lack of culture in my life, so I started paying a history teacher's wife two dollars an hour to teach me how to play the piano. She was very nice and patient, but I could tell she didn't think she had another Horowitz on her hands.

On the third Saturday of the football season, I broke my left index finger and that was the end of my musical career.

All this flashed through my mind over the weekend and, as I stood staring at that unused piano, I got thinking of all the other little gestures I'd made in an effort to improve myself one way or another over the years.

The number of times I have silently vowed to lose weight is too depressing a statistic to recall. I don't have to eat all bananas or all carbohydrates at one meal, all sugars or all fats at others. I pass through Scarsdale on the train every day and *that* hasn't helped. I don't need any calorie-counting charts or a plan for every meal. All I need to do to lose weight is to stop overeating. If I knocked off with the ice cream alone, it wouldn't do any harm.

Then I noticed about a year ago that the bulge at the back of the upper part of my arm was getting almost as big as the bicep muscle in front, except the bulge in back was mostly fat. I went to a sports store at lunchtime and bought two ten-pound dumbbells. For three weeks I got up from the chair at my desk several times a day, walked to the table under which I kept the dumbbells and lifted them from down by my knees up to my shoulders as many times as I could. Then I'd rest a minute and do it again. I thought I'd begun to notice some firming up of my arm muscles, front and back, but I came in one morning and the dumbbells were gone, stolen probably by someone with plenty of muscle.

That was the end of that exercise in self-improvement.

I type with three fingers, one on my left hand and two on my right. This is ridiculous for someone who makes his living writing, so something like fifteen years ago I decided to correct this professional shortcoming of mine. I set out to take a typing course. It was too late. You can't teach an old dog a new way to type. I still have the books and I went to one class, but I'm resigned now to the three-finger school.

Years ago I lived in California for eight months and worked at MGM. None of the people I was involved with put in an eight-hour day, but I don't play golf and I hate lying on a beach, so I decided to learn how to fly a plane. I still have my logbook. I put in eight hours before something more pressing came along and I gave up my dream of expanding my world by learning to fly.

It's got so I hate to poke through old boxes of papers. Every time I do, I come on some bit of evidence of some plan I once had for making myself a better person. And look at me.

Simple Sensations

Every once in a while, I'm reminded of some way I used to feel or some simple sensation I used to have that I don't have anymore because I no longer do whatever it was that brought it on.

I was trying to recall some of them:

—The last time I was out of work was twenty-five years ago, but being out of work and unwanted by anyone is a feeling you never forget. Everyone else is inside with a place to go and be, and you're outside with nothing.

—I suppose there are people with outboard motors equipped with electric starters who have never wrapped that rope around the fly-wheel and yanked on it until the engine started.

—It's been a long while since I toasted a marshmallow on a stick over an open fire and even longer since I melted one in a cup of hot cocoa.

—We haven't had a power failure in our house in six years now and I miss them. If it didn't last too long, it was sort of adventurous to live by candlelight and find ways to improvise dinner.

—When you walk up to someone's front door and ring the bell and wait for someone to come, it's an uncomfortable few minutes. You don't know what they're doing in there. You don't know who is going to come to the door. You aren't sure anyone will. I haven't been in that position in years. When I go to someone's house now, I either know them so well I just walk in, or they're having a big party and the door is already open, so I don't ring.

—Filling a fountain pen from a bottle of ink was satisfying.

—In the last three years, half a dozen quick car wash places have opened for business in our area. Every time the car gets dirty now, my wife takes it over there and has it washed, and I'm left with nothing easy to do Saturday morning. Washing a car gives me a sense of accomplishment without demanding much from me.

—The way I used to save money was a lot more satisfying than the way I save it now. Every night I used to empty my pockets and put all the loose change in a big jar in my closet. Now the company takes money out of my check every week. I never see the money and don't get anywhere near the pleasure from saving that I did with the jar. I guess I'm saving more now but it isn't money, it's just a number.

—There is no more secure feeling than being inside a tent that doesn't leak when it's pouring outside.

—Nothing was ever more uncomfortable than riding on the cross-bar or the handlebars of a friend's bicycle.

—It's been years since I've heard the sound or had the satisfaction that comes from slamming a genuine wooden frame screen door. Aluminum screen doors are just not the same.

—There was something special about running a stick along an iron picket fence.

—Not once this winter have I had to shovel the snow from my side-walk, but I haven't forgotten the unpleasant feeling you get when you're sliding the shovel along to scoop up the snow and hit a crack.

—When I delivered newspapers, they were usually thin enough so I could fold them into a square. You folded them once longways and then you folded them in three equal parts and tucked one part into the other. This way you could throw them on a porch from a moving bicycle. Or *near* the porch, anyway. Mrs. Potter wouldn't pay one week because she said I put too many in the bushes.

—Cakes of ice are all an inch square now and that's too bad, because getting a fifty-pound cake to break cleanly in two with an icepick was an art.

Small Pleasures

It's too bad all of us don't have some way to remind ourselves how good life is when life is going well. We are more apt to think of it as merely average and normal.

When I was fifteen, I had an appendectomy. There was some minor complication, and I was in the hospital for almost three weeks. (It's always surprising how serious a minor operation seems when you're the one who has had it.) But I recall then appreciating the colors and the action of everyday life when I got out of the hospital. My perception of many things I had always taken for granted was razor sharp. The grass looked greener, our house looked better and my mother's cooking tasted great.

The fact is, any time we or someone we love isn't dying, it should be considered a great time in life.

Just now, in the course of writing this, I was trying to remind myself of small pleasures I enjoy almost daily:

—My shower first thing in the morning is a wonderfully pleasant and exhilarating way to start the day. I like the warmth, I like a good cake of soap, and I like the idea that I'm part of a civilization that has organized itself to get water to my house and have it warm and waiting for me when I get up. It's difficult to remember to be amazed every day, but it is amazing.

—The morning newspaper and that first cup of coffee are two things I'm sure they have in heaven if there is one. I always pick up any newspaper with a great sense of anticipation. I'm a newspaper nut. There are times when I don't find much in it that interests me, but that never dampens my enthusiasm for getting at it again the following day.

—I love my work. I love writing. I even like the physical process of hitting the keys of the typewriter with my fingers, although I only use three of them. I enjoy thinking of things to write, and there is always a vague sense of excitement about whether I can do it or not; this heightens my interest. And to finish a piece of writing is a great satisfaction. It's as good as getting a sliver out of your finger.

—By noon I'm getting hungry and feeling desk-bound. I know a hundred good little restaurants, and it is a wonderfully civilized pleasure to find a friend and go to one of them for lunch.

—In the afternoons I'm not nearly so smart as I am in the shower eight hours earlier, but if I'm not pressed to do something for a deadline, I'm just as happy. It's pleasant to browse through the mail and the debris on my desk, looking for a job easy enough for my brain to handle at that hour. Perhaps I call one of my four kids working in Boston, Washington, New York and Providence.

—By late afternoon I can't wait to get home—the same home I couldn't wait to leave that morning. It's a pleasant place. My wife is glad to see me, I'm glad to see her, and we sit down and have a drink while we watch the evening news on television.

—On Saturdays I have fresh orange juice, one of the great luxuries of my life. As I sit there sipping it, I think how lucky I am to be able to make enough money to squeeze three oranges for a drink. After a great time with coffee, toast and the newspaper, I go down to my cellar filled with tools and good wood. I've had some of the pieces of wood for twenty years. I sit and consider for the hundredth time what I might make of a wide piece of walnut. I feel it and enjoy it and decide to save it.

I am not sick or dying at all right now, and I'm determined to remind myself how good life is.

X:

ENDINGS

John Lennon

A YOUNG man I like came into the office the other morning, and I happened to be walking past the coat rack when he was fumbling with a hanger.

"Good morning," I said.

As if I had asked him how he felt, he said, "I feel terrible about this thing."

His eyes were red and tears came to them again as he turned and hung his coat. What had moved him was the murder of John Lennon.

I walked back to my office and got thinking about how little it had moved me; I felt no real sadness, only interest in it as a news story and anger over its violent nature.

I had closed my mind to the Beatles. They were a phenomenon I had been exposed to a thousand times, but they never interested me much. I liked some of their music, but I'm a musical ignoramus and didn't really appreciate how technically good they were. Nor did I get much meaning from the words of their songs. I thought they confused obscurity with depth.

Part of my negative feeling about the Beatles came not so much because I never bothered to appreciate their music, but because I thought they had made drugs look attractive to a whole generation. Many of their songs seemed to me to be invitations to go fly with them. The "Yellow Submarine" was made to look like an attractive trip for young people to take.

My young office friend's genuine sorrow made it clear to me that I'd missed something, and in the days since John Lennon's death, I've read and heard a lot more about him. I feel a lot worse now than I did the night I heard he'd been shot. No amount of reading about or listening to Elvis Presley would make me feel anything different about him, but Lennon was out of Presley's class as a musician and as a human being.

It is apparent that Lennon had been trying desperately and with a lot of success to live his way out of what he got himself into by being a Beatle. He wasn't rejecting everything that had meant to him; he was just saying it was over and he wanted to move on to something else. It was something he didn't want to be anymore, and a lot of people weren't satisfied to let him stop being it. The man who killed him was one of those.

Whatever Lennon was as a Beatle, he'd obviously been something different for the last five years. He said he liked to stay home and bake bread and take care of his five-year-old son. It is obvious that he was sincere. He said it not to create an effect on the minds of readers of that statement, but because that's honestly what he wanted to do. He had had all the fame anyone could ever wish for, and he didn't want it anymore. It's easier to be an iconoclast, of course, if you've made your two hundred million dollars, but you can't fault him for that.

We make such fools of ourselves with our heroes, that's what irritates me the most about the kind of idiotic adulation the Beatles got. Wouldn't it have been possible for that whole sixties generation to have loved the Beatles' music without chasing them up and down the streets of the world?

Almost everyone who becomes famous ends up acting the way famous people act. It isn't so much that famous people *want* to act that way; they are forced into certain patterns of behavior. John Lennon was trying to act some way other than the way famous people act, and people wouldn't let him. Most of all, his murderer wouldn't let him.

It's very sad, and I understand now my friend's tears.

Herbert Hahn

He lived only a thirty-five-cent phone call away, but I never called him. No one influenced my life more than he did. Now he's gone and I don't think I ever told him.

I worked late yesterday and didn't get home until after eight. We had a quick dinner and it was too late to start anything else, so at ten I got into bed with the newspaper I'd never taken the time to read. The economic news was bad and the Giants' coach said he wasn't discouraged. I leafed through to the obituary page and my eye caught the little headline in boldface type:

HERBERT HAHN, 75
ENGLISH TEACHER

I dropped the paper to the floor next to the bed and stared at the ceiling. Mr. Hahn was dead. *Why* hadn't I called him? I was surprised to find myself crying. I hadn't really seen Mr. Hahn for forty years, didn't even know he was "Dr. Hahn" now, but I had thought of him on almost every one of the days of those forty years.

My memory of exactly what he was like in school was incredibly clear to me. I remember every mannerism, the way he pulled at the crease at the knee of his pants when he sat on the edge of his desk. I even remember that he only had two suits in 1936. One was his old suit and one was his good suit. He wore the old one for two days every other week when the good one was at the cleaners. He only made twenty-seven hundred dollars a year teaching history in Albany, N.Y., then and clothes were not a top priority of his.

He left Albany in about 1945 to teach at a good private school in New Jersey, and I wasn't surprised that the obituary called him an English teacher. It didn't really matter what Mr. Hahn's class was called. He taught life and his subject was of secondary importance. When we were fourteen and fifteen, he talked to us as though we were human beings, not children. He talked about everything in class, and just to make sure we knew he didn't think he was omnipotent, he often followed some pronouncement he'd made about government or politics by saying, "And don't forget you heard it from the same teacher who predicted in 1932 that Hitler would get nowhere in Germany."

How many teachers do you have in your life? I lay there wondering last night. Between grade school, high school and college, if you're lucky enough to go to college, I suppose you have about fifty teachers. Is that about right?

I don't remember much about some of mine, and nothing about what they were trying to teach me, but of those fifty, I had five who were very good and two who were great. Mr. Hahn was one of those.

He didn't do a lot of extra talking, but when he talked he was direct and often brilliant. He was the only genuine philosopher I ever knew. He wasn't a teacher of philosophy, but a living, breathing philosophizer. He exuded wisdom, concern for the world and quite often a bad temper. Idiots irritated him, and it annoyed him when teenagers acted younger than he was treating them.

I went to the service for him today. I don't know why, really. There was no one there I knew, and one phone call over the years would have meant more to him. A minister spoke, but it was standard stuff, and Mr. Hahn was not what most people would call a religious person, even though he wrote a book called *The Great Religions: Interpretations*.

A young woman who taught with him spoke, and she brought the tears back to my eyes. He had touched her life in the 1970s as he had touched mine in the 1930s.

Mr. Hahn could have taught at any college in the country, but he chose to stay at the secondary level. He didn't think teaching college-age people was any more important than teaching boys and girls fourteen to eighteen. He was the kind of person who gave teachers the right to be proud to be teachers.

I just wish I'd called or written to tell him how much he meant to my life.

Mother

M y mother died today.

She was a great mom and I am typing with tears in my eyes. There were a lot of things she wasn't so good at, but no one was ever better at being a mother.

She never wanted to be anything *but* a good mother. It would not satisfy many women today. If I were a woman it would not satisfy me, but there was something good about her being one that exceeded any good I will ever do.

I think I know why she was a world champion mother. She had unlimited love and forgiveness in her heart for those close to her. Neither my sister nor I ever did anything so wrong in her eyes that she couldn't explain it in terms of right. She assumed our goodness, and no amount of badness in either of us could change her mind. It made us better.

Mother gave the same love to our four children and even had enough left for our family bulldog, Gifford. One summer afternoon at her cottage in a wooded area with a lot of wildlife, some food was left on the table on the front patio. When we came back later, part of it had been eaten, and everyone but Mother suspected our bulldog.

"It couldn't have been Gifford," Mother said. "It must have been some animal."

From the day she went into the hospital, there was never any question about her living. The doctor treated her as though she might recover, but he knew she would not. I hope he is treated as well on his deathbed.

Something has to be done about the way we die, though. Too often it is not good enough. Some of the people who have heard of Mother's death at age ninety-three and knew of her protracted illness said, "It's a blessing," but there was nothing blessed about it.

For seven terrible weeks after a stroke, Mother held on to life with a determination she would not have had if she hadn't wanted to live.

Visiting her, at first, I was pleased that she seemed unaware of anything and not suffering. I would bend over, stroke her hair, and whisper in her ear, "It's Andrew, Mom." It would not seem as though she heard, but her hand, which had been picking at the blanket in a manner distinctively her own, groped for mine. She did hear. She did know. She was in a terrible half-dream from which she could not arouse herself. She was suffering and in fear of death, and I could not console myself that she was not.

My wife stood on the other side of the bed. They got along during the twenty years Mother lived with us. Mother lifted her other hand vaguely toward her. Dying, she wished to include my wife, who had been so good to her, in her affection.

Something is wrong, though. She has something in her throat, or one of her legs is caught in an uncomfortable position. You don't dare touch anything for fear of disconnecting one of the tubes leading from the bottles hanging overhead into her. The nurses are busy with their bookwork, or they are down the hall working routinely toward Mother's room. Other patients there are caught or choking, too. The nurses know Mother will probably not choke before they get there. They've done it all before.

The nurses are very good, but without apparent compassion, and you realize it has to be that way. They could not possibly work as nurses without some protective coating against tragedy. We all have it. In those seven weeks Mother lay dying, I visited the hospital fifty times, but when I left, it was impossible not to lose some of the sense of her suffering. I knew she was still lying there picking vaguely at the blankets in that sad, familiar way, but it didn't hurt as much as when I was there, watching.

I wondered—if she was the President of the United States, what extraordinary measures would they be taking for her? How could I get them for her? She is not President, she is only my mother. The doctors and nurses cannot know that this frail, dying old woman did a million kindnesses for me. They wouldn't know or care that she was girls' high-jump champion of Ballston Spa in 1902 or that she often got up early Sunday morning to make hot popovers for us or that she drove her old Packard too fast and too close to the righthand side of the road. No stranger would have guessed any of those things looking at her there and perhaps would not have cared.

There is no time for each of us to weep for the whole world. We each weep for our own.

Pieces of My Mind

Andrew A. Rooney

JANE BRADFORD *and* NEIL NYREN *had a lot to do with the editing and organization of this book and I thank them for it.* A.R.

Contents

502   *Contents*

504   *Contents*

Preface

Writers are repeatedly asked to explain where they get their ideas. People want their secret. The truth is there is no secret and writers don't have many new ideas. At least, they don't have many ideas that a comic strip artist would illustrate with a light bulb over their heads.

New ideas are one of the most overrated concepts of our time. Most of the important ideas that we live with aren't new at all. If we're grown up, we've had our personal, political, economic, religious, and philosophical ideas for a long time. They evolved out of some experience we had or they came from someone we were exposed to before we were twenty-five. How many of us have changed our opinion about anything important after we were twenty-five because of some new idea?

Like almost everything else that gets popular, new ideas and the concept of creativity have been trivialized. People are passing off novelty for invention. Not many products have been improved with a new idea compared to the number whose quality has been diminished by inferior workmanship and the use of inferior materials. The shortage we face in this country is not new ideas, it's quality work.

Much of the progress of the world has come through genuine creativity but we've cheapened the whole concept by treating creativity as if it were a commodity that could be bought and sold by the pound.

Colleges teach courses in "creative writing" as if a course in just plain writing weren't enough. Trying to teach someone to be creative is as silly as a mother trying to teach her child to be a genius.

I don't know where we all got the thought that ideas come in a blinding flash or that we can learn how to be struck with creative new ideas. Not many ideas come that way. The best ideas are the result of the same slow, selective, cognitive process that produces the sum of a column of figures. Anyone who waits to be struck with a good idea has a long wait coming. If I have a deadline for a column or a television script, I sit down at the typewriter and damn well decide to *have* an idea. There's nothing magical about the process, no flashing lights.

Creativity is a by-product of hard work. If I never have another really new idea, it won't matter. Enough writers are already exploring the new, the far-out, and the obscure. We don't understand the old ideas yet. I'm satisfied trying to quantify the obvious.

We have our ideas. What we need now are more people who can do something good with them.

I:

IT'S ONLY A PLATE

It's Only a Plate

Do I grieve for an icebox? I do.

We're about to buy a new refrigerator—which I still tend to call "the icebox"—and I feel good and bad about it. We need a new one and it's going to be more convenient but I hate getting rid of the old one. It's been such a dependable friend in time of need to eat. I just know nothing good is going to come to it when the dealer delivers the new one and takes the old one away. He'll probably take a few parts off it and just dump the rest of it somewhere. It seems so ungrateful of me.

I was sitting in the kitchen last night, looking around. It's changing gradually from the kitchen it was when the kids were growing up. The table I made that we all ate at thousands of times has been replaced. I hated to see that go, too. It's the kind of progress I don't appreciate. Now the kitchen is in for another big change when that icebox goes. I'll bet the new one won't have as satisfying a sound when you open and close it. New refrigerators have more of a sneaky sound when they open and close. I like a refrigerator door that closes with a solid, reassuring bang. I like the sound this old one has because I associate it with all the good food that came out of it.

But I didn't set out here to write of iceboxes. The question in my mind is whether or not we should be sentimental about inanimate objects. I am incurably so. I feel terrible when I trade in a car I've liked. I even hate to throw out a comfortable old pair of pajamas that are ripped or buttonless or in some other way too disreputable to wear even in the privacy of bed.

Being sentimental about a car or a pair of pajamas or a refrigerator is ridiculous and I know it but I can't help myself. I have this irrational notion that the refrigerator has feelings and will be hurt when I cast it aside after it's given me seventeen years of good service. It will want to know what it's done wrong to deserve ending up in the dump. The car I drive for 91,000 miles before I trade it in will be heartbroken at being turned over to a new owner who will abuse it.

Some inanimate objects don't get me at all. That's lucky. For

509

instance, I retired a television set from the living room about a year ago and felt nothing for it. It was ten years old and we'd watched a lot of good and bad shows on it, but somehow it never earned my affection. It was just a piece of equipment.

My mother came to grips with this and she licked any tendency she had to be sentimental about *things*. She knew that over a lifetime, it was just too sad. Losing people was all the sadness she needed.

I remember one night in our house a guest was trying to help with the dishes. As the guest was rinsing a small, old platter under running water, she hit the platter against the faucet and it cracked cleanly in two. While my mother was dismissing the broken platter as being of no importance at all, in order to make the guest feel better about having broken it, I quietly put the pieces on a shelf. I always think I can mend a plate.

Later, after the guest had gone, I saw mother looking at the two pieces and I asked her about it.

"Yes," Mother said, "Bessie gave that plate to your Dad and me when we were married. I've had it forty-five years." She paused for just one brief, sad beat, I thought, and then she threw both pieces in the wastebasket and said, "But it's only a plate."

I hope I'm not around the house when the men come to take the old refrigerator away, though. I don't think I could stand it, and the truckers would think it was pretty strange to see a grown man standing around with tears in his eyes as they carried out a tired, seventeen-year-old icebox.

A New Kitchen

For several years now I've tried to keep my wife from talking about buying a new house by heaping unnecessarily lavish praise on her for something like the new curtains she bought for the living room or the wallpaper in the front hall.

The praise I gave her for the new carpet she had put down in the twins' room apparently wasn't excessive enough, because within just a few days she started talking about moving or having the kitchen done over.

While I hate to encourage her by giving in every time in these negotiating procedures, I am pleased to announce we are having the kitchen done over.

My wife says we don't have enough cupboard space in the kitchen but I know for sure this is an illusion. Whether a kitchen cupboard, a file cabinet or a clothes closet overflows, depends more on the person putting things into it than on its size. But "Yes, Dear" we'll get new cabinets . . . anything but move.

So they're going to tear out the old cabinets and replace the stove, which they call "the range." They're going to rearrange the lighting, do over the electrical wiring and, of course, put down a new floor. The floor isn't level enough to put one down, though, so first they'll have to take the old one up. I figure if I'm lucky, this new kitchen isn't going to cost me much more than twice what the house cost in the first place. If the President was doing as much for the unemployed as my wife is, the country would be a lot better off.

Last weekend we spent both Saturday and Sunday taking everything out of the kitchen. I don't mean *almost* everything. I mean *everything*. We spent twelve hours each day arguing about what to keep and what to throw out. I lost my last argument at eleven P.M. Sunday night, when I wanted to keep ten of those little pink birthday cake candleholders that I found drifting around in the back of a drawer.

You don't realize how much stuff piles up in those drawers, cabinets and closets in the kitchen. Some of the work of emptying them out and finding places to put the stuff temporarily was useful and satisfying. When you discover that you have three bottles of vinegar, each partly used, it's a great feeling to consolidate the vinegar into two bottles and throw out the empty one. We threw out dozens of bottles, cans and jars emptied through the process of consolidation.

I made several decisions that would have shocked any good cook and didn't even tell my wife what I was doing. For instance, I poured a quarter of a bottle of relatively inexpensive corn oil into a bottle of expensive virgin olive oil that was more than half full. I mixed a small amount of marmalade in with some apricot jam.

My wife kept saying I wouldn't throw anything out but she was wrong. I threw out a bottle that had more than two inches of ketchup in it because we seldom use ketchup. And she says I won't throw anything out.

It wasn't one of the outstanding experiences of our married life but we know now that we have fourteen cans of tuna fish, three half-used boxes of soap pads, a bag of potatoes behind the sink that have begun to sprout and more frozen leftovers in the freezer, which will shortly be disconnected, than we'll ever be able to identify, let alone consume.

For the time being at least, I think I've bought myself another few months before the subject of moving comes up again.

Casting Out Books

In the futile attempts we all make to tidy up our lives and our surroundings, nothing is more difficult than throwing out a book. I can't even bring myself to throw out a terrible book. I have all I can do to throw out a magazine. It has to be done, though, and I'm trying to develop some plan.

At about age forty, each of us should resolve to throw away or give away one book for each new book we acquire. There are books we will never part with and shouldn't. If you've read and liked a book and taken a little of it into your life, you should keep it forever. It doesn't take up much room, it's attractive on the book-shelf, it doesn't take much dusting and it provides evidence to visitors in your house that you're literate. Even though you may never actually take it down and read it again, the presence of its title staring out at you every day is a reminder of its contents.

The books we should throw out are the junk books we acquire and the books that were good in their time but which have no lasting value. This includes most popular novels. No one reads a novel twice and most of them are read as entertainment and diversion. Nothing that is merely entertaining and diverting is worth saving.

There are some serious problems when you get right down to what to throw out. We have some big, expensive, arty picture books that we never look at. They don't fit on our shelves and we never look at them, but they cost so much I can't bring myself to ditch them and they're hard to give away. No one *else* wants them either. Most of them were gifts in the first place.

Volumes of old books, gilt-edged or bound in leather, are a problem. They look good on your shelves but you've never read the collected works of Dickens and never will. They were left to you by someone in the family who never read them. As a matter of fact, none of the eight volumes has ever been read by anyone and probably ought to be given to a worthy cause, although I doubt if a worthy cause would read them either.

I'm looking at my bookshelves as I write. There's *Catch-22* up there. It's a good book but I won't be reading it again.

There's *Dr. Zhivago.* I wouldn't want Boris Pasternak to know but I never got through the whole thing. Sorry, Boris, but I think you'll have to make room for someone else.

Here's a thin hardcover book I've just taken down. It's published by the U.S. Chamber of Commerce and it's called *America's Outstanding Young Men, 1938–1966.*

Now, this is the kind of book I keep. It's dated but the names in it bring back ideas and memories that might otherwise be lost to me forever. They pick ten outstanding young men every year. Look at this! In 1938 Howard Hughes was thirty-four and they thought he showed promise. Rudy Vallee's on the list and so is Elmer Layden, the Notre Dame football coach. Orson Welles is here. He was twenty-three in 1938 and considered a genius. It seems to me it's been all downhill for Orson since he turned twenty-four. Geniuses do not make their living doing television commercials. Anyway, I'm certainly not going to throw out this little book. It'll always remind me how short life is and that I'd better keep moving.

If I had to make a few rules for which books to throw out, I'd say throw out:

1—Books of advice on how to make money, lose weight or have a happy marriage.

2—Any book whose jacket says that it's "a torrid romance."

3—Any novel whose title brings to your mind no memory whatsoever of plot or character.

4—Any book whose title begins, *The Anatomy of . . .* , *A Treasury of . . .* or *The Changing Face of . . . .*

5—All the books that have been made into movies you've seen.

This should make room for some new books on your shelves.

Old Appliances

THERE'S nothing older than an old electrical appliance. An old piece of furniture may qualify as an antique and an old piece of clothing may make a good rag, but an old electrical appliance is junk. We've got to face that fact in America.

It's not easy to accept the idea that an appliance has a defined life span. Usually the appliance is so new, so shiny, so magic and so expensive when we buy it that its mortality is no more questioned by us than our own.

In our house today, pushed to the rear of upper shelves in the kitchen, hidden behind pots in the lower cabinets and stashed away in cellar, attic and garage are dozens of dead pieces of electrical equipment. We have several electric coffee percolaters that I'd never think of using again, old irons so full of sediment from the water that they no longer steam, two or three nonworking radios, several food mixers, nine hair dryers, a record player and a black-and-white television set.

Perhaps what we need is some kind of friendly mortician who would console us on the loss of our electrical loved ones and promise to dispose of them in a dignified manner. Just tossing a Mixmaster into the trash seems so uncivilized.

The absolutely worst thing you can do with an old appliance is give it to a friend or another family member as if you were doing them a favor. This not only puts the burden of throwing it away on them but they're further burdened with the fear that you'll show up at the house and ask where it is.

We really haven't had electrical appliances for all that long, in terms of the history of the world or even the history of the United States. The first ones are just getting to the age when they're absolutely no good at all but there's a whole generation of appliances that came along in the forties, fifties, sixties and seventies that would be on Social Security now if they were people.

While people are lasting longer than they used to, appliances aren't lasting as long, so there are more people alive today and more appliances that ought to be tossed out.

The whole problem first dawned on me when a quarter-inch drill

I owned stopped working. It still looked okay but it just wouldn't work. Naturally, I decided to have it fixed. Well, as we all know, *deciding* to have an appliance fixed and actually *getting* it fixed are two different things. Most modern appliances were not designed to be fixed. They were designed to be used until they broke down and then thrown away.

Anyway, I set the drill aside to be fixed at a later date and went out and bought a new one. I can use two, I thought to myself.

That was eleven years ago tomorrow and the drill that won't work is still right where I left it, waiting to be fixed. I realize now that I should have thrown it out the day it broke. There were still a lot of parts that were not broken, I suppose, but if you don't know which are and which aren't, that does you no good at all.

In the year 3000, I suppose there might be some museum value to my son's first record player but, as things stand today, it's just one more piece of junk taking up space in the room he used to occupy, and next Saturday morning I'm going to start with that. Out it goes.

The Red Badge of Character

IF it weren't for the fact that new things are so satisfying to buy, it would be depressing how soon they start to deteriorate after you acquire them.

When I buy a new car, which isn't often, I always wait with a feeling of dread for the day I put the first scratch or dent in it. Sooner or later it has to come. Once I scraped the side of the car on the green paint of the garage door when I was putting it away in a hurry during a rainstorm. Another new car I had, got its first dent in the parking lot of a supermarket. Some fellow parked too close to me and the edge of his door banged into mine when he opened it. It wasn't much of a dent but it doesn't take much to change your attitude toward a new car. Once it happens, even if it's within the first few weeks after you bought it, the car seems used and you begin thinking of your next one, pristine and undented.

We bought a new carpet for the living room eight years ago. On the third night after we got it, I took a cup of coffee into the living room after dinner to drink while I watched television. I drank most of it but by the time I got to the last half-inch it was cold and I put the cup on the little table next to my chair. Half an hour later I reached for the second section of the newspaper and dumped the cup on the floor, spilling the cold coffee. For an instant I was pleased that the cup hadn't broken but then I saw the spot on the rug. I ran to the kitchen for damp cloths and tried to remember whether it was lemon juice or club soda you use on coffee spots (I know it's tomato juice you put on a dog that gets into a skunk). Nothing took the coffee stain out, though, and from its third day that new carpet has been just another old rug with a spot on it, that I'd like to get rid of.

When I was twelve, my mother bought me a corduroy suit. It must have been the first real suit with matching pants and jacket that I ever had. It even had a vest.

That Sunday we went to my uncle's house for dinner and I wore my new suit. I was very proud of it, especially the vest. We came home late that afternoon and our English bulldog, Spike, had been locked in the house most of the day so I took him out in the backyard to play. For some reason, I didn't bother to change my clothes first.

Spike loved to pull on a heavy leather strap we had and I started to play tug-of-war with him. He weighed almost as much as I did and it was always a close contest. Somehow he got me over by the fence at the side of the yard. He gave me a hard tug and I caught my new corduroy pants on a nail sticking out of the fencepost. It tore a jagged hole in the pants just above the knee.

As you can imagine, that was not one of the best days in my life. I felt terrible about tearing my pants and even worse about how mad my mother was. My mother sewed them up and I wore them for several years but never with any pleasure. As a matter of fact, that experience gave me a complex about new suits. Whenever I buy a new one, I'm nervous every time I wear it during its first six months. I can still see that jagged tear in the knee.

Fortunately, there are characteristics that possessions have, or acquire, that we sometimes prefer to brand-newness. If we keep a car long enough, we lose the feeling that it's a new car we banged up and start thinking of it as a somewhat battered but lovable old friend.

It's a good thing we can take as much pleasure from oldness as newness because, for the most part, we have to live with more oldness. When we buy something new, we're looking for something, unlike ourselves and our other possessions, perfect. It never stays that way for long and it's this period of disillusion and disappointment that we find so hard to live with. As the possession acquires more of the character of the owner, the owner feels easier about its defects. I wouldn't recognize my old Ford station wagon without those dents in the front fender and the missing piece of decorative stripping on the door on the driver's side. They're part of the car now and I like it, but I recall how upset I was about them for the first few years.

Sartorial Shortcomings

FROM time to time it is brought to my attention that I'm not the best-dressed man in the world. Someone wrote once that I looked as though I slept in Grand Central Station every night. I have four grown children who unfortunately aren't afraid of me and they've never hesitated to point out my sartorial shortcomings, either. The least they could do is lie a little if they really love me.

I'm relatively unaware of how I look in clothes. I usually look once in the mirror when I dress in the morning but that only shows me myself from the chest up.

I don't know where I go wrong. I buy pretty good clothes but one of us is usually the wrong shape.

Maintaining clothes in good condition is as hard as keeping a house painted and in working order. For example, it's inevitable that you're going to get a spot on a necktie or the lapel of a coat once in a while. I keep all kinds of spot remover at home and in the office and I've never had any success with any of them. That spray can, with the powder in it, just plain doesn't work for me. I've used it a dozen times on grease spots and the same thing always happens. The grease spot is gone and I'm left with a big, plainly visible splotch of white chalk imbedded in the fabric. Nothing takes that out, ever.

Most brands of spot cleaner use carbon tetrachloride. I've tried to remove a thousand spots from a thousand neckties with carbon tet. All I get is a ring bigger and more obvious than the original spot.

I've seen women remove spots successfully. They say you just have to keep rubbing in circles. I've rubbed spots in circles with carbon tet until I was blue in the face from the fumes and I still get nothing but a big ring and a smelly tie.

In the morning I often take a pair of pants, a shirt or a coat into the back room where we have an iron set up. My intentions are good. I don't want to burden my wife with my problems and I want to look neat. I don't want to embarrass my friends or my family.

I have yet to iron a pair of pants that end up with fewer than two creases down the front of each leg. I'd like to have one of those machines the dry cleaners have. They just lay a pair of pants on there any which way, they pull down that handle, there's a big whoosh of steam and presto! the pants are perfect.

Shirts? Who can iron a shirt? I've never ironed a shirt yet that didn't look worse when I finished with it than it did when I started.

Neckties are smaller but they're at least as hard to iron as a shirt. You'd think they'd be easy but if you press down on a tie, you get the imprint of the lumpy lining on the front of the tie. As a result, many of my ties look like my pants.

During the summer I often carry a tie in my pocket instead of wearing it. Many of them never recover during the winter.

It's a good thing socks don't show much because if my kids think my pants and jackets look bad, they should see my socks. I've given up trying to put them on right side out because at least half the time I don't even have a pair. I just look for two socks in the drawer that are somewhere near the same color. I haven't had pairs of socks in years.

The funny thing is that I have a clear idea in my mind what someone well dressed looks like. I know what I want to look like and sometimes I realize I'm unconsciously thinking that's what I *do* look like. Obviously I'm dreaming.

I had several friends in school who were always well dressed, and I can go around for days thinking I look more or less the way they looked. Marshall always looked just right. Then someone will casually tell me I look like an unmade bed and I'm brought back down to earth.

The only thing for me to do is take the position that clothes don't make the man.

Buying Clothes

I F I had known for sure, when I bought the clothes I own, that I was going to like them and wear them, I could have saved myself a fortune. The clothing business would be in big trouble if all of us liked everything we bought when we got it home, because we wouldn't be traipsing back to the store in a few weeks to buy something to replace it. My average is slightly below fifty percent. I like and wear less than fifty percent of everything I buy once I get it home. My clothes closets are filled with pants, jackets, shirts and shoes that seemed attractive and practical to me in the store when I bought them but haven't worked out at all.

To make up for those, I have four or five suits I've owned for ten years that I've worn and worn. I wouldn't part with them for anything. I reach for the same old things year after year. Toward the middle of spring when the weather starts to turn hot, I put away the clothes I've worn all winter and think to myself that some of those old favorites have seen their last season.

I cannot quite bring myself to throw out the old favorites, though, and I decide to give them one last summer vacation in the back of my closet.

In September, when the first nip is in the air, I reach for something warmer. I take out that old favorite, look it over and put it on. It looks fresher and better than it did at the end of last year. I can get away with it for another year, I think to myself. And another. And another.

One of the great disappointments to me about clothing is how consistently I find that the most expensive clothes I buy are the best. This doesn't seem fair or biblical. When I pay more for an all-wool suit or an all-cotton shirt by a good maker, it looks better, fits better and wears longer. When I buy a snappy-looking synthetic jacket or a pair of pants that are supposed to do everything but walk to the washing machine by themselves, I'm usually disappointed. I wear the jacket a few times and then it begins to drift to the unused end of the clothespole in my closet.

A second disappointment to me when it comes to buying clothes is that you can never repeat anything. If you buy something you like and wear it for a year and decide you'd like another similar to it, you can never get one. They don't make them that way any longer. Clothing manufacturers are a restless bunch. They don't stick with a good thing when they have it. They try something else and it's usually worse. That's fashion.

I have a pair of light brown corduroy pants that are a little thin at the knees and ragged around the pockets. I still like them and wear them Saturdays but I'd like a new pair so my wife wouldn't be embarrassed when we go to the supermarket together. I can't find those corduroy pants anywhere. They're all bell-bottomed and without belt loops this year.

In America we treat clothes the way we treat food. We spend more for food than is necessary to nourish ourselves and more for clothes than is necessary to cover ourselves. We have fun with these luxuries and I have no objection to them but I wish the manufacturers would spend a little more time thinking about quality and a little less on style.

The fact is that most of us don't wear most of the clothes or shoes we own. We just *have* them.

Dave Garroway used to have his clothes closet divided into sections by size. He was always going from 180 to 230 and back down again so in the morning he'd weigh himself to see which size suit he should wear. My weight goes up and down, too, but I don't have my clothes separated by size. When my weight is up, my clothes fit tight. When my weight is down, they hang on me.

I think it might be a good idea if we set aside one night a year when we took everything we own out of the closet and every shirt, sock and set of underwear out of our dresser drawers and tried them each on in front of a mirror.

Next to the mirror there should be a huge wastebasket.

Underwear

You have to look for good in people wherever you can find it. A very nice thing about most people is that they wear their best underwear when they get dressed up to go to a party, even though it isn't going to show. There's something basically honest about that.

One of the pleasures of a vacation is being able to wear your old underwear. I have a lot of it that's too good to throw away but not good enough to wear out into the world. On a normal, nonvacation day, there's always that thought that some emergency might arise that would cause to be revealed what you're wearing underneath. Maybe you'll be hit by a bicycle and taken to a doctor's office where you'll be told to undress. (It is quite possible that one of the reasons doctors charge so much is that they see the good underwear people are wearing and conclude they must be rich.)

The pleasure of wearing old clothes on vacation isn't limited to underwear. Another good part of my vacation is being able to wear the shirts I own that are frayed at the collar after several years of regular duty. At the beginning of my vacation, I go through my dresser drawers and remove the shirts that have seen their best days. I get a pair of scissors and cut the sleeves off just above the elbow.

I can't tell you the satisfaction I get from wearing these old friends on vacation. It gives me the feeling that I'm saving money but I also like the idea of getting everything there is out of something. Wearing a comfortable old shirt with a frayed collar on vacation is conservation at its best.

Some old clothes don't adapt themselves to being worn on vacation. I own several gray business suits that are beginning to look seedy. The pants fit and they're comfortable but I wouldn't think of wearing them to hang around in on vacation.

Most dress shoes don't take kindly to this kind of retirement, either. I have a few old pairs that I keep to hack around in but shoes that were meant to be shined never look right with paint on them. I've bought myself a pair of work shoes for vacation and I alternate between them and old sneakers that were once tennis shoes.

Vacation clothes have to be clothes that are loved. It's not a time for wearing rejects that don't fit or clothes that you've hated since you got them home from the store. Sometime last winter I bought a package of three undershirts. The label said they were "100 percent cotton."

The undershirts were good in all regards, except I noticed that when I wore them, my shoulders itched. A writer can't write if his shoulders itch so I removed my outer shirt and looked for one of those scratchy labels they often put in the neck. There was none. I put the shirt back on but my shoulders still itched.

When I undressed for bed that night, I inspected the stitches in the top of the shoulder straps of my new underwear. Aha! There were the offending threads, and I question whether or not they were cotton.

Now what do I do? I can't take the underwear back to the store and demand my money back because they make my shoulders itch. This doesn't sound like a reasonable complaint, so I put the three undershirts in the bottom of my drawer until last week. Foolishly I decided that while the undershirts weren't good enough to wear to work in the city, they'd be just the thing to wear on vacation in the country. This was a mistake. I don't want my shoulders to itch on vacation any more than I want them to itch when I'm at work.

I've put those three undershirts back in the bottom of a dresser drawer. Someday maybe I'll take them to a textile laboratory and find out whether or not the shirts are really "100 percent cotton," including those threads in the shoulders.

Clothes Make the Woman

MEN and women are doing more things the same way in our society but there's still a huge difference in their attitudes toward clothes and the way they dress. You never know what a woman's going to wear. You have a pretty good idea what a man's going to have on.

"What'll I wear?" isn't a question a man asks very often because he doesn't have that many choices.

A woman may wear a skirt one day and pants the next. You wouldn't find a man wearing pants one day and a skirt the next.

I'm not complaining. This is just a comment. I admire women's ability to adjust to this kind of change every day but I wonder if it doesn't slow them down in a hundred little ways. If I wore different kinds of clothes every day, I'd always be slipping things in a pocket that wasn't there. I become as familiar with the clothes I wear as I am with being right-handed and if I dressed differently every day, it would certainly delay me. For instance, I usually leave things in my pants pockets overnight. It saves time knowing I'm going to wear them again tomorrow.

Women have a vastly greater array of underwear than men. I don't come in contact with a lot of women's underwear but I do read the ads in the Sunday papers like everyone else and I'm amazed at the variety. I don't wonder it takes longer for the average woman to dress than for the average man. Just for a woman to decide which underwear to take out of the drawer would use up several minutes. I could have my shirt and pants on by that time.

Years ago it was just a question of whether a woman's slip showed or not. Underwear for women has come a long way since then. It ranges all the way from none to lash-ups that rival an astronaut's space suit.

I hope women understand I'm just being friendly. I just want to help. Most men have four or five pairs of shoes. A man has a couple of pairs of dress shoes, usually one black pair and one brown. He has a pair of work shoes, a pair of sneaks or running shoes and maybe a pair of heavy boots.

There are lots of women who own twenty-five or thirty pairs of shoes. These are not rich women. They may be working women or housewives who aren't fancy dressers but anyone looking in their closets at the shoes on the floor might guess they were in show business. Most women could wear a different pair of shoes every day for a month and still have some left over.

Women own more belts than men. Women have more belts than shoes. Half the dresses they own take a belt and no two dresses take the same one. A man has a couple of belts to hold up his pants. They are not considered decorator items. Some men have just two belts. They have one for when they weigh 164 pounds and another for when they weigh 187. Men don't have drawers filled with belts nor do belts drip from hooks in their closets. Having so many belts to choose from is not going to help women get ahead in the world.

There's one good thing that women and men agree on. Neither wears a hat much anymore. Hats are just for fun or special occasions now. When I was growing up, my mother didn't leave the house without a hat on and neither did my father. My father wore a fedora, one of the silliest, least efficient pieces of clothing ever designed. My mother had a selection of hats she wore, depending on the occasion and the clothes she was wearing.

I like attractively dressed women but I do have a nervous feeling that women should buy fewer clothes. If women didn't have so many decisions to make when they open their closet doors in the morning, they'd be off to a better start.

Shoes

THE single biggest step women have taken toward equality with men, since they acquired the right to vote in 1920, is in the shoes they're wearing. Fewer women are tottering around on high, spindly heels and there is no doubt that the change in footwear is going to help them stay even or get ahead of men. Up until now it's taken women longer to do everything because in the shoes they were wearing, they couldn't get anywhere as fast as men.

One of the most encouraging things I see every day is women walking to work in New York City. New York, more than almost anyplace else in the country, is a walking city. Hundreds of thousands of people walk twenty or thirty blocks from where they live uptown or downtown, into midtown where they work. Thousands of women are hustling along in good, rubber-soled sneakers. Sneakers have become so sophisticated that no one calls them that anymore but I'm sure you know what I mean. The women either carry a bag with the shoes they plan to wear in the office or they have left shoes at the office. They change into those when they get there. In most cases even their dress shoes have heels that are low compared to those women wore in the past.

I don't know how women ever got trapped into wearing spike heels. Spike heels are only slightly less arcane than the bindings Chinese women used to use to make their feet small. I say I don't know but I suppose I do know. Women's legs look sexier in high heels than in sneakers. What I really don't know is why this is so.

For some obscure reason men have got themselves thinking that a woman's leg, from the knee down, is more attractive if the calf is quite full but tapering off sharply into a thin, bony ankle. If the heel is propped up on a platform, it tends to make a lump of the calf muscle. That's the look we like.

The answer is for men to reeducate themselves about what looks attractive about a woman's leg. That shouldn't be hard. I've just about got myself to the place where a woman's leg looks better to me in a pair of sneakers than in shoes with heels.

There hasn't been much progress made in what men wear on their feet. The average man is wearing shoes that don't really come close to approximating the outline of his feet. He buys a pair of shoes that are about an inch longer than his feet so they won't pinch his toes and then he starts breaking them in. Breaking in a pair of shoes means stretching them by wearing them until they're close enough to the shape of your feet so they don't hurt much when you walk in them.

If you look at a man's foot in his shoes, you can tell the shoes don't really fit. The widest part of his foot almost always stretches the leather so that the upper part of the shoe hangs over the sole.

For years now they've been molding ski boots to fit your foot precisely and I'm waiting for that to happen with the ordinary shoes we wear. I confidently expect the time isn't far off when both men and women will be able to walk into a shoe store and have shoes made for them that exactly conform to the shape of their feet.

Molded shoes can be bought now but they are made mostly for people with orthopedic problems and they're very expensive. Even people with normal feet look funny in molded shoes because the shoes *are* the shape of their feet and we're not used to that. We're used to pretending that our feet are the shape of our shoes and they're not, of course.

Feet have gotten a dirty deal over the years. We haven't paid half as much attention to them as we've paid to our hands. Feet are what Howard Cosell would call the unsung heroes of our bodies. We ought to give them a better break and the women walking to work in sneakers or running shoes are taking a big step in that direction. If I wore a hat, I'd take it off to them.

Change the Oil and the Glove Compartment, Please

A NEW car manual tells you to have the oil changed at least every season, but it never gives you any advice about the glove compartment. The things in the glove compartment need changing at least as often as the oil in the crankcase.

I've read about states applying for national disaster relief that weren't in as bad shape as the glove compartment of my car. Yesterday I was looking for a pencil when I was in the car in a supermarket parking lot. Pencils are one of the most difficult things to keep in a glove compartment because they drift to the bottom of it and way back. Finally I took everything out of the glove compartment, put it on the passenger seat and started through it methodically.

Following is the list of contents:
—Three badly folded maps of New York State, one of Ohio and a Hertz map of the San Francisco Bay Area.
—Various envelopes pertaining to new or old car registrations.
—A parking ticket from Washington, D.C., dated March 9, 1979.
—Three screws, a small stainless steel bolt and a wavy kind of washer. These have all fallen off some interior part of the car during its lifetime but I don't know where they fell from.
—The manual of operation for the car. It says on the cover: "Instructions: Read carefully before operating." I've had the car since 1977 but I haven't read it yet.
—Three pennies and a Canadian quarter.
—Half a roll of assorted Life Savers.

—One pair of sunglasses with the earpiece broken off.

—Several old grocery lists, some envelopes and bits of paper with things written on them, all of which must have been important at one time.

There were no gloves in the glove compartment and I never did find a pencil. I quickly shoved everything back in and slammed the door shut.

The most valuable thing about many old cars is the stuff in the glove compartment and what lies behind the cushions of the front seat. If you've owned a car for five years, it's likely that at least ten dollars' worth of small change and other valuables will have slipped down there. The change mixes with old Kleenex, rubber bands, lost keys, combs, important papers and pencils. That's where the pencils go in a car, down behind the front seat where you can't get at them. Some day a car manufacturer is going to make a car with a glass-bottomed front seat so you can look down and see all the money.

The trunk of a car has many of the same kind of items in it that the glove compartment has, only bigger. One of the great things about buying a new car used to be the tool kit they gave you with it. New cars don't come with tool kits any more but there are plenty of other things that fill the trunk.

I happen to know that at this very moment the trunk of my car contains two boards, a plastic bag of clothes I've been meaning to take to the Goodwill or the Salvation Army, a snow shovel, a bundle of old *National Geographics* and a partridge in a pear tree.

What I'd like, when I start packing the trunk to go somewhere, is a car equipped with one of those compactors like they have on garbage trucks. I could open the trunk, press the button and have the trunk lid come down, slowly and with great force. It would compact everything already in the trunk. That would make plenty of room for me to dump the suitcases in there and take off.

For the time being, I guess I'll just have the oil changed.

Directions

EARLY next year I'm going to take a week off and read the directions for all the things I've bought that came with the warning READ DIRECTIONS CAREFULLY BEFORE OPERATING.

There's no sense reading directions to something before you understand a little bit about it, because they don't mean anything to you. You have to know enough about something to be confused before directions help. Once I've pressed some wrong buttons or tried to open something by pressing on it when I should have been pulling on it or sliding it sideways, then I can understand the directions.

I have a whole box of directions I've never read. Many of them are still in their plastic wrappers. When Christmas comes again, I'll probably be getting more. Last Christmas my kids gave me a new camera. I've shot ten rolls of film with it and I've made about all the mistakes there are to be made. It will be fun now to see if the directions have any good suggestions.

It is always surprising to me to see how many issues divide our population almost in half. For example, I think it's safe to say that we are about evenly divided between people who read directions before operating, as they're warned to do under threat of death, and people who don't ever read the directions. The same people who don't read the maps in the glove compartments of their cars are the ones who don't pore over the instructions for operating their new washing machine or video cassette player.

My wife drives a Saab and during the three years we've had it, I've used it a dozen times. For the life of me I can't figure out how the heater works. I almost froze last winter driving into the city one day. This summer I drove in with it on a hot day and fussed with the controls the whole hour trying to get the air conditioning to work. That night I complained to my wife about how complicated the controls were. I said I was going to read the directions about how to work the air conditioning.

"Forget it," she said. "It doesn't have air conditioning."

In spite of some bad experiences, I'm a firm believer in the trial and error method of learning. If I were asked to take the space shuttle into outer space, I'd first want to climb on board and start fooling with the controls before I read anything about it. If I do read the directions about something before I know a single thing about it, I get so discouraged I give up. If, on the other hand, I bumble along making mistakes, confident that I can always look at the directions if I have to, then I usually find out how to do it the hard way.

Direction writers have improved over the years. Even the directions that come with a piece of Japanese electronic equipment are written in better English than they used to be.

You'd think it might be dangerous to ignore written directions but usually those little red tags say something like DANGER: UNDER NO

CIRCUMSTANCES SHOULD THIS BE PUT IN A BATHTUB FULL OF WATER!

They warn you against some very obvious things. Most of us know by now that you don't put a toaster in the dishwasher and that you shouldn't drop the television set when you're bringing it in the house. On the other hand, it has been my experience that FRAGILE THIS SIDE UP can usually be ignored with no ill effects. Unless you've bought a cut-glass crystal pitcher that comes filled with champagne, there aren't many things you can't carry upside down.

I'm going to look through my box of directions for the ones about my camera but usually if I really want the directions for one specific piece of equipment, those are the directions I threw out.

Wastebaskets

WHAT would you say are the ten greatest inventions of all time?

The wheel would have to be high on the list and so would the engine, steam or gasoline. The printing press, radio, airplane, the plow, telephone, cement, the spinning wheel, the automobile and now I guess you'd have to include the computer. How many's that?

You can make your own list but don't count discoveries. Discoveries are different from inventions. Nuclear energy, for instance, isn't so much an invention as it is a discovery, like electricity or fire.

The propeller to drive a boat is a good invention although you wouldn't put it in the top ten. Someone just suggested the zipper. I reject the zipper. It's a handy gadget but it's a gadget.

One of the things you never see mentioned in the schoolbooks when they talk about inventions is, in my mind, one of the greatest developments of all time. It is the wastebasket. I could live without laser beams, the phonograph record or the cotton gin, but I couldn't do without a wastebasket.

If some historian wishes to make a substantial contribution to the history of mankind, he or she might find out who invented the wastebasket. It is time we had a National Wastebasket Day in that person's honor.

There are four important wastebaskets in my life although we have nine altogether in our house. The four are in the bedroom, the kitchen, the room in which I write at home and my office away from home.

Day in and day out, I can't think of anything that gives me more service and satisfaction than those wastebaskets.

I begin using a wastebasket early in the morning. When I'm getting dressed and I get ready to put the stuff on top of my dresser back in my pants pocket, I go through it and sort out the meaningless bits of paper I've written meaningless notes on. Those I throw in the wastebasket in order to give my pockets a clean start for the day. I make room for new meaningless bits of paper.

In my writing room, nothing is more important to me than my wastebasket. This essay takes only three pieces of paper, typed and double-spaced when it's completed. You might not think so from some of the things you read in it but I seldom finish an essay in fewer than ten pages. You get three and the wastebasket gets seven.

The kitchen wastebasket is the only controversial one. Margie and I don't always agree on what goes into it. There's a fine line between what goes into the garbage can and what goes into the wastebasket.

The young people of today have television but one of the things they're missing is the experience of burning the papers in the backyard. It was a very good thing to do because it was fun, and while you were doing it you got credit for working.

Most towns have ordinances prohibiting the burning of papers now. I approve of the law but I sure miss burning the papers. Taking the wastebaskets downstairs and out into the garage to dump them into the big trash container that the garbage man picks up, is not nearly so satisfying a way of disposing of their contents as burning them used to be.

In recent years there's been an unfortunate tendency to make wastebaskets more complicated and fancier than is necessary. Many of the good department stores and fancy boutiques have made them into gifts. A wastebasket is not a proper gift item. Many wastebaskets in these places have been decorated with flowers or clever things painted on them. A wastebasket doesn't want to be clever and it doesn't want to be so cute or gussied up that it calls attention to itself, either. Wastebaskets should be inconspicuous.

You can make your own list of the ten greatest inventions of all time but leave a place for the wastebasket.

Stop, Thief!

More people than ever are stealing things and many of those things are being taken from me.

Crime rate statistics by government agencies are impersonal numbers, but when crime hits home, it hurts. Just since I sat down at my typewriter ten minutes ago, several things have disappeared. The thieves in my life are getting so good at taking things that I didn't even notice anyone come in this room. The door is closed, the windows are down but obviously someone got in. They've taken a pen I had right here next to me, for example.

Not three minutes ago I had a pad of paper on which I'd made some notes and now that's gone. It just disappeared. Why would a thief want my notebook?

I happen to know I put that notebook right next to . . . wait a minute. Okay, my notebook is here. I'm sorry about that. I did think it had been stolen. In this one case I may have been wrong but I know that pen I had was lifted by some light-fingered person who . . . hold it. Here's the pen in my shirt pocket. Maybe that wasn't really stolen either but there are plenty of things missing around here and someone must be taking them.

I wear glasses for reading or writing and a day seldom goes by that some low-down thief doesn't steal a pair from me. The thief must be afraid because I really get mad when I can't find my glasses. Obviously he gets worried about being caught red-handed and puts them back where he knows I'll find them at a later time. My glasses will sometimes show up in a coat pocket two days later or under the Sunday newspapers on the coffee table in the living room where he's planted them. Three or four times a year the thief makes off with them for good and I have to buy new ones. I don't know why anyone would want to steal my glasses all the time.

The funny thing about all this stealing is that they don't seem to go after anything of real value. How much could a burglar get from a fence for a few pieces of leftover steak I know for sure I put way back on the middle shelf of the refrigerator the other day? Obviously someone came into the kitchen in the middle of the night and stole the steak. If he's so hungry he has to take stuff out of our icebox, I guess I can't get too mad at him. He must be really hard up, because half the time when I go look for something in the refrigerator I can't find it.

There are many times when things seem to be taken more to irritate me than for any other reason. I can understand someone stealing a car but why would anyone take just the car keys? They're always disappearing. What do thieves do with car keys?

In my shop it seems to be the little things that are always missing, too. Yesterday I was looking for a five-eighths set wrench to tighten a bolt on the lawn mower. Every other size was right there in the box where I keep them but the one I needed had been stolen. It seems like that's always the way.

My wristwatch is often taken and one day last winter I was going home on the train with a briefcase full of papers and that was stolen. I can't account for what happened any other way. I know I put the briefcase on the overhead rack before I sat down but when I got home, the briefcase was gone. I didn't have it with me. The papers were all valuable to me but apparently they weren't to the guy who took it because several days later I stopped at the lost-and-found office at the railroad station and the briefcase was there. He must have stolen it and then turned it in.

Every politician who runs for office talks about getting tough with criminals. When it comes to the thieves who are taking my personal possessions all the time, I'd like to lock them up and throw the key away. I probably wouldn't even have to throw it away. If I put it on top of my dresser for a few days, the key would disappear.

The Jeep

WHY is it when the manufacturers of an appliance or a piece of machinery decide to make a new, improved model of it, they often destroy the qualities it had that we liked?

There have been very few pieces of machinery so loved as the Jeep. Its invention was a bit of American genius. It was a simple, rugged and versatile little vehicle that did a thousand jobs, all of them well.

The Jeep was most loved by Americans who fought in World War II, but affection for it wasn't limited to those people. Everyone got to know and love the Jeep ... and then they started improving it.

The Jeep they ended up making for the civilian trade was big, comfortable, automatic and expensive. It was everything the original Jeep was not. There's a time to live and a time to die, I know, but the Jeep died an unnecessarily premature death. If there were brand new Jeeps for sale today that were built with the same design and quality of the original, I suspect there would be several hundred thousand people who'd want one.

A story out of Washington recently reported that a new vehicle designed to replace the Jeep isn't working out very well. The vehicle is nicknamed "The Hummer," a contrived abbreviation of its official designation, "High Mobility Multipurpose Wheeled Vehicle."

Even that name, "The Hummer," isn't as good as the name "Jeep." "Jeep" came about naturally, as a nickname should. Its official designation as a vehicle was "General Purpose." This was abbreviated as "GP" and thus, "Jeep."

The Pentagon tested The Hummer and announced that "Reliability was very low." No one ever said that about a Jeep.

The Army had ordered 55,000 of these new, unreliable vehicles at a cost of $20,000 each.

I checked back and found that on July 3, 1941, the Army signed a contract for the original Jeep. The price was $738.74 each.

How would you like to get yourself a brand new WWII Jeep for $738.74 today? Come to think of it, I'll take two. That would be two solid little vehicles that work for a total of $1,477.48. Ten would cost me $7,387.40.

There are hundreds of pieces of equipment I've owned and liked over the years. Invariably when I've set out to replace them, I've been disappointed with the new model. Within the past year I've had this experience with a kitchen blender, a clock radio I dropped and a watch I lost. In each case the replacement—same brand—was less satisfactory than the original.

How does a company set out to change a product for the worse? The first thing it does is have a board of directors meeting. The board decides to satisfy its stockholders by raising the margin of profit on its most successful item.

In order to accomplish this, the board can do one of two things. It can cheapen the product or it can charge more for it.

The board decides to do both. They cheapen the product *and* charge more for it.

Within a year, sales begin to drop off and the board of directors is puzzled. They blame it on the economy or interference from Washington.

At the next board meeting they take drastic steps. They decide to paint their product a different color, put it in a bigger box and make it out of plastic instead of metal.

When all this fails to improve sales, they take one last, desperate measure. They authorize the president to spend three million dollars on a huge new ad campaign featuring the once-famous Hollywood star, now looking for work, Smith Barney.

The last thing they seem to think of doing to improve sales is to go back to making the good product they had in the first place.

The Big Fix

How would it be if we picked some year in the near future and didn't buy anything new at all that year? We'd spend the entire 365 days fixing things we already have. It's gotten so everyone's thowing it away and buying a new one instead of having the old one fixed, and that seems wrong.

Wouldn't it do just as much for the economy and more for the ecology if I spent $2,500 having my old car done over instead of spending $10,000 for a new one?

There's going to be some job relocation necessary but it wouldn't do any harm at all if those people in Detroit who make cars spent a year fixing them. They might be more careful when they went back to the assembly line.

It's hard to believe our economy has to depend on selling us things we don't need. There must be another way. There are a thousand things I keep buying that I don't need. I've got four electric shavers but three of them don't work. I have three quarter-inch drills but only one is operational. There are two ice-cream freezers in the garage but the motors on both of them need work. We have two retired toasters and a closet full of gadgets that just barely don't work anymore. I don't need new models. I need someone who'll fix my old models.

I'd start not buying from the ground up. I'd have all the old shoes

I own soled and heeled and I'd put new shoelaces in them. Then I'd shine them and wear them. I wouldn't buy any new ones.

I'd go through my closet, bring out the clothes that need work and take them to the tailor or sew on a few buttons myself. The art of turning a frayed collar might be revived.

I don't think we need any new houses for a year, either. The building industry will howl but there's plenty of work for them to do. Like Detroit, they could learn a little about building new ones by fixing the old ones they put up ten or twenty-five years ago.

Everywhere I go I see perfectly good houses that have been abandoned. Why couldn't the building industry, and the people who want houses, rebuild those instead of building new ones?

Why cut down more trees when we have wooden houses rotting for want of a little care and a coat of paint?

Why dig up more iron ore to turn into cars and farm machinery when we have cars and farm machinery rusting away that only need mechanical repair and some grease?

It would be a year in which no new books would be published. Each of us would read the books we bought in past years and never read. The writers are writing faster than the readers are reading. The readers need time to catch up and I speak with firsthand knowledge when I say that it wouldn't hurt if the writers spent a little more time with their work.

No new games at Christmas! Sorry, Atari. Sorry, Trivial Pursuit! We have enough games in our closets. We'll dust off our chess, our checkers and mah jong sets and bring out the Monopoly and the Scrabble boards. Maybe we'll play Michigan.

In the back room, attic, garage or basement, there must be a lot of old Hula Hoops, roller skates, bongo boards and wagons for the kids to play with. Maybe there are even some stilts, a pogo stick, a Flexible Flyer and a yo-yo.

If no one is selling anything new, this could hurt television and newspapers which depend on advertising revenue. Newspapers might have to charge what it costs to produce them. Network television would have to find some other way to collect from us. How much would a newspaper cost if we had to pay for it directly? For all we consumers know, it might be cheaper in the long run to pay for both directly.

Well, I'm dreaming, of course. We're not going to stop buying new things but I sense something basically wrong. It's wrong to be using up the earth's resources and throwing them away as fast as possible so we can make new ones just because our economy depends on sales.

II:

HOUSE BEAUTIFUL

A Nest to Come Home to

EVERYONE should have a nest to come home to when the public part of the day is over. Having a little room with a comfortable chair to settle into is important. You should be surrounded by familiar things. You can talk or read or watch television or doze off but you're in your basic place. You're home and you don't have to watch yourself.

I'm not sure the furniture stores and the room designers are in tune with what most Americans want. We've never had a designer design anything in our house. It's all happened by accident. I like our house a lot better than I like those rooms I see in magazines that have been put together by designers. They look more like the rooms they have just outside the men's room or the ladies' room on the ballroom floor of an expensive hotel. There isn't a decorator who ever lived who could surround me with the things I like to have around me in my living room.

Decorators go for fuzzy white rugs that show the dirt, glass-topped tables you can't put your feet on and gilt-edged mirrors that only Napoleon wearing his uniform would look good in.

I like to have the windows covered so the neighbors can't see in and I agree you shouldn't just cover them with newspaper but it's very easy to carry curtains too far. When strangers come into your living room and say right away how nice the curtains are, then you know you've gone too far with the curtains. Friends who come to your house once in a while should not be able to remember what the curtains look like.

It must be difficult to sell furniture. No one in a store would sell you a chair in which the springs were beginning to sag but most chairs aren't very comfortable until that begins to happen. No one wants to pay a lot of money for a secondhand piece of furniture and yet furniture looks better when it has a well-worn look.

My green leather chair is eighteen years old now and the rest of the family complains about what it looks like but I notice they take every chance they get to sit in it. I don't take that chair when I come into the room because I'm the husband or the father. I sit in

537

that chair because it's *my* chair. It's as much mine as my shoes. If they want one like it they can have one but I like a chair I can call my own. Familiar things are a great comfort to us all.

When the Christmas catalogs begin to come in and there's a noticeable increase in the amount of mail coming into the house, I usually make a decorating change of my own. I move another little table over by my chair so I have a table on either side of me. It's a temporary thing for one time of year. When the Christmas cards start coming, I have a better way of separating the cards from the bills and the junk mail from the personal letters. If you keep the newspaper, the mail, a letter opener, a glass, scissors, three elastic bands, some paper clips, some loose change, the television guide, two books and a magazine next to you, one table next to your chair isn't enough at Christmas.

When I sit down in my chair at night, it's the one place in the world I have no complaint with. It's just the way I like it. I'm wearing comfortable clothes, my feet are up and I'm surrounded by things that are there because I choose to have them there.

I was telling my wife how quickly and how well American soldiers make a nest for themselves, no matter what their circumstances are. They can be out in a field somewhere but first thing you know they've dug a foxhole and invented some conveniences for themselves out of empty coffee cans and cardboard containers. They've made that one little spot in the world their own. It's true but I never should have told my wife.

"That's what this place looks like," she said, "a foxhole."

My Dream House

IF you had all the time and all the money you needed to build yourself the perfect house, what would it be like? I have some ideas for my dream house.

First, it would have a big, handsome, wooden front door that everyone used. No one would come in the back way or through the kitchen door as a regular thing. Most houses are designed so that the front door isn't really convenient and is only used occasionally by guests who come to dinner Saturday night or by Jehovah's Witnesses wanting to give you literature. There is no reason why a front door couldn't be put in a convenient place.

There would be a four-car garage for our two cars. This would allow space for the things we presently have in our two-car garage instead of our two cars.

There would be both a living room and what we used to call the parlor in my grandmother's house. I don't actually like parlors but they're convenient for some occasions. They provide a place to keep chairs that aren't comfortable enough to sit on, walls on which to hang gilded mirrors and pictures you don't like, and shelves on which to put knickknacks and various pieces of homely but expensive china. The bookshelves in the parlor would hold the books we never read.

The dining room would be elegant, spacious, wood-paneled and quietly lit. It would have a huge and beautiful oval table that would expand to seat twenty or contract to be comfortable for four. The extra chairs would recede into the floor at the push of a button.

The living room or family room would be small and cozy with several comfortable, worn leather chairs, a mushy couch long enough to sleep on stretched out, and a television set too big for the size of the room. It would also have a stereo record player, although we never use the one we have. It would have small windows and could be entered through only one door. More than one door ruins any room.

The kitchen would have a fireplace, an alcove with a comfortable breakfast table, at which we'd usually eat dinner, and a lot of indestructible butcher block counter tops. It would have a big, professional range with eight burners, two ovens and an open flame grill. There would be a walk-in refrigerator like the ones they have in meat markets. I'd never bend over to get something out of the bottom of the refrigerator again.

In one corner of the kitchen would be a dumbwaiter that would take things from the kitchen to the rooms upstairs and to the basement downstairs.

The cellar or basement would be divided into four parts. One part would have the furnace, washer, dryer and a bin of replacement parts for every appliance in the house. A second room would have all my woodworking equipment and would be hermetically and acoustically sealed so that neither dust nor noise could drift out of it into the rest of the house. There have been some complaints about that in our present house.

In the back, running the full length of the house, I'd have a swimming pool fifty yards long and four yards wide. I don't want to play in a pool, I just want to do laps.

The fourth part of the basement would be a small, nicely equipped gym in which I'd regularly lose weight.

Upstairs there would be five bedrooms with ten adjoining bathrooms. When there are two people in a bedroom, one bathroom per bedroom is not enough. It would be nice when all the kids are home.

Each of the many huge clothes closets would be equipped with a Disposal down which could be dumped old shoes, worn or unattractive shirts, socks with holes in them and spotted neckties.

These are some of the things I'd like in my dream house.

House Beautiful

Yᴇᴀʀѕ ago, when I was making a living the hard way, writing for magazines, I sold an article to *House Beautiful*. Every once in a while I look through the magazine to see what their writers are writing today. The magazine is attractive but I can't relate to much that's in it. The articles and the advertisements are either for things I don't buy or they're so elaborate they scare me off. If this is House Beautiful, I live in House Homely.

Here's a two-page ad for a Jacuzzi whirlpool bath. There's an attractive woman lying on a pillow on the tile floor. The tub itself is sunk into the floor and she, I judge, is about to get in. Behind the woman on the bathroom floor, there's a sink, a toilet, a bidet and a fireplace with burning logs. Overhead is a crystal chandelier.

I don't like to discourage attractive advertising like this but Jacuzzi ought to know that my attention is more attracted to the barely clad woman on the floor and to the fireplace behind her than it is to the whirlpool bath they're trying to sell. My mind wanders away from commerce in the presence of nudity. I'm wondering whether she'll climb in facing the fire or with her back to it. Will she lie back, up to her pretty neck in suds, and gaze at the crystal chandelier?

Here's another good-looking ad in *House Beautiful* for "The 100 Greatest Books Ever Written." They're bound in genuine leather and cost thirty-five dollars each. Among the books shown are *The Mill on the Floss*, *The Scarlet Letter* and *Faust* by Goethe. I had to read *The Mill on the Floss* when I was sixteen and it is my opinion that it isn't even one of the 10,000 best books ever written. A book in leather is an awful burden to lay on someone anyway. Generation after generation has to take those leather-bound books with them whenever they move and no one ever reads them. A book should live or die by what's inside it, not what's outside.

It takes a while to get to the articles in a magazine like *House Beautiful* these days if you start from the beginning. If you like ads, of course, that doesn't matter. There are 178 pages in this issue and of those, about 100 are ads.

One of the articles is about a doctor and his wife in New Orleans who like to entertain.

"Once a year," the article says, "the Ochsners give a buffet reception for 200 . . ." There are wonderful pictures of the Ochsners' attractive home all fixed up ready for a party, but it's difficult for me to translate their party in terms of one we could give in our house.

The Ochsners put dining tables everywhere to handle the crowd. They put one table out by the pool, for instance. We don't even have a pool if you can imagine anyone that poor. They put tables on the patio. We don't have a patio, either. I suspect that if *House Beautiful* ever saw our house they wouldn't want to have anything to do with me. They'd certainly be embarrassed to find their magazine on the coffee table in our living room.

One problem Mrs. Ochsner says she has when there are 200 people for dinner is finding enough silver forks for all of them. I can sympathize with Mrs. Ochsner here. We'd have that trouble, too. My wife's family left us twelve but one went out with the garbage, and another was mangled in the Disposal so we'd be 190 silver forks short.

Just to prove all their houses aren't filled with froufrou, *House Beautiful* has an article about what they call "A Magnificent Hand-Hewn Log Cabin." It is magnificent, too. The picture of the living room shows a fireplace like the one in the bathroom in the Jacuzzi ad and a bookshelf. I can't read the titles in the book shelf but I imagine that somewhere up there is a complete set of "The 100 Greatest Books Ever Written," bound in leather.

Things to Do Today

For a while after I got in bed, I couldn't think where the day had gone. Then it started coming back to me, slowly but clearly.

I definitely remember starting to make a list that morning after I'd read the paper and had a second cup of coffee. "TTDT" I'd put at the top of the page of a blank sheet of paper. It stands for "Things to Do Today." I always put that at the top of the page. It's a little joke I have with myself. I remember most of the items on the list:

—Clean leaves out of gutter.

—Put storm door on back door.

—Rake leaves out of ivy at front.

—Clean out garage so we can get both cars in when the snow comes.

—Split logs brought down from the country so they'll fit into small wood stove in kitchen.

—Cover ventilating fan in attic.

—Take air conditioner out of kitchen window.

—Take lawn mower that hasn't worked in three years to dump.

—Put tools where they belong.

Sitting there at the breakfast table Saturday morning I felt very contented with my list. Just putting down the things I ought to do gave me some of the same kind of satisfaction that actually doing them would have. Nothing is too much for me to do Saturday morning at the breakfast table when I'm planning my day. It isn't until I get started that I run into trouble.

Last Saturday I got so little done on my list that I lay in bed that night trying to reconstruct my day and as I did I realized where I went wrong. I picked the wrong job to do first. I had picked the fifth item on my TTDT list, "Split Logs."

I had gone to the garden shed to get an axe, a light sledgehammer and a wedge. I set the first heavy log on my chopping block and felt the blade of the axe. It needed sharpening. I do that on a small belt sander I have in the basement so I went there with the axe in my hand.

It would have taken no more than five minutes except that I had removed a worn sandpaper belt from the machine and had to replace it with another. In loosening a screw on the sander, I dropped a critical washer on the floor and it rolled under my worktable along with quite a bit of debris. It was forty-five minutes before I got back out in the yard to the chopping block.

Now my axe was sharp, I was sharp and the first log was ready to be split asunder. I arched back with the axe dropped low behind my back. Holding it at the end of the handle like a baseball bat, I brought the axe over my head and down with all the might I could muster. Thuck! That was the noise the axe made as it buried itself no more than an inch into the log. I had assumed it would cleave it with one mighty swipe.

What I had forgotten was that the log was elm and elm is susceptible to the dread disease that has killed almost all the trees but it's highly resistant to being split with an axe.

An hour later I had the axe, the wedge, a good wood chisel, two screwdrivers and a small crowbar buried in that log. They were trapped and I was no closer to splitting it than when I started.

It was almost noon before I got everything free and by that time I was hungry again. I put the tools away, went in and made myself a grilled cheese sandwich.

I looked at the rest of my TTDT list. Nothing I couldn't do next Saturday, I thought to myself, so I watched some football on television, took a little nap and then went to the store and bought a new suitcase.

That's where last Saturday went.

Lifting

M EN enjoy lifting things. They don't like carrying them anywhere once they've lifted them but it's satisfying for them to pick up a heavy object. Last weekend was very satisfying for me. I was helping someone move out of an apartment and there was a lot of lifting to be done.

There's something macho about lifting. Men like the idea of being able to lift heavier objects than women can. It seems like a harmless thing to feel superior about. We can't have babies. It's little enough to leave us.

I can't think why else men would enjoy lifting things if it isn't to prove that they can lift more than women. Once they've lifted something, men often don't know what to do with it. Women have a better idea of where to put something down once it's been lifted.

There are half a dozen heavy objects around our house that I've been lifting for twenty-five years and it's going to be interesting to see how old I am before I can no longer pick them up. Once a year, for example, I put an air conditioner in the kitchen window and another in our bedroom window. Once a year I take them out, so I lift each one twice a year. I don't know how much they weigh but it's plenty. My gauge for weight is a bag of cement which is about 100 pounds. The air conditioners are at least that heavy and very cumbersome. There's no place to hang on as you lift. The one in the kitchen is toughest because the windowsill is chest-high and I have to get it up to that. I've seen these champion weight lifters put barbells over their heads but they have it easy. I'd like to see them put my kitchen air conditioner over their heads. They wouldn't know where to grab hold of it and lifting it chest-high is only part of it. It doesn't fit into the window neatly so I have to jockey it into position while I'm lifting. Let's see them make air-conditioner lifting an Olympic event.

I'm worried now about next year. We were having some work done around the house last month, so my wife had two men put the air conditioners in. I hate to get out of shape by missing a year like that. I remember the cowboy theory that if you lift a calf on the day it's born and continue to lift it every day, you'll still be able to lift the animal when it's full-grown. My air conditioners aren't getting any bigger, but I am.

Big television sets are in the same category as air conditioners. They often put a handle on top and call them "portable" but they aren't really. Television sets share a common fault with a lot of other objects in a house that you occasionally have to move to another room. They are almost always about the same width as the door you have to take them through. This means that there's no room for your hands if you go through the door straight and if you turn sideways, you have to get yourself and the television set through the door at the same time.

When I'm carrying something heavy and bulky down a pair of stairs in the house, my wife is always properly solicitous of my welfare. She keeps saying things like "Be careful." I suspect I'm sharing her concern with the object I'm carrying. She may not want me to hurt myself but she doesn't want me to drop what I'm carrying, either.

To tell you the truth, I've never found that the advice "Don't hurt yourself" has helped me as far as getting hurt is concerned. Either I do or I don't. I don't mind if someone says things like that to me but what I do object to is when they try to help. I'll have something heavy delicately balanced on my shoulder and I'll start walking with it. My wife decides it's too heavy. She wants to help so she lifts the back end of it.

There are some things I don't enjoy lifting. Bringing the groceries in from the car is no fun. They aren't heavy enough to be challenging and there's no place to put them down when you get inside.

Putting the garbage out is another lifting job I don't get much of a kick out of. A full garbage can, one of those big ones, is hard to lift because it's awkward. There's nothing to do but lean over and grab the handle on either side. I bet the move accounts for half the back problems in America.

I've seen all these books advising women on how to get along with a man. My advice would be for them to flatter men at least once a month by saying, "Dear, will you please lift this for me?"

A Trip to the Dump

THE President says this country is in desperate need of a moral revival. He isn't the first one to say it, either. Almost anyone who says anything has been saying it for years. The trouble is, no one knows how to revive us morally.

I have a simple idea that might just do the trick. I say we should all take our own garbage to the dump. Every able-bodied person in the country would set aside an hour twice a week to dispose of trash and garbage. There would be no exceptions. The President would pack up whatever waste was produced in the private rooms of the White House and take it to the dump just like the rest of us. A President should keep in touch with reality, too.

Going to the dump is a real and exhilarating experience. It is both satisfying and educational. It makes you acutely aware of what you have used in your home and what you have wasted. There's no faking it with garbage.

In a family, dump duty would be divided up. The kids would take their turns going to the dump with the adults. A kid can get to be voting age without knowing that the wastebasket or the garbage pail isn't the end of the line if he or she has never been to the dump. Children too young to drive would, of course, be accompanied by an adult to the dump.

The first thing you realize when you go to the dump is that we should be a lot more careful in separating what professional garbage collectors call "wet garbage" and just trash. All garbage is not the same. Trash is cans, bottles, papers, cardboard boxes and broken electrical appliances. "Wet garbage" comes from the kitchen.

Next, you have to get over that natural feeling of revulsion that garbage tends to induce. Keep in mind that coffee grounds, watermelon rinds, potato peels and corncobs were not revolting before we made them what they are today and mixed them together in our garbage pail. Think of them separately and in their original state and make a little game of breaking down the odor into its component parts.

It is possible to be overcome by a sense of your place in history at the dump. You are, at that moment, a part of the future of the universe. You are helping to rearrange the planet Earth. Man has always considered himself separate from Nature but a trip to the garbage dump can make him aware that he is not. In the millions and millions of years Earth has existed, there have been constant changes taking place. You probably live in a city that was once a lake or an ocean. The mountains you see may have had their cliffs sheared clean by a glacier when it moved relentlessly through your area an eon ago, dropping rich, loamy topsoil in the valley when it melted. Now, like the glaciers, you are doing your part to rearrange the location of the elements on Earth.

Little by little, we are taking up material from the ground in large amounts in one place, making something of it, shipping it across the country to other places, using the things, turning them into trash or garbage and burying them in ten thousand separate little piles called dumps in other places. In the process, we often ruin both places, of course, but that's another story.

If being in on this cosmic kind of cosmetics doesn't interest you to think about the dump, there are other pleasures. There is a cathartic pleasure to be enjoyed from getting rid of stuff at the dump and there is a camaraderie among neighbors there that doesn't exist at the supermarket. Everyone at the dump feels he is doing a good and honest thing and it gives him a warm sense of fellow feeling to know that others, many with more expensive cars, are doing the same grubby, down-to-earth job.

Nowhere is morality higher in America than at the dump Saturday morning and I recommend a trip there as a possible cure for what so many people think ails America, morally.

The Real Homecoming

AFTER a vacation it's traditional to tell your friends "It's great to be home." It may be great to *be* home but *coming* home is no fun at all. Most of us take a summer vacation and some weekend trips and ever since I was a kid I've hated that part where you arrive home at ten o'clock Sunday night.

It doesn't matter what time of year you take a vacation, coming back to your house is a miserable experience. If it's in the winter, the house is cold and dank. If it's in the summer, the house is hot and dank.

Out front the mail has piled up and wet newspapers are scattered all over the lawn. You've probably left a light on to convince the burglars there's someone there, but that one lonely light burning every night might as well be a neon sign flashing "NOT HOME! NOT HOME! NOT HOME!" Burglars may be dishonest but they aren't dumb.

In the driveway there are fliers from the local grocery chains telling you about this week's specials which, by this time, are two weeks old. There are weeds everywhere and the place looks as if it hasn't been lived in for six months. You've been gone two weeks and you've got a ghost house on your hands.

All I ever want to do when I get home from vacation is sit down and rest or go to bed but I never can because there are too many things to do. I expect magic when I open the door but I never find it. I always expect things to be perfect. It seems to me the house should have corrected itself while we were away. It should look the way I'd like it to look, not the way we left it.

If you left in a hurry, which you probably did, there are clothes scattered around the area where you packed. They are things you forgot or decided at the last minute not to take.

If you had a quick breakfast or just a cup of coffee before you pulled out, the chances are the dirty dishes and cups are still in the sink. Even if burglars came while you were away, they wouldn't have taken the dirty dishes.

We had a particularly nasty shock coming home after our first weekend away this summer. Last year I installed one of those big exhaust fans in the roof. It's been good for cooling down the upstairs rooms by bringing the outside air in through an opened downstairs window. The trouble came because this winter we put a small wood-burning stove in our kitchen fireplace. The attic fan goes on automatically at a certain temperature whether we're home or not and when we're away with all the doors and windows closed, the fan has only one place from which to draw air. It draws it down the chimney and through the wood stove. Anyway, when we returned home this time, the whole house smelled as if it had burned down several weeks ago. It was permeated with the smell of the wood stove and the chimney.

One of the ten worst jobs in life is emptying the trunk of the car after a trip. There's trash that should be thrown out. There are suitcases, paper bags and loose packages of things you bought while you were away. There may be fruits and vegetables that seemed attractive when you bought them at the country stand but seem unnecessary now.

Things in the trunk of a car have a way of intermingling with the handle of the jack or they get trapped back up in there with the light wires and they're hard to reach. It often takes me five trips to empty the car and there are still things left in it.

I'll bet the President doesn't have to empty the trunk of his car when he gets back to the White House after a trip. No wonder people want to be President.

When the car is mostly empty, I take the suitcases upstairs and that's another unpleasant experience, unpacking a suitcase you've been living out of for a week. It's mostly dirty underwear, socks and shirts and mine smells of the cheap perfume that comes from the little bars of soap I take when I leave a hotel.

Once I've got things cleared away enough to go to bed, I usually decide to take a shower. I get undressed, turn on the shower and then remember that I turned off the hot water heater before we left. Now I have to put on some clothes, go down cellar, turn on the oil burner and wait twenty minutes for hot water.

Sometimes coming home is such a pain in the neck I wonder whether going away is worth it.

Showered with Perfection

So many things in life are bent, broken, empty, leaking, worn-out or otherwise unsatisfactory that it's always a pleasure to report something that's perfect the way it is.

Things are going very well in the shower in our house this year. We've finally got things the way we want them.

Next to falling into your own warm bed on a cold night when you're dog-tired, the most comforting thing to do is to take a long, hot shower.

A hot shower is like eating peanuts. You can't stop. I have to use a lot of will power every morning to get myself out of the shower and into my clothes.

About three years ago we took the tub out of the upstairs bathroom and had a tile shower installed. It's big enough to turn around in comfortably and there are two little shelves high in the back corner where the spray doesn't hit. An assortment of shampoos, brushes and some miscellaneous junk is kept on the shelves. There are some items up there I don't understand but who knows what anyone else does in the shower?

The new shower wasn't completely satisfactory at first. It wasn't the shower's fault. For a while the thermostat on the heater in the basement wasn't working properly. Halfway through my shower, the water would turn tepid, then cool and finally cold. There's nothing worse than getting lathered up and then having the hot water give out.

The first shower head the plumber put on wouldn't adjust the way I wanted it to, either. I was never happy with it. I like heavy streams of water with a fairly small radius. I don't like pinpoint needles of water that hit me in the head and the feet at the same time. I like to be able to control which part of me is getting hit with water.

We replaced the first shower head and this one is just right. It's almost too good. It's costing me a few minutes' sleep every day because the shower's so nice now I'm staying in it longer and I have to get up earlier in order to catch my train.

The biggest improvement the new shower has over the old one in the bathtub is the glass door. It doesn't let any water leak out onto the floor and it ends the necessity for a shower curtain. The curtain was the worst thing about our old shower. Water was always getting on the floor and if you didn't leave the curtain pulled all the way open when you finished, it got moldy where it was folded against itself.

The best new development in my shower-taking life is a tiny electric heater I've put in the bathroom. It has a small fan behind the coils and does a good job of heating the room. But wait, don't go away! Here's the best part. I've got it on a timer.

The timer in the bathroom is set to start the little heater five minutes before my radio alarm goes off in the bedroom every morning. Now, when I get out of bed and tiptoe barefoot and shivering to the bathroom, I open the door on a wonderfully warm little room. It took me a long time to get the timer set to go off at exactly the right moment and I dread daylight saving time coming again in the spring because I'll have to reset it.

There's a radio in the bathroom and I always turn that on. I get up early and the first thing I hear, usually, is the London gold price. I don't care what the price of gold is in London but the familiar voice with the familiar information gives me some assurance that the world is still out there just the way I left it before I went to bed the night before.

The only things that go wrong these days with my morning shower are my own fault. Occasionally I get in and get wet before I realize I forgot to move my towel from the rack where I can't reach it to the little hook outside the shower door. I have to get out of the shower, wet and dripping, and get the towel.

If I ever retire and find myself looking for ways to have a good time, I think I'll just take three or four good, hot showers every day.

Neighbors

A man in Cambridge, Mass. took his neighbor to court because the neighbor hadn't cut his grass in fourteen years. This is the kind of story that interests me. There are something like sixty million single family homes in the United States and I'll bet ninety percent of the people living in those houses are having some kind of trouble with their neighbors.

The uncut grass in Cambridge is typical of the sort of thing that causes friction. No one likes the house next door to look worse or a lot better than his own. It's one thing to have a house of your own that needs painting but, knowing your own finances the way you do, you learn to live with it. When the house *next door* needs a coat of paint, that's a different matter. It can be a constant source of irritation. "Why doesn't that lazy bum paint it himself it he can't afford to have it done professionally?"

We have friends who are mad at their neighbors because they leave an old car in the driveway all the time instead of putting it away in the garage. I can understand that. If you have a nice-looking house and you keep the grounds in good condition, a piece of machinery like a seven-year-old automobile is not what you want to see all the time. As thoroughly well as I understand my friends' position on this matter, however, I usually leave the car in the driveway myself. As a matter of fact, I have two cars and a two-car garage but it has been fourteen years since there was room in it for both cars. One is tight.

If you basically like your neighbors, you don't make an issue of the things that bother you. If he hadn't cut his grass for fourteen years you might mention it, but smaller things you let slide in the interests of peace.

We have an almost ideal neighbor. We're friendly and would help each other in any emergency but we don't talk much and over a period of more than twenty-five years have had no confrontations.

Bill, my neighbor, works hard around his place and the only thing that ever bothered me wasn't really his fault, although I harbored a resentment toward him because of it.

For years I had watched him make a compost heap every year so I decided to compost my own leaves and grass cuttings. I built a wire mesh bin up against the fence between our properties and filled it with good stuff. I turned it over after four months and watered it regularly to hasten the rotting process.

After it had been there about two years and had diminished to a quarter of its original size, I decided to use some of it. The first few shovelfuls were rich and dark but then I struck trouble. It turned out that Bill's maple tree had discovered *my* compost heap and was eating from it. Small, fibrous tree roots had invaded the whole thing and I couldn't penetrate it with a spade. I finally gave up and today the location of my compost heap is a small hill over by the fence, dense with thriving tree roots.

It wasn't Bill's fault that his maple tree roots had gone out foraging for food but that's how neighborly feuds begin. You see *their* cat waiting to pounce on *your* birds. The outside light over *their* garage shines in *your* bedroom window. They leave *their* garbage cans out by the road all day after the garbage has been picked up in the morning.

You never know, of course, what *you've* done to annoy your neighbors. Tom, my neighbor across the street, is a nut in my opinion. He's out there mowing, seeding, raking and manicuring his place every time I look out the window. I get up at 7:30 Saturday mornings and he's already at it. I have to guess that my place bothers anyone that fussy. In the fall I don't rake the leaves much and they blow all over his property. Kids going by in cars often throw beer and soft drink cans out front where our two properties are closest and even when the cans are on my side, he picks them up.

That's the way it is with neighbors. If they're neater about their grounds than you are, they're fanatics. If they don't keep their place as well as you do, you think of them as bringing down real estate values.

My grass would never go fourteen years without being cut. Tom would sneak over when we're not home and cut it himself.

Building Satisfaction

FOR most of the last month I've been putting up a small building. I am not experienced in putting up buildings. My new structure is just behind the building we call the garage at our summer place. I don't know why we call that the garage, though, because it used to be an icehouse and has been full of tools for several years.

If Americans have a little bit of land near their house, they're possessed to put buildings on it. Most American farms, where there's plenty of land, are a cluster of haphazardly erected little buildings adjacent to the house and the barn. Most of the buildings were put up by someone who had an idea for their use at the time but that time has passed and they are now mostly used for what could only be called miscellaneous.

When I started my building I was going to use it for storing garden tools and a small tractor/lawnmower but now I think I may use it as a place in which to write. I'm getting to like it too much to just keep garden tools in.

My building is five-sided, eight feet tall at the sides and twelve feet tall at the crown of the roof in the middle. It's about twelve feet across although in a pentagon no side is directly opposite any other side so it's hard to measure that dimension. The base is on heavy, flat stones and the timbers are treated five-by-fives. The uprights and the roof members are two-by-fours. The sides are three-quarter-inch plywood, which I covered with tarpaper and then red cedar shingles. The floor is rough oak I bought from a farmer who has a little sawmill, and now I think if I'm going to use it as an office, I'll insulate and panel the interior.

Don't ask me why I decided on a five-sided building and don't get thinking I'm any expert. I've bungled so many things putting it up that I'd be embarrassed to have a real carpenter see it. But it's up and it's mine and I built it and I had a wonderful time doing it.

It was very hard work. Every morning I'd get up at 6:15 and go to the garage/icehouse and write until about 8:30 and then go into the house and have breakfast. After breakfast I'd start on my building. Every evening at about 6:30 my wife would yell out the back

door for me to quit. I'd work a little while longer, trying to anticipate how long I could stretch it out before she got really mad at me,
then I'd go to the house, dripping wet with perspiration. I'd take a
shower, have a drink, eat dinner and by 10:30 drop into bed.

It isn't often that I mix that much manual labor with writing and
it got me thinking about which of the two is more satisfying. Writing is a great satisfaction to me but it's a wonderful feeling to go
to bed dog-tired and twitching in every muscle after a long day's
physical work in which you accomplished something. It always
strikes me as surprising that it's so pleasurable to be physically tired
from having used your muscles excessively. It makes me wish writing involved some kind of manual labor more strenuous than typing.
If I got stiff writing, it might be even more satisfying.

Standing back and looking at my odd-shaped buildng, I've been
impressed with how much like my writing it is. It's a little crude
and not very well finished but it's direct and original.

My satisfaction in making it springs from the same well, too. For
a man or a woman to take any raw material like lumber or words
and shape these formless materials into a pattern that bears the stamp
of his or her brain or hand, is the most satisfying thing to do in the
whole world. It's what's wrong with cake mixes.

When, out of a scrambled mess of raw materials, some order
starts to emerge and it is an order you have imposed on those
materials, it's a good feeling. It was nothing and now it's something.

For me, writing in the early morning and working on my building the rest of the day was the ultimate vacation and I never worked
harder in my life.

Now I'm back at work and I can relax a little.

III:
WORKING

Procrastination

IT isn't working that's so hard, it's getting ready to work.

It isn't *being* up we all dislike in the morning, it's *getting* up.

Once I get started at almost any job, I'm happy. I can plug away at any dull job for hours and get some satisfaction from doing it. The trouble is that sometimes I'll put off doing that job for months because it's so tough to get started.

It doesn't seem to matter what the job is. For me it can be getting at writing, getting at mowing the lawn, getting at cleaning out the trunk of the car, making a piece of furniture or putting up a shed. It's a good thing I wasn't hired to build the Golden Gate Bridge. I'd never have figured out where to put that first piece of steel to make it possible to get across all that water.

There is some complex thing going on in our brains that keeps us from getting started on a job. No matter how often we do something, we always forget how long it took us to do it last time and how hard it was. Even though we forget in our conscious mind, there is some subconscious part of the brain that remembers. This is what keeps us from getting at things. *We* may not know but our subconscious knows that the job is going to be harder than we think. It tries to keep us from rushing into it in a hurry.

There is a war going on between different elements of our brain. If I consciously remembered how difficult something was the last time I did it, I'd never do it again. The wonderful thing about memory is that it's just great at forgetting. Every Friday afternoon in summer I drive 150 miles to our summer house in the country. I always look forward to *being* there and I always forget how much I hate *getting* there. My subconscious remembers. It keeps me fiddling around the office Friday afternoons, putting off leaving. The drive can take anywhere from three to four hours, depending on the traffic, and I hate it so much that sometimes I spend two of those four hours contemplating selling the place.

The following Friday, I can't wait to leave the office for the country again but my subconscious puts it off. It keeps me from getting started. *It* remembers the drive even if I don't.

557

One of the jobs my subconscious is best at putting me off getting at is painting. My subconscious is absolutely right. I probably shouldn't start it even though I enjoy it once I get going. Once again, my subconscious remembers what I forget.

I look at a door or a fence or a room and I say to myself, "I ought to give that a coat of paint. It'll take two quarts of paint. I'll need some turpentine and a new brush. No sense fooling with those old brushes."

My subconscious sometimes puts me off the paint job for months but eventually, against its better judgment, I buy the paint, the turpentine and the brush. I put on my old clothes, get a screwdriver to remove the top of the paint can and then I look more carefully at the room. Now I begin to see what my subconscious saw all along.

There are many things to do before I start to paint. I have to move everything out of the room, I have to replace a piece of the baseboard that is broken and I have to scrape and sand the places where the paint is peeling. And I better go back to the hardware store to get some spackle to fill the cracks in the ceiling. While I'm there, I'll pick up some undercoater for the new piece of baseboard and the spackled cracks. I'll have to let it dry overnight so I can't start painting today.

It is quite probable that it is this wonderfully intelligent subconscious part of our brain that makes us want to stay in bed another hour every morning. *We* want to get up. *It* knows that just as soon as we get up, the trouble will start all over again.

A Microchip on My Shoulder

RECENTLY I was talked into buying a magic new machine called a Teleram Portabubble word processor. It's basically an electronic typewriter that doesn't produce anything on paper. It's all on a little screen in front of you. The good part of it is that by pressing a few buttons and putting the telephone in the cradle provided on top of it, you can send what you've written anywhere in the world in a very few minutes. Of course, you have to want to send what you've written somewhere for it to be much use to you.

The Teleram is unique in that it stores what you've written on a memory that doesn't involve any disk or moving parts. It's portable, too, weighing only eighteen pounds, and can be plugged in anywhere.

I had no natural aptitude for the word processor but after four months, I'm thoroughly familiar with it. I've written five books and hundreds of radio and television broadcasts on my Underwood No. 5 typewriter, circa 1920, and I continue to use it as my basic writing tool. It was given to me by my uncle who was a lawyer. He had used it for twenty years before me. In the past thirty-five years I spent twelve dollars on it once to have it oiled and cleaned.

Although I'm embarrassed to tell you, it's important to the story to say that I paid $5,640 for my word processor.

Several months after I bought it, I got a letter from Arline D. Walpole, Manager, Sales Administration, the Teleram Corporation. The letter informed me that my warranty was almost up and asked if I wanted to sign up for their annual flat-fee service contract.

I have written the following letter:

Dear Miss Walpole:

I have some questions regarding the letter you sent informing me that the fee for the annual service contract for my Teleram Portabubble-81 is $660.

Do I understand that $660 is the Teleram Corporation's best estimate of what it will cost to keep one of their machines in operating condition for one year?

Could you please advise me what type failure I can expect within a year of my purchase of the word processor? I had a demonstration model belonging to your salesman for about five weeks and some kind of logjam occurred that made it necessary for me to erase and lose everything in the memory to make it operative again. Is this common? I now have the Teleram with the 260,000-character memory. What is the likelihood that I can complete the storage of that amount of material without another breakdown in your machine that would necessitate total erasure?

According to your letter, your charge for straight-time, on-site field repair is $73 an hour. Your only repair depots are in Randolph, N.J., Washington, D.C. and Dallas, Texas. None of these is in my neighborhood. Travel time for your repair men is $53 an hour, plus costs. Weekday overtime is $90 an hour and Sunday and holiday on-site double time is $120 an hour. I estimate that if one of your repairmen works a 40-hour week plus four hours overtime and four hours double time, he could make $3,760 a week or $195,520 a year. In the event one of your repairmen worked a straight 40-hour week at your factory (at

$53 per hour) with no travel and no overtime, he would only make $110,240 a year. Do you have any openings?

I have enjoyed owning my Teleram. However, if it ceases to operate, I will simply abandon it and conclude that word processors have not reached the state where they are reliable enough to be economically feasible for me to own.

I do not want the service contract you offer for $660 a year. "Prices subject to change without notice."

Sincerely,
Andrew A. Rooney

Hometown

My hometown newspaper is going to start running my essays.
I view this with mixed feelings. I'm pleased that the people I know will be able to read what I write but I'm a little apprehensive about it, too. It's a small community in Connecticut and my wife and I know most of the people. We bought our house here in 1952 for $29,500 and we've brought up four children in it.

I'm apprehensive because I suspect it's better if readers don't know a writer personally. A writer ought to give readers the impression he knows what he's talking about and it's difficult for anyone to take a writer seriously if they've been watching him put the garbage out for twenty years.

A writer only has so much and it seems like less if you know where it comes from. I have what I've lived. I draw from what I see around me, from the people I know, from what I read and from the feelings I get from all these things. There's no magic. The trick in attracting people to read the kind of thing I write about is to strike a universal chord. I try to write about things almost everyone knows about. If I write about politics, it isn't from any inside knowledge I have or any special ability to interpret what's happening. I just try to put down on paper some of the thoughts that have crossed my mind because I'm average enough so they've probably crossed the reader's, too.

Knowing a writer makes you look at what he or she has written in a different way. It's like sitting way down front at a play in a theater where you can see what's going on in the wings.

If you live in one of the 350 cities or towns that carry my column but not my name in the phone book, you can read it in blissful ignorance of the fact that I'm not any smarter than you are. Friends and neighbors in my community can't do that. They know different. They've seen me bungle too many jobs to believe I have any special knowledge or ability. They saw what I did when I tried to rehang my garage doors and finally had to call a professional. They know I don't even mow my own lawn. I don't have any special standing with them except as a friend. From now on, I'm going to have to be more careful what I write and how I write it.

Up until today a lot of you strangers out there have suspected, on occasion, that I didn't know what I was talking about but you couldn't be sure. These people I've known for thirty years will know for sure.

I've always wondered how the novelist who draws heavily on his personal life—as all novelists must—handles it Saturday nights with old friends that he's used. They must recognize some of the characters in his book and they must sometimes see themselves in an unfavorable light.

I have so many friends in our community with so many problems, who often behave in such a bizarre manner that I couldn't write about them honestly and conceal their identity or maintain their friendship. I like them but they wouldn't think so if they realized I know them as well as I do. If I write about them now that they can read it, I'll have to camouflage their character. I don't want to lose the bizarrest among them.

No writer is immune to the pleasure of seeing his words in print so I'm pleased that my local paper is going to print mine. I just want all of you to understand the new note of caution and restraint you may find here. In the future I won't be able to go off half-cocked with impunity. My neighbors will be watching.

Electronic Journalism

THERE is no business so secure that the people who work in it don't worry about its future. Usually there is some technological improvement lurking in a laboratory or on a drawing board nearby that threatens the routine operation of any commercial enterprise. I suppose the manufacturers of lead pencils thought it was the end of their world when fountain pens were invented. The owners of radio stations panicked when television started moving in but I notice they're still making lead pencils and radio seems to be surviving.

More often than not, the threat is worse than anything that actually comes of it. In other cases, change comes so slowly that everyone adapts and gets in on it.

There are times, though, when an invention hits with such impact and suddenness that it threatens to destroy a business. It happens that way just often enough to keep us all worried for good reason.

The business I worry about is news. I know some of you don't really like or trust people in the news business but I like them above all others. They are my friends. When I am in a strange city and go to the newsroom of a newspaper or a television station, I am instantly on familiar ground even though I have never been in that room before. I am among friends even though I have never met any of them.

The men and women in newsrooms across the country all know the same things I know. We share common problems and we have common goals. We start our conversations further along than you normally start a conversation with someone you've never met, because of this feeling of common knowingness.

I was in Denver this year and was taken to the press club. Once inside I could have been in any one of a hundred press clubs around the world. The look of the place, the look of the people and the sounds and the atmosphere of the place were as familiar to me as home. The newspapermen and women of Denver were indistinguishable from those standing at a bar or eating their lunch, in violent conversation with friends, in Hong Kong, Chicago, London or San Francisco.

Most newspaper people are as worried now about the various forms of technology creeping in on their business as carbon paper manufacturers must have been when offices started installing Xerox machines. I'm worried about it myself even though I don't depend solely on my newspaper work for my living.

Too many newspapers are in financial trouble today and too many cities that have had healthy competition between two or more good, fighting newspapers are in danger of losing one of them. It is not clear to me why this is nor do I think all the newspaper experts know for sure. In most instances it is the afternoon paper that is in most trouble. It seems that people who once settled down with the afternoon paper after six in the evening, are now settling down to watch their news on television.

You won't find me knocking television news, nor could anything I say conceivably have any effect on a trend but television news never has been and never will be a substitute for a newspaper. Even a bad newspaper does some things better than a good television news program.

Newspapers haven't been left behind when it comes to technology. The whole process of producing a newspaper has changed more in ten years than has the process of producing a television news broadcast. Newspaper reporters have adapted to writing on a display terminal instead of a sheet of yellow copy paper but there are other innovations lurking in the shadows that worry them. If the time comes when the newspaper itself is not a paper at all but an image that can be called up on the screen of a computer in a person's home, a lot of what they love about the business will be gone. There won't be much reason for them to hold out against switching over to television, where the journalism may be worse but the pay better. Newspapermen and women wouldn't sit around the Denver Press Club eating, drinking and arguing about a product that didn't really exist anywhere but in the memory bank of a computer.

What's News?

A YOUNG reporter I talked with last weekend said he was in trouble with his readers and with the police because of a story he'd written.

His newspaper is in a medium-sized city in the Northeast and the incident involved a holdup of a small grocery store. The two men who did it were chased into a dead-end alley and caught by three men who heard the grocer yell for help as the thieves ran out of his store.

The two men were not armed and when they were caught, they were pinned to the ground while someone called the police.

The reporter heard of the chase over his police radio and raced to the scene, arriving at about the same time as the cops.

The two suspects were released by their captors and they stood up to face the police. One of them made a smartass remark in answer to one of the cop's questions and the cop instantly pistol-whipped him to the ground and went after him again with his feet.

At this point one of the three men who had originally captured the robber pulled the cop off and told him to cool it.

When the reporter got back to the office, he realized there were three ways to write the story. It could be the grocer's story of the robbery, it could be the story of the three citizens capturing the thieves or it could be the story of the cop beating one of the robbers.

The reporter wrote the story of the policeman beating the thief.

"You wrote the wrong story," a cop said to him after the story appeared. "Those two guys were guilty as hell."

The reporter has since been reprimanded by several cops he knows and by half a dozen letter-writing readers.

A lot of newspaper readers and almost all cops would agree that the story should have been about the holdup and the capture, not about police brutality. Not many newspaper editors would, though. They'd agree the emphasis should have been where this reporter put it: MAN BITES DOG.

It seems to me there's a news crisis in the world. The crisis has nothing to do with world events but with events in the news business itself. It has become such a big business that there is inevitable pressure for the product to make money.

This is a reasonable enough expectation for owners and stockholders but most newsmen and women like to think that news is more important than money. To increase profit on a product, you have to increase its popularity. Making news more popular is the last resort of a dying news operation.

If news is treated like any other product being sold for money, then it will be made the way people like it. Newspapers will print what people want to read, not what they ought to know. Reporters will ignore stories of police brutality because no one likes to read about it. "Those two had it coming to them."

In London during the Falkland Islands war, Margaret Thatcher complained about a BBC news broadcast that suggested that the death of a husband was just as sad for a woman in Argentina as it was for the wife of a British sailor.

Margaret didn't like that.

"The case for our country is not being put with sufficient vigor by certain journalists," she said.

Mrs. Thatcher was answered by a spokesman for the BBC.

"It is not the BBC's role to boost troops' morale or to rally

British people to the flag," he said. "What we are about is not propaganda but information."

Whether a journalist is reporting a war or a grocery store holdup, it is not his business to consider whether the story will do good or harm. He has to have faith that in the long run, the truth will do good. The policeman did beat the thief. It was unusual. *It* was the news story.

The reporter was my son, Brian, too.

The Journalist's Code of Ethics

To what standards do newsmen and women adhere and how should everyone be made to adhere to them?

It is unlikely that reporters and editors are any more or less honest and ethical than doctors but I envy doctors their Hippocratic Oath, the creed they swear to when they become physicians. It's a little out of date but it has a grandeur to it that is timeless.

"I swear by Apollo, the physician," it begins.

That's not much of a beginning, but it improves even though it needs rewriting.

The Hippocratic Oath asks the young doctor to take care of the physician who taught him as he would take care of his own parents. Most young reporters don't feel all that kindly toward the editors who taught them their profession.

The Hippocratic Oath also asks the young doctor to do only what is right for his patients and to do nothing that is wrong. He promises to give no patient deadly medicine and not to induce an abortion for any pregnant woman.

The young doctor promises not to seduce any males or females and not to reveal any secrets.

If journalists had an oath of their own, it would differ from the doctor's.

The journalist certainly wouldn't start by swearing to Apollo and probably not even to Walter Lippmann or Ed Murrow. The oath should be simple and direct. I was thinking of some things that ought to be in it.

Here are some suggestions for "The Journalist's Code of Ethics":

—The word "journalist" is a little pompous and I will only use it on special occasions.

—I am a journalist because I believe that if all the world had all the facts about everything, it would be a better world.

—I understand that the facts and the truth are not always the same. It is my job to report the facts so that others can decide on the truth.

—I will try to tell people what they ought to know and avoid telling them what they want to hear, except when the two coincide, which isn't often.

—I will not do deliberate harm to any persons, except to the extent that the facts harm them and then I will not avoid the facts.

—No gift, including kind words, will be accepted when it is offered for the purpose of influencing my report.

—What I wish were the facts will not influence what investigation leads me to believe them to be.

—I will be suspicious of every self-interested source of information.

—My professional character will be superior to my private character.

—I will not use my profession to help or espouse any cause, nor alter my report for the benefit of any cause, no matter how worthy that cause may appear to be.

—I will not reveal the source of information given to me in confidence.

—I will not drink at lunch.

It needs work but it's a start on an oath for reporters and editors.

Farmers

THERE are two groups of people whose handling of money mystifies me. They are bankers and farmers.

Farmers have always been the most admired people in our country. They were an honest, independent, hard-working bunch. More than any other single group, they have made this country what it is, great.

Little by little, though, farmers are becoming less admired than they once were. They got their good reputation in the days when they were simple, self-reliant people who raised their own food and sold what they had left over in order to buy a few things they couldn't grow or make themselves.

Everyone in town knew which were the good farmers and which were the poor farmers because the good farmers' kids were better dressed and their places were better kept. You could tell just from driving by. The farmer's standard of living depended on how hard he and his family worked.

It used to be that farmers were on their own. We let them sink or swim. If they had a drought or if the economy went bad, they sank. If there was enough rain but not too much rain and the economy was good, they could get rich. In the 1930s we decided farmers were too important to be left to the mercy of the elements and a free economy, so the government got into the business of helping them. Now it can't get out and, as a result, farmers are no more independent of government than a lot of other Americans.

The farmer who isn't very good at farming and is lazy gets just as much government money today as the good farmer does. A farmer these days is often rich or poor for reasons that have nothing to do with his ability or industry. Most farmers' families don't even eat anything they grow anymore.

Last year I visited a farmer with a reputation for being one of the best in all of Kansas. He grew wheat. I went into his farmhouse half expecting a wood stove and a few rocking chairs in the living room. Instead he had two television sets, a tape recorder and a stereo record player. I asked him how much he thought the farm equipment in his yard was worth.

"Maybe million and a half, two million," he said, "but the bank owns a lot of it."

I turned to his wife standing next to the electric range in the kitchen and asked if she made bread from the wheat her husband grew.

She broke into merry laughter.

"I've never made bread in my life," she said. "John likes Wonder Bread."

Farmers these days aren't any less dependent on the rest of the world than city people, either. John grows wheat that he sells to Russia and buys Japanese television sets with the money.

There aren't any homemade pickles in *his* cellar.

Farmers seem to be victims of their own virtues. They have worked so hard and been so smart in using new scientific methods and better farm machinery that they've produced themselves out of work. We not only have a surplus of the things farmers grow, we have a surplus of farmers.

It's both sad and strange that some of the world's population is starving to death while we have more food than we can eat. Why can't we work this out?

Our farmers are growing so much that they've created a problem we don't know how to solve. The government has come up with all sorts of ingenious plans. None of them really work. Last year the government paid farmers not to grow corn. The government paid the farmers with surplus corn it had bought from them the year before. It's a form of welfare, even though farmers hate to have the word applied to them.

My only real knowledge of farming comes from the fourteen-horsepower John Deere tractor I own. I've been wondering if I could get the government to pay me for not mowing my lawn with it next year.

A Broken Water Hose

PEOPLE who really know how to do something and have the ambition to do it are hard to find.

Several weeks ago I was driving the old station wagon home on a hot summer Sunday night. I started to smell something burning. You know how that is. You hope it's the car next to you or something from the outside air. Finally I couldn't deny that it emanated from under my very own hood. I pulled off the highway into a combination gas station, grocery store and garage. It wasn't the kind of place that gives you any confidence that they know much about cars. I judged my chance of getting anything done there at seven o'clock Sunday evening to be near zero but it was the only choice I had.

Not wishing to irritate the attendant by making him come out to ask what I wanted, I shut off my steaming engine, hurried out of the car and went inside. A paunchy, balding man in his middle forties was closing the cash register on the change he had just collected from the sale of a bag of potato chips.

"Yeah?" he said in a tone that suggested he didn't have time for me.

I told him my problem. He came out to the car and as I unlatched the hood, he lifted it and was instantly engulfed in a cloud of steam.

When the fog cleared he just shook his head.

"I dunno," he said. "You got a broken water hose here."

He went back into the store, sold two Hostess Twinkies and then went into the one-pit garage connected to the store.

I waited, uncertain about whether he'd abandoned me or not. Pretty soon he emerged with a length of hose. I was tense. He tried to fit the piece of hose on the pipe leading from the radiator but it wasn't close to the right size.

"May not have it," he said.

I was fifty miles from home. I had about twenty-seven dollars on me and didn't know anyone nearby I could call.

The man disappeared into the garage again and this time I was sure he'd lost interest in my case. When he finally emerged he had two more pieces of hose. Neither of them fitted but I knew by now that I had someone special here. This fellow had taken on my problem for his own and he was sticking at it. It was a dirty little job but he was helping me.

For the next forty-five minutes he'd wrestle with a piece of hose under my hood for a while and then go in and sell something or pump fifteen gallons of gas, but he always came back to me.

I had been there perhaps an hour when he finally found a length of hose that fit. I was happy, relieved and grateful. I could hardly believe this fellow had kept at the job until he got it done.

Next, of course, I was worried about my twenty-seven dollars. I would have been happy to pay him one hundred and twenty-seven dollars if I'd had it, but I didn't, and there was no way of knowing what he'd charge.

He went into the store area as I followed along like a faithful dog, grateful for anything my master was doing for me. Inside he took a greasy parts book down off the shelf behind him. When they go for the parts book, I'm nervous.

His finger went up and down several pages, as he uttered an occasional grunt. I don't want to suggest this fellow was a lot of fun, but by now I liked him and hoped I'd be able to pay him what he asked. Finally his finger came to rest on a serial number with a price after it.

"2749–16 JDT," he said. "I'll just charge on the cost of the hose. That'll be ten dollars and eighty-five cents."

I have no aberrant tendencies but I could have kissed this man.

"Listen, I said. "It's worth more than that to me. I've only got twenty-seven dollars. Please take the twenty dollars. I'll keep the seven dollars to get to work on in the morning."

Since that episode, I've thought of him a hundred times. Does he make as good a living as he would if he'd told me to get lost, as so many would have under similar circumstances? I hope so. I hope he gets his reward in satisfaction but I hope it turns out that it's also a good way to run a business.

Not many people are running them that way.

Getting Ahead

Do you want to get ahead in business? Are you young, just starting out and ambitious to get to the top as quickly as possible? Take some advice from someone who has seen a lot of people pass him by on the way up: Get yourself an assistant.

If you're determined to be taken seriously in business, it is absolutely essential that you have an assistant in addition to your secretary. No matter how little you actually have to do, get someone to help you do it.

Don't start thinking small. If you think you don't have enough work to do for both a secretary and an assistant, you're thinking small. Don't forget that as soon as you add one more body around the office, the time it takes to do many jobs doubles. It means getting more coffee, working out more vacation schedules and finding more office space and office equipment.

I've seen hundreds of executives and the ones who get furthest fastest are the ones who make fewest mistakes. One way to make fewer mistakes is to make fewer decisions. Get an assistant who makes mistakes for you! If you use your head, you can make it appear as though you have a very important job without ever really doing anything at all. Send your assistant to meetings. If someone wants to come to your office to talk, tell him to see your assistant. Give every visitor the impression that you have someone more important waiting to see you.

To get ahead in business you have to put yourself in a position of power and to have power you must have people working for you. The minute a person gets an assistant, his own job takes on new importance.

When you get your assistant, make sure he or she has a good job title. It won't help your stature if you're only in charge of a helper or a gofer. Your assistant should, at the very least, be called "Executive Assistant." Go to your boss once in a while and make the grand gesture. Ask for a raise or a new title, not for yourself but for your assistant. Don't forget, the more important your assistant is, the more important you are.

If you've chosen your assistant wisely, he'll come to you after a few months on the job, close the door and say he has something important to ask. He thinks *he* needs an assistant.

This could be the beginning of something big for you because if your assistant gets an assistant, the whole plan for the offices on your floor will have to be worked over to make room for your assistant's assistant. Someone else will be moved out of your area to a smaller office down the hall and you're on your way to the top. You're starting a little empire within the company.

The next step is a big one and an important one. After an assistant has made a lot of mistakes on decisions you should have made yourself, you're going to have to fire him. Firing an assistant is just one more positive way of giving yourself added stature in a company. Go to your boss, tell him how bad you feel about it but say you feel it's best for everyone if your assistant gets the axe. This instantly says to the boss that all those mistakes he's noticed in your department must be the fault of your aide. You've just been too nice a guy to say anything about it until now.

Nothing succeeds like success unless it's having people afraid of you, and if they know you can fire someone, you have acquired a new power. Having people afraid of you is absolutely the best way to acquire power and don't ever forget it. If you doubt that, just look at the former vice-president or the former general manager who has been relegated to a lesser position. Everyone knows management hoped he'd retire. His power is gone because people are no longer afraid of him. He is afraid himself.

Many of America's best companies are heavily staffed with assistants that aren't really necessary, and if you're going to be successful in business, you'd better get yourself one.

Conventions

ONE of the things businessmen love to do is get together with other people in the same business and talk business.

This great interest they have in what they're doing has created another big business, conventions. Most hotels, a lot of resorts and even some cities wouldn't make it if they didn't have conventions.

I can't figure out whether the average convention is an honest business meeting or a boondoogle wrapped as a Christmas present from the executives to themselves once a year. The money seems wasteful but if it's a corporation that's making hundreds of millions of dollars, who am I to criticize? Obviously they know more about how to do business than I do. Conventions keep a lot of nice hotels and restaurants in business, too. That isn't all bad.

Still, I can't get used to the money I see big companies spending on conventions. I went to one in San Francisco where the company hired the Goodyear blimp equipped with a big electric signboard to flash welcome messages down to the participants having a lavish outdoor party below.

Some corporations spend money on conventions as if it came from a Parker Brothers game. A company that is trying to save money back at the home office by putting a cheaper brand of paper towels in the men's and ladies' rooms, will pay first-class air fare to bring four hundred of their executives or salesmen across the country and put them up in hotel rooms that cost a hundred dollars a night.

At the reception before the banquet the final night, there are always 350 pounds of shrimp on platters around the room and piles of literature about the business on the tables. Participants eagerly grab up both. They go inside to tables with fresh flowers, have dinner with two kinds of wine and are informed, amused or entertained by an orchestra and a speaker who is being paid something like ten thousand dollars for half an hour of his time.

The business meetings are dull if you don't know anything about the business but the participants love every dull minute of them. The speakers from various divisions of the company are terrible.

They drone on with charts or other visual displays that don't make anything very clear and they tell the people in the room nothing but things they already know. If they don't know, they don't care.

A typical convention speech starts like this:

"Thanks for that introduction, Ed. I'm glad you were able to be with us today after last night's party."

This is the kind of little joke that suggests Ed is a real hell-raiser and everyone laughs. The truth is that Ed had only two weak Scotch and sodas over a four-hour period the night before and he was in bed by 10:15.

The speaker then goes on to make the following points:

—Competition will be more intense this year than ever before.

—There are difficult times ahead but he's confident the company is ready to meet the challenge of the future. (No speech would be complete at one of these meetings if it didn't mention "the challenge of the future.")

—He is confident the company will maintain its leadership position in the industry in spite of the difficult economic environment in which they operate today.

—The management team is in place. ("In place" is the most popular new phrase in business speeches.)

—Last year was one of the most difficult in the company's history but, in spite of certain setbacks with which you're all familiar, it had a record they could all be proud of.

—Nothing could be further from the truth. (This is in reference to a story in the industry that the company is in trouble.)

—Because of the ongoing efforts of this great team, they're going to take a bigger share of the market next year. He's confident it is an ever-expanding market.

—The company is fortunate in having such a forward-looking leader as its President. (This is where the speaker says nice things about his boss. Then he lists some other people who have contributed so much to the success of the company and finishes by saying "the list goes on and on." I've always wondered what the people thought whose names weren't mentioned but who were relegated to the anonymous on-and-on list.)

I have a feeling that sometime, long ago, someone wrote a convention speech and with a few name changes the same speech is still being used ten thousand times a year.

Speechmaking

Iᶠ you've ever talked in front of a group of more than ten people, you know how nervous you get. In the past few years I've spoken about twenty times to large audiences and I was as nervous before the last one as I was before the first. Being nervous before speaking just doesn't seem to go away.

There are some things I've learned about speechmaking:

—Sitting at the head table, waiting for your turn while everyone eats dinner for several hours, is the hardest part of making a speech at a banquet.

—A lot of organizations that ask you to speak don't care what you talk about as long as you show up on time and don't talk for too long.

—You have to give a longer speech when the event is held in an auditorium than you do when you're speaking at a dinner, because in an auditorium those people came for the single purpose of hearing you.

—If you make a half-hour speech, it takes about three weeks. It takes a day to get there, a day to get back, a couple of days to prepare it and several weeks to worry about it.

—It's strange to be "introduced" by someone you never met.

—The worst thing that can happen is if they give out awards, citations, trophies or plaques before you speak. Those presentations take forever and after they're over everyone's ready to go home, not listen to you speak.

—If the speech is at a dinner, you usually sit next to the wife of the president. She's almost always bright and friendly. I usually like her better than the president. It's difficult to make small talk when you're nervous, though.

—The toughest audience is at a banquet where they're all sitting at round tables. There are ten or twelve people at a table and the tables are widely separated so the waiters can get through. It's late, everyone's been drinking and eating and they can't hear what you're saying very well anyway.

—Getting dressed in a hotel room before a speech, I almost always find there's something wrong with my clothes. There's a button missing on my shirt, I brought brown socks and I'm wearing a blue suit or there's a spot on my necktie.

—Usually the podium on the speaker's platform is high enough so you don't have to worry about having your pants pressed.

—The worst introductions are when the person introducing you tries to be funny. The best introductions are invariably the shortest. I've had introductions that were as long as my speech. There really isn't that much to say about me.

—Even when I'm the main speaker, there's almost always someone on the program who speaks better than I do.

—The strange thing about speaking is that you only know for sure that you've made a point with an audience when you say something funny and they laugh. If you make what you hope is a good, serious point, there's no way for them to let you know.

—They always give you a glass of water but I never drink any.

—When there are questions afterwards, there's always one person who gets up and embarrasses everyone else by asking a really stupid question.

—No matter how bad I may have been, someone always comes up to me and tells me I was great. If most people are polite but distant when you're leaving, you know you bombed out as a speaker.

—Someone always thanks you profusely for coming even when they've paid you to do it.

—There are few pleasanter times in life than when you've finished speaking.

The Nonworking Week

A LOT of people know for sure whether they're on the side of management or labor, but I don't have a side. I vacillate. One day I'm angry at the high-handed, anything-for-a-profit corporation which is paying big dividends and small salaries, but the next I'm angry at employees who take money from the company without putting in a day's work. There's plenty to dislike on both sides.

I'm not in a position where I hire or fire people but occasionally I get so far behind on mail and paperwork that Jane Bradford, who works with me regularly, and I decide to hire a temporary secretary for a few weeks to help us get caught up.

Over the years we've had about ten. With a couple of exceptions, this is the way it goes:

Linda hears we're looking for a typist so she comes to my office to talk. She's bright, young, attractive and she knows how to type. She wants the job desperately, she says, so she can pay her part of the rent for the apartment she shares with a roommate. I don't ask about the roommate.

Linda seems like what we need so I tell her to show up Monday mornng at 9 A.M.

Monday morning at 9:22, Linda waltzes in. The bus was late, she says.

First Linda puts her pocketbook down on the desk. She notices the IBM Selectric typewriter she's going to use and complains that it's an old model which she may not be able to work on.

Next she asks Jane where the ladies' room is. I know where it is too but she doesn't ask me.

Ten minutes later she reappears with a fresh makeup job. She wants to make a good impression on me, I guess.

"Is it okay if I go down to the cafeteria and get a cup of coffee?" she asks.

I had assumed that by quarter of ten she'd already had breakfast but I want to be Mr. Nice Guy with Linda, so I, of course, say sure.

Linda is in the cafeteria long enough to have fresh-squeezed orange juice, pancakes and sausage and a third cup of coffee, but when she comes back she's carrying a bag with coffee and a Danish in it. She spreads her little breakfast out on the desk and proceeds to have it while she reads the newspaper. This is not the kind of help Jane and I had in mind.

I finally put some things on her desk that I want typed. She asks me a few questions about the material and then says is it okay if she makes a phone call first.

Mr. Nice Guy says sure.

I hear her talking to her mother. She's been on the payroll for an hour and a half now and she hasn't done anything at all for me yet but she's telling her mother how good I am to work for.

It turns out Linda is a telephone junkie. She spends more time making personal phone calls than she does drinking coffee or going to the ladies' room, and by the end of the third day she's getting more incoming calls than Jane, Bob Forte, the editor, and I put together.

Several days later Linda confides in Bob, who tells me, that she really hates this kind of work. She wants to be an actress and only took the job in hopes she'd see Walter Cronkite or Dan Rather in the halls. She'd like to meet Dan because if she can't make it on Broadway, she wants to be the first anchorwoman on the network evening news show.

On Friday of the first week, Linda calls in at 11 A.M. and says she's going to be a little late because she has a dental appointment she forgot to tell me about. All the temporary secretaries I've ever had, have an awful lot of dental work done and their buses are later than anyone else's.

I thought of all this because I've read where, when unemployment is high, the absenteeism rate in industry goes way down. Workers don't goof off as much. I hope it's true even though I know it could mean less business for dentists during a recession.

Unemployment

LOOKING for work is one of the worst things to have to do. There's nothing good about it. You don't really know how to get started, you feel like a jerk and it's demeaning every step of the way.

There aren't many of us who haven't looked for work at some time in our lives. There are ten million Americans doing it at almost any time and I feel terrible for them. I feel almost as bad for them because they have to *look* for work as I do because they're *out* of work. Being out of work is bad enough but having to look for it is even worse.

If you aren't working, it's almost impossible not to feel a little ashamed of yourself. If you're a man, you feel a little less of a man; if you're a woman, I don't know how you feel.

Considering that just about everyone has looked for work, it's amazing how mean the people *with* the jobs are to the people without them. You'd think they'd never looked for jobs themselves. You'd think they were born with jobs.

Once a person gets to be in the position of hiring or firing someone, he or she seems to forget what it's like to be unemployed. Why is that?

When you fill out the form for the personnel department, the man or woman who takes it from you always makes you feel like dirt. It's as if they don't like associating with someone who doesn't have a job.

The person who interviews you always acts as if he or she was president of the company. You know darn well it's just a flunky's job but you don't dare let on you know that because your application could end up in the wasketbasket. When he turns away from you and walks to a desk or a file cabinet, you feel like giving him a swift kick in his smug tail.

I remember the first time I looked for work. There were hundreds of classified ads in the paper under the Help Wanted heading and I figured it was going to be easy.

Well, it didn't take me long to find out that the number of Help Wanted pages in the classified section of the newspaper has very little to do with getting a job.

First you count out all the ads looking for nuclear physicists, registered nurses, animal trainers and, if you don't know anything about computers, you count out the ads looking for computer programmers. I mention that because there seem to be a lot of ads for them these days. I don't know what they do but I assume it's a terrible job that doesn't pay much. If it wasn't, there wouldn't be so many ads for them under Help Wanted.

As soon as you get some experience looking in the classified section, you get discouraged. You begin to read the classifieds the way you read the phone book when you're looking for one number. You know all those hundreds of listings don't mean anything. You get to spot the ones looking for door-to-door salesmen to work on commission only. There's usually only one or two categories that mean anything to you and if anything is listed there, you're probably too late for it.

Unemployment is as much of a mystery as cancer and almost as bad. I've never understood why there should be any real unemployment. Do we mean there isn't any work to be done anywhere in the country? Do we mean people have everything they want to eat? Everything they need by way of housing? All the clothes, cars and creature comforts they want? Of course not. Then why isn't there work for everyone?

What we need is a President who can figure out a way to match up those ten million unemployed with the ten million Help Wanted ads. And when that's done, I hope everyone fires those miserable people in the personnel offices so they have to go out and look for work themselves.

Economic Indicators

Yesterday, for the first time, I noticed I've been using two tissues or paper handkerchiefs instead of one. I think I've been using two more often than one for some time now but I never thought about it until yesterday. It's a sign of the times. They're making smaller, cheaper paper handkerchiefs.

Will we ever reverse the present trend in which everything gets smaller, of less quality and more expensive? Is there a company in America that has improved its product and given us more for our money this year than it did last year? There are some, of course, but they're far outnumbered by the ones giving us less for more.

Each of us has his or her own scale on which the past economy is measured against the present. We have our own personal equivalents of the government's Gross National Product and economic indicators. It may be the price of a cup of coffee, a bus ride or a pair of stockings. (I hate to tell you but thirty-five cents for a movie is one of my standards. That's what we used to pay when we went to a cowboys and Indians double feature at the Madison when I was a kid.)

I can understand having to raise the price of a product when the cost of labor and materials goes up but how do they explain the deterioration in the quality of the product? That shouldn't have anything to do with inflation. And why is it that when the economy is good and everyone's working, prices go up but when the economy's bad and people are out of work, prices still go up?

When a well-known watch company first started making something other than the old-fashioned spring watch, I bought one. They had obviously put a lot of research and technique into it. It was the first watch I ever had that operated on a tiny battery and it was just great. It kept near-perfect time and the quality of the workmanship was first-rate. I retired my trusty old Hamilton railroad watch with a few tears and gave way to progress. The new watch gave me ten years of good service before I finally left it in a locker at the place where I play tennis and lost it.

From loyalty to the company and because I wanted another good watch, I went back to the jeweler. Well, they don't make that model anymore. The jeweler conceded their new equivalent isn't as good.

You can't tell me razor blades last as long as they did ten or twenty years ago, either. How in the world does a company make razor blades that aren't as good? That must take real technical know-how.

The gasoline we buy for our cars isn't as powerful as it used to be. Forget about the increase in price. Maybe they had to raise the price from the thirty-three cents a gallon we were paying not so long ago but did they also have to lower the octane rating so that one gallon of gas won't push a car as far? A lot of gas sold now is only eighty-seven octane and the highest octane you can buy is ninety-three. An octane rating in the nineties used to be regular gas and high test could be ninety-nine octane.

For the past ten years I've had a popular brand-name suitcase. It's been the best suitcase I ever owned even though, for a while, it looked like everyone else's suitcase. It's been all over the world and back and it's a little shabby so last month I decided to retire it. I was going to stay at an expensive hotel and I didn't want to embarrass the bellboy who would have had to carry my battered bag to the room so I went to a luggage store to buy another like it. Three guesses? They don't make it any longer. The one they do make to replace it is shoddy by comparison.

Every time a big company takes over a smaller one in this country in order to promise its stockholders a bigger return on their investment, the product suffers. They raise the price and make it cheaper. I'm not a Communist, and I own some stocks but I'd gladly settle for a little more quality as a consumer and a smaller dividend as an investor.

IV:
MONEY

A Cash Standard

THERE's something about having a thick stack of money in your pocket that gives you a feeling of well-being. I smile more when I have money in my pocket. Even too much change will do it for me if the change is mostly in quarters and quite heavy.

It occurs to me to mention this today because I've noticed that the more money I make, the less I use. I'm talking about actual cash, green paper money. Earlier in the week I took an overnight trip from New York to Washington. Before I left, I cashed a check for a hundred and fifty dollars. When I got back to New York late the next afternoon, I still had more than a hundred dollars. The surprising thing was that I had that little left because I hadn't really paid for anything. The fifty dollars went out in petty cash for tips, taxis and newspapers. I charged my air fare, my hotel room and my meals.

Like most people, when I sign for something on my credit card I consider it to be free. Paying for the item is postponed to some indefinite time in the future. The bill will come in a lump sum and will bear no relationship in my mind to any service or goods that I actually got for that amount.

The trouble with doing all these things with numbers instead of with real money is that it takes the fun and the satisfaction out of the exchange process. What's rewarding is to work hard to make money and then to take that money and buy something with it that makes life pleasant or easier.

There used to be a joke about a wealthy recluse who went to his bank once a week and made them show him his money. He wanted to make sure it was still there.

We all know our money isn't really in the bank, it's in the book-keeping machinery, but I feel the way that old guy did. I'd like to see my money in real life once in a while. Those numbers they send me aren't any fun at all.

I can't get over how little I see of my money these days. One summer when I was in college I worked at a paper mill for forty dollars a week. Every Friday afternoon they gave me my pay in an

583

envelope and I've never made money that was as satisfying to me as that. I don't care how big my check is, it can't match that forty dollars I got in cold cash.

Today the company mails my check directly to the bank. After a while, the bank mails me a slip of paper saying the check has been deposited. When I owe someone something, I write out a check and my bank deducts that from my account. It's all terribly unsatisfactory. Collecting money or paying it out can be a rewarding experience but bookkeeping is no fun at all. If I had my way, I'd have every penny I earned turned over to me in cash and I'd pay most of the people I owe with the money in my pocket.

I understand perfectly well that it wouldn't be practical sometimes but it would be more satisfactory and, furthermore, if the federal government handled its accounts in cash, there'd be a lot less waste. It's one thing for a government official to sign his name to a piece of paper transferring a billion dollars from one place to another, but it would be quite different if he had to show up with the actual money in dollar bills and hand it over. Just counting it would make everyone think twice and there'd surely be cameras around to record the event.

Money ought to be more tangible than it is today, not less. We're treating it too lightly because we can't see it. I don't understand the ramifications of a return to the gold standard but I have a feeling pennies ought to be copper, dimes ought to be silver and it wouldn't do any harm if we had some little fifty or hundred-dollar gold coins in circulation. We need money that's really worth something.

The money game is being played with numbers that are too big for most of us to comprehend. Only lawyers, bankers, computer experts and government officials understand money as a statistic. Most of us get no kick at all from a computer printout of a bank's idea of our net worth. What we want is that lump in our pocket.

Broke

Has everyone been desperately broke?

Maybe not. I always assume that there are very few experiences or emotions that aren't universal. I've been seriously broke twice in my life.

It's a feeling you never forget and although it's been twenty-six years since I didn't know which way to turn for money, I never see anyone out of a job and without a dollar in his pocket without knowing how he feels.

There are still times when I think about being broke. At night when I empty the change out of my pocket and put it on top of my dresser, I often recall, in those terrible old days, adding up my change to see if I had two dollars.

There are chronically poor people who would laugh at what I went through because it wouldn't seem very bad to them. My wife and I were never hungry. My father was retired but he had made a comfortable living even during the Depression, and my wife's father was a doctor. They wouldn't have let us get to the point where we were out on the street and without food, but you know how that is. There's an unwritten code. There are people you don't ask for money and my father and my wife's father were two of them.

I don't know who makes those rules but we all know them. Certainly if I'd asked, either would have given me money. Maybe that was it. They'd have given it to me, not loaned it to me. They would have been disappointed that I had to ask.

My father's brother was a salt-of-the-earth lawyer in a small town in New York State, fighting petty political corruption and providing free legal services to people who couldn't afford to pay him. He and my aunt never had children and I was the closest thing to a son he had. When he came to visit us when I was a child he would often slip me a five-dollar bill as he was leaving. You don't forget an uncle like that.

In desperation one year, I went to him and asked for five hundred dollars. One of the terrible memories of my life is that I never repaid him. He died three years later without ever having been able to take pleasure from thinking that his favorite nephew was a responsible person. He didn't need the money but he must have looked for some token payment from me and I never made it. I always meant to but I never did.

About fifteen years ago we were doing better but we needed $2,500 to help pay for one of the kids' college tuition and my wife went to the bank for a loan. Banks are a better place to go for a loan than an uncle is. They aren't disappointed if you don't pay them back. They get you.

By this time I was making enough money so we weren't in desperate need of the loan, so as the joke goes, we didn't have any trouble getting it. The interest was probably seven percent.

A year or so later I asked my wife if we were going to pay off the loan in a lump sum, or just continue paying the seven percent interest each year. Being in no way a business tycoon, I had the feeling we should pay it off. She does all our bookkeeping and banking, and she didn't think we should. She was right. I'm not sure to this day if we ever paid off the loan.

Now, of course, I appreciate that it's the only good joke we ever played on a bank. We won because interest rates rose. If we have the $2,500, and it's invested, maybe in the same bank's money-market fund, and we get nine percent interest, we are beating the bank for two percent on $2,500. It is not at all like failing to pay back my uncle.

This all occurred to me today because yesterday an old friend asked me to loan him money. Of course I'll loan it to him but I wish he hadn't asked. It breaks the unwritten law. It changes our relationship. I don't want to think about it every time I see him and I don't want him feeling uneasy about it when he sees me but that's what will happen.

Being broke is a terrible feeling but it's probably an experience everyone ought to have once in a lifetime. If you've never been really broke, you can't possibly understand how nice it is to have a little money in the bank.

Money in Stress

I WAS listening to one of those financial experts being interviewed on the radio the other day and he used the term "money in stress." I never heard the phrase before and I don't know what it means but I think it's where my money is. It's in stress because I don't know where else to put it.

Now that the kids are out of college and the mortgage is paid off, I'm making more money and don't need as much.

Wasn't money easier to deal with ten years ago than it is now? I don't remember hearing about a "money-market fund" until five years ago. It used to be that the solid citizens kept most of their paycheck to pay bills with and put what they had left in the savings bank. Their savings account paid four percent interest and they just let it accumulate year after year, secure in the knowledge that they had a little nest egg. It was the American way.

There was less wheeling and dealing going on and it must have been better for the average person, because when there's a lot of wheeling and dealing, the only ones who get rich are the wheeler-dealers.

Handling money has become complicated, even for someone with a modest income. If a person makes $35,000 a year, he or she could easily spend full time figuring out what to do with it. The trouble is, if you spend full time figuring out what to do with the money you're making, you couldn't keep the job that pays you the $35,000. It's so complicated for most of us that we just give up.

This year I've saved some money and because it doesn't interest me that much, I never got around to doing anything with it. At lunch with a friend last week we were talking about money and I said I had quite a bit in my checking account. He went to work on a paper napkin and figured out how much I was losing every week by having it in the checking account instead of invested in something else.

When I got back from lunch I called a woman at the bank who's been helpful to me over the years—she calls and says I'm overdrawn instead of bouncing checks when I write one for more than I have—and she suggested Treasury notes. Or, at least I think she said Treasury notes. I next called someone at the bank who deals in that kind of thing.

"Were you interested in Treasury bonds, Treasury bills or Treasury notes?" he asked. "If you put your money in ninety-day Treasury notes at five point six percent with a real earning of six point five percent . . ."

"Listen," I said, interrupting what he was telling me, "I've got another call I have to make but I'll get back to you on this."

The money is still in the checking account.

Most of us aren't that interested in getting rich—we just don't want to get poor. We want to stay even. It's very difficult for anyone whose chief interest in life isn't money to do that. If we're surrounded by people who have a serious interest in acquiring money, they usually get it. I've always thought it was unfair for anyone to try to get rich.

On the train I take to work, I often see people going to their offices in the financial district. For them, money is both business and hobby. It's all they want to read about. The only newspaper they buy is *The Wall Street Journal*. If the world ever comes to an end, I'm sure that paper will carry news of the event in a brief, well-written story summarizing the effect Doomsday will likely have on the Dow Jones average, long-term bond rates and pork belly futures. The people who follow money will have had advance inside information about it so they'd have done a lot of late profit taking the day before.

My life's savings, on the other hand, will be "money in stress."

Paying Bills

PAYING a bill isn't just a matter of having the money. Like writing a letter, there's more to paying a bill than just thinking you ought to do it. Paying a bill is easy to put off even if your bank account is in reasonably good shape. I pay my bills now slower than I did when I was broke.

If you've ever talked to a small businessman, or if you are one, you know how slow people are to pay. Most slow payers aren't dishonest or broke. They just don't get at it. That doesn't make it any easier for the small businessman, of course.

Doctors always have a lot of unpaid bills. They often have so many deadbeats that they overcharge the patients that do pay what they owe, to make up for those who don't. I, personally, don't like a lot of talk about money when it involves a doctor. I think of doctors as being above the idea of money. I'm crazy, of course.

A lot of people pay the doctor last and this strikes me as strange because you have a first-person relationship with a doctor that you don't have with the power company. It would be difficult to rush into the doctor's office in an emergency if you still owed him for the last two visits you made a year ago.

You and I may live with a vague kind of guilt over bills we haven't paid that are more than thirty days old but not paying bills quickly is a way of life for some businesses. The longer a business puts off paying what it owes, the longer it can keep its money in the bank making big interest.

Recently there was a story about what Yale University and a lot of other educational institutions are doing with their government grants. Yale, for example, was getting $82 million from the federal government for research grants, contracts and loans. The money came to Yale on the twentieth of each month. By holding on to half of it and investing it for only ten days, until the end of each month, the university made $535,000 on it over a year's time. Obviously it pays not to pay.

Some businesses have turned the tables on slow payers. They charge high interset rates on any unpaid amount and they make so much money on the interest that they don't care whether you pay on time or not. They like it better when you don't pay quickly. For example, I have a VISA card but I've learned not to use it any more often than I have to, because when my bill comes from them it's so confusing I can't figure out how much I owe. I think they do it intentionally. If I don't pay what I owe on time, they charge me high interest on that amount and on any new items I charge. They seem to do everything possible to keep me from paying my bill on time because they make more money by charging me eighteen percent interest for every twenty minutes I'm overdue.

We have a good system for paying bills in our house. My wife and I divide up the responsibilities. I open the mail and give her the bills to pay. If we get a second bill the next month, it's my responsibility to say to her, "Haven't you paid that yet?"

Yesterday I got a postcard from our town water department saying they hadn't been paid because they had not been able to get in to read our water meter for more than ninety days. When I get home tonight, I'm going to take care of that bill so I don't have to feel guilty taking a shower tomorrow morning.

I'm going to say to my wife, "How come you haven't let them in to read the water meter so they can bill us and you can pay the water bill?"

I know her. She'll say, "The water bill will be for about twelve dollars and ninety-five cents. I'm in no hurry to pay because I have it in a high interest-bearing money-market account."

Banks and Jesse James

Banks have discovered that people are a waste of time. They've discovered that money is a waste of time, too, so they're phasing out both people and money. They don't want to have anything to do with either. All they want is their computers computing away.

Banks are already trying to discourage people from coming in to get fifty or a hundred dollars in cash by keeping customers waiting a long time. They also don't keep as much cash around as they used to. If Jesse James were reincarnated in 1990, he might have to go on welfare because the tellers wouldn't have enough money on hand to make it worth his while holding them up. If he stood in line often to rob banks, he could end up making less than the minimum hourly wage.

Our daughter, Ellen, lives and works in New York. She's been saving some money for a down payment on a cooperative apartment. A while ago things started coming together for the deal and she had to give the owners a certified check for ten thousand dollars. It's hard for me to get used to the idea that a daughter of mine would *have* ten thousand dollars, but that's another story.

On the day she had to pay the money, she went to the bank where she had it stored and asked the teller to give her a bank check for ten thousand dollars. It was normal banking procedure except the bank told her their check "wouldn't clear" for three days. In other words, it couldn't be collected immediately by the people she was giving it to.

You know real estate people. They wanted it that day. My daughter, having been brought up right, said to the bank teller, "Okay then. I'll take my ten thousand in cash."

It was forty-five minutes and three vice-presidents later that she walked out with her money, much of it in one-dollar bills. They were either short of cash or trying to teach her a lesson.

A retail trade in any business is irritating because people can be so difficult. Big deals are where the money is. Obviously banks are tired of the retail trade. They can make more money loaning ten billion dollars to a bankrupt nation that can't pay them back than they can from solid citizens with modest bank accounts.

The handwriting is on the wall. All of us are going to be handling fewer dollars in the future. When we buy something the cashier will punch up our code on a machine and that will transfer money electronically from our account to the store's. The cashier won't deal in cash.

There's a lot we could all learn from banks. I've been awfully slow learning. I could kick myself for all the bills I've paid on time. Banks are teaching us it isn't the way to do business. The way to do business is to put off paying a bill until the very last minute.

Today, in many large city banks, if you deposit money in your checking account with a check written by someone else on a bank next door to yours, you cannot withdraw any of that money for ten days. That banking practice ought to be illegal.

In the past, banks have said it takes two or three days for a check "to clear." Exactly when they actually get the money no longer has anything to do with when you can have it. They hold your money, sometimes for more than a week, and won't let you use it. Of course, they make interest on your money while they withhold it from you.

It's almost impossible to find out when a bank actually collects on a check. When I deposit a check written to me by a major company on a bank within two blocks of my own bank, I can't believe it takes more than two days for them to get the money.

Why can't I use it for a week?

Companies have already learned from banks. The accounting departments of many corporations routinely stall on paying bills because every day they hold onto the money, they're making interest on it.

I recall, from some of those old movies, that Jesse James wasn't all bad. He did have a code of honor. If Jesse James were around today, it wouldn't surprise me to hear that he was refusing to do business with some banks by holding them up because their shoddy business ethics didn't meet his standards.

The Ultimate Cigarette

THE other night I turned in my ticket at a parking garage in midtown New York and waited for them to extricate my car from the pile upstairs.

A man in his mid-thirties came over and stood beside me. He had a briefcase with him and before he spoke to me I could tell he was going to speak to me.

"You're Andy Rooney, aren't you?" he said.

I don't deny that, except under extreme circumstances, so I admitted it although I was sure I didn't want to hear what he was going to say next.

"Would you like to see an idea I just presented to one of the biggest ad agencies in town?" he asked.

I shrugged. I didn't have any interest at all in seeing it but before I answered he opened his briefcase and unfolded a glossy page of paper.

"The ultimate cigarette," it said, "for people to whom money is no object."

He had a name for the cigarette but I forget it.

"My idea," he said, "is to make this cigarette a status symbol. The package will be black and the cigarette itself will be black. That way everyone will know when you pull out this pack of cigarettes that you smoke the most expensive cigarette in the world. It'll give you instant class."

"Did they like the idea?" I asked.

"Have to like it," he said. "How they not gonna like an idea this surefire. Listen. We got Cadillacs and Rolls-Royces for people who want to spend a lot on a car. We got swimming pools for status symbols for a house. We got Countess Mara neckties. We got status symbols for everything except cigarettes."

"How will you make them so expensive?" I asked. "Will the tobacco be better? Could they make a really great cigarette if they wanted to?"

"They won't be any different," he said. "That isn't my business though. I don't know how they'd make them. The big thing is, they'd be really expensive. That's what'll get people to buy them. Expensive."

My car came and it was a good thing because about then I felt like wrestling this guy to the ground and kicking him in a sensitive place.

I think you'll believe that story because it's not the kind of story I could invent. Not only that, I wouldn't be surprised if we all see his expensive black cigarette on the market in another year or so. They could probably make the cigarette a lot quicker than that. It's laying out the advertising campaign that will take the time.

The cigarette industry is representative of a lot of businesses that depend more on their advertising than on their product for sales. Cigarette brands are not very different, one from another. It's their advertising, not their tobacco, that counts. If they take on this guy in the garage with the expensive black cigarette, and get the right advertising campaign going, he won't be getting his own car out of the garage next time I see him. He'll have a chauffeur waiting.

This fellow in the garage said he was suggesting they sell his new cigarettes for two dollars a pack. I admit it could be a very effective sales gimmick. There are idiots who'll buy anything as long as it costs enough.

Made in Japan

I LOVE America. I salute the flag and I go around saying "We're the greatest!" but I'd be lying if I said I wasn't worried.

The funny thing is, unlike my government and some of my friends, I'm not worried about the Russians. I'm a little worried about the Chinese, I'll never get over worrying about the Germans, and the Japanese make me nervous but the people I'm most worried about are ourselves. We aren't doing it.

In 1950 we were making seventy-five percent of all the cars driven anywhere in the world. Now thirty percent of all the cars sold just in this country alone are made somewhere else. They're not only made somewhere else, they're made very well in Japan, Germany, France, Sweden. I've driven Russian cars and they're no threat.

Only 25 years ago airlines throughout the world were all flying America-made Boeings, Douglasses and Lockheeds. Now, the more you travel on the smaller airlines both in the United States and abroad, the more you see commercial planes made in other countries.

Our computers, our television sets, our electronic games and much of our office equipment is made in Japan. It may have the name of some fine old American company on it but don't let them kid you, the chances are the component parts come from Japan.

Our steel mills are running less than half capacity and that's partly because of the economy but even more because other countries have better technology for making steel than we do. Did you ever think it would happen? It's cheaper, even for American companies, to buy foreign steel and have it shipped here.

The same auto companies in Detroit that have workers demanding that the rest of us buy cars made in America, are producing cars they call "American" in foreign countries. Even the cars that are actually assembled in Detroit are often put together with some parts made in Japan. They're about as American as chopsticks.

Statistics show that for the first time in our history, more people are employed in service industries than in production. Today seventy-three percent of the work force deals in services. Only twenty-seven percent work in the production of goods. In other words, more people are selling it than making it.

"Service" may sound like a good word but a lot of what goes under that heading is duplicating order forms on Xerox machines, selling insurance and figuring out interest rates on bank loans.

I recognize the need for bankers, financial experts and figure jugglers but there's just so long the money-manipulators can keep their numbers in the air while they make money off each exchange. Eventually someone has to come up with a product, without which all the statistics in the world mean nothing.

If it's hard to do, we aren't doing it anymore. We buy it from someone else, double the price and sell it back to ourselves at a profit. No wonder we're in trouble. In the last three months we spent 13.1 billion dollars more in foreign countries buying their goods than they spent here buying ours. Oil is something we can't help but machinery and manufactured goods are things we ought to be able to produce better than anyone else in the world.

The basis for everything is not money but hard work. You don't have to be a Communist to believe that Wall Street doesn't deal in that kind of work and the Dow Jones average doesn't reflect it from day to day. The engineers, the chemists, the architects, the scientists, the designers ought to be predominant in our society. If anyone's going to get rich, it ought to be them. The mechanics, the carpenters, the electricians, the construction experts, the plumbers and the repair people and all the other craftsmen who really know how to do something ought to be making it, too.

The only subject you read about or hear about is money. It's as if the products on which all money is based don't make any difference at all. Why are so many foreign goods selling so well here? Usually it's because those products are being made cheaper and better than comparable products made in America.

Why shouldn't I be worried?

Automobile Costs

IT costs us almost a quarter for every mile we drive a car. That's what the government says in a study it issued called "Cost of Owning and Operating Automobiles."

The actual figure is 23.8 cents a mile and the government includes everything in that. It includes how much you paid for the car, your insurance, your gas, oil and even your parking fees. The only thing it hasn't included is parking tickets.

The study says the average car in the United States is now six years and six months old, but they base their overall statistic on a car that is twelve years old and has been driven 120,000 miles. I'd like to see the government keep all its cars for twelve years and drive them 120,000 miles.

If I thought about the fact that it was costing me a dollar for every four miles I drove, I'd probably walk more. I've always enjoyed trying to save money on a car but I've never been very successful. Last month, just after I decided to keep my old one for another year, the muffler went. I went to a Midas shop and paid $247 for a new one. Do you think I got taken? The muffler itself was only about $45 but they hit me for $125, for something called a crossover pipe. I don't think I've ever heard Midas mention a crossover pipe in their advertising.

It's difficult for most of us to know when we're getting taken by a garage mechanic. You just have to find a good one and trust him. The chances are that even an honest one will add a little on for something he didn't do to make up for something else that took him longer than he expected for reasons he couldn't possibly explain to you unless you were a mechanic.

The people who give advice say to get a written estimate from a garage but if I were a mechanic and you asked me to tell you exactly how much a job was going to cost, I'd tell you to get lost. It's like asking a doctor to tell you exactly how much it's going to cost to make you well again. When I get a bill for work done on my car, it's always twice what I thought it would be but I don't notice a lot of rich mechanics.

Driving bores me but I get a kick out of saving money in little ways on my car. It's dumb that I waste so much money on so many things and get such petty pleasure from saving thirty-five cents on a quart of oil by buying it at a department store and adding it myself, instead of having them do it at the gas station.

The most expensive thing I ever paid for was a car wash. Two weeks ago I took the car to one of those automatic car wash places. They didn't have a sign out front and I should have been suspicious but when I got to the cashier he asked for six dollars. It was too late to turn back but that's the last professional car wash I'll be getting. It's satisfying to wash a car anyway and now that I know it costs six dollars to have it done, it's going to be twice as satisfying for me.

I spend less time in gas stations than most people because I don't go in as often. I don't make many pit stops. Some people get nervous when the gas indicator shows the tank is down below half full. They always fill it before it reaches the quarter mark. I, on the other hand, seldom buy gas before it gets exciting to consider whether I'm going to make it to the next gas station or not. It keeps me awake on the road. I've only run out of gas once with my present car and after you've done it once, you know exactly how far you can go with the tank registering "Empty."

If the government knows of a good mechanic who can keep my car going until it's twelve years old, I'd like to hear from them.

Money and Sports

You can't watch the World Series on television without thinking about money. The same thing happens watching pro football Sunday afternoon.

Money is dominating sports. People are tired of it and I don't know what's going to happen. Nothing, probably. People are tired of a lot of things that don't change.

The commercials in the World Series aren't as annoying as those during the football games because it's easier to make room for a commercial during a baseball game. It isn't the real commercials that most people object to, anyway. They aren't bad. Some of them are even good, and we accept a certain number of commercials as fair exchange for what we're getting free.

The trouble comes when the broadcasters start stealing a little time here and a little time there. It's all those minor promotional intrusions that are making games on television seem like one long interruption. I don't want to be told during the World Series how different Peter Jennings is or how wonderful Dan Rather and Tom Brokaw are during football games. Leave me alone.

The networks snip away at program content on the theory that viewers won't notice the loss of a mere ten seconds or thirty seconds here and there. After a while, though, we do notice.

In an attempt to build a rating for a show of its own later in the day's schedule, the network will often interrupt the flow of the game with a promotional tease for a situation comedy "coming up at nine." They'll cover the time it takes for the batter to walk to the plate with their little in-house ad. On the football field, the promo is superimposed while the team huddles and they don't take it down until the ball is ready to be snapped.

It ought to be mandatory for a broadcaster to superimpose a dollar sign over any picture or announcement which is not a commercial but which is specifically designed to produce income for the network.

Broadcasters don't seem to understand that watching the batter walk to the plate is part of what people enjoy about baseball. Neither do fans want to watch only the part of a football game that takes place while the ball is being run or thrown. Everything that happens down there is part of the game and we want to see it. We are not interested in knowing what mediocre situation comedy is coming up later. We don't want to be lectured to about how bad drugs are for us while our quarterback is flat on his back after being blind-sided by a 270-pound tackle.

Broadcasters are lucky that team owners are as greedy as they are. The owners and associated businessmen in the sports world make the games so unpleasant to attend in person that people would rather be irritated by television in the comfort of their own homes. I speak with authority because I go to all the New York Giants home games.

The parking lot is so badly organized that it can take an hour to get into it and an hour to get out.

My ticket for a seat in the end zone costs $14 a game. If I want to know the names and numbers of the players on the other team, I have to buy a fat magazine with a lot of dull stories, which they erroneously call a program, for $1.50.

If I get thirsty, beer in a paper cup costs $1.90. If I'm very thirsty, a large beer costs $2.75.

A box of Cracker Jacks is $1.00 and a hot dog costs $1.35. They don't sell peanuts in the ball park anymore because they don't like paying to have someone sweep up the shells. They'll have to rewrite the words to "Take Me Out to the Ball Game" and eliminate the peanuts.

Ball park owners have even found a way to annoy fans electronically, too. They now have electronic scoreboards with commercials interspersed with phony exhortations for the home team.

It'll be interesting to see how far they can go with money before they kill sports.

Charity Is Never Easy

Iғ you have your health, some happiness, a job, a place to live and some money in the bank, you don't need help. The chances are you ought to be helping someone who does need help. I have those things but whom do I help and how?

At least twice a week I feel guilty as I drop some letter asking for a contribution into the little wicker wastebasket next to my chair. Do I not care about the blind? Don't I want to help wipe out cancer? Am I in favor of muscular dystrophy? What about the school and college I attended? Am I ungrateful to them because I don't always give them as much as they want?

There are so many people and organizations that need and deserve help that it's more than I can stand to think about sometimes. I'm eating too much and there are people starving. It would be better for all of us if I split what's on my plate with them but how do I do that? It is not easy to be charitable.

One of the difficult things about charity is deciding whom to give to. You can't give to everyone who asks and sometimes those who don't ask need help worse than those who do. I don't give to the blind beggar with the dog on the sidewalk outside Saks Fifth Avenue because he demeans every blind man who does not beg. Where *do* I make my contribution?

The United Way has been a partial answer to the problem of how to give but most of us aren't satisfied with such an impersonal charitable contribution. We'd like to do something in a more direct way for a person or for some specific organization. At the time of year when I begin to get my tax stuff together, I'm often embarrassed to see how little I've given compared to how much I have.

We all want to know for sure that any charitable contribution we make is not stolen or wasted and it's impossible not to look for some kind of appreciation from others who know we've given.

"Take heed," it says somewhere in the Bible, "that ye do not give alms before men, to be seen of them."

I always look with suspicion on the people who give to that blind man outside Saks. I can't read the looks on their faces but I think they're taking some smug satisfaction from giving where so many people can see them give. They may drop a quarter in his tin cup in a crowd but I wonder how much they give to the United Way in private?

A lot of rich people make wills and keep everything they have for themselves until they die. This comes mostly from the fear of not ending up with enough, I suppose. I've always thought—and I suppose everyone has thought this—that if I ever became really rich, I'd give away everything except what I needed to live on. Not being really rich, that's easy for me to think. And, of course, each of us gets to define what's really rich. If I had what I have now twenty years ago, I'd have considered myself "really rich."

Very few of us "give 'til it hurts." We wait until we have enough so it doesn't hurt much, then we give. We find ways to let ourselves off. We say to ourselves that we're suspicious of how this charity spends its money or we don't like the new policy of this school or that organization. It's easy to find an excuse for not giving and, of course, it's necessary that we have excuses. It is true that we can't give to everyone.

The mayor of New York once complained that too many New York neighborhoods are selfish. They only want good things for themselves, he said. The Mayor, a Jew, said it in a synagogue and made a wonderfully strong, honest, almost familial complaint. He said no synagogue in New York was providing a single bed for the homeless.

It isn't easy, the Mayor said, to care for the sort of people who need a bed for overnight.

Charity is never easy. So many of the people who need it don't seem to deserve it and that provides a wonderful excuse for all of us not to give much.

Place Your Bets

THE gambling casinos in Atlantic City took 193 million dollars from people visiting that city in one month last year.

That is one of the most disgraceful and sad figures I've ever seen. For gambling casinos to be legal is disgraceful; for people to be dumb enough to go to them and lose 193 million dollars in a month is sad.

If it's mandatory for people to wear seat belts in an automobile for their own protection, how come the government doesn't protect its citizens from losing their money by strapping it into their wallets when they go to Atlantic City?

The thing that bothers me most about it is that when people gamble away their money, they don't spend it on an honest product that someone has worked to make. There's only so much money and if it is lost at a gambling table, it is taken out of the productive part of our economy. Whom would you rather see employed, a blackjack dealer in a casino in Las Vegas or a machinist at an automobile assembly plant in Detroit? Who contributes most to what's good about American life?

It's estimated that the casinos in Atlantic City will take two billion dollars in profit this year. The State of New Jersey takes eight percent of the casinos' profit. This amount is what government exacts in exchange for issuing a license to steal.

I was surprised to read that Atlantic City is now grossing more than Las Vegas. I didn't think anything could be as gross as Las Vegas. Las Vegas estimates it will only take one billion seven hundred and fifty million from customers this year. (I've spelled that out so there won't be any mistake with zeros.)

That means that between the two cities they'll haul in three billion seven hundred and fifty million dollars from customers. Make it an even four billion.

I've been doing some arithmetic, figuring out what could be bought for four billion dollars.

Here are some suggestions:
—It would buy 500,000 Chrysler Le Barons at $8,000 each.
—Four years in an average college costs roughly $30,000 for tuition, room and board now. It would buy a college education for 133,000 young Americans.
—People could buy 308,880,300 copies of this book to give each other for Christmas. This would make one writer very happy.
—One hundred sixty million Americans could each buy a new pair of shoes for $25.
—You could rent an apartment at $350 a month for 952,380 years.
—It would build 66,666 new homes for $60,000 each or 26,666 expensive homes at $150,000 each.
—Two million couples could spend an all-expense-paid week in Hawaii, including air fare.
—It would feed a lot of hungry Americans. That amount would

provide food stamps for 1,326,259 families of four, for an entire year.

The slot machines account for about half of a casino's take. The dumbest money goes into those and into something called the Big Six Wheel. It's referred to as the Idiot Wheel because it takes about forty-five cents of every dollar bet on it.

The blackjack tables take fifteen to eighteen percent from a player and the craps tables, twelve percent. The roulette tables take close to twenty-five percent.

The players with the most money play baccarat. They're the smart ones. They only lose twelve percent of their money on an average evening.

The casinos refer to the money that they don't take from the customers as "the drop." The money they take is called "the hold."

Some day I'd like to rent a huge billboard on the outskirts of Atlantic City with a simple Dante-like announcement:

"Abandon hope all ye who enter here!"

Over all, the gambling casinos take eighteen percent of everything bet so there's no chance whatsoever of anyone winning over a period of time. It isn't a gamble, it's a sure thing. You lose.

V:

YOUR
WASHINGTON
REPORTER

Your Washington Reporter

I WENT to the Capitol in Washington the other day to check on things for you.

With press credentials I was able to eat in the congressional restaurant, where I had a bowl of warm milk with six oysters in it for $2.50. It had been advertised as "oyster stew" on the menu but was so unsatisfying that I also ordered a hamburg. That cost $2.75 and was barely fair. I'm telling you about lunch because you may have thought your congressman has a better place to eat lunch than you do.

It was 2:10 when I walked into the gallery of the Senate chamber. The Senate was in session but I didn't think so at first because there were exactly four senators down there on the floor. Three of them, Howard Baker, John Stennis and Russell Long, were debating whether they ought to allow television cameras into the Senate and the fourth, Orrin Hatch of Utah, was Acting Speaker.

The three senators were no more than fifteen feet apart. Senator Stennis was speaking and the stenotypist, with his machine on his chest, hanging from a broad strap around his neck, stood too close to him. The stenotypist looked like the accordionist in a bad restaurant . . . the one you hope doesn't come to your table.

Senator Stennis has never been a favorite of mine but as I sat there, I was impressed with how good he was making his case against televising Senate debate.

"All these empty seats . . ." he was saying. "All these empty seats . . . someone's gonna have to explain 'em . . . make an explanation of where these senators are. This is a dishonest picture. It doesn't tell the story of what's going on . . . all these senators doin' their work in committee meetings somewhere else."

He had a point, I thought. I'd walked in there a few minutes earlier and my first impression was that four senators were working and the other ninety-six were goofing off. It wasn't true, of course. Probably only twenty-five were goofing off and the rest were working elsewhere.

Senator Stennis went on to say how distracting television would

be. He said he was easily distracted although he didn't look as if he
would be.

He gave an example:

"It takes a lot of wind out of me," he said, "if I'm talkin' and I
look up and see the Speaker chattin' with someone else. I think
maybe I've said something good that caught his attention and he's
talkin' to that other person about it . . . but probably not."

What a wonderfully funny and human thing for this tough old
warhorse to say. I liked him better.

Senator Baker got up when Senator Stennis had finished. The
stenotypist, with his machine on his chest, moved toward Baker to
catch every word.

Baker spoke as if he was excerpting little phrases out of old
speeches he remembered but he said some good things in favor of
televising Senate proceedings.

"The Senate is a microcosm of America," Baker said. "We are
what we are and America's entitled to watch. The business of the
Senate is to do the public's business in a public place!"

"Hear, hear!" I would have shouted but I didn't want to get
thrown out.

Senator Long, the third man in the debate, had already betrayed
his opinion of the public's IQ by saying that if television was allowed in, Senate debates would have to be tailored "to appeal to the
most common denominator, let us say those with a fourth-grade
education."

During the debate, Senator Robert Byrd walked in. He paid no
attention to anyone, walking between Baker and Stennis and taking
his seat near the Speaker's platform. Senator Dole and one or two
others had drifted in and were standing in back at the fringe of the
chamber. When the debate about television coverage had come to
an end, Baker stood up, walked over to Long's desk and as they
laughed about something, Long offered Baker a cough drop. Baker
took it, put it in his mouth and wandered up the aisle toward the
back. They'd been through it all before.

At this point, Senator Byrd stood up, asked for the floor and
addressed almost no one with a perfunctory message about protecting the American eagle as our national symbol.

I didn't understand whether he was for it or against it but if I
know Senator Byrd, he was for it.

I left.

This concludes my report from the nation's Capitol.

Is Politics Child's Play?

I'M a Democrat," an eleven-year-old girl wrote me in a letter the other day.

An eleven-year-old probably doesn't know whether she's a Democrat or a Republican but that doesn't make her much different from the rest of us. We may think we know and we may announce what we think we are at regular intervals but don't ask us for a list of the differences between the two parties.

When I was a kid, my father always voted Republican but I don't think he had a lot of well-thought-out reasons for it. Like most people, he picked a couple of little things he thought the Republicans stood for and that he agreed with and concluded from those that he was one of them. People fall in love with the idea that they're either Republicans or Democrats.

When I asked my father the difference between the two, he told me the Democrats wanted to lower the import taxes on the things foreign countries shipped here to sell, and the Republicans wanted to raise the taxes to keep foreign goods out. Even way back in the 1930s, he worked for a company that was in competition with the Japanese. A person's bread and butter usually has more to do with his political affiliation than his ideals do.

You can't trust anyone's definition of what a Republican or a Democrat is. Each party likes to pretend it has hard-and-fast economic, social and philosophic principles that are cast in stone but they don't.

Generally speaking, the Democrats have always been thought of as being on the side of labor and the Republicans are thought of as being on the side of business. Obviously that isn't the way things really are or we'd never have had a Republican president. There are always going to be more working people than businessmen and women but we've elected sixteen Republican presidents and only thirteen Democratic ones.

The funny thing that happened in recent elections in both England and the United States is that a lot of blue-collar working people teamed up with a lot of white-collar business people and elected Republicans. (In England, the Republicans are called the Conservatives.) These two groups at opposite ends of the social and economic scale—low-income workers, high-income executives— agreed on politics.

The people who voted for the Democratic or Liberal party candidate in each country were all the rest and it wasn't enough. It seems as strange to have a young, college-educated businessman making $35,000 a year supporting a Democrat as it is to have a truck driver with less than a high school education making $35,000, supporting Reagan. I'm not knocking it in either case but it does seem funny. Why would the bricklayer and the owner of the construction company agree on such issues as abortion, prayer in schools, busing and the ERA Amendment?

It's all very confusing and I have an idea it's better that way. As soon as a nation's political parties begin to get too orderly and predictable, there's trouble. I'm pleased that there are no deep, sharply defined party principles the Democrats and Republicans swear by. During an election year we listen to a lot of campaign oratory that gives the impression the world will come to an end if the candidate speaking isn't elected. Someone is always beaten, though, and the world never ends because of it. When our candidate is defeated we swallow the defeat and go about our business again, confident that things won't really change much.

I don't know what to tell that eleven-year-old girl who wrote me. I don't want to discourage her interest in politics but I would like to point out to her that she probably hasn't thought out why she thinks she's a Democrat with any more clarity than why she thinks she's a Methodist, a Catholic, a Buddhist or none of the above. People fall in love with their religious affiliation for reasons that are about as well thought out as their political ones.

Imputing Motives

In the past year something like twenty congressmen or high-ranking public officials in Washington have quit politics. They have quit either because they aren't satisfied with the money they can make in government as compared to private business or because they don't like having every decision or statement they make inspected under a microscope by the public and the press.

Senator Howard Baker of Tennessee said, when he announced he was retiring, that a lot of the pleasure he used to get out of public service was gone.

"I think that news is so current," Senator Baker said, "and so often analytical and so frequently wrong, imputing motives that really don't exist in many cases, that a lot of people are just getting tired of it."

Senator Baker's decision not to run for office again was a loss for all of us. Most of us are either not capable, too selfish or not ambitious enough to help in the process of governing ourselves. We'd rather sit back and criticize the people who do involve themselves in politics. Senator Baker was one of the best. We were lucky to have had him. He's nice, honest and competent. He has simply decided he doesn't want to take all the heat he's been taking any longer. He's going to look into what he calls "a delicious range of things to do."

Print and broadcast journalists have had a lot to do with the decision many government officials have made to get out of politics, Senator Baker says.

"I can't think of a single case where someone decided to run for public office because of investigative reporting. But I can sure think of people who decided not to run because, day in and day out, they don't like having to explain the reasons for their votes."

The public, the courts and government officials have almost always been in favor of freedom of the press in the abstract and against it in the particular. The public complains about politicians who get rich from dishonest deals while they're in office and the public complains about the press reporting such incidents because news of dishonesty is so depressing. I'm disappointed that Senator Baker, one of the good guys in my opinion, has joined the popular complaint that the press is too negative. It is exactly the same as the know-nothing attitude you hear from so many uneducated people talking about politicians as being "all a bunch of crooks."

Politicians are not all a bunch of crooks but there are some crooks among them and the public has a right to know who they are. Politicians have no more right to expect perfection from journalists than the public has any business expecting perfection from politicians. They're all people and there are going to be roughly the same number of good guys and bad guys in both professions. They both have to be watched.

The best journalists assume that if all the facts are revealed, it will be a better world. Politicians often honestly believe that the public is best served if it *doesn't* know everything. This is where the battle lines are drawn between politicians and the press. For some reason that always puzzles journalists, the public agrees with the politicians. If it's bad news, they don't want to hear it even if it's true.

By retiring, Senator Baker made a politically expedient move if he wants to be President someday and by suggesting that a tough press is part of the reason for his retirement, he's getting himself a little bonus. Maybe the press will take it easier if it thinks it's driving good men like him out of politics.

Senator Baker would, I'm sure, say that I am being "analytical and frequently wrong, imputing motives that really don't exist."

Andy Rooney for President

THE candidates for office seem to have so much fun trying to kill each other with television commercials that I've decided to run for office myself. In light of this decision, I'm asking each and every one of you to make a small sacrifice in the interests of better government and mail me $10,000 so that I can start a campaign fund.

It's illegal to contribute more than $1,000 to any one person's campaign so you'll have to find some way to work this out. Check around and learn how it's being done by others. You might consult one of your local Political Action Committees, known familiarly as "PACS."

If only 2,500 of you respond to this appeal for campaign funds, it will provide me with $25 million with which I'll buy my first two thirty-second commercials on network television. Through these commercials, I hope to make my position as well-known to America as Preparation H.

Because you have a right to know where I stand on the issues before you commit $10,000 to my campaign, I'll give you a preview of the two commercials. Here are the scripts.

(CANDIDATE, DRESSED IN BUSINESS SUIT WITH VEST, IS SEEN STAND-ING BEHIND IMPORTANT-LOOKING DESK. BEHIND HIM ARE SHELVES FULL OF IMPORTANT-LOOKING BOOKS, BOUND IN RED LEATHER.)

"Good evening. I'm Andy Rooney, the Middle-of-the-Road Party's candidate in this important election.

"Are you familiar with the voting record of my opponent? Do you know where he stands on crime, for instance?

"My opponent is in favor of crime. He has supported crime in the past and will continue to do so if reelected. For more than forty years now, ever since I was twenty, I have been against crime.

"Taxes. My opponent seems to feel that the solution to every problem is higher taxes. If you want higher taxes, vote for my opponent.

"My opponent thinks the rich are an underprivileged class. He's against the working man. He hates farmers. He's never been seen in church and he locks his dog out at night even when it's cold.

"This is where I stand and I hope I can look forward to your support on election day."

That's the first commercial. If it runs a little longer than thirty seconds, I may take out the part about the dog. Here's the second script prepared for me by the same advertising agency that writes them for my opponent.

(CANDIDATE IS FOUND SITTING ON THE COUCH IN A MODEST LIVING ROOM INTERVIEWING AN ACTOR, AN ACTRESS AND TWO CHILD ACTORS. THEY ARE POSING AS THE TYPICAL AMERICAN FAMILY OF GEORGE AND BETTY MORGAN.)

ANDY: I'm here today with George Morgan and his wife, Betty. How are things going, George?

GEORGE: Terrible, Andy. I've been out of work for an hour and twenty minutes. I can't make the payments on any of our cars and the man won't come and clean our swimming pool because I still owe him for last time.

ANDY: How are you going to vote this year, George?

GEORGE: You're the kind of leadership we need in America, Andy. You're honest, forthright, fair, hard-working, easygoing, patriotic and you go to church Easter. You're going to lower taxes, raise Social Security benefits, cut inflation and reduce unemployment.

CHILD AT TABLE: I'm hungry, Mommy.

BETTY MORGAN: Hush, Linda. We can't have dinner until Mr. Rooney is elected and gets the economy going again so Daddy can get a job.

ANDY: Thanks for inviting me into your home, George and Betty. You're good Americans. Good Americans will be voting for me this election day.

The preceding political announcements have been paid for by the Committee to Elect Andy Rooney.

The Elected Official Speaks

Good evening. This is your Elected Official speaking. I've bought this one last television commercial because now that you've elected me, I'm going to tell you the truth.

"It will come as no surprise to many of you to hear that most of what I said when I was trying to get elected was pure baloney. Those commercials, for instance, were someone else's idea. I just came into the studio and read them. They wanted me to sound folksy and honest and I had to do them over about ten times before I sounded folksy and honest enough. How'd you like the one where I was in shirtsleeves and suspenders? The media consultant who did the commercials brought the suspenders to the studio for me. They were his uncle's.

"He produced the commercials for my opponent, too. They used the same suspenders on him but I think I sounded folksier and more honest. That's why I won.

"But I've given you so much doubletalk during the campaign that tonight I thought I'd level with you. Here's where I really stand on the issues.

"Taxes. You didn't really believe me when I said I wasn't going to raise your taxes, did you? If you did, you deserve what you're going to get. I'm going to raise taxes and I'm going to do it as soon as possible. That way, you may have forgotten it by the next time I run for office.

"Crime. Let's face it, voters. We got a lot of weirdos out there who'll do anything to anyone to get themselves some cash for a drug fix. I told you I'm against crime and I am but I'm not a magician. My advice to you is lock your doors at night and watch where you walk after dark.

"Social Security. I'm sorry to have to tell you this but if you're very social, you don't have much security. If you're retired, I hope you got rich while you were working because if you didn't, there's no way in hell you're going to be able to live on what you get from Social Security. You can't get blood from a stone, you know.

"Abortion. To tell you the truth, I was so scared of this issue I forget what I told you I was for or against. I figured there was no sense making a lot of enemies by coming out on either side. The truth is, I haven't thought much about abortion.

"Gun control. I hedged on this, too, but actually I'm in favor of gun control. If I had my way, no one in the United States would own a handgun except me.

"Unemployment. We have a lot of unemployment in this country and I feel sorry for some of those people but let's face it, you know and I know some of those bums wouldn't work if you drove them to the job in a Rolls-Royce. Unemployment's only bad for the people who aren't working and more than ninety percent of you are working. You're the ones who voted for me.

"In the next few weeks I'll be making a lot of appointments to important, high-paying jobs in my Administration. Those jobs are going to the people who contributed the most money to my campaign. Why should I lie to you now?"

The Queen and the President

Every few years an American president and the king or queen of some country meet on a formal occasion.

It's always been a mystery to me what a Queen and a President talk about when they have dinner together. Everything about it must be awkward, even the way they're seated. They're almost always seated side by side instead of across the table from each other and right there you have a problem. They can't look each other in the eye easily and it's difficult to bring anyone else into the conversation. The person on the President's other side can't talk to the Queen without leaning over and talking across the President's dinner, and the person on the other side of the Queen can't talk to the President for the same reason. If the person on the other side of the Queen wanted to talk to the person way on the other side of the President, he'd have to yell or get up and walk around behind him. This would probably bring the Secret Service and the Queen's Guards to their feet. It must limit the conversation.

It would be bad form, I should think, for the President to stop talking to the Queen and turn to someone else but they really don't have that much they can talk about except horses, if it's the Queen of England. There are things they *could* talk about but wouldn't.

I've been thinking about some examples of things they wouldn't talk about. This is a conversation that would never take place between Queen Elizabeth and our President:

PRESIDENT: How are all the kids these days?

QUEEN: Fine thanks. You know, they can be a pain in the royal tail sometimes but they're good kids.

PRESIDENT: Let's see, you have two . . . or is it three?

QUEEN: Four. Charles, Anne, Andrew and Edward. Everyone forgets Edward.

PRESIDENT: It must be tough on Edward, the youngest boy. How does he feel about having so little chance of ever being King?

QUEEN: We've never talked about it.

PRESIDENT: That seems to be a nice girl Charles has. Is Andrew seeing anyone?

QUEEN: Yes, and I could just kill him.

PRESIDENT: That would give Edward a better chance of getting to be King.

QUEEN: Not funny, Mr. President. He's been chasing after this road company Playboy bunny. It's awfully hard to explain to Mother, I'll tell you that. He must have gotten it from Philip's side of the family.

PRESIDENT: Maybe. At least Wallis Warfield Simpson was always well dressed.

QUEEN: You really know how to hurt a Queen, Mr. President.

PRESIDENT: It certainly wasn't intended that way. Can I get you more champagne?

QUEEN: If it's French, yes. If it's more of that California, no.

PRESIDENT: Hey, if you want to play rough I'll ask you what you do with your old hats . . . the ones your mother gave you?

QUEEN: I *wear* them, sir! At least Philip doesn't put on a pair of those macho cowboy boots you wear everytime you get within four miles of a horse. And how often do you get the grease changed in your hair?

PRESIDENT: Boy, you got a sharp tongue, lady.

QUEEN: Let me ask you this. If you could be King or President, which would you be?

PRESIDENT: Hmmm . . . of the United States or Great Britain?

QUEEN: The United States.

PRESIDENT: The way things are going I'd like to be Queen for a Day and then quit the whole mess!

We'll never know what the Queen and the President talk about when they meet, but you can bet it must set some kind of world's record for dull.

Presidential Friendship

By the time you've done all the things the President's been doing all his life, you get to know a lot of people. You've even gotten to like a lot of people and consider them to be friends. Do you send them all Christmas cards? Do you sit down with your wife in the private quarters of the White House and make a list?

There are some things a President can delegate but making a list of friends is a strictly personal matter. How do you handle old friends?

Say you're President and your best friend from high school calls. Somehow he gets through the outer layer of secretarial protection a President has and gets to one of your personal secretaries. This is a kid whose house you used to go to after school. He even stayed at your house one week when his parents were away.

What instructions does your secretary have for handling this kind of a call? If she pokes her head in the Oval Office door and asks if you want to speak to Billy Reidy, do you pick up the phone or do you tell her to brush him off politely?

Handling any kind of personal relationship would be one of the most difficult things about being President.

Do you have a telephone in the private quarters of the White House with a number you've given only a few close friends? I don't mean important congressmen or Cabinet officials. I mean do you have a number you've only given real friends, not just important people?

What about money? If you're President do you keep track of what you have in the bank? What about domestic problems? Aren't there some problems with the house at the ranch that ought to be taken care of personally? Something out there must be falling apart that no one knows about but you.

If you're the President in Washington and you notice there's a crack in the tiles around the shower in your house in Santa Barbara, do you call someone to have it fixed? Whom do you call? Even calling someone takes more time than a President has.

In 1965, Walter Cronkite was interviewing President Lyndon

Johnson. There were, as always, a lot of serious problems facing the President. There was also a minor problem with the White House staff. They'd been asking for a raise for some time and just that morning it had finally been approved and signed by President Johnson.

At one point in Cronkite's talk with Johnson, a senior aide to the President came in and interrupted.

"That raise for the staff," the aide asked, "will it be retroactive to the first of the year?"

Lyndon Johnson flushed with anger, pointed his finger at the aide and started to sputter.

"I'm the President of The United States, I've got a war in Vietnam, I've got the weight of the world on my shoulders, I'm talking to this important man here and you come in with a chicken s—— question like that."

Presidents must often feel that way.

Some U.S. presidents have been accused of working only four or five hours a day, but even if it's true, I wouldn't complain. There's no way in the world one person could sit in the Oval Office all day worrying about the life and death of the universe. A President would almost have to find a way to shut out some of the problems pressing in on him or he'd go crazy.

I often have a guilty feeling going past a hospital. I know how many sick and dying people there are in those rooms and yet how long can any one of us feel sad about everyone in trouble in the world? We have to shut out the thought of some of what we know is going on and proceed with our lives.

The President must do that. Once in a while when an old bit-part player in a movie they made together called the White House, Ron must have answered the phone and said, "Hey, I'm not doing anything. Why don't you come over and we'll shoot the breeze . . ."

The National Academy of History

I'M not at all satisfied with history the way it's being written. We've all taken history courses in school and most of us were skeptical of some of the information given us as historical fact.

There's a lot more history piling up on us every day but we ought to be gaining on it, because with pictures and sound recording it's easier to preserve original documents than it was a hundred or a thousand years ago. Everyone five hundred years from now ought to know everything about us. They won't though because too many of the things being saved as history won't present an accurate picture of what was going on this year.

I propose we establish a National Academy of History. It would be this group's job to pass on to the future exactly what happened and what we were like in our years here on earth. I even have some specific suggestions for how the National Academy of History (NAH) would go about the job.

For example, it would insist that Presidents Reagan, Carter, Ford and Nixon get together for a long weekend at Camp David, with no one else around, and let their hair down. (In Gerald Ford's case, I'm speaking figuratively.) They'd be promised that nothing they said would be released for fifty years.

The four of them would be given anything they wanted to eat or drink but they'd also be given an occasional shot of sodium pentothal, the drug that makes people blab the truth.

There are, as I write, six living wives of Presidents, Jackie, Lady Bird, Pat, Betty, Rosalynn and Nancy. These women have a view of history that is different and more accurate in many specific details than any historian will ever get. The girls ought to get together while the boys are at Camp David. If they'd relax, they'd probably like each other. If they'd talk, we'd have some real history.

This newly established NAH of mine would organize all kinds of groups to get at and preserve the details of history that are being lost now. It wouldn't be simply the history of power. It would be the history of Us.

We study the day before yesterday looking for clues about how to behave so we'll be happier tomorrow. That's what history is for and we haven't been keeping it accurately enough. There are dozens of reasons why history doesn't ring true to us.

Too many historians aren't reporters looking for facts, they're theoreticians. They have some idea about the grand sweep of history and they write their books, choosing only the facts that support their theories.

Historians like to promote the idea that there's a rhythm to history and that events follow a pattern. They're often more interested in the pattern they think they see than the facts. They can't stand the thought that there might not be a pattern and that a lot of important things happened in history, not by the design of a king, a president or a dictator, but because of some insignificant unrecorded incident or accident that started things going one way instead of another.

It's difficult to make people from one century intelligible to the people of another and if reporters can't find out what's going on right now in our own country, how can we expect the historians of ten, fifty or a hundred years from now to know anything at all that's true about us?

Russian Bombs/Russian Hotels

You can go into a strange restaurant and make a good guess about how the food is going to taste long before they've actually served you any of it. There are telltale signs that give you advanced warning. When the rolls or the bread comes, you know for sure how the whole meal is going to be.

This idea can be extended to everything and everybody. You can tell a lot about the whole from a small part. You can tell a lot about how a person does everything from watching him or her do just one thing. We are all victims of our own character and we find it impossible to do something that isn't characteristic of us.

This idea applies to whole countries just as certainly as it applies to individuals. We keep doing things like Americans, the Germans keep doing things like Germans, the French like the French.

The President said the other night that the Soviet Union has "a definite margin of superiority" over the United States in nuclear arms. Using my theory about being able to tell a lot from a sample, I doubt it. I've spent a good deal of time in Russia and hold some opinions about the people and the nation that no one can talk me out of.

One of my firmly held beliefs is that the Russians are not naturally mechanical people. They may acquire the ability and they may be better at it than they used to be but working with machinery does not come naturally to the average Russian. They have a great heritage in music and literature and the arts in general but they build terrible automobiles and don't know how to fix them when they break down.

One of the most incredible travel experiences I've ever had is a week in a Russian hotel in Moscow. The second time I stayed there they had installed telephones in every room but the telephones were not connected through any hotel switchboard. There was no way for anyone to call the hotel and be connected with me by phone in my room. It had a number just like any other telephone in a home in Moscow.

Does this sound like a country that is apt to be ahead of us in nuclear weapons?

The Russians, in their desperate attempt to get hard, Western currency away from tourists, opened what they call "Dollar Stores." They put their best merchandise in these small shops located in their best hotels and offer it for sale in exchange for dollars, not rubles. Russian citizens can't buy there.

I've bought nail clippers, razors, razor blades and ballpoint pens in those dollar stores and I've carefully inspected such items as cameras, camera lenses, binoculars, cigarette lighters, scissors and watches there. The best Russian goods are poor by our standards. The workmanship is inferior and the design is either imitative or just bad.

This isn't being written by some blindly anti-Russian nut. I don't hate the Russians. I hate their oppressive government. As a matter of fact, I kind of like the Russians. They're often wonderfully free-spirited and fun to be with but, for whatever facet of their national character it is, they do a lot of things badly. From what I've seen of their binoculars and their ballpoint pens, I'd guess nuclear weapons would be one of the things they make poorly. There are things Americans don't do well, either, but these are different things.

Obviously the Russians have learned how to do some things. Their space program is not as sophisticated as ours but it works. I have no doubt that their nuclear bombs go off with a big bang and I'm also sure they've built rockets that will take their missiles to New York. What I can't believe, from what I know firsthand about the Russians, is that they have more and better nuclear weapons than we do.

I can't help myself from thinking that the President is just trying to scare us into approving a huge defense budget. If the Russians could build great nuclear bombs, their hotels wouldn't be as poorly constructed as they are. I go into a place for a week and judge a whole country by one hotel. The Russians would be accurate in saying that's the kind of person I am.

Spies

THIS has been a bad year for spies. Every couple of days you read in the paper where they've caught some of ours or we've caught some of theirs. The French, for instance, recently expelled forty-seven Soviet Embassy people because they said they were spying. Forty-seven is a lot of spies.

It would be interesting to know what secrets all those Russian agents got from the French. They'd have to get an awful lot of secrets to make it worthwhile because keeping forty-seven agents in Paris, at those prices, isn't cheap. Even spies have to eat. I've eaten in Paris and I've eaten in Moscow and if all forty-seven of those Russians were really spies, and were smart, they'd have been trying to steal the secret of French cooking.

Being a spy in Paris must be one of the most desirable jobs any spy could have. The living is good and the French don't take spies that seriously. You could probably go to a cocktail party in Paris and discuss what you did without surprising anyone.

"What is your business, Mr. Standoffsky, if I may ask?"

"I'm in espionage. I spy for the Russian Government."

"How interesting. You must meet so many fascinating people when you're a spy."

"True, and most of them are other spies."

Recently, a Soviet citizen was apprehended (spies are "apprehended" not "caught") while he was in the process of picking up some rolls of film from the trunk of a hollow tree in Maryland. It shows that Russian spies know little about this country. Everyone knows you pick up your film at the drugstore.

We never get any information about what it is spies find out. It's always suggested that the information they take back to their country will have grave consequences on ours but I'd like more specific information. I suspect that in the past twenty-five years the most serious information one country has gotten about another is a list of its spies.

There must be a lot of wasted effort in the spy business, too. Scientists working on new developments don't have any contact with the CIA or the KGB. I can imagine a spy working for years to get hold of the plans for a new aircraft and by the time he gets them, he finds they've already been printed in *Popular Mechanics*. Or a spy might come running home with what he thinks is a secret formula for a new chemical weapon only to discover that U.S. and Soviet scientists had exchanged that information at a meeting in Sweden three years ago.

Spies are having a tough time of it everywhere and I wouldn't be surprised to see them organize and form a union. Soviet and U.S. spies would all belong to the same labor organization but in different locals. Soviet spies would have to honor the picket lines of U.S. spies and vice versa.

Any espionage union would probably make several demands on behalf of its members. It would certainly demand the right for them to be double agents. Spies, like professional athletes, ought to have the right to become free agents after a certain length of time, too. If the Russians have a really good spy, he should have the right to bargain and switch his allegiance if another country offers him more money.

An espionage union would certainly take up the matter of women's rights. Women seem to have been almost completely frozen out of the spy business ever since the unfortunate demise of Mata Hari. That could have happened to anyone. Mata Hari just happened to be a woman.

I don't have a very high regard for spies. I think we should keep track of what's going on in other countries in a general way but I don't think we need the blueprints for their nuclear energy plants or even the formula for their chemical warfare weapons. Their World Almanac is all we need.

Americans have never been very good spies. It's something we can all be proud of.

VI:

FAMILIAR THINGS

A Place to Stare

THERE'S a major renovation going on in the building I work in and it looks as if I may have to move out of my office.

The people in any company who assign offices are always thinkings of reasons why people should move. Everyone should resist them. Their reasons are usually not good enough and they don't understand what a serious effect moving an office can have on a person's life.

I've known some people who don't seem to mind moving. They're usually executives with better-organized minds than mine. They know where everything is in their office and they can move it to another and still find things. That would not be the case with me. I know that if I have to move, there are things I'll never find again in my whole life. They'll be lost at the bottom of a packing box and some survivor of mine down the road will have to go through the box and throw the stuff out. He won't dare throw anything out without looking through it because I often hide a ten-dollar bill in a book or envelope around my office so I'll have emergency money the day I come to work without a nickel.

I don't know what's wrong with me but I take inanimate objects in my life too seriously. I get to have quite an affection for a car that's given me good service and I've always hated to turn one like that over to the secondhand dealers. I feel terrible thinking of someone who doesn't care, buying it and then abusing it. How can I be so disloyal?

That's the way I feel about my office. To the building planners it's nothing more than some marks on a blueprint. It's four walls that need painting, a worn carpet and a radiator that spits water from a bad valve when the heat is up. As far as the planner goes, my office is just another secondhand car. He'll get what he can out of it without a thought for what it has meant to me.

I can remember every office I've ever had. In 1962 I had one I wrote a book in. Everyone called the office "the submarine" because it didn't have any windows and was buried in a basement area of the building but I liked it. The temperature was easy to control and it wasn't on anyone's way to their own office so people didn't drop in and chat a lot. If you're trying to write a book, it's better if you don't chat much.

The office in which I sit at this moment is one I've occupied for ten years. That's my personal world record for office occupancy and I've not only been in it longer than any other but I like it better. I've had more professional success in the years between 1972 and 1982 than I ever had before and naturally I give a lot of the credit for it to this office. If anyone gives me an award of any kind and asks me to make a speech, I'm going to mention this office when I modestly start passing credit around. "Without this office," I'll say, "I never would have been able to do what I've done." That's what I'll say and all the people at the awards dinner will applaud me for passing the credit around and congratulate my office for its contribution to my success.

No one will ever know this office as well as I do this moment. I can't tell you how many times I've leaned back in my chair, propped my feet against the angle where my desk meets the attached typing table, and simply stared at some part of my wall or ceiling. If anyone goes past my door when I'm staring, they get the impression I'm thinking about something but I'm not. I'm just staring. A writer has to get quite a bit of staring out of his system before he goes to work.

I hate the thought of moving. This office has been a great old friend to me. Losing it is going to be like a death in the family. Building planners don't understand that. They don't understand why I'm not pleased.

"The one you're going to get is bigger than this," they tell me. "Got two windows and we'll put down new carpet. It's a better office."

What do they know about staring?

Elevators

IF you've ever worked or lived in a building where you had to use an elevator, you know that it becomes part of your life. It's often as much a barrier between you and the ground, or the ground and your office or apartment, as an open drawbridge.

No one is ever completely comfortable in an elevator. There's something about them we don't trust. Lurking in the back of our memory is the story we once read about the twelve people who were stuck between the seventh and eighth floors for nine hours. We look around, imagining what it would be like to be stuck with the people now on our elevator.

There's an uncertainty in our minds about the engineering principles of an elevator. We've all had little glimpses into the dirty, dark elevator shaft and seen the greasy cables passing each other. They never look totally safe. The idea of being trapped in a small box going up and down on strings induces a kind of phobia in all of us. There we are, standing on a platform, enclosed on all six sides, that could drop to the bottom of the building in an instant if any of the strings and the emergency brakes failed.

There's a predictable sequence to the little drama of an elevator ride. If you arrive at the elevator door first and the elevator is on another floor, you press the button and stand there with absolutely nothing to do. Usually someone else arrives before the elevator does. Depending on your relationship with that person, you say nothing, nod or say hello.

Invariably the second person, and subsequent persons who arrive, stand there for ten seconds and then step forward and press the button themselves.

I've never been sure what motivates a person to press the button when I'm already standing there. Does he think I'm so dumb I was standing there without pressing it myself?

More often I think it's just a little action that relieves the embarrassment of standing there close to another person without saying anything. It's something to do. Often it's done with an impatient gesture, designed to produce a rapport among the standees, by suggesting a mutual disapproval of the machinery.

I work on the sixth floor of a building. I know some of the elevator riders well. Others I have only that nodding acquaintance with and some are total strangers.

I prefer riding with the strangers. Those elevator friends whose names I'm not always sure of aren't comfortable with the silence, but we don't know each other well enough to talk about anything of substance. The conversation often turns to the elevator itself.

If it stops at more than one floor, they'll say, "We've got a local here."

I suppose that remark has been made in my presence in that elevator a thousand times.

Any other conversation is limited to three topics and they begin with a question. Those are:

1—"They keepin' you busy?"
2—"What's new with you?"
3—"Is it hot (cold) enough for you?"

My inclination is to just nod and smile when these are directed at me. I don't want to be unfriendly but I'm not going to make a fool of myself by answering a question that wasn't really meant to be one.

Escalators have always been more fun than elevators, although most women approach them gingerly. Years ago I talked to a hotel architect named William Tabler who had just designed a new Hilton in New York. He'd put in lots of elevators but he'd connected three meeting-room floors with escalators.

"They're really slower even if you have to wait for the elevator," he said, "but people like to be moving."

This week I've decided to get in shape by walking up and down the six flights in my building. It's something I've decided to do three or four times a year for the last ten years. My resolve disappears in a few days in a fit of heavy breathing and I go back to the elevator.

Hotels and Motels

A HOTEL or motel can be a pleasure to stay in for a night or two. You don't have to do the dishes, there isn't a mess in the garage you ought to be cleaning out, and whatever needs fixing isn't your problem.

For more than a night or two, though, hotels and motels are less satisfactory. They begin to get on your nerves and you yearn for the familiar disarray of home. I've been staying in a lot of hotels and motels recently. They've ranged from seedy motels that I stayed in for convenience because they were near the airport, to a very expensive, high-class hotel in Houston.

What follows are some random notes I've made on hotels and motels:
—If you're traveling and only want a night's sleep, a motel is better than a hotel. I call it a motel if there's no elevator and you carry your own bags to your room.
—The coffee shop doesn't open until too late in most places. Seven

A.M. is too late if you want to return to your room after you eat and still get going early.

—I'm always surprised that hotels don't make more of a point of having you turn in the key when you pay the bill. I often walk off with the key by accident.

—It isn't easy to read in a motel room. The light over the bed is never where you want it and all the bulbs are low-powered. Charles Kuralt carries a hundred-watt bulb in his suitcase when he's "On the Road."

—If you're only staying one day, it's hard to wash socks and underwear at night and have them dry in time to pack them in the morning. When my socks don't dry, I drape them over the lampshade while I go have breakfast. If they still aren't dry when I come back, I put them in a plastic bag and put that in my suitcase.

—I can never bring myself to use two bars of soap. I open one for the sink but then in the morning, when I take a shower, I use that one again instead of opening the bigger one they gave me for the shower. It doesn't save me any money but it seems wasteful to use two.

—I never eat where I sleep. Motel restaurants aren't usually very good. The best restaurants are owned and run by individuals. I prefer to take a chance on one of them when I'm in a strange city. On the other hand, I usually stay in a motel that's part of a big chain instead of taking a chance on a privately owned, local motel.

—The pile rug in the bathroom of the hotel I stayed in last night was so thick the bathroom door didn't clear it and that made it difficult every time I opened or closed the door. You'd think a hotel with 250 rooms would have worked that out. They must have 250 bathroom doors that are hard to open because of the carpet.

—It's gotten so you can hardly pay cash for a motel room anymore. They insist on a credit card when you check in.

—There ought to be a law standardizing the controls for hot and cold in hotel and motel showers. It's easy to burn yourself or freeze before you catch on to how they work.

—Most places have those hangers you can't steal now. They don't have a hook on the end. The hook is attached to a bar and a little knob on the hanger fits into the hook. I hate them.

—Hotels and motels cover every flat space in the room with literature and picture folders telling you how wonderful their place is and how good their services are. I always dump these in a drawer. I need the space myself. I figure while I'm paying for the room, I shouldn't have to read their advertisements.

Some Sound Ideas

A FEW minutes ago, walking back from lunch, I started to cross the street when I heard the sound of a coin dropping. It wasn't much but, as I turned, my eyes caught the heads of several other people turning too. A woman had dropped what appeared to be a dime.

The tinkling sound of a coin dropping on pavement is an attention-getter. It can be nothing more than a penny. Whatever the coin is, no one ignores the sound of it. It got me thinking about sounds again.

We are beseiged by so many sounds from every side these days that it isn't the loudest sounds that attract the most attention. People in New York City seldom turn to look when a fire engine, a police car or an ambulance comes screaming along the street.

When I'm in New York, I'm a New Yorker. I don't turn either. Like the natives, I hardly hear a siren there.

At home in my little town in Connecticut, it's different. The distant wail of a police car, an emergency vehicle or a fire siren brings me to my feet if I'm seated and brings me to the window if I'm in bed.

The people who drive cars or trucks equipped with sirens ought to be more careful about when they use them. I'm often suspicious of ambulances that careen down the street with sirens wailing. It can't always be a matter of life and death and if they're used when it isn't, they're less effective when it is. I suspect quite a few broken legs have gone through a lot of red lights rushing too fast and too loud to an emergency room where they waited two hours for a doctor to set them.

It's the quietest sounds that have most effect on us, not the loudest. In the middle of the night, I can hear a dripping faucet a hundred yards away through three closed doors. I've been hearing little creaking noises and sounds which my imagination turns into footsteps in the middle of the night for twenty-five years in our house. How come I never hear those sounds in the daytime?

Some people, of course, never hear anything in the middle of the night. There are light sleepers and heavy sleepers and they always seem to sleep together. One gets up in the middle of the night to check the noises; the other hears nothing. The sleeper awakens four hours later to ask, "What happened?"

"Nothing happened, dear. There was a burglar downstairs walking around in hobnailed boots, the oil burner exploded and two cars hit head-on in front of the house. The cops came, the fire engines were here and the ambulance picked up the injured. Everything's all right now. Go back to sleep."

In a book by W. S. Gilbert I had when I was a kid, there was a character named King Borria Bungalee Boo, "an African swell ... whose whisper was a horrible, horrible yell."

There are people who find it impossible to whisper or even talk softly. For some reason, they're the ones who try to do most of it. There's nothing more embarrassing than to have someone whisper to you about someone else in the room, in a voice everyone in the room can hear.

Car horns are an irritating noise. There are very few times when it's important to blow the horn of a car. When someone on our street parks out in front of someone else's house and blows the horn, I feel like throwing rocks.

I'm quite clear in my mind what the good sounds are and what the bad sounds are.

I've turned against whistling, for instance. I used to think of it as the mark of a happy worker but lately I've been associating the whistler with a nervous person making compulsive noises.

Walking through the woods in the fall of the year, with the leaves up around your ankles, is a great sound.

Someone else in the room sniffling and without a handkerchief is an annoying sound.

The tapping, tapping, tapping of my typewriter as the keys hit the paper is a lovely sound to me. I often like the sound of what I write better than the looks of it.

Let It Rain

IT is raining as I write. I'm snug and comfortable here in this room. I'm surrounded by familiar things and tools like this typewriter that I know how to use. The rain can't get at me. I'm dry. Being warm and dry inside when it's cold and wet outside is one of the few victories man scores over Nature. We ought to enjoy it. This isn't a wet cave I've crept into in order to avoid the worst of the storm. This is a comfortable home where I can forget all about the rain if I choose to.

I've never understood why Longfellow wrote that famous line of his or why it's famous. You remember:

> Into each life some rain must fall,
> Some days must be dark and dreary.

It's clear that Longfellow associated rain with all the bad things that happen to us. I don't associate rain with that at all. Maybe it was raining when I was born. Rain is as important to people as it is to plants. I've lived in climates where they don't have much rain and hated it. I'm not the cactus type. The human brain needs a good, hard rain at least once every two weeks ... snow if it's cold. You can't keep going out in the bright sun every day without having it get on your nerves and dry you up. Maybe smog is nature's way of protecting Los Angelenos from all that sun they used to get.

One of the few lines I remember from what little Chaucer I read is better than Longfellow's. I never really understood Chaucer's olde English spelling but even that adds flavor to the lines he wrote about rain:

> Lord, this is an huge rayn!
> This were a weder for to slepen inne.

That has a wonderful feel to it and it evokes memories of all the good Saturday mornings I've decided to turn over and sleep for another hour under the lulling rhythm of the rayn on the roof.

People are always knocking rain but I don't think they mean it. It's just pass-the-time-of-day weather talk. We're all expected to make negative comments about a rainy day. "It's raining cats and dogs," someone will say. I've never understood what that means or where the phrase came from. No rain ever reminds me of cats and dogs coming down from the clouds and I don't know why we keep saying it.

I went to a football game in the rain earlier this year and had the time of my life. I had rubber shoes, a sailor's rubber, foul-weather suit and a wide-brimmed rain hat that kept the water from going down my neck. In addition, I had a four-foot-square rubber sheet that I brought along to keep on my lap. Under that I kept my program, my lunch and a thermos bottle filled with hot chicken broth. There I sat in a dry little island, surrounded by a sea of rain trying unsuccessfully to get at me. I was happily isolated from every outside distraction except the good game on the lighted playing field below me.

The players on the field were as happy as I was although it would be hard to explain that to anyone who has never played football. Football players don't mind rain at all unless they're quarterbacks or pass catchers. Once a player gets sloppy and wet all over, it's fun slopping around in the mud. It's John Madden's kind of football weather.

Nothing is perfect, of course, and there are one or two little things that keep me from being totally enthusiastic about rain. First there's that persistent leak in the back corner of the basement by my woodworking shop. It isn't much but a small puddle always forms on the cellar floor after a hard rain and I can't seem to find a way to stop it.

The only other thing I don't like about rain is that eight or ten inches of pants between the tops of my shoes and the bottom of my raincoat that always get soaked when I go out in a downpour.

Other than those two minor inconveniences, I say, let it rain!

The Greenhouse Effect

THE Earth is going to get a lot warmer in the near future, according to an announcement from a government agency in Washington. Our temperatures will be rising an average of nine degrees by the year 2100.

This comes as a surprise to me, because I've always assumed that the Earth would get colder, not warmer. The fire up there has to go out sooner or later, but apparently it's going to be later. First the Earth's going to get hot because of a gas barrier of carbon dioxide that's drifted up into the atmosphere from all the stuff we burn. If you always thought smoke just went up, up and away, you were only half right. It goes up but it doesn't go away. The barrier it forms lets the sun in but prevents heat from leaving the Earth.

The Environmental Protection Agency, which made the announcement, says that New York City could end up with Daytona Beach's temperatures.

If that's true, it proves beyond a doubt that there is a God and that everything works out okay in the end. For the past fifty years, residents of the Northeast have worried because so many people and so much industry has left for the Sun Belt. All kinds of industries with aging factories have been abandoning their old red brick plants in New England and moving to cinder block buildings in the South.

During the oil shortage, the exodus reached epidemic proportions. Factory operators and ordinary people who didn't like the cold wanted to go where heat didn't cost so much.

Now, apparently, the cycle has come around and it will be the Northeast's turn to prosper. If it gets warm in New England, all those factories that moved south will be moving back. They'll want to move out of the Sun Belt because they're spending too much on the electricity they need for all the air conditioning the unions require in their contracts.

The State of Maine, which has always handled its poverty with more grace than other poor states, may prosper. Maine could become the new Sun Belt. If New York has the temperature of Daytona, Maine ought to get what North Carolina has. That would be a big improvement over what Maine has now and would certainly bring industry and prosperity to it.

The thing that worries me about this warming trend is that people don't work as hard when it's warm. Most of the good work of the world has been accomplished in temperate, not tropical, climates. People work better when it's cold than when it's hot. Bad weather brings out the good in people so I hope this warming trend doesn't mean we're in for a lot of nice weather. We can't lie around in the sun if we're going to stay ahead of the Japanese.

The Environmental Protection Agency only predicted what results this warming or "greenhouse effect," as they call it, will have on the United States. It never mentioned the potential effect on world affairs.

What temperatures will the Soviet Union get?

Will Moscow be like Miami Beach or more like San Francisco?

If the Russians have San Francisco weather, will they become nicer people, like San Franciscans?

If Paris ends up with temperatures like Zambia, will Yves Saint Laurent be presenting a new collection of designer loincloths in his fall collection?

They say the polar ice cap will melt as the Earth warms. Is this the end of the igloo as we know it today?

Will Eskimos be living in thatched-roof cottages?

The environmental experts predict that the ocean could rise four feet. This is bad news for the people living in the expensive houses right on the shoreline but it's good news for me. Our house is one hundred yards from the water now and if the ocean rises, we could end up with valuable property right on the beach.

Insects

Why are there flies? I suppose they have as much right in the universe as we do but if they have their place in the grand plan of things, I don't know what it is and I'd be just as pleased if no one told me.

Yesterday I went for a walk in the woods and what might otherwise have been a very pleasant time of admiring nature and thinking good thoughts, was ruined by a couple of horseflies that took the walk with me. They're so infernally clever, those flies. They know I don't have eyes on the top of my head so they stay low over my hair, making passes at my ears in order to get the maximum effect out of their irritating little buzz. I swipe at them but I seldom hit one and if, by some lucky accident, I make contact with a waving arm and knock one to the ground, he just gets up again and buzzes off.

I not only fail to understand what flies are for but I'm not sure why they're as annoying as they are. That noise they make isn't really loud and they don't bite much. Even if they do bite, it isn't like a broken arm. There's a better reason to hate mosquitoes than flies.

Because I couldn't think of anything else on my walk, with the flies around me, I got thinking of some of the other creatures we live with that bring out some latent desire to kill in the mildest-mannered of us. We have a house in the country with both chipmunks and mice around. They are, after all, about the same size and if you were describing them to someone who'd never seen either a mouse or a chipmunk, they'd sound the same. They're awfully close to being the same thing for such a difference in my opinion of them. I'd hate to hurt a chipmunk but I've caught quite a few mice by the neck in that cruel little trap.

Ants don't bother me much. At certain times of year we have

some ants in the kitchen but I don't have any primal urge to kill them. I wish they'd go away but they don't bug me the way flies do. Maybe I'm more irritated with the fly because he's superior to me in the way that an ant isn't. The ant can't hover over my head, buzzing in my ears and tantalizing me with his ability to evade every swipe I take at him.

Keep in mind I am reconstructing this from the memory of the thoughts that came to me yesterday on my walk. I got thinking about an experience I had with a couple of ants just the day before. I saw a black ant on my workshop floor trying to run off with a smaller, red ant. They were all tangled up together and I suspected all sorts of things might have been going on there but as I watched, I decided that it was the red ant who was attacking the black ant and the black ant was trying to get away. The red ant had attached himself (or, according to my darkest thoughts *herself*) to him. I got the two of them on a piece of paper and dropped them into an empty coffee can. The two came apart and seemed to ignore each other and I left them trying to scramble up the shiny walls of the can while I went to do something else, at which I probably had about the same chance of success as they had of getting out of the can.

I came back an hour later and learned a lesson about black and red ants. I had been wrong. The red ant was in six or eight little pieces and the black ant was still trying to get out. I felt terrible about having left that little red ant in there with that black killer but how was I to know? Imagine the terror the red ant felt when I left him or her alone in the can with the black ant!

I don't suppose you could teach one of those black ants not to kill a red one. You can't teach a cat not to kill birds. Why do cats do it? Maybe it's a matter of territory. The black ants want to preserve their homeland and the red ants think they ought to have one for themselves. It seems to me there's room enough for all the ants on my workshop floor but what do I know?

I don't understand what's going on in nature anymore than I understand what's going on among people in the world and I certainly can't say why I was determined to kill those harmless flies buzzing around my head in the woods yesterday.

Matches

KEEP this page out of the reach of young children because it's about matches.

With the possible exception of pennies, nothing piles up in places where you don't need them and disappears from places where you could use them faster than packs of paper matches. I have a little drawer in my dresser, next to the one I keep my clean socks in, and there must be a hundred packs of matches in it. They'd be handy except that I never light a match looking for socks.

I've never smoked cigarettes and we have a range with pilot lights so I don't really use many matches. I want to be honest with you though. I played with matches as a kid and I've never gotten over the fascination they had for me then. I still play with matches. For instance, if I light one for anything, I always try to burn it all the way to the end. After it has burned halfway, I wet the tip of my thumb and forefinger and grab hold of the hot, bulbous end to see if I can burn the whole match.

We have a grill in the backyard and I use matches most often starting the fire for cooking there in the summer. That's where I do most of my thinking about matches.

I wish the people who make matches wouldn't be so protective of us. They keep thinking up new safety features that make matches more inconvenient and no safer. I don't think many fires are set accidentally by people using matches for a good purpose and I don't appreciate some of the ways match makers try to protect us from ourselves.

For instance, I have a strong aversion to book matches that have the striking pads on the opposite side from where the cover lifts open. They aren't handy at all and I doubt if they've ever prevented one fire. I'm careful to throw them all away without looking at the advertising displayed on them.

Last weekend I cooked out for the first time this season. I use a combination of those commercial charcoal briquettes and a few pieces of wood from the dead limbs of several hickory and maple trees we have. The charcoal briquettes are not really what I call charcoal at all, of course. They're made mostly of coal dust and a binding material like clay or starch, but they're handy.

While I was buying the bag of briquettes that morning, I also bought a box of wooden matches. It is my habit to keep matchboxes on the mantelpiece over the fireplace when I'm starting a fire in the backyard. That's what I did last weekend but after setting the fire with newspapers underneath, I couldn't get the match to light.

I went back inside to look at the box the matches came in and, of course, they were called "safety" matches. They couldn't be struck just anywhere. They had to be scratched on the strip on the side of the matchbox.

Well, when I go out to the backyard, I don't want to take the whole box of matches with me and I'd be pleased if the wooden match makers wouldn't try to make life so safe for me. There are even laws in many states making it illegal to sell matches that will strike anywhere. There are states in which you can buy a rifle at the hardware store but not a box of matches that will strike on the seat of your pants.

Most of us are fascinated with fire and it isn't hard to understand why. We're suspicious that the world will eventually grow cold and fire is a great comfort to us because of the heat it produces. The fact that it's dangerous only makes it fascinating. Civilization's ability to use fire may be the most important thing it has learned how to do.

In the movie version of Mark Twain's *A Connecticut Yankee in King Arthur's Court*, Will Rogers saved his life by amazing the king with his cigarette lighter. A dream or fantasy that often recurs in my mind is one in which I'm the only person in the world with matches. If I had lived a thousand years ago and had no other possession than those book matches in my dresser drawer, I wouldn't have needed anything else.

Of course, with my luck, I'd have gone before King Arthur with my life on the line and discovered, when I reached into my pocket to amaze him by lighting a wooden match, that they were safety matches and I'd left the box home.

Dislikes

LIFE is pleasant most of the time but there are some things it would be better without. I've made a partial list of things I dislike:

—Special or clever license plates with the owner's nickname on them.

—Magazines that hide their index where you can't find it. The index to a magazine belongs inside the first page after the cover.

—Television commercials for hemorrhoid cures, toilet paper, sanitary pads or dental adhesives. Newspaper ads for these same products don't bother me.

—Flip-top beer and soft drink cans.

—People who take up two parking spaces with one car.

—Anything stapled together.

—Announcements in the mail that I'm the potential winner of a million-dollar sweepstakes.

—A space that's too small on a form where I'm supposed to put my signature. I scrawl when I write and if I have to put it in a little space, it isn't really my signature.

—Having to open a new can of coffee when I only need two tablespoons more.

—Telephone answering machines with messages at the beginning that are too long or too cute.

—Newspapers with sections that have different numbering systems from the main news sections. There may be no good way to handle this problem but that doesn't stop me from disliking it.

—The middle seat in a crowded airplane.

—Trunks of cars that have to be opened with a key. Why can't I leave the trunk of my car unlocked if I want to?

—Religious quacks on radio and television thinking up new ways to take money from ignorant listeners and incidentally from legitimate churches.

—Dirty magazines prominently displayed at a newsstand.

—A cart in the supermarket with a wobbly wheel.

—Waiting in line to pay for anything.

—Secretaries who say, "May I ask what this is in reference to?" when you call their boss.

—Admonitions from weathermen to "drive safely." All I want to know from them is whether it's going to rain or not. I'll decide how to drive.

—Recipes in a bag of flour that you can't remove without spilling flour all over.

—Hot-air hand dryers in public washrooms. I'd rather use my shirt-tail.

—People who play radios in public places.

—Baseball or basketball scores on the radio for teams I don't care anything about.

—People who stand too close to my face when they're talking to me. I think they're cousins of the people who move you gradually over toward the buildings when you walk down the street with them.

—Screws with slots that aren't deep enough so that they tear when you twist with the screwdriver.

—Having to check a shopping bag when I go into a store. I know shoplifting is a problem but I don't like the idea of being a suspect.

—Cars with too many red taillights.

The Flu

THIS isn't going to be easy. As I write, I'm having the flu. The brain seems to be thinking all right but I can't keep it thinking about one subject for long. My body is quaking just enough so that when I go for the *h* on my typewriter, I'm often hitting the *g* or *j* on either side of it.

This is my fourth day. That's the longest I've ever had what they used to call the forty-eight-hour virus. I think I may be pulling out of it because this morning I was interested enough in life again to read the newspaper for a little while. My daily paper is one of the great pleasures of my life and when I'm not interested in it, I know I'm sick.

Strange things happen to time when you're sick. The minutes and the hours seem interminably long when you're lying in bed tossing and turning . . . 2:35 A.M. . . . 2:50 A.M. . . . my gosh, is it only 3:15? But then in the morning it all seems so condensed. You have no point of interest to which the memory can attach itself so the night is all one brief unpleasant blur.

In regard to time, I'm furthermore convinced that there is definitely some state in between sleep and wakefulness that we don't identify very often. There have been times over the past four days when I would have sworn in court that I never fell asleep between midnight and five A.M., but looking back at it rationally, I suspect that if I was not really asleep I was for part of the time, at least, in a state of suspended animation. This can happen to anyone who simply isn't sleeping very well even if they don't have the flu. When a husband or wife claims not to have slept all night, the partner is often tempted to ask what all the snoring was about then.

Considering the flu is not usually a serious disease, it sure is uncomfortable. I lie in bed wondering how I'd feel if this were a disease I'd never get over. At noon of the second day Margie said I ought to eat a little chicken broth. I said I didn't want any. I didn't feel like it and I was afraid it would make me sick to my stomach. She brought some upstairs to the bedroom anyway and in deference to her concern and effort, I drank some of it. I was soon sick to my stomach. It's a tough way to prove a point.

All day Margie kept bringing me things I didn't want. I don't suppose there was a single thing in the world I could name that I wanted except my health back. I didn't even want to turn over in bed when I ached from lying on one side for too long. When I had to go to the bathroom, I kept putting it off, thinking I might be in better shape to get up in another half hour.

You get very aware of the parts of your body lying in bed with it for four days. You get very aware of its shortcomings and dissatisfied with it. In the bathroom, I look in the mirror, unshaved, hair uncombed, face drooping and I think, "My God, this is what I really look like when I'm not fixed up."

One of the things I notice that's wrong with my body is that there's too much of it. I've been thinking about all the food I would have eaten that I haven't eaten in the past four days. I'm still alive. I have no desire for food. Why can't I have this attitude toward food when I'm well?

It's the old story, I know. It's easy to decide not to eat so much when you feel the way I do. As a matter of fact, it's difficult to remember how you felt when you were well while you're sick; and difficult to recall how you felt when you were sick when you're well.

Yesterday the inevitable happened. Margie got it. She had been so good to me that I dragged myself out of bed and started bringing her hot tea, which she likes. I noticed she didn't drink her tea. The next morning she came in to see how I was. She brought me tea and said she felt stronger.

It made me feel terrible to have her waiting on me again. She said she felt much better today but I couldn't help wondering if some people aren't just better at being sick than others.

I hope you don't get anything from reading this.

Coughing

My life has been dominated for the past four days by coughing. I must have coughed almost as often as I've exhaled.

Coughing is one of the least attractive things we do in public and I hate to do it but I can't stop myself. I have a cold or a virus or some flu bug and it seems to have settled in the spot just below my throat where that indentation is between the collarbones.

When I was young and people coughed as much as I have the last few days, they were said to have "consumption." I don't know where the word came from. The more knowledgeable word was "tuberculosis."

I don't have either of those. I have a cough. I don't smoke cigarettes and I know my body well enough to be sure I don't have any dread disease.

I was in Florida over the weekend. The temperature hit ninety degrees one day and Florida when it's ninety degrees is the worst place to be with a coughing cold. It's humid and when you're inside you need air conditioning. Air conditioning, as we all know, is a cold's best friend. A cold loves air conditioning.

Friends have been sympathetic enough about my cold. They've been properly worried and they keep saying things like "You ought to take care of yourself," but it hasn't helped. Not only that, even though I can tell they genuinely feel sorry for me, I've noticed a certain edge in their voices a couple of times. They wouldn't say it but I know what they want to say. They want to burst out loud and yell, "Will you *for goodness sake* stop that infernal coughing!"

It's irritating to have someone around you coughing all the time. No matter how much you try to keep yourself from thinking it, you always have the sneaking suspicion they could stop if they wanted to.

When I was a kid I coughed a lot when I had a cold and even now I have an annoying way of clearing my throat when I'm not sick. I'm more aware of this than I used to be because two of my four grown children do it. Drives me crazy. "Stop clearing your throat," I want to yell at them, as I clear my throat.

I've never found a legal cough syrup or cough drop that did anything at all for a cough. There was one ten or fifteen years ago that helped but it had more codeine in it than the law allows now so you can't buy it today without a prescription. I don't go to a doctor when I have a cold, no matter how bad it is. I've probably had more colds than he has and I know just as much, maybe more, about them. All the doctor can do in a case like that is give you medicine that's stronger than is good for you. I don't take much medicine, not because of any religious conviction or anything like that but because anything you can buy without a prescription probably doesn't work.

As kids we used to argue about whether the black licorice Smith Brothers Cough Drops were best or whether the menthol ones in the yellow package were.

In desperation the other day I bought a package of Luden's Menthol Cough Drops. That's a familiar old package I remember with affection, too, and I thought perhaps over the years they'd learned how to sneak something into their cough drops that would really help a cough.

I paid thirty-five cents for fifteen cough drops. That's only a little more than two cents each and you can't expect a miracle drug for that. The front of the package says they're "MEDICATED." I don't know what that word could be broadened to include but when you look further on the package for all the active ingredients, there are just two. Luden's Menthol Cough Drops are made of sugar and menthol. Menthol is the principal ingredient of peppermint. It's obtained from oil of peppermint. It sounds like candy to me.

Considering how good our bodies are at curing themselves of the worst things that happen to them all but once, it's interesting that none of us is ever totally free of every single malady or irritation. If we check closely, there's always something that isn't quite right. It may be nothing more than a hangnail but there it is, stopping our bodies just short of perfection.

I'm not going to eat any more of these cough drops. (I think "eat" is a better word than "take.") I'll put them in a dresser drawer. Next time I get a hangnail, I'll see if sugar and peppermint helps that.

Pacemakers

EVERY three or four years it occurs to me that my heart has been beating away about seventy times a minute night and day, day after day but most of the time I don't pay any attention to my heart. It's the same with breathing. If you start getting conscious of the fact that you're taking air in and pushing it out again 28,000 times a day, it can be disconcerting.

I got thinking about my heart and all our hearts the other day when I read a story about pacemakers. A Senate study found that doctors and pacemaker makers may have overcharged patients a billion dollars a year for putting the device in their hearts. About 150,000 people are having them put in every year and they are charged as much as $10,000 each. Medicare pays most of that cost and the average American's attitude is that if Medicare pays for it, it's free. If it's free to the patient, he or she doesn't care much what it costs Medicare.

Most of us are so naïve it wouldn't occur to us that there was any hanky-panky going on between the manufacturers of this really wonderful little device and the doctors who put it in. It's really disheartening to hear that while we're thinking about our hearts, some doctors and pacemaker businessmen are thinking about money. There's no reason they shouldn't think about money. It's just that the rest of us like to think the world is nicer than that.

Now that I know how aggressive these pacemaker salesmen are in selling their product to doctors, I've thought of a couple of new ways for them to get rich. They can have this idea free.

There ought to be a huge market for pacemakers that control the speed at which other parts our bodies operate. My heart is pumping away in perfectly satisfactory condition and it doesn't give me any trouble but I could sure use a pacemaker for my brain. If these pacemaker people could come up with a little device they could implant in some inconspicuous place to control the speed at which I think, I'd be mighty pleased. Maybe they could get one in my earlobe, in which case I might take two. One brain pacemaker would control the right side of my brain, the other the left.

I'd want a dial on my brain pacemaker so I'd be in control of it.

Sometimes I want to think faster than other times. When I sit down to write, I'd turn it up to full speed so my brain would be thinking its very fastest. In the evening, when I'm home watching television, I'd turn it down to idle. There's no sense having your brain thinking fast when you're watching "Dallas" or "The A Team."

As I understand the heart pacemaker, it provides a small, regular electrical impulse that controls the speed of the heartbeat. Is there anyone alive who wouldn't like one of these for his or her brain? If I went to a party where there were a lot of people I should know, I'd set my brain pacemaker for medium speed. If I saw someone whose name I should know but couldn't remember, I'd simply pinch my earlobe and turn my variable speed brain control up a few notches.

"Hey! If it isn't my old friend George Forbisher! How you been, fella! How's Grace? And the kids George Junior, Marybeth, Sarah and Walter?"

I don't want to get too clinical but there are a lot of parts of my body I'd like to have a pacemaker for. Some parts work too fast and some don't work fast enough. I'd like to be in control of all of them. If they could work something out to speed up my fingers when I'm typing, I'd be mighty appreciative. I'm a slow reader and I wouldn't mind picking up the pace of the movement of my eyes. Often my feet don't move as fast as I want them to. A couple of little pacemakers inserted somewhere near the anklebones might help. I know for certain I'd like to be able to speed up the digestive process going on down there in my stomach. I'm always eating dinner too late and then having indigestion in the middle of the night.

If the pacemaker makers get at some of these auxiliary aids, maybe they could stop overselling the heart pacemakers.

My New Lifestyle

You may have seen something about a report issued by the National Academy of Sciences saying that half of us die when we do, not because of old age but because of our lifestyle. The people from the Institute of Medicine who issued the report recommend that if we want to live longer, we ought to change our lifestyle. The NAS and IOM give official advice to the federal government.

I want to live a good long while so I've been thinking about following these recommendations. What's the sense of paying someone like your government to help you if you won't take their advice?

The problem I have with trying to change my lifestyle is that I don't think of my life as having any particular style. The word "style" to me is something that appears in certain sections of the newspaper and in magazines like *Vogue*. I just plod along, living day after day and having a pretty good time doing it, too, but it isn't what anyone would call stylish. Whatever it is though, I'm thinking of changing the way I do it to conform to government recommendations.

The report says a lot of us die from things that are unnecessary. We die from driving cars, eating too much of the wrong food, drinking too much of the wrong liquids, smoking and generally living at too fast a pace.

I don't know where to start breaking up this style the government thinks my life has. I guess I'll start with breakfast. I know the government wouldn't want me to eat bacon and eggs although it would be afraid to say so because of all the farmers who make their living selling them. I'll have a simple breakfast of two slices of plain toast without butter. I won't toast the bread much because that nice brown color comes from carbon and carbon has been found to be a potential cause of cancer. My grandmother gave me milk toast once for breakfast when I was sick. It was terrible but it must be good for you or my grandmother never would have given it to me, so maybe I'll start the day with milk toast. Of course, it won't give me much incentive to get up.

I better not drive to work anymore. The report says too many of us die before our time in automobile accidents. I don't know how I'll get to work. It's too far to walk and anyway, the government also says too many of us are killed as pedestrians. I was thinking maybe I won't go to work at all because I won't be needing as much money because everything I spend money for is bad for me according to this report.

The only thing I'll need really big money for is fresh fruit and vegetables. I know I'll have to be eating more of those. They cost plenty. I saw California oranges for sale in a fruit store last month and they were two for eighty-nine cents. The most remarkable thing about asking that much for two California oranges was, the store was in California. I'd like to know how the government proposes we pay for all this healthy fruit it wants us to eat.

The report says too many of us die before our time because of heart attacks brought on by stress. I guess I'll stop working so hard. I sure wouldn't mind taking a month off from writing some summer. I like to play tennis too but I suppose I'd better be safe and give that up. The government wouldn't want me dropping dead on the court unnaturally.

Life is going to be pretty quiet for me for the next fifty years. I should live that long with my new lifestyle. Long and dull, my life's going to be. When I wake up in the morning, I'll get up, go to the bathroom, brush my teeth and go back to bed to get some rest. I'll cancel the newspaper because that only creates stress by getting me all worked up. I can't eat, I can't get to work safely, I can't play and from what I gather, my government would just as soon I didn't have a drink before dinner. About all my new lifestyle calls for is devoting full time to living forever.

I don't really know whether I'm going to change my lifestyle or not. I'd feel like an awful fool if I gave up all these things I like and then choked to death lying down trying to take a vitamin pill with a glass of water.

You'll Never Have to Diet Again!!!

Do you want to lose weight without pain? Do you want to drop ten pounds in ten days?

If I were writing this for one of the ladies' magazines, I'd title it YOU'LL NEVER HAVE TO DIET AGAIN!!! (I'd have those three exclamation points in the headline.)

This morning I made the final decision to lose some weight and being a basically unselfish person, I'm going to share my foolproof weight loss plan with you. It's so simple I can't believe I never thought of it before.

I'm going to give up food as a hobby.

A hobby is defined as being an interest or pursuit outside one's regular occupation that is engaged in for relaxation. That's what food is for me. I'm interested in it far beyond the need I have for it to sustain me. I spend idle hours looking at it, shopping for it, reading about it and cooking it. I use food as a diversion from the problems of life and I'm going to stop that.

No longer will you find me in the interesting food stores along the area known as Hell's Kitchen in New York. On Saturdays I'm not going to spend all morning shopping for food, all afternoon preparing it and all evening eating it. I'm going to suppress my interest in food and in so doing, cut down on my consumption of it.

I'm a gourmand and a gourmet. They are not the same thing and I am both. A gourmand is a person who has an unusual interest in eating. A gourmet is someone who knows a lot about food. Being both is tough on the weight.

Over the years I've made a study of the best places to buy good food. I know where the best crusty loaf of Italian bread in America is made, for instance, in a real brick oven in the Bronx. In San Francisco, I know where the best sourdough is.

I've traveled all over this country and there are very few towns or cities you could mention in which I couldn't name the best restaurant. I might not remember the name of the hotel or why I ever went there in the first place, but as a collector of restaurants, I'd remember that.

That's all in the past, though. As of today, or tomorrow at the very latest, I'm dropping food as one of my hobbies. I'll eat supermarket cheese, the kind that comes with paper between the slices, on two pieces of Wonder Bread with margarine.

As things stand now I divide my free time between woodworking and food, but beginning soon I'm going to spend all of my hobby hours with my tools and my wood. I'll come up out of my workshop only when called for dinner.

I'm so devoted to food as a hobby that it isn't going to be an easy break, but once I make it, I'm sure the fat will melt away. At present I eat things long after I've finished being hungry, just because the food tastes good. No more of that. Once I've had as much food as I need, I'll quit eating. No more eating for the fun of it or to pass the time away.

One side effect this plan will have for me is that in addition to losing weight, I'll save time and money. When food is your hobby, you spend a lot of money on things you can't even eat. I have more good knives than we have drawers to keep them in and I'm always buying a new pan or a gadget.

I could write a novel with the time I'll save eliminating food as a hobby. Last weekend I didn't have any of that good Italian bread. I was determined to duplicate the brick-oven conditions in which it's baked, so I bought two of those red clay drainage pipes six inches in diameter. I cut them off so they'd fit into my oven and baked my own bread in them. That's the kind of fun I've got to stop having if I'm going to eliminate food as a pastime.

After I cut out food as a hobby, I'll probably lose so much weight that you won't recognize my picture on the cover of a book.

Corn

IT would be difficult to describe to a stranger what you talk about at the dinner table. One of the subjects that always comes up in our house, at certain times of the year, is the question of which ear of corn is best. I have the nervous feeling that they're fooling around too much with vegetables in agricultural laboratories and one of the vegetables they aren't helping is corn.

If you like corn as I do, you don't like the way they've been growing it the past few years. The kernels are getting smaller and smaller and whiter and whiter. I used to like a variety called Golden Bantam but I haven't seen any in years. Next came something called Country Gentlemen. Country Gentlemen had huge ears and small kernels. In recent years corn has been called Sugar and Spice, Salt and Pepper and Silver Queen. I yearn for the days of Golden Bantam but I'm in the minority at our dinner table.

We're still getting pretty good corn in our part of the country although the pumpkins are in the markets now, and when the pumpkins come, we know we're getting near the end of the fresh fruit and vegetable season.

It's been a fairly good season for vegetables in the Northeast quadrant of the United States. It hasn't been any *better* than fairly good, though. We had torrents of rain in the late spring and then almost nothing during July and August. At least that gets the roots headed down. That's what the farmers say anyway and all I know is what the farmers tell me.

Farming is desperately hard work and often it's so heartbreaking you wonder why anyone sticks at it. There is *always* a reason why the crop isn't as good as it should be. If there isn't too much rain, there's too little. If the amount of rain is just right, there's an early freeze. I stopped for apples last weekend and the farmer was complaining as usual.

"Too warm for this time of year," he said. "It takes all the color out of the apples. They're dropping off the trees before we can pick them. I got a couple hundred bushels of apples out there on the ground."

Last year he couldn't get anyone to pick them off the trees and the year before there was a freeze in September. For most of us weather is just a topic of conversation but for a farmer, it's his life.

In most parts of the country, we've had bumper crops of everything. There was never a better year for apples in the East. Wheat is abundant in the Midwest. I read where there are so many avocados in California that they're going to make dogfood out of them.

Avocados suffer from an image problem that corn on the cob doesn't have. Most Americans think of avocados as a very elitist food and not something you'd have more than a few times a year on special occasions. The day after I read about how many extra avocados there were, I went to the store with every intention of buying several. They were $1.29 each. Some dogfood! The farmers have trouble with the weather; the rest of us have trouble with prices.

Yesterday I had a sign as clear as a falling leaf that the season is changing. For the past few months we've been having corn several times a week at dinner and melons or berries for breakfast. Yesterday my wife said she couldn't get corn and for breakfast we had the first Florida grapefruit of the new year. They were small and sour but it was still good to have them back. Now I can't wait until the price of juice oranges comes back down to where I can afford to squeeze a few for breakfast Saturday and Sunday mornings. There's a time for melons and a time to forget melons. There's a time for corn on the cob and a time to forget corn on the cob.

Confessions of a Tea-Totaler

I HATE tea.

Tea is so universally respected that I've hardly dared say it before. To tell you the truth, I never even realized I disliked it until about four o'clock yesterday afternoon. There I was sitting at my desk drinking tea out of a Styrofoam cup and it hit me like a ton of bricks.

"I hate this stuff," I said to myself. "And I don't care much for this cup, either."

After that, I tried to remember how I got started drinking tea in the first place. I think I know how it happened. Several years ago some of us were sitting around the office thinking of ways not to do any work when one of us—I think it was me—said, "Let's have a nice cup of tea!"

We had a cup of tea and ever since then, that's what someone says almost every day around four.

"Let's have a cup of tea."

My grandmother never called it just a cup of tea. She always referred to it as "a *nice* cup of tea." It was practically all one word to her.

My grandmother would be very disappointed to hear me say I don't like tea. I also have a good friend I've been keeping the secret from for years and he may never speak to me civilly again. He's spent most of his adult life tasting tea for one of the big tea companies and he drinks the stuff all the time, even when he isn't working. Many of you will, no doubt, want to say you liked me up until now but if I don't like tea, you will never read anything I've written again. I'm sorry but there are things a man has to do, and I had to tell you I don't like tea. Please don't write.

Tea is a nervous habit. It's like chewing gum or your fingernails. A drink of tea is so close to nothing that it hardly even dirties the cup it's served in. If it had become fashionable to drink a cup of steaming hot water, tea never would have gained a foothold in America.

It's only a matter of time, too, before someone discovers that tea is bad for laboratory mice and should therefore be labeled as potentially dangerous for human consumption. Tea is one of the few things I can think of that hasn't been called a health hazard and you can bet its day is coming.

Drinking tea seems like a simple thing to do but it isn't simple at all. For an example of how confused tea drinkers are about it, consider how many different ways they think tea should be drunk. Tea drinkers are divided into three categories of roughly equal numbers. Each category further subdivides into those who like it with or without sugar.

—The first group likes tea with nothing in it.

—The second drinks tea with milk.

—The third wants tea with lemon.

There are no three tastes more different than milk, lemon and nothing . . . with and without sugar.

Keep in mind none of this has anything to do with iced tea. Iced tea is as different a drink from tea as lemonade is from hot cocoa with whipped cream. I liked iced tea but iced tea is not considered socially acceptable in the same way a cup of tea is.

You may think of tea as an innocuous beverage but historically tea has been a troublemaker. In the 1760s and 1770s, the amount of tea smuggled illegally into this country dwarfs anything ever smuggled in since. The marijuana trade is petty cash in comparison.

If anyone wishes to argue that the idea of afternoon tea is a civilized social convention, I'll accept that. In England everyone breaks for afternoon tea. That's fine. It's the beverage itself I can't stand.

It's almost four o'clock now. I've had a tough day and I could use a break. I guess I'll have a cup of tea. A *nice* cup of tea.

Milk

Wʜᴀᴛ is the fourth most popular drink in the United States? The answer to today's news quiz is one four-letter word: milk.

The three fluids other than water that Americans drink more of than milk are soft drinks, coffee and beer, in that order.

I haven't been so surprised by a statistic since I read that women buy more razor blades than men.

For years milk was associated with wholesomeness and goodness. The all-American kid came home after school, dropped his homework books on the kitchen table and had a glass of milk and a cookie. After that he went out and played for several hours until supper was ready. The kid had milk at supper, too.

According to the statistics, that has changed. Now when school is over a child buys a bottle or a can of sweet-flavored carbonated water and throws the can or bottle on someone else's lawn on the way home from school.

Nothing seems to hurt the booming sale of soft drinks. I had noticed the increasing popularity of something called Sunkist, so I bought a can of it to have with a sandwich at lunch the other day. The can, because of its name and color, gives the clear impression that the drink inside is made of orange juice. Sunkist is *not* made of orange juice. A carbonated beverage can be called "orange soda" without having any orange juice at all in it. For lawyers worried for me because of the legal implications of that statement, be advised that I have talked to the administrators of the regulation at the Food and Drug Administration in Washington, D.C., within the last four minutes. *They* told me that.

The makers of carbonated orange soda often put in orange pulp to help it masquerade as being made of orange juice and they may include an additive that gives the drink the cloudy appearance that real orange juice has but unless it says "orange juice" on its list of ingredients, it has none.

The dairy industry blames the decline in our consumption of milk on the medical profession. Doctors have suggested that too much milk produces cholesterol, the substance that clogs the pipes that carry our blood through our bodies.

There's no doubt that the American wish to cut down on fattening foods and foods that produce cholesterol has had an adverse effect on milk consumption, but I'm not convinced this is the principal reason for the decline. The medical profession has just as often attacked soft drinks for a variety of medical reasons and it hasn't hurt their sales.

The dairy industry can think what it likes but I think people aren't drinking as much milk and cream as they used to because it doesn't taste as good. They've made factories out of cows and the milk tastes more as if it were manufactured than given.

Jersey cows living in a pasture give wonderfully rich, good-tasting milk. It's dessert all by itself. The Jersey cows are a minority in America, though, because they only produce three-quarters as much milk as Holstein cows do. The Holstein's milk is about half as good.

Dairy farmers no longer chase their cows into the barn to milk them twice a day. A lot of cows live like broiler-bound chickens, in a narrow stall for most of their lives. They're fed from a trough in front of them that is resupplied from a conveyor belt and they're artificially inseminated once a year so they have calves and keep producing milk. A cow doesn't have any fun at all anymore and her milk tastes that way. Dairy farmers work hard. It's a tough way to make a living but many of them have become part-time scientists and their dairies are laboratories.

Milk processors take the milk apart, do unnatural things to it and then put it back together so it's more like orange soda than what the cow intended for her calf when she produced it.

That's why so few people are drinking milk.

Milk Again

I occurs to me that I'm not finished talking about milk. There was a recent exhibition by an organization called Dairymen, Inc., that I saw and they were showing how they're producing milk they process at such high temperature that it can be stored for months anywhere without refrigeration. You could keep a bottle in the trunk of your car all summer.

If the world of the future is going to serve me milk that can be kept for a long time out of the icebox, I won't have a glass, thank you. Is this really what people want from science? I personally like ice cream that melts and milk that turns sour after a reasonable period of time.

The words "natural" and "organic" have been overused in advertising. That's because advertisers recognize that almost anything that comes to us direct from nature is better than something we've concocted with the help of man-made chemicals. They know we know it, too, so they pretend their product is "natural."

We were all propagandized to believe from infancy that milk was the perfect food and one reason for its perfection was, it was natural. Well, those days are gone forever. The average quart of milk today is about as natural as Gatorade or a thick shake at McDonald's.

Almost all the good, natural foods we have ruined, have been ruined because some giant corporation in the food business wanted a product that was easier to handle and had a longer shelf life in the stores. The farmers don't ruin it.

Tomatoes were ruined by the companies that didn't care much what a tomato tastes like as long as it could be picked by a machine or packed and shipped in a crate without being crushed.

Bread isn't any good in this country because the big bakers undercook it to keep the moisture content high. Water is heavy and by law a loaf of bread can be thirty-eight percent water. Water is cheaper than anything else they can put in bread and that mushy, wet feeling gives people the idea the bread is fresh. The average commercial loaf of bread will stay soft and mushy in its wrapper for months. That's as long as the super-pasteurized milk stays "fresh."

The soft feeling bakers build into their bread has nothing to do with freshness.

There are surprisingly good commercial ice creams on the market. The bad ones have too much air and too many stabilizers in them. These ingredients, along with preservatives, allow ice cream to be mistreated by truckers and kept longer by store managers. If the ice cream is good, they have to treat it carefully and sell it quickly. They don't like that.

I am infuriated every time I fly on an airplane and the flight attendant pours me coffee and asks if I want cream or sugar. I always say, "Yes, I'll have cream."

The flight attendant then hands me a little container of liquid white plastic called For Your Coffee or Coffee Lightener.

This new process that will enable the big dairies to produce milk that will keep for months without refrigeration is a giant step in the wrong direction. It serves nothing but the convenience of the distributors. It will be one more technological improvement that further hurts the hurting dairy farmer by making milk less attractive to drink.

VII:

OPINIONS

Driving

JUNE is the beginning of the time of year when Americans do the most driving. I often spend 20 hours a week in my car during the summer months. It seems like an awful lot of time now that I've written it down. If I sleep for 42 hours a week and drive for 20, that means I'm not doing much of anything for 62 of the 168 hours in a week. Maybe we better get a weekend place nearer home.

The trouble with driving is that you often do it in a state of agitation. I'm not usually very relaxed when I drive because I'm mad at the guy behind me or the woman in front of me or the truck that just cut me off. As soon as I do relax, I get sleepy. I'd rather be angry than sleepy when I'm driving. I'm not a very safe driver when I'm driving slowly to be safe. When I'm mad, I drive faster but at least I'm alert to everything that's going on. I'm trying to get that dirty so-and-so who cut in front of me.

It is my opinion that the slow drivers are a greater menace on the road than the ones driving at, or slightly above, the speed limit. The slow drivers sit there, slumped way down behind the wheel, smug in the knowledge that they are safe drivers but they're wrong. They're the ones who don't know how to move. They're the ones who can't get out of their own way. They cause the rest of us to pile into something to avoid them.

You can tell I'm just off the road because I'm writing in an agitated state. I just drove 150 miles from upstate New York to New York City and it was the kind of drive that makes you wonder whether the weekend was worth it.

I confess to being a competitive driver. I'm vaguely irritated when someone passes me, even when the other driver has a perfect right to do it. The chances are, though, that he doesn't have a legal right because I'm probably driving as fast as the law allows, or faster. What irritates me on a major highway is that there are some nuts who won't let you maintain a reasonable distance between your car and the car in front of you. If you do leave a sensible opening, someone comes along and cuts into it and then you have to drop four or five car lengths behind him. You're losing ground and it makes you mad. I think this is the cause of a lot of accidents. People

659

tailgate because they don't want anyone getting in between them and the car ahead. When there's a sudden stop or slowdown, it can be too late to brake to a stop before hitting the car you're following.

The single most annoying driving habit Americans have on and off the major highways is their practice of hitting the right turn signal just after they've started to turn right. By then, you *know* they're turning right. What you would have liked is some indication of their intentions a few hundred yards back. It would have helped you make plans. Why do so many drivers think it does any good to hit the turn signal after they've started their turn?

In city driving, the principal menace for the average driver is the panel truck. I don't know where they get the people who drive panel trucks. Every year there are a lot of race drivers who fail to qualify for the Indianapolis 500. Maybe they all take jobs driving panel trucks in cities. They're trying to make enough money to enter the Indy 500 again next year.

The average driver puts 10,000 miles on his car every year, according to Federal Highway Administration statistics. One statistic I'd like to see that no one has kept is, how much I've paid out in automobile insurance in the past twenty-five years and how much I've collected. We've owned two cars for most of that time and I guess we've paid out a total of more than $20,000. The insurance company didn't get the perfect driver when they got me but they haven't done badly. During that time I doubt if they've paid out $2,000, mostly in dents.

I had all my accidents when I was driving carefully.

Dear American Airlines

Dear American Airlines:

Please accept what I am going to tell you as friendly criticism. I could probably say it just as well about United, TWA, Pan Am, Delta or any of the others but I just flew into New York on the overnight from Los Angeles and you're fresh on my groggy mind.

When we landed your flight attendant, formerly stewardess, thanked us all for "flying American." I felt guilty accepting her thanks because I choose an airline, not for its name or from my past experience with it, but because it has a plane going where I have to get to at a time I want to go there. I'm as loyal to American over TWA as I am loyal to Hertz over Avis if the line is shorter at Avis. So don't go to a lot of trouble thanking me for "flying American." I don't do it as a favor to you.

I'm probably grumpier than usual because I've only been off your plane for three hours and I haven't had either a shower or any sleep. I got about half an hour's sleep on the four-hour flight. I would have gotten more but ten minutes after I dozed off, one of the flight attendants tapped me on the shoulder to ask if there was anything I wanted. All I wanted was sleep.

It was an hour later before I fell asleep again and this time I had fifteen minutes before the captain woke us all to say we were over the Grand Canyon. I've been down in the Grand Canyon on a mule but I'm not interested in being awakened from a sound sleep to be told I'm flying over it at three A.M. New York time. Does American Airlines own a piece of the canyon or something? Why are you always promoting it? Sure it's a nice canyon.

I've read where eleven major airlines lost a total of $330 million in the first nine months of this year. *You* think you're losing money because business is bad. *I* think business is bad because people are getting so they hate to fly. A flight used to be an experience we looked forward to. Now we're being treated like cattle and a lot of us dread traveling. There used to be a difference between a flight and a trip on a Greyhound bus.

You tell us to get to the airport an hour before flight time. Is this so you won't have to hire enough ticket agents to handle the crowd comfortably?

I'm always impressed with how hard your flight attendants work. You've trained them well and they're invariably courteous under trying conditions. They're often as mad at you as we are. We hear them grumble—not at us but at you. They know better than anyone that you're cutting down on space and service and they're the ones who face an irritated public and have to smile.

They don't seem to be making that announcement much any more . . . the one where they say, "If there's anything we can do to make your flight more enjoyable, please don't hesitate to call on us." That's good judgment on their part because the attendants are so overprogrammed with jobs they absolutely have to get done now that they have no time for any personal service whatsoever, even in first class. First class is not as good as economy was ten years ago.

To tell you the truth, you got off to a bad start with me last week in New York before I ever got to the airport. I bought my ticket on a Tuesday for a Saturday flight. Round-trip economy class cost

$377 each way, a total of $754. On Friday of that week you announced the new economy ticket one way was going to cost $99, beginning in about ten days. That's a difference of $556. What does it cost to fly me to Los Angeles and back? Doesn't what you charge bear any relationship to what it costs?

I hope you can accept this in the spirit in which it was intended, the spirit of a dissatisfied customer who just had a lousy trip from L.A.

We all like you, airlines. We just don't want to see you go the way of the railroads.

Sincerely,
Andrew A. Rooney

Pilots

PILOTS are the good guys. No one hates a pilot.

Pilots are the ones who know how to do it. They're successful. They're smart, skillful and daring but careful. There's a little of Charles Lindbergh and Eddie Rickenbacker in each of them.

Commercial airline pilots are getting it in the neck now and it's too bad. You hate to see it happen to the good guys even if they were asking for it. The airlines are in such trouble and the unions, including the pilots' union, the Air Line Pilots Association, pushed salaries and benefits so high and work hours so low that the hurting airlines can't afford them.

Do the pilots deserve it? A good friend of mine flew for a major airline for thirty years. He made good money, went everywhere and on top of it, it seemed to the rest of us that he was home all the time. For four or five days a month it was work, work, work but then he'd get two or three weeks off for good behavior. He's smart enough to run the airline. When he wasn't flying, how come he wasn't pitching in at the office instead of raking leaves?

With airline deregulation, it's become easy for someone with a relatively small amount of money to start an airline. Unfortunately for the great old-timers flying for the traditional airlines, there are a lot of young-timers who also know how to fly. The new airlines, with no union contracts, are hiring them to do twice the work for half the price.

I hope the new pilots fit my pilot image. One thing I never worry about when I get on an airplane is the pilot. I may complain about standing in line at the ticket counter and I may not like the food or the cramped seating but I have absolute faith that the pilot sitting up front, whom I've never seen, is faultless. He's tall, square-shouldered and he has a faint smile on his face but a glint of steel in his eyes.

Bill Casey was the first pilot who took my life in his hands and I've felt safe with pilots ever since. Casey lives somewhere in Florida now. I hope dark glasses haven't dimmed that glint of steel in his eyes.

He was the pilot of the B-17 Banshee that took off one February day in 1943 for the first U.S. bombing raid on Germany. I was a nervous reporter who went along, up front with the navigator and bombardier, and with far too good a view of everything that was coming at us, from the flak on the ground to the Luftwaffe Messerschmitts and Focke-Wulfs in the air.

When they shot off the plastic nose of the Banshee, the bombardier froze his hands trying to stuff his jacket in the gaping hole. The navigator, his oxygen hose pierced, collapsed unconscious on his little table. I was healthy but helpless until Casey called me on the intercom.

"Take your parachute off so you can get through here," he said. "Then take twenty deep breaths, take your mask off and get back here and pick up the emergency oxygen tank for those guys."

I did what he said. I got oxygen to the navigator, he regained consciousness, we got back from the battle and all lived happily ever after.

You can see why I defer to pilots.

Even the pilots with their own small planes at the little airfields all across the country are special people. They have some unique ability to do things right.

An airline pilot's life is a strange combination of exciting and dull. Pilots seem to have a great appetite for excitement and a high tolerance for dullness. These are characteristics you wouldn't think you'd find in one person.

Commercial airline pilots constantly experience the excitement of new places. They're charged with the life or death of a lot of people but there's very little interesting in what they do most of the time. The best and biggest of the new commercial airliners practically fly themselves. The pilot sits there in the sun, knowing he can't go back to the bathroom in the main cabin or people will know he's mortal.

I like to think of pilots as better than that. Pilots may be mortal but they're the kind of people I trust my life to.

Culture Shock

It's easy for a writer in America to make people laugh by poking fun at anything cultural, artistic or intellectual. It's easy because people think they ought to understand or appreciate those things but they often don't. When someone suggests it's all nonsense anyway, they laugh with relief. The other reason it's easy to have fun with art, culture and intellectuality is that there's so much fake art, pretentious culture and so many imitation intellectuals around.

Last evening, I sat in a box at the season's first performance by the New York Philharmonic Orchestra at Lincoln Center. Because I do not appreciate or understand the great bulk of the music they play, I am tempted to appeal to readers I know are out there for jokes about it.

I'm not going to do it though because I wish I liked good music better. I am respectful of people who do and consider them superior to myself because of it. I don't know what's wrong with me.

Rudolf Serkin was the soloist last night and he's one of the greatest pianists in the world. I appreciate his technical expertise. He hits those little keys, all so close together, without ever hitting the one next to the one he's after, by mistake. I don't understand what the composer is trying to do though. How did the composer know when he was finished? What does he mean by these sounds or doesn't he mean anything? Should they make me think? If so, of what?

A box at the Philharmonic sounds better than it is. Avery Fisher Hall is rectangular and the box seats are not angled toward the stage. They face directly across the hall so you're looking, not at the stage, but at the people in the boxes across the way. There was an attractive woman over there but that wasn't what I had been invited to see, so I craned my neck to look at the orchestra.

My neck was further craned by the fact that the steel railing was directly in my line of sight with the conductor.

Inevitably I started drawing comparisons to my box seat at the New York Giants football games. My seat there is on the ten-yard line but the action moves up and down the field so sometimes it's directly in front of me and the seat is so high that I never miss any of the action anyway. Last night, the box was way back where the side meets the balcony. It was the equivalent of a seat low in the end zone at Giants Stadium and the ball never moves downfield at the Philharmonic.

At Giants games, the reaction of the audience is spontaneous. We cheer when our team is good, boo when it's bad. There is no reason to think that the members of the Philharmonic are any better musicians than the Giants are athletes but there is a strict form to the protocol of applause at the Philharmonic. You don't just applaud when you feel like it. You applaud during gaps in the music which are approved for applause. You follow the people who know where those places are. If you applaud when you feel like it, you make a fool of yourself at the Philharmonic. You never boo, no matter how badly the musicians play.

Because I did not understand the phonic subtleties of a piece by Gustav Mahler, I sat there, staring at the attractive woman across the way, thinking nonmusical little thoughts:

—Could Louis Armstrong have played in the Philharmonic? Could that Philharmonic trumpet player stay with Benny Goodman?

—If the Philharmonic were broadcast like a sports event and Leonard Bernstein were in the announcing booth, would he point out errors the conductor was making?

—Is the worst piece of Beethoven's music better than the best popular song ever written?

All symphonies end with a musical cliché. There is a lot of loud noise that makes them all sound like the *1812 Overture*.

At the end, I stood when the others stood. They shouted "bravo" and I clapped but I didn't really make much noise doing it. I wanted them to think I was one of them but I wasn't.

Movies

It's beginning to look as though I'm going to miss seeing the Academy Award-winning movie again this year. In the last few years I've missed *The Deer Hunter*, *Kramer vs. Kramer*, *Gandhi* and *Terms of Endearment*.

When I was young, there was nothing I liked better than going to the movies on a Saturday afternoon when I should have been outdoors playing. It was always a double feature and we'd come out of the Madison Theater feeling all funny from having been cooped up in the dark for so long. All the kids I played with liked the movies even if they were bad. In those days I don't ever recall having any critical opinion. It was just "the movies."

I still like the movies but I don't see more than one or two a year now. It isn't television that keeps me in. It's that I like what I do around the house when I'm not doing anything more than I like going out to the movies. Going to a movie is a small event and I don't need another event in my life. I find life itself eventful enough. (You could say the same thing about reading this book.)

A second reason I don't go to many movies is that I'm never very impressed with movies that set out to be arty. They're filled with meaning that doesn't mean anything to me. I sense their depth but cannot fathom it.

Motion-picture makers, more than most artists, have consciously set out to make their product arty and that never produces much art. Art is a by-product of an honest and successful attempt to do something well.

I hope motion pictures prosper as an art form because the best of them are wonderfully good art. There's no reason not to rank motion pictures along with opera, literature, the stage, music or sculpture and painting as legitimate art. The fact that most movies are junk doesn't enter into it. Most art in any form is junk.

Nudity in the movies is a good example of fake art. Most producers have found it good box office in the past ten years to include some sexy nakedness but they almost always pretend it's art. I don't mind the nudity but I object to the pretense that it's art. As a matter of fact, sometimes it just doesn't last long enough. I've seen some very beautiful women take all or most of their clothes off in movies. They looked just fine and I didn't turn my head away but the movie lasted for two hours and they only had their clothes off for maybe thirty seconds and the rest of the movie was terrible.

I'm not interested in wasting an hour and fifty-nine minutes and five dollars just to see thirty seconds of nudity.

Movies are better than they were when I was growing up. I wish I liked them as much as I did then. The shortcoming is more mine than theirs. They're doing their part. Movies have an important, well-done, big-time air about them. Even the worst ones don't look as though they were done by amateur film makers.

They aren't making movies I want to see, though. When I go to the movies, I want to be entertained, not educated. I don't go to the movies to learn how terribly sad life can be for a married couple who hate each other and have two children. I've seen dozens of examples of that in real life and it doesn't amuse, divert or educate me.

Setting the Rules

THE relationship between government officials and reporters has sure deteriorated since the last time I covered a war. They no longer trust each other.

The press was all over President Reagan because no reporters or cameramen were allowed to go with the invasion troops to Grenada and tell Americans back home what was happening. Information about the invasion was controlled by our government and, as we all know, governments aren't famous for handing out information that makes them look bad.

Secretly is how governments we don't like always invade a country. The issue of whether it was right to invade Grenada is completely separate from whether or not reporters should have been included in the action.

Secretary of Defense Caspar Weinberger said they were only thinking of the safety of the news people. Baloney, Caspar, if I may call you by your first name. Reporters have risked their lives and died in every war we've ever fought and there are hundreds who would have jumped at the chance to do it again. Thanks for your concern but sacrificing truth for safety is a bad swap.

Dwight Eisenhower was setting the rules when I was first a war reporter. He's my idea of a great American, a great general, an okay President and a fine human being. I was thinking about how differently reporters were treated under his direction. I was covering the Eighth Air Force bombing raids over Germany then. The story of how reporters got word that there would be a raid the following morning so that they could get from London to one of the bomber bases to cover it would seem incredible now to any admiral, general or White House press secretary:

The other people living in the various buildings in London where the correspondents lived must have thought the newsmen were very strange people. We were always getting mysterious phone calls at three or four A.M. The voice of Colonel Jack Redding or Major Hal Leyshon at the other end of the phone at Eighth Air Force Headquarters would say, "We're having a little party tomorrow and hope you can come."

The metaphor might have varied but we all got the message. At least eight trusted news people knew hours in advance that there would be an air raid on Germany. This was heavy intelligence. It would have been of crucial importance to the Luftwaffe. Reporters were no less critical of government and the military then than they are now but no one questioned their loyalty to their country.

In many official statements about the censorship of information, there is the faint, faraway suggestion that government officials are doing what's best for the country while newspaper and television reporters are only interested in getting the story for commercial reasons. It's strange how difficult it is to convince some people that the whole story is what's best for the country. If President Reagan thinks he's more of an American than the columnists who question his judgment because he talks about patriotism a lot, he's wrong.

One of the most disappointing facts of life is how effective press censorship can be. It was shocking to see those pictures from Havana showing thousands of young Cubans marching in the streets supporting Castro's statements on Grenada. It had never been so clear before how effectively Cuban citizens have been propagandized into believing that Castro's form of communism is best for them. The same is true in the Soviet Union. Any American who thinks the average Soviet citizen doesn't support his government is kidding himself. Why wouldn't the average Russian think it's great? Through the government-controlled press and television he's never heard anything but good about it. Government censorship of the news works for the government in power. No wonder every government is tempted to use it.

Income Tax

By April fifteenth, we have all paid—or avoided paying—our federal income tax and it feels so good to have it over with that it doesn't hurt as much as it ought to. I made more money last year than I've ever made before but my taxes were the most I ever paid, too. To tell you the truth, I have a feeling I paid more than my share. I suppose a lot of people feel that. There must be others, though, who know darn well they didn't pay enough. They beat the system.

I have an idea how the IRS could get more money out of the tax cheaters and it wouldn't cost the government a nickel. They would make income tax records open to everyone. Once a year the amount we each paid in tax would be posted in the Town Hall or printed in the newspaper. At the very least, the figures would be readily available to anyone who wanted to look them up. This would be the way to get better compliance with the tax laws.

People who wouldn't cheat or steal anywhere else have no hesitation about cheating on their tax returns. If they think they can get away with it. Most of those same people wouldn't cheat at all if they knew their neighbors were going to see what they'd done. They don't mind cheating the big, anonymous bureaucracy but they wouldn't steal from their friends. The fact that cheating on their tax is the same as stealing from their friends doesn't occur to them.

The government goes about trying to get us to pay our taxes the wrong way. They need the review system and I suppose they have to scare some people with the threat of a jail sentence, but the IRS has never appealed much to our sense of national pride. Americans would be proud to pay their income tax if they thought their money was not being wasted in Washington. If everyone knew what everyone else was paying, it would make it easier to be proud, too. No one gets much of a kick out of being proud in front of a computer checking a return for errors in arithmetic.

I don't know why income tax returns are secret. They're considered nobody else's business even though what we earn isn't usually much of a secret to anyone who knows us or to anyone who wants to find out. We all have a pretty good idea how much our friends and our enemies are making. We may not be able to pin it down to the dollar but unless they've found some way to steal and are hiding the money under the mattress, our friends' salary ranges are apparent to us. If they're driving a Mercedes, they're making more than we are.

If we know how much our neighbors make, what's wrong with knowing how much tax they pay? It would be a way of applying a kind of strong peer pressure that the government could never apply. We'd all be embarrassed into paying our fair share. Very likely there would be people who'd pay *more* than they had to just to keep up with the Joneses.

More than half the income of the federal government comes from taxing the salaries of individuals. Most of that comes from money that is withheld from their paycheck. No one gets rich on a salary no matter how high it is, and no one can cheat much on his tax if it's withheld, either. I'd like to see the federal government concentrate their investigative efforts toward the people whose income is derived from sources other than salary. I'd like to be able to look at the tax books and find out how much the guy with the house with the four-car garage and the chauffeur-driven Cadillac is paying because if he's getting off easier than I am, I'm damn sore about it.

A Dumb Idea, Made in Ohio

You want to hear something really dumb?

The State of Ohio has put into effect a "Buy Ohio" law, saying that any state agency has to buy things made in Ohio, even if they cost more and aren't as good as the same things made someplace else.

By implication, the law suggests that the ordinary citizens of Ohio, as well as government agencies, ought to buy products made in their own state.

The governor of Ohio explained what he thought was the necessity for the law by saying, "We have a lot of unemployment."

This makes Ohio different? Every state has a lot of unemployment.

Minnesota has a comparable law. A lot of states do. What would happen if all forty-eight states enacted similar laws of their own? What if they simply decided to strike back? What effect, for example, would a nationwide "Don't Buy Ohio!" campaign have?

What if neighbors of Ohio like Michigan, West Virginia and Pennsylvania started driving around with "DON'T BUY OHIO" bumper stickers?

If this law works for Ohio, and the others, perhaps the idea will spread. If states put up trade barriers between themselves, why shouldn't towns, counties and cities? Why should Cleveland buy products made in Akron when Cleveland has so many unemployed itself?

If that works, Berea, a relatively poor section of the Cleveland area, might start refusing to do business with Shaker Heights, a wealthy section.

Carried to its logical conclusion, this kind of economic isolation that Ohio is practicing could even spread into the home. This could be the salvation of America. If each one of us refused to do business with neighbors or anyone else, we'd all have to learn how to do things for ourselves to stay alive. We could become self-sufficient individuals again, building our own homes, growing our own food and making by hand the things we need in order to keep from doing business with anyone else. It could save the nation.

Short of that, there's nothing good about Ohio's plan to make it on its own. By asking the people of Ohio to be loyal to their state, legislators are asking them to be disloyal to the rest of the country. It's easier to be loyal to something small than something big. It's easier to be loyal to your family, your school or your town than it is to be loyal to the whole world or to the whole country. Loyalty, in the form of patriotism, has produced some good things, but it is basically an unthinking human reaction.

Under the patriotic stimulus of loyalty to the United States during World War II, this country produced better than at any time in its whole history. The only trouble with taking any pleasure from that is, Nazi loyalty to Adolf Hitler was the identical attribute. It produced the same extraordinary results, though. The fact that the effort was on behalf of evil doesn't bear on the quality of loyalty.

Loyalty to a country, a team, a family, a city, a school, without any question, isn't always good. Is it sadder that there are people in Ohio who don't have enough to eat because they aren't working than it is that there are hungry and unemployed people in New Jersey?

If our economy is going to be managed by our government, as it appears it has to be, it ought to be managed as a whole. It has to be done by the federal government, unpopular as that so often is. The economy can't be managed in little pieces, even pieces as big as Ohio.

There are good ways a government can use the enthusiasm of its citizens for their country, their state or their city, but "Buy Ohio" isn't one of them.

Revolutions

IT always amazed me that my mother lived from before the time we had automobiles until long after we had sent a spaceship to the moon. That's some life-span.

From day to day, though, progress seems slow and often we don't notice what's happening around us. I realize now that I've lived through half a dozen major social or mechanical revolutions that I didn't see occurring at the time.

When I was very young and unable to understand what it was all about, Franklin Roosevelt was changing the whole way we took care of ourselves in this country. It was one of the most important things that ever happened here and I was oblivious to it. All I knew was that the few rich friends my parents had, hated Roosevelt. All their poor friends loved him. I didn't understand why.

At about the same time my father bought his first Atwater Kent radio. He used to sit in front of it nights and get stations like KDKA, Pittsburgh. A few years later the whole family sat in the living room listening to Ed Wynn, Eddie Cantor or "Myrt and Marge," the "Dallas" of its day.

I was about ten and I accepted the radio the same way I accepted running water in the house. I didn't realize it was new magic. I didn't realize I'd been in on a revolution, the beginning of radio.

Radio broke the ground for television and because we already had sound coming to us out of nowhere through the air, I was too dumb in 1949 to be amazed when they started sending us pictures, too. All I wanted to know was who was fighting.

In retrospect it makes me mad to think of all the big changes I watched happen and didn't notice. I went through World War II with a front-seat view of it and I knew how exciting it was but I was oblivious to the fact that I was watching history being made.

I'm trying to be more alert to events now. I'm trying to notice what's happening right before me and maintain some awareness of what the event will look like in a history book. There are about five things I have my eye on. Not necessarily in order of their importance, they are:

1—The Reagan Administration's dismantling of the system of government Roosevelt started. The bureaucracy grew for almost fifty years before Reagan started taking it apart. For better or for worse, it was a turning point in history.

2—The tendency of bright young men and women to marry later, if at all, and to have fewer children, if any, is the most important hidden revolution of our time. It could have a profound effect on the makeup of the human race.

3—The dramatic rise in quality of products made in Japan. The Japanese first took the camera business away from the Germans and then ended the worldwide dominance of the United States as the maker of automobiles. When Roosevelt was President, the phrase "Made in Japan" printed on anything, meant "cheap and poorly made." America's reputation for hard work and excellence has declined in proportion to Japan's progress.

4—The gradual intrusion into broadcast television of the cable networks and smaller, local broadcasters. We may find, in ten or twenty years, that we're looking back at the good old days when ABC, CBS and NBC had a virtual monopoly on the mass market and were therefore able to attract advertisers who could pay for expensive news coverage and elaborate dramatic productions. If it happens, it will be the reverse of what happened in the 1930s and 1940s when big supermarket chains took over small, independent grocery stores.

5—Money seems to be disappearing and I suspect the time isn't far off when cash won't be used except for small purchases. The computers will take the place of our pocketbooks and money will be transferred directly from my account to yours without anything material ever having changed hands between us. If someone wants to steal from us, he won't hit us over the head, he'll simply hit a few keys on the computer.

Twenty years from now I don't want to look back and say I didn't realize these things were happening.

The Generation War

Iт seems likely that young people will be at war with old people in another fifteen or twenty years. You can see it coming in the numbers. In 1900 only one percent of the population was older than seventy-five years old and in a few years it's going to be five percent ... 13 million people.

The trouble with being seventy-five years old, if you aren't rich, is that with inflation, everyone working keeps getting more and more dollars for what they do but the dollars you've saved stay the same and are worth less. You have less money and, sooner or later, you'll need more medical care.

We try to be nice to old people in this country but very often self-interest wins out over compassion. If the Social Security system breaks down—and it appears as though it might—the old will have to depend on the young to support them. I'm not talking about a son or daughter taking care of a mother or father. The young are not only going to have to do something for their own parents and grandparents but for everyone else's, too. Do you think young working people in twenty years will stand for a tax on their income that goes to support the elderly? Will they be willing to go without something for themselves in order to provide for a whole generation of the old? I think they'll rebel against it and it'll be war.

There's always plenty of evidence of friction between ages. For example, when there is a vote in any community on an issue involving schools, the lines are drawn along age boundaries. The old people who already have their education and whose children also have theirs, don't want to raise taxes to pay for better wages for teachers or a new wing for the school. The young people with children are in favor of better schools.

If war comes between youth and age, I'm not sure who'll win. You'd think it would be youth but age has a lot of power. Because of age's growing numbers and the degree to which it is united because it shares this one problem, it will elect a lot of people to government office. It will have a lot of influence in Congress.

On the other hand, older people don't have much influence on day-to-day affairs unless they have a lot of money. As soon as someone leaves a job at a company, he becomes powerless because no one's afraid of him any longer. To be powerful, you have to scare people. No one fears the elderly because they don't control jobs or anyone's destiny.

When the young see the old no longer doing what they did best in their lives, it's difficult for the young to believe they ever did anything very well. We always tend to think that even the best brains of the centuries past are inferior to our own. You can't believe the doddering old man of ninety ever ran a race or that the wrinkled, gray and bent woman of ninety was ever a beauty. The young sometimes honor the old but in their hearts they feel superior to them. The old hate the young for it and that's why the war will begin.

Prejudice toward age, any age, changes with birthdays. The ten-year-old feels vastly superior to the four-year-old but at about age thirty it becomes apparent that the eighteen- and twenty-year-olds can do things you can't. Having lost the feeling of superiority you used to have over the young, you look elsewhere for it.

By the time people are forty, they no longer feel at all physically superior to anyone twenty so they satisfy themselves feeling superior to those fifty. This continues for life. When my mother was eighty, she spoke in disparaging terms of several women who were still playing bridge at ninety. When my mother turned ninety she was convinced her bridge was as good as ever.

I hope I'm wrong about the war between generations that could be fought over money. I like both the young and the old and I wouldn't want anything like a war to come between them.

Executions

THERE's an argument going on all across the country about the best way to kill a person. Even states that have decided on capital punishment can't decide how a prisoner should be put to death.

There are thirty-seven states that have the death penalty now. Eighteen have approved the electric chair as the nicest way to kill a murderer, nine gas them to death, four give them lethal injections, four hang them by the neck from a rope and Idaho shoots them. The Governor of New Jersey says he's leaning toward the intravenous death method because it's the most humane.

I have such a vindictive streak in me that I am surprised to find myself in opposition to the death penalty. Some days getting back at someone is the most fun I have and yet I do not approve of society putting anyone to death. Most of the people in the United States who do approve think of themselves as Christians. I wonder whether Jesus Christ would have voted for or against the death penalty. I should think the people who worship Christ would suspect that he'd be against it.

Those of you who approve of the death penalty might be able to give New Jersey some advice on what you think the best way is to execute someone. It's one of the states that can't decide. Everyone is always looking for the most humane method but if you are among the people who think the death penalty is a deterrent to crime, putting someone to death in the most humane manner isn't the best way to get what you're after. If you want to scare criminals off murder, maybe you'd want to consider a law that would call for torturing them to death.

How about burying them in sand up to their chins and leaving them out in the hot sun? I've read where they do it that way in some Middle Eastern countries. That would sure deter any would-be murderer who can't take the heat, I should think.

Another thing you should consider as a deterrent is the firing squad. It's dramatic, it's long drawn out and if you also made it mandatory for the television networks to show it on the evening news, everyone would watch and think twice or perhaps even three or four times before murdering anyone.

I wouldn't want to be in the state legislature if I had to decide which was the best way of executing someone. When I was eight I was playing marbles with Buddy Duffey and he asked me if I had to kill either my mother or my father, which would I? I remember I refused to try and decide that and I feel the same way now about the death penalty. Being against the whole thing, I don't have to decide which method of execution is best.

My objection to the death penalty doesn't come out of any sympathy I have for the murderers. What I object to is making a murderer of anyone else. My objection could be eliminated, of course, by a simple addition to the capital punishment laws. Have the executions carried out by other people on death row who are already murderers. Make them strap the victims in the electric chair and throw the switch. If death is to come by hanging, make them slip the noose over the victim's head and drop him through the trapdoor.

To make capital punishment a real deterrent, there are a lot of things that should be done differently. Why give a murderer the "last meal"? Traditionally the person about to die can have what he wants as his last meal. Suddenly we're being nice to this guy? And should a doctor be present? Why the minister or priest? A doctor is a saver of life. Does the clergyman ask God's forgiveness for the murderer? Does God give it? If God forgives him, who are people to take his life?

The Dead Land

IT is difficult to understand how people who talk as much about being religious and about loving their country as Americans do, can so consistently spoil what they've been blessed with. Too many of us throw the debris from a McDonald's Quarter Pounder out the car window. Too many young people throw their Coke or beer bottles on someone else's lawn as they drive by Saturday night and too many major American industries dig up the good things out of the earth, spit out what they can't use and produce poisonous waste by-products that are eventually going to kill the land and then us.

> "This is the way the world ends
> Not with a bang but a whimper."

T.S. Eliot wrote that in a poem called "The Hollow Men" fifty years ago and it was sadly prophetic. While the leaders of government everywhere are worrying about the Big Bomb, mankind everywhere is poisoning the ground and the waters we depend on for life.

I drive alongside the East River down the edge of the island of Manhattan on my way to work most mornings. The garbage barges are loaded high with all the sophisticated debris the twentieth century produces in such abundance. The barges will shortly be towed out into the Atlantic Ocean and dumped. And again tomorrow and tomorrow and tomorrow. It's a big ocean but we will certainly someday have ruined its clear, briny beauty with garbage.

How can anyone who professes to love this country or even the earth and life itself, *not* be an environmentalist? Maybe we need a better word than that. How can a businessman or a government official think and say that there is such a thing as environmental "extremism"? We are going to die or the inhabitants of the earth in future generations are going to die because the land and the water are all poisoned. Is anything more certain than that? Do we ignore it because for us today it is only a few people living near the Love Canal or in the dioxin-contaminated town of Times Beach, Missouri?

I don't think you blame Big Business for having dumped toxic wastes. Big Business wasn't malicious. It didn't set out with the intention of killing anyone. Big Business was just selfish and stupid, that's all. Big Business is just like the kid who throws the beer can out the car window. "What difference does one more make?" "This place is a mess anyway." He's not a bad kid.

Americans have taken most of their money out of the savings banks. They're spending it to live now and let the future take care of itself. That's what all of us everywhere are doing with the earth. We're using it up for ourselves with no thought of the future. Does anyone think oil prices are going to keep going down the next ten years? The next fifty years? There won't be any oil in one hundred years but you'd never believe it if you were from another planet watching what the people on earth are doing with what oil they have left. Those Arabs giving gold watches and hundred-dollar bills as tips to the help in the London hotels where they're staying, will have nothing but sand in abundance within the lifetime of almost all of us.

It's strange that the word "conservative" is so often applied to people who don't believe in conserving anything but money. Their environmental philosophy is consistent with their economic beliefs. They honestly believe that everything works out for the best if you let everyone get all they can for themselves. They believe this is what produces the most for all of us.

Whatever else it produces, it sure produces a lot of garbage.

VIII:

SEASONS

The Fourth of July

T HE Fourth of July is the second-best holiday. Christmas is first, hands down, but the Fourth is way ahead of anything else. After them come Thanksgiving, New Year's Day, Labor Day, Memorial Day, Washington's Birthday, Easter and the late starter, Columbus Day. I hope no one will be offended if I put Martin Luther King Day last.

Christmas is heavy with tradition and sentiment. It's a joyous time but it's often sad, too. You get thinking at Christmas so it has more depth. The Fourth is a mindless holiday. We celebrate our independence and we mean it and appreciate it but mostly July Fourth is a time to go out and have a good time.

The Fourth is nothing *but* relaxing. You don't have to give presents, you don't have to send cards, you don't have to do anything if you don't want to.

I remember the Fourth with great fondness because I'm old enough to have been a kid when it was legal to buy real fireworks. Just offhand, I don't recall ever having had more fun in my life than I had setting off fireworks. I know they're dangerous and I'd have been awfully nervous if my own children had shot them off but some of the best money my father ever spent giving me a good time was on the two dollars he put out every year on a bag of fireworks. Watching the professionals set off a display of rockets from the park or the town mall is fun but it doesn't compare with having a few four-inchers of your own.

July Fourth is the beginning of the serious goof-off time in America. The people who take their vacations in August don't break their backs working in July, either.

Along about Thursdays at noon at this time of year, people are beginning to say, "Have a nice weekend" to me. These are the same people who see me in the elevator Tuesday morning and say, "How was your weekend?"

There's no doubt about it, it takes the week longer to end in July. People who have never been sick a day in their lives often don't feel too good on Fridays in July so they don't come to work. Whatever they have lasts until Monday noon, when they show up again for work with a sunburn.

I haven't checked recently but I've been wondering what the statistics are in Detroit these days when it comes to auto workers calling in sick. It used to amount to as much as twenty percent of the work force in summer and again in the fall when thousands of suddenly sick auto workers went hunting in upper Michigan.

I don't want to be negative about long weekends. They're nice if the economy can afford them. Most companies give their workers long vacations now in addition to ten "sick" days. Calling in sick is standard procedure in many businesses and you can understand it. We all have personal problems to take care of. You certainly can't handle any personal business problem on Saturday or Sunday, so if you have personal business to conduct, there's not much to do but call in and lie by saying you're sick. There are good companies that recognize this and allow several "personal" days every year. I like that better than "sick" days. Sick days should be reserved for the days when you're sick and if you aren't sick, you shouldn't have to say you are.

The Japanese are using robots in their factories now and we have some in this country. Robots do the work that assembly-line workers used to do and I suppose the time will come in another hundred years when the robots will be getting five weeks' vacation plus ten sick days a year. Their union, the URW, the United Robot Workers, will insist on it.

The actual "Fourth" is inconvenient when it falls on a Sunday. Because that's a normal day off, we compensate for it by taking Monday. You can't plan on transacting any important business on Friday, either. Office phones don't answer.

The people I feel sorriest for on these long summer weekends are not the employers. They know where their next million is coming from. I feel sorry for people looking for work in July. How can you look for work if there's no one in at the place you go to, to look for work?

Summer—First the Good News

THERE are good things and bad things about summer and you can just about divide them in half. I've made a list.

GOOD THINGS ABOUT SUMMER: It's nice and warm.

BAD THINGS ABOUT SUMMER: It's too hot.

GOOD: If you're working, there aren't many people around the office. The boss is usually away and it's relaxing.

BAD: If you're working, there's no one around to make decisions and you can't get anything done.

GOOD: Packing up, going away and leaving all your problems behind at the office.

BAD: Having the nervous feeling while you're on vacation that you're missing something important back at work. Someone's getting ahead of you.

GOOD: Having a drink in the backyard in the evening.

BAD: Mosquitoes.

GOOD: Corn on the cob and real, ripe, red tomatoes.

BAD: Disappointingly hard peaches and tasteless melons.

GOOD: A swim in water that feels too cold when you first get in and so good after you've been in awhile that you don't want to get out.

BAD: So many people at the lake or the beach that going in the water is no fun.

GOOD: Waking up on vacation and realizing you don't have to go to work.

BAD: Waking up on vacation and realizing you only have four days of vacation left.

GOOD: Visiting places you've always wanted to go to.

BAD: Driving forever to get someplace you didn't want to go to anyway.

GOOD: An air-conditioned car on a hot day.

BAD: Getting into a car that's been closed up and parked in the sun.

GOOD: Being out in the sun and getting a tan that makes you look great.

BAD: The nervous feeling you ought not be out in the sun so much because it's bad for your skin and will make you look old sooner.

GOOD: The long hours of sunlight in July.

BAD: The realization in August that the days are getting shorter and it'll be all downhill from now on.

GOOD: Friends you don't see any other time of year.

BAD: People you can't avoid because everything's so open in summer.

GOOD: The satisfying feeling mowing the lawn can give you.

BAD: Realizing the grass is so long you have to mow it even though you don't feel like mowing the lawn today.

GOOD: Going someplace on vacation that's a complete change from home.

BAD: Leaving a perfectly good, comfortable home to stay at some resort that's too expensive and not as pleasant as what you left behind.

GOOD: An old pair of sneaks, a short-sleeve cotton shirt and cool khaki slacks.

BAD: Having to wear a hot suit and tie to work because that's how people dress at work.

GOOD: Not having to drive to work in heavy traffic during your vacation.

BAD: Leaving for a weekend in heavy traffic Friday afternoon and coming home in it Sunday evening.

GOOD: The peace and quiet and comforting sounds of crickets, bull-frogs and birds in the morning.

BAD: The blare of rock music from some kid's car radio as he drives past with his windows open and the noise of your neighbor's lawn-mower.

GOOD: Cooking outdoors. It can make tough meat taste good.

BAD: Cooking outdoors. It can make good meat taste tough.

GOOD: No snow.

BAD: No snow.

August

THE last two weeks of August are the dregs of the fifty-two weeks of the year. If we ever have to drop two weeks out of the year, we should drop these.

Everything about the end of August is depressing. There's that foreboding of the death of a season in the air. There are reminders all around us that this is the end of something good and none of us likes to see a good thing end.

From the middle of August on, the threat of Labor Day looms big in our minds. We know it's coming. We count the days. The summer is dwindling down to nothing. The grass is turning brown and the plants and flowers are just holding on. They are no longer blooming. Blooming suggests robust good health and flowers are no longer like that.

The little streams and creeks that are so attractive when they're running their merry way downhill are all but dried up at this time of year and the rocks in the bottom of the stream bed that like to be covered with water are baking in the hot sun. They're nowhere near as attractive as they are when magnified by a foot of water running over them.

There is no other time of year when we all become so aware of how quickly time passes and how soon the seasons go. At New Year's we cover the passing of time with the false gaiety of New Year's Eve but at the end of August with school and work and winter facing us, we can't hide from the fact that it's the definite end to another time of our lives. It is not a question of age. I have had this very same feeling about the end of August since I was eight years old.

"Never return in August to what you love."

That's a line from a poem by Bernice Kenyon. I often think of it when I go back to that place where I spent my summers as a kid. It's almost too sad to contemplate those times I had back then. August is such a sad time for remembering past good times and friends long gone out of your life. Funny thing is, I go back there in July sometimes and never feel depressed at all.

It's tough on all of us, though. Getting up in the morning is even harder. During June and July the sun shines in the bedroom window and you can jump out of bed with some enthusiasm for life. In August we begin to drag a little. It's been hot for too long. It's a little darker out because the sun isn't really up yet and we're more apt to lie in bed thinking bad thoughts or turn over and go back to sleep after the clock radio goes off. The birds aren't chirping the way they were earlier in the summer and all of nature seems to be tired. The birds have all found mates. They've made their nests, hatched their eggs and flown the coop. The plants and the birds and the bees and the bugs all know Labor Day's coming too and they don't like the prospects either. They have no more enthusiasm for the waning days of summer than I do.

The trouble with the last two weeks of August may be that we've gotten in the habit of looking ahead too much instead of enjoying what we've got at the moment. The end of August would be okay if we didn't keep thinking about summer being almost over but everything reminds us of its imminent ending. The stores are having half-off sales and the advertisements in the papers are for fall clothes. It's too hot for football but they're playing it and reminding us of fall. The economic news is all about "after Labor Day." How can we ignore the fact that summer is almost over? It's all this looking ahead that makes the last weeks of August so depressing.

It's not August's fault, it's our own.

Cannibals and Nuns

W<small>ELL</small>, finally. It's over. I don't have to anticipate its ending with dread any longer. It's been just one damn summer weekend after another. If summer had lasted another month I might have died from all that relaxation.

I can stand a little vacation but things are getting ridiculous. Our vacation period in America lasts from Memorial Day at the end of May until the Tuesday after Labor Day in September now.

Don't tell me you only get three weeks. That's just your *real* vacation. I'm talking about all the days off and long weekends we all take in addition to our vacation.

It hardly matters any more which three weeks or months anyone takes off. You can't find them at work when they aren't on vacation in the summer either.

The necessity of having fun in the summer is one of the most tiring things of the whole year for me. My idea of a good restful week is to get up at the same time every morning, eat breakfast with the newspaper, go to work, work, come home tired, have dinner, read, watch television and go to bed by eleven. That's what I call relaxing.

The tiring part of a vacation is planning to go somewhere, getting ready to go there, getting everyone else organized to go there and then getting there. Just as soon as you get there, you have to start planning how to get back.

I'll bet I could add ten years to my life if I didn't have to take all these summer vacations. When I'm on vacation I don't get enough sleep, I worry because I spend too much money, I do too much driving, I eat too much and drink too much. Sometimes it's two weeks after I return from a vacation or a long weekend before I feel rested again.

There used to be a game we played when I was a kid called Missionaries and Cannibals. I forget the exact rules but the situation was this:

There are three missionaries or nuns on one side of the river and two cannibals on the other. There is only one canoe and you can only carry two people in the canoe at one time. You have to get the three nuns to one side of the river and the two cannibals to the other without ever having a cannibal and a nun in the canoe together.

I'm always reminded of that game by the family logistics of a summer weekend. My wife and I go to a country house we have and often several of our children join us there. They come from different places at different times using different modes of transportation.

The problems are always these:

"What time can you leave?"

"Do you want to go with us or should Emily wait and pick you up?"

"If they're driving from Boston they can meet you at the railroad station when you come in from New York."

My wife leaves from home in her car and I leave from the office in mine. The operation is complicated by the fact that our home is an hour from my office but my office and our home are equal distances from the summer house. Every weekend we have a problem getting the nuns across the river without being eaten by the cannibals.

There are so many things about the summer that are tiring. Someone's always suggesting a picnic, for example. You have a nice house with a table to eat from and chairs to sit on and an icebox to go to, but people aren't satisfied in the summer unless they're breaking their backs having a good time. They want to rough it and go on a picnic. What you do is, you put all the food except what you forget in a basket and take it somewhere uncomfortable. Then you sit on the ground or perhaps on a hard rock and share lunch with an ant.

It feels great to have Labor Day over with. I've only been back to work a couple of days now but already I'm beginning to feel relaxed and rested.

The Best Snowstorm of the Decade

W HEN you read about a terrible storm in some other part of the country, you feel a little smug. You feel sorry for people you see on television being flooded out or blown away but you also feel superior to them. At least you were smart enough not to live in a house that could be washed away by the sea or floated downstream by a river.

Last weekend it was our turn in the Northeast to be shown to the rest of the country because of twenty inches of snow we got. Businesses shut down, roads were closed, cars abandoned on highways and the government in Washington was brought to a standstill by Friday noon. It couldn't happen to a nicer government.

Meteorologists were calling it "one of the worst snowstorms of the decade." That's what they usually call snowstorms.

Well, if you live someplace else and got any satisfaction from thinking we were having it bad, I don't want to take it away from you but I thought it was the *best* snowstorm of the decade. I loved every minute of it. Let me tell you about it.

The storm moved up the coast from Virginia and hit New York and Connecticut Friday night after most people were home from work. We had dinner and watched Robert Mitchum fight World War II for a while but I kept getting up to check the snowfall against the streetlight on the corner. It was still coming. There were none of those big, feathery, infrequent flakes that portend the end of a snow. These were those serious little ones in a hurry to get to the ground.

We live in Connecticut and by midafternoon the state weather bureau had called off the snowstorm warning it had issued earlier. That was a good sign. We all know how weather predicting has been going this year.

When I finally got up and turned off the television set—I know how World War II comes out—there was the kind of absolute silence I've only heard a few times in my life. (You do hear silence.) No car lights flashed from the street into our windows and if there were any sounds from the highway a mile away, they were muffled by a billion trillion of those magic, fluffy white geometric wonders piled ten inches deep now, outside our door. All the people who usually have to go someplace in their cars in the middle of the night, suddenly didn't have to go anyplace. Nothing moved except the snowflakes.

In the morning I went into the bathroom and looked out the window through the plants on the window shelves. The telephone wires leading into the house had three inches of snow balanced in a precarious parabola on them. Down below, the backyard looked perfect. If I ever wanted to sell the house, I'd have it look that way for a prospective buyer. Every flaw was hidden . . . the crabgrass, the old boards I'd left by the driveway, the bare spots . . . all were painted over with snow.

We had breakfast at the kitchen table looking out the window on the backyard. We had orange juice, good coffee, homemade bread toasted, with peach jam and black currant jelly. It was the same breakfast we have every Saturday but it never tasted so good.

After breakfast I pulled on my boots, put on a heavy wool shirt, a down vest and my good leather gloves. I couldn't find my old ones. I waxed the aluminum snow shovel with something I'd used on the car (I was very pleased with myself over this because the snow slid off it so quickly). My wife didn't like her shovel but you can't worry about someone else's tools.

By 5:30 we were dog-tired. We had a drink, broiled chicken, rice and broccoli. After a nap in the living room I fell into bed by nine P.M.

Every day in my life should be so satisfying and trouble-free as the day "one of the worst storms of the decade" hit us.

'Tis the Season to Be Worried

It's still early to start worrying about Christmas presents but this is the time I start to worry about them. I worry from now until somewhere around the twentieth of December before I buy anything.

First I make a list of the people I want to give presents to. There are twelve this year. Margie buys the one for my sister so that leaves me with eleven. I buy more than one for several people on my list though, so it's a lot of purchases, a lot of boxes. I take Christmas seriously.

Let me talk to you about seven categories of Christmas presents:

Jewelry—Some of the people on my list like it but it makes me nervous to buy. If it's junk jewelry with no real value except for decoration, it has to strike the person you buy it for just right. I don't think you can predict what kind of jewelry a woman will like. Real jewelry is nice to own but if it's really real, it costs more than I spend. I don't know who has money enough to buy rubies, diamonds, emeralds and pearls. I have had some success with small gold or silver jewelry.

Books—People like to get books. A book is a flattering present and so expensive now that people don't often buy them for themselves. A book suited to the person is a perfect present. In past years members of my family have given me a lot of woodworking books and I love getting them. Anyone with a hobby likes getting a good book devoted to it.

Perfume—I don't know a woman to whom I'd give perfume. I don't know a man I would either, for that matter. I remember giving perfume years ago but I guess I've changed. I don't like perfume on a woman any better than I like sitting next to a man who is smoking a cigar in a restaurant.

Cameras and electronics—I'm mildly embarrassed to tell you that in the years I've had money to spend, I've spent more of it on these things than anything else. I've given cameras, lenses, tape recorders, television sets and assorted electronic gadgets. There's no doubt what the biggest mistake in gift giving is. We always give the things we like ourselves rather than giving much consideration to what the gift getter would like. I suppose I've got to see if there's a computer I can afford to give anyone this year.

Toys—Ever since the kids passed the age of seventeen, I've been out of the toy market. I've looked in the windows of several toy stores and I don't know what I'm going to do when I have toy-age grandchildren. So many of the toys today look like junk I'd hate to waste my money on them.

Clothes—I consider my wife and my three daughters good-looking and I always think of them in some of the good-looking clothes I see in stores. The family is reluctant to hurt my feelings so they usually say the clothes I've bought them don't fit but I suspect they take them back because they don't like what I picked out. I don't know why I think I can do it. I don't recall ever getting a piece of clothing as a gift that *I* liked. As a kid, I was always disappointed to open a package and find clothes. The last thing a kid wants for Christmas is something practical.

Cooking utensils or food—These are dependable fall-back gifts when you can't think of anything else. Over the years friends have sent us oranges and grapefruit, nuts or cheese from those specialty catalogues and those items are always good to get. You have to think of those things in advance though, so I don't give fruit or nuts from catalogues. I almost always find a pot, a pan, a knife or an electric kitchen gadget to give.

As a general rule, I buy books in bookstores, hardware in hardware stores, jewelry in jewelry stores. I also buy presents from big, dependable, non-cutrate department stores. I know I don't get any bargains from the department stores but I don't get cheated, either.

Christmas Shopping

J IM hates buying anything," Ruth said when the four of us were having dinner a few weeks ago.

Jim was sitting right there and he didn't deny it, so I assumed it was true.

Ruth wasn't suggesting Jim was cheap—although Jim may be a

little cheap. She was simply saying that he doesn't like the whole process of buying something.

I do. I like buying things. It's a flaw in my character.

This Christmas I've really been buying things and it hasn't always been a wonderful experience.

Stores are incredibly different from what they were a relatively short time ago. You used to go into a store, ask the clerk for what you wanted and he or she would get it down off a shelf for you.

I wasn't talking about grocery stores when I started this but grocery stores are the most dramatic examples of change. When I was little, my mother would often send me to the grocery store. I'd stand in front of the counter, looking up at Mr. Evans, and tell him what I wanted. He'd get it off the shelf behind him, put it in a bag on the counter and hand it to me.

People never touched anything in a grocery store. If someone else came in while Mr. Evans was getting my order, they waited until he was finished.

That's the way most stores operated. It didn't matter whether they were selling clothes, hardware or candy. Everything was behind the counter and the customers didn't mingle with the merchandise.

You were waited on.

These days, and especially at this time of year, you're lucky if you can find someone in a store to take your money. It must lead to some shoplifting by people who didn't go there intending to steal.

There are at least a dozen truly great department stores in the United States and I like to do business with them. I hesitate to mention them for fear of missing some but you know which they are. In New York City, Bloomingdale's is one. It's a trend-setter among stores. Even though I don't always like the trends it sets, I love the store and often go there.

If Bloomingdale's charged admission, I'd go there just to look. There are hundreds of theaters I've paid to get into that weren't as good shows as Bloomingdale's is any day of the week.

At this time of year, I still go there but I don't always buy something. I would if I could but there's a limited amount of time I'm willing to spend finding a salesperson to push my money on and I don't have infinite patience with the store's paperwork. There are a lot of security people Bloomingdale's has hired to keep shoplifting down and it leads to a lot of protective pieces of paper.

The day is gone when you can get what you want, put the money down and leave. Sometimes it must cost the store more for the clerk's time in wages than the item itself costs.

Today I went to a store that is not one of the great ones. You'd know it. I was after a toolbox to give as a gift. In the hardware area I saw a huge sign over one with ten drawers.

"SAVE $100! REGULARLY $199. TODAY ONLY $99."

It was, typically for the store, an adequate but not first-class piece of merchandise. When I collared a clerk, I said quickly, so he wouldn't leave, "I'll take one of these."

"We'll have to see if we have one," he said.

"What do you mean 'See if we have one'?" I said. "If you don't have one in stock, I'll take this one."

"We can't sell the floor sample," he said.

"Well, you can't advertise it for sale either, then," I said, noticing that my voice was rising.

Christmas shopping hasn't been easy for any of us this year. The only thing worse than not being able to get anyone to wait on you at Christmas is having the clerks all over you at other times of the year when they aren't busy.

"Can I show you something?" they ask. Ten feet further along the aisle, the next clerk says, "May we help you?"

Sometimes I can understand why Jim feels the way he does about shopping.

No Room at the Inn

MAKING room for things in a house is never easy, but at Christmas it becomes even more difficult.

The other day I came in with some packages and looked for an easy place to put them down. There was none and I realized that even the telephone book takes up more space than it ought to. If it had a stiff cover, you could stand it up and there'd be more room on the telephone table.

When I look around the house and think about the problem, it becomes apparent to me that a lot of household items take up too much room.

The chief offender and probably the worst space hog is the vacuum cleaner. I could hide six Christmas presents in the space the vacuum cleaner takes up.

The importance of the vacuum cleaner has been exaggerated in America. A lot of people use it more from nervous habit than because anything needs vacuuming. The vacuum makes so much noise it gives them the feeling they're doing something important. It certainly takes up more space than it's worth. It doesn't take it up in a nice way, either.

The vacuum cleaner is clumsy and impossible to store in a tidy way. It comes with a lot of little attachments you don't want and several lengths of hose you don't need. You can't pack it away, so you just have to shove it in a closet where it occupies valuable space all its life.

What the world needs is a folding vacuum cleaner that fits into a shoebox.

The second biggest space hog in the average house is the chair, often antique, that no one sits on. They don't sit on it because they know that if they do, it will break. They also know it's uncomfortable.

I like to hide small Christmas presents under some things in my dresser drawers. The problem there is shirts. I have about eight good shirts but I have eight more that are too good to throw away and not good enough to wear out in public. These are Saturday morning shirts. They prevent me from burying anything but the thinnest Christmas presents among them.

There's no room for anything extra in the garage at Christmas. Over the years I've put up various hooks and hangers along the side walls but the snow shovel sticks out so far the car door bangs against it when you try to climb out carrying packages. The leaf rake and the garbage cans are no help, either.

As a result of this seasonal storage emergency, I take special measures. I put presents and other items I have to get out of sight for a few weeks in emergency storage areas.

The prime emergency storage area in anyone's house is under the bed. I put a lot of stuff under the bed at Christmas. We have six beds in our house and we could use six more. We have enough for people to sleep in but we could use more for storing things under.

In the winter I don't use the trunk of the car as much as in the summer so I end up leaving things in the car that I should bring into the house. I don't empty out the trunk of the car until Christmas Eve.

The basement and the attic of the house are about full, so the last place where there's a little emergency room is up the back stairway. If you have a back stairway, don't overlook it as a place to put some things temporarily. We don't ordinarily use the back stairway although we try to keep it clear of debris for most of the year. It has thirteen steps going up to the landing and at this time of year I turn those thirteen steps into thirteen little shelves on which I keep things. I leave about six inches on the side of each step as a place to step so I can still use them.

One warning: Keep careful track of the emergency storage areas you use for Christmas presents. A few days after July Fourth this year, I dropped a quarter under the bed and when I got down on my knees to look for it, I discovered a Christmas present I'd forgotten to give my sister in 1974.

Struck by the Christmas Lull

A STRANGE lull sets in sometime during the afternoon of Christmas Day in our house.

The early-morning excitement is over, the tension is gone and dinner isn't ready yet. One of our problems may be that we don't have Christmas dinner until about six. We plan it for four but we have it at six.

The first evidence of any non-Christmas spirit usually comes about one o'clock. We've had a big, late breakfast that didn't end until 9:30 or 10:00 and the dishes for that aren't done until after we open our presents.

Washing the breakfast dishes runs into getting Christmas dinner. The first little flare-up comes when someone wanders into the kitchen and starts poking around looking for lunch. With dinner planned for four o'clock, there's no lunch on the schedule. Margie's busy trying to get the cranberry jelly out of the molds and she isn't interested in serving lunch or having anyone get their own. To her, at this point, food means dirty dishes.

It isn't easy to organize the meals over a Christmas weekend. Everyone is always complaining about eating too much one minute and out in the kitchen looking for food the next. We might be able to get away with just two meals if we had Christmas dinner at two. I forget why we don't but we don't.

We have thirteen people this year. The lull will strike them all but each will handle it differently.

A few will sit around the living room. Someone will decide to tidy up the place by putting all the wrapping paper and ribbons in a big, empty box that held a Christmas present a few hours earlier.

I don't do any of this because I love the mess. As soon as you clean up the living room, Christmas is over.

At one end of the couch, someone will be reading the newspaper. It's usually pretty thin. There isn't much news and very little advertising. One of the editors has had a reporter do the story about what the homeless will be having for Christmas dinner at the Salvation Army kitchen, but it's slim pickin's in the paper.

My sister Nancy sits there reading out Christmas cards and looking at presents given to other people which she missed when they were being opened.

There are usually a few nappers. Someone will hog the whole couch by stretching out and falling asleep on it. The smart, serious nappers will disappear into an upstairs bedroom.

One of the kids will be working on or putting together a present he or she got. Someone will be reading a new book. (No one watches television in our house on Christmas Day.)

At some point there's a flurry of phone calls, in and out. We'll start making calls to other members of the family who can't be there or who are close but not in our inner circle. Usually one of the twins' classmates will call to see if they can get together during the few days they're both in town.

There's always someone who wants to know if the drugstore is open. They don't really want anything, they're just looking for some excuse to get out of the house.

If I've been given some new tool, I go down to the basement and try it out on a piece of wood. That's usually interrupted by a call from the head of the stairs asking if I want to go over to the indoor courts and play tennis. I'm always touched by the fact the kids want me to play tennis with them. It wouldn't be because I pay for the courts, would it?

By about four o'clock the Christmas Day lull is over. We all congregate in the living room again to have a drink. Nancy has slow-baked almonds and pecans which have been kept hidden from Brian and Ellen all day.

Everyone's relaxed again now. Dinner's ready but a Christmas dinner can be put on hold, so there's no rush. A turkey is better left at least half an hour after it comes out of the oven before it's carved. Mashed potatoes, creamed onions and squash are all easy to keep warm. The peppermint candy cane ice cream stays frozen.

I hate to have Christmas end.

Reverse Resolutions

THOSE of us who hate New Years's Eve and the necessity it brings with it to have fun, look forward to New Year's Day, when New Year's Eve is over.

For years I've been fighting a losing battle to make September first New Year's Day but no one will listen. If we had changed the date on which the new year starts, August thirty-first would be our next New Year's Eve and we wouldn't be faced with this unpleasantness on the last day of December. We always go to a good party but I don't even like good parties on New Year's Eve. I just want to be alone that night feeling miserable about all I didn't get done in the year past and all the hard jobs I have ahead of me in the following year.

Inevitably you think of any new year as a beginning . . . even if it comes at the wrong time of year.

Beginnings are exciting because we never learn. Every time we start something new, we think it's going to be better than it was last time. Fortunately, we're all optimists. We forget everything that can go wrong and concentrate on how it will be if everything goes right. We look forward to a pleasant experience.

Our optimism makes beginnings a happy time. If we knew how long it was going to take us and all the trouble we were going to have with ninety-nine percent of the jobs we start, we'd never start them. This ability we have to put past difficulties out of our minds is one of the wonders of the human brain.

Several years ago I listed some resolutions I resolved not to make. I have more this year.

—I'm not going to stop eating coffee ice cream. I resolved not to eat it two years ago and it made me miserable. This year I'm not promising myself anything in regard to ice cream. Maybe I will and maybe I won't.

—I'm not going to smoke cigarettes this year. This is the best kind of resolution for me. I can absolutely promise this is a resolution I'll keep. I've never smoked cigarettes and it isn't likely I'll start now.

—I'm not going to try to exercise very much this year. Last winter

I played twice a week with Cronkite and felt terrible. Walter's so busy since he retired that he isn't playing, either. I saw him last week and he looks in great shape. Not playing tennis must agree with him, too.

—I'm not going to try to save all the pennies I take out of my pockets every night. Three weeks ago I spent several hours one night counting the pennies I'd saved. Have you any idea how much room 2,437 pennies takes up in boxes, cans and dresser drawers? All this time I've been thinking of myself as rich because of my pennies. After counting them, I realized I had exactly $24.37.

—I'm not going to be as loyal to the company. Every time I'm loyal to the company, management changes and whatever I was being loyal to is gone. I'm left holding my loyalty.

—I'm not going to try to keep from being cynical if the situation calls for cynicism.

So, Happy New Year. If you drink, don't drive and if you drink and drive, don't do it near me.

IX:

A TIME TO WRITE

Ecclesiastes

I AM sitting, at the moment, in a hotel room in Beverly Hills. It is late but I don't feel sleepy. I have nothing to read and there's nothing on television I want to watch.

I have found the Gideon Bible in a dresser drawer next to the bed and I've opened it to Ecclesiastes. I only read parts of the Bible I already know. I've always found the Bible difficult to read and I've never started from the beginning and read it through. I don't know anyone else who has, either.

When you read the Bible in its old-fashioned, stilted English, you get the impression that you're reading the actual words as they were written or spoken so long ago. Ecclesiastes was written in Hebrew not English, of course, and I suppose this version I have in front of me represents the work of hundreds of editors and rewriters through the ages. Even so, it has a wonderful rhythm to it:

"To every thing there is a season, and a time to every purpose under the heaven:

—A time to be born, and a time to die; a time to plant, and a time to pluck up that which has been planted;

—A time to kill, and a time to heal; a time to break down, and a time to build up;

—A time to weep and a time to laugh; a time to mourn and a time to dance;

—A time to cast away stones, and a time to gather stones together; a time to embrace, and a time to refrain from embracing."

Some of that is just great but some of it needs rewriting. It has obviously been updated many times and probably should be modernized again now. "A time to cast away stones" doesn't mean much to us and there might be a better way to put "A time to kill, and a time to heal."

The world needs the wisdom the Bible has to offer but it has to be readable or not many people are going to read it. It has to pertain to our lives today as we live them and not to some ancient time we don't understand. There are biblical scholars working on revising the Bible right now in both England and the United States and I respectfully suggest there's some work to be done on Ecclesiastes.

Here are some additions I'd like future editors of the Bible to consider including in Ecclesiastes:

—There is a time to travel and a time to stay home and not go anywhere at all.

—A time to play basketball which shall be in the wintertime and a time to knock it off with basketball which shall be as the wintertime comes to an end and not in June.

—A time to play the radio too loud and a time to turn the radio and television set off and let silence pervade all the house.

—A time to gather together wordly goods and a time to throw stuff away.

—A time to make telephone calls and a time to get off the telephone and go to work.

—There is a time to get up in the morning even if you don't feel like getting up and a time to go to bed at night even if you don't feel like going to bed.

—There is a time for exercise and a time for lying down and taking a little nap.

—A time for putting chocolate sauce on vanilla ice cream and a time for eating vanilla ice cream without chocolate sauce.

—A time to go to the movies and a time to watch the movies on television and a time not to watch movies at all.

—A time to read the sports pages and a time to turn away from the sports pages and read what's really going on in the world.

—There is a time to have a dog and a time not to have a dog.

—A time to walk, a time to run, a time to take a train or a plane and a time to let your fingers do the walking.

—A time to start writing and a time to finish writing.

An Interview with Andy Rooney

ANYONE attracted to the rugged features of his handsome countenance might at first glance fail to observe the piercing intelligence of Andy Rooney's steel-blue eyes."

That's the way I'd like to have an article about me begin. In the past year I've been interviewed twenty times by reporters and none of them has started a piece that way. The articles have been friendly and many of them well done but no one who reads anything about himself is ever totally satisfied. Do they have to point out I'm grumpy? Must the reporter mention that my clothes are unpressed? Is it necessary to say that I'm overweight and getting gray?

What follows are some guidelines for reporters who wish to interview me in the future. I'd like to have the report go more like this:

"Rooney, who wears his expensive but tasteful clothes with a casual grace that conceals his position as one of the style setters in the men's fashion world, talked to this reporter in his hotel suite where he draped his taut, muscular frame over an easy chair.

"Considered by critics to be the leading essayist in print and broadcasting, Andy was disarmingly diffident when this reporter compared his work with that of Mark Twain, Hemingway, Robert Benchley, E. B. White, Walter Lippmann and Art Buchwald.

" 'Shucks,' he said modestly as he dug his toe into the deep pile rug of the carpet in his penthouse suite, 'I don't know about that.'

"Although it is not widely publicized," this article about me would continue if I had my way, "Andy Rooney might well be known as a modern-day Chippendale, were his mastery of the cabinetmaker's art not overshadowed by his genius with the English language.

"On the tennis court, Andy's serve has often been compared to that of John McEnroe. He moves with a catlike quickness that belies his age.

" 'Andy is wonderful to work with,' says his wife, Marguerite. 'He's always good-natured and a joy to have around the house. I can't recall an argument we've had in all the years of our marriage.'

"Rooney's four children, Ellen, Martha, Emily and Brian, are all perfect, too.

"On the average day, Andy rises at 4:30 A.M. By 6 A.M., because of his unusual ability to read 600 words a minute, he has finished two newspapers and *Time* magazine. His photographic memory enables him to store anything he has read for long periods of time and it is partly this ability that makes it easy for him to turn out three interesting, accurate, informative and perceptive essays each week.

"Of his friend, Harry Reasoner says, 'I only wish I could write as well as Andy does.'

"During our interview, Rooney got several telephone calls. William Buckley called to ask his advice on a point of grammar. There was a call from someone identified only as 'Ron' asking for advice on the economy. A third call came from E. F. Hutton asking Andy how he thought the stock market would behave in the days ahead."

I'm going to clip this out of the newspaper now and carry it with me wherever I go. If a young reporter wishes to interview me, I'll show it to him, just to give him some idea how I think his report should read. There's no sense having reporters waste a lot of time getting the facts.

Graduationese

THE headline reads, GRADUATES TO FIND JOBS SCARCE.

How many times have you read that story?

I don't offhand recall any year that wasn't the most difficult there ever was for graduating seniors to find jobs.

Each of us, at one time or another in our lives, has had a tough time finding a job, so we're sympathetic. We want to help. We don't want to give them a job, but we want to help.

The speakers at high school and college graduation ceremonies want to help by giving advice. I've been reading excerpts from some of the speeches.

For some reason, giving a commencement address brings out the worst in a speaker. Otherwise bright, normal, nice people turn themselves into pompous asses for the day. Years ago I spoke to the graduating class at the high school I attended, and I shudder to think what I told them and what my attitude was while I did it.

Pompous speeches are not necessarily the speaker's fault. That's what a commencement speech is supposed to be. The speaker is there to give the ceremony some importance so he or she has to say some important-sounding things.

(I don't know who makes the decision about whether to call it "graduation" or "commencement." There's a big difference in attitude between the two words. "Graduation" suggests students have finished with something and "commencement" suggests they're just starting.)

President A. Bartlett Giamatti of Yale University gave one of the speeches I read. Except for the fact that he uses the "A." that way for his name, Dr. Giamatti is a brilliant, down-to-earth scholar.

Normally what I see of his writing is so much smarter than I am that I'm discouraged by it, so naturally I was happy to note that he's only human. When he wrote this, he fell into the rhythm of the traditional graduation speech cliché, proving he's mortal.

There are some easily identifiable clues by which a graduation address can be detected.

First, the speaker starts with some light, often deprecating remark about either himself or commencement speeches in general. Dr. Giamatti did that:

"Commencement speeches are often as difficult to endure as to deliver," he said, "and you are, I trust, relieved that Yale doesn't have one."

That's a good remark for its kind but it is of a kind. And, of course, Yale *does* have a commencement address and he was giving it.

"Commencement speakers who have mastered the genre," he said, "manage to be at once condescending and conspiratorial . . ."

The key cliché there is the phrase "at once." You'll find it several times in most graduation speeches. Dr. Giamatti went for it again a few lines later when he referred to something as "at once satisfying and singular." That's perfect graduation speech language, too, because it's a little obscure and sounds at once important and euphonious.

Look for the word "indeed." This indicates that the speaker has had another idea for padding out his talk.

"Indeed to blend pomp and independence . . ." Dr. Giamatti said.

"Indeed I think a healthy family . . ."

He also told the Yale graduates that "no small challenge lies ahead."

This must mean he thinks there's more of a challenge than if he'd said simply, "A big challenge lies ahead."

No matter how the speaker says it, challenges always lie ahead in graduation addresses.

The meat of Dr. Giamatti's speech, though, came toward the end of it:

"I do not bring you any easy answers," he said.

I was frankly disappointed with that. It costs $50,000 to put a kid through Yale. For that much money, the least their president could do when they graduate is give them a few easy answers.

Numbers, Numbers, Numbers

It's never been clear to me whether the brain clogs up or not when you put too much in it.

Would I be able to think better about other things if I hadn't filled my head with a lot of information I never use?

For instance, I've inadvertently memorized a lot of numbers I don't need. If I did need them, it would be almost as quick to look them up or work them out. The multiplication table is handy to have in your head, and I even wish my teacher hadn't stopped at 12 × 12, but there are too many numbers I know that aren't any help at all. I was thinking of some of the numbers I know:

There must be at least twenty-five telephone numbers rattling around in my brain, taking up space.

I know our street address and the street addresses of at least ten friends and family members. I've memorized some ZIP codes and even a few telephone area codes. As a good example of mind clutter, I realize I know that the area code for Indianapolis is 317.

What am I doing storing numerical garbage like that in my brain? I haven't made more than three phone calls to Indianapolis in my life, I don't plan to make another soon and it would be better out of my head. But there it is, taking up valuable space that could just as well be occupied by the names of people I forget when I meet them on the street.

There are numbers in everyone's life that stand out as landmarks. The number 204 is a big one for me. When I was a kid we lived at 204 Partridge St. I suppose 204 has more meaning for me than any other number between 100 and 1,000 although I no longer have any use for it. For the past thirty years I've lived at number 254 on another street but 254 has never assumed the same prominence in my memory as 204.

Most people who served in the Armed Forces know their Army serial number. I remember mine but I've never memorized my Social Security number. That comes up often and my Army serial number never does.

Not knowing my Social Security number is something I've put

my mind to. I'm a little perverse about it. I don't want to be numbered by the government. They can make me take a number but I'll be damned if they can make me memorize it. I think we all owe it to ourselves to keep from memorizing as many numbers as we can. Facts and ideas are what our heads should be filled with.

It isn't easy rejecting a number. I remember Frank Gifford was No. 16 although he hasn't played for twenty years. I know Joe DiMaggio was No. 5 and I don't even like baseball.

Which numbers you remember and which you forget, don't seem to make any sense. I don't know the license plate number on my car but I remember that the battery in my watch was put in last January 9th. I keep the combination numbers to the lock on my locker at the indoor tennis court on a little slip of paper because I can't ever remember it, but the combination on my Dudley lock in high school in 1938 was 23-8-13. Why can't I delete that from my brain and replace it with the combination I'm using now?

It's difficult to understand why we don't have more control over what we recall and what we forget. It's a shortcoming our brains have. Each of us ought to be able to make a conscious effort to remember or to forgot something and have that decision stick.

The computer salesmen talk about storage capacity. I'm not so interested in storage. It's that "erase" or "delete" feature a computer has that I like. My brain runneth over with numbers I no longer use. I keep remembering things I'd rather forget and forgetting things I'm trying to remember.

Intelligence

Iғ you are not the smartest person in the world, you usually find some way to be satisfied most of the time with the brain you've got. I was thinking about all this in bed last night because I made a dumb mistake yesterday and I was looking for some way to excuse myself for it so I could go to sleep.

The thing that saves most of us from feeling terrible about our limited intellect is some small part of our personality or character that makes us different. Being uniquely ourselves makes us feel better about not being smart. It's those little differences we have that keep us from committing suicide when we realize, early in life, that a lot of people have more brains than we have.

There are two kinds of intelligence, too. One can be measured in numbers from tests but the other and better kind of intelligence is something no one has ever been able to measure. The second kind is a sort of understanding of life that some of the people with the most intelligence of the first type, don't have any of. They may have scored 145 in the I.Q. tests they took in school but they're idiots out in the real world. This is also a great consolation to those of us who did *not* score 145 in our I.Q. tests.

It almost seems as though the second type of intelligence comes from somewhere other than the brain. A poet would say it comes from the heart. I'm not a poet and I wouldn't say that but it does appear as though some of the best decisions we make spring spontaneously to our minds from somewhere else in our bodies.

How do you otherwise account for love, tears or the quickened heartbeat that comes with fear? All these things strike us independently of any real thought process. We don't think things through and decide to fall in love or decide to cry or have our heart beat faster.

There is so much evidence that there's more than one kind of intelligence that we can relax, believing that we have a lot of the less obvious kind. I prefer to ignore the possibility that someone with a higher I.Q. than mine might also have more of the second kind of intelligence. One person should not be so lucky as to have intelligence of both the brain and the heart.

I wish there was some way to decide who the five smartest people are in the world because I've always wanted to ask them the five hardest questions. I haven't decided who the five smartest people are and I haven't settled on all five questions, either.

One question I've considered for my list is this:

"Are people smarter than they were a thousand years ago?"

It's a hard one. Athletes are running faster, jumping farther and lifting heavier weights. This suggests our brains must also be performing better.

On the other hand, are our eyes and ears any better than the eyes and ears of the Romans who watched the lions eat the Christians in the year 200 A.D.? Probably not. My guess would be that our eyes and our ears haven't changed for better or for worse except as we abuse them through misuse.

If our eyes and ears haven't changed in size or improved in performance, the chances are our brains haven't either. I forget when they invented the wheel but did it take any less intelligence to invent the wheel centuries ago than it took this century to invent the windshield wiper, the ballpoint pen or the toaster oven?

It must have been 2:30 before I finally fell asleep.

Of Sports and Men

Iᴛ's hard to guess what sports will be like in fifty or a hundred years. Two race car drivers were killed recently, one of them hit a wall head-on in a car going 187 miles an hour. The car disintegrated and the driver was killed instantly.

At Indianapolis this year, several drivers have qualified for the Indianapolis 500 at speeds of more than 200 miles an hour. Where are we going with records? The average qualifying speed for the Indianapolis 500 this year was 197 miles an hour. In 1970 the average qualifying speed was 167. In 1960 it was 144 and in 1950 it was 131.

My question is this: What will it be in the year 2032? Will it be 300 miles an hour? 400? And if it is, how many drivers will be killed hitting walls head-on?

For automobile racing the solution is easy: put a limit on engine size so that racing becomes a contest solely of drivers and mechanics, not cars. But what's going to happen to records in other sports and how are average young athletes going to compete against the supermen we seem to be breeding?

Twenty years ago, Wilt Chamberlain was one of the few seven-foot basketball players around. Today there are fourteen National Basketball Association players at least that tall. A couple of them are heading for eight feet. Every high school has a few players six foot three inches and in college the short fellows who are only six feet tall don't have any better chance of making the team than the Indianapolis driver who only averages 175 miles an hour. The six-footer today isn't tall enough and the 175-mile-an-hour driver is too slow.

My father took me to a track meet at Madison Square Garden when I was young and I watched a man set the world's record in the pole vault at 14' 4". Today the record is 19' 2".

The sports page of my newspaper last week carried a small-type listing of the results of a high school track meet and I noticed that the boy who finished third in the high jump, cleared the bar at 6′ 6″. Fifty years ago that was the world's record. Today a jumper doesn't win anything if he can't clear 7′ and the record is 7′ 8¾″.

If the record keeps going up at that rate, approximately one foot every fifty years, does that mean some athlete will be jumping ten feet high in 2082?

The question is: Is there any limit to human capacity and if there is a limit, what is it? If an athlete can jump ten feet high in a hundred years, will athletes be jumping twenty feet high in five hundred years?

In track and field some of the records can be attributed to better equipment but the basic improvement in every case has been in the athletes themselves. They're bigger, stronger, faster and have more endurance. Football players have gotten heavier and stronger the way basketball players have gotten taller. When a defensive lineman from a good college team gets to the pros weighing only 235 pounds these days, he's made into a line backer because he's too small to play end or tackle.

One of the most encouraging things about all this is that while the human race has never been subjected to any kind of selective breeding, it seems to be improving physically and mentally.

On the other hand, horses have been bred selectively for hundreds of years in an attempt to produce ones that run faster but horses aren't much faster than they ever were. The horse race records at various distances haven't improved anywhere near as dramatically as human records have.

In 1882 the world's record for a man running a mile was 4:21. In 1942 it was 4:04. Today it is down under 3:50.

In 1941 Whirlaway won the Kentucky Derby, a distance of a mile and a quarter, in 2:01. In the past five years it has been run in 2:02 or more.

This is perhaps the strongest case that can be made against racism and Adolf Hitler's kind of superrace theories. It seems the kind of random breeding the human race does, produces a better strain than that produced by scientists or dictators deciding, as horse breeders do, who should breed with whom and who shouldn't breed at all.

If the human race continues to improve as sports records indicate it has, someone in the year 2100 will run the mile in a minute, swim 100 yards in 30 seconds and basketball players will all be ten feet tall.

I'd love to be around to watch but I was probably born a little too early to live to be 180.

A Penny Saved Is a Waste of Time

WHAT follows is some advice I forgot to give our kids before they left home:

—There is a Santa Claus but he doesn't always come.

—Being well dressed is like being six feet tall. You either are or you aren't and there isn't much you can do about it.

—Learn to drink coffee without sugar.

—Throw away the can of paint after you've finished painting something, no matter how much there is left in the can.

—Don't keep your watch five minutes fast.

—Go to bed. Whatever you're staying up late for isn't worth it.

—Don't expect too much from the company you work for even if it's a good company.

—You're almost always better off keeping your mouth shut, but don't let that stop you from popping off.

—There are few satisfactions in life better than holding a grudge. Pick them carefully but hold them.

—Don't fuss a whole lot with your hair.

—You're better off missing a bus or an airplane once in a while than you are getting there too early all the time.

—Don't save string. If you need string, buy it.

—Don't save pennies, either. They don't add up to anything.

—If you can't find comfortable shoes that are good-looking, buy comfortable shoes that aren't, but don't buy good-looking shoes that are uncomfortable.

—Don't call in sick except when you're sick.

—You aren't the only one who doesn't understand the situation in the Middle East.

—Nothing important is ever said in a conversation that lasts more than three minutes.

—Very few things you buy will be the answer to the problem you bought them to solve.

—There's seldom any good reason for blowing the horn on your car.

—If you work moderately hard you'll find a lot of people aren't working as hard as you are.

—It is unlikely that you'll have any success gluing a broken chair together.

—If you buy a book and feel like making marks in it with a pen or pencil, make them. It's your book and it doesn't ruin it for anyone else anyway.

—Be careful but don't be too careful.

—In a conversation, keep in mind that you're more interested in what you have to say than anyone else is.

—If nothing else works, take a hot shower.

—Don't keep saying, "I don't know where the time goes." It goes the same place it's always gone and no one has ever known where that is.

—If you own something useless which you like, don't throw it away just because someone keeps asking what you're keeping it for.

—The fewer, the merrier.

—Don't believe everything you read in the newspaper but keep in mind almost all of it is true.

—Keep the volume down on everything. It's like salt. You can get used to less of it.

—Money shouldn't be saved for a rainy day. It should be saved and spent for a beautiful day.

—Language is more important than numbers.

—Don't make a date for anything more than a month in advance.

—It's *i* before *e* except in the following words: "Neither leisure foreigner seized the weird height."

—Travel just for the sake of going somewhere is usually a disappointment.

—Use profanity sparingly and don't use any obscenities at all.

—If you can't afford the expensive one, don't buy it.

—Try to be aware of how you're being.

—You'll be better off in the long run making decisions quickly even if a lot of them are wrong. They probably won't be wrong any more often than if you took a lot of time making them.

—When you cross a street, look both ways ... even on a one-way street.

The Power of Negative Thinking

THIS is It, Readers! I think I've found the secret for eternal optimism. I've discovered how to keep from getting down on myself and I'm going to pass it along to you. I may even expand this article and write a book called *The Power of Negative Thinking*!

—All my life I've suffered from periods of depression because I got thinking about how much better a lot of people do things than I do. All that's behind me now. Today I'm concentrating on the negative. When I do something badly, all I'm going to think about is the great number of people who probably would have done it even worse. Concentrate on other people's shortcomings. Compare yourself with the worst and forget about the best.

When I reread something I've written in the past, I often feel terrible about it. It isn't as profound as Walter Lippmann. It isn't as well phrased as E. B. White. It isn't as funny as Art Buchwald or Russell Baker.

Well, I'm not going to compare myself with those masters any longer. I read the other day where twenty percent of all Americans can't read or write. Now when I get worrying about how inadequate my writing often is, I'm going to think of them. Twenty percent must be almost fifty million people and I certainly write better than they do.

—I enjoy cooking and often entertain the notion that I do it well. When people come to my house for dinner they tend to flatter me about my cooking but when I go to France or eat in a good restaurant or even at the home of a few friends who are truly good cooks, I'm ready to quit the kitchen. I'm a mediocre cook with high ambitions and no real talent.

Well, I'm through comparing myself with gourmets and master chefs. Yesterday I came through the turnstile at our supermarket and I looked at what other people had in their shopping carts. I saw precooked frozen cherry tarts, boxes of sugar-coated cereal, Brand X hot dogs made of who-knows-what and packaged TV dinners. By comparison to these people, I'm Julia Child in the kitchen.

—On the tennis court I start thinking I'm playing better and then someone in the family comes along with a camera and takes a picture of me serving. A week later they show me the picture and it gets a good laugh all around. My tennis is obviously a joke. I watch Jimmy Connors on television and his tennis is to mine what Einstein's mathematics is to my arithmetic.

With my new theory of negative thinking, I'm going to stop watching Jimmy Connors and concentrate on the people who play tennis *worse* than I do. There are some. If I watch the people playing in a public park, I can always spot players I could beat. I'm through worrying about my tennis. As a matter of fact, if there was a National Ranking for men over sixty years old, under five foot nine and weighing more than two hundred pounds, I bet I'd be in the top one hundred.

—Looking in the mirror mornings can be a disheartening experience for most of us. The trouble is we're comparing ourselves to the models in the store windows. I'm forgetting the beautiful people. From now on I'm checking my features, my form and my manner of dress against the people I see with the frozen TV dinners at the checkout counter in the supermarket.

—I don't read fast and when I'm reading over someone's shoulder, they finish before I do but I'm through worrying about it. When I was in the Army at Fort Bragg it took half the guys five minutes to read a twenty-word note on the bulletin board from the First Sergeant. I read faster than most of them. And I write better than my First Sergeant did, too.

Each one of us has got to start thinking about all the people who do things worse than we do. The United States is full of people who aren't doing things very well at all. These are the people against whom we should measure our own achievements if we want to feel good. (If we don't want to feel good, we shouldn't of course, but that's another book.)

A Rich Writer

WHAT does your husband do?" I asked a young woman I met at a wedding last weekend.

"He's a writer," she told me.

"What does he write?" I asked and I noticed that as I did, the tone of my voice turned ever so slightly away from conversational to reportorial.

"All sorts of things," she said. "Novels, short stories and . . . you know."

One of the surprising things about being a writer is that a person need not actually write anything to be one.

On further gentle prodding, it turned out that in addition to being a writer, the young woman's husband had also inherited a lot of money. That's the kind of writer I've always wanted to be.

If there is one thing I know a lot about, it's how to keep from writing. For those of you who want to call yourselves writers, here are some tips on how to be a writer without the drudgery of actually putting words on paper.

1—Only write when your mind is free and clear of any other responsibility. Don't try to write if there's something else you could be doing. Finish all your chores first. Sweep out the garage, clean out your bottom drawer and file those papers and old checks.

2—Work in comfortable surroundings. These should be a couch in your office. If you're sleepy or want more time to think through your idea, relax on the couch for a while. Have yourself a little nap if you think it will help.

3—If, after you awake from your little nap, you find that it's almost lunch or dinner time, close up shop. There's no sense trying to write on an empty stomach. And don't try to write on a full stomach, either.

4—Don't try to write with equipment that is anything less than perfect. Nothing physically wrong with your typewriter, paper supply, pencils, pens or paper clips should come between you and the clear flow of an idea. If, just for example, the holes in the *o*'s, *e*'s or *a*'s on your typewriter are clogged with dried ink from your ribbon and are producing a shaded area there on paper instead of a clean blank spot, bend out the end of a paperclip and pick out the clot of ink embedded in the keys.

5—If there's a telephone call you ought to make, make it before you write anything. If you think of an old friend you might call, call him. Make all your calls before you write.

6—There is nothing more distracting for a writer than for him to have the feeling that he's missing out on something good. If you hear the television set on in some other part of the house, go see what it is.

7—A writer ought to have a work area that is free of other materials. If there are letters you haven't read on your desk or copies of old Sunday newspaper sections, *Harper's* magazine, *Playboy* or last week's issue of *TV Guide*, read them and throw them away before you start to write.

8—Smoking can be a big help in not writing. Cigarettes are good but the pipe is far and away the favorite smoke for the writer who isn't going to actually write anything. A pipe can keep a writer busy all morning just cleaning, packing, lighting and relighting it.

9—Don't write unless the temperature is right. You can fuss with the thermostat and if that doesn't work, change your clothes for more or less warmth.

10—All of us need plenty of time to worry. There simply are not enough hours in the day for each of us to do all the worrying there is to be done. If you have a lot of worrying to do, put off writing until you've done some of it.

By following these simple rules, and inheriting a million dollars, you too can be a rich writer.

Swimsuits

THERE are a lot of sexy bathing suit advertisements in the newspapers and magazines and you have to admit they add a little to the printed page that advertisements for computers and specials on mayonnaise do not. I have never understood some things about advertising though. How do pictures of suntanned male models sitting on horseback help sell cigarettes? How do pictures of beautiful young women with great figures in teeny-weeny brief bikinis help a store sell bathing suits to the average woman?

You can never underestimate mankind's ability to fool itself and I suppose that's what the advertisers know that the rest of us don't. They know that even though the average woman *knows* she isn't going to look like the girl in the ad wearing the bikini, there still remains the faint, faraway dream that she might look a *little* like her.

I imagine there are a lot of bathing suits in dresser drawers across the country that have never been worn in the water or anywhere near it. A woman buys the suit but in the cold light of the mirror in her own bedroom, she realizes she doesn't dare go out in public wearing it. I have a few pieces of clothing of my own that fall in that category. They seemed like a good idea when I bought them but I've never worn them.

Last Sunday I saw an ad for a bikini and another item they called "the barest cover-up" for it. The woman who wanted to appear modest on the way to the water could wear this fishnet garment over her bikini. From what I could see in the ad—and I could see just about everything—the cover-up garment didn't really cover anything except, perhaps, the manufacturer's overhead.

Modesty or lack of it is an interesting subject. A great many women who modestly cover their knees when they sit down and cross their legs while wearing a skirt, pantyhose and underpants, have no hesitation about going to the beach or pool in two pieces of cloth no bigger than one small handkerchief.

Modesty is mostly what any civilization says it is. On many of the beaches in France, it is common practice for women to go topless. They wouldn't dream of wearing a skirt without a top on the street but on the beach they seem perfectly at ease wearing just the bare bottom of a bikini. They're a lot more at ease wearing so little than I am watching them wear it.

I don't really know why women have traditionally covered their breasts in our society. It hasn't been so long since men used to, too. My first five bathing suits covered me from thigh to chest and the shoulder straps always made swimming more difficult. Even in championship swim meets, men were required to wear full bathing suits. Johnny Weissmuller set all his records in one.

When men started wearing just swim trunks, a lot of people didn't think it was any more acceptable than the average person would think topless women were acceptable at the beach today. Many clubs with pools and beach committees posted signs in the 1930s and 1940s saying that men were expected to wear full bathing suits.

It's strange that bare-chested men are accepted now and bare-breasted women are not. There really isn't that big an anatomical difference. Men's breasts look about the same as women's except they don't protrude as much and are not considered sex objects.

I can't make much of a logical case against nudity or near-nudity and yet I have the feeling women's bathing suits have gone too far with revelation. I've been following the trend closely with a purely academic interest for years now and it seems to me that the advertisers and the people selling these minimal bathing suits are headed for trouble. There is just so much design a top designer can give a piece of cloth the size of a handkerchief and if they get any smaller, the designers are going to find they don't have room on them to put their names. "Cole of California" must be in trouble already. And the next step for women would, of course, put all of them out of business.

Dogs

THERE are forty million dogs in the United States. That's probably too many but don't suggest to anyone who has one that he or she ought to get rid of it. Most dog owners are very loyal. The dog may be man's best friend but very often man is dog's, too.

For almost no reason at all except that she felt sad and wanted to write someone, a woman in Orlando, Florida, wrote me a touching letter about the death of her boxer, Maximilian. She describes him as a wonderful dog and says that she still cries when she thinks of him.

"I can't even bring myself to make Jello anymore," she says, "because whenever I made it Maximilian stood around waiting for his share."

Anyone who has ever lost a dog knows exactly how this woman feels even though they may have reservations about Jello. We all say the same thing. "He was like a member of the family."

I've lost two dogs in my lifetime and it was so sad that I don't think I'll ever lose another because I'll never have another. Spike and Gifford were both English bulldogs. I grew up with Spike and my children grew up with Gifford. They were some dogs. Like most owners—although I don't like to use that word—we thought our kind of dog was best. I don't think there is another dog in the world so kind, so gentle and with as much personality to love as an English bulldog. I'm glad most people with dogs feel the same about their breed. It's good that we're loyal. If the dog is a mixed-breed mutt, the owner usually thinks mixed-breed mutts are best.

It is in memory of Spike and Gifford that I almost always speak to a dog on the street. I may ignore the person he's with but I speak to the dog. With the exception of a chow, an Airedale named Bim, several German shepherds and the bad-mannered dog of a good friend I don't want to offend by naming, I've never met a dog I didn't like.

I wouldn't want a Chihuahua, a Pomeranian or a Doberman pinscher but that's probably because I've never really known one. I didn't like poodles, either, until I got to know several and then I realized what the people who have them are always raving about.

Big dogs appeal to me the most but it would probably be better if there were fewer big dogs. Big dogs need more exercise than any of us have time to give them and unless you live on a farm, there aren't many places a dog can be free to roam and run. Next to the bulldog my favorites are golden retrievers and Labradors but I hate to see people walking them early in the morning in New York City. You just know the dog has been sleeping all night and at seven or eight in the morning he'll get a five-minute walk because the owner is in a hurry to get to work. For the rest of the day these real outdoor dogs will be in an apartment waiting for another five-minute walk in the evening.

You often see people acting foolishly with their dogs but I suppose other people would have thought I was foolish with Gifford. In the evening I'd often get down on the living room floor and lie there with him, watching television. He'd paw at me or chew on my hand affectionately and I'd roll him over and pat his stomach.

We only had a couple of rules for Giffy. We didn't feed him from the table and we didn't let him up on the furniture. Sometimes, in a moment of wild exuberance, in the morning, he'd leap up on the bed and start biting at me through the blankets. He knew he was wrong but he was having such good fun I never said much to him about it.

Some dogs are so cruelly treated that we don't even like to think about them but, for the most part, dogs and people provide as much happiness and friendship as Maximilian and the lady in Orlando provided for each other. Our behavior with dogs isn't always very adult but we express an affection for them that we often withhold from our human companions. It's nice.

Photography

As someone who has taken a lot of bad pictures I feel experienced enough to give some advice and make some observations on photography:

—The great World War II *Life* magazine photographer Bob Capa gave the best advice I ever heard. He said, "If your pictures are no good, you weren't close enough." Ironically, Bob was killed getting too close, but it doesn't alter the truth of his statement.

—It's a great temptation to take pretty pictures, but try to resist it. The only pictures that interest you a year after you take them are those of people. If you travel, don't bother with the familiar landmarks. People have already taken better pictures than you'll ever get of Rockefeller Center, the Eiffel Tower, the Taj Mahal, Notre Dame cathedral, the pyramids, Stonehenge and the Grand Canyon. If you want pictures of those, buy postcards.

—Try to remember that it is unlikely anyone but you will ever be interested in looking at your pictures, unless they're in them. Only take pictures you'll want to look at more than once.

—Don't take pictures you hope will impress people with where you've been. They don't care where you've been or what pictures you took while you were there.

—Most pretty good cameras come with a 50mm lens. This refers to the width of a picture. The smaller-numbered lenses such as a 28mm lens take a wider view but make things look more distant from the camera. The higher-numbered lenses are called telescopic lenses. They bring objects closer but cover a smaller field. You need one wide-angle lens and one medium-long lens. You don't need the all-purpose lens that comes with the camera.

—The second-best advice I ever heard was a general rule about lens openings or *f*-stops, as they're called. The rule is "sunny day, small hole, cloudy day, big hole." (If you don't know anything at all about a camera, that's not a joke.)

—Professional photographers have a difficult time. There are so many people who own good cameras and are at least reasonably competent with them, that they often get as good pictures by accident as the professionals do on purpose.

—There are some pretty good inexpensive cameras made in the United States but we have never made one that could compete with the best made in Germany or Japan. Why is that?

—When you get your pictures back, throw half of them away. If you have two almost the same, pick the best one and discard the other. Be tough on yourself when you edit your pictures.

—If you're taking pictures of people, get to know enough about your camera so you can take them quickly. Pictures of people waiting to have their pictures taken are usually poor.

—Write names and dates on the back of the pictures you keep. You're so sure who everyone is the day you get your pictures back, that it's hard to believe you'll forget some of their names a year from then. You will though, and in ten years you'll be lucky to remember half of them.

—When you see a man taking a picture of the woman he's with on vacation, offer to take a picture of both of them standing together. It's one of the small, nice things to do in life.

—Don't put pictures in an album. Put them in a box. Albums don't hold enough.

—If you're showing pictures to people, don't hand the pictures over one at a time with a speech. Give them the whole batch and let them go through the pictures like a deck of cards. This way they can decide how long they want to look at each one. Don't do too much explaining about where you were or what was happening at the time. Remember, everyone has a low tolerance for anyone else's pictures.

—When you go on a trip, don't make the decision about whether to take a camera along lightly. Having a camera and taking pictures is a very intrusive element on a trip. Make sure it's worth it. There's a lot to be said for leaving a camera home sometimes.

Letters Not Sent

Following are some letters I wish I'd mailed.

Mr. Michael Vishniac
Acme Plumbing Co.
Dear Mr. Vishniac:

I know what a busy man you are and I hate to bother you but I am writing in the hopes of being able to make an appointment with you to fix the faucet in our downstairs bathroom. It has been dripping for five months. I have called your plumbing company but all I get is an answering service. I understand you have been wintering in the Bahamas.

If it isn't convenient for you to make a house call to fix the faucet, would it be possible to make an appointment for me to bring the sink over to you to be fixed?

Sincerely, Andrew A. Rooney

Leslie Cartwright
Abraham Lincoln Grade School
Dear Mrs. Cartwright:

How wonderful it was of you to ask all thirty-one students in your fourth grade English class to write me individually for details on how I got started writing, how I get my ideas, who has influenced me most as a writer and what a young person who wants to be a writer should study.

I was so touched that I'm going to set aside the other work I had planned to do in the next three or four days and answer all thirty-one of your students.

I have to go now because many of the students told me to please get my answers back to them quickly as you told them their assignment was due next Thursday.

Ethel Washoure
Wentzville, Missouri
Dear Ethel:

Thank you for writing but I don't seem to remember you from the sixth grade. My father's name was not Arthur. It was Walter. I did not have a brother named Terrence who became an Eagle Scout. Obviously you have me mixed up with some other Andrew Rooney because I've only been to St. Louis twice in my life and I didn't get out to Wentzville either time.

Lester Grantham, Chairman
Whiteville, Section B,
Bowling League Speakers Selection Committee
Dear Mr. Grantham:

Thank you for your invitation to address the annual banquet and dinner dance of the Whiteville, Section B, Bowling League on October 4, 1987. I will be unable to accept your invitation because of a previous engagement on that date. I promised my wife I'd have dinner with her in the kitchen that night.

Mrs. Franklin Z. Welles
Glenmont Library Charity Assn.
Dear Mrs. Welles:

I would like to contribute an article of old clothing for your auction to raise money for the new sidewalk in front of the Glenmont Library but am unable to do so. I wear my old clothes.

William Wilson
Orlando, Fla.
Dear Mr. Wilson:

It was kind of you to write to say how much you dislike me and my column and that you are canceling your subscription to the newspaper and will never read it again. It is independent Americans like you who have made this country great, Mr. Wilson. May I also say that it made me feel good to know you sent a copy of your letter to the editor of the newspaper. I like an editor to know how readers feel about me. If you're ever in New York, look me up.

Sincerely, Andy Rooney

X:

THE SWEET SPOT
IN TIME

The Sweet Spot in Time

I'M lukewarm on both yesterday and tomorrow. Neither science fiction nor nostalgia interests me as much as today. I am tempted by the promise of all the great things coming up tomorrow, of course, and I do enjoy all the good memories and the graceful, simple and efficient artifacts of yesterday, the antiques, but this moment is the moment I like best.

These thoughts inevitably come at Christmas time. It's easy to get sentimental about the memories of Christmases past and years past and the people you spent them with. The advertising for gifts with which to commemorate the season, on the other hand, often emphasizes the new technology. "Buy her a computer, the tool of the future!"

So I feel a certain ambivalence toward both the past and the future. I dislike retyping a piece to correct mistakes or rearrange paragraphs. My son, Brian, said that if I got with it and bought myself a word processor, I wouldn't have to do those things. He said that if I tried one for just a few days, I'd never go back to my ancient Underwood #5.

Well, I did buy a word processor and I've tried it for a year but I still write primarily on my old machine. There are times when it's best for all of us to close our eyes to the future. There's just so much progress we have time for in our lives. Mostly we are too busy doing it the old way to take time to learn a new way. I do close my eyes to progress when it comes to typewriters. This may spring, in part, from a deep feeling I have that it's wrong to try to impose efficiency on a writer.

My antipathy for too much nostalgia can probably be traced to several hundred little antique shops where I have stopped to talk with conniving antiquaries. It seems as though every time people find out there's money in something, they ruin it. The good antique shops are outnumbered by the bad ones.

The revival of the style of the 1920s and 1930s has helped turn me off nostalgia. They call it Art Deco but to me it was the ugliest era that progress ever took us through. It's all phony frou-frou. Its ashtray art and gilded replicas of the Empire State Building put me off. The emphasis was on how it looked and not much on how it worked. Except for being old it has no virtue and it isn't even very old. Being old isn't reason enough to originate a revival of anything anyway. Age is no guarantee of quality in objects or people.

Too many of the revivals in art forms are fads based more on commercial enterprise than artistic worth. Someone stumbles across an obscure style in architecture, painting or furniture practiced by an appropriately unknown artist and they revive that style because they know where they can lay their hands on fifty examples of it and make themselves a quick buck. Art doesn't enter into it and nostalgia works as well for the dealer as fear does for the insurance salesman.

It isn't easy to live in the present. The temptation to sit thinking about the past or dreaming of the future is always there because it's easier than getting up off your tail and doing something today.

I love the electronic gadgets that promise a magic future in which we can do the hardest jobs with the touch of a button. It's just that experience has taught me that the promise usually precedes the product by so many years that it's better to put off anticipating it until it's actually in the store window.

I like old movies, old music, old furniture and old books but if I had to choose between spending the day with dreams of the future or memories of the past or this day I have at hand, I think I'd take pot luck with today.

Reunion

THERE's just so much sentimental baggage you can carry through life. I'm not much for reunions. Anyone who has reached the age of sixty could easily spend the rest of his days just sitting around, remembering.

I've returned to an old U.S. Eighth Air Force Base near Bedford, England, though, because members of the 306th Bomb Group were having a reunion and I flew with them on the first U.S. bombing raid on Nazi Germany in February 1943. It's sentimental baggage I carry easily and with great pride.

It's been forty years now since these men flew their four-engined B-17 Flying Fortresses out of here. They're the kind of men Americans like to think are typical Americans but they're better than typical. They're special. A lot of World War II Air Force men were.

It was a terrible war for them, although during this reunion they're managing to recall a lot of the good things about it. It would be too sad if they didn't. It was terrible because so many of them were killed. One evening they'd be sitting around their huts talking, worrying, playing cards and writing letters home. The next evening, if there had been a bombing mission that day, the bed next to theirs or the one next to that—and maybe both—might be empty, its former occupant, their pal, dead. Perhaps he had come down in a parachute that caught fire. "Who burned Bailey?" MacKinlay Kantor wrote. "Was it you?"

It was a great and terrible war for me because as a young reporter for the Army newspaper, *The Stars and Stripes*, I was in a strange position. I came to this base often when the bombers went out and when they returned—if they returned—I talked to the crews about what had happened. Then I'd return to London and write my story. I often felt ashamed of myself for not being one of them. I was having the time of my life as a newspaperman and they were fighting and dying. That's how I came to fly with them to Wilhelmshaven. It made me feel better about myself.

Looking out at the crumbling remains of the old runways at the airfield, I'm haunted by flashes of memory. Often the bombers came back badly damaged and with crew members dead or dying. In April of 1943 I was here when they came back from a raid deep in Germany and one of the pilots radioed in that he was going to have to make an emergency landing. He had only two engines left and his hydraulic system was gone. He couldn't let the wheels down and there was something even worse. The ball-turret gunner was trapped in the plastic bubble that hung beneath the belly of the bomber.

Later I talked with the crewmen who survived that landing. Their friend in the ball turret had been calm, they said. They had talked to him. He knew what they had to do. He understood. The B-17 slammed down on its belly . . . and on the ball turret with their comrade trapped inside it.

There are funny stories, too. Everyone here remembers the eccentric gunner Snuffy Smith, Sergeant Maynard Smith. He was an oddball kind of guy but he did his job well in the air. The Air Force loved to give medals and they had good reason in Snuffy Smith's case. On one occasion, Henry Stimson, then called Secretary of War, came to England and officials, thinking this would be a good time for publicity for the Air Force and the Secretary, arranged to give Snuffy Smith the Medal of Honor. The whole entourage came to this base with the Secretary and a dozen generals but the hero was nowhere to be found. It turned out he was in the kitchen washing dishes. He was on KP being disciplined for some minor infraction of the base rules.

Any reunion is a bittersweet experience. Last evening I had a drink at a bar where there was a gathering and a strong-looking weatherbeaten man came over and quietly said he'd like to buy me a drink. He's a Nebraska farmer now. He had been the tail gunner on the *Banshee*, the B-17 I flew in over Wilhelmshaven. We'd been hit that day and it was a terrifying trip but it made a good story for me. We laughed and talked together and he paid for the drink. As we lifted our glasses in a mutual toast, I noticed that two fingers on his right hand were missing. It often happened to crewmen who stuck by their guns while their hands froze.

And he was buying *me* a drink.

Friendship: Handle with Care

Six months ago I was talking to a friend on the telephone. We used to talk two or three times a week and we often had lunch. For about the fiftieth time he started telling me about some money he was trying to get from his father's estate. (After his mother had died, his father remarried a schoolteacher. Later his father died and the schoolteacher took up with another man and my friend thinks this fellow is after the money.)

I didn't really know or care about all the details and finally I said, "Charley, if you'd spent as much time working in the past years as you've spent trying to get that money, you'd be rich."

It seemed like half a joke and half a sharp remark that I could make to my old friend but I was wrong.

"Who needs a friend like you," he said, and slammed down the receiver. I haven't talked to Charley since and may never. I made one attempt to call him but he was out and I haven't tried again.

I suspect I violated the first rule of a friendship. To stay friends with anyone you have to avoid saying anything unforgivable and in

Charley's mind, what I said was unforgivable. I embarrassed him.

The funny thing is that real differences of opinion about important matters like religion, money or politics don't damage a good friendship. It's those little things that come up that kill one. I've often thought I should have remembered that old quotation when I was talking to Charley: "Instead of loving your enemies, try treating your friends a little better."

We all know old friends are the best friends but we don't knock new friends. We need them. We have to replace all the Charleys we lose as we go along.

This year I've been to three reunions and that's two too many. I went to a high school reunion, a college reunion and the bomber crew reunion. In each case there were about a hundred people present. I could reminisce with all of them but I really only enjoyed seeing three or four in each group. I noticed that the ones I liked seeing most were the ones I did the least old-time talking with. We talked about what we were doing now.

There's no way to figure out why you make friends with some people and not with others. I meet as many people I dislike as I meet people I like. There can be something equally hard to define that puts you off.

There seems to be some little trick of mind each of us has that matches up with some people and not with others. Something goes on between friends that doesn't go on between acquaintances even when neither person is saying anything. You don't have to say everything to a friend for both of you to understand what you mean.

The funny thing about your good friends is that sometimes you don't enjoy being with them. One of my best and dearest old friends is about the most cantankerous, aggravating, negative SOB I ever met. I don't know why I've put up with him all these years but if someone had me make out a list of my best friends, he'd be right up there near the top.

Politicians abuse the words "good friend" by using them to describe someone they met once for thirty seconds at a cocktail party in Washington. I object to that but I concede that it's possible to consider someone a good friend whom you've never spent much time with. It depends on the intensity of the time you did spend. There are people I've known for twenty-five years that I don't really know at all. On the other hand, there are people I don't see more than once every ten years whom I consider good friends.

Maybe I ought to try calling Charley again.

Wally

I SEE a lot of my friend Wally in the summer. Wally is the best old friend I ever had. I haven't known him for long but he's eighty-two. That's an old friend. My relationship with most people I've known who were that age has been distant. I felt separated from them. I've loved some, admired many and felt sorry for quite a few older people but I never had a pal eighty years old until I met Wally.

Wally and his wife have a place in the little village where we spend much of our time in the summer. Our house is on top of the hill about a mile out of town. What Wally and I have in common, in addition to that indefinable sense of understanding one another that friends have, is an interest in woodworking. We travel around the countryside together looking for good pieces of cherry or walnut in some of the little sawmills and we swap tools and exchange problems. Wally's idea of a good time is to drive into the city and buy a new tool. That's my idea of a good time, too. Each of us has more wood and more tools than we know what to do with.

Wally's real name is Wellington and he has the stature to handle that kind of a name, although no one ever calls him by it. Wally is six foot five, a giant of a man and still strong. When I go down to his workshop with a problem, he'll dig out one of his cabinetmaker's books that explains what to do in detail. He goes to the book more often than I do. He'll come out of his workshop and put the book on top of his car parked in the driveway at the side of the house and start looking for the answer to my problem. He points to some page in the book. The problem is, he's eight inches taller than I am so my eyes are only on a level with the top of his car. He's looking down on the book. Last week, for instance, I was trying to find out how to bend a piece of oak by steaming it and Wally read me how to do it from his book on top of the car.

Later in the day I came by again and Wally was worried because he couldn't remember where he'd put the cabinetmaking book we'd been looking at. He was afraid he might have absentmindedly left it on top of the car and that his wife had driven off with it up there. Wally's very aware of his age and he thinks he's more absentminded and forgetful than he used to be. I don't know, of course, but I suspect he's always been about the way he is now. Forgetfulness seems to come very naturally to him.

"There are three things bad about getting old," he says. "One, you can't remember anything ... and I forget the other two." He laughs. Wally likes old jokes.

Early in the summer when we first came here, I went down to greet Wally. We talked about our winters and then he said, "Hey, come in here a minute."

We went to his crowded workshop and he pointed to a pile of pieces of cherry on his workbench. There were four carefully turned and fluted legs, several small pieces that had been dovetailed or rabbited and one wide board that looked like the top of something.

"Look at this stuff," Wally said. "I did this at the end of last summer and left it here and now I can't remember what the hell I was making."

Wally has better tools than I have but his workshop is just as much of a mess. He says he waits until the sawdust reaches his knees before he cleans it out. Last week I loaded up my station wagon with scraps of wood and two barrels of sawdust to take to the dump. Wally went with me but when we got there the people in the little office at the entrance to the dump said I had to have a sticker on my car to prove we were residents.

I filled in a form but I had to go outside to look at my license plate number. "Hey, Eddie," I heard one of the men say to another. "How about that. He don't even know his license plate number."

Wally decided he ought to get a dump sticker too so he came back into the office with me. He started filling out the form and when he came to the license plate question he looked up at the dump man and said, "I don't know my license plate number." The man shook his head and gave a knowing look at Eddie. To him it was evidence that we were two dumb city slickers, neither of whom knew his license number. To me it helped explain why Wally and I are such good friends.

When Wally was known as Wellington, he was vice-president of a very big corporation. He must have been good at his work to have been so successful but I suspect Wally never did anything better in his life than he does being eighty-two years old.

The Art of Conversation

The best conversationalists are people whose stories or ideas have a definite beginning and a definite ending. The bores are the ones who talk on and on without ever making a point.

The other night we had Pranas Lape, an old friend, to dinner and I got thinking afterwards that he's one of the best conversationalists I know. He has original ideas, serious thoughts and usually punctuates them with a twist that makes everyone laugh.

Pranas lives a monastic existence on the coast of Maine, painting huge canvases of abstract art and living off the fish he catches, the vegetables he grows and the mushrooms he finds in the woods. He buys an occasional bottle of ketchup toward the end of winter when the things he froze don't taste as good as they did when they were fresh. He can live, he says, on three thousand dollars a year.

Pranas left Lithuania as a young man thirty years ago and he still speaks with a heavy accent. He uses the English language with great directness but with very little regard for traditional grammar. When he speaks there's no doubt about what he means although the words are never arranged the way I would have arranged them.

"He is already going for long time with this program," Pranas will say of President Reagan. "Ven vill it do something except bad?"

I have never liked Pranas's paintings but I think that's more my shortcoming than his. I simply don't understand the ideas he's trying to express with his shapes and colors. I've never dismissed him as a painter, though, because I assume he has as many good ideas when he's painting as when he's talking.

"Put all the MX missiles together in one six-pack on a remote island in the Pacific Ocean," he says. "Make them so they could be shot off by remote control from someplace else. Tell the Russians exactly where the island is. Keep a few nuclear weapons on board submarines and heavy bombers. If the Russians ever declare war on us, they'd first have to destroy that island with all our missiles six-packed on it.

"Our missiles would be destroyed but no American would be killed and no city would be destroyed but at the instant the island was destroyed, we'd know we were at war with Russia and we could strike with our other weapons."

Everything at dinner reminds Pranas Lape of a story. He has a Lithuanian friend who exchanges letters with her family in her Russian-dominated homeland. The letters are often censored so the woman arranged a code with her family. They include pictures with their letters. If the picture shows the family standing, things are going well. If the family is sitting, things are not so good.

"Last time she get letter," Pranas says, "they are lying on floor."

We had wine with dinner and even that reminded Pranas of a story. A summer neighbor of his, Roger Fessaguet, is one of the fine chefs in America and owner of La Caravelle restaurant in New York. Roger invited several other chefs to Maine for a weekend and Pranas was asked to dinner. One of the chefs, a renowned wine expert, had brought several rare old bottles of Bordeaux. When the first bottle was opened, each guest tasted it. Some expressed doubt about the wine. Others, not wishing to offend their friend who had brought it, withheld their opinion.

When the chef who had brought the wine tasted it, he quickly spit it out.

"Undrinkable vinegar!" he declared.

A second bottle was opened. Each chef tasted it and their reaction was good this time. Then the expert who brought it swished it around in his mouth.

"Magnificent," he said. "One of the best I have ever tasted."

"So," Pranas said at our dinner table, "I taste both wines. I try first one, then other. I cannot tell difference. Both same!" He roars with laughter.

If every table had a conversationalist like Pranas, we wouldn't need television.

"You Aren't Going to Tell That Old Story Again?"

No one ever said married life was easy and if anyone ever did say it and I missed it, they were wrong. Young people getting married listen to the for-richer-for-poorer-in-sickness-and-in-health talk but not many of them understand the real pitfalls in sharing a whole life with someone else.

Over the weekend I was thinking about one cause for divorce that wouldn't occur to a young couple just starting married life. I think they ought to be warned about it in the wedding ceremony. If you're going to be married to someone for a long time, you have to be prepared to listen to them repeat the same stories over and over again hundreds of times during your life. You'll find from experience that every time a husband or a wife is in a conversation with a few people around, they'll find a way to be reminded of one of their favorite stories.

Telling an old story is taking a calculated risk. If there are eight people listening to you at the dinner table, for instance, and your wife and two other people at the table have heard it before, it's probably a wise idea not to tell the story again. If, on the other hand, your husband or wife is the only one who has heard it, you sacrifice whatever respect you may lose from your spouse and go ahead with it.

The wedding ceremony ought to be rewritten to make certain both parties understand that they are not only "to love, honor and obey" but also "to listen, laugh and approve." It isn't easy to laugh at a story you've heard 183 times before but a good wife or husband should put her or his mind to it and try.

This comes to my mind now because we had some good friends at the house for dinner last weekend. The subject of speeding tickets came up because someone at the table got one on the way to our house.

"I'll never forget a ticket I got years ago," another good old friend said.

"Dear," his wife said looking at him with a pained expression, "you aren't going to tell that story again, are you?"

There were eight people at dinner and three of them admitted they'd heard my friend, Bill, tell the story before. Several of the others who hadn't heard it or didn't remember hearing it before, urged him to continue with it. One of the three who had heard it several times before is always nice to everyone. He said, "Oh, that's a great story. Go ahead. Tell Brian what happened when the cop pulled you over when you were on your way to give a speech at the dinner for the Police Commissioner."

"It was way back when I was doing a radio show," Bill began.

Bill's wife dropped her eyes to her plate and toyed with a few pieces of lettuce.

Bill is a great story teller and he's had so much practice with this one that he really tells it well.

"And so," he concluded after five minutes, "this cop says to me,

'Well, holy mackerel then, you better get over there in a hurry. Here, give me your license and registration. This won't take a minute.' "

Everyone laughed, and when the laughter subsided I didn't want the conversation to die so I said, "That reminds me of the time I was driving through this little town in Georgia."

"You told that story last time Bill told that story," my wife said.

"I haven't told it as often as you've told the one about what happened in the shooting gallery on board the ship when your parents took you to Europe when you were seventeen," I said.

"Tell us what happened on the ship, Marge," the friend who is always nice to everyone said.

I decided to clear some of the dishes off the table. If I couldn't tell my story about being arrested in the little town in Georgia, I wasn't going to sit through that story about the shooting gallery on the ship again.

The Wedding

T HE beautiful daughter of good friends of ours was being married last Saturday in a local church. Her father is the most successful businessman among our old friends and her mother is one of the most attractive and charming people we know. If you were invited, it was a wedding with reception party afterwards that you didn't miss. I missed part of it.

At five A.M. Saturday morning I awoke and rushed for the bathroom. I knew I was ill. Having just recovered from the flu, I couldn't believe I had it again. The day before I'd had lunch with a camera crew at a big, sloppy Italian restaurant. The food tasted good at the time but I noticed that when I thought about the eggplant parmigiana, my stomach turned over. This is usually a clue.

By nine Saturday morning, I talked myself into thinking I felt better and went downstairs to do some odd jobs. By noon I knew I was kidding myself. I had something. Not going to the wedding was unthinkable and I put that out of my mind. One way or another I had to go. Usually you can take a shower, pull yourself together and do something if you really have to, even when you're sick.

The wedding was a formal affair. My wife had bought a new dress and I was to wear a tuxedo. I went upstairs to lie down but first decided to see if my tuxedo was pressed. I could not find my tuxedo. My wife could not find my tuxedo. She called the cleaners and the cleaners could not find my tuxedo.

Because my tuxedo was twenty-five years old, worn and ill-fitting anyway, I decided to buy a new one. It is not easy to buy a tuxedo at two P.M. Saturday and wear it that evening, particularly if you are somewhat misshapen, as I am.

I need a tuxedo two or three times a year and I hate to pay twenty-five dollars to rent one so, still feeling absolutely terrible, I drove twelve miles to a good men's store. I am ill at ease with clothing store salesmen. They are always so nice they make me suspicious. The salesman was not only nice to me, he found a tuxedo that practically fit. The sleeves were a little long but I was in no position to look for a perfect fit. The tailor agreed to shorten the pants then and there and I walked out with a $250 tuxedo thirty minutes later. You can see I wasn't taking this wedding lightly.

The wedding was at 6:30. The thought of the church ceremony was torture but my wife has always made it clear to me that you don't go to the party afterwards if you don't go to the wedding itself. It was then about five P.M. and I had to lie down. I spent the next hour between the bed and the bathroom. Then I gritted my teeth, took the shower, dressed and left for the church. I kept thinking how different my situation was from the bride's.

We didn't arrive at the church until 6:25 and the bride's mother was already standing in the back of the church with her entourage. She greeted me and I had a terrible decision to make. As affectionate old friends, we usually kiss. I didn't have time to say, nor would she have been interested in knowing, that I had either food poisoning or the flu. "She'll be kissed by a hundred people today," I thought to myself, "and one more won't hurt. I'll stay way up on her cheek, away from her mouth and my germs will never get to her." I kissed her.

Until Saturday I had never realized how much you sit and stand during the standard wedding ceremony, which, incidentally, is in serious need of being rewritten. It seemed as though the minister had us bobbing up and down for hours when all I wanted to do was ask the people next to me to move over so I could lie down in the pew.

After the ceremony, we walked back to the car. It was obvious I couldn't make it to the country club for the party. We don't have a bathroom in our car. All I wanted to do was go home to bed. My wife agreed I should. It's okay, I guess, to go to the wedding and not the party.

Every time you go any place where there's a crowd, I suppose someone is in the condition I was. I sure hope the bride's mother noticed my new tuxedo and that I didn't give her anything.

Trust

Oꜱᴇ day I was driving in a city I don't know very well. I came to a major crossroads where I wanted to turn right but the light was red so I stopped.

I'm still not totally comfortable with the law that lets you turn right on red, and there are so many exceptions that when I'm on a street I'm not familiar with, I'm never sure whether I can go or not.

A car pulled up behind me with its right blinker on, and as I looked up into my rearview mirror, my eyes met the eyes of the driver. He quickly took his right hand off the wheel, raised it with his palm toward his face as though his hand were a Stop sign and nodded twice.

The motion wasn't any standard form of sign language but I understood perfectly what he meant. There was no suggestion of irritation on his part. He simply understood my confusion and was indicating to me that it was okay to make the turn.

It wasn't much but it struck me as very nice and I had a brief sensation of warm, friendly fellow feeling. Two strangers had understood and trusted each other. We had exchanged a little moment of understanding. He had helped me and thus himself and then we'd each gone our own way, never to meet again.

There are more people in the world than all of us can be friends with but friendliness seems to be a disappearing quality of life. Friendliness and trust go together and while I suppose we can do without friendliness, we can't do without trust. We have to have some confidence in each other or everyone is going to end up living in a fenced-off world of his or her own.

The most valuable thing the bad guys have stolen from the rest of us is not money but trust. We're suspicious of everyone.

We're suspicious of strangers because we know they might steal or attack us.

We're suspicious of government because we've read about the dishonest politicians and know they may be cheating us.

We're suspicious of products because we know that what some dishonest companies say about them in their advertisements is not true.

In the building where I've worked for twenty years, there's a guard desk at the door and everyone is asked to show an identification card. It's common now in most offices and factories.

I detest the new distrust. The basic assumption is that people are no damn good.

In many stores in big cities, you're expected to check the bags you have with you. Before you've even been in the place, you're suspected of being a thief.

I know there are shoplifters but I don't go in stores that make you check your bags. If they don't trust me, I don't trust them. I don't like wandering through a store knowing the management thinks I'm trying to steal. Civilization rests on trust. Without friendliness and the understanding that we're all in this thing together, one of us is going to drop the bomb.

In the parking lot of the supermarket my attention is often attracted to a person locking a car door. I know it may be the sensible thing to do but I never feel friendly toward the people doing it.

Last week I was reading the paper and feeling pretty bad about all the devious, dishonest work our Central Intelligence Agency feels it's necessary for it to do in Central America. After I read the paper I drove over to a hardware store and lumberyard in a nearby town and then I felt better.

I went into a back room where they keep small pieces of hardware and picked out a selection of screws and carriage bolts and took them to the front desk.

"How many carriage bolts you got here?" Lou, the man at the desk, asked.

"Twenty," I said.

"Twenty times thirty-three . . . that'll be six sixty," Lou said.

He didn't count the carriage bolts. Lou trusts me and I suspect he has less stolen from him at the hardware than they have at those places in the city where they make you check your shopping bags at the door.

Letting the Experts Decide: What Could Go Wrong?

RECENT Presidents have hit on an interesting new way to deal with the problems of government. When faced with an issue so difficult that it seems to have no solution, they appoint a committee to look into the matter and report back to them with a recommendation. I'm so impressed with this presidential method that I'd like to apply it to my own life.

Today I'd like to appoint a committee of experts to come up with the answer on what to do with my old station wagon. Just as Central America is too much for a President to figure out, that station wagon problem is too much for me. Should I keep it another year? Should I spend a lot of money getting it fixed? Should I bother to have the dent taken out of the right rear fender where I mashed it in against the side of the garage door?

I'm going to let the committee decide.

For the committee on station wagons, I think I'll appoint Lee Iacocca as chairman. He's with Chrysler, and the station wagon's a Ford, but he won't let that interfere with his judgment. He'll be fair as presidential committees always are.

Just as soon as the Iacocca Commission gets back to me, I'll take action. In the meantime, I'm just going to drive the car, as always. Of course, I may just drive it as always after the commission gets back to me, too, no matter what their recommendation is.

I'm going to appoint another commission to study my financial condition. The commission will be headed by the economic expert Alan Greenspan and will have such members as Milton Friedman and Paul Volcker. It will report back to me within ninety days on whether or not I can afford to buy the new power saw I have my eyes on.

In addition to the question of the saw, it will explain to me things like the money market, tax-free municipal bonds and whether it really matters to me what the price of gold is in Zurich.

We're having some people in for dinner Saturday night and I'm going to appoint another commission to come back within three days with a fair, honest and bipartisan report on what we ought to serve. Once that report is made, no one else will have any grounds on which to complain. The decision on the food will have been made, not by me, but by the experts.

The Saturday Night Dinner Commission will be headed by the great executive chef Pierre Franey. He will have on his commission André Soltner, chef at America's best restaurant, Lutèce, and food writers Mimi Sheraton and Craig Claiborne. Craig and Mimi don't speak to each other but I'm sure they can put aside their differences for the good of our dinner party on this important occasion, just as members of the President's commissions have.

If the food commission advises anything for dinner Saturday night that's too expensive, I'm going to turn over its recommendation to the financial committee and let the two committees argue it out between them. I'm tired of making decisions. The answer obviously is to appoint a committee.

In the event that there are any disagreements between two committees, I'll appoint an Arbitration Committee whose sole job will be to decide which of the two committees is right.

I'm going to appoint a commission on overweight to study the problem of why I can't eat ice cream and still get thin. For this committee, I'm going to look through *Family Circle*, the *Reader's Digest*, *Redbook*, the *National Enquirer*, the *Ladies' Home Journal* and all the book best-seller lists and find the best diet writers.

I anticipate that once these committees report back to me, I'll have my life as well organized as any of our Presidents have organized the country.

Self-Improvement Week

I THINK I'll improve myself this week.

I ought to do more reading. Maybe I'll buy an important book tomorrow and read that and learn something I didn't know. As a matter of fact, why don't I decide to do that every week. I'll read one good book a week. That would improve me.

It wouldn't do any harm if I stopped eating so much, either. I'll cut down on butter and stop eating so much ice cream. For breakfast I'll just have half a grapefruit and some dry toast.

If I cut down on what I eat and start jogging in the morning before I go to work, I could lose some weight and really get into shape. My tennis would improve if I was in better shape. Maybe I'll start jogging a half mile at first and work up to two miles. That's what I'll do. I'll do two miles every morning, take a shower, read a chapter or two of a good book and have half a grapefruit before going to work.

I'm going to stop wasting so much time watching television, too. Half of what I watch is junk and I'm only watching because I'm sitting there and it comes on. I'm going to start turning off the television set. I'll go to bed earlier and get more sleep. That'll be good for me, more sleep.

There are a lot of exercise books on the market. I'll get one of those. It wouldn't hurt if I tightened up my stomach muscles. They say you can do some of those exercises anywhere. I heard a man on radio say it's a good idea to get used to tensing and then relaxing muscles wherever you are. He said you could even stretch some muscles while you were brushing your teeth. That sounds easy and I haven't been brushing my teeth enough anyway. I'll start brushing my teeth for longer and tensing up some muscles while I do it.

My fingernails don't look too good. I ought to be more careful cutting them and then I ought to file them a little. My toenails are much too long and I've got to start cutting them more often so they don't keep poking holes in my socks.

Speaking of my fingers, I'm going to learn a new skill with them. I've always thought it would be great to know how to take notes in shorthand so I'll enroll in a secretarial school for an hour at noon instead of eating a big lunch or maybe I'll go evenings, instead of watching television. If I can find a simple course in accounting, I'll take that too. It'll make it quicker and easier to pay bills and keep track of bank accounts. If they have a computer course, I might as well take that while I'm at it.

I ought to be more careful about my clothes. I have a reputation for not being very neat. It would be a good idea if I got my pants pressed more often. I don't even change a shoelace when it breaks. I pull the lace through so it's even again and just tie the short ends in a regular knot instead of a bow. It looks terrible and I'm determined to stop doing that. If my pants are pressed and the rest of my clothes are neat and tidy, I ought to get a haircut more often. There's nothing that looks worse than someone who needs a haircut. I've got to stop letting my hair come over my collar in back the way it does now.

What I ought to do is organize my time better so that I can do more in a day. I'll set aside one hour in which to read the newspaper, for instance. Instead of this hit-or-miss way I read the paper now, I'll start on page one and go right through the paper until I've read the whole thing.

After I jog and eat my grapefruit and do my exercises and brush my teeth and read the newspaper, press my pants and cut my fingernails, I'm going to take a few minutes to relax, meditate and plan my day. I read somewhere that everyone should plan his day in advance and not just start out willy-nilly in the morning so that's what I'll do.

I'm just sick and tired of myself the way I am. In the near future, if I follow these plans I'm making to improve myself, I'm going to be smart, efficient, muscular and in beautiful shape. I can hardly wait to see myself in the mirror.

I Did It Again—Nothing

PROBABLY I'll learn this week but why has it taken me so long? Perhaps, if not this week, next week? Or by the year 2000 at the latest?

I know I haven't learned yet because I did it again this year. I went away on vacation, took along a lot of paperwork and didn't do any of it. I did the same thing last year, the year before that and for as many years back as I can remember. I took mail to be answered, bills to be paid and notes on things I wanted to write. Nothing. I took two boxes of papers and a full briefcase this year and haven't opened any of them except to get out a pen I left in the briefcase.

In the middle of my vacation I had to go to Chicago for two days and I took the briefcase with me because I thought I'd have some extra time at night. I returned from Chicago with the briefcase unopened. I didn't even look for another pen in there. Now, when I go back to the office shortly, I'll take the briefcase and the two boxes of papers with me in the exact condition they were in when I left, without the pen, of course.

That I've never learned is one of the first rules of life. Everything takes longer than you think it's going to. Even vacations take longer and are harder work than you thought they were going to be.

If I did all the work I've taken home with me nights or taken on vacation with me, I might be President. I'd be rich, relaxed and without a worry in the world. I wouldn't have that nagging feeling all the time that there were things I should have done and didn't. My life and everything in it would be organized and up to date.

If I'd done all my homework I'd have written the letter to my aunt with a little gift in plenty of time for her to have received it before her birthday, not three days after it. I'd have personally answered hundreds of good letters I've received. No one would think I was rude or that I considered myself a big shot too busy to respond to a nice letter. My loans would be all paid up and my dues would be paid to the Writers' Guild, the Directors' Guild and AFTRA, the American Federation of Television and Radio Artists and the Authors' League. I'd have checked my bank balance against my canceled checks and I'd have found a new, cheaper insurance company for my car. I'd have filled in all the forms you have to send in to get your guarantee for the things you buy. I'd be some great person.

I can understand just plain not doing something but what I don't understand is how I can so consistently fool myself into thinking I'm *going* to do something when life's experience should remind me that there isn't a chance in the world I'll do it. I remember when I was in high school, I took five or six books home with me every night. I had briefcases to carry them in, I had special bags sometimes and one year I had a thick strap. I always worried about how to carry my books home. I should have worried more about doing something with them when I got them there. Tonight was always going to be different. Finally I'd get at doing all my homework. I never did and it was a habit I carried over with me into college. I must have carried a cumulative total of ten tons of books home from school over the years without ever having read more than a few pounds of them.

My genius for thinking I'll do more than I can do is nowhere more apparent than with the reading I plan to do and don't. I buy books, magazines, newspapers and I save all the good Sunday supplements and put them aside for when I have more time. I have never once in my whole life had more time and I don't know why I think I ever will. If I did read all the books on our shelves, all the magazines I've subscribed to and all the newspapers I've put aside for a rainy day, I'd be one of the best-informed people in the world. If it ever rains for long enough for me to get all my rainy-day reading done, I'll be reading on board an ark.

Safe at Last

DID you ever have one of those days when nothing goes right? It sounds like the beginning of a joke but it's no joke, and the thing that worries me is that I'm running into the second day.

Yesterday I was in Hershey, Pa., talking to 2,500 school kids who had gathered in an auditorium. The people running the event flattered me by pointing out how many kids had come to hear me. But I'm not that old. When you're in school and you get a chance to break the regular classroom routine, you'll do anything different that's offered to you.

As I was leaving, someone who runs an inn near Hershey presented me with a little wicker hamper of delicacies they thought I might eat for lunch on my way back to New York. They thought I was driving, but I flew. At the airport I ate a delicious little shrimp salad in the basket and a piece of apple tart. There was a bottle of sparkling cider which was too good to leave but I couldn't drink it all so I decided to take it home with me. I carried it on board the plane and put it in the overhead rack with my coat.

I was dozing on the flight to New York when there was a sudden commotion from the seats ahead of me and as I awakened something started dripping into my lap from above. The cabin of the small commuter plane was poorly pressurized and the cork had popped out of my sparkling cider, spraying the passengers in front of me.

It was embarrassing and there was no sense trying to convince them it was cider, not champagne. I turned the bottle over to the stewardess and she poured what was left into cups and gave them to the wet passengers as a consolation prize.

My car was in the parking lot at La Guardia Airport in New York. When I got to the booth where they take the money, I couldn't find the parking ticket. They're used to that but still it took almost half an hour to fill out the forms they demanded before they'd let me leave with my car.

On the highway home I pass through two toll gates. The exact-change lanes are much quicker than the manned gates. I fished change out of the ashtray where I keep it and drove up. I stopped and reached out to flip the quarter into the basket. My hand hit the edge of the window which I hadn't rolled down all the way and the quarter fell to the pavement. There were no more quarters in the ashtray and as I reached in my pocket to look for another, the horns behind me started blowing.

I got out and started looking under the car for my quarter. The exasperated driver behind me finally gave me one. It wasn't kindness, it was impatience but I thanked him profusely.

It was 11:00 when I got to bed last night .My clock radio is set to go on early, 5:37 A.M. When I finally awoke without its assistance this morning, it seemed lighter than usual. I looked at my watch on the table next to the bed. It was 6:20 A.M. and I'd already missed my regular train.

"I meant to tell you," my wife said. "The power went off for a little while yesterday." That's why the clock radio didn't go on.

I dressed hurriedly and as I yanked on my right shoelace, I got the end of it in my hand. Threading a frayed, broken shoelace through a small eyelet is not a job to be done in a hurry.

When I finally boarded a later commuter train, I thought my troubles were over. I got a seat and opened my newspaper, safe at last.

Ten miles down the track, the train ground to an ominous halt. After about fifteen minutes the conductor's voice came over the intercom.

"We're having trouble with the braking system, ladies and gentlemen. They're going to pull another train up alongside us and you'll get off and board that."

The train that came alongside was already filled. By the time perhaps 1,500 people from our train were loaded on it, there wasn't room for anyone who might have fainted to fall down. Reading the paper was out of the question.

I'm at the office now, two hours late, typing and waiting expectantly for my typewriter to break down. It's been dependable for forty years but if it's ever going to go, this'll be the day.

Florence Nightingale Never Would Have Said That

O N the last day of my vacation I was fixing the roof, standing on the top rung of a ten-foot ladder, when the rung broke.

The only good thing to say about the fall is that it was a better way to end a vacation than it would have been to begin one.

I came down through the uprights of the ladder and caught my ribs on the second rung from the top. My ribs broke the second and third rungs of the ladder. The ladder broke my seventh and eighth ribs. If this column isn't as clear as usual today, it's because I'm hitting the keys of my typewriter lightly in order not to jar my frame.

It happened quickly, like an auto accident. I didn't slide off the roof, I dropped like a stone. My wind was knocked out when my ribs hit the oak rung which, for an instant, delayed my plunge to the ground. The rung caught me under my left arm toward my back and temporarily paralyzed my breathing muscles. As I lay there, stunned and gasping, a lot of things went through my mind.

"I think I'm hurt," I remember grunting to myself. I even remember thinking how strange it was I'd taken time to think that. I wondered, too, whether I'd get any air into my lungs before I suffocated.

After three or four minutes I got my wind back and pulled myself up. My elbow was bleeding and I could tell my left leg was bruised from ankle to hip but the only thing that really hurt was my ribs.

I hobbled to the kitchen and called upstairs.

Margie came down and because I was such a sorry-looking sight and in obvious pain, she was instantly tender and solicitous.

She got me to lie down on the kitchen floor, pulled my shirt off and put a dish towel filled with ice on my ribs. Florence Nightingale couldn't have done more . . . for five minutes.

When I finally got myself up off the floor and onto a kitchen chair, it must have appeared to her as though I was going to survive because her attitude changed abruptly.

"What were you doing up on the ladder anyway?" she asked,

critically. There wasn't a tender inflection in her mouth.

"I had one of those caulking guns," I said. "I was trying to fix the leak."

"You're too heavy to be standing on the top rung of a ladder at your age," she said, stabbing me twice in one sentence. Tender people can be so cruel when they aren't being tender. Florence Nightingale never would have said that to a person as wounded as I was.

That night I hurt so much that there was no part of my body I could lie on and I spent much of the time sitting in a chair.

The following morning it seemed likely that I was more than scraped and bruised so we drove thirty miles to the hospital for X rays.

You never know for sure whether you're making more of a fuss about pain than you ought to, so naturally I was pleased when the doctor came back with the pictures a few minutes later and announced that I had two broken ribs. Not that knowing your ribs are broken does you any good.

"The woman over there at the cashier's desk will take care of you," the young doctor said next.

"Isn't there anything you do?" I asked.

"We don't strap ribs any more," he said. "I'll give you some pills for pain. You'll be uncomfortable for about a month."

I paid for the diagnosis and left.

When I got home I'd traveled sixty miles, spent two hours in the emergency room and a fair amount of money, and I hurt exactly as much as before I'd gone to the hospital.

In the days following that first five minutes on the kitchen floor, I've sought consolation from people other than my wife. I haven't gotten much. For one thing, I haven't run into a single person who hasn't interfered with me telling them about my broken ribs by them telling me about theirs. Everyone, it seems, has broken a rib.

Three days later, all I'm getting is advice on how not to fall off ladders, or pessimistic talk about how long it takes ribs to heal. All I want is for them to kiss it and make it better and they're giving me advice.

I don't feel like doing much work these days but at least I'm not on vacation. I'm at the office where I don't have to.

Jenny Kissed Me

Teachers are no longer making pupils memorize things as much as they used to. Those in favor of making kids memorize things, hold up your hands. Those against?

When I had to memorize things, I thought it was stupid. It didn't seem to me as though learning something by heart had anything to do with an education. The phrase "to learn by heart" suggests that memorizing has nothing to do with the part of the brain we think with, and yet today I'm not so opposed to memorizing a few things as I used to be.

It may be idiocy to learn something by heart but there's a great comfort in knowing all the words to a long, well-written passage. Like an old friend, familiar words are nice to have around sometimes. It was probably true that the worst teachers made you do the most memorizing but once you've done it you have something that stays with you. Maybe it's only to laugh about with your classmates when you meet twenty years out of school, but you have it.

Nothing in the world could convince me that the quality of mercy is strained, for example. I learned that the quality of mercy is *not* strained when I was about fourteen and I've never forgotten it. Furthermore, it droppeth as the gentle rain from heaven, upon the place beneath. I could no more forget that than forget my name.

If you start thinking about it, you'll be surprised at how many things you learned by rote. In my school we started with the alphabet and the multiplication tables. Sometimes now I have to stop and think for a minute whether nine times seven is fifty-six or sixty-three but I can always start from the beginning and get the right answer. I'm told that some schools aren't even making kids learn the multiplication tables any more. They all have computers!

I hate myself for having turned so conservative about some things but I don't think it's a bad idea to make kids memorize a little good literature. I don't know as Henry Wadsworth Longfellow does much for them but the preamble to the Constitution is pretty good stuff to have permanently in your head.

"We, the People of the United States, in order to form a more perfect union ..." are magnificent words expressing a profoundly important idea and we shouldn't forget them.

Most of us have in our heads hundreds of fragments of poems and long segments of prose. We don't use them much but they're nice to have up there. They're like the chairs in a room you don't sit in very often. They're good for special occasions.

In my high school poetry book there were two poems on one page written by Leigh Hunt. We had to memorize "Abou Ben Adhem" (may his tribe increase), and I hated it. The second poem on the same page is one I loved and have never forgotten.

> Jenny kissed me when we met,
> Jumping from the chair she sat in;
> Time, you thief, who love to get
> Sweets into your list, put that in!
> Say I'm weary, say I'm sad,
> Say that health and wealth have missed me,
> Say I'm growing old, but add,
> Jenny kissed me.

The things you memorize inadvertently, as I memorized that, are probably better than the things you have to memorize.

One of the things in my repertoire now is Lincoln's Gettysburg Address. I learned it not in school but working with Harry Reasoner. When you're filming something, the sound man asks the person doing the talking for a voice level so that he can adjust the dials on his recorder. Some people, when asked to do this by the sound technician, merely count off: "Testing, one, two three ... testing, testing, one, two, three."

Harry always gave the sound man Lincoln's Gettysburg Address. "Fourscore and seven years ago our fathers brought forth ...," he'd say. Sometimes he'd only get through a few lines before the technician stopped him and said, "That's fine." Sometimes, though, he'd go the whole way through it and after listening to Harry recite it several hundred times, I learned the whole thing myself.

If you're ever over to my house for dinner, I'll give you the Gettysburg Address, Lewis Carroll's "Jabberwocky," half a dozen short poems by Robert Browning and "Jack and Jill" in Latin.

"Jack et Jill quaerentes fontem/Ascendebant parvum montem" is the way it begins.

Tarawa

WHEN the President spoke at a luncheon for 125 Medal of Honor winners, my thoughts turned to war and to one Marine who never got a medal.

The year was 1943. No one knows who he was. He came wading into the beach at Tarawa with a rifle held high over his head. When he hit the beach, he was one of only four left from the group of twenty Marines who had been dumped off the small blue Higgins invasion boat, 600 yards out on the coral reef beyond the shallow lagoon.

A Japanese machine gun had dropped all but those four men into the lagoon, dead or so badly wounded that they drowned with the seventy-five pounds of equipment on their backs.

The Marine lay still for five minutes. His khaki started to dry out and turn light again, except where the blood oozed out near the shoulder.

Finally he raised his head. He could make out the Japanese machine-gun position concealed in a nest 100 feet to his right. It was four feet above him, behind a line of coconut logs that formed a barricade the length of the beach.

The Marine looked back. He saw men pile out of other landing boats off the atoll. He knew they were going to get it from the same machine gunner who got the men who started in with him. As the Marines waded closer, he could see bullets kicking up the water around them. The bullets came from the position just up the beach from where he lay.

Some Marines were hit. First he saw their helmets, then their rifles, sink below the surface.

Marines on the beach with him who told the story saw him get to his knees. They knew what he was going to do even though they could see a sticky splotch of red where blood still flowed from the wound on his shoulder.

He quickly pulled himself up over the log barrier so that he was on the sandy plateau above the beach, on a level with the Japanese gunners.

The others lost sight of him as he moved inland a little, behind a tangle of brush.

Suddenly there were wild shouts in English mixed with Japanese. Then there was a short burst of machine-gun fire and, almost simultaneously, an explosion. Then, silence.

When the other Marines made their way to the scene, there were pieces of two Japanese machine gunners blown apart by the Marine's grenade. In front of them, there lay the Marine, cut in two through the middle by the last burst of machine-gun fire as he hurled his grenade.

Out in the lagoon, Marine reinforcements waded in safely. They never knew why the machine-gun fire had stopped. The men who knew never had time to tell them. That's the way the battle for Tarawa began forty years ago.

During the fight for one square mile of coral in the Pacific, 4,690 Japanese soldiers were killed. Seventeen were taken prisoner. None escaped.

There were 1,026 Marines killed, 2,296 wounded.

It was war at its disgusting worst and not all the Marines were heroes, either. There were huge pyramid-shaped cement barriers that the Japanese had built in the shallow waters to prevent landing craft from getting to shore. Some of the wading Marines stopped and hid behind the barriers while the braver among them waded onto the beach in the face of enemy fire. It's always that way and who among us is certain what he'd do under the circumstances.

There were other horrors. One live Japanese soldier would often lie among a pile of his own dead, wait until the Marines had passed by and then rise and attack them from behind. It led to the unpleasant Marine habit of firing their automatic weapons into any pile of dead Japanese they passed.

There should be better ways to settle differences among us.

XI:

PASSING

The War Correspondent

He was Hollywood's idea of what a war correspondent should be when I first met him, a kind of James Bond of journalism. He was quick, bright, tough and good-looking in his belted trench coat. To me, he was one of the Big Guys. He knew the story he was after and when he'd written it, he'd sell it for a lot of money to the *Saturday Evening Post, Collier's* or the *Reader's Digest*.

His name doesn't add anything to the tragedy and I'm not going to use it. The last time I heard from him he needed money. He always needed money. We all have friends who have borrowed and we may have done some of it ourselves but this man was an all-time, world-class borrower. He'd borrowed money from everyone he'd ever heard of and he'd touched the best—men like Budd Schulberg and Walter Cronkite.

He had different ways of asking for money from different people and he never suggested you were giving him anything. He was going to pay you back next Thursday. He had sold an article to the *Reader's Digest* and they'd told him the check was in the mail so it was just a matter of a few days to tide him over, he'd say.

His name appears in more than one hundred entries in the *Readers' Guide to Periodical Literature* for articles he wrote for America's most prestigious magazines ... but the last entry is one he wrote for *Coronet* magazine in 1958. It had been downhill ever since.

In the beginning this peerless borrower did things in a big way. He ran up tabs of hundreds of dollars at the best drinking places in New York. When he was poor, he didn't mingle with the poor. He went to the 21 Club and mingled with the rich. In the beginning he'd ask for loans of a thousand or fifteen hundred dollars, but in recent years he reduced his demands to a hundred dollars or less. The last time he called me was just six weeks ago. He was suffering from a rare blood disease, he told me, and desperately needed thirty dollars for medicine. It was so like him to make it thirty dollars instead of twenty-five because it sounded more believable.

I didn't give it to him.

Still fresh in my memory was the time ten years ago when he'd come to my office with tears streaming down his cheeks. His son, he'd told me, had a rare eye disease and would I loan him two hundred and fifty dollars so he could take his son to Boston where there was a doctor who knew how to treat the problem. Too late, I'd found out that the story of the ailing son was pure fiction.

Yesterday I was sitting in the back seat of a car with Walter Cronkite and he pulled a letter out of his pocket.

"Dear Walter," the letter began, "your friend is dead." The letter mentioned his name. "He died December first in the library at 11 East 40th Street or just outside in the cold. Positive identification was made at the City Morgue.

"I've known him for the past five years," the letter continued. "I'm a bartender at McAnn's on Third Avenue.

"Over the past five years he would speak about his World War II days with you. He was quite good at telling anecdotes. We spent many hours talking about many subjects under the sun. He brightened up many days which would have been otherwise boring for me. I thought you would want to know."

The bartender's letter to Walter was a warmer and more sincere obituary than anyone else could have written.

"I consider it a privilege to have known him," he wrote. "Unfortunately I met him in the twilight of his life. He died of a rare disease, the name of which I can't even pronounce."

Henry Fonda

I'D never met Henry Fonda before and I never saw him again but in the late spring of 1975 I spent five intense hours with him while he read a script of mine for a television show. Until that day I had considered Henry Fonda's success an accident of birth that had given him a special and charming way of being. From that day on I understood that Fonda's success came to him mostly because he was a talented and hard-working professional actor.

When television has a documentary to which it hopes to attract a large audience, it often asks some famous person to lend his name to it by reading the script. I've never approved of the system and I didn't like the idea of hiring Henry Fonda to read my script on

Franklin Roosevelt called *FDR: The Man Who Changed America.*

It was out of my hands, though, and the date was made for Fonda to narrate the film on camera. About three minutes before his appointed hour, Henry Fonda walked into a barnlike New York television studio carrying a suitcase not much bigger than a briefcase. Three or four of us introduced ourselves and Fonda immediately asked to see the director.

Vernon Diamond, one of television's top news directors, identified himself and Fonda put his little suitcase on a bare table on stage and opened it to reveal four new shirts and eight neckties.

"I didn't know what your background or lighting would be so I brought a selection," Fonda said to the director. "What do you want me to wear here?" he said, pointing to the open suitcase.

It was a small thing but it was the beginning of one of the most pleasant, low-key, professional performances I have ever seen.

Fonda said very little but he made several small jokes about his pacemaker and about the fact that he was hard of hearing. He seemed at ease with himself and with us. He gave us no impression that he felt he was among strangers. He assumed we were as professional as he was, which was giving most of us a break.

What I really recall is how malleable he was. I realized then that unless an actor is a one-part player who goes around being himself in every role he plays, he must be able to adjust to how others want him to be or think he ought to be for the part.

He had been given my script several days earlier and I was curious about whether he would have bothered to read it in advance. He had not only read it, he had marked it throughout with heavy pen lines. I was nervous about whether he liked it or not and I never got any satisfaction from him in this regard. It did not seem to enter his mind to make any judgment about whether my script was good or bad. That was not his business. His business was to make what I had written sound as good and as much like the way I intended it to sound as he was able.

Vern Diamond sat Fonda on a stool in the middle of a barren stage with a circle of light on him.

"If you are fifty years old," Fonda started to read, "Franklin Delano Roosevelt was President for almost a quarter of your life. If you were born after 1945, he was already gone when you got here."

I was sitting to the side and Fonda stopped and turned toward me. He knew my name now.

"How do you want me to read that, Andy? Do you want it like that or like this?" He read it again, changing the rhythm and emphasis of his voice to give it another nuance of meaning.

For the rest of those five hours Henry Fonda kept turning to me to ask how I wanted something read and what I had in mind when I wrote this or that.

It was the last time I ever thought of Henry Fonda's art as an accident of birth. I have never seen anyone so thoroughly professional work so hard to do a good job.

"I'm going over to the hospital now," he said as he left the studio. "Need a new battery for my pacemaker."

Jud

IT's strange about friends. You don't even like some of them, you just have them.

Jud was my friend and I liked him. He was fifteen when we first met, sitting on the bench just outside the locker room, lacing up our football shoes. Jud's parents were moving to our city and Jud was transferring to our school. He was the new kid. We'd heard he was already six feet tall and weighed 185 pounds, so we had high hopes he could help us beat Albany High School.

Fifteen-year-old kids don't talk much under those circumstances. We just laced up our shoes, but even so, I remember liking him.

Jud and I played next to each other on the football team for three years. He was a tackle and I was a guard and we had an understanding between us about the moves we'd make that no one else would have understood. It was just between us.

We shared all kinds of good times growing up and we've had fun remembering them ever since. Remembering can be pleasant if you don't do too much of it. A few days ago Jud was remembering the telephone number of a girl named Peggy he was in love with for two months in 1937. He had a great memory for trivia like that.

It was a pretty, blue dress that finally came between him and Peggy. She came to dancing class wearing it one night. She looked beautiful, but Jud said he realized right then that she was the only girl who wore a brand-new dress to dancing class every week. That worried him about her, and things were never the same.

Summers, Jud's family went to Speculator, a small town near Lake Placid, where he had a horse. The horse was well along in years but Jud loved it. To help pay to feed the animal, he let other people ride it for a dollar an hour.

One summer Max Baer, the World Heavyweight Champion, and his younger brother, Buddy, were training in Speculator. Buddy weighed 240 pounds and he liked to ride horses. One day he rented Jud's horse. The next morning the horse was so tired he could hardly stand up and Jud felt terrible. After that when Jud saw Buddy Baer coming down the road, he'd run in and take his horse out the back door of the barn and hide him in the woods until Buddy left.

Now it's forty-seven years later. We've stayed as close as we were when we played football together. We never played the same games again but we always understood each other's moves.

Jud became a B-17 pilot during World War II. He had the kind of coordinated grace it took to fly a four-engined bomber. Learning how to fly came more easily to him than the irregular verbs we'd tried to master sitting side by side in Mr. Sharp's French class.

After the war, nothing came easily to Jud for a while. He got a job selling Cadillacs on commission and we used to laugh about it. In 1945 the dealer he worked for had back orders for fifty cars, but General Motors was still switching over to peacetime production and Jud's dealer was only getting two Cadillacs a month. There were four salesmen who had seniority.

I don't know why we remained such close friends. We had little in common but memories and understanding. Jud ended up owning a liquor store in New York and I knew as little about his work as he knew of mine. We called each other two or three times a week and said almost nothing.

On Christmas Eve, Jud had a heart attack. On the day he was to be released from the hospital, doctors discovered what they referred to as "a spot on his lung." He recovered from his heart attack and went back to work. A month ago they operated on Jud's lung. It was not a spot. The malignancy was pervasive and surgery was a mistake. He had nine of what were to have been twenty-one cobalt treatments and Friday he went home to have lamb chops.

Sylvia called me this morning at 6:25. Our phone does not ring at 6:25 with good news.

"Jud's dead," she said.

Andrew A. Rooney writes a column three days a week for the Tribune Company Syndicate that appears in more than 350 newspapers nationwide. In addition, his television essays have won him four Emmys, six Writers' Guild Awards, the Peabody Award and a host of other honors.

He began his writing career as a correspondent for *The Stars and Stripes* during World War II and went on to become a radio and television writer for Arthur Godfrey, Garry Moore and others before joining Harry Reasoner in a collaboration—Rooney writing and producing, Reasoner narrating—that produced notable essays on chairs, hotels, bridges and the English language. In 1971 he began reading his own material with "An Essay on War" on NET's "The Great American Dream Machine" and since then has produced such acclaimed specials as "Mr. Rooney Goes to Washington" (1975), "Mr. Rooney Goes to Dinner" (1976), "Mr. Rooney Goes to Work" (1977) and "Andy Rooney Takes Off" (1984) as well as his weekly "A Few Minutes with Andy Rooney" on "60 Minutes."

Andy Rooney is the author of numerous books, including *The Story of The Stars and Stripes*, *Air Gunner* and *Conqueror's Peace* (all with Bud Hutton), *The Fortunes of War*, and the best sellers *A Few Minutes with Andy Rooney*, *And More by Andy Rooney*, *Pieces of My Mind*, *Word for Word*, and *Not That You Asked*.